CONTENTS

Introduction

Chapter 1

"IT'S GOING TO CHANGE YOUR LIFE"

Chapter 2

NURSERY NECESSITIES: CRIBS, DRESSERS & MORE

Chapter 3

BABY BEDDING & DECOR

Chapter 4

THE REALITY LAYETTE: LITTLE CLOTHES FOR LITTLE PRICES

Chapter 5

MATERNITY/NURSING CLOTHES & FEEDING BABY

Chapter 6

AROUND THE HOUSE: BABY MONITORS, TOYS, BATH, FOODS, HIGH CHAIRS, AND SWINGS

Chapter 7

CAR SEATS

Chapter 8

STROLLERS, DIAPER BAGS, CARRIERS AND OTHER TO GO GEAR

Chapter 9

Affordable Baby Proofing

Chapter 10

The Best Gifts for Baby

Chapter 11

Etcetera: Catalogs, The 'Net, Child Care & More

Chapter 12

Conclusion: What Does It All Mean?

ICONS

Getting Started

Money-Saving Secrets

Sources

Best Buys

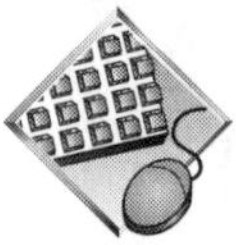

Parents In Cyberspace

The Name Game

What Are You Buying?

Do it By Mail

Safe & Sound

Email from the Real World

Smart Shopper

More Money Buys You . . .

Wastes of Money

Bottom Line

NEW!

4th edition

BABY BARGAINS

SECRETS

to saving 20% to 50% on babyfurniture, equipment, clothes, toys, maternity wear and much, much more!

Denise & Alan Fields
Authors of the Best-seller Bridal Bargains

Copyright Page, Credits and Zesty Lo-Cal Recipes

Saxophone, lead guitar and breast-feeding by Denise Fields
Drums, rhythm guitar and father stuff by Alan Fields
Congas on "Grandparents" by
Max & Helen Coopwood, Howard & Patti Fields
Cover/interior design and keyboard solo by Epicenter Creative
Baby-sitting and harmony vocals by Kirsten Bock
Screaming guitar solos on "(Let's Go) Perego" by
Charles & Arthur Troy
Additional guitar work on "Diaper Changing Blues"
by Ed Robertson and Steven Paige
Backing vocals on "(She's Got A) Five-Point Car Seat" by Ric Ocasek
Band photography by Moses Street

This book was written to the music of the Barenaked Ladies, which probably explains a lot.

Distribution to the book trade by Publisher's Group West, Berkeley, CA 1-800-788-3123. Thanks to the entire staff of PGW for their support.

To order this book, call 1-800-888-0385. Or send $15.95 plus $3 shipping (or, in Canada, $25 plus $4 shipping) to Windsor Peak Press, 436 Pine Street, Boulder, CO 80302. Questions or comments? Please call the authors at (303) 442-8792. Or fax them a note at (303) 442-3744. Or write to them at the above address in Boulder, Colorado. E-mail the authors at authors@babybargainsbook.com.

Updates to this book are on the web at www.BabyBargainsBook.com

Library Cataloging in Publication Data

Fields, Denise
Fields, Alan
Baby Bargains: Secrets to saving 20% to 50% on baby furniture, equipment, clothes, toys maternity wear and much, much more/ Denise & Alan Fields
470 pages.
Includes index.
ISBN 1-889392-09-X
1. Child Care–Handbooks, manuals, etc. 2. Infants' supplies–Purchasing–United States, Canada, Directories. 3. Children's paraphernalia–Purchasing–Handbooks, manuals. 4. Product Safety–Handbooks, manuals. 5. Consumer education.
649'.122'0296–dc20. 2002.

We miss you Dee Dee.

Version 4.1

CHAPTER 1

"It's Going to Change Your Life!"

That had to be the silliest comment we heard while we were pregnant with our first baby. Believe it or not, we even heard this refrain more often than "Do you want a boy or a girl?" and "I'm sorry. Your insurance doesn't cover that." For the friends and relatives of first-time parents out there, we'd like to point out that this is a pretty stupid thing to say. Of course, we knew that a baby was going to change our lives. What we didn't realize was how much a baby was going to change our pocketbook.

Oh sure, we knew that we'd have to buy triple our weight in diapers and be subjected to dangerously high levels of Thomas the Tank Engine. What we didn't expect was the endless pitches for cribs, gear, toys, clothing and other items parents are required to purchase by FEDERAL BABY LAW.

We quickly learned that having a baby is like popping on the Juvenile Amusement Park Ride from Consumer Hell. Once that egg is fertilized, you're whisked off to the Pirates of the Crib ride. Then it's on to marvel at the little elves in StrollerLand, imploring you to buy brands with names you can't pronounce. Finally, you take a trip to Magic Car Seat Mountain, where the salespeople are so real, it's scary.

Consider us your tour guides—the Yogi Bear to your Boo Boo Bear, the Fred to your Ethel, the . . . well, you get the idea. Before we enter BabyLand, let's take a look at the Four Truths That No One Tells You About Buying Stuff For Baby.

The Four Truths That No One Tells You About Buying Stuff for Baby

1 **BABIES DON'T CARE IF THEY'RE WEARING DESIGNER CLOTHES OR SLEEPING ON DESIGNER SHEETS.** Let's be realistic. Babies just want to be comfortable. They can't even distinguish between the liberals and conservatives on "Meet the Press," so how would they ever be able to tell the difference between Baby Gucci crib bedding and another less famous brand that's just as comfortable, but 70% less expensive? Our focus is on making your baby happy—at a price that won't break the bank.

2 **YOUR BABY'S SAFETY IS MUCH MORE IMPORTANT THAN YOUR CONVENIENCE.** Here are the scary facts: 65,000 babies per year are injured (and 87 deaths are caused) by juvenile products, according to government estimates. Each chapter of this book has a section called "Safe & Sound," which arms you with in-depth advice on keeping your baby out of trouble. We'll tell you which products we think are dangerous and how to safely use other potentially hazardous products.

3 **MURPHY'S LAW OF BABY TOYS SAYS YOUR BABY'S HAPPINESS WITH A TOY IS INVERSELY RELATED TO THE TOY'S PRICE.** Buy a $200 shiny new wagon with anti-lock brakes, and odds are baby just wants to play with the box it came in. In recognition of this reality, we've included "wastes of money" in each chapter that will steer you away from frivolous items.

4 **IT'S GOING TO COST MORE THAN YOU THINK**. Whatever amount of money you budget for your baby, get ready to spend more. Here's a breakdown of the average costs of bringing a baby into the world today:

The Average Cost of Having a Baby

(based on industry estimates for a child from birth to age one)

Crib, mattress, dresser, rocker	*$1500*
Bedding / Decor	*$300*
Baby Clothes	*$500*
Disposable Diapers	*$600*
Maternity/Nursing Clothes	*$1200*
Nursery items, high chair, toys	*$400*
Baby Food / Formula	*$900*
Stroller, Car Seat, Carrier	*$300*
Miscellaneous	*$500*
TOTAL	**$6200**

The above figures are based on buying name brand products at regular retail prices. We surveyed over 1000 parents to arrive at these estimates.

Bedding/Decor includes not only bedding items but also items like lamps, wallpaper, and so on for your baby's nursery. Baby Food/Formula assumes you'd breastfeed for the first six months and then feed baby jarred baby food ($400) and formula ($500) until age one. If you plan to bottle-feed instead of breastfeed, add another $500 on to that figure.

Sure, you do get an automatic tax write-off for that bundle of joy, but that only amounts to about $2800 for 2001 (plus you also get an additional $500 tax credit, depending on your income). But those tax goodies won't nearly offset the actual cost of raising a child. And as you probably realize, that chart is missing some expensive "extras" . . . like medical bills, childcare, saving for college and more. Here's an overview of what can add to the tab:

◆ ***Medical/adoption bills.*** Yes, for most couples, conceiving a child is free (although some may argue about that). But not everyone is that lucky—fertility treatments for the estimated 6% to 11% of woman who can't conceive naturally can run $10,000 to $12,000 a try. Yes, health insurance providers pick up some of that cost, but many have been cutting back.

Besides the normal prenatal visits to the doctor, the biggest medical bill is for the birth—about $6400 for a "normal" delivery at a hospital. The same study pegs the cost of a Caesarian at $11,000. Medical bills for first year routine check-ups and immunizations can cost $700 or more. Yes, insurance typically picks up most of those costs, but there are many children (15% of the total births this year) that are born without any coverage. So, if you have insurance, count yourself among the lucky.

Couples who adopt a baby typically face fees and expenses that range from $15,000 to $25,000. There is a federal tax credit that offsets some adoption expenses—check with your tax preparer for details. One bargain for parents who are considering an overseas adoption: some airlines now offer adopting parents a break on airfares. Both Northwest and British Airways offers 65% discounts off full coach fares (the ones adopting parents have to use, as most adoptions are done on short notice). The baby's one-ware fare back home is also discounted. Always ask the airline you want to use if they have an adoption fare deal.

◆ ***Child care.*** According to the Department of Agriculture, the average cost of childcare for a 3 to 5 year old child is $1260 per year. But those costs seemed low to us—our research on child care costs (detailed in Chapter 11, Etcetera) revealed family daycare runs $3000 to $10,000 and center care can cost up to $13,000. What about a nanny? Most run $10,000 to $20,000 in average cities, but that depends on whether they are live-in or not. In high cost cities like New York or San Francisco, childcare costs for wealthy families can top $30,000 a year.

◆ ***Housing.*** Those neighborhoods with the best schools aren't cheap. The government estimates the average middle-class family with one child will spend an *extra* $53,310 on shelter until the child is 18. The average annual cost of housing one child is $2300 to $5000, according to government estimates.

◆ ***Transportation.*** Yes, a brand new minivan today tops $20,000 and some models approach $30,000. All those trips to daycare (and later, the mall) add up–the government says average parents will spend $34,920 to transport a child to all those required activities until the age of 18.

◆ ***And more.*** Additional expenses that parents face include health care (the government says even the average, healthy child can rack up $20,757 in medical bills for the first 18 years), clothing (if you think baby clothes are pricey, check out the $22,063 bill the average kid racks up in clothes until age 18), and education (private school, anyone?).

The bottom line. If you're still with us, let's see what the government says is the GRAND TOTAL of expenses to raise a baby to age 18. Are you sitting down? Try $301,183. And that's for middle class Americans. More affluent parents spend $437,869. Yes, there are economies of scale if you add more children–but there's a limit to the savings. On average, each additional child costs just 24% less than a single child.

But wait! The government leaves two critical costs out of its equation: saving for college and lost wages from a parent who stays at home. Let's look at both:

◆ ***College.*** Price college tuition lately? Even if you forget about Harvard, the cost of attending a state school today is staggering. And with college costs expected to continue to rise in the future, you'll have to put away $350 each month for baby's college fund if you start at birth to pay for the average state school's four-year program. Wait longer to get started and the costs rise rapidly. Quicken.com has an excellent free "college planner" feature on their web site that lets you compare savings plans for public versus private schools.

◆ ***Lost wages.*** Having a baby is a financial double-whammy–not only are your expenses rising, but your income drops. Why? At least one parent will have to take off time to care for the baby. Yes, lost wages could be a short six-week maternity leave . . . or the next 18 years for a stay-at-home parent.

Hence, when you add in saving for college and lost wages for a stay-at-home mom for 18 years, the cost of raising an average middle class child to age 18 will run $1,455,581. Amazing, eh?

(Source: the above numbers are from the 1999 "Expenditures on Children by Families" by the US Dept of Agriculture and US News & World Report's "The Cost of Children", March 30, 1998).

Reality Check: Does it Really Cost that Much to Have a Baby?

Now that we've thoroughly scared you enough to inquire whether the stork accepts returns, we should point out that children do NOT have to cost that much. Even if we focus just on the first year, you don't have to spend $6200 on your baby. And that's what this book is all about: how to save money and still buy the best. Follow all the tips in this book, and we estimate the first year will cost you $3740. Yes, that's a savings of over $2400!

Now, at this point, you might be saying "That's impossible! I suppose you'll recommend buying all the cheap stuff, from polyester clothes to no-name cribs." On the contrary, we'll show you how to get *quality* name brands and safe products at discount prices. For example, we've got outlets and catalogs that sell all-cotton baby clothing at 20% to 40% off retail. You'll also learn about web sites that sell car seats and strollers for 40% off. And much more. Yes, we've got the maximum number of bargains allowed by federal law.

A word on bargain shopping: when interviewing hundreds of parents for this book, we realized bargain seekers fall into two frugal camps. There's the "do-it-yourself" crowd and the "quality at a discount" group. As the name implies, "do-it-yourselfers" are resourceful folks who like to take second-hand products and refurbish them. Others use creative tricks to make homemade versions of baby care items like baby wipes and diaper rash creme.

While that's all well and good, we fall more into the second camp of bargain hunters, the "quality at a discount" group. We love discovering a hidden factory outlet that sells goods at 50% off. Or finding a great web or mail-order source that discounts name-brand baby products at rock bottom prices. We also realize savvy parents save money by not *wasting* it on inferior goods or useless items.

While we hope that *Baby Bargains* pleases both groups of bargain hunters, the main focus of this book is not on do-it-yourself projects. Books like the *Tightwad Gazette* (check your local library for a copy) do a much better job on this subject. Our main emphasis will be on discount catalogs, web sites, outlet stores, brand reviews and identifying best buys for the dollar.

What? There's No Advertising in This Book?

Yes, it's true. This book contains zero percent advertising. We have never taken any money to recommend a product or company and never will. We make our sole living off the sales of this and other books. (So, when your friend asks to borrow this copy, have them buy their own book!) Our publisher, Windsor Peak Press, also derives its sole income from the sale of this book and our other publications. No company recommended in this book paid any consideration or was charged any fee to be mentioned. (In fact, some companies probably would offer us money to leave them *out* of the book, given our comments about their products or services).

As consumer advocates, we believe this "no ads" policy helps to ensure objectivity. The opinions in the book are just that–ours and those of the parents we interviewed.

We also are parents of two small children. As far as we know, we are the only authors of a consumer's guide to baby products that actually have young kids. We figure if we actually are recommending these products to you, we should have some real world experience with them. (That said, we should disclose that our sons have filed union grievances with our company over testing of certain jarred baby foods and that litigation is ongoing.)

Of course, given the sheer volume of baby stuff, there's no way we can test everything personally. To solve that dilemma, we rely on reader feedback to help us figure out which are the best products to recommend. We receive over 100 emails a day from parents; this helps us spot overall trends on which brands/products parents love. And which ones they want to destroy with a rocket launcher.

Finally, we have a panel of moms who also test new products for us, evaluating items on how they work in the real world. One bad review from one parent doesn't necessarily mean we won't recommend a product; but we'll then combine these tests with other parent feedback to get an overall picture.

What about prices of baby products? Trying to stay on top of this is often like attempting to nail Jell-O to a wall. Yet, we still try. As much as we can confirm, the prices quoted in this book were accurate as of the date of publication. Of course, prices and product features can change at any time. Inflation and other factors may affect the actual prices you discover in shopping for your baby. While the publisher makes every effort to ensure their accuracy, errors and omissions may exist. That's why we've established a web site where you can get the latest updates on this book for free (www.babybargainsbook.com). You can also talk directly to us: call (303) 442-8792 or e-mail us at authors@BabyBargainsBook.com to ask a question, report a mistake, or just give us your thoughts. Finally, you can write to us at "Baby Bargains," 436 Pine Street, Suite 700, Boulder, CO 80302.

What about the phone numbers listed in this book? We list contact numbers for manufacturers so you can find a local dealer near you that carries the product (or request a catalog, if available). Unless otherwise noted, these manufacturers do NOT sell directly to the public.

So, Who Are You Guys Anyway?

Why do a book on saving money on baby products? Don't new parents throw caution to the wind when buying for their baby, spending whatever it takes to ensure their baby's safety and comfort?

Ha! When our first son was born in 1993, we quickly realized how darn expensive this guy was. Sure, as a new parent, you know you've got to buy a car seat, crib, clothes and diapers . . . but have you walked into one of those baby "superstores" lately? It's a blizzard of baby stuff, with a bewildering array of "must have" gear, gadgets and gizmos, all claiming to be the best thing for parents since sliced bread.

Becoming a parent at the turn of the century is both a blessing and curse. The good news: parents today have many more choices for baby products than past generations. The *bad* news: parents today have many more choices for baby products than past generations.

Our mission: make sense of this stuff, with an eye on cutting costs. As consumer advocates, we've been down this road before. We researched bargains and uncovered scams in the wedding business when we wrote *Bridal Bargains*. Then we penned an expose on new homebuilders in *Your New House*.

Yet, we found the baby business to be perilous in different ways—instead of outright fraud or scam artists, we've instead discovered some highly questionable products that don't live up to their hype—and others that are outright dangerous. We were surprised to learn how most juvenile items face little (or no) government scrutiny, leaving parents to sort out conflicting safety claims. In addition, in recent years new "discount" baby product web sites have failed to live up to their own promises of prompt delivery and customer service.

So, we've gone on a quest to find the best baby products, at prices that won't send you to the poor house. Sure, we've sampled many of these items first hand. But this book is much more than our experiences—we interviewed over 1000 new parents to learn their experiences with products. We also attend juvenile product trade shows to quiz manufacturers and retailers on what's hot and what's not. The insights from retailers are especially helpful, since these folks are on the front lines, seeing which items unhappy parents return.

Our focus is on safety and durability: which items stand up to real world conditions and which don't. Interestingly, we found many products for baby are sold strictly on price . . . and sometimes a great "bargain" broke, fell apart or shrunk after a few uses. Hence, you'll note some of our top recommendations aren't always the lowest in

What you need, when

Yes, buying for baby can seem overwhelming, but there is a silver lining: you don't need ALL this stuff immediately when baby is born. Let's look at what items you need quickly and what you can wait on. This chart indicates usage of certain items for the first 12 months of baby's life:

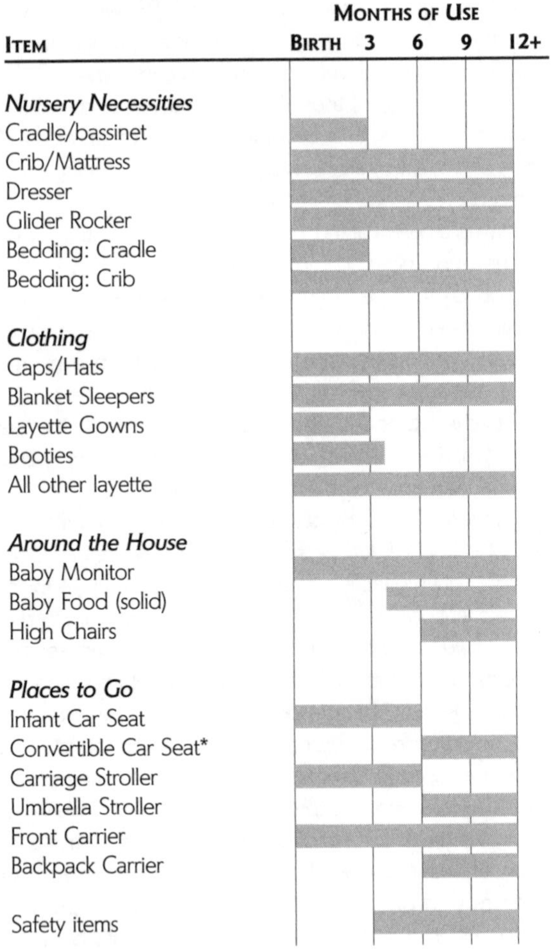
MONTHS OF USE
ITEM
BIRTH
3
6
9
12+
Nursery Necessities
Cradle/bassinet
Crib/Mattress
Dresser
Glider Rocker
Bedding: Cradle
Bedding: Crib
Clothing
Caps/Hats
Blanket Sleepers
Layette Gowns
Booties
All other layette
Around the House
Baby Monitor
Baby Food (solid)
High Chairs
Places to Go
Infant Car Seat
Convertible Car Seat*
Carriage Stroller
Umbrella Stroller
Front Carrier
Backpack Carrier
Safety items

**You can use a convertible car seat starting immediately with that first ride home from the hospital. However, it is our recommendation that you use the infant car seat for the first six months or so, then, when baby grows out of it, buy the convertible car seat.*

price. To be sensitive to those on really tight budgets, we try to identify "good, better and best" bets in different price ranges.

We get questions: the Top 5 Questions & Answers

From the home office here in Boulder, CO, here are the top five questions we get asked here at *Baby Bargains*:

1 DO YOU HAVE A BOOK FOR OLDER CHILDREN? WHY DOESN'T BABY BARGAINS COVER PRODUCTS FOR OLDER CHILDREN LIKE POTTIES, TOYS OR BICYCLES? *Baby Bargains* focuses on products for babies age birth to 2. We did this to a) keep this book from becoming 800 pages long and b) to maintain our sanity. We realize there is a whole universe of products out there that parents buy for older kids. By the time you read this, we hope to have special reports for sale on our web page (www.BabyBargainsBook.com) that focus on such topics as booster seats and other toddler purchases. Meanwhile, the *Baby Bargains* book will continue to focus on the under-two set.

2 HOW DO I KNOW IF I HAVE THE CURRENT EDITION? We strive to keep the *Baby Bargains* as up-to-date as possible. As such, we update it periodically with new editions. But if you just borrowed this book from a friend, how do you know how old it is? First, look at the copyright page. There at the bottom you will see a version number (such as 4.0). The first number (the 4 in this case) means you have the 4th edition. The second number indicates the printing—every time we reprint the book, we make minor corrections, additions and changes. Version 4.0 is the initial printing of the 4th edition, version 4.1 is the first reprint of the fourth edition and so on.

So, how can you tell if your book is current or woefully out of date? Go to our web page at www.BabyBargainsBook.com and click on "Which version?" There we will list what the most current version is. (One clue: look at the book's cover. We note the edition number on each cover. And we change the color of the cover with each edition). We update this book every two years (roughly). About 30% to 40% of the content will change with each edition. Bottom line: if you pick up a copy of this book that is one or two editions old, you will notice a significant number of changes.

3 WHAT IF I SEE A NEW PRODUCT IN STORES? HOW CAN I FIND INFO ON THAT? First, make sure you have the latest edition of *Baby Bargains* (see previous question). If you can't find that product in our latest book, go to our web page at www.BabyBargainsBook.com. There you will find a treasure trove of information. First, check out the "News" section with updates on industry trends and, yes, new products. Second, search the "Reader Mail" section to see if other readers have tried out the product and reported to us on their experiences. If that doesn't work, go to the "Message Boards" and post a query for other parents to respond to. Of course, you can email us with a question as well (see the How to Contact Us page at the back of this book). Be sure to sign up for our "Free E-Newsletter" to get the latest news on our book, web page, product recalls and more. All this can be done from www.BabyBargainsBook.com.

Even though we have a treasure trove of FREE stuff on our web page, please note that we do not post the entire text of *Baby Bargains* online (hey, we have to make a living somehow). If a friend gives you a ten year-old edition of this book, you can't go online and just download all the changes/updates for free. Yes, someday soon, we will probably offer "e-book" versions of our book to download from our web page but there will still be a cost.

4 **I AM LOOKING FOR A SPECIFIC PRODUCT BUT I DON'T KNOW WHERE TO START! HELP!** Yep, this book is 400+ pages long and we realize it can be a bit intimidating. But you have a friend in the ***Index***–flip to the back of the book to look up just about anything. You can look up items by general category, brand name and more.

If that doesn't work, try the Table of Contents. We sort the book into major topic areas (strollers, car seats, etc). In some chapters, we have "also known as" boxes that help you decode brand names that might be associated with other companies (for example, Eddie Bauer car seats are made by Cosco).

Don't forget the handy Telephone/Web Site Directory in the back of the book as well. You can pop to any company's web page to find more details about a product we review in *Baby Bargains*.

5 **WHY DO YOU SOMETIMES RECOMMEND A MORE EXPENSIVE PRODUCT THAN A CHEAPER OPTION?** Yes, this is a book about bargains, but sometimes we will pick a slightly more expensive item in a category if we believe it is superior in quality or safety. Sometimes it makes sense to invest in better-quality products that will last through more than one child. And don't forget about the hassle of replacing a cheap product that breaks in six months.

To be sure, however, we recognize that many folks are on tight budgets. To help, we offer "Good, Better, Best" product suggestions that are typically sorted by price (good is most affordable, best is usually more expensive). Don't torture yourself if you can't afford the "best" in every category; a "good" product will be just as, well, good.

Another note: remember that our brand reviews cover many options in a category, not just the cheapest. Don't be dismayed if we give an expensive brand an "A" rating—such ratings are often based on quality, construction, innovation and more. Yes, we will try to identify the best values in a category as well.

What happens when our advice conflicts with other publications like *Consumer Reports*? See the following box for more on this.

Baby Bargains versus Consumer Reports

First off, let us say right here and now that we are BIG fans of *Consumer Reports* (CR) magazine. The magazine (and now books and web site) are the gold standard of consumer journalism.

That said, we often get deluged with email from readers when CR reviews and rates a baby product category. Many folks ask us why we at *Baby Bargains* sometimes come to different conclusions than *Consumer Reports*.

First, understand that we have different research methods. *Consumer Reports* often lab tests products to make sure they are safe and durable. At *Baby Bargains*, we rely on parent/reader feedback to make our recommendations. Yes, we do hands-on inspections of products and meet with manufacturers at trade shows to demo the latest gear, but the reader feedback loop is our secret sauce.

Not surprisingly, most of the time we actually agree with *Consumer Reports*. In recent articles on strollers in CR and in our book, we both picked the same three of four brands as best. Yet, sometimes there are differences—we might pick a model as a "best bet" that CR thinks is only a second runner-up. And vice versa. We suppose you can chalk up the differences in rating to our research methods.

Another issue: out of date reports. We love CR, but sometimes they are WAY behind when it comes to reviewing baby products. Since they don't focus on baby products, it can be YEARS between reports for certain categories. Models and brands change very quickly in this industry. Trying to compare a five year old report in a CR back issue with a current edition of this book isn't very helpful.

Of course, we don't take everything *Consumer Reports* says as the gospel truth. They (like us) make mistakes; we always try to verify results if CR determines a product is unsafe. In cases where we differ with CR, we'll point that out in our book and on our web site.

Let's Go Shopping!

Now that all the formal introductions are done, let's move on to the good stuff. As your tour guides to BabyLand, we'd like to remind you of a few park rules before you go:

1 **NO FEEDING THE SALESPEOPLE.** Remember, the juvenile products industry is a $5.4 BILLION DOLLAR business. While all those baby stores may want to help you, they are first and foremost in business to make a profit. As a consumer, you should arm yourself with the knowledge necessary to make smart decisions. If you do, you won't be taken for a ride.

2 **KEEP YOUR PERSPECTIVE INSIDE THE VEHICLE AT ALL TIMES.** With all the hormones coursing through the veins of the average pregnant woman, now is not the time to lose it. As you visit baby stores, don't get caught in the hype of the latest doo-dad that converts a car seat to a toaster.

3 **HAVE A GOOD TIME.** Oh sure, sifting through all those catalogs of crib bedding and convertible strollers will frazzle your mind. Just remember the goal is to have a healthy baby–so, take care of yourself first and foremost.

What's New in This Edition?

As usual, we just couldn't leave well enough alone. With the fourth edition of *Baby Bargains*, you'll notice some additions and improvements. First, there is a brand new section on bassinets and cradles, plus a slew of brand new reviews of cribs in Chapter 2, Nursery Necessities.

In Chapter 4 (Reality Layette), there is a new section on mail-order diapers, plus a handy chart that compares the cost of such options. Looking for plus-size maternity clothes? We've beefed up our sources for these items in Chapter 5, Maternity/Nursing.

Chapter 6 (Around the House) includes an update on baby food and monitors, plus the latest research on the safety of walkers and stationary play centers. We also review the latest high chair models in that chapter.

In this new edition, we have split the car seat and stroller chapters into two parts. Now, car seats have their own chapter (7), as do strollers/carriers and other on-the-go gear (chapter 8). Read the latest on new LATCH/ISO-FIX car seats in Chapter 7, along with all the newest infant and convertible models.

This must be the Year of the Jogging Stroller, with a huge collection of new models coming on the market. We'll review many of the options, including the first tandem jogger in Chapter 8. Also new in that chapter: travel system strollers by Peg Perego and other brands that will debut this year. We've also added more to the section on carriers.

In Safety (Chapter 9), you'll notice a brand new section on pool alarms along with beefed up coverage of safety gates. We've updated our list of top gifts and baby announcements with new options and web sites.

Speaking of the web, you'll notice a myriad of new web sites in this edition, from places that sell strollers online to the latest info on car seat compatibility. See Chapter 11 for a run-down of the best web sites, catalogs and other mail-order options.

But that's not all—we also added a killer feature to this book: a sample baby registry. Planning to register at a store like Babies R Us? Now, you can find a sum-up of our ALL recommendations in Appendix B so you can zip through those baby registries. We also have updates for our Canadian readers (Appendix A) and a new section on recommendations for parents of twins (Appendix C).

Of course, we've kept all the things you liked about past editions of *Baby Bargains*. You'll find those handy comparison charts for cribs, strollers, car seats and more—all updated to reflect the latest models. Don't forget the handy phone/web directory in the back of the book. With one glance, you can see the phone numbers and web site addresses for all the companies and contacts we reference in the book (Appendix D).

So, buckle your seat belts and secure all loose items like sunglasses and your sanity. We're off to BabyLand.

CHAPTER 2

Nursery Necessities: Cribs, Dressers & More

How can you save 20% to 50% off cribs, dressers, and other furniture for your baby's room? In this chapter, you'll learn these secrets, plus discover smart shopper tips that help clarify all those confusing crib options and features. Then, you'll learn which juvenile furniture has safety problems and a toll-free number you can call to get the latest recall info. Next, we'll rate and review over 30 top brands of cribs, focusing on quality and value. Finally, you'll learn which crib mattress is best, how to get a deal on a dresser, and several more items to consider for your baby's room.

Getting Started: When Do You Need This Stuff?

So, you want to buy a crib for Junior? And, what the heck, why not some other furniture, like a dresser to store all those baby gifts and a changing table for, well, you know. Just pop down to the store, pick out the colors, and set a delivery date, right?

Not so fast, o' new parental one. Once you get to that baby store, you'll discover that most don't have all those nice cribs and furniture *in stock*. No, that would be too easy, wouldn't it? You will quickly learn that you have to *special order* much of that booty.

To be fair, we should note that in-stock items vary from shop to shop. Some (especially the larger chain stores) may stock a fair number of cribs. Yet Murphy's Law says the last in-stock Millennium Crib with that special chartreuse trim was just sold five minutes ago. And while stores may stock a good number of cribs, dressers are another story—these bulky items almost always must be special-ordered.

Most baby specialty stores told us it takes four to six weeks to order many furniture brands. And here's the shocker: some imported cribs can take 12 to 16 weeks. It's hard to believe that it takes this long for companies to ship a simple crib or dresser—we're not talking space shuttle parts here. The way it's going, you'll soon have to order the crib *before* you conceive.

Obviously, this policy is more for the benefit of the retailer than the consumer. Most baby stores are small operations and they tell us that stocking up on cribs, dressers and the like means an expensive investment in inventory and storage space. Frankly, we could care less. Why you can't get a crib in a week or less is one of the mysteries of modern juvenile product retailing that will have to be left to future generations to solve. What if you don't have that much time? There are a couple of solutions: some stores sell floor models and others actually keep a limited number of styles in stock. Discounters also stock cribs—the only downside is that while the price is low, often so is the quality.

Here's an idea given to us by one new mother: don't buy the crib until *after* the baby is born. The infant can sleep in a bassinet or cradle for the first few weeks or even months, and you can get the furniture later. (This may also be an option for the superstitious who don't want to buy all this stuff until the baby is actually born.) The downside to waiting? The last thing you'll want to do with your newborn infant is go furniture shopping. There will be many other activities (such as sleep deprivation experiments) to occupy your time.

So, when should you make a decision on the crib and other furniture for the baby's room? We recommend you place your order in the sixth or seventh month of your pregnancy. By that time, you're pretty darned sure you're having a baby, and the order will arrive several weeks before the birth. (The exception: if your heart is set on an imported crib, you may have to order in your fourth or fifth month to ensure arrival before Junior is born).

Cribs: Sources to Find

There are five basic sources for finding a crib, each with its own advantages and drawbacks:

1 **BABY SPECIALTY STORES.** Baby specialty stores are pretty self-explanatory—shops that specialize in the retailing of baby furniture, strollers, and accessories. Some also sell clothing, car seats, swings, and so on. Independents come in all sizes: some are small mom and pop stores; others are as large as a chain superstore. Some indie retailers join together in "buying groups" to get volume discounts on items from suppliers—these groups include Baby Express, Baby News and USA Baby stores. On the plus side, specialty stores have a good selection of the best name brands. Generally, you get good service—most stores have knowledgeable staffers (usually the owner or manager) who can answer questions. We also like the extra services, like set-up and delivery. The downside: you often pay for that service with higher prices.

Another bummer: some specialty stores only carry the most expensive brand names. Later, we'll give you some money-saving tips if you want to go this route.

2 THE CHAINS. There are two types of chains that sell baby products: specialty chains like Babies R Us that focus on juvenile products and general discounters like Wal-Mart, Target, and K-Mart that have baby departments. We'll discuss each more in-depth later in this chapter. The selection at chains can vary widely—some carry more premium brands, but most concentrate on mass-market names to appeal to price-conscious shoppers. Service? Fuggedaboutit—often, you'll be lucky to find someone to help you check out, much less answer questions.

3 DEPARTMENT STORES. Traditional department stores like Sears still have baby departments that carry furniture, clothing and equipment. Prices aren't typically as low as the discounters, but occasional sales sometimes bring bargains.

4 THE WEB/MAIL-ORDER CATALOGS. You can mail order many items for baby, but furniture is somewhat tricky. Why? Shipping bulky items like cribs and dressers is prohibitively expensive. There's also the risk of damage from shipping. But that doesn't keep some catalogs from trying: JCPenney (800-222-6161) has a catalog with nursery items and, yes, you can even buy a crib or dresser. Baby product web sites like those reviewed in Chapter 11 and catalogs like Pottery Barn also sell a limited number of cribs. Be careful of exorbitant shipping charges for cribs; one catalog (Eddie Bauer) we noted adds a whopping $125 shipping charge onto a crib that is already $850. Other sites refuse to ship furniture items to Alaska, Hawaii or Canada. As a result of shipping costs and challenges, most mail order catalogs and web sites concentrate more on selling nursery accessories—glider rockers, changing tables, decor, etc. And if you find a crib for sale online, it will usually be for a more obscure brand (like Delta, MIBB, Angel Line or Million Dollar Baby's DaVinci line—all of these are reviewed later in this section).

5 REGULAR FURNITURE STORES. You don't have to go to a "baby store" to buy juvenile furniture. Many regular furniture stores sell name-brand cribs, dressers and other nursery items. Since these stores have frequent sales, you may be able to get a better price than at a juvenile specialty store. On the other hand, the salespeople may not be as knowledgeable about brand and safety issues.

Parents in Cyberspace: What's on the Web?

There are an amazing number of sites out there where you can look at cribs and get safety information. Unfortunately, actually BUYING a crib or dresser online is another matter. As we discussed above, the sheer bulk and weight of furniture typically limits mail-order options to a few peripheral items like glider-rockers, bassinets and the like. Here are the best sites for both buying and info:

Danny Foundation

Web site: www.dannyfoundation.org
What it is: The best source for crib safety info.
What's cool: Founded in 1986, the Danny Foundation's mission is to educate parents about crib dangers and to warn the public about the millions of unsafe cribs still in use or storage. You can read the latest recalls with cribs and portably play yards (which often have a bassinet feature) on the site. Danny Foundation's excellent crib safety checklist is a must read.

◆ **Other sites.** The best selection of Dutailier rocker-gliders and ottomans has to be on ***Baby Catalog*** (www.babycatalog.com), the online offshoot of a Connecticut store and catalog. We love the prices, but the site requires many clicks/scrolls to get pricing and ordering info on the gliders.

The smallish collection of cribs on ***Baby Style*** (www.babystyle.com) does include brand names like Million Dollar Baby/DaVinci and Evenflo. But we were amazed at the prices for the wrought-iron cribs from Corsican that run an eye-popping $1350. On the plus side, we loved the "Themed Nurseries" section on Baby Style. Here the site pairs cribs, bedding, lamps and other décor accessories for a complete look. Very cool . . .even if you don't buy anything the ideas are interesting.

Burlington Coat Factory's ***Baby Depot*** (www.coat.com) has ten different styles of cribs available on their site, all by Delta (see review later). Prices are affordable ($99 to $229) and shipping is reasonable (about $30, depending on the style). But we have been put off by the site's nutty organization that requires you to sift through several menus and sub-menus to actually see products. The selection of other nursery items (dressers, glider-rockers, etc.) is also a bit thin.

As we were going to press, we noticed the ***Pottery Barn Kids*** catalog was planning to launch an "online store" and "design studio" in spring 2001 at www.PotteryBarnKids.com. We review the mail-order catalog later in this chapter; meanwhile, keep an eye out on the web for their new online store, which sounds interesting.

Looking for a comprehensive listing of web sites that sell baby products? Check out Chapter 11 (Etcetera), which has reviews of the biggest baby sites.

What Are You Buying?

While you'll see all kinds of fancy juvenile furniture at baby stores, focus on the items that you really need. First and foremost is a crib, of course. Mattresses are typically sold separately, as you might expect, so you'll need one of those. Another nice item is a dresser or chest to hold clothes, bibs, wash cloths, etc. A changing table is an optional accessory; some parents just use the crib for this (although that can get messy) or buy a combination dresser and changing table. Some dressers have a removable changing table on top, while others have a "flip top": a hinged shelf that folds up when not in use.

So, how much is this going to cost you? Crib prices start at $100 for an inexpensive metal crib at a discounter like Wal-Mart. A hardwood crib by such domestic manufacturers as Simmons or Child Craft (see reviews later in this chapter) starts at about $200 and go up to $500. Import brands (Pali, Ragazzi, Status) can range from $250 to $600. At the top end, designer cribs from posh stores like Bellini and catalogs like Pottery Barn can soar to $700, $800 and more.

Fortunately, mattresses for cribs aren't that expensive. Basic mattresses start at about $50 and go up to $150 for fancy varieties. Later in this chapter, we'll have a special section on mattresses that includes tips on what to buy and how to save money.

Dressers and changing tables (known in the baby business as case pieces) have prices that are all over the board. A basic four-drawer dresser (made from laminated particleboard) sells for $100 to $200, while name brand, all-wood styles run $400 to $600. We've seen five-drawer dressers by the Canadian manufacturer Ragazzi top $750! If you want to go all out, Ragazzi even has an armoire for baby at a whopping $1000+.

If you want a "flip-top" dresser/changing table combination, expect to spend another $50 to $100 over the price of a regular dresser. A better solution may be the "combo" (also called hi-lo) dressers/changers pioneered by Rumble Tuff (see review later this chapter). Such styles run $500 to $600. If you want a separate changing table, expect to spend $85 to $180 for basic styles, and up to $300 for fancy brands.

So, you can see that your quest for a crib, mattress, dresser, and/or changing table could cost you as little as $300 or more than $1000.

More Money Buys You . . .

Here's a little secret most baby stores don't want you to hear: ALL new cribs (no matter what price) sold in the U.S. or Canada must meet federal safety standards. Yes, the governments of both the U.S. and Canada strictly regulate crib safety and features—that's one reason why most cribs look alike, no matter the brand or price. So, whether you buy a $100 crib special at K-Mart or a $700 Italian design at a posh specialty boutique, you are getting a crib that is equally safe.

Now, that said, when you spend more money, you do get some perks. First: double-drop sides (cheaper cribs have only a single drop side). Spend a bit more and you also get an under-crib storage drawer. But the biggest thing you get for more money: styling and a quieter release. The more money you spend, the fancier the crib's design (thicker corner posts, fancy colors, etc.) And more expensive cribs tend to have quieter drop-sides (cheap cribs can be noisy when you raise or lower the side rail).

Safe & Sound

Here's a fact to keep you up at night: cribs are the third-biggest cause of injuries and deaths among all nursery products. In the latest year for which statistics are available, over 10,000 injuries and 35 deaths were blamed on cribs alone. Altogether, nursery equipment and furniture account for over 65,000 injuries serious enough to require emergency room treatment each year.

Now, before you get all excited, let's point out that the vast majority of injuries related to cribs were caused by *old* cribs. Surprisingly, these old cribs may not be as old as you think—some models from the 1970s and early 1980s have caused many injuries and deaths. (Safety standards cribs were first enacted in 1973 and 1976; these rules were revised in 1982). Nearly all *new* cribs sold in the United States meet the current safety standards designed to prevent injuries. In fact, the annual death rate for cribs (35) is dramatically below that in the 1970's, when nearly 200 children died each year from crib hazards.

These facts bring us to our biggest safety tip on cribs:

◆ ***Don't buy a used or old crib.*** Let's put that into bold caps: **DON'T BUY A USED OR OLD CRIB.** And don't take a hand-me-down from a well-meaning friend or relative. Why? Because old cribs can be death traps–spindles that are too far apart, cutouts in the headboard, and other hazards that could entrap your baby. Decorative trim (like turned posts) that look great on adult beds are a major no-no for cribs–they present a strangulation hazard. Other old cribs have lead paint, a dangerous peril for a teething baby.

Another hazard to hand-me-down cribs: missing parts and directions. It only takes one missing screw or bolt to make an otherwise safe crib into a death trap. Without directions, you can assemble the crib wrong and create additional safety hazards. So, even if your friend wants to give/sell you a recent model crib, you could still have problems if parts or directions are missing.

It may seem somewhat ironic that a book on baby bargains would advise you to go out and spend your hard-earned money on a new crib. True, we find great bargains at consignment and second-hand stores. However, you have to draw the line at your baby's safety. Certain items are great deals at these stores–toys and clothes come to mind. However, cribs (and, as you'll read later, car seats) are no-no's, no matter how tempting the bargains. And second hand stores have a spotty record when it comes to selling safe products. A recent report from the CPSC said that two-thirds of all US thrift/second-hand stores sell baby products that have been recalled, banned or do not meet current safety standards (specifically 12% of stores stocked old cribs). Amazingly, federal law does not prohibit the sale of cribs (or other dangerous products like jackets with drawstring hoods, recalled playpens or car seats) at second hand stores.

Readers of the first edition of this book wondered why we didn't put in tips for evaluating old or hand-me-down cribs. The reason is simple: it's hard to tell whether an old crib is dangerous just by looking at it. Cribs don't always have "freshness dates"–some manufacturers don't stamp the date of manufacture on their cribs. Was the crib made before or after the current safety standards went into effect in 1982? Often, you can't tell.

Today's safety regulations are so specific (like the allowable width for spindles) that you just can't judge a crib's safety with a cursory examination. Cribs made before the 1970's might contain lead paint, which is difficult to detect unless you get the crib tested. Another problem: if the brand name is rubbed off, it will be hard to tell if the crib has been involved in a recall. Obtaining replacement parts is also difficult for a no-name crib.

What if a relative insists you should use the "family heirloom" crib? We've spoken to dozens of parents who felt pressured into using an old crib by a well-meaning relative. There's a simple answer: don't do it. As a parent, you sometimes have to make unpopular decisions that are best for your child's safety. This is just the beginning.

◆ ***Cribs with fold-down railings or attached dressers are a major safety hazard.*** Most cribs have a side rail that drops to give you access to an infant. However, a few models have fold-down railings–to gain access to the crib, the upper one-third of the railing is hinged and folds down.

What's the problem? Actually, there are two problems. First, the folding rail can be a pinch point (see Baby's Dream review later in this chapter for details on a recall that addressed this very issue).

The second problem: toddlers can get a foothold on the hinged rail to climb out of the crib, injuring themselves as they fall to the floor. Attached dressers pose a similar problem. Children can climb onto the dresser and then out of the crib. One mother we interviewed was horrified to find her ten month-old infant sitting on top of a four-foot-high dresser one night. (Child Craft still makes one of these models, the 16670 Crib N Bed, although they've been de-emphasizing this product line in recent years).

So what's the appeal of these cribs? Well, manufacturers like Baby's Dream (whose Crib 4 Life has a fold-down rail) say the design lets you easily convert the crib into a youth bed (a small size bed that uses the crib mattress). We say big deal–most children can go directly from a crib to a twin bed, making the "youth" bed an unnecessary item. Another point to remember: if you plan to have subsequent children, you can't use the crib again (because the older child is using its frame for his bed).

And the prices of these items are amazing–most of these crib models sell for $600+. For that kind of money, you can buy a decent (and safe) crib with a normal drop-side release *and* a twin bed. Yet our biggest beef with these products comes down to safety. We urge the Consumer Products Safety Commission to initiate an investigation as to whether cribs with fold-down side rails should be banned.

◆ ***Metal beds.*** Metal cribs are cheap (under $100 retail), but we have safety concerns with these products. First, sloppy welding between parts of the crib can leave sharp edges. Clothing can snag and fingers can get cut. Remember that when your baby starts to stand, she will be all over the crib–chewing on the railing, handling the spindles, and more. We've also noticed that inexpensive metal cribs tend to have inadequate mattress support. In many models, the mattress is held up with cheap vinyl straps.

◆ ***Forget about no-name cribs.*** Many less-than-reputable baby stores import cheap cribs from foreign countries whose standards for baby safety are light years behind the U.S. Why would stores do this? Bigger profits–cheap imports can be marked up big-time and still be sold to unsuspecting parents at prices below name-brand cribs. Take the Baby Furniture Outlet of Marathon, Florida. These scam artists imported cribs and playpens that grossly failed to meet federal safety standards. From the construction to the hardware, the cribs were a disaster waiting to happen. As a result, 19 babies were injured, and the Consumer Products Safety Commission permanently banned the items in 1987. Sold under the "Small Wonders" brand name at the Baby Furniture Outlet (and other outlets nationwide), parents were undoubtedly suckered in by the "outlet" savings of these cheap cribs. Instead of recalling the cribs, the company declared bankruptcy and claimed it couldn't pay to fix the problem. (By the way, this company is not related to Baby Furniture Outlet of Canada, which is mentioned later in this chapter).

There is one exception to our advice to avoid no-name cribs—JCPenney's catalog sells several "private label" cribs that are made exclusively for Penney's and sold under names like Bright Future. Penney's has strict standards that makes these cribs a decent buy, despite their lack of a brand name.

◆ ***Watch out for sharp edges.*** It amazes us that any company today would market a baby furniture item with sharp edges. Yet, there are still some on the market. We've seen changing tables with sharp edges and dressers with dangerous corners. A word to the wise: be sure to check out any nursery item carefully before buying—look in less-than-obvious places, like the bottom edges of a dresser or the under-crib drawer.

◆ ***Be aware of the hazards of putting a baby in an adult bed.*** Co-sleeping (where a baby sleeps in an adult bed) has been linked to 515 deaths of babies from 1990 to 1997, says the Consumer Products Safety Commission. Of those deaths, 23% were reportedly due to a parent rolling on top of the baby while sleeping. Other deaths were caused by strangulation when a child's head became entrapped between a bed and the headboard. We are alarmed by these deaths and urge any parent who is considering co-sleeping to consult with a pediatrician before going forward. (For the record, we should note that a product we recommend later in this book, the Arm's Reach Co-sleeper, is safe since a baby doesn't actually sleep in the adult bed when using this product.)

◆ ***Italian cribs can make bumper tying impossible.*** Those thick corner posts on Italian cribs sure look pretty, but they can create problems—using a bumper pad (a bedding item discussed in the next chapter) on these cribs can be darn near impossible. Why? Many bumper pads have short ties that simply don't fit around thick corner posts. And some Italian cribs (particularly Pali,

Sorelle/C&T, and Bonavita) have side rails that preclude use of many bumper pads. Why? The side rail release mechanism is designed in such a way that you can't move the rail down with a bumper tied to the corner post. So, what's the solution? First, we should note that other cribs with thick corner posts don't have this problem with the side rail—domestic makers like Child Craft/Legacy and Canadian maker Morigeau have bumper-friendly crib designs. Second, there are two bedding companies that have designed bumpers to overcome the Italian problem; bumpers from Judi's and Luv Stuff (reviewed in the next chapter) each work on Italian cribs. Finally, we should note that some Italian crib makers (particularly Pali) have pledged to redesign their cribs in 2001 to fix the problem. (Check with a retailer before you buy to get an update on this). And some folks think bumper pads themselves aren't really necessary, as we'll discuss in the next chapter.

◆ ***When assembling a crib, make sure ALL the bolts and screws are tightened***. A recent report on *Good Morning America* pointed out how dangerous it can be to put your baby in a mis-assembled crib—a child died in a Child Craft crib when he became trapped in a side rail that wasn't properly attached to the crib. How did that happen? The parent didn't tighten the screws that held the side rail to the crib. All cribs (including the Child Craft one here in question) are safe when assembled correctly; just be sure to tighten those screws!

◆ ***Recalls: where to find information***. The U.S. Consumer Product Safety Commission has a toll-free hotline at (800) 638-2772 and web site (www.cpsc.gov) for the latest recall information on cribs and other juvenile items. Both are easy to use—the hotline is a series of recorded voice mail messages that you access by following the prompts. You can also report any potential hazard you've discovered or an injury to your child caused by a product. Write to the U.S. Consumer Products Safety Commission, Washington, D.C. 20207.

Another good source: Toys R Us posts product recall information at the front of their stores. Although they don't sell much in the way of furniture, you will find recall information on a myriad of other products like high chairs, bath seats, and toys.

Finally, consider subscribing to our free e-newsletter. We send out updates on product recalls and other matters to our readers on periodic basis. Go to www.BabyBargainsBook.com and click on "Free Newsletter" to subscribe.

Smart Shopper Tips

Smart Shopper Tip #1

Beware of "Baby Buying Frenzy."

"I went shopping with my friend at a baby store last week, and she just about lost it. She started buying all kinds of fancy accessories and items that didn't seem that necessary. First there was a $50 womb sound generator and finally the $200 Star Trek Diaper Changing Docking Station. There was no stopping her. The salespeople were egging her on–it was quite a sight. Should we have just taken her out back and hosed her down?"

Yes, you probably should have. Your friend has come down with a severe case of what we call Baby Buying Frenzy–that overwhelming emotional tug to buy all kinds of stuff for Junior, especially when Junior is the first child. And baby stores know all about this disease and do their darndest to capitalize on it. Check out this quote from *Juvenile Merchandising* (October 1993) advising salespeople on how to sell to expectant parents: "It's surprising how someone who is making a purchase (for baby) sometimes can be led into a buying frenzy." No kidding. Some stores encourage their staff by giving them bonuses for every additional item sold to a customer. Be wary of stores that try to do this, referred to in the trade as "building the ticket." Remember what you came to buy and don't get caught up in the hype.

Smart Shopper Tip #2

The Art and Science of Selecting the Right Crib.

"How do you evaluate a crib? They all look the same to me. What really makes one different from another?"

Selecting a good crib is more than just picking out the style and finish. You should look under the hood, so to speak. Here are our eight key points to look for when shopping for a crib:

◆ ***Mattress support.*** Look underneath that mattress and see what is holding it up. You might be surprised. Some lower-end cribs use cheap vinyl straps. Others use metal bars. One crib we saw actually had a cardboard deck holding up the mattress–boy, that looked real comfortable for baby. The best option: a set of springs that provide both mattress support and a springy surface to stand on when Junior gets older. Remember, your infant won't just lay there for long. Soon, Junior will be standing up in the crib, jumping up and down, and causing general mayhem.

◆ ***Ease of release.*** At least one side of the crib has a railing that lowers down so you can pick up your baby. There are four types of crib rail releases:

1 **FOOT-BAR.** You release the crib drop side by depressing a foot bar. This used to be the most common rail release type, especially on American-made cribs. But domestic makers Child Craft and Simmons have abandoned the foot-bar in recent years for alternatives like the knee-push (see below). The negatives to the foot-bar seemed to spell its doom—some parents find the foot-bar release awkward, requiring them to balance on one foot while lowering the rail with one hand. Another negative: the foot-bar release requires exposed hardware (rods, springs, etc.) that can be noisy and seems unattractive. While we think there is no safety concerns with the foot-bar release or exposed hardware, Canada has banned the use of the foot bar release. As a result, you'll see less and less of the foot-bar in the market in coming years. Million Dollar Baby and Angel Line (see reviews later) are two of the few hold-outs still using the foot-bar release.

2 **KNEE-PUSH.** By lifting and pushing against the rail with a knee, the drop side releases. We first saw this release on more expensive cribs imported from Europe or Canada, but in recent years nearly all crib makers (both domestic and imported) use this type of release. This is probably the quietest release, although that can vary from maker to maker. Another plus: the hardware is hidden inside the crib posts, so there are no rods and springs like the foot-bar release. We should note that one version of the knee-push (most notably used by Ragazzi) has exposed plastic brackets on the crib posts. The Italian crib makers are more likely to have the completely hidden hardware.

3 **DOUBLE TRIGGER.** This release is used on low-price cribs from makers like Stork Craft and Delta. The drop side is released by simultaneously pulling on two plastic triggers on either side of the rail. Crib makers that use this type of release tout its safety (only an adult can release the rail) and the lack of exposed hardware like that used on foot-bar releases. However, we see two major drawbacks: first, you need two hands to operate the release, not any fun if you have a baby in your arms. Also, the double trigger release uses plastic hardware that can be a problem if you live in a dry climate. Why? The wood posts can shrink, causing the plastic hardware to crack.

4 FOLD DOWN. Rarely used in the market today, the fold-down rail release does what is sounds like—instead of lowering, the rail has a hinge that allows the top portion to fold down. The biggest user of the fold-down release is Baby's Dream. As we'll mention in the review of Baby's Dream later in this chapter, we're not big fans of fold-down rails—we believe the hinge can be a pinch point, as well as an opportunity for larger toddlers to gain a foothold to climb out of the crib.

◆ ***Mattress height adjustment.*** Most cribs have several height levels for the mattress—you use the highest setting when the baby is a newborn. Once she starts pulling up, you adjust the mattress to the lowest level so she won't be able to punt herself over the railing. You have two choices when it comes to this topic: bolt/screws or a hooked bracket. The first system requires you to loosen a bolt or screw that connects a strap to each of the four posts. Then you lower the mattress and screw the bolt back to the post. The only problem with the bolt/screw method: cheap cribs use uncoated bolts that over time can strip the holes on the post, weakening the support system. The bolt/screw is used on cribs with knee-push or double trigger rail releases. The alternative is the hooked brackets—the mattress lays on top of springs, anchored to the crib frame by hooked brackets. Child Craft, Simmons and other makers use this system on their cribs with foot-bar releases. Yet, as we mentioned, those makers are phasing out the foot-bar release and, with it, the hooked bracket hardware.

◆ ***How stable is the crib?*** Go ahead and abuse that crib set up in the baby store. Knock it around. The best cribs are very stable. Unfortunately, cheap models are often the lightest in weight (and hence, tend to wobble). Cribs with a drawer under the mattress are probably the most stable. Unfortunately, all this extra stability comes at a price—models with this feature start at $400 and can go up to $500 or $600. Keep in mind that some cribs may be wobbly because the store set them up incorrectly. Check out the same model at a couple of different stores if you have stability concerns.

◆ ***Check those casters.*** Metal casters are much better than plastic. We also prefer wide casters to those thin, disk-shaped wheels. You'll be wheeling this crib around more than you think—to change the sheets, to move it away from a drafty part of the room, etc. One solution: if you find a good buy on a crib that has cheap casters, you can easily replace them. Hardware stores sell heavy-duty metal casters for $10 to $20—or less.

◆ ***How easy is it to assemble?*** Ask to see those instructions—most stores should have a copy lying around. Make sure they are not in Greek. The worst offenders in the lousy assembly directions department are the importers (from Asia and Europe). Poorly translated directions and incomprehensible illustrations can frustrate even the most diligent parent.

◆ ***Compare the overall safety features of the crib.*** In a section earlier in this book, we discuss crib safety in more detail.

◆ ***Consider other special needs.*** As we noted above, noisy crib railing release mechanisms can be a hassle—and this seems especially so for short people (or, in politically correct terms, the vertically challenged). Why? Taller folks (above 5′ 8″) may be able to place the baby into a crib *without* lowering the side rail (when the mattress is in the highest position). Shorter parents can't reach over the side rail as easily, forcing them to use the release mechanism more often than not. Hence, a quieter release on a more expensive brand might be worth the extra investment.

Disabled parents also may find the foot bar difficult or impossible to operate. In that case, we recommend a crib that has a "lift and push" rail release, described earlier.

Wastes of Money

1 **SURPRISE COSTS WITH "CONVERTIBLE" CRIBS.** Convertible to what, you might ask? Manufacturers pitch these more expensive cribs as a money-saver since they are convertible to "youth beds," which are smaller and narrower than a twin bed. But, guess what? Most kids can go straight from a crib to a regular twin bed with no problem whatsoever. So, the youth bed business is really a joke. Another rip-off: some manufacturers sell cribs that convert to adult-size beds. The catch? You have to pay for a "conversion kit," which will set you back another $30 to $200. And that's on top of the hefty prices ($400 to $600) that many of these models cost initially. (There is good news to report on the price front, though. In the past year or so, several crib makers have rolled out new, lower-price convertible cribs. We'll discuss such models later in this chapter in the manufacturer reviews). Another negative to convertible cribs: if you have more than one child, you'll have to buy another crib, because the older child is using the "convertible" crib frame for their bed.

2 CRADLE. Do you really need one? A newborn infant can sleep in a regular crib just as easily as a cradle. And you'll save a bundle on that bundle of joy—cradles run $100 to $400. Of course, the advantage of having the baby in a cradle is you can keep it in your room for the baby's first few weeks, making midnight (and 2 am and 4 am) feedings more convenient. If you want to go this way, consider a bassinet instead of a cradle (bassinets are baskets set on top of a stand, while cradles are miniature versions of cribs that rock). We priced bassinets at only $40 to $180, much less than cradles. Is it worth the extra money? It's up to you, but our baby slept in his crib from day one, and it worked out just fine. If the distance between your room and the baby's is too far and you'd like to give a bassinet a try, see if you can find one at a consignment or second-hand store. We'll discuss good buys on bassinets later in this chapter.

3 CRIBS WITH "SPECIAL FEATURES." It may be tempting to buy a special crib (like the round cribs from Little Miss Liberty, reviewed later in this chapter), but watch out. A special crib may

E-MAIL FROM THE REAL WORLD

Get all the details on delivery before you mail-order furniture

A mom-to-be in Chicago discovered Sears was a much better deal than JCPenney for her nursery furniture. Here's her story:

"While I was searching for baby furniture, I thought JCPenney's would be a good choice. The catalog gave me a large selection to choose from and it would be less time consuming than hitting all the little shops. So, I put in an order for a crib and mattress and a four-drawer dresser. The prices on the furniture were pretty good (about $150 less than in other stores). However, the furniture has to be shipped directly from the warehouse to your home. Shipping and handling would have been $110 and the shipping company would only drop off the material at the front door—not into the home (or, in our case, a second floor apartment!) I could hardly believe it! If I had to spend over a hundred dollars extra on shipping, I would rather spend it on a higher quality crib and dresser than on shipping and handling. Hence, the search continued.

"So, next I went to Sears where they had the 'Sculptured' series Child Craft crib and the matching flip-top dresser. The prices were reasonable, you could pick the delivery day (including Saturdays) and they would deliver for just $25! They had these items in stock, so we got it in two days. Even if it did have to be shipped from the main warehouse, however, we would still only be charged the $25 fee and would have to wait at most four weeks. Needless to say, we bought the crib and dresser at Sears!"

require additional expenses, such as custom-designed mattresses or bedding. While Little Miss Liberty includes a round foam mattress with every crib it sells, the round bedding is extra . . . prepare to spend as much as $800. And since few companies make bedding for round cribs, your choices are limited. The best advice: make sure you price out the total investment (crib, mattress, bedding) before falling in love with an unusual brand.

4 **CHANGING TABLES.** Separate changing tables are a big waste of money. Don't spend $70 to $200 on a piece of furniture you won't use again after your baby gives up diapers. A better bet: buy a dresser that can do double duty as a changing table. A good example are the hi-low or combo dressers (pioneered by Rumble Tuff, reviewed later in this chapter) which start at $500 (not much more than a regular dresser). Best of all, a hi-low dresser doesn't look like a changing table and can be used as a real piece of furniture as your child grows older. Another solution: buy a dresser with a flip-top changing table. Child Craft makes one for about $340. Other parents we interviewed did away with the changing area altogether—they used a crib, couch or countertop to do diaper changes.

Money Saving Secrets

1 **GO FOR A SINGLE INSTEAD OF A DOUBLE.** Cribs that have a single-drop side are usually less expensive ($50 to $100 cheaper) than those with double-drop sides. Sure, double-drop side cribs are theoretically more versatile (you can take the baby out from either side), but ask yourself if your baby's room is big enough to take advantage of this feature. Most small rooms necessitate that the crib be placed against a wall—a double-drop side crib would then be a tad useless, wouldn't it?

2 **FORGET THE DESIGNER BRANDS.** What do you get for $600 when you buy a fancy crib brand like Bellini or Ragazzi? Safety features that rival the M-1 tank? Exotic wood from Bora Bora? Would it surprise you to learn that these cribs are no different than those that cost $180 to $300? Oh sure, "Italian-designed" Bellini throws in an under-crib drawer for storage and Canadian-import Ragazzi has designer colors. But take a good look at these cribs—except for fancy styling, they are no better than cribs that cost half as much.

3 CONSIDER MAIL ORDER. Say you live in a town that has one baby shop. One baby shop that has sky-high prices. What's the antidote? Try mail order. JCPenney and Sears sell such famous (and quality) name brands as Child Craft and Bassett. Granted, they don't sell them at deep discount prices (you'll find them at regular retail). But this may be more preferable than the price-gouging local store that thinks it has a license from God to overcharge everyone on cribs and juvenile furniture. You can also check the web sites (reviewed earlier in this chapter) for discount quotes on crib and other nursery items. One note of caution: be sure to compare delivery costs and policies. See the box "E-Mail from the Real World" about a story on this subject earlier in this chapter. (One important note: Sears does NOT have a catalog; some Sears stores carry juvenile furniture. You can also buy nursery furniture from Sears.com).

4 SHOP AROUND. We found the same crib priced for $100 less at one store than at a competitor down the street. Use the manufacturers' phone numbers and web sites (printed later in this chapter) to find other dealers in your area for price comparisons. Take the time to visit the competition, and you might be pleasantly surprised to find that the effort will be rewarded.

5 GO NAKED. Naked furniture, that is. We see an increasing number of stores that sell unfinished (or naked) furniture at great prices. Such places even sell the finishing supplies and give you directions (make sure to use a non-toxic finish). The prices are hard to beat. At a local unfinished furniture store, we found a three-drawer pine dresser (23" wide) for $100. while a four drawer dresser (38" wide) was $175. Compare that to baby store prices, which can top $300 to $600 for a similar size dresser. A reader in California e-mailed us with a great bargain find in the Bay Area: "Bus Van" has two locations in San Francisco (900 Battery, 415-981-1405 and 244 Clement 415-752-5353) that sell unfinished furniture. She found a five-drawer dresser in pine for just $109 and other good deals on glider-rockers. Another idea: Million Dollar Baby (see review later in this chapter) is one of the few crib makers to offer unfinished crib models (the Alpha and a Jenny Lind, M0301). While unfinished cribs are somewhat rare, naked furniture stores at least offer affordable alternatives for dressers, bookcases, and more.

6 HEAD TO CANADA. A weak Canadian dollar has created some incredible cross-border bargains. Thanks to NAFTA, it's now even easier to shop in Canada—there are no duties or taxes. The best deals are on juvenile furniture actually made in Canada (as opposed to imported from Asia). If you want to explore this tip, first start by calling a Canadian manufacturer to find the names of both U.S. and Canadian dealers (the numbers/web sites are in our manufacturer review section later in this chapter). Then compare prices over the phone.

What if you don't live near Canada? Can you just call up a Canadian baby shop and have a crib shipped to the US? Well, you *used* to be able to do this about a year ago. Since then, Canadian crib makers have cracked down on this practice, fearing that cross-border shipping was cutting down on their lucrative sales to US baby retailers. (So much for NAFTA—we guess free trade is a one-way street for some Canadian crib makers). As a result, only a few brands (such as Morigeau/Lepine) permit their Canadian retailers to ship across the border. Also, we should note Dutailier (the glider/rocker company reviewed later in this chapter) does permit cross-border shipping; sites such as Baby Furniture Outlet in Canada (800-613-9280, 519-649-2590, www.babyfurnitureoutlet.com), BabyCatalog.com, CribNCarriage.com and Good Night Ben (www.goodnightben.com) sell their rocker-gliders online at great prices. Shipping for a glider-rocker is usually in the $30 to $40 range; the savings usually far outweigh that fee.

7 CHECK OUT REGULAR FURNITURE STORES FOR ROCKERS, DRESSERS, ETC. Think about it—most juvenile furniture looks very similar to regular adult furniture. Rockers, dressers, and bookcases are, well, just rockers, dressers, and bookcases. And don't you wonder if companies slap the word "baby" on an item just to raise the price 20%? To test this theory, we visited a local discount furni-

"Exclusive" cribs hard to shop

When you visit a local baby store and see a particular crib style, you might think you can price shop this furniture online, or at least, at another store across town. But sometimes it isn't that easy. That's because juvenile furniture makers sometimes make "exclusive" cribs and dresser styles for certain groups of baby stores like NINFRA's Baby Express group or the USA Baby stores. These exclusive models aren't sold to other stores or online. In fact, you can't even look them up on a manufacturer's web site. The reason is clear: baby stores know you can't price shop the crib and that means fatter profits for them.

ture store. The prices were incredibly low. A basic three-drawer dresser was $56. Even pine or oak three-drawer dressers were just $129 to $189. The same quality dresser at a baby store by a "juvenile furniture" manufacturer would set you back at least $300, if not twice that. We even saw cribs by such mainstream names as Bassett at decent prices in regular furniture stores. What's the disadvantage to shopping there? Well, if you have to buy the crib and dresser at different places, the colors might not match exactly. But, considering the savings, it might be worth it.

8 **SKIP THE SLEIGH CRIB.** Lots of folks fall in love with the look of a sleigh-style crib which looks like, well, a sleigh. The only problem? Most sleigh cribs have solid foot and headboards. All that extra wood means higher prices, as much as $100 to $300 more than non-sleigh crib styles. If you have your heart set on a sleigh style, look for one that doesn't have solid wood on the ends. Such models sold in the JCPenney's catalog and web site aren't much more than non-sleigh styles.

9 **CONSIDER AN AFFORDABLE CONVERTIBLE CRIB.** Now, we stress the word is "affordable." Earlier in this chapter, we derided most "convertible" cribs for their high prices and expensive conversion kits. But there is good news: several companies have rolled out affordable convertible cribs. Take Child Craft's Crib and Double Bed (36101), for example. For $540, you get a decent crib that converts to a toddler bed and then to a real-size double bed with the addition of simple bed rails. There are no conversion kits to buy; and the design has a true headboard and shorter foot board (many low-end convertible cribs cheat on this point by having the same size head and foot boards). The only quirk to this model–there is no under crib drawer and the side rail is fixed (it doesn't move up or down).

10 **CHECK FOR REBATES.** Some of the companies we review later in this chapter have rebates on products. One good example: Cosco. Their web site (www.coscoinc.com) has an entire page of rebates that include links to an online form you can print out to send in.

Best Buys: Baby Superstores

What a long strange trip it's been.

When we wrote the first edition of this book back in 1993, a new breed of baby stores was emerging: the superstore. With

30,000 or more square feet, these big box stores promised to stock everything a new parent needed, at prices that were below that of specialty stores. Instead of visiting multiple stores and shops to buy for baby, superstores promised one-stop convenience.

There was no shortage of competitors in this category. Baby Superstore was first in the market in 1991 and held sway in the Southeast, with rapid expansion planned nationwide. LiL' Things was launched in Texas in 1993 and quickly spread to California, Arizona and Colorado. KidsSource launched superstores in Florida. Even the big boys got into the act: Toys R Us rolled out "Babies R Us" stores and the Burlington Coat Factory put "Baby Depot" departments in its stores, as well as launching free-standing Totally for Kids stores.

Experts predicted these big box baby stores would steam roll the competition (namely, independent juvenile retailers), blanketing the country with locations selling discount furniture and equipment.

Fast forward to the present day. As it turns out, only one store survived: Babies R Us. Baby Superstore was bought out by Toys R Us in 1996 and absorbed into their Babies R Us operation. LiL' Things went bankrupt and eventually closed all its stores in 1998. Kids Source failed, closing all locations. Burlington Coat Factory scrapped plans to roll out more Totally for Kids stores (though they have increased Baby Depot departments in their regular stores).

What happened? Well, the giants found the baby business tougher than they anticipated. While each failure had its own peculiarities, there was one common thread: not enough profits. You might think selling baby products in a booming economy would be a no-brainer, but the chains discovered a truth about big box retailing–it doesn't help to have a narrow market. Unlike other superstores that sell one product (office supplies, say) to a wide market (small business, big business and everything in between), baby superstores had the opposite strategy–sell a wide range of goods to a narrow market. In the end, there wasn't enough room in the market for more than one superstore concept.

As a consumer, there's no reason to be glum about the demise of these baby superstore concepts. In the place of these bricks-and-mortar discounters has come a new way to save: the Internet. Yes, the web has evolved into a giant discount bazaar, complete with web sites that sell everything from cribs to high chairs, car seats to cloth diapers at bargain prices. The lure of e-commerce hasn't escaped the notice of the big boys either; both Toys R Us and Wal-Mart (among others) have rolled out web sites with online ordering.

And entrepreneurs haven't given up on the baby superstore concept. One of the most promising new entrants into the field is Buy Buy Baby, which is run by the sons of the family that founded the Bed, Bath & Beyond chain. Yes, they only have four locations

(Scarsdale, NY 914-725-9220, Huntington Station, NY 631-425-0404, Rockville, MD 301-984-1122, Paramus, NJ 201-599-1900), but it's possible they may expand. Readers rave about Buy Buy Baby's selection, service and prices, so if there's one near you, check it out. (You can also shop the chain's web site, www.BuyBuyBaby.com, but it only carries a limited selection of items from the store).

Here's a look at the key players that are left in the field:

Babies R Us

To find a store near you, call 888-BABYRUS. Over 100 locations.

What's Cool: We love the selection of this store, which includes everything from diapers to car seats, cribs to clothes. Unlike Toys R Us' puny baby departments, Babies R Us actually carries good-to-better brand names like Peg Perego strollers, Carters clothing and Child Craft cribs. Some of the best buys are their in-house brands for diapers and wipes. What about the rest of the prices? Yes, you can find better deals on the web or at Wal-Mart, but Babies R Us is generally competitive. Overall, the baby registry gets good marks from parents we've interviewed.

Needs work: Did someone say service? Unfortunately, that's not Babies R Us' strong suit. Our reader email is filled with stories of inconsistent service at Babies R Us, and our own personal experiences echo that sentiment. Sometimes we find helpful, friendly salespersons who can give you basic facts about products. On other visits, however, we're lucky to find someone to check us out, much less answer questions. We realize stellar service ain't exactly what made parent Toys R Us famous, but is it too much to ask to have some warm body on the floor with an IQ higher than a rutabaga?

Web: www.babiesrus.com Babies R Us was late to the web, but they've made for lost time with an excellent site that can be searched by category, brand, nursery theme and more. The site doesn't sell many furniture or nursery items online, but we did see a nice selection of high chairs, monitors, car seats and strollers. Each section includes thumbnails of the product, a brief description and (this hard to believe) stock status! The product info pages were very well designed, complete with larger views of the product and even fabric swatches. Best of all, Babies R Us web site lets you tap into their baby registry system–you can view and purchase gifts online. Coming soon, the site promises you will be able to create or even update a registry online. Also unique: BabiesRUs.com has a resource center with a baby name finder, due date calculate, new parents checklist and more. The Safety Corner has tips and advice, as well as a link to product recalls.

Baby Depot (Totally for Kids)

To find a store near you, call 800-444-COAT. 220 locations.

What's Cool: The Burlington Coat Factory has 280 locations, but only 220 have "Baby Depot" departments. The company also operates two free-standing baby stores (one is called Totally For Kids; the other Baby Depot–check their web site at www.coat.com for a store locator, which also tells you which location has what). Baby Depot's strength is their low prices, often lower than competitors like Babies R Us and even Wal-Mart. Yes, a Baby Depot is smaller than a Babies R Us, but we're always amazed at the top-quality brands they sell, including Combi, Peg Perego and Chicco. Baby Depot's furniture selection is also impressive–crib brands include Simmons, Child Craft, Basset, Delta, C&T and Babi Italia. Baby Depot also has added a maternity section and carries a small but decent layette area. New to Baby Depot: a national gift registry that offers a 5% rebate of purchases made for you. And look for Burlington's in store magazine with coupons for select items. And some Entertainment coupon books will have a $10 off deal when you purchase $50 worth of stuff at Baby Depot.

Needs work: "Inconsistent" would be a charitable way to describe the Baby Depot experience. Some Baby Depots have the ambience of a decrepit warehouse, while others are bright and cheerful. Obviously, much of the blame on this can be pinned on parent Burlington Coat Factory, which doesn't seem to have a clue about marketing strategy and hence operates in widely disparate locations (outlet malls, power centers, free standing stores, etc). Our last visit to Baby Depot was disappointing–the drone of the harsh florescent lights was only matched by the apathetic sales help and disorganized aisles. And watch out for Baby Depot's return policy, which is among the worst in North America. Basically, there are no cash refunds–if you buy something that doesn't work or breaks, that's tough. All you get is store credit. As a result of that return policy, we would recommend passing on Baby Depot's gift registry. As a side note, we did have an employee of Baby Depot email us with some "inside" info on the return policy. She told us if you have a miscarriage or stillbirth, Baby Depot will give you a cash refund on returned purchases–but only if you go through their corporate headquarters. Wow, how nice! (See the following email from the real world on the next page for more on Baby Depot's return policy.)

Web: www.coat.com. Burlington's web site has come along way in the last year or so. Besides the standard online store locator, you can shop from several "baby" categories, like Nursery, Baby Travel, Maternity and more. But we still found the site very hard to use–you have to click through numerous menus just to get to something to buy. Shipping costs are also missing on each product page (you have to add the item to your shopping cart to find out this important detail). Another bummer: you can't access your gift registry online to make changes or to see what's been bought.

The Discounters (Target, Wal-Mart, K-Mart)

What's Cool: Any discussion of national stores that sell baby items wouldn't be complete without a mention of the discounters: Target, Wal-Mart, K-Mart and their ilk. In recent years, the discounters have realized one sure-fire way to drive traffic—discount toys and baby stuff in order to get parents to walk by all those high-margin items. As a result, you'll often see formula, diapers and other baby essentials at rock-bottom prices. And there are even better deals on "in-house" brands.

E-MAIL FROM THE REAL WORLD
The world's worst return policy?

Baby Depot's draconian no-cash refund policy draws harsh criticism from our readers:

"Add yet another dissatisfied Baby Depot customer to your list. I was aware of their awful return policy, but somehow, I lost my mind, and we ordered a Simmons crib from them anyway. Four weeks after we ordered, we get a message saying that our order was in at Baby Depot. But when we went to the store to pick it up not only could they not find the crib we had ordered, our order had been listed as "combo unit", not a crib, and had been marked as "picked up" on the same day that we ordered it. So not only did we have to wait for 30 minutes while the lone salesperson in that department searched for our item, we have to find some way to spend $50 of store credit at a store we never want to set foot in again."

"We bought a Century car seat at Baby Depot, got it home, and opened the box only to discover that the wrong car seat was in the box! We took it back to Baby Depot, and were told that we could be issued a store credit, but that's it. They don't give refunds. We were also told the model we wanted has been discontinued. After the rude treatment we received at the store, I am not inclined to purchase anything else there."

A word to the wise: make sure you REALLY want an item before buying it at Baby Depot. And check carefully for any damage (open boxes, confirm the right thing is in the box, etc.) before giving them your money.

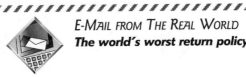

Of all the discounters, we think Target is best. Their baby department is just a notch above Wal-Mart and K-Mart when it comes to brand names and selection. Yes, sometimes Wal-Mart has lower prices—but usually that's on lower-quality brands. Target, by contrast, carries Perego high chairs and a wider selection of products like baby monitors. The best bet: Super Targets, which have expanded baby products sections.

Needs work: If you're looking for premium brand names, forget it. Most discounters only stock the so-called mass-market brands: Graco strollers, Cosco cribs, Gerber sheets, etc. And the baby departments always seem to be in chaos when we visit, with items strewn about hither and yon. K-Mart is probably the worst when it comes to organization; Wal-Mart the best. We like Target's selection (especially of feeding items and baby monitors), but their prices are somewhat higher than Wal-Mart. What about service? Forget it—you are typically on your own.

Web: Each of the major discounters sells baby products online. Here's an overview of each site:

◆ ***WalMart.com:*** This redesigned site is easy to use, complete with a "baby" tab at the entry page. Moving into the Nursery category, we noticed the site had a smattering of furniture, bedding and other products for sale. We like the detailed info for each product, including weight, dimensions, shipping info and more. Yet, in some cases, the brand names for items were omitted. And the selection was quite small—just five bedding patterns? Two infant car seats? We thought WalMart.com could do better than this, although prices were very competitive.

◆ ***Bluelight.com*** is K-Mart's online outpost and it is a winner—we liked the bright graphics and easy navigation. But we were also puzzled by the site's classification system. When we clicked on "Furniture" in the Baby & Toddler section, all we got was a crib light, a step stool and a tape player. Curiously absent was any actual furniture. The selection of other items (notably strollers, carriers and car seats) was better—and we liked the fact that you can sort the items on a page by name, brand or price. The product description pages were very informative, but we would have liked to see shipping info upfront (you have to add items to your shopping cart before finding out about shipping charges).

◆ ***Target.com*** has probably the coolest looking web site of all the discounters—click on the "baby" section and then select from sections like furniture, safety or strollers. Yet, like Bluelight.com, when we clicked on "furniture" we got a nice mix of swings, playpens and other decidedly non-furniture items. On the plus side, we noticed Target.com has a selection of accessories for nurseries, including lamps, an organizer cart and mobiles. Best of all, the sections include large thumbnails of each product with a name and price. The product description pages were good and included dimensions and other shipping info. Again, shipping costs are absent until you add an item to your shopping cart (but Target does give you several shipping options, including rush and express).

Outlets

There may be dozens of outlets that sell kid's clothing, but when it comes to furniture the pickings are slim. In fact, we found just two major manufacturers (Child Craft and Cosco) and two catalogs that have outlets.

One of the biggest outlets is ***Cosco's*** outlet in Indiana. Located in the Prime Outlet Mall in Edinburgh, IN, (812) 526-0860 about 30 minutes south of Indianapolis, the Cosco outlet sells cribs, high chairs, play pens and more. In fact, the store carries nearly every product with the Cosco name on it. Cosco's metal cribs are $79 and up. In general, prices are up to 50% off retail; all the products are new and first-quality. As we mentioned in the Name Game, we're not really wild about their cribs, but their other products are good buys.

Child Craft has a strange arrangement for their outlet stores. First, there is the "official" (and only) Child Craft factory outlet. Then there are two semi-official outlets (blessed by Child Craft) that are

Baby registries disappoint

The Internet age was supposed to make this so easy—just register for gifts at a baby stores and the computers do the rest. Your guests can buy things online and some registries even let you create/change your registry via the web. Sounds so easy? Not so fast. Baby gift registries generate a big number of complaints, judging from our reader email. The gripes: duplicate gifts, out of stock items, backorders and other frustrations. And it doesn't seem to matter the size of the registry—we hear complaints about small retailers' registries and those of the big chains and web sites. (The exception: Buy Buy Baby, mentioned earlier in this section, seems to have figured out how to do it right). We don't know what the problem is here. Perhaps retailers should take their web programmers out back, give them 30 lashes and withhold the Starbucks for a week. Until they can figure out how to work their computer systems, we urge caution with all baby gift registries.

operated by CC dealers in Kentucky and Massachusetts.

First, the official outlet: Child Craft quietly opened this location in Indiana last year to sell their discontinued and overstock furniture. Located 30 minutes south of Indianapolis in Uniontown off I-65 (exit 41, 812-524-1999), the outlet sells only first-quality merchandise including discontinued pieces. While there is little damaged merchandise, some of the pieces are "off color." Prices are discounted 30% to 70%—cribs start at $179 and most are $200 to $400 or so.

A reader who scoped out the outlet for us said she was a little disappointed with the selection (none of the fancier models were in the outlet at the time she visited) but the "prices were terrific." She also pointed out that a nearby Child Craft dealer in Louisville, KY (Kiddie Kastle) was so miffed at the official outlet that they convinced the manufacturer to let them open their own Child Craft Outlet. The ***Kiddie Kastle Warehouse Outlet*** is at a different location than the main store (502-499-9667) and is only open limited hours (mainly Fridays, Saturdays and Sundays—call first). But the deals are great—"the selection is small but there are some very desirable models." She found a cherry sleigh crib (original $600) for just $350. And the same outlet also carries bedding at very good prices.

Live in the Northeast? Check out ***Baby Boudoir,*** a baby store in New Bedford, MA. (800-272-2293, 508-998-2166) that is also authorized by Child Craft to sell their discontinued furniture at wholesale prices or below. Baby Boudoir has 60-75 cribs in stock at any one time at prices that start at $139 and up. The store also carries glider rockers, bedding and other baby products at 30% to 70% off retail.

Pottery Barn Kids has an outlet for their kids catalog in Memphis, TN (901-763-1500). A reader found some good deals there, including a changing table for $99 (regularly $199) and a rocker for $199 (down from $700). The outlet also carries the PBK bedding line at good discounts.

Finally, don't forget that ***JCPenney*** has 15 outlet stores nationwide. The stores carry a wide variety of items, including children's and baby products (always call before you go to confirm selection). Check out the web site Outlet Bound (www.outletbound.com) for a current listing of locations.

The Name Game: Reviews of Selected Manufacturers

Here is a look at some of the best-known brand names for cribs sold in the U.S. and Canada. There are over 100 companies in the

U.S. that manufacture and/or import cribs, but, because of space limitations, we can't review each one. We decided to concentrate on the best and most common brand names. If you've discovered a brand that we didn't review, feel free to share your discovery by calling or emailing us (see our contact info at the end of the book).

How did we evaluate the brands? First, we inspected samples of cribs at stores and juvenile product trade shows. With the help of veteran juvenile furniture retailers, we checked construction, release mechanisms, mattress supports, and overall fit and finish. Yes, we did compare styling among the brands but this was only a minor factor in our ratings (we figure you can decide what looks best for your nursery).

Readers of previous editions have asked us how we assign ratings to these manufacturers–what makes one an "A" vs. "B"? The bottom line is quality *and* value. Sure, anyone can make a high-quality crib for $500 or $800. The trick is getting that price down to $300 or less while maintaining high quality standards. Hence, we gave our highest ratings to manufacturers that make high-quality cribs at prices that don't break the bank.

What about the crib makers who got the lowest ratings? Are their cribs unsafe? No, of course not. ALL new cribs sold in the U.S. and Canada must meet minimum federal safety standards. As we mentioned earlier in this chapter, a $100 crib sold at Wal-Mart today is just as safe as a $700 designer brand sold at a posh boutique. The only difference is styling, features and durability–more expensive cribs have thick wood posts, fancy finishes, features like "hidden hardware" on the rail release, under-crib storage drawers and durability to last through two or more kids.

Ratings here only apply to cribs; many of these manufacturers also make dressers and other furniture pieces. Later in this chapter, we'll discuss our brand recommendations for these items.

Please note: we've included phone numbers and web addresses in this section so you can find a local dealer. These manufacturers do NOT sell directly to the public. Some (but not all) may have catalogs or brochures to send out; others have web sites that feature a selection of their cribs.

The Ratings

A **EXCELLENT**–*our top pick!*
B **GOOD**– *above average quality, prices, and creativity.*
C **FAIR**–*could stand some improvement.*
D **POOR**–*yuck! could stand some major improvement.*

Angel Line *17 Peak Place, Sewell, NJ 08080, Call (800) 889-8158 or (856) 863-8009 for a dealer near you. Web: www.angelline.com* This low priced line offers good quality even though the styling is rather boring. Their entry-level Jenny Lind-style crib sells for $150, but other more contemporary styles are in the $200 to $340 range. Typical of the plain vanilla styling is the Angel II crib with curved headboard and single drop side (all Angel Line models have single drop sides). Available finishes are natural, white, maple, white wash, oak and cherry. As for the quality, we liked the overall construction (they use a spring mattress platform, for example) and large casters. One negative: most of Angel Line's cribs featured exposed rail hardware and a foot-bar rail release mechanism, which most of their competition has abandoned in recent years. On the plus side, Angel Line is one of the few crib brands you can buy online (see the Cyberspace section earlier in this chapter for a list of sites that sell cribs). New this year at Angel Line is an Italian-style line of cribs with hidden hardware on the rail releases and under-crib storage drawers for $350. Angel Line (whose parent is Longwood Forest Products) also makes canopy cribs, changing tables, cradles, rockers and high chairs, all made in Taiwan. The company's detailed web site features extensive info on their cribs (even size and weight), as well as thumbnail pictures of each model (which can be enlarged for viewing). ***Rating: B-***

A.P. Industries *346 St. Joseph Blvd., Laurier Station, Quebec, Canada, Call (800) 463-0145 or (418) 728-2145. Web site: www.apindustries.com* There must be a traffic jam at the U.S./Canadian border somewhere near Vermont, where Quebec-based crib makers are all lined up three miles deep to bring their goods to the U.S. The latest in a long string of Canadian furniture makers to debut in the U.S. is A.P. Industries (also known as Generations). Their stylish cribs and case pieces are available in five styles in nine different collections. All the items are made in Quebec of solid birch (although one collection is made of beech). Sample price: $500 to $600 for a crib with hidden hardware and a knee-push rail release. We thought A.P had the best look of all the Canadian cribs we reviewed, although the rail release does make a rather loud "click" when it is locked into position (at least on one model we tested). Another plus: A.P. makes some very affordable dressers; a reader spied an A.P. hi-low dresser for just $309 at Baby Depot. If you plan to splurge on a crib, this is a good choice. ***Rating: A-***

Baby's Dream *PO Box 579, Buena Vista, GA 31803, Call (800) TEL-CRIB or (912) 649-4404 for a dealer near you. Web: www.babysdream.com* Baby's Dream's claim to fame is their "Crib 4 Life," a design that converts from a crib to a youth bed to a twin bed to an adult bed to, finally, a thermonuclear weapon. Just kidding on that last one. But seriously . . . some parents are fans of these cribs, citing their functionality and stability. Well, they should be stable–weighing in at a whopping 120 pounds, these monsters can't be lifted by mere mortals. And that functionality comes at a price: Baby's Dream "Generations" crib in oak runs a whopping $500 to $700 (depending on the finish). Not bad for all those uses, you think? Hold it–in order to morph the crib into a twin or adult bed, you have to buy a separate "conversion kit." This could set you back another $130. In the end, you've probably spent just as much as, or more than, the cost of a simple crib and twin bed.

Of course, Baby's Dream does make some less expensive models (all of which are made in Georgia). Many styles are in the $300 to $500 range; one reader reported seeing a simpler crib model for $250, with the conversion kit running just $70. But, that crib was in pine, wood that easily nicks and scratches. Hence, we recommend sticking with Baby's Dream's other woods (oak, sycamore, beech).

Safety is another concern with these cribs. While Baby's Dream likes to tout its safety reputation (they're JPMA certified), we have serious concerns about their rail release. Unlike other crib brands that use a rail that drops down, the majority of Baby's Dream cribs use a folding design, where the rail folds down to give you access to the baby. We find this dangerous for two reasons: the risk of finger entrapment and the possibility that an older baby might be able to climb out of the crib. As your baby starts standing up, she can use this extra ledge (the rail's hinge) to get a foothold to climb out. And our fears of finger entrapment were unfortunately verified by the CPSC: in February 1998, the government ordered the recall of 13,000 Generation cribs for this very reason. Baby's Dream received eight reports of babies' fingers being trapped in the rail release's "drop gate," including seven reports of severe lacerations. To correct the problem, Baby's Dream replaced the crib's four small hinges with a piano-style hinge that runs the entire length of the drop gate.

Making matters worse, the CPSC charged that Baby's Dream failed to "timely report defects" with the suspect cribs. To settle those charges, Baby's Dream agreed to pay a $200,000 fine.

So, it's hard for us to recommend this company's cribs. If you go for this style of crib, we suggest the model that doesn't have the fold-down rail (the Eternity, made of beech wood). While we realize many parents will consider this brand because of its convertibility, the hefty initial investment and later "conversion" kit expenses makes this crib no bargain. Finally, the recent recall and CPSC fine against Baby's Dream led us to lower their rating this time out. ***Rating: C+***

Hotel cribs: hazardous at $200 a night?

Sure, your nursery at home is a monument to safety, but what happens when you take that act on the road? Sadly, many hotels are still in the dark ages when it comes to crib safety. A 2000 survey by the CPSC found unsafe cribs in a whopping 80% of hotels and motels checked by inspectors. Even worse: when the CPSC invited hotel chains to join a new safety effort to fix the problem, only the Bass Hotel chain (Inter-Continental, Holiday Inn, Crowne Plaza) agreed to join. That chain pledged to have their staffs inspect all cribs, making sure they meet current safety standards. We urge other hotels to join this effort, as research shows children under age two spend more than seven MILLION nights per year in hotels and motels. And if you find yourself in a hotel with your baby, don't assume the crib you request is safe–check carefully for loose hardware, inadequate size sheets and other problems.

Babi Italia This is a special brand made by Bonavita for chain stores. See the Bonavita review later in this section for more info.

Babies Love by Delta See the review of Delta later in this section.

Bassett *3525 Fairystone Park Hwy, Bassett, VA 24055. Call (540) 629-6000 for a dealer near you. Web: www.bassettfurniture.com* Bassett cribs are sold to chain stores like JCPenney, which features the cribs in their baby catalog. A Bassett crib with solid head and foot boards with wainscot detailing in pine with a single drop side is $350, not a bad value. The quality of these cribs is average–most are made of wood from New Zealand and Australia, although other parts are made in such diverse places as Indonesia and Slovenia. Final assembly is in the U.S. at Bassett's factory in Virginia. Bassett cribs feature exposed crib release hardware (rod and cane) and foot-bar releases, which is a bit behind the times. In recent years, Bassett has launched its own retail stores called "Bassett Furniture Direct." At this writing, there are 45 Bassett stores, with a goal of 200 in the next few years. The stores don't sell cribs, but do carry other juvenile furniture like dressers, bunk beds, twin beds and the like. ***Rating: B-***

Bellini *Call (805) 520-0974, (800) 332-BABY or (516) 234-7716 for a store location near you. Web: www.bellini.com* When Italian cribs were hard to find in the early 1990's, Bellini had the market

JUVENILE
PRODUCTS
MANUFACTURERS
ASSOCIATION

CERTIFIED

THIS MODEL TESTED BY AN
INDEPENDENT LABORATORY
FOR COMPLIANCE TO ASTM
SAFETY STANDARDS

Certifications: Do they really matter?

As you shop for cribs and other products for your baby, you'll no doubt run into "JPMA-Certified" products sporting a special seal. But who is the JPMA and what does its certification mean?

The Juvenile Products Manufacturers Association (JPMA) is a group of over 400 companies that make juvenile products, both in the United States and Canada. Twenty years ago, the group started a testing program to help weed out unsafe products. Instead of turning this into a propaganda effort, they actually enlisted the support of the Consumer Products Safety Commission and the American Society of Testing and Materials to develop standards for products in several categories: carriages/strollers, cribs, play yards, high chairs, safety gates, portable hook-on chairs, and walkers (which we think are dangerous, but more on this later).

Manufacturers must have their product tested in an independent testing lab and, if it passes, they can use the JPMA seal. To the group's credit, the program has been so successful that the JPMA seal carries a good deal of credibility with many parents we interviewed. But does it really mean a product is safe? Well, yes and no.

First, as with any product, you must carefully follow instructions for assembly and use. Second, realize the testing program (and standards) are voluntary. Since certification can cost $10,000 or more, some smaller manufacturers claim they can't afford to test their products.

Furthermore, many Canadian and European manufacturers do not certify their products through the JPMA. They claim that safety standards in Canada and Europe are already more strict than the U.S. or JPMA's rules, so they believe the certification process is unnecessary. Hence, you're more likely to see the JPMA seal on domestically-made cribs from brands like Simmons

One important point to remember: ALL cribs sold in the U.S. must meet government safety standards. Yes, the JPMA certification rules for cribs are slightly stricter than the government's rules, but the difference is negligible. And most of the JPMA's standards for other products (like high chairs, strollers, etc.) are merely labeling requirements. For more info on the JPMA program or to get a list of certified products, you can call (856) 439-0500 or check out their web site at www.jpma.org. A safety brochure (in both English and Spanish) is available online.

to themselves. With 50+ locations (mostly on the East and West coasts), Bellini made a killing selling expensive cribs, furniture and other products to the monied crowds in California and New York. Cribs at Bellini are $500, $600 and more. Yet today you can find Italian cribs with similar styling and features in Babies R Us for a fraction of the Bellini price. Heck, even offerings from Pali and Bonavita look affordable next to Bellini. So, what's the appeal of Bellini today? Fans cite the customer service, but detractors of Bellini say it can be inconsistent (each Bellini is independently owned). Whether the service makes it worth the high prices is up to you, but we find the snob appeal of the chain a turn-off. Another major negative: Bellini uses the outdated double-trigger method for its rail releases. Most crib makers (and especially the Italian crib competition) have long moved to the knee-push rail release. ***Rating: C+***

Berg *(908) 354-5252. Web: www.bergfurniture.com.* In business since 1984, Berg recently branched out into juvenile furniture. The company offers several different crib models. Solid pine cribs (made in Russia) run $349 to $449, while convertible cribs (that convert to twin beds; made in the U.S.) run $649 to $849. That is pricey, but the convertible models do include the conversion kit. Quality is good, although this brand is so new to the juvenile market we don't have much feedback on them yet. We liked the hidden hardware on the knee-push rail releases, but the attached dressers on their "Crib N Beds" were a turn-off (for safety reasons, as we discussed earlier). ***Rating: B***

Bonavita *125 Jackson Ave., Edison, NJ 08837. Call (888) 266-2848 or (732) 346-5150 for a dealer near you. Web site: www.bonavita-cribs.com, www.issi-gallery.com.* Italian importer Bonavita has been expanding in recent years, launching a low-end line called Babi Italia in chain stores like Babies R Us. On the upper-end, the new "Issi" line debuted in 1999 with high-price "architectural" style cribs. In the middle, both style and price-wise, are their "Bonavita" cribs and case pieces. Like all Italian cribs, all Bonavita cribs feature hidden hardware rail releases, solid beechwood construction and undercrib storage drawers (in most models). The basic difference is styling. The simple Babi Italia cribs run $280 to $370, a great buy for the dollar. (Babi Italia is also sold under the name LaJobi in some stores). A step-up in detailing are the Bonavita cribs, which start at $350 and go to $600. Want an Issi crib? Expect to shell out $450 to a cool $1000 for the "Chesterfield," a crib with huge column posts. New this year is a convertible crib in the Bonavita line for $500. While we have to give Bonavita bonus points for style, we thought the Issi cribs were a bit over the top, both design and value-wise (hence the slightly lower rating). The best buys remain the Babi Italia cribs, although the entry-level Bonavita models might be worth the trade-up in price. The quality is good, although Bonavita's release isn't the quietest on the market—that might change in 2001 when the company plans to debut a new drop side release that promises to fix that minor issue. One final caveat to Babi Italia: one reader emailed us about the "pure hell" they experienced trying to assemble a Babi Italia crib, blaming the "millions of parts, fuzzy drawings and unhelpful directions." ***Ratings—Bonavita: A-, Babi Italia: A, Issi: B.***

Bridgeport Cosco makes wood cribs under this name and Jardine. See Jardine for a full review. (See Cosco's review for contact information and web site).

Bright Future *See the JCPenney catalog (800) 222-6161, web: www.jcpenney.com.* This is a private label brand made for JCPenney and imported from Asia. A recent Penney's catalog featured a single drop side crib for $250. The cribs are similar to other low-end brands in quality; on the plus side, the newer models have knee-push release rails and spring mattress supports. The styling is rather plain; don't look for any fancy features like under-crib drawers or cutting-edge looks from Bright Future. On the upside, Penney's cribs have a good reputation for safety and durability. The company dispatches its own representative to suppliers to make sure quality is up to snuff. Yet, you get what you pay for here—a low-end crib at a decent price. You sacrifice things like a spring mattress platform on the older models (a reader who bought a Penney's sleigh crib reported the mattress platform was made of plywood). Nonetheless, this might make a good secondary crib for grandma's house. ***Rating: B-***

C&T International This importer now sells their cribs under the name Sorelle. See their review later in this section.

Child Craft *PO Box 444, Salem, IN 47167. Call (812) 883-3111 for a dealer near you. Web: www.childcraftind.com* Founded in Salem, Indiana in 1910, Child Craft is one of the largest domestic producers of cribs in the U.S. As such, you'll see them everywhere: from chain stores like Babies R Us and Baby Depot to catalogs like JCPenney. For specialty stores, Child Craft markets a separate line of cribs and juvenile furniture called "Legacy" (reviewed separately later in this section). Styling at Child Craft runs the gamut, from traditional low-price models to elaborate canopy and convertible

E-MAIL FROM THE REAL WORLD
IKEA fans love ready-to-assemble furniture

The European furniture superstore with stylish furniture at down-to-earth prices, IKEA has 15 stores in the U.S., most of which are on the East and West Coast (plus Chicago and Houston). For a location near you, call 610-834-0180 or web: www.ikea.com. IKEA has a special baby/kids area called "Children's IKEA", a 5000 square foot area that showcases IKEA's nursery and kid's furniture as well as accessories. While our readers applaud IKEA's prices, they are mixed on the quality. Here's a sampling:

"We outfitted our entire nursery for just $300 at IKEA. The crib was $79, a basic dresser was $110, while the changing tabletop was $50. The beauty of Ikea is that many of the furnishings come flat-packed, ready to take home and assemble yourself—don't fret, though, each piece comes with easy-to-follow, logical instructions. Only drawback: IKEA furniture isn't for traditionalists. Most items are made of beech, wood veneer or laminate and particleboard. Despite this, they are very durable and of high quality."

"IKEA is a great place for changing tables—the model we purchased (Narvik) was $200 and very sturdy. It can be screwed into the wall so it won't tip over if baby decides to climb up the drawers. Another great feature: it has a flip-top shelf."

"We love Ikea but their $79 crib has no drop sides and the mattress height can not be adjusted, so it is a bit of a problem for short parents. Ikea does have a lovely crib with a drop side (double handed mechanism) and adjustable height but it's priced at around $229. They have a nice selection of inexpensive dressers, though."

Another reader wasn't impressed with IKEA's quality:

"We looked at the Ikea crib, as one of your readers did, and found it substandard—plastic hardware, shaky and thin particle board construction. Hard to imagine it even lasting through one baby."

Our advice: before you make a special trip to IKEA, first pre-shop their catalog. The 39 page catalog has a special section on kid's items. IKEA's web site also features children's furniture and accessories. If you browse the catalog or web site before you visit the store, you'll have a better idea of the offerings, prices and styles.

cribs. Child Craft's web site gives you a good overview of several collections. A best buy: style 10171, a simple maple crib with a single-drop side that sells for $200 to $250 or so. Other cribs from this company sell for $250 to $500, depending on the finish. All Child Craft's cribs are made of hard woods like maple and oak and the company has been aggressive in rolling out convertible models recently. The quality is also very good; in the past year, Child Craft has abandoned the noisy foot bar rail release for much quieter knee-push releases with hidden hardware. That eliminated one of our biggest beefs with Child Craft. Yet, the company still hawks a "Crib N Bed" which includes an attached dresser (as you know, we think these are dangerous). On the upside, the new convertible "Millennium Crib" (36101, also called the Crib and Double Bed) is a winner at $599: the crib converts to an attractive double bed without any expensive conversion kits (you just buy standard bed rails). This is probably the best looking convertible crib on the market today (although the honey oak finish is a bit too dark for our tastes; go for the golden oak finish for a better look). A couple final notes on Child Craft: don't forget about Child Craft's outlet stores in Indiana, Kentucky and Massachusetts (see the outlet section earlier in this chapter for details). ***Rating: A-***

Childesigns *Made by Generation 2 Worldwide 113 Anderson Court Suite 1, Dothan, AL 36301. For a dealer near you, call (800) 736-1140 or (334) 792-1144. Web: www.childesigns.com* This company used to be known as Nelson, a low-end crib maker that was always an also-ran in the crib market. Generation 2 has been trying to jump-start their sales in recent years with a combination of fresher styling and hardware improvements. Until recently, the company had two different brand names: Childesigns and Next Generation (each is assembled in Alabama from parts made in Asia). In the last year, the company decided to stick with one brand name (Childesigns) and expand its offerings. In addition to their basic designs which sell for $150 to $250, Childesigns is debuting a $300 crib with a more sculptured design. The company even has a $200 model with an undercrib drawer in solid wood, which is a good deal. All Childesigns cribs have knee-push rail release systems (although you might still see double trigger rail releases on a few older models). The rail release rides in exposed plastic tracks. The company calls this system "Quiet-Glide" and claims the crib rail can be raised or lowered without any squeaks or clanks. Well, we tried it out and though it was quieter than other competitors, it's still not whisper-quiet. On a positive note, all the cribs feature dual-wheeled casters and metal spring mattress supports. The more expensive models have a few more doo-dads (teething rail guards on both sides, a three versus two position mattress height adjustment, etc.). We also like the fact the cribs come pre-assembled. And Childesigns has greatly expanded its case good offerings in the past year, adding solid pine and ramin dressers sold at Wal-Mart and Target. So, we'll give Generation 2 a thumbs-up: this furniture won't win any awards for cutting-edge design, but they are well constructed and represent a decent value. ***Rating: B***

Cosco *2525 State St., Columbus, IN 47201. Call (800) 544-1108 or (812) 372-0141 for a dealer near you. Web: www.coscoinc.com.* Cosco's claim to fame is their very inexpensive metal cribs (one in four cribs sold in the U.S. is a metal crib). Cosco is probably the biggest crib maker in North America, shipping 250,000 cribs each year. One big reason: price. Most Cosco metal cribs sell for $100 to $150, among the lowest prices for a full size crib on the market. But what do you get for that money? Not much, as it turns out. Like most metal cribs, the mattress doesn't rest on a set of springs but instead sits on a series of straps or metal bars, which is inadequate in our opinion. The welding of the joints looks sloppy, and the mattress height adjustment mechanism consists of a metal bar that screws into the side post. The problem? Those screws can strip and the mattress could conceivably disconnect from the frame. Although unrelated to that potential problem, Cosco has suffered three major recalls in recent years. In 1995, the company recalled 190,000 metal cribs when it discovered the spindles of the side rails could loosen and separate from the side rail, creating an entrapment hazard. Then in 1997, Cosco warned consumers to check more than 390,000 cribs manufactured since 1995 that "may have been mis-assembled with the mattress platform being used as a side rail." The CPSC reported "Cosco has received more than 47 reports of cribs being mis-assembled with the mattress platform being used as a side rail, including 27 reports of babies becoming entrapped, resulting in one death." Apparently, the crib's confusing assembly instructions led to the mistake. Yet another child death prompted a third recall by Cosco in 1997—this time, the CPSC found that mattresses Cosco sold with their metal cribs could compress and be pushed between the bars on the crib's platform. Cosco received 12 complaints of mattress compression (where babies slipped between the crib's platform and became entrapped) including one 11 month old baby boy who died after becoming entrapped. As a result of all these safety problems, we cannot recommend Cosco's metal cribs. (We should note Cosco also makes wood cribs under the names Bridgeport, Dorel and Jardine; see Jardine's review later in this section for details). ***Rating: D***

DaVinci *See Million Dollar Baby later in this chapter for contact info.* Da Vinci is the online name for Million Dollar Baby (MDB), reviewed later in this section. We guess Million Dollar Baby uses the different name for its cribs sold online so as to not offend its regular retail stores. Basically, Da Vinci cribs are just a re-packaged version of MDB's cribs–same styles, same finishes. Hence, like MDB, you'll see two price groups of Da Vinci. The lower price ones (under $200) are imported from Asia and feature foot bar releases, and simple styling. The upper-end Da Vinci cribs are similar to MDB's "Reflections" line. Styles like the Leonardo are $400 to $500 and feature knee push rail releases. And despite the Italian sounding name, most of these cribs are NOT made in Italy (a few models are made of Italian parts, but final assembly is in the U.S.). As for quality, we give Da Vinci the same rating as MDB since they are basically the same thing. You can find Da Vinci cribs online at BabyUniverse.com. ***Rating: C+***

Delta *175 Liberty Ave., Brooklyn, NY 11212. Call (718) 385-1000 for a dealer near you. Web: www.deltaenterprise.com.* Imported from Indonesia, Delta (also known as Delta Luv and Babies Love by Delta) is one of the few cribs you can find sold online. We saw Delta cribs on several sites, including Baby Age and Burlington Coat Factory (see Chapter 11 for review of these sites). The prices are sure hard to beat–most Delta cribs sell for $130 to $240. Among the hottest sellers is their convertible crib, the Millennium ($229.95 at Burlington's coat.com). This single-drop side crib converts to a full size bed with headboard and foot board. No, it is not as fancy looking as Child Craft's convertible crib, but, hey, it is half the price. So, what is Delta's quality like? Well, our biggest beef with Delta is the wood platform that form's the crib's base. Delta claims its wood platform is better for baby's back than the more common bed springs you see in other brands, but we remain unconvinced. On the plus side, Delta has eliminated the double trigger rail releases on some of its models; now all cribs will have knee push releases (although the hardware is still exposed). Also good: all Delta cribs feature hardwood construction, heavy-duty furniture-style casters and easy assembly (all models ship pre-assembled from the factory and require no tools to set up). Yes, the styling of Delta is very plain but they have introduced a few models with carved head boards that add a bit more pizzazz to the line. If you decide to go with a Delta crib, leave plenty of time however. The president of one major baby product web site told us Delta is perennially back-ordered, as the company struggles to keep up with production. ***Rating: B-***

Domasido This is a private label brand sold by JCPenney's catalog. See their review later in this chapter.

Co-sleepers

If you can't borrow a bassinet or cradle from a friend, there is an alternative: the Arm's Reach Bedside Co-Sleeper (call 800-954-9353 or a dealer near you; web: www.armsreach.com). This innovative product is essentially a bassinet that attaches to your bed under the mattress and is secured in place. The three-sided co-sleeper is open on the bed side. The result: you can easily reach the baby for feedings without ever leaving your bed, a boon for all mothers but especially those recuperating from Caesarean births. Best of all, the unit converts to a regular playpen when baby gets older (and goes into a regular crib). You can also use the co-sleeper as a diaper changing station. The cost for the basic model? $150 to $190, which is a bit pricey, considering a plain playpen with bassinet feature is about $100 to $120. But the unique design and safety aspect of the Arm's Reach product may make it worth the extra cash layout.

In recent years, Arm's Reach has rolled out several variations on its co-sleeper. The new "Universal" model ($190 to $225) is re-designed to fit futons, platform and European beds. The removable sidebar and new liner can also be positioned at the top level of the play yard to create a four-sided free-standing bassinet.

If you don't like the plastic/metal look of the original Arm's Reach co-sleeper, the company offers several wood models. The "Traditional" co-sleeper runs $250 to $375, depending on the wood, and later converts to an art easel, desk with two shelves or "juvenile couch," which is a nice plus. A simpler "Traditional" model that just converts to a desk and couch (no art easel) sells for $185 to $275. Finally, we should note that Pottery Barn sells a version of the Arm's Reach co-sleeper with a slip cover for a whopping $350. (Watch out, a reader says about the PB version—the cover isn't machine washable!).

If you like the functionality of a co-sleeper but not the look (let's be honest—they are a bit ugly), help is available. Sweet Pea (the bedding maker reviewed in the next chapter) has designed several floor-length covers that fit over the tubular frame of the original co-sleeper. The covers (available in six colors) are machine washable and sell for $60 to $125.

While we like the Arm's Reach Co-Sleeper, let us point out that we are not endorsing the concept of co-sleeping in general. Co-sleeping (where baby sleeps with you in your bed) is a controversial topic that's beyond the scope of this book. Consult your doctor and other parenting books for more pros/cons on co-sleeping.

Dorel Cosco's wood cribs are sold under this name, Bridgeport and Jardine; see the Jardine review later in this chapter for details.

Evenflo *For a dealer near you, call (800) 233-5921. Web: www.evenflo.com.* Evenflo just sells a few crib models, which they inherited from their merger with Gerry a few years back. A basic Jenny Lind style crib is available in white or oak and runs about $120 to $140. We weren't impressed with the quality of the crib, which had a footbar release with exposed hardware. New for 2000, Evenflo plans to debut a new oak model for about $180–again, this didn't impress us much. Evenflo's other major crib product, however, is a winner–a fold-away mini-crib for grandma's house. For $90, you get a basic wood crib with foam mattress that folds flat for storage. ***Rating: C***

Fisher Price This line of cribs is made by Stork Craft, reviewed later in this chapter.

Generation 2 This is the parent company of Childesigns, reviewed earlier in this section.

Golden Baby This crib is imported from Italy by C&T International. This company is reviewed under their main trade name, Sorelle, later in this section. Golden Baby cribs are sold at Babies R Us. Basically, there are very few differences between Golden Baby and Sorelle cribs.

Graco *Rt. 23, Main St., Elverson, PA 19520. For a dealer near you, call (800) 345-4109, (610) 286-5951.* Web: www.gracobaby.com. Graco entered the metal crib market last year with the "4-in-one sleep system" for $199 (in the Penney's catalog and web site). This single-drop side crib (made in China) has a knee push release and converts first into a toddler bed, day bed and finally a twin bed. While there is no conversion kit, the twin bed version only has a headboard (no foot board like other competing models). Although we promised to keep our opinions on crib styling to a minimum in this book, we do have to comment on how Graco's cribs look. They are god awful ugly. The wood trim accent on these crib's head and foot boards gives these models all the panache of the Brady Bunch's wood paneled station wagon. We realize this is Graco's first stab at this market, but we expected a bit more from such a major player as Graco. While we give Graco bonus points for value, the styling of these cribs leaves much to be desired. ***Rating: D+***

Issi This is Bonavita's upper-end line, reviewed earlier in this chapter.

Jardine (See Cosco's review for contact information and web site). Jardine/Bridgeport is the new name for Okla Homer Smith. As readers of past editions might remember, Okla Homer Smith was the troubled crib maker that was spun off by Century to Cosco after Century's merger with Graco. Realizing the crib maker suffered from a deserved black eye in the marketplace for its numerous recalls, Cosco decided to give the brand a makeover. Cosco now markets wood cribs under three names: Bridgeport, Dorel (Cosco's parent name) and Jardine. Bridgeport cribs debuted in 2000 and were priced at $220 to $350; they featured a variety of rail releases (some had knee push releases, while others were double trigger). We weren't that impressed by Bridgeport, but the Jardine (and Dorel) cribs are definitely more promising. Introduced in 2002 at Babies R Us, a typical Jardine crib runs $319 and features sturdy construction and an under-crib drawer. The negatives? The models we saw were pine, a very soft wood prone to scratches. And the knee push hardware is exposed (other cribs in this price range have hidden hardware). Jardine is too new to the market for us to get a read on their durability, so we'll give them a middle rating as we wait for more parent feedback. ***Rating: B***

Jenny Lind This is a generic crib style, not a brand name. We explain what a Jenny Lind crib is in the box below.

Kinderkraft Kinderkraft is only sold in Babies R Us; the brand was inherited by Babies R Us after they bought Baby Superstore (Kinderkraft was Baby Superstore's in-house brand). Kinderkraft's recent offerings didn't impress us much quality-wise (all the cribs are made in Central America). We saw a sleigh style crib for $200 and a "Crib & Double Bed" for $359. The latter had an attached dress-

Who Is Jenny Lind?

You can't shop for cribs and not hear the name "Jenny Lind." Here's an important point to remember: Jenny Lind isn't a brand name; it refers to a particular style of crib. But how did it get this name? Jenny Lind was a popular Swedish soprano living in the 19th century. During her triumphal U.S. tour, it was said that Lind slept in a "spool bed." Hence, cribs that featured turned spindles (which look like stacked spools of thread) became known as Jenny Lind cribs. All this begs the question—what if today we still named juvenile furniture after famous singers? Could we have Britney Spears cribs and Shania Twain dressers? Nah, bad idea.

er which, as you read earlier this chapter, we think is a safety hazard (toddlers can use the dressers to climb out of the crib). We also noticed some quality problems with a Kinderkraft armoire, which had mis-matched doors and a laminate top that was off-color. All in all, very disappointing. ***Rating: C-***

La Jobi This is the parent company for Babi Italia and Bonavita. See their review earlier in this section.

Legacy *See Child Craft for contact and web info.* How do you serve two masters? That's the dilemma faced by crib makers today, who have to keep both independent specialty stores and the giant chains happy. Small baby shops don't want to carry the same crib brands as the chains, who can often under-cut them on price. The solution? Come out with a separate "high end" label that's just sold to specialty stores (no chains allowed). That was the idea behind Legacy, launched by mass-market crib maker Child Craft in 1997. Yet it would be nice if these high-end cribs were actually better (or at least) different from the more pedestrian Child Craft cribs. Perhaps it's just the cynics in us, but these cribs didn't look much different from the stuff Child Craft sells to Babies R Us. Oh, yeah, there are some fancier finishes (cognac or pearwood, anyone?) and a few items that sport that hip Shaker look. But that doesn't justify higher prices Legacy charges ($400 to $750 for a crib, even more for dressers). Yes, there are a few small differences between Legacy and Child Craft. Most Legacy cribs are made in the U.S., although a few

Don't forget our web site, message boards

Does this sound familiar? You're reading this book, see a really cool deal or product and you call the company. "Sorry this number has been disconnected," says the voice on the other end of the phone. Or the web site gives you a dreaded 404 error message. What can you do to get updated info? The answer: go to our web site, www.BabyBargainsBook.com. There we have FREE updates posted on this book. Yes, we always try to get phone numbers and web sites correct–but sometimes we goof or the info changes after we go to press. Go to BabyBargainsBook.com, click on updates and bam! Updates for you. Also: our online message boards let you ask other readers questions about brands, products and more. Share a bargain, get advice or complain to your heart's content.

models are imported from Croatia (Child Craft cribs are made from parts made in Asia and assembled in the U.S.). Unlike Child Craft, most Legacy models have an undercrib drawer . . . but this is made of MDF, not solid wood. (Some of Legacy's upper-end competitors have solid wood drawers). As for the rail releases, both Legacy and Child Craft now use knee-push mechanisms with hidden hardware. So, bottom line, the big difference is between Legacy and Child Craft is styling. Whether you think Legacy is worth the 30% price premium over Child Craft is up to you. Yet, if you don't need the designer colors or look, save your money and buy a Child Craft. It's basically the same thing. ***Rating: B***

Little Miss Liberty *3040 N. Avon St., Burbank, CA 91504. Call (800) RND-CRIB or (310) 281-5400 for a dealer near you. Web: www.crib.com.* Little Miss Liberty has two claims to fame. First, they are one of the very few companies that makes round cribs. Second, they are the only crib maker owned by the wife of the cartoon voice of Shaggy (of Scooby Doo fame). Yes, actress Jean Kasem (who played Loretta Tortelli on "Cheers" and is the wife of Casey "America's Top 40" Kasem) is the driving force behind this company, which took over the country's largest round crib maker a few years ago. The company plays up it's Hollywood connection to the hilt, with Jean dropping celebrity client names (Melanie Griffith, Roseanne) on her many talk show appearances to plug the cribs.

So, what's so special about a round crib, except for its price tag? The company points out that the first cribs commissioned for European royalty were round or oval. In press materials, Jean says "those who want the best cribs favor the rounded shape because they don't restrict the child's view. They can focus on the whole world and they are the center of it." Uh huh.

Well, we can say one thing about Little Miss Liberty—that unrestricted worldview ain't cheap. (Warning: unless you are a dot-com millionaire or Bill Gates, you may be shocked at the following prices). A Little Miss Liberty wood round crib will set you back a cool $1000—and that doesn't include the bedding. Matching bedding sets can add another $500 to $1500 to the price.

Not expensive enough for you? How about a brass or chrome round crib? The "Biker Baby Crib" in chrome is just $3600. Brass will set you back $4400. Of course, you should buy your baby a cradle for those first few weeks. To help with this, Little Miss Liberty offers a "Swang Cradle," hand carved replica of a 16th century design, finished in cherry and gold leaf. Your bargain price today, just $4800.

It's apparent the company realized those prices were a wee bit high for those of us non-Hollywood types and has since introduced a low-price crib model (and bedding). Their new "Dura Crib" is made from molded "poly-plastic" components (the regular round cribs are made of wood) and features a canopy. The price: $570, although we've seen it online at Rainbee.com for $450 and one reader spied it on sale at Baby Depot for $300. The new bedding ("Bedding in a Bag") sells for about $250.

So, is it worth it? Well, we don't buy Little Miss Liberty's argument that round cribs are safer than rectangular ones. We monitor the federal government's reports on injuries caused by juvenile products and see no evidence that rectangular cribs are a problem. So, if you're going to go for a round crib, do it because you like the crib's aesthetics. And save up those pennies–when you add in the bedding, this investment can soar above $1000 quickly. ***Rating: B***

Why do all Italian cribs look alike?

Walk into a baby store to look at Italian cribs and you'll be hard pressed to tell any difference between the Italian brands. Heck, there is rarely *any* difference, except for the finish color. Why is that? First, understand that most Italian cribs are made by just a handful of manufacturers. All these crib makers located in the same region of Italy; in fact, they are clustered right across the street from one another. (Memo to any IRS auditor reading this book: at some point, we will have to take a business trip to Italy to confirm this fact.) Second, while manufacturers like Pali and Bonavita assemble their own cribs, they buy many component pieces (like side rails) from the same supplier. That's why the rail releases on Italian cribs are nearly identical. Finally, consider the wood used to make the cribs–nearly all the manufacturers use 100% Italian beech. (No wonder things look so alike!).

Where this gets confusing is the brand names. Most Italian manufacturers (with the exception of Pali) do not directly export to the U.S. and Canada. They sell their wares to importers like Bellini, Sorelle, Mondi and Bonavita. Then those importers sometimes slap different model names on cribs sold in discount stores or specialty stores (Bonavita's cribs in Babies R Us go under the name Babi Italia; in specialty stores, the same importer has a high-price line called Issi).

That's not to say there are no differences between the Italian crib brands. Often, the importers have different track records for delivery and customer service (we'll note who is better in this chapter). And some importers have been more aggressive than others to target the entry-level price points at stores like Babies R Us. But if you wonder why all the Italian cribs look alike, there's your answer.

MIBB *299 W. 12th St, Suite 16J, New York, NY 10014. Call (212) 279-9222 for a dealer near you.* Italian crib maker MIBB debuted in the U.S. in 1998 with a stylish set of cribs that was impressive. MIBB has been making cribs in Europe for 30 years, but is unknown to most US and Canadian consumers. As for the quality, we found it to be high–on par with other Italian cribs imported by Sorelle (C&T) and Bonavita. All MIBB cribs have knee-push rail releases and hidden hardware; the rail release is among the quietest on the market. Prices for MIBB run $450 to $550 for a crib that is made of solid beech and features an under-crib drawer. That's not a great steal, but we should note that MIBB is sold online at stores like BabyAge.com. So, it's possible you might be able to escape sales tax (although you have to pay shipping–potentially quite expensive). As for parent feedback, most give MIBB passable grades on ease of assembly. The biggest complaint: on one model (The Capri), we read a parent complaint that an "addendum" to the installation instructions required drilling holes in the headboard and foot board! Obviously, that isn't acceptable. And one parent complained to us that the side rail on her MIBB crib became stuck and inoperable. The company agreed to send out free replacement hardware. Those complaints aside, we still think MIBB is a good quality crib brand. ***Rating: B+***

Million Dollar Baby *855 Washington Blvd., Montebello, CA 90640. Call (877)600.6688 or (323) 728-9988 for a dealer near you. Web: www.milliondollarbaby.com* Hong Kong entrepreneur Daniel Fong started Million Dollar Baby (MDB) in 1990 and quickly established it as a successful maker of low-price cribs. The Los Angeles-based company is mostly known for its $99 "Jenny Lind" cribs sold in discount stores. These cribs never really impressed us quality-wise; we spoke with one baby store manager who claimed they've received returns on low-end Million Dollar Baby cribs who's spindles have broken. In recent years, Million Dollar Baby has greatly expanded their offerings to include more upper-end cribs. In 1999, they launched the "Da Vinci" line (see review earlier in this section) that is sold online. Da Vinci is just a version of Million Dollar Baby cribs that are re-packaged to be sold online. New this year is the "Reflections" line of cribs imported from Italy and Poland. These cribs (with prices between $400 and $500) feature knee-push rail release and hidden hardware. That contrasts with the rail release system used in the lower-end MDB cribs–basically, if you spend under $250 on a MDB crib, you will likely get a foot-bar release with exposed rod/cane hardware. And if we had to criticize something with this line it would be this outdated rail release. Most of MDB's competitors have abandoned the foot bar release in recent years, so it's a puzzle why MDB is sticking with it. On the plus side, Million

Dollar Baby does offer crib styles (the Alpha and Jenny Lind) in an unfinished option, which is a boon for parents who want to paint/finish a crib themselves for a small savings. And it's nice that you can actually buy one of MDB's cribs online, which is a rarity. But overall, this line is a disappointment–the styling is somewhat behind the curve. And the lack of convertible models is another missing piece in MDB's puzzle. ***Rating: C+***

Morigeau/Lepine *3025 Washington Rd., McMurray, PA 15317. Call (800) 326-2121 or (724) 941-7475 or (970) 845-7795 for a dealer near you Web: www.morigeau.com* Based in Quebec, Canada, this family-run juvenile furniture company has been in business for over 50 years. Like other Canadian manufacturers, Morigeau/Lepine's specialty is stylish cribs and dressers that look like adult furniture. The quality is impeccable, but you're going to pay for it–cribs run $500 to $700 and a simple dresser can run $600. What do you get for those bucks? Solid wood construction (Morigeau even runs its own sawmill to process the maple and birch it uses in the furniture), drawers with dove-tailed joints and cribs with completely hidden hardware and self-lubricating nylon tracks, which makes Morigeau cribs some of the quietest on the market. Safety-wise, Morigeau's dressers have side-mounted glides with safety stops. We also liked the fact that most of Morigeau's dressers are oversized with 21" deep drawers to give you extra storage. The styling of the line is quite sophisticated–in fact, this is probably the most "adult" looking baby furniture on the market today. We weren't wild about some of the new, darker finishes Morigeau has introduced in the past year, but we think some of the new, oversize pieces (like a large armoire for $2000) were rather amazing in their design. We should note that Morigeau's sister line is "Lepine," a smaller collection of cribs at slightly lower prices (cribs are $450 to $660). All in all, we liked Morigeau–the prices are high, but so is the quality. Perhaps the biggest beef we've heard about Morigeau is their slow delivery; some retailers complain it can take forever to get in special order items. ***Rating: A-***

Pali *For a dealer near you, call (877) 725-4772. Web: www.paliitaly.com* In the last edition of this book, we picked Pali as one of our top crib brands. Unfortunately, Pali didn't exactly live up to our expectations last year. In fact, if it is possible, Pali became simply *too* popular. Pali's production fell so far behind (after a surge of orders) that the company was quoting six MONTHS delivery for cribs at one point. Then, inexplicably, Pali dumped its long-time distributor (R. Levine) in July 2000, opting to set up their own distribution center in Canada. The resulting chaos was stunning–consumers complained about late orders, Pali didn't have a toll-free customer service number for parts and the web site was down for much of last year, which was inexcusable So, what's the current status? Pali has caught up on its deliveries and the new distribution center is online (as is the new web site, which we have to admit is very cool). And the cribs, of course, are still great—all cribs feature knee push rail releases with hidden hardware and solid beechwood construction. Most Pali cribs are in the $400 to $600 range, although one model even tops $800. You won't find Pali sold online or in discount stores; it's only at specialty stores, which means there is only a limited opportunity to price shop this brand. If we had one gripe about Pali's release, it would have to be the visible track inside the rail—other Italian-made cribs have completely hidden tracks. And Pali's release isn't as quiet as other Italian crib makers or even Canadian makers Ragazzi and Morigeau. Pali has pledged to fix these flaws with a new rail release in 2001, but we didn't see that yet at press time. Also new: Pali plans to launch a new high-end line of dressers, imported from Italy (up to now, Pali's case pieces were made in Canada). And there is a new line of Pali mattresses (both foam and coil) made by Jupiter Industries of Canada. So, what's the bottom line on Pali? Great cribs, nutso company. As a result, we've docked Pali half a grade, which considering the events of 2000 is quite charitable. ***Rating: A-***

E-MAIL FROM THE REAL WORLD
Layaway Pitfalls

A mom in Kentucky writes:

"I put a crib and dresser on layaway at a baby store, only to discover the items were later discontinued! The store forced me to buy used floor samples; if not, I would have lost my deposit!"

Layaway sounds like a great idea—you can freeze the price of an item and make small payments each month until it's paid off. Yet, there are many ways that layaway can turn into a consumer nightmare: products can be discontinued, items disappear out of stock rooms and more. Worse yet, some dishonest shop owners (realizing they have a big chunk of your money) may coerce you into completing the deal. If you don't take this substitute product or trashed sample, you can kiss your money good bye. As a result, we do not recommend using layaway. Besides, there's been so little inflation in recent years that "holding a price" doesn't mean much these days. If you feel compelled to use layaway, only do it for a short term (no more than 30 or 60 days). And check refund policies—some stores let you back out of a layaway for a minimal fee (say $5).

Pottery Barn *(800) 430-7373 or www.potterybarnkids.com.* We'll review Pottery Barn in depth later in this chapter in the Do It By Mail section. We should mention that Pottery Barn's cribs are made by Status and Simmons, both brands we review later in this section. Unfortunately, Pottery Barn doesn't say which cribs are made by which manufacturers–a cardinal sin in our view. Why? As a consumer, you should know the brand name of the crib you are purchasing BEFORE you buy it so you can compare safety track records, rail release methods, etc. And watch out for the exorbitant shipping charges Pottery Barn slaps on their cribs–as much as $100 or more, on top of the already high prices. Bottom line: use this catalog for décor items like bedding or lamps and skip the furniture.

Ragazzi *8965 Pascal Gagnon, St. Leonard, Quebec H1P 1Z4. Call (514) 324-7886 for a dealer near you. Web: www.ragazzi.com* Readers of past editions of this book may remember that Ragazzi wasn't our favorite crib brand (to put it charitably). Our biggest beef with Ragazzi was their high prices–many of their cribs sell for $500, $600 or more (although some of our sharp-eyed readers have seen them on sale for $400 or so). You spend that much money and get exposed hardware on the crib rails? Yeah, it is a very quiet release but if you are paying this much money, you'd least expect the Canucks to figure out how to match the Italians for their hidden hardware and styling. (Ragazzi will finally correct this long-standing deficit in 2001 with a new, completely hidden hardware system on their new models). All that said, our position on Ragazzi has softened in recent years. Parents who've bought Ragazzi acknowledge the high prices, but say the quality is worth it–they like the construction and hip styling. Like Morigeau and other Canadian-based crib makers, Ragazzi's styling emphasis is on fancy adult-like looks. Founded by the son of an Italian carpenter, Ragazzi started out in 1972 making TV consoles (of all things), then segued into cribs and juvenile furniture in 1991. The company's "3 child or 15-year warranty" is unique in the industry and we have to admit their web site is very cool. Yet, we still can't get past the snob quotient with this line–we still think the prices are too high. You can buy the same quality crib from Babi Italia, MIBB or Sorelle for at least $100 or $200 less. And those cribs would have completely hidden hardware. ***Rating: B***

Simmons *613 E. Beacon Ave., New London, WI 54961. Call (920) 982-2140 for a dealer near you. Web: www.simmonsjp.com.* Simmons (which also goes under the name Little Folks in some specialty stores and Canada) is one of the largest domestic producers of cribs and juvenile furniture. The Wisconsin-based company was started in 1917 by Thomas Alva Edison to provide wooden cabinets for one of his recent inventions (the phonograph). The company launched infant furniture in 1927. Like their domestic competitor Child Craft, Simmons produces cribs with conservative styling (some would say it's a tad boring). Quality is very good–Simmons uses hardwoods like maple and ash for its products. Like Child Craft, Simmons has abandoned the foot-bar release with exposed hardware in favor of a system it calls "Easy Glide." Now, all the cribs have this knee-push rail release. As far as prices go, we think Simmons is a very good value. We saw Simmons cribs in Baby Depot that started at $240. Other models were $300 to $350. At the top of the line is Simmons Crib N More, a convertible crib that converts into a full bed for $500. That's about what Child Craft charges for their convertible model, although we give the edge to Child Craft on styling. One caveat: Pottery Barn sells Simmons cribs at a major mark-up. One Simmons model we saw was $399 plus $100 shipping in the Pottery Barn Kids catalog–we'd rather buy this crib in stores for just $219. A sleigh-style Simmons crib in PBK's catalog is $800! Bottom line: this company won't win any styling awards, but they offer a good quality crib at a great price. Simmons has a one year warranty on their cribs. ***Rating: A***

Sorelle *170 Roosevelt Place, Palisades Park, NJ 07650. Call (888) 470-1260 or (201) 461-9444. Web: www.sorellefurniture.com for a dealer near you.* Sorelle is the new name for C&T, an Italian importer that has been on the market since 1977. In previous editions of this book, we knocked C&T for their high prices and a 1997 recall for defective side rails. Well, there is some good news. The company has addressed those quality problems and has become much more competitive on price. Now, most models are $250 to $400 retail, which makes them very competitive with other entry-level Italian cribs like Babi Italia. (FYI: Sorelle cribs are sold under the name Golden Baby at Babies R Us). Quality is now above average; all the cribs are made from 100% Italian beech wood, feature knee push rail releases and many have under crib drawers. While the cribs are made in Italy, the cradles are manufactured in Russia and Sorelle's case pieces are made in New York. The only negative we can criticize Sorelle for is their lack of models in the hot convertible crib category. We wish they had more offerings that converted into full size beds. Nevertheless, as a result of the new lower prices and improved quality, we've decided to up the rating for this company. ***Rating: A-***

Status *571 Lepine Ave., Dorval, Quebec, Canada, H9P 2R2 . For a dealer near you, call (514) 631-0788. Web: www,statusfurniture.com* Yet another Canadian juvenile furniture maker that's recently come to the U.S., Status offers several coordinating sets of cribs and dressers. We liked the neo-shaker looks, as well as the French Country motifs. New this year are several sleigh style cribs (six in all). The oversized dressers with bun feet echo similar looks in the adult furniture market. The quality of Status is very good–the cribs use a knee-push rail release and are made from hardwoods like maple and birch. Prices for a crib are $400 to $700. The only disappointment: the rail hardware isn't completely hidden (a plastic track is visible when the rail is in the lower position). Yes, it is similar to Ragazzi's rail release but we weren't impressed by that either. And watch out for some of Status' case pieces. One dresser we noticed was painted MDF (medium density fiberboard) instead of wood. While we liked the styling of this group, we'd rather get solid maple or birch wood instead of MDF at these prices. ***Rating: B+***

Stork Craft *11511 No. 5 Road, Richmond, British Columbia, Canada, V7A4E8. For a dealer near you, call (604) 274-5121. Web: www.storkcraft.com* Unlike other Canadian crib makers that concentrate on the upper-end markets, Stork Craft's cribs are priced for the rest of us. Most are in the $150 to $250 range (although a few reach $400) and are sold in such places as Babies R Us and other chain stores. Manufactured in Mississauga, Ontario (just outside Toronto), Stork Craft has three collections. The entry-level "Fisher Price" brand cribs sell for $129 to $299 and feature very simple styling, painted MDF construction (not solid wood) and wood mattress platforms (no springs). The middle-level cribs (Signature) feature mixed species of wood and a bit more fancy styling (as well as spring mattress platforms). The top-end "Diamond" cribs are solid maple. All Storkcraft cribs now feature knee-push rail release (gone are the foot-bar rail releases with exposed hardware). The hardware on Storkcraft is similar to Ragazzi and Status–the rail release glides up and down on a plastic track. As a result of the new hardware, we've decided to up Stork Craft's rating this year. ***Rating: B***

Tracers *39 Westmoreland Ave., White Plains, NY 10606. Call (914) 686-5725 for a dealer near you.* Tracers cribs are made in Israel and Macedonia (in the former Yugoslavia). The styling mimics that of Italian cribs, but we think the quality isn't quite there. Yes, all Tracers cribs feature knee-push rail releases with hidden hardware (a change from previous years when the hardware was exposed) but we found the rail releases to be quite noisy. Second, the warranty on these cribs (90 days) is among the shortest in the business. We also didn't like the metal straps that hold up the mattress and the side rails that lack teething guards. The prices are also somewhat high: the average Tracers crib sells for $400. Simple models without under-crib drawers are $340, while top-of-the-line styles run $600+. On the plus side, we liked the stability of their cribs. And Tracers dressers (made in Canada) feature solid wood drawers and sides made from 100% beechwood So, it's a mixed review for this brand. And when will Tracers join the rest of the modern world with a web site? ***Rating: C+***

Vermont Precision *249 Professional Dr., Morrisville, VT 05454. For a dealer near you, call (802) 888-7974. Web: www.vtprecision.com* This children's furniture veteran launched a crib line in 1998, winning kudos from our readers. Their handcrafted cribs boast solid wood (maple) construction that exceeds Pali and Ragazzi in quality and stability, according to recent customers we've interviewed. The cribs use the knee-push rail release and all the hardware is concealed. But the prices are steep: a crib from Vermont Precision will set you back $500 to $750. A combo maple and cherry crib this year nears $800. That's a bit disappointing, especially since you don't get an under-crib drawer for storage. But this is really an heirloom-quality piece of furniture, so some readers have felt the high price was worth it. Vermont Precision has limited distribution (about 30 stores nationwide), so it may take searching if you want to check them out. ***Rating: B***

Other crib brands. Besides the major brand names reviewed above, there are a small number of other crib brands out there. Here's a quick overview:

Coriscan Kids (800-421-6247 or 323-587-3101; web: www.corsican.com) is a California-based furniture maker that specializes in wrought iron crib designs. We found the prices ($1000 to $1300) to be hard to swallow, especially since the cribs are just single-drop sides. You can see them on BabyStyle.com.

Cara Mia (800-661-2319; www.caramiafurniture.com) cribs are made in Slovenia of 100% beech wood. We liked the hidden hardware (although a few models have exposed hardware) and optional drawer on most models. Typical price: $399, plus another $70 for the drawer. Cara Mia has good quality and stability.

Mondi (630-953-9519; web: www.mondibaby.com) is the latest Italian import to reach the U.S. Made in Italy by the same factory that turns out Bellini's cribs, Mondi cribs are similar to other Italian models you see on the market (solid beech wood, hidden hardware, under crib storage drawers). Mondi's differences: heavier side rails and more ornate carved headboards. Prices are about $300 to $550.

The recent invasion of Canadian crib companies to the U.S. continues, with several new brands debuting on the market. ***St. Ferinand/Meubles*** (418-428-3746; distributed to the U.S. by P.R.

Baby which also distributes the Mondi brand mentioned above) is a Quebec-based crib maker with three styles of cribs (made of solid birch) that sell for $450 to $500 at stores like Buy Buy Baby (mentioned earlier in this chapter). The hardware of these cribs is similar to Ragazzi. The same can be said for ***E.G. Furniture*** (418-325-2050; web: www.egfurniture.com) and ***Natart*** (819-364-3189; web: www.natartfurniture.com). Both are Quebec-based crib manufacturers that also entered the U.S. market last year—good quality, moderate prices.

Finally, in the Canadian import category, we should note that ***Forever Mine*** (800-356-2742 or 819-297-2000; web: www.forevermine.com) recently debuted their convertible cribs on the market for about $400. We weren't impressed with hinged drop-gate drop side on some of their models, but they are solid maple and made in Quebec. One unique aspect to Forever Mine: they sell direct from their web site. A reader who ordered a convertible crib, three drawer dresser with changing table and a four drawer dresser from Forever Mine was very impressed with the quality and easy of assembly. The best part: the total price was just $845 for all three pieces including shipping.

Readers have emailed us their kudos for Maine-based ***Moosehead*** (207) 997-3621 (web: www.kynd.com/~moosehed) cribs and other juvenile furniture. The company has been in business since 1947, but just started making cribs and other infant items a few years ago. Moosehead has two lines: a Shaker look made of maple and a Mission-style in ash. Prices for a crib are $349 to $499. Moosehead is sold in 200+ stores in the US, but their distribution is somewhat spotty (they are not sold in Canada).

And now for something totally different. Tired of standard cribs that look the same? Check out ***Todd Parr Furniture*** from Fun Time Designs (416-924-0766; web: www.funtimedesigns.com). This new line (sold in the Penney's catalog as well as in stores) features whimsical designs in bold colors from artist Todd Parr. The Rocket Crib ($350) is a good example, with yellow side rails and blue and red headboards. The only caveats to this line: the crib sits lower than other models so there is no drop-side. And all Parr furniture is made of painted MDF (medium density fiberboard), not solid wood. But, hey, at least they are trying to do something different. We liked all the coordinating accessories (changing table, chest, armoire and more).

Along the same lines as Todd Parr, ***Stephanie Anne's*** "Room to Grow" (888-885-6700;www.stephanieanne.com) offers whimsical cribs with pencil post designs and interesting finishes. The company (with two locations in Dallas and Houston) sells its cribs through a catalog for about $785 to $1075, depending on the finish. That's a bit pricey, considering the cribs have exposed hardware (rod and cane) rail releases, but you have to give them bonus points for styling.

Brand Recommendations: Our Picks

Good. On a tight budget? A decent single-drop side crib from domestic makers Child Craft or Simmons is a safe bet. Prices run $200 to $300 for a wood, single-drop side crib with a knee-push release. You can find these cribs in stores like Babies R Us and Baby Depot.

Better. Want to step up a bit in style? Consider the Italian crib lines Babi Italia, Sorelle or Pali. Each features all beechwood construction and hidden hardware rail releases that are a bit quieter than domestic makers. A basic Babi Italia or Sorelle crib is about $300 to $400 and is sold at chain stores like Babies R Us. A slight step up in price is Pali ($400 to $500 for an entry-level model), which is only sold at specialty stores.

Best. How about a convertible crib? Yes, they are more expensive to start with but you are actually getting two products—a crib that later converts into a full-size bed. The best bets here are Child Craft's Millennium Bed (style #36101, also called the Crib N Double Bed) for $599. Simmons offers a similar style (the Crib 'N More, sold in Penney's catalog for $500). If you don't want a convertible crib, consider something from Canadian makers Morigeau or Status. Both make very stylish cribs with undercrib drawers and hidden hardware. These will set you back $500 or so.

Grandma's house. If you need a secondary crib for Grandma's house, consider a small "portable" crib that folds up/away for easy storage. Evenflo's "Fold Away Portable Wood" crib is $90. Delta makes a similar model; we saw it for $100 at Baby Depot recently. What about portable playpens? These can be used as a crib if you are in a pinch; just make sure you are using a new model that isn't a recalled hand-me-down. See Chapter 6 for more on this topic.

Do it by Mail: The Best Mail-Order Sources for Cribs and Baby Furniture

JCPenney

To Order Call: (800) 222-6161. Ask for the catalogs baby and maternity.
Web: www.jcpenney.com
Credit Cards Accepted: MC, VISA, JCPenney, AMEX, Discover.

JCPenney has been selling baby clothes, furniture, and more for over 90 years. Their popular mail-order catalog has two free "mini-

Continued on page 68

CRIB RATINGS

NAME	RATING	COST	WHERE MADE?
ANGEL LINE	B-	$ TO $$	TAIWAN
A.P. INDUSTRIES	A-	$$$	CANADA
BABY'S DREAM	C+	$$ TO $$$	USA
BABI ITALIA	A	$$	ITALY
BASSETT	B-	$$	ASIA/USA
BONAVITA	A-	$$ TO $$$	ITALY
BELLINI	C+	$$$	ITALY
BERG	B	$$ TO $$$	RUSSIA/USA
BRIDGEPORT	C+	$$	USA
BRIGHT FUTURE	B-	$$	ASIA
CHILD CRAFT	A-	$$ TO $$$	ASIA/USA
CHILDESIGNS	B	$ TO $$	ASIA/USA
COSCO	D	$	ASIA
DAVINCI	C+	$ TO $$$	ASIA/USA
DELTA	B-	$ TO $$	ASIA
EVENFLO	C	$	ASIA
GRACO	D+	$	ASIA
KINDERKRAFT	C-	$$	CENTRAL AMERICA
LEGACY	B	$$$	CROATIA/USA
LITTLE MISS LIBERTY	B	$$ TO $$$	USA
MILLION $ BABY	C+	$ TO $$$	ASIA/USA
MIBB	B+	$$$	ITALY
MORIGEAU/LEPINE	A-	$$$	CANADA
PALI	A-	$$$	ITALY
RAGAZZI	B	$$$	CANADA
SIMMONS	A	$$ TO $$$	USA
SORELLE	A-	$$ TO $$$	ITALY
STATUS	B+	$$$	CANADA
STORK CRAFT	B	$ TO $$	CANADA
TRACERS	C+	$$ TO $$$	ISRAEL/MACEDONIA
VERMONT PRECISION	B	$$$	USA

KEY

RATING: Our opinion of the manufacturer's quality and value.

COST: $=under $200, $$=$200-400, $$$=over $400.

WHERE MADE? Where the cribs parts are made; in many cases, final assembly may be in the US. In those cases, we note the country of origin as "Asia/USA."

RELEASE: How does the crib drop-side release? For a discussion of the different releases, see the section earlier in this chapter. Note that the release type may vary by model within the same manufacturer's line.

HARDWARE: This refers to the hardware that operates the crib drop-side, whether it is concealed or exposed.

NURSERY NECESSITIES

Release	Hardware	Stability	Warranty
Foot-bar**	Exposed	Average	6 months
Knee-push	Hidden	Excellent	1 year
Fold-down*	Hidden	Excellent	1 year
Knee-push	Hidden	Excellent	1 year
Foot-bar	Exposed	Average	1 year
Knee-push	Hidden	Excellent	1 year
Double trigger	Hidden	Excellent	None
Knee-push	Hidden	Good	1 year
Foot-bar/Knee-push	Exposed	Average	1 year
Foot-bar/Knee-push	Exposed	Average	Lifetime
Knee-push	Hidden	Good	None
Knee-push	Hidden	Average	2 years
Knee-push	Exposed	Average	1 year
Foot-bar/Knee-push**	Varies	Average	15 years
Knee-push	Exposed	Average	1 year
Foot-bar	Exposed	Average	1 year
Knee-push	Exposed	Average	1 year
Knee-push	Exposed	Average	1 year
Knee-push	Hidden	Excellent	None
Double-trigger	Exposed	Good	30 days
Foot-bar/Knee-push**	Varies	Average	15 years
Knee-push	Hidden	Excellent	Lifetime
Knee-push	Hidden	Excellent	1 year
Knee-push	Hidden	Excellent	6 months
Knee-push	Hidden	Excellent	15 years
Knee-push	Hidden	Good	1 year
Knee-push	Hidden	Good	None
Knee-push	Hidden	Good	Lifetime
Knee-push	Hidden	Average	1 year
Knee-push	Hidden	Excellent	90 days
Knee-push	Hidden	Excellent	1 year

Stability: Our opinion of a crib's stability based on hands-on inspection. "Average" is the lowest rating; "good" is better and "excellent" is tops.

Warranty: Some companies don't have written warranties. Several crib makers (Simmons, Vermont Precision and Bellini) told us they "stand behind their cribs and will replace parts if they break," but that's not in writing and there are no time guidelines. Our position: if it isn't in writing, there is no warranty.

**While most of Baby's Dream models have a fold-down rail release, a few have the knee-push drop-sides.*

*** These lines have cribs with foot-bar rail release/exposed hardware; a few models also feature knee-push releases and concealed hardware.*

catalogs" that should be of particular interest to parents-to-be.

"The Baby Book" is Penney's main juvenile furniture catalog, with over 50 pages of cribs, bedding, mattresses, safety items, car seats, strollers, swings, and even a few pages of baby clothes. The crib section features such famous brand names as Child Craft, Simmons, Bassett and more. Basic wood cribs from name brands start at about $250, although convertible models can top $500. If you buy a mattress, Penney's will discount the crib by $15.

We should also note that Penney's sells their own private label cribs under the name Bright Future. (Sometimes, Penney's catalog doesn't delineate a brand name for their in-house cribs. One clue: the catalog will just say the crib is imported from Indonesia). Many readers have asked us about these cribs. Here's our take: Penney's has an excellent safety track record for their in-house cribs. While the cribs are made in Asia and imported to the U.S., Penney's strict safety standards make them comparable to cribs made in the U.S. and Canada.

All of Penney's catalog is also available online at Penney's web site. We found the site easy to use, but you did have to click several times to get to their baby/children's section. And the descriptions of the products could be beefed up a bit. But, overall, the web site functions just fine.

Overall, prices in the Penney's catalog aren't discounted—but since most of the brands Penney's carries are affordable to begin with, we find the catalog to be a decent value. If you live in a remote area of the U.S. or Canada with few or no baby stores, however, this catalog might be a savior.

POTTERY BARN KIDS

To order call: (800) 430-7373.
Web: www.potterybarnkids.com
Credit Cards: American Express, VISA, Mastercard

You've got to give Pottery Barn credit for their excellent kid's catalog—it's rare that one catalog can actually influence an entire industry. But that's exactly what happened when this smartly designed book landed in parents' mailboxes two years ago—the "Pottery Barn" look suddenly spread from mail-order to baby stores and beyond. Even Penney's has been trying to make their baby catalog more hip in response to PBK.

So, what's all the fuss about? PBK smartly mixes hip looks (patchwork quilts; denim accents) with upscale furniture and accessories to create contemporary layouts that don't scream "baby."

The best bets: those cute rugs, lamps and other accessories. And we generally found the bedding to be high quality (see review in the next chapter). But what about the furniture? Grossly overpriced, we're sad to say. As we mentioned earlier in this chapter, the cribs Pottery Barn sells are good brands (Status, Simmons, etc.). But the prices! What are these guys thinking? A sleigh crib for $800? Plus $100 shipping? The huge mark-ups on these items are obscene. Our advice: go buy a Status or Simmons crib in a regular baby store, pay retail and still save 30% over this catalog.

So, it's a mixed review for PBK–love the looks, but the furniture is a no go. Use this catalog as design inspiration for your nursery, even if you decided to buy items elsewhere. And we wish PBK didn't have to be so secretive as to who makes their cribs–we noticed the catalog omits any details on this and operators refuse to say when asked.

(One note: PotteryBarnKids.com was under construction when we went to press, but it should be online by the time you read this).

Other catalogs. *Ethan Allen* has jumped into the kid's market with their EAKid's catalog (1-888-EAHELP1; web: www.ethanallen.com). We loved the catalog (which is available in any of their 300 stores nationwide), although the prices are a bit steep–$700 to $900 for a basic crib? We don't think so.

A few other catalogs also sell an occasional cribs and nursery furniture, including ***Eddie Bauer*** (see review in Chapter 3 for contact info). Like Pottery Barn, however, we found these catalogs better for soft goods (bedding) and accessories instead of furniture.

Finally, a reader recommended a source for dressers from Canada: ***Mother Hubbard's Cupboard*** (416) 661-8201. This Toronto-based furniture maker offers a four drawer dresser for $377 and an armoire for $599; quality is very good. The reader was especially pleased that the Mother Hubbard dresser she was considering matched her crib's finish.

Bassinets/Cradles

A newborn infant can immediately sleep in a full size crib, but some parents like the convenience of bassinets or cradles to use for the first few weeks. Why? These smaller baby beds can be kept in the parent's bedroom, making for convenient midnight feedings especially if the baby's room is not next door.

What's the difference between a bassinet and a cradle? Although most stores use the terms interchangeably, we think of bassinets as small baskets that are typically put onto a stationery stand. Cradles, on the other hand, are typically made of wood and rock back and forth.

A third category of bassinets/cradles are "Moses baskets," basically woven baskets with handles that you can use to carry a newborn from room to room. (A web site with a good selection of Moses baskets is Babies Boutique, www.babiesboutique.com).

As for prices, we noticed a Badger Basket bassinet (a rather common brand, www.badgerbasket.com) runs about $40 at Babies R Us, but that price doesn't include the "soft goods" (sheets, liners, skirts and hoods). Models that include soft goods typically run closer to $90 and up to $180. Cradles, on the other hand, run about $100 to $400 but don't need that many soft goods (just a mattress, which is usually included, and a sheet, which is not). Moses baskets run $100 to $250.

So, which should you buy? We say neither. As we mentioned at the beginning of this section, a newborn will do just fine in a full-size crib. If you need the convenience of a bassinet, we'd suggest skipping the ones you see in chain stores. Why? Most are very poorly made (stapled together cardboard sheets, etc) and won't last for more than one child. One reader said the sheets with her chain store-bought bassinet "were falling apart at the seams even before it went into the wash" for the first time. And the function of these products is somewhat questionable. For example, the use of a Moses basket, while pretty to look at, can be easily duplicated by an infant car seat carrier, which most folks buy anyway.

Instead, we suggest you get a portable playpen with a bassinet feature. We'll review specific models of playpens in Chapter 6, but basic choices like the Graco Pak 'N Play run $100 to $130 in most stores. The bassinet feature in most playpens (basically, a small insert that creates a small bed area at the top of the playpen) can be used up to 15 pounds, which is about all most folks would need. Then, you simply remove the bassinet attachment and voila! You have a standard size playpen. Since many parents get a playpen anyway, going for a model that has a bassinet attachment doesn't add much to the cost and eliminates the separate $100 to $200 expense. (See the next chapter for a discussion of bassinet sheets).

Of course, you can also go for the Arm's Reach Co-Sleeper (reviewed earlier in this chapter) as an alternative to the bassinet as well.

Mattresses

Now that you've just spent several hundred dollars on a crib, you're done, right? Wrong. Despite their hefty price tags, most cribs don't come with mattresses. So, here's our guide to buying the best quality mattress for the lowest price.

Safe & Sound

Babies don't have the muscle strength to lift their heads up when put face-down into soft or fluffy bedding—some have suffocated as a result. The best defense: buy a firm mattress (foam or coil) and DO NOT place your baby face down in soft, thick quilts, wool blankets, pillows, or toys. (Futon mattresses are also a no-no). Never put the baby down on a vinyl mattress without a cover or sheet since vinyl can also contribute to suffocation. In addition, you should know that several studies into the causes of Sudden Infant Death Syndrome (SIDS) have found that a too-soft sleep surface (such as the items listed above) and environmental factors (a too-hot room, cigarette smoke) are related to crib death, though exactly how has yet to be determined. Experts therefore advise against letting infants sleep on a too-soft surface. Another important tip: make sure you put your baby to sleep on her back. Studies suggest that babies who are put to sleep on their stomachs have an increased risk of SIDS.

Another point to remember: while mattresses come in a standard size for a full-size crib, the depth can vary from maker to maker. Some mattresses are just four inches deep; others are six. Some sheets won't fit the six-inch thick mattresses; it's unsafe to use a sheet that doesn't snuggly fit OVER the corner of a mattress and tuck beneath it.

Smart Shopper Tips

Smart Shopper Tip #1
Foam or Coil?

"It seems the choice for a crib mattress comes down to foam or coil? Which is better? Does it matter?"

Yes, it does matter. After researching this issue, we've come down on the foam side of the debate. Why? Foam mattresses are lighter than those with coils, making it easier to change the sheets in the middle of the night when Junior reenacts the Great Flood in his crib. Foam mattresses typically weigh less than five pounds, while coil mattresses can top 20 pounds! Another plus: foam mattresses are less expensive, usually less than $100. Coil mattresses can top out at $150.

We get quite a few calls from readers on this issue. Many baby stores only sell coil mattresses, claiming that coil is superior to foam. One salesperson even told a parent that foam mattresses aren't safe for babies older than six months. Please. We've consulted with pediatricians and industry experts on this issue and have come to the conclusion that the best course is to choose a *firm* mattress for baby—it doesn't matter whether it's a firm coil mattress or a firm foam one. We suspect some stores only sell coil because they can get fatter profit margins from such items.

Bottom line: foam mattresses can be hard to find. As a result, we'll recommend mattresses in both the coil and foam categories just in case the baby stores near you only stocks coil.

Smart Shopper Tip #2

Coil Overkill and Cheap Foam Mattresses

"How do you tell a cheap-quality coil mattress from a better one? How about foam mattresses—what makes one better than the next?"

Evaluating different crib mattresses isn't easy. Even the cheap ones claim they are "firm" and comparing apples to apples is difficult. When it comes to coil mattresses, the number of coils seems like a good way to compare them, but even that can be deceiving. For example, is a 150-coil mattress better than an 80-coil mattress?

Well, yes and no. While an 80-coil mattress probably won't be as firm as one with 150 coils, it's important to remember that a large number of coils does not necessarily mean the mattress is superior. Factors such as the wire gauge, number of turns per coil and the temper of the wire contribute to the firmness, durability and strength of the mattress. Unfortunately, most mattresses only note the coil count (and no other details). Hence, the best bet would be to buy a good brand that has a solid quality reputation (we'll recommend specific choices after this section).

What about foam mattresses? The cheapest foam mattresses are made of low-density foam (about .9 pounds per cubic foot). The better foam mattresses are high-density with 1.5 pounds per cubic foot. Easy for us to say, right? Once again, foam mattresses don't list density on their packaging, leaving consumers to wonder whether they're getting high or low density. As with coil mattresses, you have to rely on a reputable brand name to get a good foam mattress (see the next section for more details).

One good, basic test for crib mattresses firmness: take the mattress between your two hands and push your hands together. Okay, that sounds silly but you'll notice some differences in firmness right off the bat.

Sleep positioners and special mattresses: Helpful products or SIDS scare tactic?

The baby products industry is good at churning out products that pray on parents' fears. Case in point: the "sleep positioner." Most parents have heard the warnings about Sudden Infant Death Syndrome (SIDS), which claims about 3000 lives a year. SIDS is a real danger and safety advocates have done a good job explaining to parents how to lessen its occurrence; yet the baby products industry sometimes can't stop itself sometimes from creating "helpful" products that are, at the least, a waste of money and at their worst, dangerous frauds.

On the waste of money end are the "sleep positioners." SIDS advocates recommend putting babies to sleep on their backs as a proven way to reduce SIDS. Between 1992 to 1998, the number of babies placed their stomachs to sleep plunged from 70% to 21%. This corresponded with a reduction in the death rate from SIDS by 38% in the same years. To "help" parents put babies to sleep on their backs, the baby product industry has come out with "sleep positioners," basically foam blocks that sell for $10 to $15.

Do babies really need sleep positioners? No, most babies that are put on their backs to sleep will stay there throughout the night. Most infants simply don't have the muscle strength to roll over yet. And if baby does start rolling over, you can use a low-tech solution to keep them on their backs: rolled up towels. Two small rolled up towels (placed below the waist) will do the trick at no cost.

Last year, a host of "SIDS prevention" products were recalled by the CPSC. Turns out many of these "breathable mattresses" and other contraptions simply didn't work. Worse still, parents who used such devices might have been lulled into a false sense of security about SIDS, perhaps even putting baby to sleep on her stomach.

The only SIDS product tested that actually worked was the Halo Crib Mattress (218-525-5158; web: www.halosleep.com). This mattress has a small built-in fan that quietly re-circulates air around a baby. Cost: about $200.

Readers who bought the Halo Mattress praise it overall, although with some caveats. One reader pointed out that you should be certain your crib is large enough for the mattress, since it is not as flexible as regular mattresses (apparently the first crib she bought didn't work). "The mattress is much quieter than we though it would be," she said, but the bumper pad that comes with the mattress should be skipped (it makes the sheets harder to put on). A couple of readers complained that the company didn't promptly answer its emails. That aside, the product is a winner overall.

For more information about SIDS check out the excellent web site for the SIDS Alliance (www.SidsAlliance.org).

Smart Shopper Tip #3

Flatulent foam mattresses?

"I read on the 'net that some foam mattresses have an out-gassing problem. Is this true?"

We've noticed that several eco-catalogs have raised concerns that standard crib mattresses are a possible health hazard. One even went on to say that such mattresses are "unhealthy combinations of artificial foams, fluorocarbons, synthetic fibers and formaldehyde, all materials that give off toxic fumes." The solution? Buy *their* organic cotton crib mattress for a whopping $650 and your baby won't have to breathe that nasty stuff.

Hold it. We checked with pediatricians and industry experts and found no evidence that such a problem exists. While it is possible that a foam or coil mattress might give off a few vapors when you first take it out of the packaging, there's no ongoing fume problem in our opinion. There are also no medical studies linking, say, lower SAT scores to kids who slept on foam mattresses as babies. While it is possible that a few children who have extreme chemical sensitivities might do better on "organic" mattresses, it's doubtful such products will make any difference to the vast majority of infants. We think it's irresponsible of such eco-crusaders to raise bogus issues intended to scare parents without providing corresponding proof of their claims.

Top Picks: Brand Recommendations

When it comes to mattresses, it's best not to scrimp. Go for the best mattress you can afford. Besides, the price differences between the cheap products and the better quality ones are often small, about $50 or less.

◆ **Foam Mattresses.** Our top brand recommendation for foam mattresses is ***Colgate*** (call 404-681-2121 for a dealer near you; web: www.colgatekids.com). This Georgia-based company makes a full line of foam mattresses which range from $50 to $125. Among the best of Colgate's offerings is the "Classic," a group of five-inch foam mattresses with varying firmness. The Classic I was top-rated by *Consumer Reports* and is available in discount stores and mail order catalogs like Baby Catalog of America (1-800-PLAYPEN; web: www.babycatalog.com) for $90. Of course, just about any Colgate foam mattress will do the trick; the company has several different lines but we found little difference among them. One caution to Colgate mattresses: they can be hard to find. The company's distribution is a bit thin in places around the U.S.—check their web site for the current list of dealers.

◆ ***Coil Mattresses.*** We liked the ***Sealy*** (by Kolcraft) 150 coil mattress for $60 at Babies R Us as a best buy for the dollar. Also good: ***Simmons*** "Baby Beauty" 104 coil mattress for $70 and Simmons Super Maxipedic 160 coils for $80 (again at Babies R Us). We also liked the Evenflo's "Serta" line, sold at Baby Depot and other stores for $60 to $110.

If you can find the Colgate brand, they too make a decent coil mattress—a 150 coil model is about $100.

In the next year, we expect to see a bit more competition in the crib mattress category—both ***Child Craft*** and ***Pali*** are rolling out their own mattress lines. Child Craft will offer both a foam and coil mattress under the Legacy and Child Craft names at $50 to $150. Pali is teaming with Canadian mattress maker Jupiter Industries (www.BoPeepNurseryProducts.com) for their new line. Among the unique features for Pali's mattresses: antibacterial covers and a combo foam/coil mattress. Prices will be high, however (about $190).

Bottom line: there isn't much difference between coil mattress brands—each does a good job. Stick with the ones at 150 coils (80 is too little; 250 is overkill).

Still can't decide between foam or coil? Well, Colgate has a solution—a "2 in 1" mattress that is half foam and half coil. The company suggests the extra-firm foam side for infants. When your baby reaches toddlerhood, you flip the mattress over to the coil side. The price: $120 to $130.

E-Mail from The Real World

Colic remedy turns mattress into magic fingers.

Colic, that incessant crying by young infants at night, can drive parents to distraction. A mom in Tennessee writes about one solution she found:

"After several relatively sleepless nights with our 2 week old infant, I found a product called the Sleep Tight Infant Soother. This product basically makes sleeping in the crib similar to riding in the car. A vibration device attaches underneath the mattress and you can either get a sound box for the crib which plays white noise or get a 90 minute cassette tape. If you opt for the sound box, the price is $129; it is $89 if you go for the cassette tape. The product has a 15 day trial period and can be ordered online at www.colic.com or by calling 1-800-NO COLIC. The FDA has approved it as a medical device so insurance may reimburse the cost."

Dresser & Changing Tables

The juvenile trade refers to dressers, changing tables, and the like as "case pieces" since they are essentially furniture made out of a large case (pretty inventive, huh?). Now that you've got a place for the baby to sleep (and a mattress for her to sleep on), where are you going to put all those cute outfits that you'll get as gifts from Aunt Bertha?

And let's not forget that all too important activity that will occupy so many of your hours after the baby is born: changing diapers. The other day we calculated that by our baby's first birthday, we had changed over 2400 diapers! Wow! To first-time parents, that may seem like an unreal number, but babies actually do go through 70 to 100 diapers a week for the first six months or so. That translates into ten to 15 changes a day.

What are You Buying

1 **DRESSERS.** As you shop for baby furniture, you'll note a wide variety of dressers—three drawer, four drawer, armoires, combination dresser/changing tables, and more. No matter which type you choose, we do have two general tips for getting the most for your money. First, choose a dresser whose drawers roll out on roller bearings (located on the drawer sides). Cheap dressers have drawers that simply sit on a track at the bottom center of the drawer. As a result, they don't roll out as smoothly and are prone to come off the track. Our second piece of advice: make sure the dresser top is laminated. If you're in a rush and put something wet on top, you want to make sure you don't damage the finish. Also, unlaminated tops are more prone to scratches and dings. Look at the drawer sides—the best furniture makers use "dove-tailed" drawer joints (they look like interlocking fingers) where the side panel meets the front of the drawer.

What about wood substitutes like medium density fiberboard (MDF)? MDF by itself isn't necessarily good or bad. It really depends on the overall construction (drawer glides, joints, etc.), not so much the wood content. Yes, some high-price furniture makers tout their "all wood" construction (where even the sides and backs of the dresses are wood), but that might be overkill. How often will you be looking at the back of your child's dresser anyway? While you should avoid dressers made of cheap laminate, we've seen several good MDF dressers by makers like Status that were impressive.

2 CHANGING AREA. Basically, you have two options here. You can buy a separate changing table or a combination dresser/changing table. As mentioned earlier, we think a separate changing table is a waste of money (as well as a waste of space).

A better option is the combo package, a dresser and changing table all rolled into one. These come in two varieties: the flip-top and the hi-low (also called combo units). Flip-top dressers have a top unit that flips forward to provide a space to change the baby. Some of these models convert to regular dressers (the changing tabletop detaches and can be removed). A good example is Child Craft's flip-top dresser (about $350 at Babies R Us). The large changing surface of this changing table would be great for parents of twins. The only downside? It's kind of a pain to flip the changing area over each time you want to use it. Also, there's a limited area for changing supplies in the small space under the flip-top.

Hi-low dressers are another popular option. These dressers (also called "combo" or "castle" units) were pioneered by Rumble Tuff, reviewed later in this section. The two-tier design of these dressers provides a convenient space to change diapers while not looking like a diaper-changing table. Most parents keep diaper-changing supplies in the upper drawer, while the lower dresser functions as clothing storage, etc. Hi-low dressers start at $450 and range up to $600. As an option, some manufactures offer a hutch that attaches to a hi-low dresser to give you shelf space.

Let's say you're on a really tight budget. What should you do? Forget the diaper changing station altogether! Some mothers we interviewed just change their baby in the crib or on a countertop. Of course, there are a couple of disadvantages to this alternative. First, there's not a convenient place for diapers and supplies. A rolling storage cart could solve this (cost: about $25 in many catalogs and stores; we saw one for $18 at the Container Store 800-733-3532; web: www.containerstore.com; Sam's Club has a plastic "six drawer mini chest" for $24). Another disadvantage: if you have a boy, he could spray the crib sheets, bumper pads, and just about anything else in the crib with his little "water pistol." Hence, you might find yourself doing more laundry.

One mom sent us an e-mail with a solution to the changing table dilemma—she bought a "Rail Rider," changing table that fits across a crib and can be removed when the baby is sleeping. For $40, it did the trick. Made by Burlington Basket Company (for a dealer near you, call 800-553-2300 or 319-754-6508) and sold online at Baby Catalog (www.babycatalog.com), the Rail Rider does have a few drawbacks: it doesn't fit all cribs and shorter folks find it more difficult to use.

Safe & Sound

Safety doesn't stop at the crib–also consider the nursery's other furniture items when baby-proofing.

◆ ***Anchor those shelves.*** A nice bookcase (whether on the floor or on top of the dresser) can become a tip-over hazard as the baby begins pulling up on objects. The best advice is to attach any shelves to a wall to provide stability.

◆ ***Baby proof the diaper station.*** If your diaper changing area has open shelves, you may have to baby proof the bottom shelves. As the baby begins to climb, you must remove any dangerous medicines or supplies from easily accessible shelves.

◆ ***Choose a dresser that doesn't have drawer pulls.*** Those little knobs can make it easy for baby to open the drawers–and it's those open drawers that can be used as a step stool to scale the dresser. A good tip is to buy a dresser without drawer pulls; quite a few styles have drawers with grooves that let you open them from below. While this isn't totally baby proof, it reduces the attraction for baby. Another good tip: anchor the dresser to the wall. In case baby does find a way to climb it, at least the unit won't tip over.

◆ ***Air out all that new nursery paint, furniture and decor.*** A University of Maryland School of Medicine study suggests new parents should air out freshly painted or wallpapered rooms before baby arrives. New furniture and mattresses also "out-gas" fumes, so consider ventilating the nursery when they arrive as well. How much ventilation? The study suggested four to eight weeks of open window ventilation, which seems a bit excessive to us. But it makes sense to do some air-out of the nursery before baby arrives. Another idea: look for environmentally friendly paints that have lower out-gas emissions. If you install new carpet in the house, leave during the installation and open the windows (and turn on fans) for two days.

Our Picks: Brand Recommendations

As previously noted in this chapter, many of the crib makers also manufacture "case pieces" (dressers, armoires, etc). For contact information on these brands, refer to the reviews earlier in this chapter. Here's a round up:

Good. The dressers from domestic manufacturers ***Simmons, Bassett*** and ***Child Craft*** are good entry-level options. A simple four dresser from Bassett is $290; the same item from Child Craft is $350 (both available at Babies R Us). Hi-low combo dressers are a bit more ($540 to $600 from Simmons and Child Craft) but do offer more flexibility. As for quality, we noted Simmons uses solid wood drawer sides, while Child Craft's drawer sides are pressed wood. The only bummer: most drawers in this price range lack dovetail joints and feature plain styling.

Better. If you're looking for better quality and more style, check out the offerings from Canadian manufacturers. ***Morigeau, Ragazzi*** and ***Status*** make dressers with hip adult looks like bun feet and shaker styling. Quality is better, but you're going to pay for it: most dressers start at $500 and go up to $700 or more.

Morigeau has a hi-low combo dresser for $600, while a simple four drawer dresser with hutch runs $750. Status' basic three-drawer dresser with changer top is $500. In this "better" category, we'd also put the brands like Pali, Bonavita and Sorelle/C&T. Most of these dressers are made in Canada; quality is excellent but you will pay for it with a 30% premium over domestic makers you'd see at Babies R Us.

Best. Our top pick for juvenile furniture is an obscure Utah-based company that doesn't even make cribs—they concentrate solely on case pieces (dressers, bookshelves and more). ***Rumble Tuff*** (for a dealer near you, call 800-524-9607 or 801-226-2648; web: www.rumbletuff.com) is also a best buy—their prices are often 10% to 25% less than the competition. Their strategy is to knock-off the big guys, making similar furniture styles in the exact same finishes as the crib makers so everything will match. (Well, to be fair, they don't match EVERY last finish offered by crib makers, but darn close).

Rumble Tuff's claim to fame is their popular combo dresser. This unit combines a three-drawer dresser/changing table and a taller base cabinet and drawer. Price: $500 to $600, depending on the finish. These combo units have proven so popular that other furniture makers have knocked them off. In fact, Simmons and Child Craft have tried to match Rumble Tuff on price for their combo units, but you'll note that the competition is still much higher when you look at accessories like book shelves, desks and so on.

All in all, Rumble Tuff makes 30 different pieces, in both contemporary and traditional finishes. The quality is excellent: all of Rumble Tuff's drawers feature roller bearings. Every dresser is made of solid wood like maple and oak (except for the sides and tops, which are veneers). Best of all, the furniture comes in 20 different colors; you can mix and match color accents for knobs or tops to your heart's content.

While the drawer sides are not solid wood, we found the overall construction to be good. We bought a Rumble Tuff dresser and bookshelf unit and have been very happy—it matches our Child Craft crib exactly and we saved over $100.

One caveat to Rumble Tuff: the brand can be difficult to find, as their distribution is spotty in places like New England. Go to their web site to find a list of dealers.

Another brand to consider: Readers write to us to say ***Camelot Furniture*** of Anaheim, Calif. (714-283-4194) has some great deals on dressers and other case pieces. "The infant and case pieces by Camelot gave me the most bang for the buck, not to mention a perfect match in color for my Pali crib," says a reader. Yes, it's made of laminate but the drawer glides have a lifetime warranty and the prices are great—$479 for an armoire, $198 for a book shelf.

Even More Stuff To Spend Money On

Just because to this point you have spent an amount equivalent to the gross national product of Peru on baby furniture doesn't mean you're done, of course. Nope, we've got four more items to consider for your baby's room:

1 **ROCKER-GLIDER.** We're not talking about the rocking chair you've seen at grandma's house. No, we're referring to the high-tech modern-day rockers that are so fancy they aren't mere rockers—they're "glider-rockers." Thanks to a fancy ball-bearing system, these rockers "glide" with little or no effort.

Quebec-based ***Dutailier*** (call 800-363-9817 or 450-772-2403; web: www.dutailier.com), is to glider-rockers what Microsoft is to software—basically, they own the market. Thanks to superior quality and quick delivery, Dutailier probably sells one out of every two glider rockers sold in the U.S. and Canada each year.

Dutailier has an incredible selection of 45 models, seven finishes, and 80 different fabrics. The result: over 37,000 possible combinations. All wood is solid maple or oak and features non-toxic finishes. You have to try real hard to avoid seeing Dutailier—the company has 3500 retail dealers, from small specialty stores to major retail chains.

Prices for Dutailier start at about $200 for a basic model. Of course, the price can soar quickly from there—add a swivel base, plush cushions or leather fabric and you can spend $500. Or $1000. (The fancier Dutailier's are in the "AvantGlide" line).

If we had to criticize Dutailier on something, it would have to be their cushions. Most are not machine washable (the covers can't be

E-MAIL FROM THE REAL WORLD
Antique bargains

A reader reminds us that antique stores can be great sources for baby furniture.

"You might remind readers not to overlook the local antique store when shopping for nursery furniture. We found a great English dresser from the 1930s with ample drawer and cupboard space for $325 that has a lot more character than anything we've seen in baby stores, plus it can be easily moved to another room/use when our baby outgrows it."

zipped off and put into the washing machine). As a result, you'll have to take them to a dry cleaner and pay big bucks to get them looking like new. A few of our readers have solved this problem by sewing slip covers for their glider-rockers (most fabric stores carry pattern books for such items). Of course, if the cushions are shot, you can always order different ones when you move the glider-rocker into a family room.

It can take 10-12 weeks to order a custom Dutailier rocker, but the company does offer a "Quick Ship" program—a selection of 17 chair styles in two or three different fabric choices that are in stock for shipment in two weeks.

Unfortunately, Dutailier's web site lacks a product catalog. But there is good news: Dutailier is one of those products that is easy to research (and buy) online. Several sites carry the brand at a discount, including BabyCatalog.com. Two sites that have a great selection of Dutailier are CribNCarriage (www.cribncarriage.com) and Rocking Chairs 100% (www.rocking-chairs.com; 800-4-ROCKER), a web site offshoot of the Corte Madera, CA store of the same name. The latter site is easy to navigate, with thumbnails of different models and little color chips for available colors. A reader also recommended American Health & Comfort's site (www.ForYourBaby.com; 800-327-4382) for deals on Dutailiers.

An optional accessory for glider rockers is the ottoman that glides too. These start at $99 without a cushion, but most cost $125 to $150 with cushion. We suggest forgetting the ottoman and ordering an inexpensive "nursing" footstool (about $30 to $40 in catalogs like Motherwear 800-950-2500 or on line). Why? Some moms claim the ottoman's height puts additional strain on their backs while breastfeeding. While the nursing footstool doesn't rock, it's lower height puts less strain on your back.

Is a glider-rocker a waste of money? Some parents have written to us with that question, assuming you'd just use the item for the baby's first couple of years. Actually, a glider-rocker can have a much longer life. You can swap the cushions after a couple of years (most makers let you order these items separately) and move the glider-rocker to a family room.

Of course, there are several other companies that make glider-rockers for nurseries. Here are some alternatives to Dutailier:

◆ ***Brooks*** *Call 800-427-6657 or 423-626-1111 for a dealer near you.* Tennessee-based Brooks has been around for 40 years, but only entered the glider-rocker business in 1988. Their glider-rockers retail for $169 to $399, while the ottomans are $100-$150. Unlike Dutailier, all their fabrics are available on any style chair. Brooks chairs feature solid base panels (Dutailier has an open base), which the company touts as more safe. While we liked Brooks' styles and fabrics, one baby storeowner told us he found the company very disorganized with poor customer service.

◆ ***Conant Ball/Shermag*** *In the U.S., call 800-363-2635 for dealer near you or 800-556-1515 or 819-566-1515 in Canada.* We saw this brand at chain stores (which is also sold under the name Shermag). The gliders retail for $240 to $350 (with cushions) while ottomans start at $80. The quality is better than average and Conant Ball offers a good selection of cushions. Conant Ball is manufactured in Sherbrooke, Quebec.

◆ ***Relax-R*** *Call 800-850-2909 for a dealer near you.* Relax-R is a Vermont company that makes leather glider rockers that swivel, glide and recline. New to the market, Relax-R also offers another unique feature: heated massage. We tried out a Relax-R rocker recently and were impressed–they were very comfortable, require no assembly and feature several leather choices. The downside? First, they're pricey: $500 for a basic model (add $100 for the massage option). Second, they're kind of ugly. The overstuffed cushions and armrests win points for comfort but not style.

◆ ***Towne Square*** *Call 800-356-1663 for a dealer near you; web: www.gliderrocker.com.* Hillsboro, Texas-based Towne Square has a lifetime warranty for all its glider-rockers. They feature a "long-glide" rocking system that has no ball bearings that can wear out. Towne Square's gliders sell for $300 to $500. Their "nursing ottoman" is low to the ground at a height that the manufacturer claims is "ideal for nursing" and gives you control over the chair's rocking motion. Like Brooks, Towne Square gliders feature solid sides as a safety measure (to keep little hands out of the rocking mechanism). As for looks, we'd put Towne Square in the "traditional" category–if you want a contemporary look, this probably isn't for you.

◆ ***And more ideas.*** One reader emailed in this great idea–check out "assembly required" glider-rockers for under $100 at home centers like Home Base (call 949-442-5000 for a store near you; web: www.homebase.com). Unfortunately, Home Base only has locations in the Western part of the U.S., but you can always check another home center near you for any glider-rocker kits. "My husband had to put it together and the cushions aren't as soft as the ones I've seen in baby stores, but at $80 it is far more reasonable and I absolutely love it!"

What about plain rocking chairs (without cushions)? Almost all the glider-rockers we recommend above can be ordered without cushions. Of course, just about any furniture store also sells plain rocking chairs. We don't have any preference on these items–to be honest, if you think you want a rocker, we'd go for the glider-rocker with cushions. Considering the time you'll spend in it, that would be much more comfortable than a plain rocking chair with no padding.

2 **CLOSET ORGANIZERS.** Most closets are a terrible waste of space. While a simple rod and shelf might be fine for adults, the basic closet doesn't work for babies. Wouldn't it be better to have small shelves to store accessories, equipment and shoes? Or wire baskets for blankets and t-shirts? What about three more additional rods at varying heights to allow for more storage? The solution is closet organizers and you can go one of two routes. For the do-it-yourself crowd, consider a storage kit from such brands as Closet Maid (call 800-874-0008 for a store near you; web: www.closetmaid.com), Storage Pride (800) 441-0337 or Lee Rowan (800) 325-6150 web: www.leerowan.com. Closet Maid's web site (closetmaid.com) is particularly helpful, with a useful "Design Selector" and how-to guide. Two catalogs that sell storage items include Hold Everything (800) 421-2264 web: www.holdeverything.com and the Container Store (800) 733-3532 web: www.containerstore.com. A basic storage kit made of laminated particle board ranges from $50 to $120 (that will do an average size closet). Kits made of coated wire run $30 to $60.

What if you'd rather leave it to the professionals? For those parents who don't have the time or inclination to install a closet organizer themselves, consider calling Closet Factory (call 800-692-5673 for a dealer near you; web: www.closetfactory.com) or California Closets (call 800-274-6754 for a dealer near you; web: www.californiaclosets.com). You can also check your local phone book under "Closets" for local companies that install closet organizers.

Professionals charge about $400 to $500 for a typical closet.

While a closet organizer works well for most folks, it may be especially helpful in cases where baby's room is small. Instead of buying a separate dresser or bookshelves, you can build-in drawer stacks and shelves in a closet to squeeze out every possible inch of storage. Another idea: a deep shelf added to a closet can double as a changing area.

We invested in a closet organizer for our youngest child's room and were more than pleased with the results.

3 **STEREO.** During those sleep deprivation experiments, it's sure nice to have some soothing music to make those hours just whiz by. Sure, you could put a cheap clock radio in the baby's room, but that assumes you have decent radio stations. And even the best radio station will be somewhat tiring to listen to for the many nights ahead. Our advice: buy (or get someone to get you as a gift) one of those CD/cassette boom box radios that run $100 to $300 in most electronics stores.

4 **DIAPER PAIL.** Well, those diapers have to go somewhere. Sure you could buy a basic diaper pail, but we like the Diaper Genie, that wonderful invention by a parent who apparently smelled one too many diaper pails. In Chapter 4, we'll explore the Eighth Wonder of the World: The Diaper Genie.

A safety note on this subject: many basic diaper pails come with "deodorizers," little cakes that are supposed to take the stink out of stinky diapers. The only problem: many contain toxic chemicals that can be poisonous if toddlers get their hands on them. A new solution to this problem comes from Sassy (616) 243-0767 web: www.sassybaby.com. This Michigan-based company makes a "no touch" diaper pail deodorizer that is completely non-toxic.

5 **A CUTE LAMP.** What nursery would be complete without a cute lamp for junior's dresser? A great catalog for lighting fixtures is Shades of Light (800) 262-6612; web: www.shades-of-light.com. While most of the catalog focuses on fixtures for the rest of the home, there are a few options for baby's room (look on their web site under "Odds and Ends".

The Bottom Line: A Wrap-Up of Our Best Buy Picks

For cribs, you've got two basic choices: a simple model that is, well, just a crib or a "convertible" model that eventually morphs into a twin or full size bed. In the simple category for best buys, Child Craft's 10171 is a simple maple crib with single-drop side for just $200 to $250. In a similar vein, a basic Simmons model at Baby Depot ran $240.

Other features that are nice (but not necessary) for cribs include a double drop side, a quiet rail release and hidden hardware. If you fancy an imported crib, there are few bargains but we found Sorelle/C&T and Babi Italia have reasonable prices ($250 to start) for above average quality.

The best mattress? We like the foam mattresses from Colgate ($90 for the Classica I). Or, for coil, go for a Sealy (Kolcraft) 150 coil mattress for $60 at Babies R Us.

Where to buy a crib and other nursery furniture? Our readers say chains like Babies R Us and Baby Depot have the lowest prices, but the web can be a great source for discounts on non-bulky items like rocker gliders. Good ol' JCPenney has the best mail order catalog for nursery deals–use it if there are no good baby stores nearby. For design inspiration, consider the Pottery Barn Kids catalog for ideas (but few deals).

Dressers and other case pieces by Rumble Tuff were great deals–they exactly match the finishes of Child Craft and Simmons, but at prices 10% to 25% less than the competition. We liked their three-drawer combo unit that combines a changing table and a dresser for $450 to $600. Finally, we recommend the Dutailier line of glider-rockers. At $200 to $300, their basic models are well made and stylish. A matching ottoman runs $110 to $180.

So, let's sum up some of our recommendations:

Simmons single drop-side crib	$240
Sealy 150 coil mattress	$60
Rumble Tuff Hi-Lo dresser	$500
Dutailier glider-rocker	$250
Miscellaneous	$200
TOTAL	$1250

By contrast, if you bought a Bellini crib ($600), a 200-coil mattress ($160), a Ragazzi dresser ($750), a fancy glider-rocker ($500), separate changing table ($200) and miscellaneous items ($200) at full retail, you'd be out $2410 by this point.Of course, you don't have any sheets for your baby's crib yet. Nor any clothes for Junior to wear. So, next we'll explore those topics and save more of your money.

CHAPTER 3

Baby Bedding & Decor

How can you find brand new, designer-label bedding for as much as 50% off the retail price? We've got the answer in this chapter, plus you'll find nine smart shopper tips to help get the most for your money. We'll share the best web sites and mail-order catalogs for baby linens. Then, we'll share nine important tips that will keep your baby safe and sound. Finally, we've got reviews of the best bedding designers and an interesting list of seven top money-wasters.

Getting Started: When Do You Need This Stuff?

Begin shopping for your baby's linen pattern in the sixth month of your pregnancy, if not earlier. Why? If you're purchasing these items from a baby specialty store, they usually must be special-ordered—allow at least four to eight weeks for delivery. If you leave a few weeks for shopping, you can order the bedding in your seventh month to be assured it arrives before the baby does.

If you're buying bedding from a store or catalog that has the desired pattern in stock, you can wait until your eighth month. It still takes time to comparison shop, and some stores may only have certain pieces you need in stock, while other accessories (like wall hangings, etc.) may need to be special ordered.

Sources

There are six basic sources for baby bedding:

1 **BABY SPECIALTY STORES.** These stores tend to have a limited selection of bedding in stock. Typically, you're expected to choose the bedding by seeing what you like on sample cribs or by looking through manufacturers' catalogs. Then you have to special-order your choices and wait four to eight weeks for arrival. And that's the main disadvantage to buying linens at a specialty store: THE WAIT. On the upside, most specialty stores do carry high-quality brand names you can't find at discounters or baby superstores. But you'll pay for it—most specialty stores mark such items at full retail.

2 DISCOUNTERS. The sheer variety of discount stores that carry baby bedding is amazing—you can find it everywhere from Wal-Mart to Target, Marshall's to TJ Maxx. Even Toys R Us sells baby bedding and accessories. As you'd expect, everything is cash and carry at these stores—most carry a decent selection of items in stock. You pick out what you like and that's it; there are no special orders. The downside? Prices are cheap, but so is the quality. Most discounters only carry low-end brands whose synthetic fabrics and cheap construction may not withstand repeated washings. There are exceptions to this rule which we'll review later in this chapter.

3 DEPARTMENT STORES. The selection of baby bedding at department stores is all over the board. Some chains have great baby departments and others need help. For example, JCPenney carries linen sets by such companies as NoJo and Cotton Tale (see the reviews of these brands later in this chapter), while Foley's (part of the May Department Store chain) seems to only have a few blankets and sheets. Prices at department stores vary as widely as selection; however, you can guarantee that department stores will hold occasional sales, making them a better deal.

4 BABY SUPERSTORES. The superstores reviewed in the last chapter (Babies R Us, Baby Depot, etc.) combine the best of both worlds: discount prices AND quality brands. Best of all, most items are in-stock. Unlike Wal-Mart or Target, you're more likely to see 100% cotton bedding and better construction. Yet, the superstores aren't perfect: they are often beaten on price by online sources (reviewed later in this chapter). And superstores are more likely to sell bedding in sets (instead of a la carte) which included frivolous items.

5 THE WEB. If there was a perfect baby product to be sold online, it would have to be crib bedding and linens. The web's full-color graphics let you see exactly what you'll get. And bedding is lightweight, which minimizes shipping costs. The only bummer: you can't feel the fabric or inspect the stitching. As a result, we recommend sticking to well-known brand names when ordering online.

6 MAIL-ORDER CATALOGS. In the last few years, there's been a marked increase in the number of catalog sellers who offer baby linens, and that's great news for parents. Catalogs like Pottery Barn, Land's End and Company Kids offer high quality bedding (100% cotton, high thread counts) at reasonable prices. Best of all, you can buy the pieces a la carte (eliminating unnecessary items found in sets) while at the same time, mixing and matching to your heart's content. If you want "traditional" bedding sets, JCPenney's catalog won't disappoint. We'll review these and more catalogs later in this chapter.

Parents in Cyberspace: What's on the Web?

Burlington Coat Factory Direct (Baby Depot)

Web site: www.bcfdirect.com

What it is: The online version of discounter Burlington Coat Factory's Baby Depot.

What's Cool: This site offers good discounts (about 20% to 30%) on bedding from such famous names as Lambs & Ivy, Cotton Tale, KidsLine, Brandee Danielle and more. Best of all, you can order a la carte if you don't want a complete set—each page lists a plethora of matching accessories for each grouping plus you can click on thumbnail swatches for a closer look. In our last edition we criticized the site for not having a shopping cart feature. We're pleased to say they've fixed that part of the site. Finally, Baby Depot lets you know how long each item takes to ship and the shipping costs are reasonable.

Needs work: We're a bit disappointed with the navigation on this site. It takes a tremendous number of clicks to see all the bedding offerings. We had to navigate through four menus to get to the bedding list. Even more confusing: the site mixed in general categories like "boy" and "girl" with specific manufacturers like Baby Guess. Once you do choose a brand name, all you get is a list of collections without any thumbnails. This means you either have to know which collection you want or you have to go through all the patterns to see what's up, a very time consuming process.

Baby Bedding Online

Web site: www.babybeddingonline.com

What it is: The online outpost for bedding manufacturer Carousel.

What's cool: Carousel used to sell its line of bedding exclusively through retail stores at about $250 to $300 per set. A couple years ago, however, they decided to sell directly to the public via their web site, Baby Bedding Online. The prices have taken a huge drop as a result. For example, their four piece Gingham collection used to sell for $269. Online it's a modest $149. Can't beat the prices for an all cotton bedding line. And best of all, Carousel doesn't do this half way: the web site offers free fabric swatches, free shipping on orders over $100 and other goodies. Lastly, Baby Bedding Online has an outlet store as well. Check the web site to find out when the outlet store is open.

Needs work: The main page for each collection just includes a photo of the item. You have to click again to get details and prices. And this site isn't going to win any awards for design innovation either. It's basically a text driven site with very simple graphics, however it still gets the job done.

Best For Babies

Web: www.bestforbabies.com, see Figure 1 below.
What it is: The online offshoot of a Maryland baby store, First Step.
What's cool: This site has an excellent selection of high quality name brands like Patchkraft, Wendy Belissimo and more. And prices are great. One reader said she found a Sumersault set for only $273. Other sites were selling the same pattern for $350. Another plus: they offer close ups of fabric swatches when you click on thumbnails. Not only do they sell bedding, but the site also offers clothing, strollers, car seats and more.
Needs work: Well, we can't find much to complain about with this site. They have secure order forms, a wish list option and accept all major credit cards.

◆ ***Other web sites to check out:*** Don't forget manufacturers' web sites—one of the best is ***Brandee Danielle's*** (www.brandeedanielle.com). Their entire catalog is online so you can surf to your heart's content. Since most baby stores only carry a few patterns from any one manufacturer, it's informative to see the *entire* collection.

Of course, there are more than just big manufacturers online. The small guys are there too—one of our readers recommended

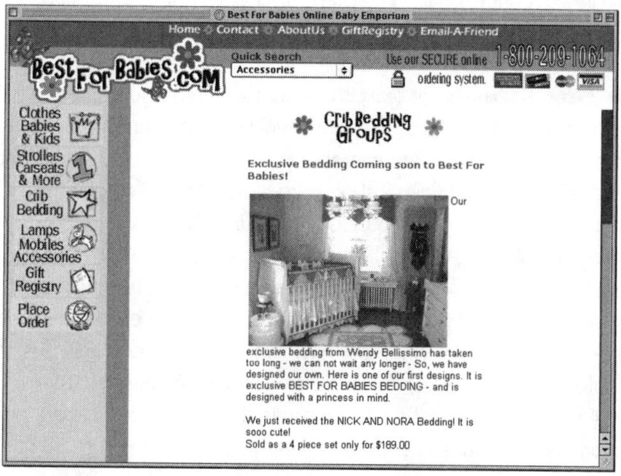

Figure 1: BestForBabies.com discounts the better brands of crib bedding by 20% to 30%.

custom-bedding maker ***Kid's Etc*** (949-495-5828; web: www.kids-etc.com), a small California-based company that sells whimsical 100% cotton linens. Our only gripe: some of the photos are a bit fuzzy. Prices are about $400 per set, on the high side.

For parents looking for accessories and bedding with a Beatrix Potter theme, check out ***Country Lane*** (www.countrylane.com). This site has just about every accessory and bedding piece available in the Beatrix Potter pattern. Unfortunately, the organization could use some improvement. Be sure to check for discontinued items (click the "specials" link). The discounts are up to 40% off.

Finally, one of the better sites for upper end bedding is ***Baby Style*** (www.babystyle.com). With designers like Amy Coe, Wendy Belissimo and CoCaLo the prices are a bit on the higher side, although they do a limited discount. The selection is smaller, but they offer free shipping for sales over $100 and various coupons for new customers.

What Are You Buying?

Walk into any baby store, announce you're having a baby, and stand back: the eager salespeople will probably pitch you on all types of bedding items that you MUST buy. We call this the "Diaper Stacker Syndrome," named in honor of that useless (but expensive) linen item that allegedly provides a convenient place to store diapers. Most parents aren't about to spend the equivalent of the Federal Deficit on diaper stackers. So, here's our list of the absolute necessities for your baby's linen layette:

◆ ***Fitted sheets***—at least three to four. When it comes to crib sheets, you have three choices: woven, knit and flannel. Woven (also called percale) sheets are available in all cotton or cotton blend fabrics, while knit and flannel sheets are almost always all cotton. As to which is best, it's up to you. Some folks like flannel sheets, especially in colder climates. Others find woven or knit sheets work fine. If you plan to use a bassinet/cradle, you'll need a few of these special-size sheets as well. One tip: look for sheets that have elastic all-around the edges (cheaper ones just have elastic on the corners). See the "Safe & Sound" section for more info on crib sheet safety issues.

If you need bassinet sheets or cradle sheets, your choices are pretty limited. They are often found together in the same section, so be sure to get the right size for your mattress. You'll usually find solid color pastels or white. Some linen manufacturers do sell bassinet sheets, but they can get rather pricey. And you may find complete bassinet sets that come with all the linens for your baby. Just be sure to check the fabric content (all cotton is best) and washing instruction. By the way, one mom improvised bassinet sheets by putting the bassinet mattress inside a king size pillow case. You may want to secure the excess fabric under the mattress so it doesn't un-tuck.

◆ ***Mattress Pads/Sheet Protector.*** While most baby mattresses have water-proof vinyl covers, many parents use either a mattress pad or sheet protector to protect the mattress or sheet from leaky diapers. A mattress pad is the traditional way of dealing with this problem and is placed between the mattress and the crib sheet. A more recent invention, the sheet protector, goes on top of the crib sheet.

E-MAIL FROM THE REAL WORLD
Sheet savers make for easy changes

Baby bedding sure looks cute, but the real work is changing all those sheets. Karen Naide found a solution:

"One of our best buys was 'The Ultimate Crib Sheet.' I bought one regular crib sheet that matched the bedding set, and two Ultimate Crib Sheets. This product is waterproof (vinyl on the bottom, and soft white cotton on the top) and lies on top of your regular crib sheet. It has six elastic straps that snap around the bars of your crib. When it gets dirty or the baby soils it, all you have to do is unsnap the straps, lift it off, put a clean one on, and that's it! No taking the entire crib sheet off (which usually entails wrestling with the mattress and bumper pads)... it's really quick and easy! While the white sheet may not exactly match your pattern, it can only be seen from inside the crib, and as you have so often stated, it's not like the baby cares about what it looks like. From the outside of the crib, you can still see the crib sheet that matches your bedding. Anyway, I think it's a wonderful product, and really a must."

Note: The Ultimate Crib Sheet is made by Basic Comfort (call 800-456-8687 for a store near you; web: www.basiccomfort.com). It sells for $16 to $19 and is available at Babies R Us or we've seen it for as little as $13 on web sites like www.BabyAbby.com. Of course, there are several other companies that sell similar sheets; we've seen them in general catalogs like One Step Ahead and Baby Catalog of America. Another sheet saver is made by Kiddopotamus (800) 772-8339 (web: www.kiddopotamus.com).

A sheet protector has a rubber backing to protect against leaking. And here's the cool part: it Velcro's to the crib's posts, making for easy removal. If the baby's diaper leaks, simply pop off the sheet protector and throw it in the wash (instead of the fitted crib sheets). You can buy sheet protectors in most baby stores or catalogs. See an "Email from the Real World" on the previous page for information on one brand of sheet saver, the Ultimate Crib Sheet.

◆ ***A Good Blanket.*** Baby stores love to pitch expensive quilts to parents and many bedding sets include them as part of the package. Yet, all most babies need is a simple cotton blanket. Not only are thick quilts overkill for most climates, they can also be dangerous. The latest report from the Consumer Product Safety Commission on Sudden Infant Death Syndrome (SIDS) concluded that putting babies face down on such soft bedding may contribute to as many as 30% of SIDS deaths (that's 1000 babies) each year in the U.S. (As a side note, there is no explanation for the other 70% of SIDS cases, although environmental factors like smoking near the baby and a too-hot room are suspected). Some baby bedding companies have responded to these concerns by rolling out decorative flannel-backed blankets (instead of quilts) in their collections.

But what if you live in a cold climate and think a cotton blanket won't cut it? Consider crib blankets made from Polartec (a lightweight 100% polyester fabric brushed to a soft fleece finish) available in most stores and catalogs. For example, Company Kids sells a polar fleece crib blanket for $19. Land's End has one for $22. Of course, polar fleece blankets are also available from mainstream bedding companies like California Kids (reviewed later in this chapter). Or how about a "coverlet," which is lighter than a quilt but more substantial than a blanket? Lightweight quilts (instead of the tradition thick and fluffy version) are another option for as little as $70 in mail order catalogs.

Finally, we found a great product to keep baby warm and avoid a blanket altogether. Halo Sleep Systems (www.halosleep.com), the manufacturer of Halo crib mattresses, also makes a product called the Sleep Sack. This "wearable blanket" helps baby avoid creeping under a blanket and suffocating. Available in three sizes and two fabrics, the Sleep Sack is $30. A portion of the sale price goes to the SIDS Alliance.

◆ ***Bumper Pads.*** In a previous edition of this book, we called bumper pads "an important safety item." We've since changed our mind and now consider them to be an optional accessory. Why the change of heart? All the warnings about SIDS and soft bedding (see previous paragraph) make us wonder whether any fluffy, soft bedding should be in a crib, even if bumpers are designed as a "safety item." After having two babies of our own, we also question their usefulness, since you're suppose to remove them after baby begins pulling himself up (so he doesn't use them as a stepstool to get out of the crib). Besides, most parents have heeded SIDS warnings and now put baby to sleep on their back, making it tougher for them to do much moving around in the crib. On the other side of the debate are parents who think bumpers keep antsy babies from knocking into the side rails (some babies move around the crib more than others). Bumpers can also keep little arms and legs inside a crib, so they don't get lodged in the space between spindles.

If you choose to purchase bumpers, don't buy the ultra-thick kind. Check to see if you can machine-wash them—thinner bumpers can be popped into a washing machine, while ultra-thick bumpers may have to be dry-cleaned. Some parents are concerned that the chemical residue from dry-cleaning might be harmful to their baby. (As a side note, federal law requires the fill in bumpers be 100% polyester).

More Money Buys You . . .

Baby bedding sets vary from as little as $40 in discount stores up to nearly $1000 in specialty stores. The basic difference: fabric quality and construction. The cheapest bedding is typically made of 50/50 cotton-poly blends with low thread counts (120 threads per inch). To mask the low quality, many bedding companies use cutesy licensed cartoon characters. So what does more money buy you? First, better fabric. Usually, you'll find 100% cotton with 200 thread counts or more. Better quality bedding sets include more substantial bumpers with more ties. Some may even have slipcovers removable for easy cleaning. Cheap quality crib sheets often lack elastic all the way around and some shrink dangerously when washed (see Safe and Sound later in this chapter for details). Beyond the $300 price point, you're most likely paying for a designer name and frilly accessories (coordinating lamp shade, anyone?).

Safe & Sound

While you might think to cover your outlets and hide that can of Raid, you might not automatically consider safety when selecting sheets, comforters, and bumpers. Yet, your baby will be spending more time with these products than any others. Here are several safety points to remember:

◆ ***Make sure the crib sheets snugly fit the mattress.*** Never use a sheet that has shrunk so much it no longer can be pulled over the corners of the mattress. Unfortunately, some sheets shrink more than others. See the section below for more info on this hazard. Another web site to check out for info on this issue is www.babysheets.com. The site offers its own sheet called the Stay Put safety sheet. Finally, Baby Sleep Safe (www.babysleepsafe.com) makes a crib sheet anchor that helps keep a crib sheet snug to the mattress. A six-point harness attaches to the sheet from the underside of the mattress.

The Crib Sheet Controversy

It's one of the ironies of safety regulation: the government regulates the places where babies sleep but NOT what they sleep on. Cribs must meet specific design and construction safety rules, but when it comes to crib BEDDING, anything goes.

Take crib sheets, for example. If the sheet doesn't fit the mattress properly (that is, pull completely over the corner and tuck under the mattress), a toddler may be able to tug it loose and possibly become entangled in the sheet. Sheets can also pop off when baby tosses and turns in the night.

In a November 1998 article ("The Crib Sheet Catastrophe"), *Good Housekeeping* magazine reported three incidents of babies who have died since 1986 when they became entangled in their crib sheets. What's the main culprit of ill-fitting sheets? Shrinkage. After repeated washings, the simple fact is that many "fitted" crib sheets no longer fit the mattress. Parents who continue using the sheets are unknowingly creating a hazard for their child.

To see how widespread this problem is, the Good Housekeeping Institute tested 23 sheets from 14 manufacturers by washing and drying them according to manufacturer's care instructions. The result? After five washings (the point after which shrinkage is less of an issue), seven sheets shrunk so much they didn't fit over the mattress corners. Another eight sheets could barely be tucked under the mattress. The balance (eight sheets) fit correctly, with at least two inches of fabric tucked under mattress.

The magazine didn't stop there. Next, they measured how easy it would be to pull sheets off the mattress. Obviously, the smallest sheets (after washing) were easy to pull off. Another sheet (the

◆ ***All linens should have a tag*** indicating the manufacturer's name and address. That's the only way you would know if the linens were recalled. You can also contact the manufacturer if you have a problem or question. While this is the law, some stores may sell discounted or imported linens that do not have tags. Our advice: DON'T buy them.

◆ ***Recent studies of Sudden Infant Death Syndrome*** (SIDS, also known as crib death) have reported that there is an increased incidence of crib death when infants sleep on fluffy bedding, lambskins, or pillows. A pocket can form around the baby's face if she is placed face down in fluffy bedding, and she can slowly suffocate while breathing in her own carbon dioxide. The best advice: put your infant on her back when he or she sleeps. And don't

Simmons 100% cotton sheet) used such poor elastic that it too pulled off with very little force.

(We have reprinted the original chart from the 1998 article on our web site at www.BabyBargainsBook.com in the "Updates" section. In 2000, *Good Housekeeping* updated this info by evaluating an additional 50 crib sheets with their "pull test." This chart is also on our web site).

The results of the study: as you might expect, the cheapest sheets performed the worst. Low-quality brands sold in discounters like Wal-Mart for $7 to $14 rank near the bottom of the list. The best sheets were $16 to $30, many of which were sold by mail order catalogs like Lands End, the Company Store and Eddie Bauer.

We discussed this issue with bedding makers and found that many of the better brands over-sized their 100% cotton sheets to allow for shrinkage and use elastic to encircle the ENTIRE sheet, not just the ends (or corners). Others use fabric that is pre-shrunk. Sadly, some of the poorest-performing crib sheet makers admit they make a product for a price–and that low price means they can't use expensive elastic or extensive fabric to allow for shrinkage (they also deny there's a safety problem with their products).

The bottom line: as a parent, you must take responsibility for your baby's safety. First, spend a few more bucks on quality sheets that won't shrink. And if you find that a crib sheet has shrunk so much it can no longer be tucked under the mattress, do NOT use it.

Yes, the government should mandate crib sheet standards for length and shrinkage (amazingly, *Good Housekeeping* reported unwashed sheets varied by as much 8" in their tests). But we'll all grow old waiting for that happen–and in the meantime, you have to take action on your own.

put pillows, comforters or other soft bedding or toys inside a crib.

In 1999, the Consumer Product Safety Commission issued new guidelines regarding SIDS and soft bed linens. They recommend that parents not use any soft bedding around, on top of, or under baby. If parents want to use a blanket, tuck a very thin blanket under the mattress at one end of the crib to keep it from moving around. The blanket should then only come up to baby's chest. Safest of all: avoid using any blankets in a crib and put baby in a blanket sleeper and t-shirt for warmth. (More on blanket sleepers in the next chapter). Finally, one mom wrote to tell us about a scary incident in her nursery. She had left a blanket hanging over the side of the crib when she put her son down for a nap. He managed to pull the quilt down and get wrapped up in it, nearly suffocating. Stories like that convince us that putting any soft bedding in or near a crib is risky.

◆ ***Beware of ribbons or long fringe.*** These are possible choking hazards if they are not attached properly. Remove any questionable decoration.

◆ ***If you decide to buy bumper pads,*** go for ones with well-sewn ties at the top and bottom (12 to 16 total). Ties should be between seven and nine inches in length. That's the industry's voluntary standard for safety–ties that are too short can't be tied correctly around a crib post. If ties exceed nine inches, they can be a choking hazard. We should note that while that's the standard, our investigation of baby bedding found many manufacturers exceed the limit–one even had ties that were 14" in length! As a defense, we should note that expensive bedding makers claim their customers put their bedding on expensive Italian cribs, whose thick corner posts require longer ties. We think that's a weak excuse–14" is too long, even for cribs with the thickest posts. If you buy bumpers with ties that exceed 9", we recommend cutting off any excess length after you install them on the crib. (See the previous chapter's Safe & Sound section for a discussion of Italian cribs and bumper pads).

A related issue to the length of the ties is their location: some companies have ties on BOTH the top and bottom of bumpers. If there are just ties on the top of bumper (as most companies use), baby may scoot under the bumper and get trapped. If you fall in love with bedding that has ties only on the top, consider adding additional ties yourself. Just be sure to sew them on securely. A chart later in this chapter will compare the tie length and location among different brands.

◆ ***Never use an electric blanket/heating pad.*** Babies can overheat, plus any moisture, such as urine, can cause electric shock.

◆ ***Avoid blankets that use nylon thread.*** Nylon thread melts in the dryer and then breaks. These loose threads can wrap around your baby's neck, fingers or toes or break off and become a choking hazard. Cotton thread is best.

◆ ***Look out for chenille.*** It's the hip new thing and sort of like the shag carpeting of fabric—chenille is all over the market (sweaters, blankets, etc.) and now it's come to baby products. At a recent trade show, we saw many bedding manufacturers who had chenille groupings. Some used chenille as an accent on bumpers, while others have chenille blankets. Yet, some safety advocates wonder if chenille is safe for baby's bedding—with some chenille, you can actually pull out chenille fibers from the fabric backing with little effort. And that might be a choking hazard for baby.

◆ ***Travel.*** Now that you've created a safe nursery at home, what about when you travel? Parents who frequently travel are often frustrated by hotels, who not only have unsafe cribs (see previous chapter) but also questionable sheets. We've been given queen size bed sheets to use in a crib! A solution: one reader recommended bringing a crib sheet from home. That way you know your baby will be safe and sound. (When you reserve a crib find out if it is a portable crib or a standard crib so you know what size sheet to bring.)

Smart Shopper Tips

Smart Shopper Tip

Pillow Talk: Looking for Mr. Good Bedding

"Pooh and more Pooh—that seemed to be the basic choice in crib bedding at our local baby store. Since it all looks alike, is the pattern the only difference?"

There's more to it than that. And buying baby bedding isn't the same as purchasing linens for your own bed—you'll be washing these pieces much more frequently, so they must be made to withstand the extra abuse. Since baby bedding is more than just another set of sheets, here are nine quality points to look for:

1 **RUFFLES SHOULD BE FOLDED OVER FOR DOUBLE THICKNESS—INSTEAD OF A SINGLE THICKNESS RUFFLE WITH HEMMED EDGE.** Double ruffles hold up better in the wash.

2 **COLORED DESIGNS ON THE BEDDING SHOULD BE PRINTED OR WOVEN INTO THE FABRIC, NOT STAMPED** (like you'd see on a

screen-printed t-shirt). Stamped designs on sheets can fade with only a few washings. The problem: the pieces you wash less frequently (like dust ruffles and bumpers) will fade at different rates, spoiling the coordinated look you paid big money for. In case you're wondering how to determine whether the design is printed rather than stamped, printed fabrics have color that goes through the fabric to the other side. Stamped patterns are merely applied onto the top of the fabric.

3 **MAKE SURE THE PIECES ARE SEWN WITH COTTON/POLY THREAD, NOT NYLON.** Nylon threads will melt and break in the dryer, becoming a choking hazard. Once the thread is gone, the filling in bumpers and quilts can bunch up.

4 **CHECK FOR TIGHT, SMOOTH STITCHING ON APPLIQUÉS.** If you can see the edge of the fabric through the appliqué thread, the appliqué work is too skimpy. Poor quality appliqué work will probably unravel after only a few washings. We've seen some appliqués that were actually fraying in the store—check before you buy.

5 **HIGH THREAD-COUNT SHEETS.** Unlike adult linens, most packages of baby bedding do not list the thread count. But, if you can count the individual threads when you hold a sheet up to the light, you know the thread count is too low. High thread-count sheets (200 threads per inch or more) are better since they are softer and smoother against baby's skin, last longer and wear better. Unfortunately, most affordable baby bedding has low thread counts (80 to 120 thread counts are common)—traditionally, it's the design (not the quality) that sells bedding in this business. But there is good news on this front: there are several upstart brands (reviewed later) who are actually touting high thread counts for their sheets.

Another tell-tale sign of a quality sheet is the elastic. The best sheets will have elastic that encircles the entire sheet. See our box on The Crib Sheet Controversy earlier for more information.

6 **FEEL THE FILLING IN THE BUMPER PADS.** If the filling feels gritty, it's not the best quality. Look for bumpers that are soft when you squeeze them (Dacron-brand filling is a good bet).

7 **THE TIES THAT ATTACH THE BUMPER TO THE CRIB SHOULD BE BETWEEN SEVEN AND NINE INCHES IN LENGTH.** Another tip: make sure the bumper has ties on both the top and bottom and are securely sewn. For more discussion on this issue, see "Safe & Sound" earlier in this chapter.

8 THE DUST RUFFLE PLATFORM SHOULD BE OF GOOD QUALITY FABRIC—or else it will tear. Longer, full ruffles are more preferable to shorter ones. As a side note, the dust ruffle is sometimes referred to as a crib skirt.

9 REMEMBER THAT CRIB SHEETS COME IN DIFFERENT SIZES—bassinet/cradle, portable crib, and full-size crib. Always use the correct size sheet.

Wastes of Money/Worthless Items

"I have a very limited budget for bedding, and I want to avoid spending money on stuff that I won't need. What are some items I should stay away from?"

It may be tempting to buy every new fad and matching accessory. And you'll get a lot of sales pressure at some stores to go for the entire "coordinated" look. Yet many bedding items are a complete waste of money—here's our list of the worst offenders:

1 DIAPER STACKER. This is basically a bag (in coordinating fabric, of course) used to store diapers—you hang it on the side of your crib or changing table. Apparently, bedding makers must think stacking diapers on the shelf of your changing table or storing them in a drawer is a major etiquette breach. Take my word for it: babies are not worried if their diapers are out in plain sight. Save the $30 to $50 that bedding makers charge for diaper stackers and stack your own.

2 PILLOWS. We are constantly amazed at the number of bedding sets that include pillows or pillow cases. Are the bedding designers nuts, or what? Haven't they heard that it's dangerous to put your baby to sleep on a pillow? What a terrible safety hazard, not to mention a waste of your money. We don't even think a decorative pillow is a good idea. Forget the pillow and save $20 to $30.

3 SETS OF LINENS. Sets may include useless or under-used items like those listed above as well as dust ruffles and window valances. Another problem: sets are often a mixed bag when it comes to quality. Some items are good, while others are lacking. Many baby stores or even chains will sell bedding items a la carte. That way you can pick and choose just the items you need—at a substantial savings over the all-inclusive sets.

4 CANOPIES. Parents-to-be of girls are often pressured to buy frilly accessories like canopies. The emphasis is on giving her "everything" and achieving a "feminine" look for your nursery. Don't buy into it. The whole set-up for a canopy is going to be more expensive (you'll need a special crib, etc.)–it'll set you back $75 to $175 for the linens alone. And enclosing your baby's crib in a canopy won't do much for her visual stimulation or health (canopies are dust collectors).

5 ALL-WHITE LINENS. If you think of babies as pristine and unspoiled, you've never had to change a poopy diaper or clean spit-up from the front of an outfit. I'm amazed that anyone would consider all-white bedding, since keeping it clean will probably be a full-time job. Stick with colors, preferably bright ones. If you buy all-white linens and then have to go back to buy colored ones, you'll be out another $100 to $200.

6 TEETHING PADS FOR CRIB RAILS. Most new, name brand cribs will already have plastic teething guards on the side rails, so adding pads (cost: $20 extra) is redundant. One store owner pointed out that if your baby has nothing better to teeth on than the crib railing, he is spending too much time in the crib anyway.

7 HEADBOARD BUMPERS. Whatever side you come down on in the bumper debate (some parents think they're a good safety item; others worry about the suffocation risk), there is a certain bumper that definitely is a waste of money–the headboard bumper. This bumper is designed to cover the entire headboard of the crib. Regular bumpers are just a six to nine-inch tall strip of padding that goes around the crib . . . and that's all you need if you want bumpers. Headboard bumpers are more expensive than regular bumpers, running another $25 to $75, depending on the maker.

Money Saving Secrets

1 IF YOU'RE ON A TIGHT BUDGET, GO FOR A GOOD BLANKET AND A NICE SET OF HIGH THREAD-COUNT SHEETS. What does that cost? A good cotton blanket runs $10 (even fancy Polartec ones are only $20), while a fitted sheet runs $15 to $20. Forget all the fancy items like embroidered comforters, duvet covers, window valances, diaper stackers and dust ruffles. After all, your baby won't care if she doesn't have perfectly coordinated accessories.

2 DON'T BUY A QUILT. Sure, they look pretty, but do you really need one? Go for a nice cotton blanket, instead—and save the $50 to $200. Better yet, hint to your friends that you'd like receiving blankets as shower gifts.

3 SKIP EXPENSIVE WALL HANGINGS—DO DECOR ON THE CHEAP. One of the best new products we've discovered for this is "Transfer-Mations" by Camp Kazoo (call 303-526-2626 for a store near you; web: www.boppy.com). These innovative iron-on transfers let you create paint-by-number masterpieces in your baby's room. Paint an eight-by-ten foot mural or just add some decorative borders. Cost: $30 (plus the cost of paints). For even less effort you can buy Transfer-Mations Easy Stick for $18 to $45. These are peel and stick decals require no painting.

Of course, crafts stores are another great source for do-it-yourself inspiration. Michaels Arts & Crafts (800-MICHAELS; web: www.michaels.com) sells stencils and supplies for nursery decor.

4 MAKE YOUR OWN SHEETS, DUST RUFFLES AND OTHER LINEN ITEMS. Think it is too complicated? A mom in Georgia called in this great tip on curtain valances—she bought an extra dust ruffle, sewed a curtain valance from the material and saved $70. All you need to do is remove the ruffle from the fabric platform and sew a pocket along one edge. I managed to do this simple procedure on my sewing machine without killing myself, so it's quite possible you could do it too. A good place for inspiration is your local fabric store—most carry pattern books like Butterick, Simplicity and McCalls, all of which have baby bedding patterns that are under $10. There are other pattern books you can purchase that specialize in baby quilts—some of these books also have patterns for other linen items like bumpers. Even if you buy good quality fabric at $8 per yard, your total savings will be 75% or more compared to "pre-made" items.

5 SHOP AT OUTLETS. Scattered across the country, we found a few outlets that discount linens. Among the better ones were House of Hatten and Carousel (also known as www.babybeddingonline.com)—see their reviews earlier in this chapter. Another reader praised the Pottery Barn Outlet. They have three locations: Jeffersonville, OH (740) 948-2004, Dawsonville, GA (706) 216-5211 or (706) 216-6465, Memphis, TN (901) 763-1500. The discounts start at 50% and only get better from there. They have cribs, bedding and other furniture on sale..

6 DON'T PICK AN OBSCURE BEDDING THEME. Sure, that "Exploding Kiwi Fruit" bedding is cute, but where will you find any matching accessories to decorate your baby's room? Chances are they'll only be available "exclusively" from the bedding's manufacturer–at exclusively high prices. A better bet is to choose a more common theme with lots of accessories (wall decor, lamps, rugs, etc.). The more plentiful the options, the lower the prices. Winnie the Pooh is a good example (see the box on "Pooh at a discount" later in this chapter), although you'll find quite a few accessories for other themes like Noah's Ark, teddy bears, rocking horses, etc.

7 GO FOR SOLID COLOR SHEETS AND USE THEMED ACCESSORIES. Just because you want to have a Beatrix Potter-themed nursery doesn't mean you have to buy Beatrix Potter bedding. A great money-saving strategy: use low-cost solid color sheets, blankets and other linen items in the crib. Get these in colors that match/compliment theme accessories like a clock, poster, wall paper, rugs, etc. (Hint: register for these items, which make nice shower gifts). You still have the Beatrix Potter look, but without the hefty tag for Beatrix Potter bedding. Many of the mail-order catalogs we review later in this chapter are excellent sources for affordable, solid-color bedding. Another bonus: solid color sheets/linens from the catalogs we recommend are often much higher quality (yet at a lower price) than theme bedding.

8 SURF THE WEB. Earlier in this chapter, we discussed the best web sites for baby bedding deals. Later in this chapter you'll find additional mail-order sources for bedding on a budget. The savings can be as much as 50% off retail prices. Even simple items like crib sheets can be affordably mail ordered. Next up: the best outlets for saving on baby bedding.

Outlets

GARNET HILL

Location: Historic Manchester Outlet Center, Manchester, Vermont. (802) 362-6198.

Love the look of the Garnet Hill bedding catalog but think the prices are hard to swallow? Then check out this outlet in Vermont, which features first-quality overstock items from the current catalog like flannel sheets, quilts, blankets, children's clothing and more. The savings is 30% to 50% and the outlet welcomes phone inquires and ships nationwide.

HOUSE OF HATTEN

Location: 3939 IH-35, Suite 725, San Marcos, TX. (512) 392-8161.

Perhaps the only thing more beautiful than a great quilt is a great quilt on sale. That's why we love House of Hatten's fantastic outlet store in San Marcos, Texas—the only one like it in the country. You can find their quilts, as well as mobiles, bumper pads, dust ruffles, and sheets at 50% off retail. The store also sells their clothing line, which features smocked outfits for girls and boys (starting at 3-6 month sizes). You can find a nice selection of gift items like rattles, bibs, pillows and more. Look for their sales near holidays for additional savings. The outlet offers mail-order service and ships nationwide. All items are discontinued, and some are imperfect or flawed.

THE INTERIOR ALTERNATIVE

Locations: 9 locations, most of which are in the East, Midwest and South. Call (413) 743-1986 for a location near you.

Looking for fabric to decorate your baby's room or do-it-yourself bedding projects, but shocked at retail fabric store prices? Then seek out the Interior Alternative, a fantastic fabric outlet. We visited their Dallas location and were amazed at the deals—literally THOUSANDS of bolts of fabric in just every imaginable pattern. If you like

CyberOutlet: Overstock.com

What happens when those high-flying dot-coms crash down the earth? Liquidators move in to sell their warehouses stuffed with unsold goods. Since they pay pennies on the dollar, these liquidators can turn around and sell you the goods at substantial discounts and still make a buck. (And how do liquidators sell distressed inventory from dot-coms? The Internet, of course). Case in point: Overstock.com, the premier liquidator of dot-coms. This company has an excellent web site that sells brand new merchandise at 50% off and more. A recent visit to the site turned up some interesting baby items. How about a designer four-piece set of all-cotton crib bedding that retails for $235, you pay just $99 and free shipping? We also saw crib mobiles for $34 (originally $56), toys, baby clothes, shoes and more. To see what's available for babies at Overstock.com, go to the "Gifts & Seasonal" section, then to General Gifts and finally Baby Gifts.

Waverly patterns, you'll find them here for just $8 a yard. There's also wall paper, borders, upholstery, pre-made curtain valances (for just $20) and more. Everything here is factory seconds, but we couldn't see any flaws. If you buy the entire bolt, you can take 10% off their prices.

LAURA ASHLEY

Location: Potomac Mills, Prince William, Virginia (703) 494-3124.

This famous British designer has scaled back her outlets in recent years–in fact, this one (about 30 minutes south of Washington DC) is all that's left. Yet, if you're in the neighborhood, it might be worth the trip. You can save 20% to 50% off Ashley's baby bedding and children's clothes.

◆ ***Another outlet.*** *Nojo* announced in 2000 that they were closing their outlet store in Rancho Santa Margarita, CA (949-858-9496). Yet, apparently the company has decided to keep it open (it was operating as of press time). A reader said she found great deals there–a four piece bedding set for $59.95 (regularly $200), matching valences at half price and Nojo's baby sling for only $9 (regularly $40). "Mismatched" crib bedding was going for as low as $4 a piece! We're not sure if and when this outlet will be operating, but if you are in the area you might call to see if it is still around.

Have you found an outlet store for baby bedding that's not listed above? Call us at 303-442-8792 or e-mail us with your find at authors@BabyBargainsBook.com.

The Name Game: Reviews of Selected Manufacturers

Here are reviews of some of the brand names you'll encounter on your shopping adventures for baby bedding. Note: we include the phone numbers, web sites and addresses of each manufacturer–this is so you can find a local dealer near you (most do not sell directly to the public, nor send catalogs to consumers). We rated the companies on overall quality, price, and creativity factors, based on an evaluation of sample items we viewed at retail stores. We'd love to hear from you–tell us what you think about different brands and how they held up in the real world by calling us at (303) 442-8792 or emailing authors@BabyBargainsBook.com.

The Ratings

A **EXCELLENT**–*our top pick!*
B **GOOD**– *above average quality, prices, and creativity.*
C **FAIR**–*could stand some improvement.*
D **POOR**–*yuck! could stand some major improvement.*

Amy Coe *For a dealer near you, call (203) 221-3050. Web: www.amycoe.com.* Designer Amy Coe turned her hobby of collecting vintage fabrics into a business when she launched her eponymous baby bedding line in 1993. The result is a linen collection with a flair for nostalgia: Coe takes fabrics that replicate patterns from the 1930's to 1950's and crafts a full line of bedding items. We previewed the collection recently and were impressed: we liked the flannel ticking stripes, gingham checks and cotton chambrays. New, Amy has added chenille throws ($104-$116), flannel blankets ($37), and waffleweave blankets ($56).Quality is high (everything is all-cotton), but so too are the prices–a single sheet is $30 and a set including the bumper, bed skirt and coverlet was a whopping $395 on BabyStyle.com. Despite the cost, we still like Coe. While the rest of the market has knocked off the vintage prints idea, Amy Coe still has some interesting designs that might be worth a look. ***Rating: B+***

Baby Guess *Manufactured by Crown Crafts. For a dealer near you, call (714) 895-2250. Web: www.crowncraftsinfantproducts.com.* Baby Guess has sure made the rounds since their baby bedding first came on the market. The license has been sold to a series of manufacturers over the years, most recently by bedding giant Crown Crafts who bought the brand along with NoJo bedding (see their review later in this section). After a few real design duds, Baby Guess finally seems back on the fashion track with simple designs in muted colors plus 100% cotton fabrics (knits and weaves). Baby Guess is available widely at discounters like Baby Depot and Babies R Us at prices ranging from $180 to $240 for a four piece set. ***Rating: B***

Baby Martex This brand is distributed by CoCaLo. See their review later in this section.

Bananafish *For a dealer near you, call (800) 899-8689 or (818) 727-1645.* "Sophisticated" and "tailored" is how we'd describe this California-based bedding maker. Bananafish's emphasis is on all-cotton fabric with adult-like finishes (such as pique) and muted color palettes. It's not cheap—prices range from $240 to $400 at retail for a four-piece set. We weren't really wild about the styling (a bit too dull for our tastes) but the quality is high. ***Rating: B***

Beatrix Potter This brand is licensed by Crown Crafts. See their review later in this section.

Beautiful Baby *For a dealer near you, call (903) 295-2229. Web: www.bbaby.com.* Next to Nava's (reviewed later), this is probably the most over-the-top bedding in the market today. There's nothing subtle about Beautiful Baby's linens, which feature satin, lace and tulle. The bumpers are so huge they're like king-side pillows sewn together (okay, that's an exaggeration, but trust us, they are BIG) but they do have the most bumper ties of any manufacturer (26). A plus: their sheets all have safety straps, an added feature we applaud. With over 130 styles to choose from, Beautiful Baby says it takes four to six weeks to ship most orders. Prices are very high: expect to shell out $500 to $800 for a four-piece set, which is somewhat surprising since some of the groupings are made of blended fabrics. ***Rating: B-***

Bedtime Originals This brand is made by Lambs & Ivy. See their review later in this section.

Blue Moon Baby *For a dealer near you, call (626) 455-0014.. Web: www.bluemoonbaby.com.* In business for five years, California-based Blue Moon Baby specializes in chenille bedding. Their seven collections feature chenille in a variety of patterns and designs for both boys and girls. One of the best bets: The Cowboy Collection with its red bandanna trim and denim accents, along with a chenille cowboy. For girls, the Cotton Tail collection featured cute pink bunnies that are sure to draws ooh's and aah's from grandparents. Blue Moon Baby also sells coordinating furniture, stuffed animals and other decorative accents. Prices are about $400 for a three-piece set which includes bumper, skirt and quilt (Blue Moon Baby doesn't sell sheets). The fabric is all cotton. We thought the quality was very good and we really like the unique designs—no one is doing sculptured chenille designs. On the downside, the price is rather high for what is just a three-piece set of bedding. Blue Moon Baby also makes bassinet bedding in four designs. ***Rating: B***

Blueberry Lane *Call (413) 528-9633 for a dealer near you. Web: www.blueberrylanehome.com.* Designer Diane Sorrell uses textured blends to give Blueberry Lane's baby bedding a unique look. Quality is good; the bedding is sewn in North Carolina and

Affordable Artwork

Framed artwork for baby's room has to be expensive, right? Nope, not if you buy a framed print from Creative Images (call 800-784-5415 or 904-825-6700 for a store near you; web: www.crimages.com). This Florida-based company makes framed prints, growth charts, wall hangings and more at very affordable prices–just $20 to $80. Each print is mounted on wood and laminated (no glass frame) so baby can enjoy it at eye-level (just sponge it off if it gets dirty). Best of all, there are hundreds of images for any theme to choose from: Pooh, Beatrix Potter, Noah's Ark, plus other collections of animals, sports and pastels. Check out their web site for samples.

Massachusetts. Blueberry Lane offers "total room concepts" that pair bedding with coordinating hand-painted furniture pieces and window treatments. Price for the bedding run $350 to $520 for a four piece set. ***Rating: B+***

Brandee Danielle *For a dealer near you, call (800) 720-5656, (714) 957-1240. Web: www.brandeedanielle.com.* Despite its feminine-sounding name, Brandee Danielle is one of the few makers that designs bedding with "boyish" themes. One pattern, "Dumpin' Dirt," even featured a series of construction equipment illustrations for the little handyman-to-be. They've added some new feminine patterns like "Princess Pink" ($330 set) to round out their selection. Brandee Danielle is one of the few companies that sews all its bedding in-house (most use outside contractors). The bedding is widely available at chain stores (Babies R Us, Baby Depot) and specialty shops. Prices are $290 to $390 for a four piece set. Even at that price level, it's a pretty good buy; most of the fabrics are 100% cotton. As a side note, Brandee Danielle also makes car seat covers, stroller pads, and bedding for round cribs (which runs $600). New this year is a silk dot blanket and they've added coordinating summer weight blankets to their accessories options. ***Rating: A-***

California Kids *For a dealer near you, call (800) 548-5214, (650) 637-9054.* One of our favorite bedding lines, California Kids specializes in bright and upbeat looks. New this year, they've added a "Princess Collection" of more girl oriented themes. They've even added a line of coordinating drawer pulls. Also look for their Waverly prints and matching rugs plus the new sports-themed groupings. The quality is excellent; everything is 100% cotton and made in California. Prices run $250 to $350 for a five-piece set (the average is about $300). With an amazing array of options (60+ patterns were available at last count), California Kids is available in specialty stores and upper-end department stores. Available accessories include wall hangings, lamp shades and fabric by the yard. ***Rating: A***

Carter's *Made by Riegel. Call (800) 845-3251 or (803) 275-2541 for a dealer near you. Web: www.carters.com or www.parentinformation.com.* Carter's is one of the biggest names in baby products–you'll find clothes, high chairs, strollers and even bedding sporting the name. One big reason: clever design, like the runaway success of the John Lennon Real Baby collection. The collection (which also includes coordinating clothing and accessories) is based on a series of drawings Lennon made for his youngest son, Sean. We were impressed with the quality of this whimsical bedding–100% cotton, 200 thread count with sewn appliques. That's not what we expect from a brand known for its affordable sleepers. And, amazingly enough, the price isn't that high–a four-piece set of Lennon baby is $160.

If you don't like the Lennon look, Carter's has two other bedding lines: Baby Basics, a mix and match coordinates line in 100%, 200-thread count cotton and the Emu line, designed by Emu Namae, a blind Japanese artist famous for his children's illustrations. The Baby Basics line runs about $60 for a four piece set while Emu is similar in price to the Lennon line.

We are impressed with the improvements to the Carter's line. We think the Baby Basics are an amazing value (although the bumpers are a bit skimpy) and the flexibility of buying just what you need is terrific. ***Rating B+***

Celebrations *Call (310) 532-2499 for a dealer near you. Web: www.baby-celebrations.com.* This bedding maker offers 32 styles with feminine, sophisticated looks–we saw patchwork motifs, eyelet laces, chenille trim and layered dust ruffles. The all-cotton linens range from $300 to $590. Quality is excellent; we noticed the bumpers sported ties on the top and bottom (16 total). ***Rating: B+***

CoCaLo *Call (714) 434-7200 for a dealer near you. Web: www.cocalo.com.* You could say baby bedding runs in the family at CoCaLo. Owner Renee Pepys Lowe's mother (Shirley) founded Nojo in 1970 and Renee worked at the family business before it was sold to Crown Crafts a couple of years ago. Since then, Renee branched out on our own, launching the CoCaLo line in 1999 (the

LICENSE TRANSLATOR

Who makes what brand of bedding

One of the hottest trends in crib bedding is licensed characters–just about every cartoon character imaginable has been licensed to one of the big bedding makers for use in juvenile bedding. But how can tell you tell who makes what? Here is a list of popular licensed characters and their bedding makers:

LICENSE	SEE BEDDING MAKER
Baby Guess	Crown Crafts
Baby Gund	Lambs & Ivy
Baby Looney Tunes	Crown Crafts
Baby Looney Tunes	Gerber
Baby Martex,	Cocalo
Beatrix Potter	NoJo
Blues Clues	Crown Crafts
Hello Kitty	Quiltex
Lennon Baby for Carter's	Riegel/Mt. Vernon Mills
Laura Ashley	Sumersault
My First Thomas	Quiltex
Osh Kosh B'Gosh	Cocalo
Precious Moments	Crown Crafts
Raggedy Ann & Andy	Lambs & Ivy
Rainbowfish	Kidsline
Save the Children	Quiltex
Sesame Street	Mt. Vernon Mills
Snoopy	Lambs & Ivy
Studio Spot	Infantino
Suzy's Zoo	Gerber
Todd Parr	Quiltex
Winnie The Pooh	Crown Crafts

name comes from the first two letters of Renee's daughters, Courtenay and Catherine Lowe). CoCaLo is made up of four lines: Euro Baby, Osh Kosh, Baby Martex and an eponymous collection. The lowest price (and largest) group is Osh Kosh, with prices ranging from $230 to $300 for a five-piece set. Unfortunately, not all of this collection is all-cotton (some sets are blends). Step up to the

Euro Baby line and you'll find 100% cotton fabric imported from Holland. Prices for Euro Baby are about $350 per set. Finally, CoCaLo has their own line of bedding that features overstuffed bumpers and extra long ruffles for $340 per set. Design-wise, the Osh Kosh line features their trademark denim look in most groupings, while Euro Baby is more whimsical, in muted hues. Baby Martex is simpler with checks, plaids and seersucker looks, although one grouping also showcased vintage floral prints. Quality-wise, we were impressed with CoCaLo, although Osh Kosh is a bit pricey for a grouping that is 50/50 cotton-poly. We'd stick with the 100% cotton selections. ***Rating: B+***

Company Kids This bedding is sold via mail order in the Company Store catalog. See the "Do it By Mail" section later in this chapter for details. ***Rating: A***

Cotton Tale *Call (800) 628-2621 or (714) 435-9558 for a dealer near you.* What most impressed us about Cotton Tale was their originality. There are no licensed cartoon characters or trendy fabrics like chenille here. Instead, you'll see hand-painted looks in

The Marketing of Baby Linens: Dangerous Impressions?

Flip through any bedding catalog or web site and you'll see decked-out cribs, stuffed with sumptuous linens. Some linen companies like Baby Martex even use long-ago recalled cribs (with dangerous corner posts) to market "antique" looking patterns. Yet, in their haste to market their products, baby linen makers may be sending a wrong (and dangerous) message to parents—that it's OK to put soft bedding items like pillows, comforters and the like in cribs. Safety advocates clearly warns against this, but it still amazes us to see bedding brochures with many offending items loaded into cribs, some of which are missing a drop-side (in order to show the merchandise more clearly, of course). The reason why this happens is clear: linen manufacturers make fat profits off of such "decorative" accessories. And what better way to sell such items for baby than to deck out cribs? But we wonder if this sends the wrong message to parents—some folks may think that's how their crib should look. Yeah, many bedding makers include warning labels (in six-point type) that says you shouldn't put such items in a crib—but that's usually in the fine print if it exists at all. All bedding makers should eliminate this practice at once.

beautiful soft pastels, all made in the U.S. We loved the whimsical animal prints and the feminine touches. One standout design: "Aruba" complete with a rainbow of cabana stripes. Best of all, Cotton Tale's prices are affordable–most range from $200 to $400 with an average of $275 for a four piece set, a bit of a rise in prices from years past. All of the fabrics are 100% cotton. New this year at Cotton Tale is a beautiful cotton organza collection called "Paper White" for $310. They've also added lots of seersucker, plaids and even an animal print. Look for whimsical decorations like fabric dragonflies, stick horses and memory boards as well. You can still buy coordinating sponge paint kits as well. Cotton Tale bedding is available just about everywhere. . . even in the JCPenney catalog and Babies R Us. ***Rating: A***

Crown Crafts *Call (800) 421-0526 or (714) 895-9200 for a dealer near you. Web: www.CrownCraftsInfantProducts.com.* Baby bedding behemoth Crown Crafts seems to have snapped up every possible character license you can imagine. For example, Crown Crafts now makes Beatrix Potter, Precious Moments, Baby Guess, Winnie-the-Pooh, and Blues Clues crib bedding and more. The offerings range from the low-price Fisher Price bedding sold in discount stores to the upper-end Waverly bedding sold in Babies R Us. Crown Crafts also owns sub-lines NoJo, Little Bedding and Red Calliope (see later reviews for details on some of these lines). The word that best sums up Crown Crafts is CHEAP. Cheap prices–but also cheap fabric and quality. Yes, the Waverly line is the exception with all cotton, high thread count fabrics, but most of the licensed character bedding is cotton/poly blends with low thread counts. And the prices correspond. For example, a three piece screen printed Blues Clues set in cotton/poly blend is a mere $67. On the high end, Baby Guess four piece sets are as much as $300, a bit pricey compared to similar brands. Bottom line, you get what you pay for with this manufacturer. Stick with the Waverly or all cotton sets and avoid the cheap-o licensed sets. ***Rating: C+***

Eddie Bauer. This bedding is sold via mail order in the Eddie Bauer catalog. See the "Do it By Mail" section later in this chapter for details. ***Rating: A***

Euro Baby This brand is licensed by CoCaLo. See their review later in this section.

Fisher Price. This bedding is made by Crown Crafts; see review above.

Gerber *For a dealer near you, call (800) 4GERBER Web: www.gerber.com.* While Gerber offers some cute patterns in their bedding line and they're available almost everywhere, the company scored incredibly low on the Good Housekeeping shrinkage test (see article earlier). Gerber's biggest licenses are Suzy's Zoo and Baby Looney Tunes, but the quality just isn't there. Okay, the prices are cheap—a three piece set of Baby Looney Tunes from Babies R Us is a mere $40. But the designs are screen printed on cotton/poly fabrics. ***Rating: D***

Glenna Jean *For a dealer near you, call (800) 446-6018 or (804) 561-0687.* We liked Glenna Jean's designs—as long as you stick with non-appliquéd patterns. The quality and sewing construction of the appliqués just wasn't very impressive. Glenna Jean is big on teddy bear designs and accessories, although most of the colors tend toward the darker side. A four-piece set runs $150 to $750 with an average of $280 per set. Six of their collections are designed by Tamara Tilles (known as Tamara), a famous California designer of celebrity baby bedding. Her designs are at the high end of the price range. New this year are some pretty, textured fabrics, chenille accents and a denim patchwork design. Overall, the best bets in the Glenna Jean line are the 100% cotton patchwork and floral print designs (only certain groupings are all-cotton; the rest are blends). ***Rating: B-***

Hoohobbers *For a dealer near you, call (773) 890-1466. Web: www.hoohobbers.com.* The quality of this brand was impressive—all of the comforters are made duvet-style with Velcro enclosures. The result: it's easy to remove the cover for washing. Even the bumpers feature zippered covers. Hoohobbers 16 designs tend to be bright and bold with surprising color combinations (although there are a few muted options as well). Prices for all their four-piece collections are $375; that's expensive, but everything is 100% cotton and well-constructed (the sheets feature all-around elastic, for example). The good news is you can see and buy any of their patterns on their web site. They're also planning to open company stores soon (check the web site for the latest locations). Finally, we should mention Hoohobbers' bassinets and Moses baskets come in coordinating fabrics as well. In fact, the company makes a wide range of accessories including cribs and other furniture, bouncer seat covers and more. ***Rating: B+***

House of Hatten *For a dealer near you, call (800) 5-HATTEN (542-8836) or (512) 819-9600.* House of Hatten's specialty is beautiful appliquéd and embroidered quilts. When we first reviewed this manufacturer, we saw mostly pastel and white designs. While they still have a few of those designs (most notably the Nursery Rhyme and Hearts and Flowers patterns) they've added a number of bolder looks. Our favorite this year is the Enchanted Orchard with bold red cherries offset by a cute-as-a-button bunny. Even brighter: check out the Picture Book collection with unbelievable primary colors and simple appliques. Finally, accessories for each collection are extensive–you'll see matching clocks, picture frames, light switch plates and toys among others. Quilts are $80 to $150; a four-piece set that adds a sheet, dust ruffle and bumper runs about $210 to $400. All of the fabrics are 100% cotton. As a side note, House of Hatten has a discount outlet in Texas; for more info, see the Outlet section earlier in this chapters. ***Rating: B+***

Infantino *Call (800) 365-8182 or (858) 689-1221 for a dealer near you.* Last year brought a raft of changes at bedding maker Infantino. First, they bought themselves out from Dorel, the parent company of Cosco. Then Infantino purchased bedding manufacturer Judi's Originals (see separate review below). Finally, the company decided to expand their own bedding offerings including adding a new license from former My Dog Spot designer Pattie McDonald. This line is called "Studio Spot." While the designs don't include the wonder dog himself, the three Studio Spot collections are cute and whimsical. We liked Stacking Cows best with it's, well, stacked cows. The four piece sets retail for $180 to $260. Overall, we think this first effort by Infantino is promising–the quality was above average. ***Rating (for Studio Spot): B***

Judi's Originals *For a dealer near you, call (800) 421-9433. Web: www.judis.com.* Three-dimensional appliqué work is the trademark of Judi's, a family run baby bedding manufacturer in business since 1968. One of their all-time best sellers is "Judi's Jungle," which features whimsical 3-D animals in bright purple, pink and green hues. While that grouping is 100% cotton, unfortunately that's the exception to the rule: most are 50-50 blends. As such, Judi's prices are a bit high: a four-piece set runs $140 to $570. We were also somewhat disappointed with the quality of appliqué work (we'd stick with the non-appliquéd groupings to be on the safe side). On the plus side, the company has introduced several all-cotton groupings in recent years (although they are in the $275 to $300 range). We also liked Judi's web site, which includes an online catalog and extensive information (FAQ's) on their bedding and accessories. As we were going to press, Judi's announced they were being acquired by Infantino (see review above). It was unclear what changes Infantino has in mind for Judi's. ***Rating: C+***

KidsLine *151 W. 135th St., Los Angeles, CA 90061. Call (310) 660-0110 for a dealer near you. Web: www. Kidslineinc.com.* In the last edition of our book, we criticized KidsLine for overly cutesy designs and prices that were no bargain. There's good news to report this time around–in the last year or so, the company has expanded its design options to include more stylish prints, although the Rainbow Fish license still plays a big part in KidsLine's offerings. And prices are a bit more reasonable ranging from $140 to $200 for a six piece set. A few upper end sets (mainly the jacquard patterns and round bedding options) price out above $200. So how's the quality? We noticed that most of KidsLine patterns are poly-cotton blends. And even many of the all-cotton options featured low thread (below 200) counts. So what you're paying for with KidsLine is the design, not so much the fabric. But those designs are colorful and playful. Bottom line: we've raised their rating and think they're a good mid-priced brand. ***Rating: B***

Kimberly Grant *Call (714) 546-4411 for a dealer near you. Web: www.kimberlygrant.com.* West Coast designer Kimberly Grant started her business by selling art prints and then added matching bedding sets. We liked the sophisticated look (floral prints, plaids) and fabrics (velvets, satins, cotton), all in a bright palette. Prices run $379 to $515 for a four-piece set. Pricey but good quality. ***Rating: A-***

Lambs & Ivy *For a dealer near you, call (800) 345-2627 or (310) 839-5155. Web: www.lambsivy.com* Barbara Lainken and Cathy Ravdin founded this LA-based bedding company in 1979. Their specialty: fashionable baby bedding that is sold in discount and mass market stores (you'll also see them sold in JCPenney's catalog and on many web sites). This year they've added some whimsical looks along with vintage prints and licensed characters. In fact, they've expanded their Snoopy license to include two options now and added a Raggedy Ann and Andy option. New this year: a Baby Gund design with three-dimensional furry bear. They've really improved the quality of their stamped designs by using a photo quality heat transfer technology. This is a clever way of achieving a nicer look without big cost (you have to see the bedding in person to note the difference). Prices are still reasonable at $150 to $200 for a four piece set. Bedtime Originals, a sub-line of Lambs & Ivy, is slightly lower in price and quality. We'd rank the overall quality of Lambs & Ivy a bit ahead of other mass-market bedding brands. Yes, most of the fabrics are blends (50-50 cotton/poly), but the stitching and construction is a cut above. ***Rating: B+***

Little Bedding This is a sub-line of Crown Crafts. See their review earlier in this section.

Lands End This bedding is sold via mail order in the Lands End catalog. See the "Do it By Mail" section later in this chapter for details. ***Rating: A***

Laura Ashley This is a licensed line of Sumersault. See their review later in this section.

Luv Stuff *Call (800) 825-BABY or (972) 278-BABY for a dealer near you.* Texas-based Luv Stuff's claim to fame is their unique, hand-trimmed wall hangings, which match their custom bedding. You can mix and match to your heart's content (all items are sold a la carte). The quality is high: the company makes their own fabrics, which are mostly 100% cotton and high thread count plus all their collections are made in house in Texas. As you might expect, however, all this quality isn't free–a four-piece ensemble (sheet, comforter, bumper, dust ruffle) runs $400 to $500. And Luv Stuff's bumpers aren't very consumer friendly–they are dry clean only. Despite this, we liked the brand's unique and bold styles. This bedding is a tour de force of color and contrast. ***Rating: B***

Martha Stewart *Kmart's version is made by Riegel (see comments at the end of this section) Web: www.kmart.com. Another version is sold on line at www.marthastewart.com.* Martha is an interesting contradiction. On her eponymous web site, she offers one of the most expensive crib bedding sets out there. Her matte lasse collection is $268 for a three-piece set. A crib sheet is a hefty $42. And the set is only available in white (you can bet your baby will inaugurate that bedding quickly!). By contrast, Martha's Kmart brand of bedding is on the other end of the cost universe. While it's still 100% cotton, 200 thread count, the quality otherwise is disappointing: the applique and stitching are only average, the bumper has only six ties on the top and the elastic does not go all the way around the sheet. Okay, the prices are a great deal ($40 for a three-piece set), but it's obvious Martha cut some corners to bring the bedding in at that price. The colors are generally muted with patchworks and ginghams. You'll even find coordinating chenille blankets, diaper stackers, receiving blankets and more. These sheets ($8 to $10) have to be cold water washed which makes us wonder if they are shrinkage prone. On the plus side, the design and styling of Martha's bedding is a cut above what you usually expect to find at Kmart. But nagging quality issues lead us to give this brand (the Kmart version) only an average rating. ***Rating: C***

Nava's Designs *For a dealer near you, call (818) 988-9050. Web: www.navasdesigns.com.* Speaking of over the top, you can't talk about super-expensive bedding without mentioning Nava's Designs. But unlike My Dog Spot, we found the designs less innovative and more over-priced. A typical example: a pattern like "Promises," a patchwork of yellow, blue and white plaid with touches of chambray. The price? Are you sitting down? How about a whopping $780 to $940 for a set. A major negative (besides the price): some designs don't wash well and may even have to be dry-cleaned (check the washing instructions carefully). On the upside, the fabrics are very heavy, high-quality cottons, and the stitching is excellent. Among the stand-outs in Nava's line are her floral prints, lushly rendered with large cabbage roses, delicate lace and shimmering rope piping. This might be the bedding in Bill Gates' baby's nursery (we're only guessing, but he's the only one who could afford it), but Nava's just doesn't impress us. ***Rating: C+***

NoJo *Noel Joanna Inc. For a dealer near you, call (800) 854-8760 or (310) 763-8100. Web: www.nojo.com* NoJo was founded in 1970 and made just one product–a quilted infant car seat cover. Since then, NoJo has expanded into a wide range of bedding and nursery products (the company was acquired in 1997 by textile giant Crown Crafts, which also owns Red Calliope). Nojo is sold everywhere, from discounters like Baby Depot and Wal-Mart to specialty stores and chains like Babies R Us. In the past year, Crown Crafts has repositioned NoJo as more of a 100% cotton "better" bedding line. Prices for a four-piece, all-cotton set are about $180 to $240. We did notice Nojo bedding online at sites like www.comfortliving.com that sold for as little as $120, but these were 50/50 cotton blends. Design-wise, the line is moving away from the licensed characters like Babar, Paddington Bear and Spot. Instead you see more simple patchwork and gingham designs and subtle colors like violet. In the past we've criticized NoJo's cheaper bedding for poor quality, but with the repositioning of the brand, we've decided to raise the rating a bit. ***Rating: B***

OshKosh B'Gosh This brand is licensed by CoCaLo. See their review earlier in this section.

Patchkraft *Call (800) 866-2229 or (973) 340-3300 for a dealer near you. Web: www.patchkraft.com* Patchkraft has one of the best web sites of any bedding manufacturer. They have done a terrific job of showcasing their extensive bedding line with clear thumbnails and enlargements that even include a swatch of fabric in many case. While there is no substitute for feeling the fabric first-hand, the site helps you picture how these well made, 100% cotton bedding collections look in real life. Besides the web site, we were also impressed with Patchkraft owner Paula Markowitz's commitment to safety. All their bumpers feature ties on the top and bottom and the company provides detailed safety and care instructions to its customers. We also liked the fact that Patchkraft has eliminated the comforter from some of its sets (instead, they substitute a flannel blanket; the quilt is now an optional accessory). You do have to pay for all that quality at prices ranging from $300 up to $500 for a four piece set, but it is a good brand if you want to splurge. Most designs are in the $380 to $400 range. New this year you'll see some lightweight velour fabrics and flannels among the patchwork designs. They've also added a wall paper line in addition to borders. Our only gripe: we wish Patchkraft had more entry-level options below $300 (they have two as of this writing). Despite that criticism, we'll give them our highest rating based on safety, quality and design. ***Rating: A***

Pine Creek *Call (503) 266-6275 for a dealer near you. Web: www.pinecreekbedding.com* In the last year, Oregon-based Pine Creek Bedding has moved away from their signature look (darker, flannel designs) to emphasize more contemporary colors and fabrics. In a preview of their new collections, we saw ginghams and stripes in watercolor hues. A good example: "Sparkle," a design that is bordered by contrasting ginghams. All the fabrics are 100% cotton. Considering the quality, we thought Pine Creek's prices were reasonable at $280 to $360 for a four-piece set, a bit of a price increase over past years. Pine Creek also sells accessories like lamp shades and curtain valances, plus fabric is available by the yard. New this year are wallpaper borders and some velour fabric accents. ***Rating: A-***

Pooh Classic Pooh and Disney Pooh bedding are made by Crown Crafts subsidiary Red Calliope; see review below.

Pottery Barn See review later in this chapter. ***Rating: B+***

Quiltex *For a dealer near you, call (800) 237-3636 or (212) 594-2205.* Quiltex is famous for their licensed bedding items, including Hello Kitty, Todd Parr (Outer Space), Save the Children and our son's favorite, Thomas the Tank Engine. Style-wise, we'd put Quiltex into the "cutesy, baby-ish" category—the groupings are heavy on the pastel colors and frilly ruffles. Unfortunately, most of the line is blends (50/50 cotton-poly fabric). The quality of the Quiltex designs is middle-of-the-road: some appliqué work leaves a bit to be desired, while other designs are merely stamped on the fabric. Their prices ($130 to $240 for a four-piece set) are a bit more reasonable this year, on the upside. ***Rating: B-***

Red Calliope *For a dealer near you, call (800) 421-0526 or (310) 763-8100. Web: www.redcalliope.com* Red Calliope is a division of Crown Crafts, the billion dollar bedding behemoth that also owns Nojo. And like Nojo, Red Calliope is sold just about everywhere and offers bedding in a wide variety of stores. The bread and butter designs at Calliope are Pooh—that's Winnie the Pooh. To say that Calliope's Pooh bedding has been a run-away best-seller would be an understatement. Winnie the Pooh has been such a blockbuster for Calliope that the company has been very busy rolling out various Pooh spin-offs in several price points. To understand the Pooh line, you have to realize there are two different Pooh's: "Disney Pooh" and "Classic Pooh." The way you can tell the difference is Pooh's wardrobe—Disney Pooh wears a red shirt, while Classic Pooh is shirtless. Disney's Winnie-the-Pooh designs (sometimes made by Red Calliope's Little Bedding subsidiary) are priced for the mass market at $39 to $80 for a three-piece set (sheet, bumper, comforter). In the past year, Red Calliope has expanded Disney Pooh to include a few upper end patterns that now sell for as much as $224 per four piece set. Just to confuse you, Red Calliope also sells "Classic Pooh" which runs $220 to $300 and features designs from the original Pooh book by A. A. Milne. Quality-wise, you get what you pay for—the least expensive sets have 50-50 cotton/poly fabrics and fewer embellishments. New to the Classic Pooh line this year is "Timeless Memories" a 100% cotton 220 thread count design as well as a cotton knit collection and a matte lasse design. The bottom line: while it's understandable why Pooh is so popular, the quality of most of Calliope's Pooh bedding is just not worth the price. If you want to do a Pooh theme, we suggest following the money-saving tip mentioned earlier in this chapter—decorate your baby's room with Pooh accessories and decor, but choose solid (non-Pooh) bedding. You can find 100% cotton sheets, blankets and other linen items in matching colors from a variety of sources. ***Rating: C+***

Sumersault *Call (800) 232-3006 or (201) 768-7890 for a dealer near you. Web: www.sumersault.com* Owner Patti Sumergrade imports beautiful fabrics from Portugal and other European countries to create this top-shelf bedding line. We loved the plaids, which featured off-beat colors that match the richer wood tones popular for cribs in New England and the Northeast. Sumersault does few appliqués and leaves most of the cutesy touches to optional wall-hangings. A four piece set retails for $325 to $400. We should note that Sumersault also makes the Laura Ashley Mother and Child bedding collection which sells for $250 to $350 for four pieces. We've also noticed that Sumersault has experimented with even lower price points in the past year. Sears is offering a set of their bedding for just $175, although Sumersault claims the quilt in the set is no where near as fancy as their upper end collections. As for the designs, this year Sumersault rolled out more muted pastel themes. If you like the Hey Diddle Diddle nursery rhyme theme, they offer three sets to mix and match. Look for coordinating hand painted lamps this year as well. Overall, we like the quality of Sumersault and are pleased to see the brand at lower price points. As a side note; you may have noticed Sumersault's sheets scored low in the Good Housekeeping shrinkage tests (see the chart on our web site, www.BabyBargainsBook.com in the Updates section). We spoke to Sumersault about his and they said the tested sheets were discontinued patterns from 1993. In 1996, the company redesigned its sheets to address this problem–the new sheets are now oversized to allow for shrinkage and feature high-quality elastic. ***Rating: A***

Sweet Pea *Call (626) 578-0866 for a dealer near you.* You gotta like Sweet Pea . . . their fun and funky fabrics are imported from places like the Vatican (which we didn't realize exported anything other than Popes). Sweet Pea's 100% cotton bedding features a variety of very-adult finishes including jacquards, satins and even crushed velvets. If you don't like the damask-woven fabric, consider a floral chintz that looks like Laura Ashley on acid. One impossibly over-the-top design featured mix-and-match cabbage roses, corded piping trim and ribbon accents. Unfortunately, the prices are also over-the-top: five piece sets *start* at $400 and can top $1000. Ouch. While the quality is high, the prices are way out of the ballpark. ***Rating: B***

Waverly See Crown Crafts review earlier in this section.

Wendy Bellissimo Baby N Kids *Call (818) 348-3682 for a dealer near you. Web: www.wendybellissimo.com.* Wendy Bellissimo is a hot young designer from California whose bedding is often seen at upper-end baby stores like Bellini. The look: beautiful, sophisticated patterns made with 100% cotton fabrics. Accents include velour, appliques and lace touches. All Bellissimo's bumpers are slipcovered so you can wash them separately. So what does all this quality and cache cost you? We saw prices at BabyStyle.com ranging from $360 to $660 for a four to five piece set (some sets include a second dust ruffle for a layered effect). Whoa! And if you don't have a pricey baby boutique nearby, you can buy all these designs online from her web site (which is a bit of a surprise). The web site also lets you see large swatch samples of the fabrics and tells you if the designs are in stock. One unique feature to this line: boutiques that carry Bellissimo also may participate in her computer-assisted custom design options. Finally, you'll find accessories including diaper covers and swaddling blankets as well as Moses baskets ($230 to $280) and bassinets. While the prices are no bargain, the designs are interesting and the quality is exceptional. ***Rating: B+***

◆ ***Other brands to consider: Simmons*** (the crib maker) also makes bedding ranging from $130 to $280. The designs are simple with patchwork accents in some cases. They have quite a wide range of accessories to go with each collection and they are discounted heavily on the web and in chain stores.

Riegel (800) 845-3251 or (803) 275-2541 (web: www.parentinformation.com) made by Mt. Vermont Mills is a big player in the bedding market–but you might not recognize the name. Riegel is the company behind the in-store bedding brands at discounters like Target and Wal-Mart. The company also sells two collections under their own name, makes the Carter's Lennon Baby (reviewed earlier, ($150 for a four-piece 100% cotton 200 thread count set) and the Carter's Coordinates ($60 for four pieces in 100% cotton). Finally, Riegel manufacturers Sesame Street crib bedding for $40 for a four-piece set. While the Carter's line is good quality, the Sesame Street and Riegel collections are poly/cotton blends intended for mass market discount stores. Just to confuse you more, Riegel is also the manufacturer of Kmart's Martha Stewart brand (see review above).

Springs (call 212-556-6300 for a dealer near you; web: www.springs.com) has three patterns available in their collection. Wamsutta Baby is a standout with 100% cotton sheets and matte lasse finish on the coverlet and bumpers. Entry-level bedding sets sell in Wal-Mart for $40 and go up to $100 for a four-piece set.

The upper-end of the baby market has been booming in recent years. A good example is bedding from ***Ruby & Coco*** (800-316-2772 or 610-869-4830; web: www. rubycoco.com). This company started out as a baby boutique in Newark, Delaware and evolved into a "couture" bedding line with prices from $440 to $650 per four piece set. ***Bebe Chic*** (201) 941-5414 (www.bebechic.com) is a New Jersey-based designer who says their bedding combines "old world charm (with) soft textures, jacquards and quilted solids." Their prices: $200 to $300 for a comforter, $40 to $60 for a single sheet. Their designs are available in Bellini stores.

Finally, if Marcia Brady were designing baby bedding, we'd bet her collection would look like ***Groovy Baby*** (973) 748-0606. The 100% cotton psychedelic flowers and surfer dude designs will really get your baby grooving for $340 to $410 per four piece set. Another neat touch: Stretchy sheets made of cotton spandex. Cool!

Do It By Mail

Here's an overview of several catalogs that offer baby bedding. In most cases, the catalogs carry private label merchandise (with the

Winnie the Pooh at a Discount

Who's the hottest bear in baby bedding? Why, it's Pooh, Winnie the Pooh to be exact. Sales of Pooh bedding have been off the charts for the past several years and it seems like there's no stopping that silly old bear. But with the price for a basic four-piece set running close to $200 (or more), how can you get Pooh at a discount?

Unfortunately, there's only one company that makes Pooh crib bedding (Crown Crafts' Little Bedding, reviewed earlier in this chapter), so you can't choose among several suppliers to get a better deal. On the upside, the bedding is widely available, so you can get it on sale (at places like JCPenney) or regularly discounted from a mail order sources or web sites (see later in this chapter for possibilities)/

While many parents like Pooh, some told us they are less than thrilled with the quality of the Pooh bedding. In the past, much of this bedding was poly/cotton blends with low thread counts. But there is good news: recently, Red Calliope has added several 100% cotton collections, albeit at rather stiff prices ($300+).

So what can you do? Here's an idea: who says you have to have Pooh bedding to do a Pooh-themed nursery? Our advice: buy solid color matching sheets and linens and then accessorize with Pooh items. Fortunately, a myriad of companies make Pooh licensed accessories. For example, Michel & Co/Charpent (310) 390-7655 makes Pooh lamps, clocks and other accessories, Beacon (828) 686-3861 makes Pooh cotton blankets and throws, Couristan (800) 223-6186 makes hand-hooked Pooh-themed rugs, Sunworthy Wallcoverings (800) 535-7811 makes Pooh wall boards and wall paper and Gund (800) 448-4863 (web: www.gund.com) makes Pooh plush and soft toys.

exception of JCPenney, Baby Catalog, etc., which sell name brands). In general, we find that the bedding from most mail-order catalogs is very high quality and unique in design. Another big plus: you can find affordable basic items like solid color sheets and blankets.

BABY CATALOG OF AMERICA

Call (800) PLAYPEN or (203) 931-7760; Fax (203) 933-1147.
Internet: www.babycatalog.com
Accept: all major credit cards
Order by mail or visit the Baby Club of America Warehouse Outlet, 719 Campbell Ave., West Haven, CT 06516.

How can you get name-brand bedding at a big discount? Unfortunately, most catalogs sell bedding at full retail and baby stores are loath to discount fancy brands.

Well, here's the good news: Baby Catalog of America is a one-stop source for brand new bedding, linen, decor and other accessories at prices 20% to 50% off retail. And we're not talking about just the low quality bedding brands either. Baby Catalog of America sells a wide variety of premium brands, including Sumersault and Pine Creek.

What about accessories? You can find lamps, wall decor, and other nursery items at good prices too. There's a big selection of Pooh items as well as basics like solid color sheets and blankets.

If those prices weren't low enough, Baby Catalog will give you another 10% off each purchase if you buy an annual membership ($25). And that's just the beginning: the catalog also sells strollers, car seats, accessories and more. The only caveat to using this catalog and web site is we don't recommend using their baby registry. We've received many complaints from past readers about this service.

COMPANY KIDS

To Order Call: (800) 323-8000
Web: www.companykids.com
Shopping Hours: 24 hours a day, seven days a week.
Or write to: 500 Company Store Rd., La Crosse, WI 54601.
Credit Cards Accepted: MC, VISA, AMEX, Discover.

A subsidiary of the Company Store, Company Kids now offers a complete catalog catering to the bedding whims of parents and little ones alike. Basically, Company Kids offers a selection of quilts for infants, which can then be paired with sheets in solids or checks. There are also some bedding sets (sold a la carte with matching bumpers, sheets and dust ruffles) as well. You can also buy comforter covers and comforters to go together.

Sheets run $12 to 19 each while comforters range from $50 to $88 each. A four-piece set is about $170. Not a bad deal at all for 100% cotton percale, flannel or knit bedding fabrics.

Bottom line: we think Company Kids continues sells high quality baby bedding at great prices. We also liked their web site, which is easy-to-navigate and features clearance items for even bigger savings. If you're in the vicinity of The Company Store's outlet store, don't miss it. One reader found the prices amazing including sheets at only $5 each.

EDDIE BAUER

To Order Call: (800) 426-8020; Web: www.eddiebauer.com
Shopping Hours: 24 hours a day, seven days a week.
Or write to: PO Box 182639, Columbus, OH 43218.
Credit Cards Accepted: MC, VISA, AMEX, Discover.

Eddie Bauer offers a decent selection of crib sheets, blankets, and quilts, as well as complete sets. Most of the sets are made exclusively for the catalog by Sumersault (reviewed earlier), so you know the quality is high (100% cotton fabric, etc.). "Crazy Quilt" is a colorful pattern that runs $269 for a three-piece set (quilt, bumper, dust ruffle). All cotton flannel sheets are $19 while percale sheets are $22. A flannel blanket is $19. Prices can be a bit high, but the quality is top of the line.

Eddie Bauer's web site is a joy to use—you can easily zip from one section to another. The weekly specials and clearance items are especially good deals. Speaking of deals, a reader emailed to say that Eddie Bauer offers two promotional events each year, with 20% discounts off. The first is the Friends and Family sale which occurs in June and November; the second is the Corporate event. Each event lasts four days. Although it is supposed to be limited to the stores only, our reader said the catalog will often honor the sale price if you ask nicely. And don't forget: if you order from the in store phones at your local Eddie Bauer store, shipping is free.

GARNET HILL

To Order Call: (800) 622-6216; In Canada, call (603) 823-5545.
Shopping Hours: 24 hours a day, seven days a week.
Or write to: Garnet Hill, 231 Main St., Franconia, NH 03580.
Credit Cards Accepted: MC, VISA, AMEX, Discover.
Outlet: Historic Manchester Outlet Center, Manchester VT (802) 362-6198.

If you want to spend the big bucks on bedding, check out

Continued on page 126

BEDDING RATINGS

NAME	RATING	COST
AMY COE	B+	$$$
BABY GUESS	B	$$
BANANA FISH	B	$$ TO $$$
BEAUTIFUL BABY	B-	$$$
BRANDEE DANIELLE	A-	$$
CALIFORNIA KIDS	A	$$
CARTERS	B+	$
CELEBRATIONS	B+	$$ TO $$$
COCALO	B+	$$
COMPANY KIDS	A	$
COTTON TALE	A	$$
CROWN CRAFTS	C+	$ TO $$
EDDIE BAUER	A	$$
GERBER	D	$
GLENNA JEAN	B-	$ TO $$$
HOOHOBBERS	B+	$$
HOUSE OF HATTEN	B+	$$ TO $$$
INFANTINO	B	$ TO $$
JUDI'S	C+	$ TO $$$
KIDSLINE	B	$ TO $$
LAMBS & IVY	B+	$ TO $$
LANDS END	A	$
LUV STUFF	B	$$$
MARTHA STEWART	C	$
NAVA'S DESIGNS	C+	$$$
NOJO	B	$ TO $$
PATCHKRAFT	A	$$ TO $$$
PINE CREEK	A-	$$
POTTERY BARN	B+	$$
QUILTEX	B-	$ TO $$
RED CALLIOPE	C+	$ TO $$
SUMERSAULT	A	$$ TO $$$
SWEET PEA	B	$$$
WENDY BELLISSIMO	B+	$$ TO $$$

KEY

*** N/A.** In some cases, we didn't have this information by press time.

COST: Cost of a four-piece set (comforter, sheet, dust ruffle/bed skirt, bumpers) $=under $200; $$=$200 to $400; $$$=over $400

FIBER CONTENT: Some lines have both all-cotton and poly/cotton blends–these are noted with the word "Mix."

FIBER CONTENT	BUMPER TIES	TIE LENGTH
100% COTTON	TOP/BOTTOM	10″
100% COTTON	TOP	8″
100% COTTON	TOP	6″
MIX	TOP/BOTTOM	8″
MIX	TOP	7″
100% COTTON	TOP/BOTTOM	10″
100% COTTON	*	*
100% COTTON	TOP/BOTTOM	9″
MIX	*	*
100% COTTON	*	*
100% COTTON	TOP	7.5″
MIX	TOP	8″
100% COTTON	*	*
POLY/COTTON	*	*
MIX	TOP	10″
100% COTTON	TOP	6″
100% COTTON	TOP/BOTTOM	8.5″
MIX	*	*
MIX	TOP	7″
MIX	TOP/BOTTOM	7″ TO 9″
POLY/COTTON	TOP	10″
100% COTTON	TOP/BOTTOM	*
MIX	TOP	11″
100% COTTON	TOP	*
100% COTTON	TOP/BOTTOM	14″
MIX	TOP	7″
100% COTTON	TOP/BOTTOM	9″
100% COTTON	TOP/BOTTOM	8″
100% COTTON	*	*
POLY/COTTON	TOP	7″
MIX	*	*
100% COTTON	TOP	7″-9″
100% COTTON	TOP/BOTTOM	10″
100% COTTON	TOP/BOTTOM	*

BUMPER TIES: refers to the location of bumper ties, top and bottom or top only.
TIE LENGTHS: the length of the bumper ties; these are approximate estimates and may vary from style to style.

Garnet Hill. This catalog makes a big deal out of its "natural fabric" offerings, and they do sell products we haven't seen elsewhere. But you'll pay for the privilege.

Garnet Hill sells woven, knit and flannel crib bedding. Fitted sheets range from $22 to $28 each and the designs are attractive—we especially like the "Ballerina" and "Farmyard" patterns. The quality is high: all sheets are 200 thread count and some are made of Egyptian cotton. One reader emailed her thoughts on Garnet Hill's flannel sheets: "A big thumbs up," she said, adding that "even though the price was high, the sheets were very high quality, soft and didn't pill." She wasn't as thrilled with their bumper pads, which only have ties at the top and the filling "got a bit munched in the washing machine."

The catalog's patchwork quilts are quite beautiful and cost $78 to $98. Good news: the Wall St. Journal's Catalog Critic rated a Garnet Hill crib quilt as Best Overall. High praise indeed.

GRAHAM KRACKER

To Order Call: (800) 489-2820; Fax: (915) 697-1776
Web: www.grahamkracker.com; Credit Cards Accepted: MC, VISA.

This mail order company specializes in custom bedding. You can mix and match your own selections from 17 styles or choose from five ready-made collections. Or you can provide your own fabric. The price? A whopping $450 for a five-piece set, which includes a headboard bumper and baby pillow (don't use this in the crib please!). The prices have gone up a bit in the last year, making their custom option on the expensive side. But, everything is 100% cotton and there are all sorts of matching accessories. Most of the choices are bright, cheerful colors, but not too cutesy. Shipping time is two to three weeks.

JCPENNEY

To Order Call: (800) 222-6161. Ask for the "Pennies from Heaven" catalog.
Web: www.JCPenney.com/shopping
Shopping Hours: 24 hours a day, seven days a week.
Credit Cards Accepted: MC, VISA, JCPenney, AMEX, Discover.

JCPenney carries quite a wide range of name brand baby bedding from manufacturers like Simmons, Carter's (Lennon Baby), Baby Loony Tunes, Nojo, Lambs & Ivy, Judi's Originals, Glenna Jean, KidsLine and Red Calliope (Disney Pooh). While Penney's prices aren't always affordable (we compared some designs to other mail-order sources and found Penney's to be a few dollars higher), they do offer the most accessories we've ever found. For example, they carry every accessory available for the "Pooh" line. The catalog carries valances, wallpaper borders, mobiles, and wall hangings for these and other bedding designs. If you want a "complete look," give Penney's a call. The only bummer: Penney's web site is hard to use–we couldn't find any of the juvenile items on a recent visit. When we clicked on "Bedding & Coordinates," the site popped up a picture of a Kitchen Aid mixer! Your best bet is to use the search function to find crib bedding. Then you'll get where you want to go.

The Land of Nod

To Order Call: (800) 933-9904. Web: www.landofnod.com
Shopping Hours: Mon-Fri 7:30am to 9:00pm, Weekends 9am to 5pm
Or Write to: PO Box 1404, Wheeling, IL 60090
Credit Cards: MC, VISA, AMEX, Discover.

This stunning catalog features sumptuous layouts of baby's and kid's rooms, replete with expensive linens and accessories. Even if you don't buy anything, the Land of Nod is a great place to get decorating ideas.

Crib bedding is sold in sets or a la carte. A four-piece set runs $370, while a single sheet can cost $40. We loved the color palette, which ranged from patchwork denim to bright pastels. Check out the whimsical lamps and other accessories. We wish they had their whole catalog up on their web site instead of just a few samples of their collection. It's a bit disappointing–all you can do is email a catalog request or order one of ten sample items via the (800) number. Memo to the Land of Nod: the Internet thing is here to stay, so get with it.

Lands' End.

To Order Call: (800) 345-3696; Web: www.landsend.com
Shopping Hours: 24 hours a day, seven days a week.
Or write to: Lands' End Inc., 1 Lands' End Ln., Dodgeville, WI 53595.
Credit Cards Accepted: MC, VISA, AMEX, Discover.
Retail Outlets: Lands' End has 20 outlet stores, mostly in the Midwest and Northeast–call the number above for the nearest location to you.

The Lands' End "Coming Home" catalog offers a three bedding options for infants: cotton percale (a woven sheet), flannel (brushed cotton weave) and knit (feels like a t-shirt). We found the prices to be a good deal, given the quality (Lands' End's sheets scored very well in Good Housekeeping's shrinkage tests). Solid color flannel sheets are $32 (sold in packs of two), while bumpers are $48 and a dust ruffle is $28, and coverlets are $32. We love these Lands' End "coverlets" (which are more substantial than a blanket but not as thick as a quilt/comforter) instead of those huge quilts sold by other manufacturers. The Polartec blankets ($22) are also a good option for parents in cold climates.

While the offerings change each season, Land's End designs have tended toward the simple, with no cartoons or appliques to clutter up the simple look. Another bonus: Lands' End web site has fantastic overstock deals, posted twice weekly.

Pottery Barn Kids

To Order Call: (800) 430-7373. Web: www.potterybarnkids.com
Shopping Hours: 24 hours a day, seven days a week.
Or write to: P.O. Box 379909, Las Vegas, NV, 89137.
Credit Cards Accepted: MC, VISA, AMEX.
Outlet Stores: Jeffersonville, OH (740) 948-2004, Dawsonville, GA (706) 216-5211 or (706) 216-6465, Memphis, TN (901) 763-1500.

No catalog has shaken up the baby bedding and décor business in recent years like the Pottery Barn Kids (PBK) catalog. Their cheerful baby bedding, whimsical accessories and furniture have overrun the rest of the industry. PBK isn't cutesy-babyish or overly adult. It's playful, fun and bright. And hot. We get more questions about this catalog than any other.

So let's answer a few of those questions. PBK's bedding is 100% cotton, 200 thread count. The sheets have 10" corner pockets and elastic that goes all the way around the edge. In general, the quality is good, although several readers have complained about the bumpers, which are knocked as "thin and insubstantial." One reader even complained that the ties kept pulling off her bumper.

Prices for quilts range from $70 to $90, bumper sets are $40 to $80, sheets are $18 to $25 and dust ruffles are $40 to $60. Not bad for the quality. Compared to other bedding manufacturers, Pottery Barn is a pretty good deal. Frequent sales make more expensive items like lamps and rugs even more affordable. The best deal: PBK's outlet stores. One reader saw sheets on sale for $8, duvet covers for $15 and even a crib for $175 at the outlet (see above for locations).

What really seems to be PBK's strong suit is accessories. The catalog is stuffed with so many rugs, lamps, storage options and toys, you can shop one place for a complete look. For example, how about a nursery theme with flowers and butterflies? You can find the bedding ($148 for the bumper and quilt) plus a coordinating butterfly lamp ($49), rug ($79-$200) butterfly stamps and paint to match ($35 and $16) and more.

Overall, we like PBK. One caveat: their success has led to some growing pains. You may find some items back-ordered. Our advice: order early to be sure you get what you want on time.

◆ ***Other Catalogs to Consider.*** Here are several other catalogs that carry basic linens and supplies:

Kid's Club	(800) 363-0500
The Right Start	(800) 548-8531
One Step Ahead	(800) 274-8440

The following catalogs offer many of the same linen items but with an eco-friendly angle:

Natural Baby	(800) 388-BABY
Seventh Generation	(800) 456-1177

The Bottom Line: A Wrap-Up of Our Best Buy Picks

For bedding, we think Cotton Tale and Lambs & Ivy combine good quality at a low price. If you can afford to spend more, check out the offerings from Patchkraft, Sumersault, and California Kids. And if money is no object, try Wendy Bellissimo. Of course, there's no law that says you have to buy an entire bedding set for your nursery—we found that all baby really needs is a set of sheets and a good cotton blanket. Catalogs like Lands' End and Company Store sell affordable (yet high-quality) basics like sheets and blankets. Instead of spending $300 to $500 on a bedding set with ridiculous items like pillows and diaper stackers, use your creativity to decorate the nursery affordably and leave the crib simple. The iron-on Transfer-Mations are a great example of cheap chic—create a mural or decorative border in your baby's nursery for just $30 (plus paints).

And if you fall in love with Pooh, don't shell out $300 on a fancy bedding set. Instead, we recommend buying solid color sheets and accessorizing with affordable Pooh items like lamps, posters, rugs, etc.

Who's got the best deals on bedding? If it's a set you desire, check out web sites like Baby Depot (www.coat.com) for discounts of 20% to 40%. If you're lucky to be near a manufacturer's outlet, search these stores for discontinued patterns.

Let's take a look at the savings:

Lands' End 100% cotton fitted sheets (three)	$64
Cotton coverlet blanket from Lands' End	$36
Miscellaneous (Transfer-Mations, lamp, other decor)	$100
TOTAL	$200

If you live in a cold climate, you might want to get a Polar fleece blanket from a catalog like the Company Store for $20.

In contrast, if you go for a designer brand and buy all those silly extras like diaper stackers, you could be out as much as $800 on bedding alone–add in wall paper, accessories like wall hangings, matching lamps and you'll be out $1100 or more. So, the total savings from following the tips in this chapter could be as much as $800 to $900.

Now that your baby's room is outfitted, what about the baby? Flip to the next chapter to get the lowdown on those little clothes.

CHAPTER 4

The Reality Layette:
Little Clothes for Little Prices

What the heck is a "onesie"? How many clothes does your baby need? How come such little clothes have such big price tags? These and other mysteries are unraveled in this chapter as we take you on a guided tour of baby clothes land. We'll reveal our secret sources for finding name brand clothes at one-half to one-third off department store prices. Which brands are best? Check out our picks for the best clothing brands for your baby and our nine tips from smart shoppers on getting the best deals. Next, read about the many outlets for children's apparel that have been popping up all over the country. At the end of this chapter, we'll even show you how to save big bucks on diapers.

Getting Started: When Do You Need This Stuff?

◆ ***Baby Clothing.*** You'll need basic baby clothing like t-shirts and sleepers as soon as you're ready to leave the hospital. Depending on the weather, you may need a bunting at that time as well.

You'll probably want to start stocking up on baby clothing around the seventh month of your pregnancy. It's important to have some basic items on hand (like sleepers or stretchies) in case you deliver early; however, you may want to wait to do major shopping until after any baby showers to see what clothing your friends and family give as gifts.

Be sure to keep a running list of your acquisitions so you won't buy too much of one item. Thanks to gifts and our own buying, we had about two thousand teeny, side-snap shirts by the time our baby was born. In the end, our son didn't wear the shirts much (he grew out of the newborn sizes quickly and wasn't really wild about them anyway), and we ended up wasting the money we spent.

◆ ***Diapers.*** How many diapers do you need for starters? Are you sitting down? If you're going with ***disposables***, we recommend

600. Yes, that's six packages of 100 diapers each (purchase them in your eighth month of pregnancy, just in case Junior arrives early). You may think this is a lot, but believe us, we bought that much and we still had to do another diaper run by the time our son was a month old. Newborns go through many more diapers than older infants. Also, remember that as a new parent, you'll find yourself taking off diapers that turn out to be dry. Or worse, you may change a diaper three times in a row because Junior wasn't really finished.

Now that you know how many diapers, what sizes should you buy? We recommend 100 newborn-size diapers and 500 "size one" (or Step 1) diapers. This assumes an average-size baby (about seven pounds at birth). But remember to keep the receipts—if your baby is larger, you might have to exchange the newborns for sizes one's (and some of the one's for two's).

If you plan to use a diaper service to supply ***cloth diapers***, sign up in your eighth month. Some diaper services will give you an initial batch of diapers (so you're ready when baby arrives) and then await your call to start up regular service. If you plan to wash your own cloth diapers, buy two to five dozen diapers about two months before your due date. You'll also probably want to buy diaper covers (6 to 10) at that time.

Even if you plan to use disposable diaper, you should pick up one package of high-quality cloth diapers. Why? You'll need them as spit-up rags, spot cleaners and other assorted uses you'd never imagined before becoming a parent.

Sources

There are ten basic sources for baby clothing and diapers:

1 Baby Specialty Stores. Specialty stores typically carry 100% cotton, high-quality clothes, but you won't usually find them affordably priced. While you may find attractive dressy clothes, play clothes are typically a better deal elsewhere. Because the stores themselves are frequently small, selection is limited. On the upside, you can still find old-fashioned service at specialty stores—and that's helpful when buying items like shoes. In that case, the extra help with sizing may be worth the higher price.

As for diapers, you can forget about it—most specialty baby stores long ago ceded the diaper market to discounters and grocery stores (who sell disposables), as well as mail-order companies (who dominate the cloth diaper and supply business). Occasionally, we see specialty stores carry an offbeat product like Tushies, an eco-friendly disposable diaper. And some may have diaper covers, but the selection is typically limited.

2 **DEPARTMENT STORES.** Clothing is a department store's bread and butter, so it's not surprising to see many of these stores excel at merchandising baby clothes. Everyone from Sears to Nordstrom does baby clothes and frequent sales often make the selection more affordable.

3 **SPECIALTY CHAINS.** Our readers love the Gap's Old Navy (see money-saving tips section) and Gap Kids. Both sell 100% cotton, high-quality clothes that are stylish and durable. Old Navy's (3580 stores nationwide and soon to open stores in Toronto) selection of baby clothes is somewhat limited compared to Gap Kids (with 1885 stores in the US). Other chains to check out include Gymboree, and Talbots for Kids. All are reviewed later in this chapter.

4 **DISCOUNTERS.** Wal-Mart, Target and K-Mart have moved aggressively into baby clothes in the last decade. Instead of cheap, polyester outfits that were common a decade ago, most discounters now emphasize 100% cotton clothing in fashionable styles. Even places like Toys R Us now stock basic layette items like t-shirts, sleepers and booties.

Target has vastly expanded their baby clothes with their in-store brand, Cherokee, and others like B.U.M. Not only have they expanded, but the quality is terrific in most cases. We shop Target for all cotton play clothes and day care clothes. They seem to last pretty well with the active play our kids indulge in.

Diapers are another discounter strong suit—you'll find both name brand and generic disposables at most stores; some even carry a selection of cloth diaper supplies like diaper covers (although they are the cheaper brands; see the diaper section later in this book for more details). Discounters seem to be locked into an endless price battle with warehouse clubs on baby care items, so you can usually find the prices to be rock bottom.

5 **BABY SUPERSTORES.** Both Babies R Us and Baby Depot carry a decent selection of name-brand clothing at low prices. Most of the selection focuses on basics, however. You'll see more Carter's and Little Me than the fancy brands common at department stores. We've noticed in recent years that places like Babies R Us have "dumbed-down" their clothing section, trading fancy dress clothes and brands for more staples at everyday low prices. In that respect, Babies R Us has ceded the hip, stylish market to specialty chains like Gap Kids.

Diapers are a mixed bag at superstores. Babies R Us carries them, but Baby Depot doesn't. When you find them, though, the prices are comparable to discounters. We've seen diapers priced 20% to 30% lower at Babies R Us than grocery stores.

6 WAREHOUSE CLUBS. Members-only warehouse clubs like Sam's, Price/Costco and BJ's sell diapers at rock-bottom prices. The selection is often hit-or-miss—sometimes you'll see brand names like Huggies and Pampers; other times it may be off-brands. While you won't find the range of sizes that you'd see in grocery stores, the prices will be hard to beat. The downside? You have to buy them in "bulk," huge cases of multiple diaper packs that might require a fork lift to get home.

As a side note, we've even seen some baby clothes at warehouse clubs from time to time. We found very good quality blanket sleepers at Sam's for $8 each during one visit. Costco has also greatly improved their kid's clothing offerings in recent years. We love Costco's 100% cotton pajamas for toddlers at $10 a pair (compare at $28 a pair in catalogs). Costco also has infant-size play clothes and sleepers at bargain prices.

7 MAIL-ORDER. There are a zillion catalogs that offer clothing for infants. The choices can be quite overwhelming, and the prices can range from reasonable to ridiculous. It's undeniably a great way to shop when you have a newborn and just don't want to drag your baby out to the mall. Another mail order strength: cloth diapers and related supplies. Chains and specialty stores have abandoned these items, so mail order suppliers have picked up the slack. Check out "Do it By Mail" later in this chapter for the complete low-down on catalogs that sell clothing and diapers.

8 THE WEB. Baby clothing sales on the 'net have been somewhat slow to take off. We suspect this might have to do with the glut of mail order catalogs that vie for parents' attention, as well as the fact that clothing's relative low prices make the discounts less dramatic. As for diapers, several web sites have popped up in recent years to offer discount disposables. We'll discuss the best bets in cyberspace in the next section.

9 CONSIGNMENT OR THRIFT STORES. You might think of these stores as dingy shops with musty smells—purveyors of old, used clothes that aren't in great shape. Think again—many consignment stores today are bright and attractive, with name brand clothes at a fraction of the retail price. Yes, the clothes have been worn before, but most stores only stock high-quality brands that are in excellent condition. And stores that specialize in children's apparel are popping up everywhere, from coast to coast. Check out SecondHand.com (www.secondhand.com) for a directory of resale shops. Later in this chapter, we'll tell you how to find a consignment store near you.

10 **GARAGE/YARD SALES.** Check out the box on the next page for tips on how to shop garage sales like the pros.

Baby Clothing

So you thought all the big-ticket items were taken care of when you bought the crib and other baby furniture? Ha! It's time to prepare for your baby's "layette," a French word that translated literally means "spending large sums of cash on baby clothes and other such items, as required by Federal Baby Law." But, of course, there are some creative (dare we say, sneaky?) ways of keeping your layette bills down.

At this point, you may be wondering just what does your baby need? Sure you've seen those cute ruffly dresses and sailor suits in department stores—but what does your baby *really* wear everyday?

Meet the layette, a collection of clothes and accessories that your baby will use daily. While your baby's birthday suit was free, outfitting him in something more "traditional" will cost some bucks. In fact, a recent study estimated that parents spend $12,000 on clothes for a child by the time he or she hits 18 years old—and that sounds like a conservative estimate to us. That translates into a 20

CPSC Issues Thrift Shop Warning

Do second-hand stores sell dangerous goods? To answer that question, the Consumer Product Safety Commission surveyed 301 random thrift stores in 2000, looking for recalled or banned products like clothing with drawstrings (an entanglement and strangulation hazard). The results: 51% of stores were selling clothing (mostly outerwear) with drawstrings at the waist or neck. This is particularly disturbing since 22 deaths and 48 non-fatal accidents since 1985 are attributed to drawstrings. If you buy clothing at a consignment or thrift store or from a garage sale, be sure to avoid clothes with drawstrings. Another disturbing finding: about two-thirds of the stores surveyed had at least one recalled or banned product on the shelves.

billion (yes, that's billion with a B) dollar business for children's clothing retailers. Follow our tips, and we estimate that you'll save 20% or more on your baby's wardrobe.

Parents in Cyberspace: What's on the Web?

Little Prince & Princess

Web: www.royalbaby.com. Toll-free (866) 855-1945.
What it is: A giant online store with infant/toddler clothing, footwear and more.

Garage & Yard Sales Eight Tips to Get The Best Bargains

It's an American institution—the garage sale.

Sure you can save money on baby clothes and products at an outlet store or get a deal at a department store sale. But there's no comparing to the steals you can get at your neighbor's garage sale.

We love getting e-mail from readers who've found great deals at garage sales. How about 25¢ stretchies, a snowsuit for $1, barely used high chairs for $5? But getting the most out of garage sales requires some pre-planning. We interviewed a dozen parents who call themselves "garage sale experts" for their tips:

1 **CHECK THE NEWSPAPER FIRST.** Many folks advertise their garage sales a few days before the event—zero in on the ads that mention kids/baby items to keep from wasting time on sales that won't be fruitful.

2 **GET A GOOD MAP OF THE AREA.** You've got to find obscure cul-de-sacs and hidden side streets.

3 **START EARLY.** The professional bargain hunters get going at the crack of dawn. If you wait until mid-day, all the good stuff will be gone. An even better bet: if you know the family, ask if you can drop by the day before the sale. That way you have a first shot before the competition arrives. One trick: if it's a neighbor, offer to help set-up for the sale. That's a great way to get those "early bird" deals.

4 **DO THE "BOX DIVE."** Many garage sale hosts will just dump kid's clothes into a big box, all jumbled together in different

What's cool: This well-designed site features high-quality brands (such as Mother Maid and Alexis) at decent prices. For example, the Teddy Toes blanket with feet is just $45 here. Clothing brands include Jack Rabbit Creations, Farmer Jones Kidswear and North American Bear (booties). Frequent sales add to the deals. There's a selection of footwear, toys and gifts for under $10 plus links to other parenting sites. A clearance area featured mark-downs of 20% to 30%. We loved their "No Risk Guarantee"—you can return any item within 60 days of purchase for a full and complete refund (including the original shipping costs).

Needs work. Well, there is no shopping cart feature—if you want an item, you have to go to a separate order form page to fill out

sizes, styles, etc. Figuring out how to get the best picks while three other moms are digging through the same box is a challenge. The best advice: familiarize yourself with the better name brands in this chapter and then pluck out the best bets as fast as possible. Then evaluate the clothes away from the melee.

5 **CONCENTRATE ON "FAMILY AREAS."** A mom here in Colorado told us she found garage sales in Boulder (a college town) were mostly students getting rid of stereos, clothes and other junk. A better bet was nearby Louisville, a suburban bedroom community with lots of growing families.

6 **HAGGLE.** Prices on big ticket items (that is, anything over $5) are usually negotiable. Another great tip we read in the newsletter *Cheapskate Monthly*—to test out products, carry a few "C" and "D" batteries with you to garage sales. Most swings and bouncing seats use those type batteries, so you want to make sure they're working before buying.

7 **DON'T BUY A USED CRIB OR CAR SEAT.** Old cribs may not meet current safety standards. It's also difficult to get replacement parts for obscure brands. Car seats are also a second-hand no-no—you can't be sure it wasn't in an accident, weakening its safety and effectiveness. And watch out for clothing with drawstrings, loose buttons or other safety hazards.

8 **BE CREATIVE.** See a great stroller but hate the fabric? Remember that you can buy stroller seat covers from companies like Nojo (see a review of this company in the bedding chapter earlier in this book). For a small investment, you can rehabilitate a stroller into a showpiece.

the details. Yes, you can also order via an 800#, but we were surprised that such an easy-to-navigate site would overlook the shopping cart. Shipping is reasonable (but calculated on dollars spent, not weight). And the selection of clothing is pretty small. Finally, the ultra-cute pink and blue text gets a bit annoying after a while.

Patsy Aiken

Web: www.patsyaiken.com or www.chezami.com
What it is: The online arm of the well known clothing manufacturer.
What's cool: We've always loved Patsy Aiken's clothes, but their distribution is limited to fancy baby boutiques. The good news: their site now sells the entire collection online. The US-made clothes are all 100% cotton with amazing embroidery, applique and smocking. You'll find adorable lambs, sailboats, and more in pale pastels. They also offer beautiful holiday outfits for those family portraits. Prices average around $25 to $30 for a typical bubble, dress or pantsuit. Not cheap but the quality is terrific.
Needs work: While the site is fine, we thought the layout lacked interest–basically it is just row after row of outfits. You can enlarge the thumbprints, but some of the detail is still hard to see.

One of a Kind Kid

Web: www.oneofakindkid.com, see Figure 1 on the next page.
What it is: Discount outlet offering huge deals on high-quality kids clothes closeouts.
What's cool: This site specializes in the upper-end clothes you see in Nordstrom and Neiman Marcus. We saw brands like Florence Eisman, Wes & Willy and Hartstrings among others. One of a Kind Kids sells all their clothes at 70% off, a great deal only topped by the flat $6 shipping fee. Gift wrap? That's free. New items appear weekly so checking back frequently is a good idea.
Needs work: Unfortunately, the site notes that many of the items on their site are "one of a kind." This means if you see something you like, you may have to order it on the spot. While the thumbnails of the clothes are expandable, their tiny size makes it hard to get a quick read on what's available.

◆ ***Other great sites. Preemie.com*** (www.preemie.com) is a wonderful oasis for preemie parents. You'll find items like hospital shirts, basics, sleepwear, caps and booties. Not to mention, they have a selection of diaries and books as well as preemie announcements. If you've got a preemie, this is the site for you.

While ***SuddenlyMommies*** (www.suddenlymommies.com) doesn't have a huge selection of baby wear, it sure is cute stuff. All white with colorful ribbon borders, the outfits are generally all

Baby and Children's Clothing and Gifts at One...
GIRLS - infant, toddler, 4-6x, 7-16 | BOYS infant, toddler, 4-7, 8-16 | INFO my order store info
New Arrivals!
Special Occasion
Lilly!
Baby Gifts & Layette
Christening Outfits
Infant Girls
Infant Boys
Toddler Girls
Toddler Boys
Girls 4-6x
Boys 4-7
Girls 7-16
Boys 8-16
Customer Care
Show Cart
One of a Kind
The Children's Boutique & Outlet
K I D
Baby and children's clothing and gifts discounted up to 70% off original retail every day!
The best brands at the best prices!
YAHOO! SHOPPING
TOP SERVICE
Welcome to One of a Kind Kid - The Baby and Children's Boutique & Outlet! We feature discount prices on the finest European and American designer baby and children's clothes.
We carry all your favorite specialty store brands - Catimini, Cakewalk, Marese, Deux par Deux, Vive La Fete, Anavini, Maria Casero, Clayeux, Marsha, Portofino, Simi, Cozy Toes, Maggie Breen, Rosetta Millington, Wes and Willy, Nautica, Gum Boots, Carriage Boutiques, Les Bebes du Paradis, Robert Jackson, Melissa Jackson, CachCach, Feltman Brothers, Hartstrings, Kitestrings and more!

Figure 1: Great prices, high-quality brands and flat fee shipping make OneOfAKindKid.com a winner.

cotton and include booties, pants sets, diaper covers, dresses and more. Prices are a bit high. For example, a short sleeve cotton knit dress is $33.

We'd be remiss if we didn't also mention ***eBay*** (web: www.ebay.com) in this section. Their baby section is often stuffed with great deals on baby clothes. One tip: look for listings that say NWT—that's eBay-speak for "New With Tags." Obviously, these items are worth the most, yet often still sell for 50% off.

Of course, remember our mantra: never pay retail. You don't have to pay full retail for these clothes online. A great way to save is to use web coupons. See the box in the next chapter ("Coupon deals cut the cost of online shopping") for a list of sites that catalog the best web deals.

What Are You Buying?

Figuring out what your baby should wear is hardly intuitive to first-time parents. We had no earthly idea what types of (and how many) clothes a newborn needed, so we did what we normally do—we went to the bookstore to do research. We found three dozen books on "childcare and parenting"—with three dozen different lists of items that you *must* have for your baby and without which you're a very bad parent. Speaking of guilt, we also heard from relatives, who had their own opinions as to what was best for baby.

All of this begs the question: what do you *really* need? And how much? We learned that the answer to that last, age-old question was the age-old answer, "It depends." That's right, nobody really knows. In fact, we surveyed several department stores, interviewed dozens of parents, and consulted several "experts," only to find no consensus whatsoever. In order to better serve humanity, we have developed THE OFFICIAL FIELDS' LIST OF ALMOST EVERY ITEM YOU NEED FOR YOUR BABY IF YOU LIVE ON PLANET EARTH. We hope this clears up the confusion.

Feel free to now ignore those lists of "suggested layette items" provided by retail stores. Many of the "suggestions" are self-serving, to say the least.

Of course, even when you decide what and how much to buy for your baby, you still need to know what *sizes* to buy. Fortunately, we have this covered, too. First, recognize that most baby clothes come in a range of sizes rather than one specific size ("newborn to 3 months" or "3-6 months"). *We recommend you buy "3-6 month" sizes (instead of newborn) so your child won't grow out of his clothes too quickly.* Stay away from newborn to three-month sizes. If you have a premature baby or an infant who is on the small side, we have identified a couple of catalogs that specialize in preemie wear. And, if on the other hand, you deliver a 10-pounder, make sure you keep all receipts and labels so you can exchange the clothes for larger sizes–you may find you're into six-month sizes by the time your baby hits one month old!

(Along the same lines, don't wash all those new baby clothes immediately. Wash just a few items for the initial few weeks. Keep all the other items in their original packaging to make returns easier).

Remember, you can always buy more later if you need them. In fact, this is a good way to make use of those close friends and relatives who stop by and offer to "help" right after you've suffered through 36 hours of hard labor–send them to the store!

We should point out that this layette list is just to get you started. This supply should last for the first month or two of your baby's life. Also along these lines, we received a question from a mom-to-be who wondered, given these quantities, how often do we assume you'll do laundry. The answer is in the next box.

More Money Buys You . . .

Even the biggest discounters now offer good quality clothing. But with more money you tend to get heavier weight cottons, nicer fasteners, better quality embellishments and more generous sizing. At some point, however, considering how fast your little one is growing, you'll be wasting money on the most expensive clothes out there.

The "Baby Bargains" Layette

◆ ***T-Shirts***. Oh sure, a t-shirt is a t-shirt, right? Not when it comes to baby t-shirts. These t-shirts could have side snaps, snaps at the crotch (also known as onesies or creepers) or over-the-head openings. If you have a child who is allergic to metal snaps (they leave a red ring on their skin), you might want to consider over-the-head t-shirts. As a side note, you have to wait until your baby's belly button falls off (don't ask; this usually happens in a week or two) until you can use the snap-at-the-crotch t-shirts.

By the way, is a onesie t-shirt an outfit or an undergarment? Answer: it's both. In the summer, you'll find onesies with printed patterns that are intended as outfits. In the winter, most stores just sell white onesies, intended as undergarments.

HOW MANY? T-shirts usually come in packs of three. Our recommendation is to buy two packages of three (or a total of six shirts) of the side-snap variety. We also suggest buying two packs of over-the-head t-shirts. This way, if your baby does have an allergy to the snaps, you have a backup. Later you'll find the snap-at-

E-MAIL FROM THE REAL WORLD
How Much Laundry Will I Do?

Anna Balayn of Brooklyn, NY had a good question about baby's layette and laundry:

"You have a list of clothes a new baby needs, but you don't say how often I would need to do laundry if I go with the list. I work full time and would like to have enough for a week. Is the list too short for me?"

Our answer: there is no answer. Factors such as whether you use cloth or disposable diapers (cloth leaks more; hence more laundry) and how much your baby spits up will greatly determine the laundry load. Another factor: breast versus bottle feeding. Bottle-fed babies have fewer poops (and hence, less laundry from possible leaks). An "average" laundry cycle with our layette list would be every two to three days, assuming breast feeding, disposable diapers and an average amount of spit-up.

the-crouch t-shirts to be most convenient since they don't ride up under clothes.

◆ ***Gowns.*** These are one-piece gowns with elastic at the bottom. They are used as sleeping garments in most cases. (We'll discuss more pros/cons of gowns later in this chapter.)

HOW MANY? This is a toss-up. If you want to experiment, go for one or two of these items. If they work well, you can always go back and get more later.

◆ ***Sleepers.*** This is the real workhorse of your infant's wardrobe, since babies usually sleep most of the day in the first months. Also known as stretchies, sleepers are most commonly used as pajamas for infants. They have feet, are often made of flame-retardant cloth and snap up the front. While most are made of polyester, we've seen an increase in the numbers of cotton sleepers in recent years. Another related item: cotton long johns for baby. These are similar to sleepers, but don't have feet (and hence, may necessitate the use of socks in winter months).

HOW MANY? Because of their heavy use, we recommend parents buy at least four to six sleepers.

◆ ***Blanket Sleepers.*** These are heavy-weight, footed one-piece garments made of polyester. Used often in winter, blanket sleepers usually have a zipper down the front. In recent years, we've also seen quite a few "Polartec" blanket sleepers, their key advantage being a softer fleece fabric and a resistance to pilling.

HOW MANY? If you live in a cold climate or your baby is born in the winter, you may want to purchase one or two of these items. As an alternative to buying blanket sleepers, you could put a t-shirt on underneath a sleeper or stretchie for extra warmth.

◆ ***Coveralls.*** One-piece play outfits, coveralls (also known as rompers) are usually cotton or cotton/poly blends. Small sizes (under 6 months) may have feet, while larger sizes don't.

HOW MANY? Since these are really play clothes and small infants don't do a lot of playing, we recommend you only buy two to four coveralls for babies under four months of age. However, if your child will be going into daycare at an early age, you may need to start with four to six outfits.

◆ ***Booties/socks.*** These are necessary for outfits that don't have

feet (like gowns and coveralls). As your child gets older (at about six months), look for the kind of socks that have rubber skids on the bottom (they keep baby from slipping when learning to walk).

HOW MANY? Three to four pairs are all you'll need at first, since baby will probably be dressed in footed sleepers most of the time.

◆ ***Sweaters.*** HOW MANY? Most parents will find one sweater is plenty (they're nice for holiday picture sessions). Avoid all-white sweaters, since they show dirt much faster.

◆ ***Hats.*** Believe it or not, you'll still want a light cap for your baby in the early months of life, even if you live in a hot climate. Babies lose a large amount of heat from their heads, so protecting them with a cap or bonnet is a good idea. And don't expect to go out for a walk in the park without the baby's sun hat either.

HOW MANY? A couple of hats would be a good idea–sun hats in summer, warmer caps for winter. We like the safari-style hats best (they have flaps to protect the ears and neck).

◆ ***Snowsuit/bunting.*** Similar to the type of fabric used for blanket sleepers, buntings also have hoods and covers for the hands. Most buntings are like a sack and don't have leg openings, while snowsuits do. Snowsuits can be used in a car seat, while buntings are a no-no. Both versions usually have zippered fronts.

HOW MANY? Only buy one of these if you live in a climate where you need it. Even with the Colorado winter, we got away with layering clothes on our baby, then wrapping him in a blanket for the walk out to a warmed-up car. If you live in an urban city without a car, you might need two or three snowsuits for those stroller rides to the market.

◆ ***Kimonos.*** Just like the adult version. Some are zippered sacks with a hood and terry-cloth lining. You use them after a bath.

HOW MANY? Are you kidding? What a joke! These items are one of our "wastes of money." We recommend you pass on the kimonos and instead invest in good quality towels.

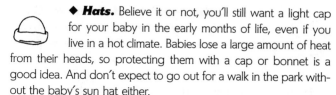

◆ ***Saque Sets.*** Two-piece outfits with a shirt and diaper cover.

HOW MANY? Forget buying these as well. We'll discuss later in this chapter why saque sets are a waste of money.

◆ ***Bibs.*** These come in two versions, believe it or not. The little, tiny bibs are for the baby that drools the volume of Lake Michigan. The larger versions are used when you begin feeding her solid foods (at about six months). Don't expect to be able to use the drool bibs later for feedings, unless you plan to change her carrot-stained outfit frequently.

HOW MANY? Skip the drool bibs (we'll discuss why later in this chapter under Wastes of Money). When baby starts eating solid foods, you'll need at least three or four large bibs. One option: plastic bibs for feeding so you can just sponge them off after a meal.

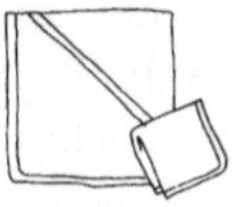

◆ ***Washcloths and Hooded Towels.*** OK, so these aren't actually clothes, but baby washcloths and hooded towels are a necessity. Why? Because they are small and easier to use, plus they're softer than adult towels and washcloths.

HOW MANY? At first, you'll probably need only three sets of towels and washcloths (you get one of each per set). But as baby gets older and dirtier, invest in a few more washcloths to spot clean during the day.

◆ ***Receiving Blankets.*** You'll need these small, cotton blankets for all kinds of uses: to swaddle the baby, as a play quilt, or even for an extra layer of warmth on a cold day.

HOW MANY? We believe you can never have too many of these blankets, but since you'll probably get a few as gifts, you'll only need to buy three or four yourself. A total of seven to eight is probably optimal.

What about the future? While our layette list only addresses clothes to buy for a newborn, you will want to plan for your child's future wardrobe as well. For the modern baby, it seems clothes come in two categories: play clothes (to be used in daycare situations) and dress-up clothes. Later in this chapter, we'll discuss more money-saving tips and review several brands of play and dress-up clothes.

Safe & Sound

Should your baby's sleepwear (that is, the items he'll wear almost non-stop for the first several months of life) be flame retardant? What the heck does "flame retardant" mean anyway?

According to the Consumer Product Safety Commission (CPSC),

items made of flame retardant fabric will not burn under a direct flame. Huh? Doesn't "flame retardant" mean it won't burn at all? No—that's a common myth among parents who think such clothes are a Superman-style second skin that will protect baby against any and all fire hazards.

Prior to 1996, the CPSC mandated that an item labeled as sleepwear be made of "flame retardant fabric." More often than not, that meant polyester. While there are a few companies that make cotton sleepwear that is chemically treated to be fire retardant, the prices of such items were so high that the de facto standard for children's sleepwear was polyester.

Then the government changed its mind. The CPSC noticed that many parents were rebelling against the rules and putting their babies in all-cotton items at bed-time. After an investigation, the CPSC revised the rules to more closely fit reality.

First, pajamas for babies nine months and under were totally exempt from the flame-retardancy rules. Why? Since these babies aren't mobile, the odds they'll come in contact with a fire hazard that would catch their clothes on fire is slim. What if the whole house catches fire? Well, the smoke is much more dangerous than the flames—hence, a good smoke detector in the nursery and every other major room of your house is a much better investment than fire retardant clothes.

What about sleepwear for older babies? Well, the government admits that "close-fitting" all-cotton items don't pose a risk either. Only flowing night gowns or pajamas that are loose-fitting must meet the flame retardancy rules today.

If you still want to go with "flame retardant" baby items, there are a couple of options beyond polyester. The Land's End catalog now sells "Polar Fleece" pajamas for babies and young children ($24.50). The fabric, while polyester, is specially woven to breathe and be more comfortable. Another option: some catalogs listed later in this chapter sell cotton clothes treated to be flame retardant.

Finally, one final myth to dispel on this topic: does washing flame-retardant clothing reduce its ability to retard flames? Nope—fabrics like polyester are naturally flame retardant (that is, there is no magic chemical they've been doused with that can wash out in the laundry). What about those expensive treated all-cotton clothes? We don't think that's a problem either. While we haven't seen any evidence to the contrary, we think those companies that sell these pricey items would be drummed out of business in a heartbeat if the flame-retardancy of their clothes suddenly disappeared after a few spins in the rinse cycle.

There is one exception to the laundry rule: if you do choose to buy flame-retardant clothing, be sure to avoid washing such clothing in soap flakes. Soap flakes actually add a flammable chemical residue to clothes. Instead, we recommend you use regular powder or liquid laundry detergent. What about other safety hazards with children's clothing? Here are a few more to consider:

◆ ***Check for loose threads.*** These could become a choking hazard, or the threads could wrap around fingers or toes, cutting off circulation. Be careful about appliqués as well. "Heat-welded" plastic appliqués on clothes can come off and cause choking. Poorly sewn appliqués can also be a hazard.

◆ ***Avoid outfits with easy-to-detach, decorative buttons or bows***—these may also be a choking hazard. If you have any doubts, cut the decorations off.

◆ ***Watch out for drawstrings.*** In recent years, many manufacturers have voluntarily eliminated such drawstrings. But if you get hand-me-downs or buy second-hand clothes, be sure to remove any strings.

Smart Shopper Tips

Smart Shopper Tip

Tips and Tricks to Get the Best Quality

"I've received several outfits from friends for my daughter, but I'm not sure she'll like all the scratchy lace and the poly/cotton blends. What should she wear, and what can I buy that will last through dozens of washings?"

Generally, we recommend dressing your child for comfort. At the same time, you need clothes that can withstand frequent washings. With this in mind, here are our suggestions for baby clothing:

1 **SEE WHAT YOUR BABY LIKES BEFORE INVESTING IN MANY GARMENTS.** Don't invest $90 in fancy sweaters, only to find baby prefers cotton onesies.

2 **WE GENERALLY RECOMMEND 100% COTTON CLOTHING.** Babies are most comfortable in clothing that breathes.

3 **IF YOU DISCOVER YOUR CHILD HAS AN ALLERGY TO METAL SNAPS** (you'll see red rings on his skin), consider alternatives such as shirts that have ties. Another option is a t-shirt that pulls on over the head. Unfortunately, many babies don't like having any-

thing pulled over their heads. Another alternative for allergic babies: clothes with plastic snaps or zippers.

4 IN GENERAL, BETTER-MADE CLOTHES WILL HAVE THEIR SNAPS ON A REINFORCED FABRIC BAND. Snaps attached directly to the body of the fabric may tear the garment or rip off when changing.

5 IF YOU'RE BUYING 100% COTTON CLOTHING, MAKE SURE ITS PRE-SHRUNK. Some stores, like Gymboree (see review later in this chapter), guarantee that their clothes won't shrink. In other cases, you're on your own. Our advice: read the label. If it says "wash in cold water" or " tumble dry low," assume the garment will shrink (and hence buy a larger size). On the other hand, care instructions that advise washing in warm water usually indicate that the garment is already preshrunk.

6 GO FOR OUTFITS WITH SNAPS AND ZIPPERS ON BOTH LEGS, NOT JUST ONE. Dual-leg snaps or zippers make it much easier to change a diaper. Always check a garment for diaper accessibility—some brands actually have no snaps or zippers, meaning you would have to completely undress your baby for a diaper change! Another pet peeve: garments that have snaps up the back also make diaper changes a big hassle.

7 BE AWARE THAT EACH COMPANY HAS ITS OWN WARPED IDEA ABOUT HOW TO SIZE BABY CLOTHES. See the box on the next page for more details.

8 BEWARE OF APPLIQUÉS. Some appliqué work can be quite scratchy on the inside of the outfit (it rubs against baby's skin). Also, poor-quality appliqué may unravel or fray after washing.

9 KEEP THE TAGS AND RECEIPTS. A reader emailed us her strategy for dealing with baby clothes that shrink: until she has a chance to wash the item, she keeps all packaging, tags and receipts. If it shrinks, she returns it immediately.

Wastes of Money

Waste of Money #1

Clothing that Leads to Diaper Changing Gymnastics

"My aunt sent me an adorable outfit for my little girl. The only problem: it snaps up the back making diaper changes a real pain.

One Size Does Not Fit All

A six month-size t-shirt is a six-month-size t-shirt, right? Wrong. For some reason, baby clothing companies have yet to synchronize their watches when it comes to sizes. Hence, a clothing item that says "six-month size" from one manufacturer can be just the same dimensions as a "twelve-month size" from another. All this begs the question: how can you avoid widespread confusion? First, open packages to check out actual dimensions. Take your baby along and hold up items to her to gauge whether they'd fit. Second, note whether items are pre-shrunk—you'll probably have to ask the salesperson or catalog representative (if not, allow for shrinkage). Third, don't key on length from head to foot. Instead, focus on the length from neck to crotch—a common problem is items that seem roomy but are too tight in the crotch. Finally, forget age ranges and pay more attention to labels that specify an infant's size in weight and height, which are much more accurate. To show how widely sizing can vary, check out the following chart. *Parenting Magazine* compared "six-month" t-shirts from six major clothing makers (we've added dimensions from three popular catalogs, Hanna Anderson, Land's End and Talbot's Kids). Here's what these six-month t-shirts really translated to in terms of a baby's weight and height:

What a six month t-shirt really means

MAKER	WEIGHT	HEIGHT
Baby Gap	17-22 lbs.	26-29"
Carter's Layette	12-18 lbs.	25"
Gymboree	18-23 lbs.	26-29"
Hanna Anderson	14-21 lbs.	26-30"
Health-Tex	13.5-19 lbs.	24-27.5"
Land's End	14-18 lbs.	25-27"
Little Me	16-17 lbs.	27-28.5"
Oshkosh	16.5-18 lbs.	27-28.5"
Talbot's Kids	11-16 lbs.	24-27"

Here's another secret from the baby clothing trade: the more expensive the brand, the more roomy the clothes. Conversely, cheap items usually have the skimpiest sizing. What about the old wives' tale that you should just double your baby's age to find the right size (that is, buying twelve-month clothes for a six-month old?). That's bogus—as you can see, sizing is so all over the board that this rule just doesn't work.

In fact, I don't dress her in it often because it's so inconvenient. Shouldn't clothing like this be outlawed?"

It's pretty obvious that some designers of baby clothing have never had children of their own. What else could explain outfits that snap up the back, have super tiny head, leg and arm openings, and snaps in inconvenient places (or worse, no snaps at all)? One mother we spoke with was furious about outfits that have snaps only down one leg, requiring her baby to be a contortionist to get into and out of the outfit.

Our advice: stay away from outfits that don't have easy access to the diaper. Look instead for snaps or zippers down the front of the outfit or on the crotch. If your baby doesn't like having things pulled over his head, look for shirts with wide, stretchie necklines.

Waste of Money #2

The Fuzz Factor

"My friend's daughter has several outfits that aren't very old but are already pilling and fuzzing. They look awful and my friend is thinking of throwing them out. What causes this?"

Your friend has managed to have a close encounter with that miracle fabric known as polyester. Synthetics such as polyester will often pill or fuzz, making your baby look a little rag-tag. Of course, this is less of a concern with sleepwear—some parents believe the flame retardancy of the fabric outweighs the garment's appearance.

However, when you're talking about a play outfit, we recommend sticking to all-cotton clothes. They wash better, usually last longer, and generally look nicer—not to mention they feel better to your baby. Cotton allergies are rare, unlike sensitivities to the chemicals used to make synthetic fabrics. You will pay more for all-cotton clothing, but in this case, the extra expense is worth it. Remember, just because you find the cheapest price on a polyester outfit doesn't mean you're getting a bargain. The best deal is not wasting money on outfits that you have to throw away after two washings.

If you get polyester outfits as gifts, here's a laundry tip: wash the items inside-out. That helps lessen pilling/fuzzing. And some polyester items are better than others—polar fleece sweatshirts and pajamas are still made of polyester, but are softer and more durable.

Waste of Money #3

Do I Really Need These?

"My mother bought me a zillion gowns before my baby was born, and I haven't used a single one. What the heck are they for?"

"The list of layette items recommended by my local department store includes something called a saque set. I've never seen one, and no one seems to know what they are. Do I really need one?"

"A kimono with matching towel and washcloth seems like a neat baby gift for my pregnant friend. But another friend told me it probably wouldn't get used. What do you think?"

All of these items come under the heading "Do I Really Need These?" Heck, we didn't even know what some of these were when we were shopping for our baby's layette. For example, what in the world is a saque set? Well, it turns out it's just a two-piece outfit with a shirt and diaper cover. Although they sound rather benign, saque sets are a waste of money. Whenever you pick up a baby under the arms, it's a sure bet her clothes will ride up. In order to avoid having to constantly pull down the baby's shirt, most parents find they use one-piece garments much more often than two-piece ones.

As for gowns, the jury is still out on whether these items are useful. We thought they were a waste of money, but a parent we interviewed did mention that she used the gowns when her baby had colic. She believed that the extra room in the gown made her baby more comfortable. Other parents like how gowns make diaper changes easy, especially in the middle of the night. Finally, parents in hot climates say gowns keep their infants more comfortable. So, you can see there's a wide range of opinions on this item.

There is no question in our minds about the usefulness of a baby kimono, however. Don't buy it. For a baby who will only wear it for a few minutes after a bath, it seems like the quintessential waste of your money (we saw one Ralph Lauren baby kimono for $39. And that was on sale). Instead, invest in some good quality towels and washcloths and forget those cute (but useless) kimonos.

Waste of Money #4

Covering Up Those Little Piggies

"I was looking at shoes for my baby the other day, and I saw a $35 pair of Baby Air Jordans at the store! This must be highway robbery! I can't believe babies' shoes are so expensive. Are they worth it?"

Developmentally, babies don't need shoes until after they become quite proficient at walking. In fact, it's better for their muscle development to go barefoot or wear socks. While those expensive Baby Air Jordans might look cute, they're really a waste of time and money.

One mother we interviewed insisted her daughter wear shoes

whenever they went out. If you, too, feel uncomfortable if your child goes shoe-less, at least look for shoes that have the most flexible soles. You'll also want fabrics that breathe and stretch, like canvas and leather–stay away from vinyl shoes. The best brands we found: OSA fabric booties, soft-sided shoes (available from the One Step Ahead catalog, 800-274-8440, web: www.onestepahead.com) run $10 and have non-skid soles. Booties, moccasins and "crib shoes" are available from many catalogs and retail stores. An excellent brand of affordable moccasins is Minnetonka (718) 365-7033, web site: www.minnetonka-by-mail.com.

Reader Teri Dunsworth recommends Canadian-made Robeez (800) 929-2623 or (604) 435-9074; web: www.robeez.com. "They are the most AWESOME shoes–I highly recommend them," she said in an email. Robeez are made of leather, have soft skid-resistant soles and are machine washable. They start at $22 for a basic pair. "My baby wears nothing else! They have infant and toddler sizes and oh-so-cute patterns." Another reader recommended New Zealand-made Bobux shoes (www.bobuxusa.com). These cute leather soft soles "do the trick by staying on extremely well," according to a reader.

What about shoes for one or two year olds? We've found great deals at Target, whose wide selection of sizes and offerings were impressive. Another good source: Gap Kids/Baby Gap. Their affordable line of sneakers are very good quality. Parents have also told us they've had success with Babies R Us' in-house brand; others like Stride Rite shoes, which are often on sale at department stores. If none of these stores are convenient, consider mail-order–see the Do It By Mail section later in this chapter for possibilities.

Waste of Money #5

To Drool or Not to Drool

"I received a few bibs from my mother-in-law as gifts. I know my baby won't need them until she's at least four to six months old when I start feeding her solids. Plus, they seem so small!"

What you actually got as a gift from your mother-in-law was a supply of drool bibs. Drool bibs are tiny bibs intended for small infants who start teething and hence drool all over everything. Or infants who spit-up frequently. Our opinion: they're pretty useless–they're too small to catch much drool or spit-up. Our solution: go for larger, more absorbent versions that you can reuse later when starting to feed solids to baby.

When you do buy bibs, stay away from the ones that tie. Bibs that snap or have Velcro are much easier to get on and off. Another good bet: bibs that go on over the head (and have no snaps or

Velcro). Why? Older babies can't pull them off by themselves.

Stay away from the super-size vinyl bibs that cover the arms, since babies can get too hot in them. However, we do recommend you buy a few regular-style vinyl bibs for travel. You can wash them off much more easily than the standard terry-cloth bibs. As for sources of bibs, many of the catalogs we review in this book carry such items.

Waste of Money #6

The Dreft Syndrome

"I see ads in parenting magazines that say an infant's clothes should be washed in special laundry detergent. Is this true?"

No, not in our opinion. We call it the "Dreft Syndrome" (after the laundry soap that claims it's better for infant clothes)—parents, typically first-timers, think if they don't wash Junior's clothes separately with expensive special soap, something bad will happen to their baby. Hogwash. Unless you have the rare child who suffers from skin allergies (and chances are, you don't), just throw baby's clothes in with the rest of the wash. And use regular laundry soap. If you're worried about perfumes or dyes, use one of the "clear" detergents free of such additives. Another idea: do a second rinse cycle to make sure all soap is removed from clothing on a first washing.

Other laundry tips: use the delicate cycle when washing baby items, since this lessens the wear and tear. Turn the clothes inside-out to protect against pilling/fuzzing. And put the clothes through an extra rinse cycle if you are using bleach or other additives.

The bottom line: Washing your baby's clothes separately in special soap is not only expensive, but you'll have to do much more laundry, since you can't throw the items in with your regular laundry.

Money Saving Secrets

1 **Two words: Old Navy.** The hip, discount off-shoot of the Gap (www.gap.com) was launched in 1994 and now has 500+ stores nationwide. Readers rave about the buys they find at Old Navy (sample: "adorable" 100% cotton onesies for just $4; gripper socks, 3 for $4.50), although most admit the selection is limited. The options change rapidly and Old Navy's sales and clearance racks are "bargain heaven," say our spies. An insider tip to Old Navy and Gap Kids: the stores change out their merchandise every six weeks, moving the "old" stuff to the clearance racks rather quickly.

2 Wait until after showers and parties to purchase clothes. Clothing is a popular gift item—you may not need to buy much yourself.

3 Stick with basics—T-shirts, sleepers, caps, socks and blankets. For the first month or more, that's all you need since you won't be taking Junior to the opera.

4 Take advantage of baby registries. Many baby stores offer this service, which helps avoid duplicate shower gifts or too many of one item. This saves you time (and money) in exchanging gifts.

5 Go for the SALES! The baby department in most department stores is definitely SALE LAND. At one chain we researched, the baby section has at least some items that are on sale every week! Big baby sales occur throughout the year, but especially in January. You can often snag bargains at up to 50% off the retail price. Another tip: consider buying for the future during end-of-season sales. If you're pregnant during the fall, for example, shop the end-of-summer sales for next summer's baby clothes.

6 Choose quality over low price for playclothes and basics. Sure that 100% polyester outfit is 20% cheaper than the cotton alternative. HOWEVER, beware of the revenge of the washing machine! You don't realize how many times you'll be doing laundry—that play outfit may get washed every couple of days. Cheap polyester clothes pill or fuzz up after just a few washings—making you more likely to chuck them. Quality clothes have longer lives, making them less expensive over time. The key to quality is thicker or more heavyweight 100% cotton fabric, well-sewn seams and appliqués, and snaps on reinforced fabric bands.

7 For sleepwear, try the affordable brands. Let's get real here: babies pee and poop in their sleepers. Hence, fancy designer sleepers are a money-waster. A friend of ours who lives in Texas uses affordable all-cotton onesies as sleepwear in the hot summer months. For the winter here in Colorado, we use thermal underwear which we've found for as little as $10.50 in Target and other stores.

8 Can't return it? Did you get gifts of clothing you don't want but can't return to a local store? Consign it at a local thrift store. We took a basketful of clothes that we couldn't use or didn't like and placed them on consignment. We made $40 in store credit or cash to buy what we really needed.

9 SPEAKING OF CONSIGNMENT STORES, HERE IS A WONDERFUL WAY TO SAVE MONEY: Buy barely used, consigned clothing for your baby. We found outfits ranging from $5 to $7 from high quality designers like Alexis. How can you find a consignment or thrift shop in your area specializing in high-quality children's clothes? Besides looking in the phone book, check out web sites like Internet Resale Directory (www.SecondHand.com) or the National Association of Resale & Thrift Shops (www.narts.org, click on the shopping icon). If you want to be cutting-edge, bid for second-hand baby items at online auction sites like eBay (www.ebay.com).

10 CHECK OUT DISCOUNTERS. In the past, discount stores like Target, Wal-Mart and Marshall's typically carried cheap baby clothes that were mostly polyester. Well, there's good news for bargain shoppers: in recent years, these chains have beefed up their offerings, adding more all-cotton clothes and even some brand names. We've been especially impressed with Target's recent offerings. For basic items like t-shirts and play clothes that will be trashed at day care, these stores are good bets. And don't forget other discounters like TJ Maxx and Ross Dress for Less. Just remember that some off price discounters will lack atmosphere (and that's

E-Mail from The Real World
Second-hand bargains easy to find

Shelley Bayer of Connecticut raved about Once Upon A Child, a nationwide chain of resale stores with 100+ locations (call 614-791-0000 for locations; web: www.OnceUponAChild.com).

"We have two locations of Once Upon A Child in Connecticut and I love them! The clothes and toys are of great quality and very affordable. The good thing about these stores is that when you take something in to be sold, they pay you cash. You do not have wait for something to be sold and keep checking your account like a traditional consignment shop."

One caution about second-hand stores—if you buy an item like a stroller or high chair at a resale shop, you may not be able to get replacement parts. One mom told us she got a great deal on a stroller that was missing a front bar . . . that is, it was a great deal until she discovered the model was discontinued and she couldn't get a replacement part from the manufacturer.

putting it lightly). Warehouse discounters like Sam's occasionally carry baby clothes as well. On our latest visit we saw Carter's fleece sleepers for only $7.

11 **DON'T FORGET ABOUT CHARITY SALES.** Readers tell us they've found great deals on baby clothes and equipment at church-sponsored charity sales. Essentially, these sales are like large garage/yard sales where multiple families donate kids' items as a fund-raiser for a church or other charity.

Outlets

There's been a huge explosion in the number of outlet stores over the last few years—and children's clothing stores haven't been left out of the boom. Indeed, as we were doing research for this section, we heard from many manufacturers that they had even more outlets on the drawing board. Therefore, if you don't see your town listed below, call the numbers provided to see if they've opened any new outlets. Also, outlet locations open and close frequently—always call before you go.

CARTER'S

Locations: Over 150 outlets.
Call (888) 782-9548 or (770) 961-8722 for the location nearest you.

It shows you how widespread the outlet craze is when you realize that Carter's has over 140 outlets in the U.S. That's right, 140. If you don't have one near you, you probably live in Bolivia.

We visited a Carter's outlet and found a huge selection of infant clothes, bedding, and accessories. Sleepers, originally $12, were available for $7, gowns were $5 (regularly $12) and side snap t-shirts were $10 for three (regularly $10).

As for baby bedding, we noted the outlet sells quilts (including the popular Lennon Baby—$65 regularly $115), bumpers, and pillows as well as fitted bassinet sheets and towels at low prices. All Carter's bedding is made by Riegal (see previous chapter for a review of their bedding line).

If you think those deals are great, check out the outlet's yearly clearance sale in January when they knock an additional 25% to 30% off their already discounted prices. A store manager at the Carter's outlet we visited said that they also have two other sales: back-to-school and a "pajama sale." Regardless of what they have on sale, the Carter's outlets sell only first quality goods—no seconds or rejects. (There's also a Carter's clearance outlet in The Marketplace in Old Bridge, NJ).

Esprit

Locations: 24 outlets. Call (415) 648-6900 for the location nearest you.

Not all of the Esprit outlets carry infant and toddler clothing, but those that do have sizes from 12 months through youth sizes (girls' designs only). The options include dresses, pants (we even saw a few pairs of flaired pants), and shorts. The prices are 30% to 70% off, and they sell only first quality overruns—no seconds. Call the outlet nearest you to see if it carries Esprit's children's line.

Flapdoodles

Location: Dillon, CO (970) 262-9351

The all-cotton designs from Flapdoodles are a great value even at retail, but you can actually find the clothes at 20% to 40% off retail in their outlet stores. With first quality merchandise and sizes from six months up to youth size 14, Flapdoodles outlet is worth a peek for long-lasting, high-quality play clothes.

Seconds are sold usually at the first of every month at their Newark, DE factory. Call (302) 731-9793 for the latest sale schedule.

Florence Eiseman

Location: Milwaukee, WI (414) 272-3222. Web: www.florenceeiseman.com

This baby clothing manufacturer closed their two outlet stores, but you can still find great deals at their factory sales in Milwaukee. A reader in Oak Park, IL emailed us this tip, adding the discounts are as much as 50% to 75% on baby and kid's clothing (which are normally sold at such stores as Neiman Marcus and Nordstrom's). Florence Eiseman specializes in party dresses and swimwear, but there is a selection of casual outfits as well. The company also sells its high-quality fabric, notions and remnants at these factory sales, which are held a couple times a year (call the above number for the latest schedule). If you're within shouting distance of Milwaukee, it might be a great sale to check out.

Hanna Andersson

Locations: Outlets Stores: Lake Oswego, OR (503) 697-1953 ; Michigan City, IN (219) 872-3183; Portsmouth, NH (603) 433-6642; Bloomington, MN (612)884-9390; Kittery, ME (207) 439-1992.

If you like Hanna Anderson's catalog, you'll love their outlet stores, which feature overstocks, returned items and factory seconds. For more information on Hanna Anderson, see "Do It By Mail" later in this chapter.

HARTSTRINGS

Locations: 15 outlets, mostly in the eastern U.S. Call (610) 687-6900 for the location near you.

Hartstrings' outlet stores specialize in first-quality apparel for infants, boys, and girls and even have some mother/child outfits. Infant sizes start at three months and go up to 24 months. The savings range from 30% to 50%.

HEALTH-TEX

Locations: 55 outlets. Call (800) 772-8336 for the location near you.

Health-Tex children's clothing is owned by Vanity Fair Corporation, which also produces such famous brands as Lee jeans, Wrangler, and Jantzen. The company operates four dozen outlets under the name VF Factory Outlet. They sell first-quality merchandise; most are discontinued items. Most of the VF outlets carry the Health-Tex brand at discounts up to 70% off retail.

JCPENNEY

Locations: 15 outlets; call (800) 222-6161.. Web: www.JCPenney.com

A reader in Columbus, Ohio emailed in her high praise for the Penney's outlet there. She snagged one-piece rompers for $5 (regularly $25) and hand-loomed coveralls for $2.99 (compared to $28 in stores). She also found satin christening outfits for both boys and girls for just $5 that regularly sell for as much as $70. The outlet carries everything from layette to play clothes, at discounts of 50% or more. (Hint: the outlet stores also have maternity clothes).

OSHKOSH

Locations: 128 outlets. Call (920) 231-8800 for the nearest location.

OshKosh, the maker of all those cute little overalls worn by just about every kid, sells their clothes direct at over 125 outlet stores. With prices that are 30% to 70% off retail, buying these play clothes staples is even easier on the pocketbook. For example, footed sleepers were $7.70 (regularly $11), and receiving blankets were $18.20 (regularly $24).

We visited our local OshKosh store and found outfits from infant sizes up to children's size 7. They split the store up by gender, as well as by size. Infant and toddler clothes are usually in the back of the store.

The outlet also carries OshKosh shoes, socks, hats, and even stuffed bears dressed in overalls and engineer hats. Seasonal ensembles are available, including shorts outfits in the summer and snowsuits ($42) in the winter. Some clothes are irregulars, so inspect the garments carefully before you buy.

Talbot's Kids

Location: 10 stores, most of which are in the Eastern U.S. Call (800) 543-7123 or (781) 740-8888. Web: www.talbots.com

A reader who calls herself a "devoted Talbot's shopper" emailed in her compliments for Talbot's outlet stores, which carry a nice selection of baby and children's clothes that didn't sell in their stores or catalog. "The deals can be fantastic, especially given the quality," she said, adding that you can get on the outlet's mailing list to get notices about additional markdowns. She estimated she saved 40% to 60% on items for her baby. Hint: Talbot's regular stores hold major sales twice a year (after Christmas and the end of June). What doesn't get sold then is shipped to the outlets.

◆ ***Other outlets.*** A great source for outlet info is ***Outlet Bound magazine***, which is published by Outlet Marketing Group ($9 plus $4 shipping, 1-888-688-5382). The magazine contains detailed maps noting outlet centers for all areas of the U.S. and Canada, as well as store listings for each outlet center. We liked the index that lists all the manufacturers, and they even have a few coupons in the back.

Outlet Bound also has an excellent web site (www.outlet-bound.com) with the most up-to-date info on outlets in the U.S. and Canada. We did a search on children's clothing outlets (you can search by location, store, brand or product category) and found several additional interesting outlets. These included outlets for Eagle's Eye Kids (two outlets), the Disney catalog outlet (11 locations) and the Oilily catalog (five outlets).

If you can't get enough of the ***Gap***, check out their outlet stores (650) 952-4400 (web: www.gaponline.com). With 88 locations nationwide, most Gap outlets have a baby/kid's clothing section and great deals (50% off and more).

Yet another outlet: ***Pingorama*** offers periodic factory sales from their Novato and Redwood, California locations. Check their web site, www.pingorama.com, (the where to buy link) for dates and directions.

Did you discover an outlet that you'd like to share with our readers? Call us at our office at 303-442-8792 or e-mail authors@ BabyBargainsBook.com.

The Name Game: Our Picks for the Best Brands

Walk into any department store and you'll see a blizzard of brand names for baby clothes. Which ones stand up to frequent washings? Which ones have snaps that stay snapped? Which are a good value for the dollar? We've got the answers, based on extensive parent feedback.

We're broken our recommendations into three areas: best bets, good but not great and skip it. As always, remember most of these manufacturers do not sell directly to consumers (those that do sell online are identified by an asterisk*). The phone numbers and web sites are included so you can locate a retailer near you who carries that brand. Here we go:

Best Bets

Alexis	(800) 253-9476	alexisusa.com
Baby Gap*	(800) GAP-STYLE	babygap.com
Cotton Tale Orig.	(800) 628-2621	
Earthlings*	(888) GOBABYO	earthlings.net
Flap Happy	(800) 234-3527	
Flapdoodles	(302) 731-9793	
Florence Eisman	(414) 272-3222	florenceeiseman.com
Gymboree*	(800) 990-5060	gymboree.com
Hartstrings	(610)687-6900	hartstrings.com
Jake and Me*	(970) 352-8802	jakeandme.com
Little Me		littleme.com
Mini Classics	(201) 569-7357	
Mother-Maid	(770) 479-7558	
Mulberri Bush (Tumbleweed too)		mulberribush.com
OshKosh B'Gosh*		oshkoshbgosh.com
Patsy Aiken*	(919) 872-8789	patsyaiken.com
Pingarama		pingarama.com
Sarah's Prints*	(888) 4-PRINTS	sarasprints.com
Skivvydoodles	(212) 967-2918	skivvydoodles.com
Sweet Potatoes/Spudz	(510) 527-7633	sweetpotatoesinc.com
Wes & Willy		wesandwilly.com

Good But Not Great

CARTER'S	(770) 961-8722	CARTERS.COM
FISHER PRICE*	(800) 747-8697	FISHER-PRICE.COM
GOOD LAD OF PHILA.*	(215) 739-0200	GOODLAD.COM
LE TOP	(800) 333-2257	
TARGET* (CHEROKEE BABY, B.U.M., BRAMBLY HEDGE, LULLABY CLUB, NATURAL BASICS)		TARGET.COM

Skip It: HEALTH TEX, GERBER, HANES.

Do it by Mail

BIOBOTTOMS

To Order Call: (800) 766-1254 or fax (540) 670-2121.
Shopping Hours: 7:00 am to 12:00 am, everyday.
Or write to: 730 E. Church St., Suite 19, Martinsville, VA, 24112..
Web: www.biobottoms.com, www.freshairwear.com
Credit Cards Accepted: MC, VISA, AMEX, Discover.

Once upon a time, when we first started writing about baby products, we discovered the Biobottoms catalog. Originally, they were based in California and started with a simple wool diaper cover. Since then they've been sold a couple times and added an incredible variety of cloth diaper options and clothing.

The catalog and web site basically showcase their bright, cheerful clothing. Baby basics include "tummy toppers" (long sleeve t-shirts) at $10, cotton coveralls ($19.50)and overalls ($32). Don't forget cute accessories like hats, socks, headbands and more. The prices aren't exactly a bargain, but the fun designs and high quality make them worth the purchase price.

By the way, Biobottoms.com showcases clothing from newborn to size 3 while FreshAirWear.com targets sizes 4 and up.

CHILDREN'S WEAR DIGEST (CWD)

To Order Call: (800) 242-5437; Fax (800) 863-3395.
Shopping Hours: 24 hours a day, seven days a week.
Or write to: 3607 Mayland Ct., Richmond, VA 23233.
Credit Cards Accepted: MC, VISA, AMEX, Discover.
Web: www.cwdkids.com
Outlet: "CWD Outlet," Gayton Crossing Shopping Center, Richmond, VA.
Also two company stores in Virginia. Call or visit the web site for more info.

If you're looking for name brands, check out Children's Wear Digest (CWD), a catalog that features clothes in sizes 12 months to 14 for both boys and girls.In a recent catalog, we saw clothes by Sweet Potatoes, Mulberribush, S.P.U.D.Z., Flapdoodles, and Sarah's Prints. Unlike other catalogs that de-emphasize brand names, CWD prominently displays manufacturer info.

Children's Wear Digest doesn't offer much of a discount off regular retail, but it does have a selection of sale clothes from time to time with savings of 15% to 25%. A best buy: CWD's web site (www.cwdkids.com) has online bargains, with savings of up to 50% on quite a few items and the latest news on their outlet store.

Chock

To Order Call: (800) 222-0020; or (212) 473-1929; Fax (212) 473-6273.
Shopping Hours: Sunday-Thursday 9:00 am to 5:00 pm Eastern.
Or write to: Chock, 74 Orchard St., New York, NY 10002.
Web: www.chockcatalog.com
Credit Cards Accepted: MC, VISA, Discover.
Retail store: 74 Orchard St., New York, NY 10002.

This small, black and white catalog focuses on basics at very good prices. You'll see name brands like Little Me, Gerber and Carter's, plus a good selection of t-shirts, caps, booties, gowns, sleepers, towels and washcloths. Best of all, the prices are discounted about 25% off the manufacturer's suggested list prices. Another plus for Chock: they always stock a supply of all-year-round merchandise, especially out-of-season items. New this year, Chock has a gift section including items from Montgomery Schoolhouse (wooden toys). The only bummer: Chock asks you to pay $2 for their catalog (but, hey, if you mention the *Baby Bargains* book, it's only $1). Instead, go on line and see the catalog for free on their web site. In fact, the web site mentions easy color coordinating options for layette.

Fisher Price

To Order Call: (800) 747-8697; Fax (608) 836-0761
Shopping Hours: 6 am to midnight Central Time, seven days a week.
Or write to: PO Box 620010, Middleton, WI, 53562
Web:www.fisher-price.com
Credit Cards Accepted: MC, VISA, AMEX, Discover.

Fisher Price might be a more familiar name to toy aisles than clothing racks, but their new catalog impressed us. We found a decent selection of layette items in 100% cotton including snap t-shirts ($10.50), playsuits ($18.50) and hat-bib-bootie sets ($18.50). Best bets: cute cardigans, jumpers, and overalls—even fleece sleep sacks! Sizes go from newborn to 7. Matching accessories like shoes, animal hats and tights compliment the whimsical designs.

HANNA ANDERSSON

To Order Call: (800) 222-0544; Fax (503) 321-5289.
Shopping Hours: 5 am to 9 pm Pacific Time, seven days a week.
Or write to: 1010 NW Flanders, Portland, OR, 97209.
Web: www.hannaandersson.com
Credit Cards Accepted: MC, VISA, AMEX, Discover.
Retail Stores: 125 Westchester Ave., Suite 3370, White Plains, NY 10601; (914) 684-2410; 327 NW Tenth Ave., Portland, OR 97209; (503) 321-5275.
Outlets Stores: Lake Oswego, OR (503) 697-1953 ; Michigan City, IN (219) 827-3183; and Portsmouth, NH (603) 433-6642.

Hanna Andersson says it offers "Swedish quality" 100% cotton clothes. Unfortunately, Swedish quality is going to set you back some big American bucks.For example, a simple coverall with zippered front was a whopping $34. While Andersson's clothing features cute patterns and attractive colors, it's hard to imagine buying a complete wardrobe at those prices.

These aren't clothes you'd have your baby trash at daycare—Hanna Andersson's outfits are more suitable for weekend wear or going to Grandma's house. One note of caution: while the quality is very high, some items have difficult diaper access (or none at all). Another negative: Hanna Andersson uses "European sizing," which can be confusing. (Yes, there is an explanation of this in the catalog, but we still found it difficult to follow). Furthermore, some items (like dresses) are cut in a boxy, unstructured way.

On the plus side, we liked their web site (www.hannaandersson.com), which features an online store, sizing info and more. The site has a sale page that offers 20% to 40% off on overstock items; you can quickly glance at the specials by category, size and price.

LANDS' END

To Order Call: (800) 963-4816,; Fax (800) 332-0103.
Web: www.landsend.com
Shopping Hours: 24 hours a day, seven days a week.
Or write to: 1 Lands' End Ln., Dodgeville, WI 53595.
Credit Cards Accepted: MC, VISA, AMEX, Discover.Discount
Outlets: They also have a dozen or so outlet stores in Iowa, Illinois and Wisconsin—call the number above for the nearest location.

Lands' End children's catalog features a complete layette line—and it's darn cute. The clothes feature 100% cotton "interlock knit," which the catalog claims gets softer with every washing and doesn't pill. Choose from playsuits, cardigans, onesies, pants, even cashmere sweaters—all in sizes three to 12 months. Most items were $10 to $26. For older babies, Lands' End all-cotton play clothes range from size 6 months to 4T. Don't look for fancy dress clothes from this catalog; instead Lands End specializes in casual playwear basics like sweat pants, overalls and hiking shoes (for toddlers no doubt).

Land's End web site is a continuation of the catalog's easy-to-use layout—you can buy items online, find an outlet store and more. Best bet for deals: check the great overstock deals, posted twice weekly.

LL Kids

To Order Call: (800) 552-5437; Fax (207) 552-3080
Shopping Hours: 24 hours a day; seven days a week.
Or write to: LL Bean, Freeport, ME 04033
Web: www.llbean.com
Credit Cards Accepted: MC, VISA, Discover, AMEX
Retail store: Freeport, ME

The baby version of big brother LL Bean, LL Kids originally emphasized outdoor gear: coats, snowsuits, hats, gloves, etc. But today the options have expanded to include pants and leggings, sleepwear, jumpers and more. Sample price: a fleece coverall that comes with zippered front and rollover mittens (and foot covers) for $40. A too-cute pair of duck rain boots was $16. Quick, grab the umbrella! Even though those prices are high, the quality of LL Kids is excellent—these items will last through several children. The web site is easy to use if you don't have a catalog handy. And if you find yourself near Freeport, Maine, check out the LL Kids store, a two-stories tall shop that resembles a Maine campground. An interactive area lets kids crawl into tents, experience a simulated mountain bike ride, scale a climbing wall and, oh yea, shop. We hear this 17,000 square foot store is quite spectacular, complete with tumbling waterfall and live trout pond.

Oilily

To Order Call: (800) 977-7736; Fax (888) 534-1120.
Or write to: 920 N. Michigan Ave. L522, Chicago, IL 60611
Credit Cards Accepted: MC, VISA, Discover, AMEX
Retail stores: 30 stores nationwide; call for a location near you.

"Subtle" is NOT the word we'd use to describe the clothes in the

Oilily catalog—you'll see bright and busy patterns that mix various textures and motifs. Sweaters can range up to $148, pants $80 and t-shirts $40. Oilily has some of the most expensive kid's clothes we've seen, so it's not a surprise this is the mail-order off-shoot of the retail chain with locations in Beverly Hills, CA and Aspen, CO. Be prepared to burn a hole in your charge card here.

Olsen's Mill Direct

To Order Call: (800) 537-4979 or Fax (920) 426-6369
Shopping Hours: 7:00 am to 11:00 pm Central Time, seven days a week.
Web: www.OlsensMillDirect.com
Or write to: Olsen's Mill Direct, 1641 S. Main St, Oshkosh, WI 54901.
Credit Cards Accepted: MC, VISA, AMEX, Discover.

One of the best organized catalogs we've seen, Olsen's Mill Direct offers an attractive selection of such famous brands as Good Lad of Philadelphia, OshKosh, and more. Another plus: the catalog has large photos of the clothes, so you can see what you're getting. Olsen's has a nice selection of newborn sleepwear ($18) from Little Me. We found the prices similar to retail list prices you'd see in stores and most items are 100% cotton. One negative note: our request for an updated catalog went unanswered. We tried to verify if prices have changed in recent months, but their web site wasn't much help.

Patagonia Kids

To Order Call: (800) 638-6464; Fax (800) 543-5522.
Shopping Hours: Monday-Friday 6 am to 6 pm Pacific; Saturday and Sunday 8 am- 4 pm Pacific Time.
Web: www.patagonia.com
Or write to: 8550 White Fir St., PO Box 32050, Reno, NV 89533.
Credit Cards Accepted: MC, VISA, AMEX, Discover.

Outdoor enthusiasts all over the country swear by Patagonia's scientifically engineered clothes and outerwear. They make clothing for skiing, mountain climbing, and kayaking—and for kids. That's right, Patagonia has a just-for-kids catalog of outdoor wear. In their recent 30-page kids' catalog, we found a few pages of clothes for babies and toddlers. They offer synchilla (Patagonia's version of polar fleece) clothes like cardigans ($46), coveralls ($48), and baby buntings ($64). We bought our baby a bunting from Patagonia and found that it had some cool features. For example, with a flick of its zipper, it converts from a sack to an outfit with two leg openings, making it more convenient for use with a car seat. It also has a neck to knee zipper (speeding up diaper changes), flipper hands, and a hood. When your baby's bundled up in this, you can bet she won't get cold.

Other gear for tots includes two-piece sets of capilene long underwear ($36), fleece pants ($18) and interesting accessories like "Baby Pita Pocket" mittens ($16) and assorted shoes, hats and booties. All of these items are also featured on Patagonia's web site (www.patagonia.com), which is easy-to-use and features an excellent online store and a section called "Enviro Action," a series of essays and info on Patagonia's environmental efforts.

The bottom line: this is great stuff. It ain't cheap, but the cold weather gear is unlike that from any other manufacturer in terms of quality and durability.

Talbot's Kids

To Order Call: (800) 543-7123.
Shopping Hours: 24 hours a day, 7 days a week.
Or write to: Talbot's Kids, 1 Talbots Dr. Hingham, MA 02043.
Web: www.talbots.com
Credit Cards Accepted: MC, VISA, AMEX.
Retail stores: 600 stores in the U.S., Canada and the United Kingdom. Talbot's also has 18 outlets–call the above number for the nearest location.

Talbot's splashes its bright colors on both layette items for infants (three months to 12 months) and toddlers (up to 4T sizes). For baby, the catalog features a good selection of t-shirts, sleepwear, and overalls. Prices, as you might expect, are moderate to expensive. We saw a cotton-footed coverall for $28, cotton t-shirts with crotch snaps for $18. New this year is a line of velour coveralls and overalls in beautiful hues. With the exception of these velour and some fleece items, nearly all of Talbot's Kids offerings are 100% cotton. The web site has made some great improvements and is easy to use.

Wooden Soldier

To Order Call: (800) 375-6002; Fax (603) 356-3530.
Shopping Hours: Monday-Friday 8:30 am to midnight,Saturday and Sunday 8:30 am to 9 pm Eastern Time.
Or write to: The Wooden Soldier, PO Box 800, North Conway, NH 03860.
Credit Cards Accepted: MC, VISA, AMEX, Discover.

If you really need a formal outfit for your child, Wooden Soldier has the most expansive selection of children's formalwear we've ever seen. Unfortunately, the prices are quite expensive–a girls' plaid dress with embroidered collar is $54; a boy's suspendered nicker set with shirt is $68. And those are for infant sized clothes!

On the plus side, the *Wall Street Journal* lauded this catalog for its high quality in a recent comparison of girl's holiday dresses from major catalogs. Wooden Soldier continues to expand their casual offerings, which now include overalls, jumpsuits and cotton sweaters.

◆ ***Other catalogs.*** Looking for licensed clothing items from Warner Brothers or Disney? Each has a catalog that can help. ***Warner Bros. Studio Store*** (800)223-6524 has a mail-order catalog with four pages of "baby wear." We saw terry cloth coveralls, sweat suits, denim overalls, and bodysuits–all emblazoned with such Looney Tunes characters as Tweety, Bugs Bunny and the Tasmanian Devil. A sample price: $26 for the denim overalls. ***Disney Catalog*** (800) 237-5751 (web: www.disneystore.com) has quite a few infant and toddler options, including Mickey fleece buntings and a wide assortment of Classic Pooh clothing, bedding, and accessories.

Fitigues (800) 235-9005 sells casual baby clothes at outrageous prices. Yes, the items are made of thermal knit or French terry with velvet trim, but we couldn't see ourselves spending $68 for a girl's dress in thermal knit. One plus: the kid's outfits do coordinate with the pricey adult clothes Fitigues offers.

If you need outdoor gear, check out ***Campmor*** (800) 226-7667 (web: www.campmor.com) or ***Sierra Trading Post*** (800) 713-4534 (web: www.sierratradingpost.com). Both heavily discount infant and children's outer-wear, including snowsuits. They also have back-packs. Since these items are close-outs, the selection varies from issue to issue.

Our Picks: Brand Recommendations

What clothing brands/catalogs are best? Well, there is no one correct answer. An outfit that's perfect for day care (that is, to be trashed in Junior's first painting experiment) is different from an outfit for a weekend outing with friends. And dress-up occasions may require an entirely different set of clothing criteria. Hence, we've divided our clothing brand recommendations into three areas: good (day care), better (weekend wear) and best (special occasions). While some brands make goods in two or even three categories, here's how we see it:

Good. For everyday comfort (and day-care situations), basic brands like Carter's, Little Me, and Osh Kosh are your best bets. We also like the basics (when on sale) at Baby Gap for day-care wardrobes. For great price to value, take a look at Old Navy and Target. As for catalogs, most tend to specialize in fancier clothes. However, Chock and Lands' End have a nice selection of everyday clothing.

Better. What if you have a miniature golf outing planned with friends? Or a visit to Grandma's house? The brands of better-made casual wear we like best include Alexis, Baby Gap, Flapdoodles, Good Lad of Philadelphia, and Gymboree. For catalogs, we like the clothes in Hanna Anderson and Talbot's Kids as good brands, as well as the better items in Biobottoms.

Best. Holidays and other special occasions call for special outfits. We like the brands of Patsy Aiken, Good Lad of Philadelphia, and the fancier items at Baby Gap. Of course, department stores are great sources for these outfits, as are consignment shops. As for catalogs, check out Wooden Soldier.

Note: For more on finding these brands, check out the Name Game earlier in this chapter. See "Do it By Mail" for more information on the catalogs mentioned above.

Diapers

The great diaper debate still rages on: should you use cloth or disposable? On one side are environmentalists, who argue cloth is better for the planet. On the other hand, those disposable diapers are darn convenient.

Considering the average baby will go through 2300 diaper changes in the first year of life, this isn't a moot issue. And that statistic is for disposable diapers—cloth diapers require even more changes. We took a fresh look at the diaper debate recently; here's a run-down of the pros and cons with cloth and disposable diapers.

Cloth. Prior to the 1960's, this was the only diaper option available to parents. Today, folks who choose cloth do so for environmental reasons. They point out that 19 billion disposable diapers (that's *three million tons*) are sent to landfills each year. If that weren't enough eco-damage, another 82,000 tons of plastic and 1.8 million tons of wood pulp (250,000 trees) are consumed to make disposables each year. Cloth diapers, on the other hand, are recyclable and reusable. Your city's municipal sewage system handles the solid waste.

Cloth diaper fans claim their babies have less diaper rash and toilet train earlier. Parents with the best of eco-intentions, however, often get frustrated with cloth diapers. The biggest problem: leaks. Cloth diapers can't hold a candle to today's super-absorbent disposable diapers. As a result, you'll be doing extra laundry even if you hire a commercial diaper service. Add in the time needed to do extra diaper changes (cloth requires twice as many changes as disposables) and you've got a significant time investment here.

Of course, there's another reason why cloth diapers aren't very popular today–most day care centers don't allow them.

Disposables. Disposable diapers were first introduced in 1961 and now hold an amazing lead over cloth–about 95% of all households that use diapers go for disposables. Today's diapers have super-absorbent gels that lower the number of needed diaper changes, especially at night (which helps baby sleep through the night sooner). Even many parents who swear cloth diapers are best still use disposables at night.

And the jury on diaper rash is still out–disposable diaper users tell us they don't experience any more diaper rash than cloth diaper users.

Besides the eco-arguments about disposables, there is one other disadvantage–higher trash costs. In some communities, the more trash you put out, the higher the bill. Hence, using disposable diapers may result in slightly higher garbage expenses.

The eco-bottom line: it's hard to convince an ardent environmentalist that disposable diapers aren't evil incarnate. But let's look at this issue in perspective–yes, all those disposable diapers are sent to landfills each year, but by weight it's only 1.5% to 2% of landfill volume. Compare that to newspapers (which account for 40% of trash volume) and you see it's small potatoes. Yes, it may take a disposable diaper 500 years to decompose in a landfill, but cloth diapers have environmental costs too–all that water, heavy chemicals and energy used to dry and deliver diapers takes its toll. Chlorine bleach used to sanitize diapers may be released into our environment through water treatment systems (although non-chlorine bleaches might be a safer alternative).

As a result, we've come to this conclusion: from an environmental view, it depends on where you live. In arid parts of this country where water is scarce and landfill space is abundant, disposable diapers may make a better eco-choice. In other parts of the U.S. and Canada, the situation is reversed–there's plenty of water but not much landfill space. The conclusion if you live there: cloth diapers may make more environmental sense.

The financial bottom line: Surprisingly, there is no clear winner when you factor financial costs into this equation.

Cloth diapers may seem cheap at first, but consider the hidden costs. Besides the diapers themselves ($100 for the basic varieties; $200 to $300 for the fancy diaper systems), you also have to buy diaper *covers*. Like everything you buy with baby, there is a wide cost variation with diaper covers. The cheap stuff (like Dappi covers at Target) will set you back $4 to $6 each. And you've got to buy several in different sizes as your child grows so the total investment could be $100+. If you're lucky, you can find diaper covers second-hand for $1 to $3. Of course, some parents find low-cost covers leak and quickly wear out. As a result, they turn to the more expensive covers–a single Mother-Ease (see later for more info on this brand) is $9.75. A Biobottoms wool cover is $20. Invest in a half dozen of those covers (in various sizes, of course) and you've spent another $200 to $400 (if you buy them new).

What about laundry? Well, washing your own cloth diapers at home may be the most economical way to go, but most folks don't have the time or energy. Instead, many parents use a cloth diaper service. In a recent cost survey of such services across the U.S., we discovered that most cost $500 to $725 a year. While each service does supply you with diapers (relieving you of that expense), you're still on the hook for the diaper covers.

Proponents of cloth diapers argue that if you plan to have more than one child, you can reuse those covers spreading out and lowering the cost. You may also not need as many sizes depending on the brands you use and the way your child grows.

So, what's the bottom line cost for cloth diapers? We estimate the total financial damage for cloth diapers (using a cloth diaper service and buying diaper covers) for just the first year is $600 to $800.

By contrast, let's take a look at disposables. If you buy disposable diapers from the most expensive source in town (typically, a grocery store), you'd spend about $600 to $650 for the first year. Yet, we've found discount sources (mentioned later in this chapter) that sell disposables in bulk at a discount. By shopping at these sources, we figure you'd spend $300 to $375 per year (the lowest figure is for private label diapers, the highest is for brand names).

The bottom line: the cheapest way to go is cloth diapers laundered at home. The next best bet is disposables. Finally, cloth diapers from a diaper service are the most expensive.

Parents in Cyberspace: What's on the Web?

All Together Diaper Company

Web: www.clothdiaper.com

What it is: Home of the all-in-one cloth diaper made in house by the All Together Diaper Company.

What's cool: We loved the simplicity of this site. In business since 1990, the All Together Diaper Company sells their own cloth diaper system in various packages. The accompanying FAQ, washing instructions and analysis of diaper costs are really helpful. While some of their price comparisons between cloth and disposable are a bit inaccurate, the information on the cost of home washing was helpful.

What about the diapers? We were impressed with the cool design—the all-in-one system has cotton inside against baby's skin, a waterproof outer shell, adjustable snaps and elastic leg openings. These diapers (the Deluxe) are $6.25 to $8.50 each or $69 to $96 per dozen. Less expensive are the Fitted diapers which do not have the waterproof shell. Price: $5.50 to $7 each or $60 to $78 per dozen. Packages of diapers do offer some savings: the Deluxe package which includes 30 small diapers, and 24 medium, large and toddler sizes runs $648.

The Baby Lane

Web: www.thebabylane.com
What it is: A comprehensive baby product and information site with a selection of cloth diapers and accessories.
What's cool: This is really the Mother of All Cloth Diaper sites. You'll find offerings from Under the Nile, Bumkins, Kushies, Aristocrats, Plushies, Imse Vimse, Alexis, Bummis and Green Earth. Kushies Ultras were $6.80 to $10.40 each (discounts available for five packs).
Needs work: Unfortunately, this site could use a little more organization. The topics list (in varying type sizes) was rather annoying.

Diapers 4 Less

Web: www.diapers4less.com, see figure 2 on the next page.
What it is: The web site for Diaper Factory Plus, a manufacturer of generic disposable diapers.
What's cool: Rock bottom prices. Even with shipping costs, this site's diapers are about 20% less than any other discount diaper sites. Rock-a-bye "premiums" have a cloth-like backing, elastic leg openings and tape closures. The price for a case of 204 small size diapers is only $26.99. Even with shipping ($8.50 on average) the cost comes to a mere 17¢ per diaper. In the chart following this section, you'll see this price compares well with wholesale clubs like Costco (and of course, these diapers are delivered to your home).

Another plus: Diapers 4 Less has a recurring delivery scheduler where you specify how much you want and they send them to you on a regular schedule and automatically bill your card. Plus you can save an additional 5% if you spend more than $30.
Needs work: The shipping costs are scaled based on how far away you are from Eau Claire, Wisconsin. Hence, higher shipping costs might make this less of a deal if you live in places that are quite a distance from Wisconsin (say, Southern California). We noticed many of Diapers 4 Less' competitors charge a flat shipping fee, which seems more fair. One final tip: as with any generic diaper source, it is always best to order a small quantity as a test before going whole hog.

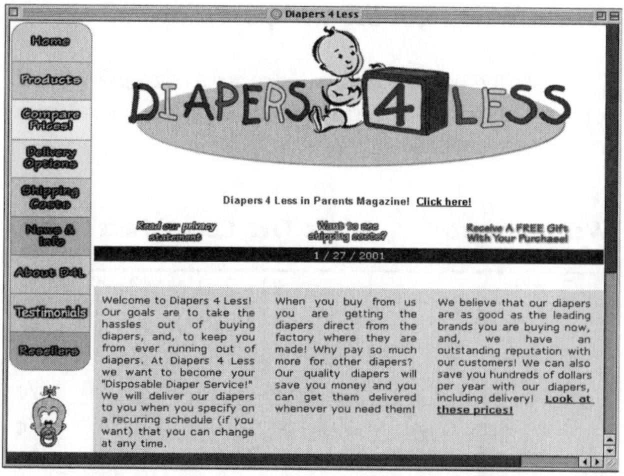

Figure 2: Even when you factor in shipping costs, Diapers4Less.com often beats grocery store prices.

◆ ***Other sites to consider.*** We found several more sites that sell disposable diapers on line. Among the best: ***Drug Emporium*** (www.drugemporium.com), ***CVS Pharmacy*** (www.cvspharmacy.com), ***Baby's Heaven*** (www.babysheaven.com), and ***Diaper Site*** (www.diapersite.com). And don't forget about the on line companions to bricks and mortar stores like ***Costco***. On www.costco.com you can purchase the same diapers at the same price (plus shipping) as you find in their warehouses.

For cloth diapers, check out ***A Bottom Line*** (www.abottomline.com). They have the most extensive selection of cloth diapers, both common brands and more obscure options. A similar site is ***Baby J*** (www.babyj.com). You'll find all-in-ones, folded diapers, wraps, liners and more with such brands as Kushies, Cotton Kids, and Bummis.

Our Picks: Brand Recommendations

Disposables. The evolution of disposable diapers is rather amazing. They started out in the 1960's as bulky and ineffective at stopping leaks. In 30 years, disposables morphed into ultra-thin, super-absorbent miracle workers that command 95% of the market.

And writing about disposable diaper brands is like trying to nail Jell-O to a wall—every five minutes, the diaper makers come out with new features and new gimmicks as they jostle for a piece of the $3.6 billion diaper market. In the seven years since the first edition of this book came out, we're amazed at the constant innova-

Who's got the cheapest diapers?

What's the best place to buy disposable diapers? We did a price comparison among several major sources, listed here from least to most expensive:

WEB SITE OR STORE	DIAPER TYPE	COUNT	PRICE	PER DIAPER
COSTCO	HUGGIES #1	240	$31.99	13¢
SAM'S CLUB	HUGGIES #1	228	$32	15¢
BABIES R US	HUGGIES #1	120	$18	15¢
COSTCO.COM	HUGGIES #1	240	$41.48¥	17¢
DIAPERS4LESS.COM	HOUSE BRAND	204	$35.49	17¢
GROCERY STORE*	HUGGIES #1	120	$18.60	18¢
BABYSHEAVEN.COM	HUGGIES #1	228	$47.98	21¢
DIAPERSITE.COM	HOUSE BRAND	100	$21.95**	22¢
DRUGEMPORIUM.COM	HUGGIES #1	80	$17.90**	22¢
CVSPHARMACY.COM	HOUSE BRAND	34	$9.50†	28¢

Price: Includes shipping.
Per Diaper: The cost per diaper.

¥ Includes shipping and tax to Colorado. If you have a Costco in your state, you will be charged sales tax.
* Checked at King Soopers, part of the Kroger chain.
** Flat shipping fee regardless how many you order.
† Free shipping over $35 purchase.

Prices checked as of March 2001.

tion in the category. Before we get to our brand recommendations, consider the three basic types of disposables:

◆ ***Basic.*** These are the cheapest diapers and also the most bulky.

◆ ***Ultrathin.*** Even though they are thinner than basic diapers, they are more absorbent, thanks to high-tech absorbent jells. Most of the diapers sold today are ultrathins.

◆ ***Premium/Supreme.*** As the name implies, these are the most expensive diapers on the market. What do you get for that 25% higher price? Well, some premium diapers have cloth-like outer covers and fancier closures like Velcro. You may also find additives like aloe to prevent diaper rash.

No matter what brand you try, remember that sizing of diapers is all over the board. The Step 2 diaper in one brand may be cut totally different than the "medium" of another, even though the weight guidelines on the package are similar. Finding a diaper that fits is critical to you and your baby's happiness.

Surprisingly, the absorbency of diapers varies little from brand to brand. A recent *Consumer Reports* test of 8000 diaper changes on 80 babies at a day care center (August 1998) found that of 13 diaper types tested, eight were judged excellent. And three more were "very good." Translation: no matter what brand you choose, you'll probably have a diaper that fits well and doesn't leak. Yes, the premium/supreme diapers scored highest in CR's tests, but the difference between them and the ultrathins was minimal (except for the price, of course).

Beware of gimmicks when diaper shopping. This market goes through fads faster than Madison Avenue. Remember gender-specific diapers? That was more hype than real benefit and now they're gone (we're back to unisex versions). The latest fad: "Pampers Rash Care," a premium diaper which "Contains the same active ingredients as many diaper rash creams" to prevent diaper rash. Next week we expect Huggies to come out with a brand that promises higher college entrance test scores (call it Huggies "SAT Boost Supreme").

Let's break down the diaper choices:

◆ ***Huggies.*** Love 'em. We used the Ultratrims and were very happy. In recent years, Huggies has added Velcro-like closures to the Ultratrims (before, it was sticky tape that sometimes stopped sticking or tore the diaper). Some folks like the Huggies Supreme, but we find them overpriced. For whatever reason, we found that brand preferences tended to split along gender lines–parents with boys favored Huggies, while those with girls like Pampers. We're not sure why, but we've seen that trend in our research. Check out Huggies web site at www.huggies.com for their complete line of six different types of diapers. You can also see what makes each type different. We loved the Huggies Boutique link which helps visitors find on line and bricks and mortar sources for their diapers. Be sure to sign up under "special offers" to receive coupons off Huggies as well.

◆ ***Pampers.*** Scored highest in *Consumer Reports* tests (specifically, the Pampers Premium) and we agree–these are great diapers. And, thankfully, they only have three products lines: Premium, Baby Dry and Rash Care. Compared to Huggies six options that's streamlined.

Pampers easy to use web site (www.pampers.com) offers a unique option for friends and family looking to give you a useful gift: Gift

Packs. Each gift pack includes gift certificates for free jumbo packs of diapers, a Fisher Price toy, a travel wipes box and gift box. You can buy one, three, six or twelve month packs. A three month pack with 8 jumbo packs of diapers runs $115 plus $5 shipping. You can also join their mailing list for coupons and special announcements.

◆ ***Luvs.*** Made by the same company that makes Pampers, Luvs are marketed as a lower-price brand (about 21¢ per diaper, compared to 25¢ to 29¢ for Pampers). Once again, we didn't see much difference between Luvs and Pampers or Huggies.

Luvs' web site (www.luvs.com) is heavy on Barney, the purple dinosaur. You can read about their "Barney Rewards" program, which lets you earn points toward free toys and other prizes. Whoopee. After you wade through all the Barney plugs, you'll note Luvs has recently added swim diapers to their line up and ultra thick wipes. Unfortunately, at the time we visited, Luvs had no coupon campaign parents could sign up for.

◆ ***Store brands.*** We've received numerous emails from parents who love store-brand diapers at Target, Wal-Mart, K-Mart and Toys R Us. Even grocery stores are getting into the game with private label diapers at prices to rival the discounters. Generally, these diapers are 20% to 30% cheaper than name brands. In the past, they were inferior in terms of features and quality but no more—most have the same ultrathin design, cloth-like covers and Velcro-closures. Toys R Us and Target's in-house brands received the highest marks from our readers; we noticed *Consumer Reports* liked Walgreens generic brand as well. Yes, there are several other obscure brands of diapers out there (among them, Drypers, Dri-Bottoms, Fitti and Tushies), but we didn't receive enough feedback from parents to form an opinion on then.

Cloth Diapers. Ask 100 parents for their recommendations on cloth diapers and you're likely to get 100 different opinions—it seems everyone has their special system or favorite. We did see one common thread amongst cloth diaper devotees: most used a variety of brands/types to make it through the day. Like a well-armed soldier going into battle, the cloth diapering parent typically has an arsenal of various products, schemes and tactics.

Because of limited space, we won't go into detail on these brands. For additional tips on this subject, check out the web site BornToLove (www.BornToLove.com). Their "World Wide Cloth Diapering Resources" is a massive index of 214 U.S. cloth diaper companies and 41 Canadian manufacturers plus links to cloth diaper books, magazine articles, associations, discussion lists, and message boards. A good book on using cloth diapers is *Diaper Changes* by Theresa Rodriquez (Homekeepers Publishing, 1997, 800-572-1826, web: www.homekeepers.com).

There are six categories of cloth diapers (plus covers):

◆ ***Flat fold diapers.*** Sold in stores like Target and Wal-Mart, these are nice for clean-up rags but rather useless for diapers.

◆ ***Standard pre-fold diapers.*** Two common brands: Dundee and Curity. Our verdict: not much more useful than flat-fold diapers. Translation: skip 'em.

◆ ***Diaper service diapers.*** Yes, you can buy the diapers used by cloth diaper services via mail order or specialty stores. Used with pins or covers, these diapers come in three sizes (newborn, standard and toddler) and run $25 per dozen. The only bummer: diaper-service diapers can be bulky when used on infants under 15 pounds. Hence, most parents use these after a baby is six months or so.

◆ ***Fitted diapers.*** The Mercedes of this category is Canada-made "Mother-Ease" (www.mother-ease.com), a brand that has a fanatical following among cloth diaper devotees. Suffice it to say, they ain't cheap but the quality is excellent. Mother-Ease sells both fitted diapers and covers; the diapers run $9 to $10 a pop, while the covers are about $9.75. Before you invest $73 to $375 in one of Mother-Ease's special package deals, consider trying their "introductory offer" (see details below in our money-saving tips section).

Other parents like Kushies (800) 841-5330 (web: www.kushies.com), another Canadian import. (For some reason, Kushies are known as "Kooshies" in the rest of the world). This brand offers several models, which sell for $5 to $7 each.

One note: both Kushies and Mother-Ease are sold via mail-order only. Yes, you can sometimes find these diapers at second-hand or thrift stores, but most parents buy them from a catalog or on the 'net. Kushies are trying to branch out into retail stores—check your local baby specialty shop.

◆ ***Terry flannel diapers.*** These are marketed to parents as the ultimate "eco-friendly" choice—terry flannel diapers are typically made of 100% organic cotton. Cost: $42 to $120 per dozen depending on the brand (these diapers are sold via web sites like www.diaperdance.com or www.daisydiapers.com). These diapers can take quite a while to dry and may be overkill for most parents. On the upside, they are contoured and less bulky, which means they fit newborn infants well.

◆ ***All-in-one diapers.*** As the name implies, these diapers combine a diaper and cover. And they aren't cheap: $6.25 to $15, depending on the brand. Most moms we interviewed say these diapers are too expensive for everyday use, but their convenience makes them handy for long trips. Once again, Mother-Ease and Kushies are two of the better brands to consider in this category. Other good all-in-one-diapers are made by All Together (801-566-7579, web: www. clothdiaper.com; $6.25 to $8.50) and Bumkins (800-338-7581 web: www. bumkins.com; $14 each). We've also received parental kudos for Indisposables (800-663-1730; sold at the BabyTown web site (www.eskimo.com/~babytown). Indisposables are cotton diapers. They will can accommodate a paper insert that can then be flushed down the toilet. Cost: $75 to $84 for a dozen. The inserts are $5.25 per roll (one roll lasts about a week).

◆ ***Inserts and liners.*** One of the criticisms of cloth diapers (fairly or not) is that they leak, especially at night. To help your baby sleep through the night and avoid those 3 am crib changes, consider adding liners or inserts to your cloth diapers. Inserts are additional absorbent pads placed in the strategic crotch area of a regular cloth diaper to soak up any extra wetness. We've seen them for between $2 and $4 per insert on cloth diaper web sites.

◆ ***Covers.*** With the exception of all-in-one cloth diapers, all other cloth diapers typically need covers, which help prevent leaks. The best diaper covers (also called wraps) not only must withstand leaks but also the washing machine–durability is a key factor.

Earlier in this chapter, we cited the wide variability in diaper cover costs, from the cheapest (Dappi covers at Target or Wal-Mart for $4 to $6) to the most expensive (wool Biobottoms at $20 each). Obviously, the cheap diaper covers wear out much quicker than the expensive ones. Realizing that fact, some parents use the cheaper covers when baby is younger and growing rapidly (the faster the growth, the less each cover is used) and switch to more pricey covers when baby is older (say over a year, when growth slows and covers are used for a longer period of time).

As for specific brands, one mom we interviewed didn't like Cottonwraps ("they leaked like crazy), Ecology Kids (the Velcro wears out too quickly) or Snappiwraps (the elastic also wears out too fast). Bumkins covers got better marks, but they have a vent panel in the back that makes it hard to put on baby. Once again, Mother-Ease received raves for their covers ($9.75 a pop), as did Kushies wraps ($6 each at the www.thebabylane.com). We also heard positive comments about Diaperwraps, although feedback was mixed on Nikki's (some loved them, others said they were overpriced). Once again, the Born to Love web page (web: www.borntolove.com) has contact info for these cover makers, as well as mail-order catalogs like Baby Bunz (800) 676-4559.

Special thanks to readers Sheila Pierson and J. Russel in Baltimore, MD for their insightful emails on this topic.

Wipes. Like diapers, you have a basic choice with wipes: name brand or generic. Our advice: stick to the name brands. We found the cheap generic wipes to be inferior. With less water and thinner construction, store brand wipes we sampled were losers. Our favorite brand is Pampers Baby Fresh, although other parents we interviewed swear by Huggies' wipes.

Money Saving Secrets

Here are some tips for saving on disposable diapers (cloth diaper bargain advice is at the end of this section):

1 **BUY IN BULK.** Don't buy those little packs of 20 diapers—look for the 80 or 100 count packs instead. You'll find the price per diaper goes down when you buy larger packs.

2 **GO FOR WAREHOUSE CLUBS.** Both Sam's (www.samsclub.com) and Costco (www.costco.com) wholesale clubs sell diapers at incredibly low prices. For example, Costco sells a 100-count package of Huggies Step 1 for just $15. We also found great deals on wipes at the wholesale clubs. Huggies Natural Care Wipes were $15 for a 576 count pack at Costco. Another warehouse club is BJ's (www.bjswholesale.com) which has over 100 locations in 15 states, most in the Eastern U.S.

3 **BUY STORE BRANDS.** As mentioned earlier in this chapter in brand reviews, many parents find store brand diapers to be equal to the name brands. And the prices can't be beat—many are 20% to 30% cheaper. Chains like Target, Wal-Mart, K-Mart and Toys R Us carry in-house diaper brands, as do many grocery stores. Heck, even Sam's wholesale club stocked a generic brand of diapers that was 26% cheaper than name brands.

4 **CONSIDER TOYS R US.** Sure, you may not have a wholesale club nearby, but you're bound to be close to a Toys R Us (or their sister division, Babies R Us). And we found them to be a great source for affordable name-brand diapers. The best bet: buy in

bulk. You can often buy diapers (both name brand and generic) by the case at Toys R Us, saving you about 20% or more over grocery store prices. As you might have noted in the earlier diaper cost comparison, Babies R Us was one of the lowest prices sources for diapers we found.

Don't forget to check the front of the store for copies of Toys R Us' latest catalog. Occasionally, they offer in-store coupons for additional diaper savings–you can even combine these with manufacturer's coupons for double savings.

5 **WHEN YOUR BABY IS NEARING A TRANSITION POINT, DON'T STOCK UP.** Quick growing babies may move into another size faster than you think, leaving you with an excess supply of too-small diapers.

6 **DON'T BUY DIAPERS IN GROCERY STORES.** We compared prices at grocery stores and usually found them to be sky-high. Most were selling diapers in packages that worked out to 20¢ to 25¢ per diaper. We should note there are exceptions to this rule, however: some grocery chains (especially in the South) use diapers as a "loss-leader." They'll sell diapers at attractive prices in order to entice shoppers into the store. Also, store brands can be more competitively priced.

7 **USE COUPONS.** You'll be amazed at how many coupons you receive in the mail, usually for 75 cents off diapers and 50 cents off wipes. One tip: to keep those "introductory" packages of coupons coming, continue signing up to be on the mailing lists of the maternity chain stores (apparently, these chains sell your name to diaper manufacturers, formula companies, etc.) or on line at diaper manufacturers' web sites.

8 **ASK FOR GIFT CERTIFICATES.** When friends ask you what you'd like as a shower gift, you can drop hints for gift certificates from stores that sell a wide variety of baby items–including diapers and wipes. That way you can get what you really need, instead of cute accessories of marginal value. You'd be surprised at how many stores offer gift certificate programs.

9 **FOR CLOTH DIAPER USERS, GO FOR "INTRODUCTORY PACKAGES."** Many suppliers have special introductory deals (Mother-Ease offers one diaper, liner and cover for $17 US; $20 Canadian, which includes shipping). Before you invest hundreds of dollars in one brand, give it a test drive first.

Do it By Mail

There are several catalogs that sell cloth diapers and diaper covers by mail. Here are some of the best:

BABY WORKS

To Order Call: (800) 422-2910.
Shopping Hours: Monday through Friday 9:00 am to 4:00 pm Pacific time.
Or write to: Baby Works, 11725 N. W. West Rd., Portland, OR, 97229.
Web: www.babyworks.com.
Credit Cards Accepted: VISA, MC, Discover.

Looking for baby products that are "gentle to the earth?" Then check out Baby Works. You'll find diaper covers like Nikkys, all-in-one diaper systems, cotton diapers, laundry products, and accessories. We saw the Bumkins all-in-one system for $12.50 per diaper. We liked all the washing instructions included on each page for the different items. Another nice feature: Baby Works has a recommended layette for cloth diapers. They even offer clothing and nursing items as well. Prices aren't anything to shout about, but the selection is good.

BIOBOTTOMS

To Order Call: (800) 766-1254 or fax (540) 670-2121.
Shopping Hours: 7:00 am to 12:00 am, everyday.
Or write to: Biobottoms,730 E. Church St., Suite 19, Martinsville, VA, 24112..
Web:: www.biobottoms.com, www.freshairwear.com
Credit Cards Accepted: MC, VISA, AMEX, Discover.

Biobottoms got their start as purveyors of cloth diapers and diaper covers. They make their own brands of diaper covers called "Original Biobottoms," and "Cotton Bottoms." Original Biobottoms are made of "felted lambs wool." The price is $20 each. The Cotton Bottoms diaper covers are made of 100% cotton, with an inner lining of polyester. Cost: $18. Either way, these covers are among the most expensive we've found.

And what about the cloth diapers you're supposed to put inside those diaper covers? Well, Biobottoms offers pre-fold diapers for $28 per 12 pack. A big plus: the catalog's sizing chart is easy to understand.

Born to Love

To Order Call: (905) 725-2559; Fax: (905-725-3297.
Shopping Hours: Monday to Saturday, 9am to 9pm (Eastern).
Or write to: 445 Centre Street S. Oshawa, ON Canada L1H 4C1.
Web: www. Borntolove.com.
Credit Cards Accepted: MC, VISA, AMEX.

This Canadian catalog and web site has won numerous fans for their low prices. You'll see page after page of cloth diaper systems (including such name brands as Bummis and Babykins). Heck, there are even 14 pages of accessories, plus selections of nursing bras, breast pumps, toys, safety products and more. Yes, the web site is a jumbled mess, but there's lots of useful info, articles and links when you sift through it all.

The Natural Baby Company

To Order Call: (800) 388-2229.
Shopping Hours: Monday through Friday 7:00 to Midnight EST; Saturday and Sunday 9:00 am to 9:00 pm EST.
Or write to: 7835 Freedom Ave., NW, North Canton, OH 44720.
Credit Cards Accepted: MC, VISA, AMEX, Discover.

The diapers available through Natural Baby Co. are not the usual square cloth diapers you see in stores. No, these have a unique hourglass shape that doesn't require any fancy folding. All this unique design doesn't come cheap. The prices range from $21 to $37 per dozen, depending on the style. Also available are pre-folded diapers ($28 per dozen), diaper doubler inserts ($10 for six), and even an all-in-one option called Reuz'm ($86 for six).

Natural Baby used to sell a wider variety of covers and diapers including Nikki's, but they seem to have cut back a bit on this area. Prices are also a disappointment compared to other options.

The Nurtured Baby

To Order: (888) 564-BABY.
Or write to: 4004 Keble Drive, Charlotte, NC 28269.
Web: www.nurturedbaby.com
Credit Cards Accepted: MC, VISA, Discover.

The Nurtured Baby sells their own "Cotton-Baby" diaper system. They claim its energy efficient design enables quick drying (only 25 minutes in the dryer). Cost: $60 to $65 for a box with six to eight diapers. The catalog sells Bumkins all-in-one cloth diapers and Kushies flushable liners.

◆ ***More sources for diaper covers.*** *TC Kidco* (888) 825-4326 is a Canadian catalog that sells "Indisposables" all-in-one cloth diapers and diaper covers (mentioned earlier). You can buy from the catalog or from their direct representative. The catalog also has nursing bras, blankets, bibs and more.

The ***Weebees*** web site (www.weebees.com) sells a wide variety of cloth diapers, covers, and accessories. We even saw Australian Nappies which they claim are the most absorbent diapers they've ever seen. Another cool item: Little Squirt. This device is a power sprayer that hooks up to your toilet plumbing. It allows you to spray off baby's bottom and the waste goes directly into the toilet. It even has a toddler proof handle for $50.

The Bottom Line: A Wrap-Up of Our Best Buy Picks

In summary, we recommend you buy the following layette items for your baby (see chart on next page):

Quantity	Item	Cost
6	T-shirts/onesies (over the head)	$22
6	T-shirts (side snap)	$25
4-6	Sleepers	$64-$96
1	Blanket Sleeper*	$10
2-4	Coveralls	$40-$80
3-4	Booties/socks	$12-$16
1	Sweater	$16
2	Hats (safari and caps)	$30
1	Snowsuit/bunting*	$20
4	Large bibs (for feeding)	$24
3 sets	Wash cloths and towels	$30
7-8	Receiving blankets	$42-$48
TOTAL		$335 to $417

** If you live in a cold climate.*

These prices are from discounters, outlet stores, or sale prices at department stores. What would all these clothes cost at full retail? $500 to $600, at least. The bottom line: follow our tips and you'll save $100 to $300 on your baby's layette alone. (Of course, you may receive some of these items as gifts, so your actual outlay may be less.)

Which brands are best? See "Our Picks: Brand Recommendations" earlier in this chapter. In general, we found that 100% cotton clothes are best. Yes, you'll pay a little more for cotton, but it lasts longer and looks better than clothes made of polyester blends (the exception: fleece outerwear and sleepwear). Other wastes of money for infants include kimonos, saque sets, and shoes.

What about diapers? We found little financial difference between cloth and disposable, especially when you use a cloth diaper service. Cloth does have several hidden costs, however–diaper covers can add hundreds of dollars to the expense of this option although the cost can be spread out among additional children.

For disposables, we found that brand choice was more of a personal preference–all the majors did a good job at stopping leaks. The best way to save money on disposable diapers is to skip the grocery store and buy in bulk (100-diaper packages) from a warehouse club or Babies R Us. Diapers from discount sources run about $300 to $375. The same diapers from grocery stores could be $600 or more. Another great money-saver: generic, store-brand diapers from Wal-Mart, Target, K-Mart and like. These diapers performed just as well as the name-brands at a 20% to 30% discount.

CHAPTER 5

Maternity & Nursing

Love 'em or hate 'em, every mother-to-be needs maternity clothes at some point in her pregnancy. Still, you don't have to break the bank to get comfortable, and, yes, fashionable maternity items. In this chapter, we tell you which sources sell all-cotton, casual clothes at unbelievably low prices. Then, we'll review the top maternity chains and reveal our list of top wastes of money. You'll learn which outlet stores offer tremendous savings on career wear. Finally, learn all about breastfeeding, including seven sources for help, and the lowdown on which breast pumps work best.

Maternity & Nursing Clothes

Getting Started: When Do You Need This Stuff?

It may seem obvious that you'll need to buy maternity clothes when you get pregnant, but the truth is you don't actually need all of them immediately. The first thing you'll notice is the need for a new bra. At least, that was my first clue that my body was changing. Breast changes occur as early as the first month and you may find yourself going through several different sizes along the way.

Next, your belly will begin to "swell." Yes, the baby is making its presence known by making you feel a bit bigger around the middle. Not only may you find that you need to buy larger panties, but you may also find that skirts and pants feel tight as early as your third month. Maternity clothes at this point may seem like overkill, but some women do begin to "show" enough that they find it necessary to head out to the maternity shop.

If you have decided to breastfeed (more on this later in this chapter), you'll need to consider what type of nursing bras you'll want. Buy two or three in your eighth month so you'll be prepared. You may find it necessary to buy more nursing bras after the baby is born, but this will get you started. As for other nursing clothes, you may or may not find these worth the money. Don't go out and buy a whole new wardrobe right off the bat. Some women find nursing shirts and tops to be helpful while others manage quite well with regular clothes. More on this topic later in the book.

Sources

1 **Maternity Wear Chains.** Not surprisingly, there are quite a few nationwide maternity clothing chains. Visit any mall and you'll likely see the names Pea in the Pod, Motherswork, Mimi Maternity, and Motherhood, to mention a few. More on these chains later in the chapter.

2 **Mom and Pop Maternity Shops.** These small, independent stores sell a wide variety of maternity clothes, from affordable weekend wear to high-priced career wear. Some baby specialty stores carry maternity wear as well. The chief advantage to the smaller stores is personalized service—we usually found salespeople who were knowledgeable about the different brands. In addition, these stores may offer other services. For example, some rent formal wear for special occasions, saving you big bucks. Of course, you may pay for the extra service with higher prices.

3 **Consignment Stores.** Many consignment or thrift stores that specialize in children's clothing may also have a rack of maternity clothes. In visits to several such stores, we found some incredible bargains (at least 50% off retail) on maternity clothes that were in good to excellent condition. Of course, the selection varies widely, but we strongly advise you to check out any second-hand stores in your area.

4 **Discounters.** When we talk about discounters, we're referring to chains like Target, Wal-Mart and K-Mart. Now, let's be honest here—these discounters probably aren't the first place you'd think of to outfit your maternity wardrobe. Yet, each has a surprisingly nice selection of maternity clothes, especially casual wear. Later, we'll tell you about the incredible prices on these all-cotton clothes.

5 **Department Stores.** As you might guess, most department stores carry some maternity fashions. The big disadvantage: the selection is usually rather small. This means you'll often find unattractive jumpers in abundance and very little in the way of fashionable clothing. Department stores like Penney's and Sears often have end-of-the-season sales with decent maternity bargains.

6 **WEB/MAIL-ORDER.** Even if you don't have any big-time maternity chains nearby, you can still buy the clothes they sell. Many chains offer a mail-order service, either from printed catalogs or online stores. We also found several mail-order catalogs that have a selection of maternity clothes. In the "Do It By Mail" section of this chapter, we'll give you the run-down on these options.

7 **NON-MATERNITY STORES.** Maternity stores don't have a monopoly on large-size clothes—and you can save big bucks by shopping at stores that don't have the word "maternity" in their name. Later in this chapter, we'll give you some specific examples.

8 **YOUR HUSBAND'S CLOSET.** What's a good source for over-sized shirts and baggy sweaters? Look no further than the other side of your closet, where your husband's clothes can often double as maternity wear.

9 **OUTLETS.** Yes, there are several outlets that sell maternity clothes and the prices can be a steal. We'll discuss some alternatives later in this chapter.

10 **YOUR FRIENDS.** It's a time-honored tradition—handing down "old" maternity clothes to the newly pregnant. Of course, maternity styles don't change that much from year to year and since outfits aren't worn for a long time, they are usually in great shape. Just be sure to pass on the favor when you are through with your pregnancy.

Parents in Cyberspace: What's on the Web?

Motherwear

Web: www.motherwear.com
What it is: The online version of the nursing clothes catalog.
What's cool: "This catalog makes the best clothes for nursing!" gushed one mom in an email to us and we have to agree—this is a great catalog and web site. Prices aren't cheap (a long sleeve nightshirt is $38), but the quality is excellent. And they have a clearance section with additional bargains—that aforementioned nightshirt was last seen marked down to $29 (a 20% savings). Don't forget to check their weekly specials as well. A cool feature: want to see what the nursing openings look like on each garment? Just click on the little icon and a window pops open with clear photos of each opening.

Medela

Web: www.medela.com
What it is: A treasure trove of info on breastfeeding.
What's cool. Medela's web site is a great example of what makes the 'net so helpful—instead of a thinly veiled pitch for their products, Medela stuffs their site with reams of useful info, tips and advice. Yeah, you can read about their different breast pumps, but the site is full of general breastfeeding tips, links to other sites and more. "Problems and Solutions" is an excellent FAQ for nursing moms. New this year: online chats with a breastfeeding expert.
Needs work: When we first reviewed this site, the navigation was disorganized and difficult to use. We're pleased to see they've cleaned it up for the most part. It may take a few clicks to get to the info you need, but it's a lot better. We'd still like to see approximate retail prices for Medela's products on the site.

eStyle

Web: www.estyle.com
What it is: A "lifestyle" retailer targeting pregnant women and new moms with fashions, tips and information.
What's cool: A fast-loading, color-saturated site with easy navigation, it's easy to see why eStyle is a favorite among new and expecting parents. Not only can you shop for maternity fashions, you'll also find tips, calendars, sizing and style suggestions and more. The brands they feature include Belly Basics, Diane Von Furstenburg, Belly Beautiful and more. They even have their own in-house brand, Private Collection. All the clothing we saw was quite stylish.
Needs work: But don't expect cut rate prices for all that fashion. How 'bout a pair of twill stretch pants for $78? Or our favorite, plether pants for a mere $138? We were sweating just thinking about wearing that. If you really want to buy something here, check for their specials and deals.

◆ ***Other sites:*** While most towns only have a handful of maternity stores, the web is teeming with possibilities. ***Anna Cris Maternity*** (www.annacris.com) sells such quality brands as Japanese Weekend and Belly Basics.

While most folks know ***Gap*** as a great place for kids clothes, few realize that Gap also does maternity. Not in the store, mind you—you have to go online to their web site (www.gap.com, see Fig. 1). You'll find classics like cardigans and jeans as well as stretch silk shirts, capri pants and more. Check frequently for sale items—they seem to offer more sales than most maternity retailers. Readers have been impressed with the quality of Gap maternity, according to our email.

Little Koala (www.littlekoala.com) was also recommended by

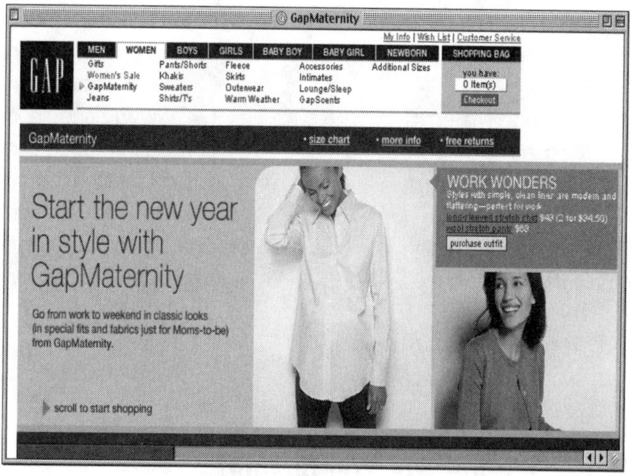

Figure 1: Sold only online, Gap Maternity has one cool feature: you can return items to Gap stores, free of charge.

a reader. They sell a decent selection of maternity clothes including undergarments, plus infant clothes, diaper bags and carries/slings.

Maternity 4 Less (www.maternity4less.com) received yet another reader recommendation, this time for speedy delivery. Our reader reported that they exchanged a pair of maternity pants for her in only a matter of days, not the usual weeks other mail order sources take. They carry the gamut of maternity and nursing clothes and accessories.

For a wide range of styles and sizes (up to 3X plus talls and petites), check out ***Mom Shop*** (www.momshop.com). With great full size photos and an easy to use site, we think MomShop.com is a top site.

Nursing clothes are where ***One Hot Mama*** (www.onehotmama.com) got their start, but they have expanded into maternity clothes as well. Either way, they attempt to showcase hip styles from manufacturers like Japanese Weekend. Just don't read the sermons from the site's owners. It's a bit irritating and disconnected.

For our Canadian readers, check out ***Thyme Maternity*** (www.maternity.ca), recommended by a reader in Ontario. She thought the styles were more "real world," the sizing was great and prices were reasonable. They do ship to the U.S. although it can take up to three weeks.

We could go on and on with all these maternity/nursing web sites, but let's condense it a bit for you. The following are yet more options to check out for maternity and nursing clothing:

Fit Maternity	www.fitmaternity.com
From Here to Eternity	www.fromheretomaternity.com
Just Babies	www.justbabies.com
Lattesa	www.lattesa.com
Liz Lange Maternity	www.lizlange.com
Mothers In Motion	www.mothers-in-motion.com
Naissance Maternity	www.naissancematernity.com
On'na Maternity	www.onnamaternity.com
Pumpkin Maternity	www.pumpkinmaternity.com
Style Maternity	www.stylematernity.com
That Glow	www.thatglow.com
Thyme Maternity (Canada)	www.maternity.ca
Twinkle Little Star	www.twinklelittlestar.com

What Are You Buying?

What will you need when you get pregnant? There is no shortage of advice on this topic, especially from the folks trying to sell you stuff. But here's what real moms advise you to buy:

◆ ***Maternity Bras.*** Maternity bras are available just about everywhere, from specialty maternity shops to department stores, mail-order catalogs and discount chains. More on this topic in the box on the next page "News from Down Under: Maternity Bras for the Real World."

HOW MANY? Two in each size as your bust line expands. I found that I went through three different sizes during my pregnancy, and buying two in each size allowed me to wear one while the other was washed.

◆ ***Sleep Bras.*** What do you need a bra to sleep in for, you ask? Well, some women find it more comfortable to have a little support at night as their breasts change. Toward the end of pregnancy, some women also start to leak breast milk (to be technical, this is actually colostrum). And once the baby arrives, a sleeping bra (cost, about $10) will keep those breast pads in place at night (to keep you from leaking when you inadvertently roll onto your stomach—yes, there will come a day when you can do that again). Some women just need light support, while others find a full-featured bra a necessity.

HOW MANY? Two sleep bras—one to wear, one to wash.

◆ ***Underpants.*** There are two schools of thought when it comes to underpants. Traditional maternity underwear goes over your tummy, while bikini-style briefs are worn under the belly. Some women like the traditional maternity briefs, while others find bikini-style underwear more comfortable. Whichever style you choose, be sure to look for all-cotton fabric, wide waistbands and good construction—repeated washings take their toll on cheap undies. See "Our Picks: Brand Recommendations" later in this section for the best bets.

HOW MANY? I don't like to do lots of laundry, so I bought eight pairs. Since you may be wearing them even after your baby is born for a few weeks, get some that will last.

◆ ***Nursing Bras.*** What's the difference between a nursing bra and a maternity bra? Nursing bras have special flaps that fold down to give baby easy access to the breast. If you plan to nurse, you should probably buy at least two during your eighth month (they cost about $20 to $35 each). Why then? Theoretically, your breast size won't change much once your baby is born and your milk

Plus-size Maternity Clothing

What's the number one frustration with maternity wear? Finding decent plus-size maternity clothes, say our readers. Some maternity clothing manufacturers think only women with bodies like Cindy Crawford get pregnant. But what to do if you want to look attractive and your dress size starts at 16 or above? Our readers have recommend the following sites:

Baby Becoming	www.babybecoming.com
Baby Becoming	www.babybecoming.com
Expecting Style	www.expectingstyle.com
IMaternity	www.imaternity.com
JCPenney	www.jcpenney.com
Maternal Instinct	www.maternal-instinct.com
MomShop	www.momshop.com
Motherhood	www.maternitymall.com
One Hot Mama	www.onehotmama.com
Plus Maternity	www.plusmaternity.com
Plus Size Mommies	www.plussizemommies.com

What about petites and talls? They are generally more easily available on most of the sites we recommend in this chapter. If we run across sites or catalogs that specialize in these sizes, we'll let you know.

comes in. I'd suggest buying one with a little larger cup size (than your eighth month size) so you can compensate for the engorgement phase. You can always buy more later and, if your size changes once the baby is born, you won't have invested too much in the wrong size. If you want more advice on nursing bras, you can call ***Playtex*** (800-537-9955) for a free guide or check out their cool web site at www.playtex.com. Click on the apparel section, then "Products" and finally "Expectant Moment." You'll find info on bras and you can go to the "Fit" section for advice on sizing.

HOW MANY? Buy two to three bras in your eighth month. After the baby is born, you may want to buy a couple more. Another good tip: buy two to three pairs of breast pads (to prevent leaks) before the baby is born.

◆ ***Career Clothing.*** Our best advice about career clothing for the pregnant mom is to stick with basics. Buy yourself a coordinating outfit with a skirt, jacket, and pair of pants and then accessorize.

News from Down Under: Maternity Bras for the Real World

What makes a great maternity bra? Consider the following points while shopping:

◆ *Support–part I.* How much support do you need? Some women we interviewed liked the heavy-duty construction of some maternity bras. For others, that was overkill.

◆ *Support–part II.* Once you decide how much support you need, consider the type of support you like. The basic choice: underwire bras versus those that use fabric bands and panels. Some moms-to-be liked stretchy knit fabric while others preferred stiffer, woven fabric.

◆ *Appearance*. Let's be honest: some maternity bras can be darn ugly. And what about the bras that claim they'll grow with you during your pregnancy? Forget it–expect to go through several sizes as the months roll along.

◆ *Price.* Yes, the best maternity bras can be pricey. But I've found it doesn't pay to scrimp on underwear like bras and panties. Save money on other items in your maternity wardrobe and invest in comfortable undergarments.

Now, we know what you're saying. You'd love to follow this advice, but you don't want to wear the same old thing several times a week–even if it is accessorized. I don't blame you. So, go for a couple dresses and sweaters too. The good news is you don't have to pay full price. We've got several money-saving tips and even an outlet or two coming up later in this chapter.

At some point, you'll notice that regular clothes just don't fit well, and the maternity buying will begin. When this occurs is different for every woman. Some moms-to-be begin to show as early as three months, while others can wait it out until as late as six months. But don't wait until you begin to look like a sausage to shop around. It's always best to scope out the bargains early, so you won't be tempted to buy outfits (out of desperation) at the convenient–and high-priced–specialty store.

By the way, thanks to the casual trend of office wear, pregnant woman can spend hundreds of dollars LESS than they might have had to five or ten years ago. Today, you can pair a knit skirt with a sweater set for the office. Gone are the days of the power suit, thank goodness.

◆ ***Casual Clothes.*** Your best bet here is to stick with knit leggings or sweat pants and big tops. You don't necessarily have to buy these from maternity stores. In fact, later in this chapter, we'll talk about less-expensive alternatives. If you're pregnant in the summer, dresses can be a cooler alternative to pants and shorts.

◆ ***Dress or Formal Clothes.*** Forget them unless you have a full social calendar or have many social engagements associated with your job. Sometimes, you can find a local store that rents maternity formalwear for the one or two occasions when you might need it.

◆ ***Nursing Clothes.*** You may not think so (especially at 8 1/2 months), but there will come a day when you won't need to wear those maternity clothes. But what if you want to nurse in public after baby is born? Many women swear by nursing clothes as the best way to be discreet, but others do just fine with loose knit tops and button front shirts. If you want to experiment, buy one or two nursing tops and see how they work for you.

Looking for something comfortable to sleep in that allows you to nurse easily? Check out ***Majamas*** (www.majamas.com). One of our product testers tried out their cotton/lycra t-shirt with her newborn and thought it was great, worthy of a recommendation. They allow you to sleep without wearing a nursing bra since they have pockets for holding breastpads and have easy nursing access.

More Money Buys You . . .

Like any clothing, the more you spend, the better quality fabric and construction you get. Of course, do you really need a cashmere maternity outfit you'll wear for only a few months? Besides fabric, you'll note more designer names as prices go up. For example, Lilly Pulitzer, Nicole Miller and Vivian Tam are making maternity clothes now. You can even buy maternity clothes from Laura Sara M, the designer for Hollywood stars.

Smart Shopper Tips

Smart Shopper Tip #1
Battling your wacky thermostat

"It's early in my pregnancy, and I'm finding that the polyester-blend blouses that I wear to work have become very uncomfortable. I'm starting to shop for maternity clothes—what should I look for that will be more comfortable?"

It's a fact of life for us pregnant folks—your body's thermostat has gone berserk. Thanks to those pregnancy hormones, it may be hard to regulate your body's temperature. And those polyester-blend clothes may not be so comfortable anymore.

Our advice: stick with natural fabrics as much as possible, especially cotton. Unfortunately, a lot of lower-priced maternity clothing is made of polyester/cotton blend fabrics. To make matters worse, you may also find that your feet swell and are uncomfortable as your pregnancy progresses. As a result, wear shoes that have low heels for maximum comfort.

Smart Shopper Tip #2
Seasons change

"Help! My baby is due in October, but I still need maternity clothes for the hot summer months! How can I buy my maternity wardrobe without investing a fortune?"

Unless you live in a place with endless summer, most women have to buy maternity clothes that will span both warm and cold seasons. The best bets are items that work in BOTH winter or summer—for example, light-weight long-sleeve shirts can be rolled up in the summer. Leggings can work in both spring and fall. Another tip: layer clothes to ward off cold. Of course, there's another obvious way to save: borrow items from friends. If you just need a few items to bridge the seasons (a coat, heavy sweater, etc), try to borrow before buying.

Our Picks: Brand Recommendations for Maternity Undergarments

Thank goodness for e-mail. Here at the home office in Boulder, CO our e-mail (authors@BabyBargainsBook.com) has overflowed with great suggestions from readers on maternity undergarments.

God bless Canada—those Maple Leaf-heads make one of the best maternity bras in the world. Toronto-based ***Bravado Designs*** (for a brochure, call 800-590-7802 or 416-466-8652; web: www.bravadodesigns.com) makes a maternity/nursing bra of the same name that's just incredible. "A godsend!" raved one reader. "It's built like a sports bra with no underwire and supports better than any other bra I've tried . . . and this is my third pregnancy!" raved another. The Bravado bra comes in three support levels, sizes up to 42-46 with an F-G cup and a couple of wonderful colors/patterns (you can also call them for custom sizing information). Available via mail order, the bra costs $32 U.S. (or $33.50 Canadian). Another plus: the Bravado salespeople are knowledgeable and quite helpful with sizing questions. Some of our readers have criticized the Bravado for not providing enough support, especially in the largest sizes. If you have doubts, just try one at first and see if it works for you before investing in several. We even found a discount site for Bravados at www.boebabybiz.com. The day we visited they were charging $24 (regular price $26).

The ***Natural Baby Catalog*** (800) 388-2229 (web: www.kidsstuff.com) sells an "awesome" maternity bra, says another reader. The all-cotton bra has five hooks in back and is available in off-sizes ("just try finding a 38-40 B bra that doesn't have a cup that looks like a D," she says). Available in underwire and plain with cup sizes up to H. Cost: $27 to $30.

One Hanes Place (800) 300-2600 (www.onehanesplace.com) is a great catalog with 50% off maternity hose and nursing bras (more on this later in this chapter). Readers rave about this catalog, which features name brands like Playtex and L'Eggs. Be forewarned: selection can vary widely from time to time.

The web is a great place to look for nursing bras: Kelly Prince of Atlanta, Georgia recommended a great site: ***Decent Exposures*** (www.decentexposures.com; 800-524-4949) which sells the "Un-bra" among other finds. They've added a new "Dri-Release" fabric option to their line of Un-bras. Lined or unlined, this might be a great sleep bra for the leaking mom.

Looking for maternity shorts/tights for working out? One of the best is ***Fit Maternity*** (www.fitmaternity.com; 530-938-4530). They offer an unbelievable assortment of workout clothes including unitards, tights, swimsuits and more. Also check out their books and work out tapes. On the same subject, the catalog Title Nine Sports (510) 655-5999 offers a few items. Pants are $59 and have a belly band for extra support. The catalog also carries shorts and sports bras, which some women find is a more comfortable alternative to maternity bras.

What about underpants? The best I wore were ***Japanese Weekend*** (800) 808-0555 (web: www.japaneseweekend.com), a brand available in stores and via mail order (see review later in this chapter). Their "OK" bikini-style underwear boasts 100% thick cotton fabric and an extra-wide waistband that cradles your belly. Although they aren't cheap (three for $30), I found them incredibly comfortable *and* durable, standing up to repeated washings better than other brands. The company also carries tights and nursing bras.

Wastes of Money

Waste of Money #1
Maternity Bra Blues

"My old bras are getting very tight. I recently went to my local department store to check out larger sizes. The salesperson suggested I purchase a maternity bra because it would offer more comfort and support. Should I buy a regular bra in a larger size or plunk down the extra money for a maternity bra?

We've heard from quite a few readers who've complained that expensive maternity bras they've bought were very uncomfortable and/or fell apart after just a few washings. Our best advice: try on the bra before purchase and stick to the better brands. Compared to regular bras, the best maternity bras have thicker straps, more give on the sides and more hook and eye closures in back (so the bra can grow with you). Most of all, the bra should be comfortable and have no scratchy lace or detailing. I've had luck with the ***Olga*** "Christina" maternity bras (sold in department stores) and the Bravado bra, mentioned earlier in this chapter. Readers tell us that a good sports bra can also be a fine alternative.

Waste of Money #2
Orange You Going to Wear Hose?

"Have you seen the horrendous colors available in maternity hose? I can't wear those orange things to work!"

Don't. You don't have to buy ugly maternity hose—those thick, itchy horrors only sold in four shades of orange (Ugly, Sheer Ugly, Super-Duper Ugly, and Son of Ugly). Maternity hose must have been invented by a third world country looking for a new torture device; they take their rightful place next to the bridesmaid's dress as one of the most dreaded apparel items for women.

Fortunately, there is some good news on this front. ***The One Hanes Place catalog*** (800-300-2600; www.onehanesplace.com) carries L'Eggs Sheer Energy and Playtex maternity panty hose in several colors *besides* orange and at great prices.

If you'd prefer a fancier brand, we found ***Hue*** (made by Leslie Fay Co.; call 212-947-3666 for a store near you) comes in several attractive colors and retails for about $10 a pair.

What about large-size panty hose? A mother-to-be in Georgia e-mailed us a recommendation for "Just My Size." This special line for larger-size woman is manufactured by L'eggs and sold for half the price of "official preggo" pantyhose, she said.

Yo, Expect THIS!

We realize we might be tarred and feathered as heretics at the next bookseller's convention for saying this, but sometimes parenting books can be BIG wastes of money. And the biggest offenders are the so-called "spin-offs" books. Yeah, your first book was so good, why don't you write Chicken Soup for the Vertically Challenged? One of our favorite all-time stinkers was by the sister team that wrote the "What to Expect" books. Yes, *What to Expect When You're Expecting* is a classic, but you need no more evidence of spin-off disease than to read *What to EAT When You're Expecting* (our emphasis). The centerpiece of this book is the authors' diet "advice"—and we use that word loosely. The "Best Odds Diet" is similar to the regimen used by prisons in third-world countries to torture inmates. Although the advice has merit (avoid high-fat foods, eat lots of vegetables), just take a look at this piece of advice: "The Best Odds diet recommends eating no refined sugars at all during pregnancy." Excuse me? Are they kidding? While many expectant mothers aspire to cut back on sweets, going nine months without an ice-cream cone just doesn't happen in the real world. Their recommended fat intake is another shocker—the authors advise restricting this to two tablespoons of fat a day. Basically, one bagel with cream cheese would shoot your fat allowance for the whole day. File this book under "Fiction" at your local bookstore.

Of course, there is another solution to the maternity hose dilemma: don't buy them. With a few modifications, you may be able to wear regular hose during *most* your pregnancy. Try rolling the waistband down under your tummy. It works, believe me. When I was six months pregnant and invited to a formal occasion, I wore regular hose in that manner and had no problem. Or you may find that cutting the waistband of your hose gives you some breathing room for a few months. If you wear only long skirts and dresses, knee-hi hose are an option; no one will know you're not wearing full hose. Some women swear by self-supporting thigh-high stockings, the kind with rubber-like grippers around the bands. While a few pregnant moms find them uncomfortable (check with your doctor if you have concerns about blood circulation in your legs), this tip worked for others we interviewed.

Waste of Money #3

Over the Shoulder Tummy Holder

"I keep seeing those 'belly bras' advertised as the best option for a pregnant mom. What are they for and are they worth buying?"

Belly bras provide additional support for your back during your pregnancy. One style envelopes your whole torso and looks like a tight-fitting tank top. No one can argue that, in many cases, the strain of carrying a baby (and the additional weight) is tough even on women in great physical shape. So, if you find your back, hips, and/or legs are giving you trouble, consider buying a belly bra.

However, in our research, we noticed most moms don't seem to need or want a belly bra. The price for one of these puppies can range from $35 to an incredible $55. The bottom line: hold off buying a belly bra or support panty until you see how your body reacts to your pregnancy. Also, check with your doctor to see if she has any suggestions for back, hip, and leg problems.

If you need one of these, check out the general catalogs we recommend in the Do It By Mail chapter later in this book. For example, we noticed the ***One Step Ahead catalog*** (800) 274-8440 sells the Mom-EZ support belt for $42.95. Another reader spotted a belly/back support belt in a Motherhood maternity store (reviewed later in this chapter) for $13.

Waste of Money #4

Overexposed Nursing Gowns/Tops

"I refuse to buy those awful nursing tops! Not only are they ugly, but those weird looking panels are like wearing a neon sign that says 'BREASTFEEDING MOM AHEAD'!"

"I plan to nurse my baby and all my friends say I should buy nursing gowns for night feedings. Problem is, I've tried on a few and even though the slits are hidden, I still feel exposed. Not to mention they're the ugliest things I've ever seen. Can't I just wear a regular gown that buttons down the front?"

Of course you can. And considering how expensive some nursing gowns can be ($35 to $50 each), buying a regular button-up nightshirt or gown will certainly save you a few bucks. Every mother we interviewed about nursing gowns had the same complaint. There isn't a delicate way to put this: it's not easy to get a breast out of one of those teenie-weenie slits. Did the person who designed these ever breastfeed a baby? I always felt uncovered whenever I wore a nursing gown, like one gust of wind would have turned me into a centerfold for a nudist magazine.

And can we talk about nursing shirts with those "convenient button flaps for discreet breastfeeding"? Convenient, my fanny. There's so much work involved in lifting the flap up, unbuttoning it, and getting your baby positioned that you might as well forget it. My advice: stick with shirts you can pull up or unbutton down the front. These are just as discreet, easier to work with, and (best of all) you don't have to add some expensive nursing shirts (at $30 to $50 each) to your wardrobe.

If you want nursing shirts, check out ***Motherwear*** (800-950-2500; web: www.motherwear.com). While they aren't cheap, they do have the biggest, best selection and the quality is great.

Another tip: try on any nursing clothing BEFORE you buy. See how easy the buttons are to open. You might be surprised how easy (or difficult) an item can be. Imagine as you are doing this that you have an infant that is screaming his head off wanting to eat NOW, not five seconds from now. You can see why buying any nursing clothes sight unseen is a risk.

Money-Saving Secrets

1 CONSIDER BUYING "PLUS" SIZES FROM A REGULAR STORE. Thankfully, fashion styles of late include leggings and oversized tops and sweaters. This makes pregnancy a lot easier since you can buy the same styles in larger ladies' sizes to cover your belly without compromising your fashion sense or investing in expensive and often shoddily made maternity clothes. We found the same fashions in plus-size stores for 20% to 35% less than maternity shops (and even more during sales).

One drawback to this strategy: by the end of your pregnancy, your hemlines may start to look a little "high-low"—your expanding belly will raise the hemline in front. This may be especially pronounced with skirts and dresses. Of course, that's the advantage of buying maternity clothes: the designers compensate with more fabric in front to balance the hem line. Nonetheless, we found that many moms we interviewed were able to get away with plus-size fashions for much (if not all) of their pregnancy. And how much can you save? We priced a pair of cotton-blend leggings from Mimi Maternity at $44. Meanwhile, we found that Eddie Bauer carries cotton/spandex leggings for only $24 to $30—and we'd hardly call Eddie Bauer a discount store. And Eddie Bauer sells leggings through their catalog in petites, talls, extra large, and extra, extra large sizes (see box below).

2 DON'T OVER-BUY BRAS. As your pregnancy progresses, your bra size is going to change at least a couple times. Running out to buy five new bras when you hit a new cup size is probably foolish—in another month, all those bras may not fit. The best advice: buy the bare minimum (two or three).

3 DON'T SKIMP ON MATERNITY BRAS AND UNDERWEAR. Take some of the money you save from other parts of this book and invest in good maternity underwear. Yes, you can find cheap underwear for $3 a pair at discount stores, but don't be penny-wise and pound foolish. We found the cheap stuff is very uncomfortable

E-Mail from The Real World
Two thumbs up for Eddie Bauer

Annie M. of Brooklyn, NY found great deals at Eddie Bauer on clothes that can work as maternity fashions:

"Eddie Bauer is my salvation. I'd marry the man if I weren't so damn fond of my husband. The XL and XXL leggings are $24 to $30 and they last and last. The shirts are all available in petite through XXL sizes, the lengths are good for short or tall people, and they have many styles that are suitable for late in pregnancy without looking 'smocky.' I also know that I'll be able to wear most of the stuff again and again after I have the baby. Eddie Bauer's generously cut sundresses wear wonderfully and are accommodating me beautifully into my sixth month (with lots of room to grow). And another plus: they also have great sales!"

and falls apart, forcing you to go back and buy more. Investing in better-quality bras and underwear also makes sense if you plan to have more than one child—you can actually wear it again for subsequent pregnancies. Another obvious tip: if you like bikini style underwear, you may not need to buy special "maternity" bikini style undies—just use your regular underwear.

4 **CONSIDER TARGET, WAL-MART, K-MART FOR CASUAL CLOTHES.** Okay, I admit that I don't normally shop at K-Mart or Target for my clothes. But I was surprised to discover these chains (and even department stores like Sears) carry casual maternity clothes in 100% cotton at very affordable prices. Let's repeat that—they have 100% cotton t-shirts, shorts, pants, and more at prices you won't believe. Most of these clothes are in basic solid colors—sorry, no fancy prints. At Target, for example, I found a 100% cotton white t-shirt (long sleeves) for $10. Stretch twill pants were only $23 as were jeans. Even a knit long skirt was a mere $15. If you buy from one of these discounters, just be sure that you check the fabric and try everything on before you buy. You don't want to have to lug the stuff back to the store.

While the discounters don't carry much in the way of career wear, you'll save so much on casual/weekend clothes that you'll be ecstatic anyway. Witness this example. At A Pea in the Pod, we found a cotton knit tank top and shorts outfit in solid yellow. The price: a heart-stopping $82. A similar all-cotton tank top/shorts outfit from Target was $20. Whip out a calculator, and you'll note the savings is an amazing 75%. Need we say more? Not to mention that casual is the rule for office wear these days anyway.

5 **RENT EVENING WEAR—DON'T BUY.** We found that some indie maternity stores rent evening wear. For example, a local shop we visited had an entire rack of rental formalwear. An off-white lace dress (perfect for attending a wedding) rented for just $50. Compare that with the purchase price of $175. Since you most likely would need the dress for a one-time wearing, the savings of renting versus buying would be $125.

6 **CHECK OUT CONSIGNMENT STORES.** You can find "gently worn" career and casual maternity clothes for 40% to 70% off the original retail! Many consignment or second-hand stores carry only designer-label clothing in good to excellent condition. If you don't want to buy used garments, consider recouping some of your investment in maternity clothes by consigning them after the baby is born. You can usually find listings for these stores in the phone book. (Don't forget to look under children's clothes as well.

Some consignment stores that carry baby furniture and clothes also have a significant stock of maternity wear.) Two web sources to find consignment shops are www.secondhand.com and www.narts.org.

7 **FIND AN OUTLET.** Check out the next section of this chapter for the low-down on maternity clothes outlets.

8 **GET THE ONE HANES PLACE CATALOG.** This is our favorite catalog (800) 300-2600 (web: www.onehanesplace.com) for maternity hose, Playtex nursing bras, and more. Some items are "slightly imperfect," but we couldn't find any visible flaws. Best of all, prices are 40% or more below retail.

9 **BE CREATIVE.** Raid your husband's closet for over-sized shirts and sweat pants. One mom we interviewed found a creative use for her pre-pregnancy leggings. She simply wore them backwards! The roomier backside gave her space for her expanding tummy.

10 **SEW IT YOURSELF.** A reader in California emailed in this recommendation: she loved the patterns for nursing clothes by Elizabeth Lee Designs (435-454-3350; web: www.elizabethlee.com). "I would think anyone with a bit of sewing experience could handle any of the patterns, which don't LOOK like nursing dresses or tops." Elizabeth Lee has both a catalog and web site; in addition to patterns, they also sell already-made dresses and tops. Another bonus: the company has one of the largest selections of nursing bras we've seen, including Bravado Bras.

11 **BEG AND BORROW.** Unless you're the first of your friends to get pregnant you know someone who's already been through this. Check around to see if you can borrow old maternity clothes from other moms. In fact, we loaned out a big box after our second baby was born and it has made the rounds of the whole neighborhood. And don't forget to be generous after your baby making days are over too.

Outlets

MOTHERHOOD MATERNITY OUTLETS

Locations: 76 outlets (13 are called Maternity Works). For location info, call (800) 466-6223.

The offspring of the catalog and retail stores of maternity giant Motherhood Maternity (see review later in this chapter), Maternity

Works outlets have started springing up in outlet malls across the country. On a recent visit, the outlet featured markdowns from 20% to 75% on the same top-quality designs you see in their catalog or retail stores.

For example, we noticed a cotton knit jumper at Motherhood Maternity for $59 that was regularly priced at $98. Knit stirrup pants were on sale for $39, almost 20% off the regular price of $48. A suit jacket was priced at a mere $39 (regularly $158), and the matching skirt was only $29 (regularly $58). That's right, you could pick up this whole outfit for just $68, instead of the $226 retail price. The outlet also carried a decent selection of party dresses, undergarments, and casual wear.

MOTHERTIME

Location: Secaucus, NJ (773)481-3180; Web: www.mothertime.com

This is Dan Howard's outlet store, which operates under the separate name "Mothertime." Their NJ location carries casual and career maternity clothes, as well as a selection of children's clothing (from newborn to 24 months). The discounts are rather slim, however, averaging about 20% off retail. But there are ongoing sales with higher discounts. At the time of this writing their web site was still under construction.

MOTHERWEAR

Location: Northampton, MA (413) 586-2175.

The Motherwear catalog has a factory outlet that is open just Wednesday, Thursdays, Fridays and Saturdays. They sell returned merchandise, seconds, overstock and discontinued items. "Great bargains—worth the trip," says a reader who visited the outlet.

The Name Game: Reviews of Selected Maternity Stores

Usually this section is intended to acquaint you with the clothing name brands you'll see in local stores. When it comes to maternity wear, however, the biggest players are actually the stores themselves. National chains like MothersWork and Dan Howard have their own store brands. Here's a wrap-up of what's available. We've also included Japanese Weekend, which is a maternity brand sold in department and specialty stores and via mail order.

The Ratings

A **EXCELLENT**–*our top pick!*
B **GOOD**– *above average quality, prices, and creativity.*
C **FAIR**–*could stand some improvement.*
D **POOR**–*yuck! could stand some major improvement.*

Dan Howard *Call (312) 263-6700 to find a store near you or (800) 966-6847 for a catalog. Web: dan-howard.com* A manufacturer of maternity career, dress and casual fashions, Dan Howard sells its clothes in 100 locations in the U.S. and Canada that they call "factory outlets," with alleged savings of 25% to 50%. Yet our sharp-eyed readers noticed the prices weren't anything special. Dan Howard marks all their clothes with tags that compare their prices to "suggested retail," yet the latter prices seemed inflated to us. Nevertheless, the quality of the clothes is OK; besides career clothing, we noticed leggings, bike shorts, undergarments and even bathing suits. Dan Howard's web site is only fair. Their online catalog features a wide selection of items but it takes several clicks to order an item, which seems a bit primitive. We also tried to buy a white t-shirt, but it wouldn't place it in our shopping cart even after clicking "Buy" three times. Thankfully, they've added clearance items in their outlet section and weekly specials. We have received complaints on Dan Howard from readers who feel the quality isn't great for the price. Others slam their horrible return policy–even damaged items can't be returned for refund (see "Watch out for return policies" box later in this chapter. ***Rating: D***

Japanese Weekend *To find a store near you that carries this brand of clothing, call (800) 808-0555, (415) 621-0555, or write to 22 Isis St., San Francisco, CA 94103. You can also ask for a catalog. Web: www.japaneseweekend.com* Japanese Weekend (JW) is a line of maternity clothing that emphasizes comfort. They are best known for their unusual "OK" belly-banded pants, which have a waistband that circles *under* your expanding tummy for support (rather than cutting across it). In recent years, JW has expanded its line beyond pants to include jumpers, tops, catsuits, nightgowns, and skirts. We really like the simple, comfortable style of the clothes and highly recommend them. For once, a company has created all-cotton clothing for moms-to-be, avoiding the all too common polyester blends. One nice plus: JW will send you a list of stores that carry their clothes (call the above number for more information). In addition, the designer has a company store in San Francisco (415-

Watch out for return policies!

Have you bought a maternity dress you don't like or that doesn't fit? Too bad–most maternity stores have draconian return policies that essentially say "tough!" Most don't accept returns and others will only offer store credit. A word to the wise: make sure you REALLY like that item (and it fits) before you give any maternity store your money.

A reader in Brisbane, California emailed us with the most horrific return story we've ever heard about maternity stores' return policies. "I recently visited a Dan Howard maternity store in San Francisco and was shocked to find their return policy stands even when you haven't left their store yet! They overcharged me for a sale item that was mismarked and then said all they could give me was store credit for the difference! I hadn't stepped one foot outside the store! They refused to credit my charge card, so now I'm stuck with a $65 store credit for a place I despise!"

989-6667). As for JW's web site, it's visually stunning but a bit difficult to navigate. They have added a shopping cart function, but it takes a while to figure out how to find the items you want. Prices are expensive, but on the up side, there is a "sale page" with a nice selection of goods at 50% off list price. ***Rating: A***

Mothercare *Call (312) 263-6700 for a store near you. Web: www.imaternity.com* Mothercare Maternity stores offer moderately-priced maternity clothing with a wide selection of casual and work clothes. For example, we saw a striped cotton shirt for $30, paired with matching blue stirrup pants for $24. Considering that we've seen leggings and stirrups for as much as $50 in other maternity shops, Mothercare is a bit easier on the pocketbook. Dresses and suits are also available. A crepe floral print dress was only $38. Undergarments and swim suits are also reasonably priced. As an interesting side note, Mothercare is owned by the same parent company that operates Dan Howard (reviewed earlier). The web site showcases quite a few sale items as well. ***Rating: B***

Motherhood *For a store near you, call (800) 4-MOM-2-BE. Web: www.maternitymall.com.* Motherhood is the Microsoft of maternity wear–they dominate the market and can be found in just about any mall in North America. Their three chains (A Pea in the Pod, Mimi Maternity, Motherhood Maternity) have 580+ locations

nationwide, plus Motherhood operates leased maternity stores in Macy's and Lazarus department stores. Each store carries a similar mix of casual and career wear, albeit at different price levels. Motherhood's eponymous stores seem to have more emphasis on casual clothing, while Pea in the Pod is the company's "upper-end" concept. Mimi Maternity is the hip, young store—you'll see this name in hot, hip malls. What about prices? Well, the good news is prices are down from years past, at least for the Motherhood line. For example, you can buy a navy jacket from Motherhood for $40, a matte jersey skirt ($30), or a pinstripe stretch skirt ($20). Motherhood also carries plus-size clothes. A simple long sleeve all-cotton t-shirt at Mimi Maternity is $28. At A Pea in the Pod, however, the emphasis is on designer wear. We noticed a Lilly Pulitzer silk embroidered cardigan for $220 and matching pants for $195. Ouch! On the upside, the quality is generally good—most items are natural fabrics and stylish. What about the service? Well, it's a mixed bag. We found generally helpful salespeople at most Motherhood stores, yet the folks at A Pea in the Pod can get a little pushy. Like static cling, one saleswoman followed me around and asked one too many questions about my pregnancy. As soon as you walk in, it takes less than five seconds for someone to offer you spring water—a contrived, albeit nice, gesture. The bottom line: stick with Motherhood or Mimi Maternity stores. A Pea in the Pod is incredibly pricey. And check out the web site. We've noticed Motherhood has offered big discounts online (see review earlier in this chapter).
Rating: B

Do it By Mail

GARNET HILL

To Order Call: (800) 622-6216, (603) 823-5545; Fax (888) 842-9696.
Web: www.garnethill.com
Shopping Hours: Mon-Fri 7 am-2 am; Sat and Sun 8 am-midnight, Eastern.
Or write to: Garnet Hill, 231 Main St., Franconia, NH 03580.
Outlet: : Historic Manchester Outlet Center, Manchester, VT. (802) 362-6198.
Credit Cards Accepted: MC, VISA, AMEX, Discover.

Unfortunately, Garnet Hill is a good example of how expensive maternity clothes can get. Sample impressions from a recent catalog: a fleece maternity cardigan runs $74, a cotton knit maternity jumper $54 and cotton knit pants $58. There's even a selection of nursing bras. The good news: while those prices are still somewhat high, they are a bit lower than in years past. We're glad Garnet Hill has tried to keep its prices closer to reality in recent catalogs. And at least the clothes are stylish. If you're looking for sale items, you'll be hard pressed to find any maternity deals either in the sale catalogs or on line.

JCPENNEY

To Order Call: (800) 222-6161. Ask for "Maternity Collection" catalog.
Web: www.JCPenney.com/shopping
Shopping Hours: 24 hours a day, seven days a week.
Credit Cards Accepted: MC, VISA, JCPenney, AMEX, Discover.

JCPenney offers a free "mini-catalog" called "Maternity Collection." A recent edition featured 36 pages of maternity clothes, plus a small selection of nursery items.

Perhaps the best aspect of Penney's offerings is their wide range of sizes—you can find petites, talls, ultra-talls and womens sizes. It's darn near impossible to find womens sizes in maternity wear today, but Penney's carries sizes up to 26W.

What most impressed us about Penney's maternity catalog was their career clothes. For example, we saw a "three-piece wardrobe" suit (v-neck top with gold accents, matching skirt and pants) for just $60 to $70. This acetate/rayon outfit was available in every conceivable size. Another stand-out: Penney's "Dividends Maternity Set," a complete wardrobe of five pieces (pullover jumper, tunic, skirt, t-shirt and leggings) in cotton/lycra spandex for $99. New this year, Penney's has expanded the wardrobe-in-a-box concept with ultra-talls available.

While most of the career wear is blends of rayon and polyester, Penney's casual maternity clothes feature more all-cotton fabrics. We saw a wide array of affordably-priced cotton maternity shirts and jeans, as well as denim dresses and jumpers. A selection of nightgowns, swim suits, nursing shirts and lingerie round out the offerings.

One bargain hint: Penney's has quite a few unadvertised sales and discounts on maternity wear. When placing your order, inquire about any current deals.

Nursing fashions in Canada: The Toronto-based Breast is Best catalog sells a wide variety of nursing tops, blouses and dresses as well as maternity wear. For a free catalog and fabric swatches, call (877) 837-5439 toll free or check out their web site online at www.breastisbest.com.

Breastfeeding

Suppose we told you that you could take a miracle pill during pregnancy that would do amazing things for your baby.

What things? How about a higher IQ? Yes, this miracle drug would do that, as well as lessen your child's chance of respiratory and gastrointestinal infections. The same pill would mean fewer and less severe allergies, and your baby would have better jaw and tooth development. Speech problems and ear infections in childhood? This pill would help eliminate them, as well as provide protection from illnesses like rubella, chicken pox, bronchitis, and polio. If that weren't enough, taking this pill would even reduce the chance your child would be obese as an adult. Not only would this miracle pill do all that for your baby, but it would also lower the chance of breast cancer and heart disease in you, the mother.

E-MAIL FROM THE REAL WORLD
Stay fit with pregnancy workout videos

Margaret Griffin e-mailed us with her opinions of several popular workout videos tailored for the pregnant woman. Here are her thoughts:

"As a former certified aerobics instructor, I have been trying out the video workouts for pregnancy. I have only found three videos available in my local stores, but I wanted to rate them for your readers.

"***Buns of Steel 8 Pregnancy Workout*** with Madeleine Lewis ($10) gets my top rating. Madeleine Lewis has excellent cueing, so the workout is easy to follow. Your heart rate and perceived exertion are both used to monitor your exertion. There is an informative introduction. And I really like the fact that the toning segment utilizes a chair to help you keep your balance, which can be off a little during pregnancy. Most of the toning segment is done standing. This is a safe, effective workout led by a very capable instructor and I highly recommend it." The average customer review on Amazon.com: 4 1/2 stars out of 5.

"A middle rating goes to ***Denise Austin's Pregnancy Plus Workout*** ($15). Denise has a good information segment during which she actually interviews a physician. She also provides heart rate checks during the workout. However, there are a couple of things about this workout that I don't particularly like. First, during the workout, there are times when safety information is provided regarding a particular move. This is fine and good, but instead of telling you to continue the movement and/or providing a picture-in-a-picture format, they actually change the screen to show the safety information and then cut back into the workout in progress. Surprise! You were supposed to keep doing the movement.

Surprise! There is no pill that does all that! But there is something you can do for your baby that does everything described above and more: breastfeeding.

Certainly, comparing breastfeeding to taking a pill during pregnancy isn't entirely fair. While breastfeeding may be a piece of cake for some moms, most have to work to get it right—and those first few days can seem like hell. So, it's important to know how to find help. This section will provide you with tips and tricks to successfully breastfeed, including a list of products and organizations that can make the process easier.

What if you can't or don't want to breastfeed your baby? If you have a medical/work situation that precludes breastfeeding, you may choose to bottle feed. For such parents, we've also included an expanded section in the next chapter on infant formula, bottle systems and other necessary accessories.

Second, Denise Austin is a popular instructor, but I personally find that her cueing is not as sharp as I prefer and sometimes she seems to be a little offbeat with the music. My suggestion is get this video to use in addition to other videos if you are the type who gets easily bored with one workout."

"The video I recommend that you skip altogether is the ***Redbook Pregnancy Workou***t led by Diane Gausepohl. I have nothing positive to say regarding this workout. I did the workout once and immediately retired the tape. The instructor has poor cueing skills and does not keep time with the music well at all. This makes the workout hard to follow. My husband was actually laughing at the instruction, it was so poor. I also don't like the fact that it includes toning exercises that can be done (and are demonstrated) lying on your back. We all know that by the fifth month of pregnancy, the weight of the uterus can restrict the blood flow in the inferior vena cava, so you should not lie flat on your back. Even though these exercises can be modified I think it is better to avoid the temptation altogether. There are plenty of other toning exercises that are effective that do not require you to lie on your back at all. My advice is to skip this video altogether." Th average customer review on Amazon.com: 1 1/2 stars.

Another reader, Sheri Gomez, recommended Yoga Zone's video ***Postures for Pregnancy****. She told us it was* "wonderful for stretching and preventing back problems. It's beginner friendly and not too out there with the yoga thing." *Her only complaint: there is no accompanying music, so she played her own CD's along with the tape.*

Editor's note: Amazon.com is a great source to find these videos at a discount. Also: Madeleine Lewis now has a post-pregnancy video called Buns of Steel 9.

Breastfeed Your Baby and Save $500

Since this is a book on bargains, we'd be remiss in not mentioning the tremendous amount of money you can save if you breastfeed rather than use formula. Just think about it: no bottles, no expensive formula to prepare, no special insulated carriers to keep bottles warm/cold, etc.

So, how much money would you save? Obviously, the biggest money-saver would be not having to buy formula. Even if you were to use the less expensive powder, you would still have to spend nearly $12 per 16-ounce can. (For reference, we used our local grocery store's price of $11.98 per can as a price point.) Since each can makes 118 ounces of formula when mixed with water, the cost per ounce of formula is about 10¢.

That doesn't sound too bad, does it? Unless you factor in that a baby will down 32 ounces of formula per day by 12 weeks of age. Your cost per day would be $3.25. Assuming you breastfeed for the first six months, you would save a grand total of $546. Not only is breastfeeding better for your baby's health, it is much kinder to your wallet.

To be fair, there are some optional expenses that might go along with breastfeeding. The biggest dollar item: you might decide to get a piston electric breast pump. The cost? About $50 per month to rent or $200 to buy (plus a kit–one time cost of about $40).

If $546 doesn't sound like a lot of money, consider the savings if you had to buy formula in the concentrated liquid form instead of the cheaper powder. A 32-ounce can of Similac ready-to-eat liquid costs about $4.10 at a grocery store and makes up only 4 bottles. The bottom line: you could spend over $650 on formula for your baby in the first six months alone! And that doesn't even include the cost of bottles, sterilizers and other accessories. Even if you ignore the fantastic health benefits from breastfeeding your baby, it's hard to argue against the money it saves.

What's a Breastfeeding Mom's Biggest Misconception? "I'm not making enough milk"

In some ways, a mom who feeds her baby formula has it easy. She measures out a certain amount of formula and can see her baby's progress as she empties the bottle. Breastfeeding, however, is based a little more on faith. You can't see how much milk you have, nor can you tell how much milk your baby has consumed. The truth is most women make plenty of milk. The nagging fear that your baby isn't eating enough is often just that: a fear.

To be frank, however, we should note that in a small number of cases mothers may not have enough milk to breastfeed their babies. According to a report in the *Wall Street Journal*, "insufficient-milk syndrome may occur as much as 5% of the time, affecting about 200,000 mothers a year in the U.S. Some physicians say certain breasts are structurally incapable of producing enough milk; in addition, women who have had breast surgery are at risk. Some infants, meanwhile, are incapable of learning how to breast-feed."

The result: mothers with the best of intentions can actually starve their babies. Since the signs of dehydration can be subtle, the best advice may be to see your doctor immediately if your think your baby is not getting enough milk in the first few days. Close contact with a pediatrician or lactation consultant may make the difference between success or failure. Of course, failing to breastfeed your baby does not mean that you're a failure as a mother.

Fortunately, this syndrome is quite rare. Most women have no problem producing enough milk for their baby. The biggest obstacle to breastfeeding may be psychological. Many moms start out with the best of intentions, only to abandon breastfeeding because of lack of support or self-confidence. In fact, a November 2000 government report found that the goal of having 75% of new mothers breastfeed newborns isn't being met. Only 64% of new mothers are breastfeeding, which is better than the 50% statistic of a decade ago but still disappointing. The main reason given for this

How to Make Breastfeeding Universal

Here's a depressing statistic: only 29% of all mothers breastfeed their babies until they are six months old. While we applaud the government's new goal that by 2010 half of all mothers breastfeed exclusively until age six months, we can't help but offer some of our own suggestions. So here they are:

If the government can subsidize bottle feeding by the distribution of formula through welfare programs (to the tune of $2.7 BILLION a year nationwide), why not breast pumps? The purchase of a breast pump should at least be fully tax deductible; better yet, why not a tax credit?

How about mandating a more breastfeeding-friendly environment at workplaces? We're talking adequate breaks and private rooms for pumping. That way new mothers could be encouraged to pump and freeze breastmilk. The government should also come out and clearly discourage the use of bottles or pacifiers until an infant is at least six weeks of age. After six weeks, infants can easily shift between breast and bottle without suffering from nipple confusion. Discouraging bottle use for the first six weeks lets babies become efficient at breastfeeding.

failure: lack of support from fathers, grandparents and doctors. So where do you find support if you can't get it from your doctor or family? The Sources section of this chapter addresses this problem.

Sources: Where to Find Help

The basis of breastfeeding is attachment. Getting your new little one to latch onto your breast properly is not a matter of instinct. Some babies have no trouble figuring it out, while many others need your help and guidance. In fact, problems with attachment can lead to sore nipples and painful engorgement. Of course, you should be able to turn to your pediatrician or the nurses at the hospital for breastfeeding advice. However, if you find that they do not offer you the support you need, consider the following sources for breastfeeding help:

1 **La Leche League** (800) LA LECHE or web: www.lalecheleague.org. Started over 35 years ago by a group of moms in Chicago, La Leche League has traditionally been the most vocal supporter of breastfeeding in this country. You've got to imagine the amount of chutzpah these women had to have to buck the bottle trend and promote breastfeeding at a time when it wasn't fashionable (to say the least).

In recent years, La Leche has established branches in many communities, providing support groups for new moms interested in trying to nurse their children. They also offer a catalog full of books and videotapes on nursing, as well as other child care topics. Their famous book *The Womanly Art of Breastfeeding* is the bible for huge numbers of breastfeeding advocates.

Although we admire the work La Leche League has done to help nursing mothers and to change society's attitudes toward them, we disagree with some of the group's tenets. For example, their approach toward parenting includes an unhealthy dose of negativism when it comes to working moms. Let's get real, folks. The latest stats indicate that currently 59% of woman who have children under one year of age work outside the home (compared to 33% in 1976). To have such a prestigious organization as La Leche dissing moms who work outside the home is quite anachronistic.

Of course, this is a minor point of disagreement. All in all, La Leche provides an important service and, coupled with their support groups and catalog of publications, is a valuable resource.

2 **Nursing Mothers' Council** (408) 272-1448, (web: www.nursingmothers.org). Similar in mission to La Leche

League, the Nursing Mothers' Council differs on one point: the group emphasizes working moms and their unique needs and problems.

3 **LACTATION CONSULTANTS.** Lactation consultants are usually nurses who specialize in breastfeeding education and problem solving. You can find them through your pediatrician, hospital, or the International Lactation Consultants Association (703) 560-7330 web: www.iblce.org. Members of this group must pass a written exam, complete 2500 hours of clinical practice and 30 hours of continuing education before they can be certified. At our local hospital, resident lactation consultants are available to answer questions by phone at no charge. If a problem persists, you can set up an in-person consultation for a minimal fee (about $40 to $90 per hour, although your health insurance provider may pick up the tab).

Unfortunately, the availability of lactation consultants seems to vary from region to region. Our research shows that, in general, hospitals in the Western U.S. are more likely to offer support services, such as on-staff lactation consultants. Back East, however, the effort to support breastfeeding seems spotty. Our advice: call area hospitals before you give birth to determine the availability of breastfeeding support.

4 **HOSPITALS.** Look for a hospital in your area that has breastfeeding-friendly policies. These include 24-hour rooming in (where your baby can stay with you instead of in a nursery) and breastfeeding on demand. Pro-nursing hospitals do not supplement babies with a bottle and don't push free formula samples. Their nurses will also respect your wishes concerning pacifier usage, which is important if you are concerned about nipple confusion.

5 **BOOKS.** Although they aren't a substitute for support from your doctor, hospital, and family, many books provide plenty of information and encouragement. Check the La Leche League catalog for titles.

6 **THE WEB.** We found several great sites with breastfeeding information and tips. Our favorite was ***Medela*** (www.medela.com), which is a leading manufacturer of breast pumps. Medela's site features extensive information resources and articles on breastfeeding, as well as advice on how to choose the right breast pump. Of course, you can also get info on Medela's breast pumps and other products, find a dealer near you and more.

The catalog ***Bosom Buddies*** (www.bosombuddies.com or call 888-860-0041) has a web site with a good selection of breastfeeding articles, product information and links to other breastfeeding sites on the web.

If that weren't enough, there's even a news group dedicated to the subject, news: misc.kids.breastfeeding. Moms post questions, swap stories and trade information about which products work best.

7 YOUR HEALTHCARE PROVIDER. Contact your healthcare provider as soon as you become pregnant. They often have a variety of services available to policy holders, but you have to ask. One reader told us her Aetna US Healthcare has a "Lil' Appleseed" program. You qualify for two to three visits from a registered nurse after the birth of your baby, a real boon if you're having trouble with nursing or anything else. Our reader also told us you are assigned a case manager ("a real live person" she said) for your entire pregnancy and, if you ask for the registration kit, you get reimbursement for childbirth classes and a discount catalog. Wow!

Parents in Cyberspace: What's on the Web?

MedRino

Web site: www.breastpumps-breastfeeding.com
What it is: A medical supply company with a selection of breast pumps and accessories.
What's cool: What's not? Here's a site with a huge selection of breast pumps from Medela at discount prices. For example, MedRino claims the Pump In Style Professional sells for $277 retail, but they sell it for $250. Granted, not a huge discount, but when you order the Pump In Style, they give you free 2nd Day Air delivery (free UPS ground for all the other models). Wow! When you pull up a product you're interested in, the site has clear photos, details on the product and a price grid with retail and sale prices. You'll also find breast shells, pads, storage products and more on the site.
Needs work: The site should sell more brands than just Medela. How about Avent and Ameda Egnell as well?

Nursing Mothers Supplies

Web: www.nursingmothersupplies.com
What it is: An extensive nursing supply resource.
What's cool: Not only does this site carry breast pumps and supplies from Medela, Avent and Ameda Egnell (among others), they offer support to customers after they buy. Nursing Mothers Supplies has an excellent online FAQ as well as the opportunity to contact a counselor for one-on-one help. Prices are regular retail

(the Purely Yours was $198), but they offer free shipping for all orders over $75 and a portion of the sale goes to UNICEF (nice touch). Nursing pillows, storage options (the Mothers Milk Mate is $25), slings, Avent bottles and pads are also available.
Needs work: Not much to complain about here. The site is a bit primitive in design, but it does the job—loads fast, has a shopping cart feature, clear photos, etc. We also like the gentle approach to encouraging breast feeding. These guys aren't too preachy.

◆ ***Other web sites:*** Check out some of the general baby product web sites for breast pumps. These include ***Baby Catalog*** (www.babycatalog.com), ***Baby Style*** (www.babystyle.com), ***The Right Start*** (www.rightstart.com) and ***One Step Ahead*** catalog (www.onestepahead.com). More on these sites in Chapter 11.

Smart Shopper Tips

Smart Shopper Tip #1
Pumped Up

"My husband and I would really like to go out to dinner sometime before our daughter is 15 years old. I've been looking at different breast pumps—which really work best?"

Expressing milk is a science in itself. You'll notice a wide variety of pumps, from manual pumps that cost under $20 to huge, piston electric pumps that run into the hundreds of dollars (you can rent or buy these).

One caveat about pump shopping: amazingly, the government does NOT set standards for breast pumps as they do for other medical devices. It's best, in our opinion, to stick with the major brands like Medela and Ameda Egnell, who specialize in breast pumps.

Which breast pump is right for you? Check out the chart from Medela on the next page for some answers. And here's a rundown of the four options when it comes to pumps:

◆ ***Manual Expression:*** There are several good breastfeeding books that describe how to express milk manually. Most women find that the amount of milk expressed, compared to the time and trouble involved, hardly makes it worth using this method. A few women (we think they are modern miracle workers) can manage to express enough for an occasional bottle; for the majority of women, however, using a breast pump is a more practical alternative.

BREAST PUMPS

Which pump works best in which situation?

Do you need a pump for:	Manual	Mini-Elec.	Piston Elec.	Rental*
A missed feeding?	■	◆		
Evening out from baby?	■	◆		
Working part-time.	■	◆		
Occasional use, a few times a week.	■	◆		
Working full-time.			●	●
Premature or hospitalized baby?			●	●
Low milk supply?			●	●
Sore nipples/engorgement?		■	●	●
Latch-on problems or breast infection?			■	●
Drawing out flat or inverted nipples?	■	◆	●	●

Key: ■ = Good ◆ = Better ● = Best

**Rental refers to renting a hospital-grade pump. These can usually be rented on a monthly basis.*

Source: Medela.

◆ ***Manual Pumps:*** Non-electric, hand-held pumps create suction by squeezing on a handle. While they're cheap, manual pumps are generally also the least efficient—you simply can't duplicate your baby's sucking action by hand. Therefore, these pumps are best for moms who only need an occasional bottle or who need to relieve engorgement.

Recommendation: The best manual pump is the Avent "Isis" ($45, for a store near you, call 800-542-8368; web: www.aventamerica.com). Our readers love this pump, which Avent claims is as efficient as a mini-electric (it takes about eight to ten minutes to empty a breast). You can buy the Isis by itself, or as part of a kit that includes extra bottles, cooler packs and more ($60 to $75).Yes, there are other manual pumps (Medela's "Manual-Ease" $50 with adjustable vacuum control is a good second bet), but we think the Isis is tops. (One caveat to the Isis, however: a reader recommends going for the model with the reusable bottle, instead of the disposable one. Why? The reader says Avent's bottle liners for the disposable bottles are terrible—you have to double bag to freeze them or they leak).

◆ ***Mini-Electrics:*** I bought one of these, and it was a waste of money. I thought these battery-operated breast pumps would be good for expressing an occasional bottle. Unfortunately, the sucking action is so weak that I quickly discovered it took twenty minutes *per side* to express a significant amount of milk. And doing so was not very comfortable, to say the least. Why is it so slow? Most models only cycle nine to fifteen times per minute—compare that to a baby who sucks the equivalent of 50 cycles per minute!

Recommendation: The Medela Mini Electric ($102, call 800-435-8316 for a store near you; web: www.medela.com) is one of the few battery operated breast pumps that actually operates at 34 to 36 cycles per minute. Medela also has the "Double Ease" double mini-electric pump for $200. As for all the other models, once again you can find cheaper mini-electrics for, say, $30 to $50, but we wouldn't recommend them.

◆ ***Piston Electric Pumps:*** The Volvos of breast pumps—we can't sing the praises of the piston electric pumps enough. In just ten to twenty minutes, you can pump *both* breasts. And piston electric pumps are much more comfortable than mini-electrics. In fact, at first I didn't think the piston electric pump I rented was working well because it was *so* comfortable. The bottom line: there is no better option for a working woman who wants to provide her baby with breast milk.

Today, you have two options when it comes to these pumps: rent a hospital-grade pump or buy a high-end double-pump. As for rental, a wide variety of sources rent breast pumps on a daily, weekly or monthly basis. We called a lactation consultant at a local hospital who gave us a list that included maternity stores, small private companies, and home-care outfits. Another possibility is to call La Leche League (800-LALECHE; web: www.lalecheleague.org) or

Introduce the Bottle Early

If you plan to introduce a bottle to your baby so you can go out on the town or back to work, do it around the sixth week of age. Most parenting books tell you about this, but they don't stress how important it is to keep giving a bottle regularly—perhaps two or three feedings per week. In our case, we didn't give a bottle consistently, and by the time our son was about four months old, he absolutely refused to take a bottle at all. Oops! That made going out to dinner and a movie alone a lot tougher. A word to the wise: keep up the occasional bottle.

other lactation support groups for a referral to a company that rents piston electric pumps.

What does it cost to rent a hospital-grade pump? One company we surveyed rented pumps for $60 for one month or $45 per month if you rent for two or more months. In general, we found rental charges ranged from $1 to $2.60 per day, with the lower rates for longer rentals. You'll also have to buy a kit of the collection bottles, shields, and tubes (this runs about $20 to $40). Prices will vary according to where you live. Medela's Lactina Select (800) 435-8316, White River Concepts Model 9050 (800) 824-6351 and Egnell Elite (800) 323-8750 are all hospital grade pumps available for rental.

What about buying? Yes, you can buy a piston-electric pump. The two best choices are Medela's "Pump In Style" ($280) and the Ameda Egnell "Purely Yours" ($200, available from the company at 800-323-4060 or from web sites). I used the Pump In Style for my second child and was impressed–it's a fully automatic double pump that uses diaphragm action to best simulate a baby's sucking motion. Best of all, it's portable (about seven pounds) and is hidden in an attractive black leather bag for discretion.

Other moms we interviewed complimented the Ameda model, which comes with six storage bottles and carrying case. A reader said she could pump four ounces of milk in about 20 minutes. Fans of the Ameda like its lower price and weight (two pounds vs. the

Nursing Extras

The wonder about nursing baby is how simple it can be–the milk is always ready, at the right temperature, etc. Yet, breastfeeding can be made even easier (and more comfortable) with one accessory: the nursing pillow. Our readers have emailed compliments for "My Brest Friend" by Zenoff Products (800-555-5522; web: www. zenoffproducts.com). Okay, it probably qualifies as the Most Stupid Name for a Product Ever award, but it really works–it wraps around your waist and is secured with Velcro. It retails for $40, but we saw it for $32. Other parents liked Nojo's nursing pillow (www.nojo.com; see review in bedding chapter for Nojo's contact info). Got twins? Check out EZ-2-NURSE's pillow (800-584-TWIN; we saw it on www.everythingmom.com). A mom told us this was the "absolute best" for her twins, adding "I could not successfully nurse my girls together without this pillow. It was wonderful." Cost: $56. New at Walmart is a breastfeeding collection with Lansinoh products (including their amazing nipple cream). Check the special displays in the store or on their web site at www.walmart.com.

Used pumps are fine

Pop onto eBay (www.eBay.com) and you'll notice quite a few used breastpumps for sale, often for half the original retail—a bargain considering their hefty prices. Yet, major pump makers like Medela warn against using used pumps like the Pump N Style claiming they are a "single owner item" (unlike their rental pumps). So is it kosher to buy a used pump? Of course. Many readers say they've used second-hand pumps without any problem whatsoever. All of the recommended pumps in this chapter can last through more than one mom, if not several moms. Of course, you buy a new collection kit (the tubes and bottles) but an used pump itself is fine, in our opinion.

Medela at seven pounds). Another plus for Ameda: it can run on AA batteries; the Medela has that option . . . if you pay another $160 for a rechargeable battery pack.

One reader recommended the Nurture III breast pump available on line at www.baileymed.com. She claimed that the pump is made by Ameda as well (sure does look a lot like the Purely Yours) but retails for a mere $110. Quite a deal for a piston pump. Also check this web site for a great price on milk storage bags.

Recommendation: Before you invest in a retail high-end pump like the Pump In Style or Purely Yours, *rent* a hospital-grade pump first for a week or two (or a month). After you decide you're serious about pumping and you're comfortable with the double-pumping action, *then* consider buying one of your own. Given the hefty retail prices, it makes sense to buy only if you plan to pump for several months or have a second child.

There are a couple disadvantages to these retail pumps. Some woman find the sucking action weaker than hospital-grade pumps—hence, it may take *longer* to pump. I've used both the Medela hospital-grade pump and the Pump In Style and while I definitely like the Pump In Style, the hospital-grade pump was more comfortable to use. On the other hand, the portability of the retail pumps may outweigh any of their disadvantages. Hospital grade pumps are bulky and are not very portable (they weigh over 20 lbs.).

Waste of Money

Even Cows Opt for the Electric Kind

"I'm going back to work a couple of months after my baby is

Breastfeeding in public: Exposing yourself for onlookers' fun and your baby's health

Here's a controversial topic to discuss around the office water cooler: breastfeeding in public. Since our society tends to see a woman's breasts as sexual objects rather than as utilitarian milk delivery systems, we often run into disapproval of breastfeeding, especially in public. Ironically, this is one of the chief advantages of breastfeeding—it's very portable. No hauling and cleaning bottles, mixing and warming formula, and your child gets nourishment exactly when he needs it.

Amazingly, some parts of this country still manage to equate breastfeeding in public with indecent exposure. Florida just recently repealed a law forbidding public breastfeeding after several woman were cited by the "breast" police for whipping it out at a local mall. It's hard to believe that until just recently laws in this country branded one of life's most basic needs—eating—as illegal. You can call your local La Leche League or other breastfeeding sources to find out if your city or state still has laws like these. If they do, consider getting involved in trying to get them repealed.

The irony is that breastfeeding in public involves very little flashing of flesh. As an admitted public breastfeeder, I can attest to the fact that it can be done discreetly. Here are some suggestions:

1 **IF THE THOUGHT OF BREASTFEEDING IN PUBLIC IS NOT YOUR CUP OF TEA, CONSIDER BRINGING A BOTTLE OF EXPRESSED MILK WITH YOU.** We know one couple who did this and never seemed to have a problem.

born. My co-worker who breastfeeds her baby thinks manual and mini-electrics pumps are a waste of money. What do you think?"

While they may be useful to relieve engorgement, manual pumps aren't very practical for long-term pumping when you're at work. They are very slow, which makes it hard to get much milk. Mini-electric breast pumps are better but are really best only for occasional use—for example, expressing a small amount of milk to mix with cereal for a baby who's learning to eat solids. Mini-electrics do extract more milk but may be painful and still too slow.

Your best bet if you plan to do some serious pumping is to rent a piston electric pump. These monsters maintain a high rate of

2 **USE THE SHAWL METHOD.** Many women breastfeed in public with a shawl or blanket covering the baby and breasts. While this works well, you must start practicing this early and often with your baby. Otherwise, you'll find that as she gets more alert and interested in her surroundings, she won't stay under the shawl.

3 **FIND ALL THE CONVENIENT REST ROOM LOUNGES IN YOUR TOWN.** Whenever we visit the local mall, I nurse in one of the big department store's lounge areas. This is a great way to meet other breastfeeding moms as well. Of course, not every public rest room features a lounge with couches or comfy chairs, but it's worth seeking out the ones that do. We applaud stores like Babies R Us for having "breastfeeding rooms" with glider-rockers and changing tables for easy nursing.

Another creative alternative: stores will usually let you use a dressing room to breastfeed. Of course, some stores are not as "breastfeeding friendly" as others. New York City, for example, has 10 million people and about seven public rest rooms. In such places, I've even breastfed in a chair strategically placed facing a wall or corner in the back of a store. Not the best view, but it gets the job done.

4 **TRY YOUR CAR.** My son knows the back of both of our cars extremely well now. I found it easier and more comfortable to feed him there, especially when he started to become distracted in restaurants and stores. The car holds no fascination for him, so he tends to concentrate on eating instead of checking out the scenery. I suggest you keep some magazines in the car since you may get bored.

extraction with amazing comfort. A lactation consultant we interviewed said piston electric pumps can empty both breasts in about 10 to 15 minutes–contrast that with 20 to 30 minutes for mini-electrics and 45 minutes to an hour for manual pumps.

As mentioned earlier, the only manual pump to receive high marks from our readers is the Avent Isis–and even though it is a vast improvement over previous options, it still is a MANUAL pump. It may not work well for moms who plan to work part or full-time and still nurse their baby. That said, one solution is to use two pumps–a mom we interviewed uses a Pump In Style when she's tired (during the evening or night-time) and the Avent Isis at work (it's much quieter; doesn't need electricity, etc).

The Bottom Line: A Wrap-Up of Our Best Buy Picks

For career and casual maternity clothes, we thought the best deals were from the JCPenney catalog and Motherhood stores (not the other chains like A Pea in a Pod). Compared to retail maternity chains (where one suit can run $200 to $300), you can buy your entire wardrobe from these two places for a song.

If your place of work allows more casual dress, check out the prices at plus size stores. A simple pair of leggings that could cost $45 to $50 at a maternity shop are only $30 or less at "regular" stores. Another good idea: borrow from your husband's closet–shirts, sweat pants and sweatshirts are all items that can do double-duty as maternity clothes.

For weekend wear, we couldn't find a better deal than the 100% cotton shirts and shorts at discounters like Target, Wal-Mart and K-Mart. Prices are as little as $8.98 per shirt–compare that to the $40 price tag at maternity chain stores for a simple cotton shirt.

Invited to a wedding? Rent that dress from a maternity store and save $100 or more. Don't forget to borrow all you can from friends who've already had babies. In fact, if you follow all our tips on maternity wear, bras, and underwear, you'll save $700 or more. Here's the breakdown:

1. Career Wear $240

JCPenney's maternity catalog features a three-piece "maternity suit" (jacket, skirt and pants) for just $60 to $70. Buy two of these in different colors, add a couple nice dresses (another $120) and you're set.

2. Casual Clothes $100

Five outfits of 100% cotton t-shirts and shorts/pants from Target or K-Mart run $100. Or check out JCPenney's "Dividends 4 You" maternity ensemble. For $99, you get a cotton lycra jumper, tunic, skirt, leggings and t-shirt. Another plus: all Penney's clothes are also available in plus, petite and tall sizes.

3. Underwear $200 to $300

The One Hanes Place catalog features great deals on maternity underwear–$11 for a nursing bra, $3.50 for maternity panties, and $3 for a pair of maternity hose. On the other hand, we strongly suggest investing in top-quality underwear for comfort and sanity purposes. For example, a Bravado bra is $31 and Japanese Weekend "OK" bikini maternity underwear are three for $26. Either way, you need eight pairs of maternity underwear, plus six bras, including regular/nursing and sleep bras.

Total damage: $540 to $640. If you think that's too much money for clothes you'll only wear for a few months, consider the cost if you outfit yourself at full-price maternity shops. The same selection of outfits would run $1200 to $1400.

If you plan to breastfeed, we strongly recommend either renting a piston electric pump (about $45 per month) or purchasing the Medela "Pump In Style" ($275) or Ameda Egnell "Purely Yours" ($200). If all you need is a manual pump, try the Avent Isis ($50). Don't go for cheap breast-pumps–they don't work and are supreme wastes of money.

CHAPTER 6

Around the House: Monitors, High Chairs, Bottles & More

What's a "Flatobearius"? Which baby monitor scrambles its signal to prevent eavesdropping? Why do baby foods look like a sinister science experiment gone wrong? In this chapter, we explore everything for baby that's around the house. From a basic list of toys to the best bottles, we'll give you tricks and tips to saving money. You'll learn nine safety tips for toys and the tricks to saving on baby food and formula. Finally, we've got reviews of the best high chairs, advice on humidifiers, playpens and swings—and even tips for making sure pet and baby get along.

Getting Started: When Do You Need This Stuff?

The good news is you don't need all this stuff right away. While you'll probably purchase a monitor before the baby is born, other items like high chairs, activity seats, and even bath-time products aren't necessary immediately (you'll give the baby sponge baths for the first few weeks, until the belly button area heals). Of course, you still might need to register for these items before baby is born. In each section of this chapter, we'll be more specific about when you need certain items.

What Are You Buying?

Here is a selection of items that you can use when your baby is three to six months of age. Of course, these ideas are merely suggestions—none of these items are "mandatory." We've divided them into three categories: bath-time, the baby's room and toys.

Bath

1 **Toys/Books.** What fun is it taking a bath without toys? Many stores sell inexpensive plastic tub toys, but you can use other items like stacking cups in the tub as well. And don't forget about tub safety items, which can also double as toys. For example, Safety 1st (800) 739-7233 (www.safety1st.com) makes a ***Bath Pal Thermometer***, a yellow duck or tugboat with attached thermometer (to make sure the water isn't too hot) for $3. ***Tubbly Bubbly*** by Kel-Gar (972) 250-3838 (web: www.kelgar.com) is an elephant or hippo spout cover that protects against scalding, bumps and bruises. In fact, Kel-Gar makes an entire line of innovative bath toys and accessories.

2 **Toiletries**. Basic baby shampoo like the famous brand made by Johnson & Johnson works just fine, and you'll probably need some lotion as well. The best tip: first try lotion that is unscented in case your baby has any allergies. Also, never use talcum powder on your baby–it's a health hazard. If you need to use an absorbent powder, good old cornstarch will do the trick.

What about those natural baby products that are all the rage, like Mustela or Calidou? We got a gift basket of an expensive boutique's natural baby potions and didn't see what the big deal was. Worse yet, the $20-a-bottle shampoo dried out our baby's scalp so much he had scratching fits. We suppose the biggest advantage of these products is that they don't contain extraneous chemicals or petroleum by-products. Also, most don't have perfumes, but then, many regular products now come in unscented versions. The bottom line: it's your comfort level. If you want to try them out without making a big investment, ask for them as a shower gift.

3 **Baby Bathtub.** While not a necessity, a baby bath tub is a nice convenience (especially if you are bathing baby solo). As a best bet, we suggest the First Years' ***Three Stage Baby Bather*** (800) 225-0382 or (508) 588-1220–it's a $15 bath tub that features a sling for small infants and a cushioned foam pad for older babies.

If you don't have much storage in your bathroom, consider the Safety 1st Fold-up Bath ($13 at Babies R Us). Most baby stores also sell a variety of "bath cushions" that keep a baby from slipping around in a tub–these can be affordable alternatives to complete baby bath tubs at $4 to $5.

4 **Potty seat.** Since this book focuses on products for babies age birth to 2, we have traditionally left potty seats out of this chapter (most children start to potty train after age two or three). That

said, we've received quite a few requests from readers to review potty seats and other toilet training products. Look for a chapter on this topic in our new book, *Toddler Bargains*, due out in September 2002.

Baby's Room

1 **A Diaper Pail.** Yes, there are dozens of diaper pails on the market. We're big fans of the ***Diaper Genie*** ($25 to $30, reviewed later in this chapter). The only downside to the Diaper Genie: you have to buy special refill canisters, which can get a bit expensive. Nonetheless, the Diaper Genie has been a run-away success, spawning knock-offs and other similar products. Cosco, for example, markets the "Diaper Nanny" ($20) that also uses $6 refills. As an alternative, both Safety 1st and Fisher Price make "odor free" diaper pails that use regular kitchen trash bags, as does the Baby Trend "Diaper Champ."

2 **Monitor.** Later in this chapter, we have a special section devoted to monitors, including some creative money-saving tips. Of course, if you have a small house or apartment, you may not even need a baby monitor.

3 **The Changing Area.** The well-stocked changing area features much more than just diapers. Nope, you need wipes and lots of them. We discussed our recommendations for wipe brands in Chapter 4. We should note that we've heard from some thrifty parents who've made their own diaper wipes—they use old washcloths or cut-up cloth diapers and warm water.

What about wipe warmers? In previous editions of this book, we've recommended these $20 devices, which keep wipes at 99 degrees (and lessen the cold shock on baby's bottom at three in the morning). Yet, we've been concerned with safety issues about wipe warmers that have arisen in recent years.

First, Dex recalled a half million of their wipe warmers in 1997 after one alleged fire was caused by the unit (there were six instances "involving melting of the product," says the CPSC). While Dex fixed the problem in January 1997, we were so miffed about how the company handled the recall, we won't recommend them again. (See the box on the next page).

Then, we started getting complaints from readers about another brand of wipe warmers (Prince Lionheart) that were damaged dresser tops. Prince Lionheart blamed the problem on the little feet under the warmer, which were apparently leaving marks on the dresser tops when the unit warmed up. The company claims it has now fixed the problem (and denies that wipe warmers "burn" wipes—they say the heat discolors the chemicals in the wipes), but we're still leery of these products in general.

If you still want a wipe warmer, we'd go for the ones that warm wipes from the top down (Prince Lionheart has one such model). These seem to be more trouble-free than the older, bottom up ones.

Other products to consider for the diaper changing station include diaper rash ointment (A & D, Desitin, etc.), lotion or cream, cotton swabs, petroleum jelly (for rectal thermometers) and rubbing alcohol to care for the belly button area. Another excellent idea for organization: ***BabySmart's*** (800) 756-5590 or (908) 766-4900 (web:www.baby-smart.com) wipes and diaper holders. Made of lucite, each clips on to the edge of your changing table. The wipes holder is about $7 and the diaper holder is $16. If you have a Container Store nearby (800) 733-3532 (www.containerstore.com), we noticed they sell simple plastic storage containers for all those diaper changing station items at $3 to $7.

4 **PORTABLE CRIBS/PLAYPENS**. While this item doesn't necessarily go in your baby's room, many folks have found portable cribs/playpens to be indispensable in other parts of the house (or when visiting grandma). Later in this chapter, we have a special section devoted to this topic.

5 **WHITE NOISE**. Some parents swear they'd never survive without the ceiling fan in their baby's room—the "white noise" made by a whirling fan soothed their fussy baby (and quieted

How NOT to Run a Recall

If we had to give an award for the Worst Recall of a Baby Product, the winner would have to be Dex, the California-based maker of wipe warmers and other baby products. In 1997, Dex recalled a popular wipe warmer, instructing parents to call a toll-free number. First, it took FOREVER to get through to Dex's hotline after the recall was announced. Then, after reaching a human, we were instructed to call Halcyon, Dex's supplier in Canada (who actually manufactured the wipe warmer). At Halcyon, a not-too-helpful person who answered the phone told us we had to send our request for a replacement wipe warmer to Canada. The piece de resistance: the Halcyon folks didn't tell us to keep the warmer COVER, which we sent back with the recalled unit. So, the heating element they sent back sans cover was useless. The result: we curse Dex. Having your customers call your supplier in another country to fix a defective product you sold is NOT good customer service.

sounds from the rest of the house). Just about anything can generate white noise—a humidifier, ceiling fan, etc. Some parents play nature CDs or tapes on a boombox. You'll find these at stores like the Nature Company (www.naturecompany.com).

6 **HUMIDIFIER.** See the next section for tips on buying the best humidifier.

I Dream of the Diaper Genie

Excuse us for a moment while we wax rhapsodic about the Diaper Genie, the neatest invention for parents since the babysitter. This sleek white plastic can has done what years of diaper pails have failed to do: taken the stink out of stinky diapers.

Here's how it works: you pop in a disposable diaper and give the lid a twist. That's it! No brain damage! The Playtex Diaper Genie seals the diaper in airtight, deodorized plastic and stores it in the container base. There are no batteries or motorized parts to worry about: just hit a lever on the base and a chain of sealed diapers emerges for easy disposal (the container holds up to 20 diapers). Best of all, there's little or no smell and no deodorant cartridges to replace.

The Diaper Genie sells for about $25 to $30. And then you've got to buy the refill canisters that hold the plastic wrap—these retail for about between $4 and $6. One of those refill canisters wraps 150 to 180 diapers—or about two weeks worth. So, if you use the Diaper Genie for a year, your total cost would be about $150 (including the cost of the Genie itself). That isn't cheap and probably explains the resistance of some parents to the Diaper Genie, who don't want to part with that much cash to keep their nursery odor-free. (One money-saving tip: use the Genie only for the stinky diapers. Put the wet diapers in the regular trash—that will save you some in refill purchases).

Despite the cost, we've used the contraption for years and think it is worth it. It's relatively easy to use, although it does take a little getting used to. The process of emptying the diapers is relatively straightforward (you twist a cutter on top and the chain of diapers that look like sausages plops out the end), but the switching of canisters is a little more complicated. It takes a few times before you'll get the hang of it, but since you'll be changing as many as 100 diapers a week in the beginning, you'll adjust pretty fast. Best of all, the Genie is virtually pet-proof and child proof—the same can't be said for competing diaper pails.

Humidifiers

Even if you don't live in a dry climate, you might consider a humidifier for baby's room during the winter months. Why? Forced air heat or air conditioning can dry out a house quickly. When it comes to humidifiers, you have two choices:

One technical note: if you get a Diaper Genie as a hand-me down, make sure you note which version you got. The original Diaper Genie was replaced in 1997 with an improved model that holds more diapers and has a wider opening. The only bummer: the newer Diaper Genie uses different refill packages (which are marked in blue). Hence, if you get an original Diaper Genie hand-me down, you may find it difficult to find refill canisters. The deordorization has improved in the new model as well.

Of course, environmentalists tend to have a fit when we recommend something like the Diaper Genie, a device that adds insult to injury in their view–it wraps evil disposable diapers in plastic, which are then thrown into the trash to be carted off to a landfill. Granted, the Diaper Genie won't be winning any awards from the Sierra Club, but let's get real: 95% of parents use disposables and even if there wasn't a Diaper Genie, they'd still throw those diapers into a plastic trash bag. So, we don't see the big deal.

Even if you don't buy a Diaper Genie, you'll need some type of diaper pail (which run $10 to $25). And, with some models you have to replace special charcoal filters every three months to keep the odors down (at a cost of $4 to $5 each).

What about competitors to the Diaper Genie? When you shop baby stores for diaper pails, you'll note quite a few other makers (Baby Trend, Fisher Price, Safety 1st) make knock-offs of the Diaper Genie. Their key advantage: they use regular kitchen bags, so you don't have to buy pricey refills. Their key disadvantage: they don't work anywhere near as well as the Genie does at eliminating odors. So the trade-off comes down to price versus stink. We'll take the Genie, thank you. If you want to try the non-refill alternatives, the Baby Trend Diaper Champ ($30) and Safety 1st's "Odor-Less Diaper Pail" ($17) would be the next best bets.

The bottom line: we give the Diaper Genie a big "thumbs up." It's not cheap, but the convenience factor is hard to beat. (For a store near you that carries the Diaper Genie, call 1-800-843-6430 or www.playtexbaby.com).

◆ ***Cool mist.*** These models work either by evaporation (a filter traps minerals and impurities and then a fan sends the cool mist into the air) or ultrasonic (which uses an electronic transducer to create cool mist). Some folks like ultrasonic models since they are quieter; on the other hand, the fan in evaporative humidifiers generates white noise that can comfort a fussy baby.

◆ ***Warm mist.*** These humidifiers have a heating system to release warm mist into the air. Some warm mist humidifiers have a "vaporizer" feature that allows you to vaporize prescribed medicine into the baby's room (although doctors rarely prescribe that today). These models make a bit of noise when they heat up the water (usually, it's a gurgling sound), but they are quieter than cool mist evaporative models with fans.

So, should you get a warm or cool mist model? It's a toss-up. Warm mist models can raise the temperature in baby's room–that could be a plus (if your house is somewhat drafty) or a minus (if baby's room gets too warm). Each model requires regular cleaning every week and replacement of filters every four to eight weeks.

The disadvantages of humidifiers: evaporative coolers have filters that trap mineral deposits. Over time deposits can reduce the effectiveness of the wick. For ultrasonic humidifiers, mineral deposits can be dispersed through the air as "white dust" which is a cleaning hassle (and some believe a health hazard.) Yes, you can use distilled water in ultrasonic humidifiers, but that's expensive. Finally, what about warm mist humidifiers? Some doctors don't recommend these because they believe a warm, moist environment can lead to bacteria growth.

One feature we recommend: a built-in humidistat. This feature works much the same way a thermostat controls your heat or air conditioning. When the humidity in a room reaches a preset level, the humidistat shuts off the humidifier. If the humidity drops, the unit turns back on. Some cheaper humidifiers lack humidistats; we suggest skipping those models.

What are the best brands? We like the Holmes brand (which are also sold under the brand name Duracraft; 800-5-HOLMES; www.holmesproducts.com). Holmes makes both warm and cool mist models as well as ultrasonic units. They're sold at reasonable prices at discounters like Wal-Mart and Target (among many other stores).

What about humidifiers by juvenile product makers? We find them to be overpriced and under-powered. For example, Evenflo sells both warm and cool-mist 2.5 gallon models for $40 at Babies R Us. That's nice, but we've seen the same size humidifiers at discounters for $30 or less. Another benefit for Holmes: all their humidifiers are treated with "Microban" antibacterial protection in the plastic (and in the cool mist wick filters).

What's the right size humidifier? For most standard size bedrooms, a 1.5 to 2.0-gallon humidifier should do. For larger rooms, check out these guidelines:

Area Humidified (in sq. ft.)	**Room Size**	**Needed Output (gallons per day)**
500 or lower	Very Small	1.5 to 2.0
530-600	Small to Medium	2.2 to 2.5
700-800	Medium	3.0 to 3.5
900-1000	Medium to Large	4.0 to 5.0
1000-2000	Large to Whole House	7.0 to 9.0
Over 2000	Whole house	10.0 or higher

Source: www.holmesproducts.com

Toys

1 **Stacking Cups.** Once your baby starts to reach for objects, a nice set of stacking cups can supply endless hours of fun—although we had second thoughts about whether we'd later regret teaching our son to knock over objects. Sage insight or the ramblings of a first-time parent? Anyway, you can find a set of stacking cups at grocery stores, toy stores and chains like Toys R Us. Cost: about $5. Speaking of affordable toys, we also liked the ***Lamaze*** line of baby toys by Learning Curve (800) 704-8697 (web: www.learningtoys.com). These fun developmental toys (categorized by age) include a puzzle ball, soft stacking rings and more.

2 **Mobile For Crib.** Sure, a mobile sounds like the perfect accessory for any crib, but how do you choose one? Here's our best advice: look at it from underneath. It's surprising to see the number of flat two-dimensional mobiles out there—get underneath them and look from the baby's perspective and what do you see? Nothing—the objects seem to disappear! The best mobiles are more three-dimensional. Most mobiles are $40 to $60; two good, less-expansive brands for mobiles are ***Dolly*** (800) 758-7520 (www.dolly.com) and ***Infantino*** (800) 365-8182 (www.infantino.com). We've seen both online for $20 to $30. Under the "too cute to be legal" category, we should also mention the North American Bear "Flatso" mobiles (see the mention of the Flatso line later in this chapter).

3 **ACTIVITY CENTER/BUSY BOX.** Ah, the old stand-by. This venerable toy (about $15) features various spinning balls, bells, phone dialer, squeakers, etc.–all attached to molded plastic. One famous brand is the ***Fisher-Price Activity Center*** (web: www.fisher-price.com) which has been around since 1973. The center (like other toys) has a strap that enables you to attach it to the crib. We found two problems with this: first, it's hard to do, since the crib's bumper pads may be in the way. Also, such crib toys make it difficult to put the baby down to sleep–any time you touch the crib, the toy makes a sound, and the baby might wake up. Our advice: plan on using "noisy" toys outside the crib.

4 **ACTIVITY GYM.** Among our favorites is the ***Gymfinity*** by Today's Kids (call 972-404-9335 for a dealer near you; web: www.todayskids.com). What most impressed us about the Gymfinity is its versatility. First, it's an infant toy bar, which dangles high-contrast toys for the baby to play with from underneath. Then, it converts to a toddler play table, with puzzle pieces, interlocking gears, and other fun activities for kids through age three. The only drawback to the Gymfinity: its hefty retail price ($30 to $40 at stores like Toys R Us) is somewhat hard to swallow. We should also note we've seen the Gymfinity on special at local stores from time to time for as little as $30. Another company that makes a similar product is the Gymini by Tiny Love (for a dealer near you, call 800-843-6292; web: www.tinylove.com). It sells for about $40 to $60, depending on the version. The ***Activity Arch by Tiny Love*** (about $30) can either be attached over the crib (for babies under five months) or to the side of the crib for older babies.

5 **ACTIVITY SEAT/BOUNCER WITH TOY BAR.** An activity seat (also called a bouncer) provides a comfy place for baby while

Discovery Toys

When our son Jack was born, we received a box of Discovery Toys as a gift and were quite impressed. The line of developmental toys, books and games (sold through local representatives; call 800-426-4777 in the U.S. or 800-267-0477 in Canada for more information; web: www.discoverytoysinc.com) are featured in an 80+ page catalog that relates how toys develop certain skills. You'll find toys that teach "thinking/learning," "creativity," "senses and perception" and more–the catalog features little symbols to point out the skills each item promotes.

you eat dinner, and the toy bar adds some mild amusement. The latest twist to these products is a "Magic Fingers" vibration feature—the bouncer basically vibrates, simulating a car ride. Parents who have these bouncers tell us they'd rather have a kidney removed than give up their vibrating bouncer, as it appears the last line of defense in soothing a fussy baby short of checking into a mental institution.

What features should you look for in a bouncer? Readers say a carrying handle is a big plus. Also: get a neutral fabric pattern, says another parent, since you'll probably be taking lots of photos of baby and a garish pattern may grate on your nerves.

So, where can you get one of these wonder products? Fisher Price (www.fisher-price.com) makes the most popular one in the category—their ***Soothing Bouncer Seat*** is about $30 to $35 (it comes in a couple different versions). Yes, other companies make similar products (Summer makes one for $30, Combi has a $60 version, etc.) but the feedback we get from parents is that Fisher-Price is the best.

Kolcraft debuted two ***Tender Vibes*** bouncers last year for $20 to $30. The more expensive model has a music feature that is sound activated (hence, when you baby cries, strains of Led Zeppelin's "Stairway to Heaven" start to play. Just kidding. It's actually Brittany Spears). Also new: Summer's ***Double Action*** bouncer, which both vibrates and bounces and has a sound generator to play nature or womb sounds and lullabies. Price: $60.

Here's another money-saving tip: turn your infant car seat into an activity center with an attachable toy bar. Children on the Go (which is owned by Graco, for a dealer near you, call 800-345-4109; www.gracobaby.com) makes a toy bar with rattles and spinning toys for just $10 to $15. Two elastic straps attach to any brand infant car seat and the product is available in primary colors or black and white. Another plus: your baby is safer in an infant car seat carrier than in other activity seats, thanks to that industrial-strength harness safety system.

6 **TAPE PLAYER.** Gotta have something to play those Raffi tapes on. Actually, there is quite a good selection of musical tapes for babies that are less irritating than you might think. Look for a tape player designed specifically for use with small children. Such products have child-safe battery compartments and simple controls. Most of the "general" baby catalogs mentioned in this book carry a tape player or two for about $20. If your baby shows a budding interest in music, check out the ***Music Blocks*** ($70) from Neurosmith (562) 296-1100 (web: www.neurosmith.com). This smart toy lets babies create complex musical compositions. By mixing and matching the blocks, this toy cranks out a variety of harmonies and music styles.

7 SELECTION OF BOOKS. As book authors, we'd be remiss if we didn't recommend that you buy lots of books for your baby. Visit your local bookstore, and you'll find stiff board books (easier for young hands to turn or, at least, not destroy) as well as squishy cloth books. There are even books made of vinyl to make bath-time more fun. Obviously, a bookstore that specializes in children's books is a best bet. Used bookstores are another excellent source as are book sales at libraries and other charity events. If your child will be in a day care center, check to see if the school participates in the Scholastic Book Club–prices are low and sales benefit your school.

8 FLATOBEARIUS. Our hip California cousins Ken and Elizabeth Troy turned us on to this adorable line of small stuffed animal rattles. "Flatobearius" is a flat, squishy bear rattle, part of the "Flatso" series from North American Bear Co. (to find a dealer near you, call 800-682-3427 or 312-329-0020 web: www.nabear.com). Once you get hooked, you'll have to acquire the entire collection of animal rattles–Flatopup, Flatjack (a rabbit), and Squishy Fish to name a few. The small Flatso rattles are about $10 (not cheap, but worth it), and they even have a couple of larger versions ($25 to $55) and mobiles.

Safe & Sound for Toys

Walk through any toy store and the sheer variety will boggle your mind. Buying toys for a newborn infant requires more careful planning than for older children. Here are nine tips to keep your baby safe and sound:

1 CHECK FOR AGE APPROPRIATE LABELS. Yes, that sounds like a no-brainer, but you'd be surprised how many times grandparents try to give a six-month old infant a toy that is clearly marked "Ages 3 and up." One common misunderstanding about these labels: the age range has NOTHING to do with developmental issues; instead, the warning is to keep small parts out of the hands of infants because those parts can be a choking hazard. Be careful of toys bought at second-hand stores or hand-me-downs–a lack of packaging may mean you have to guess on the age-appropriate level. Use a toilet paper tube to see if small parts pose a choking hazard: anything that can fit through the tube can be swallowed by baby.

2 MAKE SURE STUFFED ANIMALS HAVE SEWN EYES. A popular gift from friends and relatives, stuffed animals can be a haz-

Are teethers a playpen peril?

How do baby product manufacturers make those soft, chewy teethers you see in every store? The answer: chemical additives known as "phthalate esters," which make poly-vinyl chloride (PVC) toys easy to chew. But should baby be putting that kind of chemical in his mouth?

Greenpeace says no. In 1997, they launched a campaign to get rid of teethers made of PVC's, calling them "toxic toys." You can read about Greenpeace's efforts at www.greenpeace.org.

Are phthalates really dangerous for kids? As you'd expect, there's no agreement on this—the chemical industry says there is no health problem. Baby product makers say the level of phthalates in teethers is so low, there's no risk. Yes, animal studies show huge doses of PVC's are dangerous, but how much does baby really ingest by simply chewing on a soft teether?

To answer that question, safety regulators in Europe have done some preliminary human studies on phthalates. Their findings: very little of the plasticizer is ingested during chewing. In late 1999, the Consumer Products Safety Commission studied the issue and arrived at much the same conclusion: few, if any, children are at risk. The amount of phthalates ingested by babies chewing a plastic toy "is below a harmful level," said the CPSC.

Nonetheless, a few European countries have moved to ban phthalates (including the Netherlands). That's prompted large European baby product makers to reformulate their teethers to remove the chemical—and that trend has extended across the Atlantic.

As publicity about the issue gathered steam, 90% of U.S. baby product makers announced they too will drop plasticizers from their teethers. A good web page with more info on this controversy (including which companies have or have not eliminated phtahlates) is Turner Toys (www.turnertoys.com/PVC_framepage1.htm). At press time, the CPSC announced it was going to continue to study the problem.

Unfortunately, this issue is still very confusing for consumers. Why? Toys and teethers that contain phthalates are NOT labeled as such. While that might change in coming years as manufacturers tout their reformulated teethers as "phthalate-free," it's hard to tell right now what's what. And not all vinyl toys contain the chemical.

Our take on this issue: we're not convinced this is a major safety problem. We'd like to see medical studies that actually indicate there's harm to chewing on a teether for a prolonged period of time. That said, we can understand why parents might err on the side of safety and try to keep such items out of baby's mouth. It's not like teethers are essential items like car seats—we'd avoid those toys with plasticizers until more evidence is in.

ard if you don't take a few precautions. Buttons or other materials for eyes that could be easily removed present a choking hazard—make sure you give a stuffed animal the once over before you give it to baby. Keep all plush animals out of the crib except maybe one special toy (and that only after baby is able to roll over). While it is acceptable to have one or two stuffed animals in the crib with babies over one year of age, resist the urge to pile on. Once baby starts pulling themselves up to a standing position, such stuffed animals can be used as steps to escape a crib.

3 **BEWARE OF RIBBONS.** Another common decoration on stuffed animals, remove these before giving the toy to your baby.

4 **MAKE SURE TOYS HAVE NO STRINGS LONGER THAN 12 INCHES**—another easily avoided strangulation hazard.

5 **WOODEN TOYS SHOULD HAVE NON-TOXIC FINISHES.** If in doubt, don't give such toys to your baby. The toy's packaging should specify the type of finish.

6 **BATTERY COMPARTMENTS SHOULD HAVE A SCREW CLOSURE.** Tape players (and other battery-operated toys) should not give your baby easy access to batteries—a compartment that requires a screwdriver to open it is a wise precaution.

7 **BE CAREFUL OF CRIB TOYS.** Some of these toys are designed to attach to the top or sides of the crib. The best advice: remove them after the baby is finished playing with them. Don't leave the baby to play with crib toys unsupervised, especially once she begins to pull or sit up.

8 **BATH SEATS SHOULD BE USED WITH EXTREME CAUTION.** It looks innocuous—the baby bath seat—but it can be a disaster waiting to happen. These seats suction to the bottom of a tub, holding baby in place while they take a bath. The problem? Parents get a false sense of security from such items and often leave the bathroom to answer the phone, etc. We've seen several tragic reports of babies who've drowned when they fell out of the seats (or the seats became un-suctioned from the tub). The best advice: NEVER leave baby alone in the tub, even for just a few seconds.

9 **DO NOT USE WALKERS.** And if you get one as a gift, take it back to the store and exchange it for something that isn't a death trap. Exactly what are these invitations to disaster? A walker suspends your baby above the floor, enabling him or her to "walk" by rolling

around on wheels. The only problem: babies tend to "walk" right into walls, down staircases, and into other brain damage-causing obstacles. It's a scandal that walkers haven't been banned by the Consumer Products Safety Commission. How many injuries are caused by these things? Are you sitting down? 9,000 a year.

To be fair, we should note the industry has tried to make walkers safer—with a large amount of prodding from the CPSC. While the government decided not to ban walkers outright in 1993, the CPSC did work to strengthen the industry's voluntary standards over the past few years. The result: redesigned walkers with safety features that stop them from falling down stairs. Some have special wheels or "gripping strips" that prevent such falls.

The result of these new safety features: walker injuries have dropped 60% since 1995. But we still think 9000 injured babies is 9000 too much. Our advice: don't put your baby into a walker, no matter how many new "safety" features are built-in.

What about walker alternatives? So called "stationery" play centers made a big splash on the baby market in recent years, led by Evenflo's Exersaucer. Most stationary play centers run $50 to $90 and are basically the same—you stick the baby into a seat in the middle and there are a bunch of toys for them to play with. (The more money you spend, the better the toys, bells and whistles). While the unit rocks and swivels, it can't move. And that's a boon to parents who need a few minutes to make dinner or use the bathroom.

So, should you get one? Well, no. We're troubled by studies that have shown infants who use walkers and stationary play centers suffer from developmental delays when compared to babies who don't use them. According to a study in the October 1999 Journal of Developmental and Behavioral Pediatrics, researchers at Case Western Reserve University found "babies who were placed in walkers were slower to sit up, crawl and walk than those raised without walkers. The mental development of the children also appeared to be slowed," according to an Associated Press article on the study.

Researchers studied 109 infants, including 53 who did not use walkers/stationary play centers. On average, babies who used the walkers were delayed at least a month on average in sitting up, crawling and walking. Non-walker using kids also scored 10% higher on mental development tests than walker users.

The researchers concluded that "restriction in a walker may exert its greatest influence on mental development during the 6- to 9-month age period, a time regarded as transformational in a child's intellectual development," according to the AP article. Noticeably, walker babies were able to catch up to non-walker children after they started crawling—and hence used the walker less often.

Why do walkers and stationary playcenters have such a dramatic effect on a child's development? Researchers speculate that the "the opaque trays placed on the newer walkers as a safety device prevent the children from seeing their legs, blocking the feedback they get from moving a limb and seeing the leg actually move," the article stated.

As a result, we don't recommend parents buy or use walkers or stationary play centers.

Wastes of Money

1 **FANCY TOYS.** We interviewed one couple who bought a fancy set of expensive toys for their infant daughter, only to be dismayed that she didn't want to play with them. What did baby really like to play with? Their keys. The lesson: sometimes it's the simple, inexpensive things in life that are the most fun.

2 **FANCY BOOKS.** Walk through any children's section in your local bookstore and you'll see a zillion children's books, all lavishly illustrated and beautifully packaged. And do you know what most babies want to do with books? Eat them. We liked the suggestion that one mom discovered when it came to books: many popular hardcover children's books come in soft-cover or paperback versions, at substantially lower prices. That way if Junior decides his favorite book looks like lunch one day, you're not out as much money. Board books and even cloth books are good to chew on too.

3 **FANCY BURP PADS.** Do you really need to spend $5 on a burp pad–a scientifically designed piece of cloth for you to put on your shoulder to keep spit-up off your clothes when Junior burps? No, just put a cloth diaper on your shoulder (average price 50¢ or less) and save the money.

4 **BLACK AND WHITE MOBILES.** Yes, they are all the rage today. True, your baby is attracted to high-contrast black and white images in the first four months, and such mobiles may be quite fascinating. But $20-$40 seems like a lot of money to be spent on an item that's used for just four months. We liked the money-saving suggestion from one dad we interviewed: he drew patterns with a black pen on white index cards and then attached the cards to a regular color mobile. The baby liked the improvised version just fine, and the parents saved $20 to $40. (One safety tip: make sure the cards are attached firmly to the mobile. And, as always, remove

all mobiles from the crib after five months when your baby sits up). Another money-saving tip: forget the mobile altogether. Some parents we interviewed said their baby got along fine without one.

5 **BABY BATHTUB.** Save the $15 to $25 that these tubs cost and just give your baby a bath in the kitchen sink. Or bring the baby into the bathtub with you. Not everyone agrees with this tip, however. One reader of our last edition wrote that she tried giving her baby a bath in the kitchen sink and found it awkward. She couldn't both hold the baby and wash him at the same time. That's true–it's best to have two people to do the job (one to hold the baby, the other to wash). If you find yourself bathing baby alone, a baby bathtub may a good investment (buy one second-hand or at a garage sale if you can). Another solution: bath cushions. We've seen these $5 two-inch thick foam cushions in baby stores or in catalogs–they support baby while you bathe her in the sink or tub. You'll save $15 or more over buying a full baby bath tub. Another reader writes with kudos for the ***EZ Bather Delux***e by Dex Products ($6, 800-546-1996; www.dexproducts.com), an L-shaped vinyl frame that keeps babies head above water in the bathtub or kitchen sink.

Money-Saving Secrets

1 **USE WEB COUPONS.** Yeah, you've heard about all the hype on great deals folks get online. But where can YOU find such deals? One of the biggest bargains online are special electronic "coupons" you can use to save big. See the box on the next page for details.

2 **DON'T FORGET CONSIGNMENT STORES.** A great item to find at second-hand stores specializing in children's products: mobiles. Most aren't handled by babies so they're in excellent condition–at prices that are typically 50% or more off retail. We found quite a few in our local baby consignment store for $10 to $20; compare that to the $50 retail price these fetch at specialty stores. Since you tend to use a mobile for such a short period of time, you can then re-consign it at the shop and get some money back! Of course, these stores sell much more than mobiles–you can pick up toys, high chairs, and, of course, clothes at tremendous savings. Check your phone book under "Consignment" or "Thrift Stores"; many are also listed under "Clothes & Accessories–Infant & Child–Retail." For a great online source to local second hand shops, check out www.SecondHand.com. Another great source for bargains:

garage sales. Refer back to Chapter 4 for more tips on shopping garage/yard sales.

3 **GO FOR REFILLABLE PACKAGES.** Take diaper wipes, for example. You can often buy refillable packages of wipes to fit into those plastic boxes. The savings: about 20% off the cost of buying a new box. And you save another plastic box from the landfill.

Coupon deals cut the cost of online shopping

How do baby product web sites generate traffic and sales? One tried and true method is the online coupon—a special discount, either in dollars or percentage off offers. Sites offers these as come-ons for new customers, returning customers . . . just about anyone. Coupons enable sites to give discounts without actually lowering the prices of merchandise. You enter the coupon code when you place the order and zap! You've saved big.

How big? Well, when the internet gold rush was on in 1998 and 1999, some sites were going nuts with coupons—like $50 off a $60 purchase for first-time customers! Or 30% off and free shipping. Things have cooled somewhat in the past few months, but good deals are still out there. How do you find them? You don't have to spend hours surfing; instead just visit the coupon web sites—these sites track deals on other sites.

A good example for baby products is DotDeals (www.dotdeals.com). Their special section on "Kids & Toys" lets you see all the current deals at a glance.. A recent scan of the site revealed $10 off a $30 purchase at a big baby products web site, 30% off any purchase at another site and even 25% off a purchase at a toy web site if you use American Express. Some deals are for first-time customers; others are for anyone. Just note the coupon code (a series of letters and numbers) and the expiration date and you're on your way.

Other web sites that track coupons include Amazing Bargains (slow to load, ugly to look at but very comprehensive at www.amazing-bargains.com) and the oddly named Flamingo World (www.flamingoworld.com).

But you say, Alan and Denise, please give us more coupon sites! Sure, here are some more. Readers have recommended Deal of the Day (www.DealOfDay.com), eDealFinder (www.eDealFinder.com), ImegaDeals (www.ImegaDeals.com), Big Big Savings (www.BigBigSavings.com), Fat Wallet (www.FatWallet.com), Clever Moms (www.CleverMoms.com), and Image Deals (www.imagedeals.com).

Now, go fire up the browser and start saving!

4 REUSE THAT MOBILE. Safety experts say crib mobiles should be removed when baby starts to sit up. Why? Those strings can be a strangulation hazard. But that doesn't mean the mobile is garage sale fodder. Instead, reuse it—we hung ours over the changing table to entertain baby during those zillion diaper changes.

5 MAKE A BABY DRAWER IN THE KITCHEN. Who needs fancy toys? Buy a $200 wagon at a toy store and chances are baby is more interested in the box. So, why fight it? Simple household items like wooden spoons, old boxes or Tupperware containers can provide hours of fun. In the kitchen, give baby a drawer of his own and fill it with some fun items.

6 ORGANIZE A TOY EXCHANGE. As one television network says, if you missed the original episode, the repeat is "new to you." The same goes for toys—pop over to a neighbor's house and you'll notice all those toys seem new and fascinating to your child. So, here's an idea: organize a toy swap with other parents in your neighborhood or playgroup. Label a dozen toys with your name and pop them in a box. Trade that box with another family for toys their children have grown bored with. Voila! Instant new toys for free. Every month, swap again, this time with another family.

7 CONSIDER CREATIVE ALTERNATIVES TO TOY BOXES. A wooden toy box can run $150 to $300. But there are ways to save. First, check out unfinished furniture stores, that have toy boxes for $100 or less. Another idea: use a rolling cart (about $18), wicker laundry baskets ($25) or other inexpensive storage ideas.

8 ONE WORD: EBAY. If you haven't discovered this fantastic bargain source, you should return your bargain shopper license—eBay is an amazing source for baby products. Samples: we popped the words "high chair" into eBay's search engine and whamo! 169 results, including a brand new, still in the box Chicco Mama high chair (reviewed later). The bids for this item were just $75, compared to the $170 retail. Another reader found a $200 breast pump for $140, again brand new. And here's a little secret to getting the best deals: look for baby product makers, catalogs and stores who are selling overstock products quietly on eBay. Yes, you can often get brand new product (still in the box, with all directions, etc.) by just careful searching. Be sure to read product descriptions with a fine tooth comb to make sure an item is new, "in the box" or damaged/used. Most sellers honestly report the condition. Once you find a baby store/catalog that is selling online, you can view all their auctions by clicking on their name.

Do it By Mail

BACK TO BASICS TOYS

To Order Call: (800) 356-5360; Fax (800) 759-8477.
Web: www.backtobasicstoys.com
Shopping Hours: 24 hours a day, seven days a week.
Or write to: 1 Memory Lane, Ridgely, MD 21685
Credit Cards Accepted: MC, VISA, AMEX, Discover.

In business since 1988, Back to Basics Toys catalog theme is "they DO make them like they used to." An excellent index lets you zero in on a certain age group of toys. The "early childhood" section featured such classics as "Rock A Stack" toy by Fisher Price for $4. Altogether, there are over 20 pages of toys for children up to five years, complete with color pictures, great descriptions and age specifications. Back to Basics Toys has a joint web site with Amazon's toy site. There you can find some pricey items like $500 wooden playhouses, but also plenty of affordable items as well. We like the retro toys (Lincoln Logs, Raggedy Ann and Andy, Radio Flyer trikes) best among the online offerings.

CONSTRUCTIVE PLAYTHINGS

To Order Call: (800) 832-0572 or (816) 761-5900; Fax (816) 761-9295.
Web: www.constplay.com
Shopping Hours: 24 hours a day, seven days a week.
Or write to: 13201 Arrington Rd., Grandview, MO 64030.
Credit Cards Accepted: MC, VISA, Discover
Retail Outlets: They have seven retail stores; call the phone number above for a location near you.

Yes, this catalog can seem cluttered, but we like the organization by age group. The "First Playthings" section, for example features infant stimulation toys, foam blocks and other affordably priced items. Heck, we didn't see much over $50 in this section, which is a contrast to other toy catalogs that seem weighted down with expensive offerings. We liked the "First Learning" section that featured a good selection of educational toys. Constructive Playthings has greatly improved their web site since our last visit—now the navigation is easy and the organization excellent. Check out the "sale products" section for the best deals.

EDUTAINMENT CATALOG

To Order Call: (800) 338-3844; Fax (800) 226-1942.
Web: www.mattelinteractive.com
Shopping Hours: 24 hours a day, seven days a week.
Internet: www.mattelinteractive.com
Credit Cards Accepted: MC, VISA, AMEX, Discover.
Canadian orders: A minimum $75 purchase is required for Canada orders.

Edutainment specializes in educational and entertainment software; the catalog was recently bought out by Mattel. You can still get the print version (which has about 90 programs) or shop MattellInteractive.com for a selection of 500 or more programs. The web site is easy to navigate with special sections dedicated to software, downloads, gifts and clearance items. In the software category, we noticed special areas for Arthur, Dr. Seuss and more. You can also search by age-appropriate level, which is nice. The downsides: the type on the web site is very tiny and the prices are not discounted. You might be able to find these titles for less on sites like Buy.com or other software discounters.

KAPLANCO.COM

To Order Call: (800) 533-2166;
Web: www.kaplanco.com
Credit Cards Accepted: MC, VISA, AMEX, Discover.

Kaplan Company bought out the Great Kids Company catalog a few years ago and discontinued the print version. But you can still shop their great selection of educational toys online at KaplanCo.com. We liked the well-designed web site, with special buttons that highlight toys by age, "exceptional children," "outdoor classroom" and more.

PLAYFAIR TOYS

To Order Call: (800) 824-7255; Fax: (303) 440-3393
Shopping Hours: 7am to 7pm Mountain time.
Or write to: PO Box 18210, Boulder, CO 80308
Credit Cards Accepted: MC, VISA, AMEX, Discover.
Web: www.playfairtoys.com
Retail store: 1690 28th St, Boulder, CO.

Yeah, the catalog's organization is a jumbled mish-mash of different age groups, but we liked Playfair's helpful product descriptions. No, this isn't a discount catalog (most of the prices are at full retail), but the large selection of arts and crafts supplies is unique.

Playfair carries Ambi toys and kids' furniture (likes desks and sofa sets). The web site is pretty basic but functional–we wish they had more thumbnails of products instead of text listings.

SENSATIONAL BEGINNINGS

To Order Call: (800) 444-2147; Fax: (734) 242-8278.
Shopping Hours: 24 hours a day, seven days a week.
Or write to: 987 Stewart Rd., PO Box 2009, Monroe, MI 48162
Web: www.sensationalbeginnings.com
Credit Cards Accepted: MC, VISA, AMEX, Discover.

Characters like Madeline and the Teletubbies are the focus of Sensational Beginnings, a well-organized catalog that includes a nice selection of infant items (play centers, activity gyms and more). We saw lots of Brio and Thomas the Tank Engine items, as well as non-toy baby products like the Baby Bjorn carrier. While the catalog's prices are regular retail, Sensational Beginnings web site features specials at 20% to 30% off. That web site, by the way, is spectacular–you can shop by age, brand, category and more. Their "Wow! Gifts" are great splurges (hint to the grandmothers reading this book). You can even find a small selection of baby products like strollers, carriers and the like.

TOYS TO GROW ON

To Order Call: (800) 542-8338; Fax: (310) 537-5403.
Shopping Hours: 24 hours a day, seven days a week.
Or write to: 2695 E. Dominguez St., PO Box 17, Long Beach, CA 90801
Web: www.toystogrowon.com
Credit Cards Accepted: MC, VISA, AMEX, Discover.

As the name implies, Toys To Grow On specializes in education toys. We liked the selection of dress-up "imagine" toys, science projects and arts and crafts supplies. There isn't a big selection of items for children under 2, but they did have some tub toys, soft rattles and blocks. The best deal: Toys to Grow On sells a train table and board for Brio or Thomas that was HALF the cost of what we saw in retail toy stores. We ordered this table from Toys to Grow On and were impressed (it was well made and easy to assemble). As for Toys to Grow On's web site, we loved the "20 under $20" section as well as their "What's Hot" section. You can shop by category (examples: Pretend Play, Bath Toys, etc.) but there are no recommendations for toys by age, unfortunately.

◆ ***More toy catalogs.*** We have to issue a warning before we discuss the next catalog. Here's what we've learned from seven years of parenthood: Thomas the Tank Engine is like an addictive drug for toddlers. Once they get started playing with it, look out—you'll soon be searching toy stores and web sites for Thomas pajamas and lunch sacks . . . and that darn obscure "Mike" train.

So, you can imagine our son's delight when the ***Totally Thomas' Toy Depot*** catalog (800-30-THOMAS; www.totallythomas.com) showed up in our mailbox. This 16 page catalog carries Thomas clothing, backpacks, toys and, of course, trains—engines, track, accessories and more. It was all we could do to rip the catalog out of his little hands to write this review. (Hint: you can learn more about Thomas on their official web site at www.thomas-thetankengine.com).

FAO Schwarz (800) 426-8697 (web: www.faoschwarz.com) is the catalog offspring of the famous toy store. You'll see lots of Elmo, Barney, giant plush toys and more, all at various price levels. The selection is much the same as you'd see in the stores, so this catalog may be best for those who don't have an FAO store nearby.

Hearth Song (800) 325-2502 (www.hearthsong.com) sells arts and crafts supplies, as well as an entire line of Peter Rabbit toys and games. The catalog also has a nice selection of seasonal items and musical instruments like guitars and lap harps.

Imagine the Challenge (888) 777-1493 (www.imaginetoys.com) boasts a section of education toys for kids under three, including a wooden workbench, a play-and-fold clubhouse, and a cute "My First Camera." Most of the items are under $50, which makes this one of the more affordable catalogs we reviewed.

Leaps & Bounds (800) 477-2189 (www.leapsandboundscatalog.com) focus on "dress up and pretend toys" as well as furniture options like desks, play tables and kid-size sofas. Leaps & Bounds is owned by the same parent company as the One Step Ahead catalog.

SmarterKids (web: www.smarterkids.com) is an excellent web site with educational toy recommendations by age and lots of bargains in their clearance section.

Finally, a reader recommends ***Earthwise Toys*** (www.natural-toys.com) for wood toys and baby basics. The site features sale items that change every week.

Monitors

For her first nine months, your baby is tethered to you via the umbilical cord. After that, it's the baby monitor that becomes your surrogate umbilical cord—enabling you to work in the garden, wander about the house, and do many things that other, childless human beings do, while still keeping tabs on a sleeping baby. Hence, this is a pretty important piece of equipment you'll use every day–a good one will make your life easier and a bad one will be a never-ending source of irritation.

Smart Shopper Tips for Monitors

Smart Shopper Tip #1

Bugging your house

"My neighbor and I both have babies and baby monitors. No matter what we do, I can still pick up my neighbor's monitor on my receiver. Can they hear our conversations too?"

You better bet. Let's consider what a baby monitor really is: a radio transmitter. The base unit is the transmitter and the receiver is, well, a receiver. So anyone with another baby monitor can pick up your monitor–not just the sound of your baby crying, but also any conversations you have with your mate about diaper changing technique.

You'll notice that many monitors have two channels "to reduce interference," and some even have high and low range settings–do they help reduce eavesdropping? No, not in our opinion. In densely populated areas, you can still have problems.

We should note that you can also pick up baby monitors on many cordless phones–even police scanners can pick up signals as far as one or two miles away. The best advice: remember that your house (or at least, your baby's room) is bugged. If you want to protect your privacy, don't have any sensitive conversations within earshot of the baby monitor. You never know who might be listening.

One solution: a few baby monitors have "privacy" features where the signal is scrambled, foiling eavesdroppers. We'll highlight which monitors have this feature later in this section..

Smart Shopper Tip #2

Battery woes

"Boy, we should have bought stock in Duracell when our baby was born! We go through dozens of batteries each month to feed our very hungry baby monitor."

Most baby monitors have the option of running on batteries or on regular current (by plugging it into a wall outlet). Our advice: use the wall outlet as often as possible. Batteries don't last long–as little as 8 to 10 hours with continual use. Another idea: you can buy another AC adapter from a source like Radio Shack for $10 or less—you can leave one AC adapter in your bedroom and have another one available in a different part of the house. (Warning: make sure you get the correct AC adapter for your monitor, in terms of voltage and polarity. Take your existing AC adapter to Radio Shack and ask for help to make sure you are getting the correct unit. If not, you can fry your monitor).

Another solution: several new baby monitors (reviewed later in this chapter) feature rechargeable receivers! You'll never buy a set of batteries for these units—you just plug them into an outlet to recharge the batteries.

Smart Shopper Tip #3

Cordless compatibility

"We have a cordless phone and a baby monitor. Boy, it took us two weeks to figure out how to use both without having a nervous breakdown."

If we could take a rocket launcher and zap one person in this world, it would have to be the idiot who decided that baby monitors and cordless phones should share the *same* radio frequency. What were they thinking? Gee, let's take two people who are already dangerously short of sleep and make them *real* frustrated!

After hours of experimentation, we have several tips. First, make sure your cordless phone has the ability to switch among ten channels to find the clearest reception. If you don't have this feature, you may find your phone and monitor are always in conflict, no matter how many times you flip that "Channel A or B" switch on the baby monitor.

Another tip: consider buying one of those new cordless phones that work on the 900 MHz or 2.1 GHz frequency—this lessens the chance of interference. (For techno-heads out there, most cordless phones and baby monitors work on the 46 to 49 MHz radio frequency). The only disadvantage to this tip is that the new cordless phones can be pricey—as much as twice the cost of regular cordless phones.

Of course, just to confuse you, we should note there are new baby monitors that work on the 900 MHz frequency. These are touted as having longer ranges (600 to 1000 feet), but those claims are hard to verify in real-world conditions. And of course, these can interfere with cordless (and cellular) phones that work on the same band.

Baby monitors have one of the biggest complaint rates of all products we review. We suspect all the electronic equipment in people's homes today (computers, fax machines, large-screen TV's the size of a Sony Jumbotron), not to mention all the interference sources near your home (cell phone towers, etc.) must account for some of the problems folks have with baby monitors. Common complaints include static, lack of range, buzzing sounds and worse—and those problems can happen with a baby monitor in any price range.

The best advice: always keep the receipt for any baby monitor you buy—you may have to take it back and exchange it for another brand if problems develop. It sure would be nice if manufacturers of cordless phones and baby monitors would label their products with the radio frequency they use, so you could spot conflicts before they happen.

Smart Shopper Tip #4

The one-way dilemma

"Our baby monitor is nice, but it would be great to be able to buzz my husband so he could bring me something to drink while I'm feeding the baby. Are there any monitors out there that let you communicate two ways?"

Yep, Evenflo, Graco and Safety 1st have models that do just that (see reviews later in this chapter). Of course, there is another alternative: you can always go to Radio Shack and buy a basic intercom for about $40. Most also have a "lock" feature that you can leave on to listen to the baby when he's sleeping. Another advantage to intercoms: you can always deploy the unit to another part of your house after you're done monitoring the baby. Of course, the only disadvantage to intercoms is that they aren't portable—most must be plugged into a wall outlet.

More Money Buys You

Basic baby monitors are just that—an audio monitor and transmitter. No-frills monitors start at $20 or $25. More money buys you a sound/light display (helpful in noisy environments, since the lights indicate if you baby is crying) and rechargeable batteries (you can go through $50 a year in 9-volts with regular monitors). More expensive monitors have transmitters that also work on batteries (so you could take it outside if you wish) or dual receivers (helpful if you want to leave the main unit inside the house and take the second one outside if you are gardening, etc.). Finally, the top-end monitors either have 900 MHz technology (which extends range) or intercom features, where you can use the receiver to talk to your baby as you walk back to the room.

The Name Game: Reviews of Selected Manufacturers

If you've ever looked at monitors, you might ask yourself, "what's the difference?" Most models have all the neat features that you want–belt clips, flexible antennas, two switchable channels. But, there are some differences as we mentioned above. We'll try to make some sense of these choices in the following reviews.

Use the phone numbers listed below to call to find a dealer near you (most manufacturers don't sell directly to the public). All these monitors can be found at stores like Babies R Us, Baby Depot and Toys R Us, as well as on the baby product web sites mentioned throughout this book (an example is BabyStyle.com).

The Ratings

- **A EXCELLENT**–*our top pick!*
- **B GOOD**– *above average quality, prices, and creativity.*
- **C FAIR**–*could stand some improvement.*
- **D POOR**–*yuck! could stand some major improvement.*

Evenflo *For a dealer near you, call (800) 233-5921 or (937) 415-3300. Web: www.evenflo.com* When Evenflo bought out Gerry Baby Products in 1997, the company inherited Gerry's baby monitors. And that was a both an asset and a liability. While Gerry had a big monitor line, it also had a quality problem–there were several recalls of their products after the monitors allegedly sparked house fires. As a result, we've always been leery of Evenflo monitors, which were just repackaged Gerry models. In the past year, however, Evenflo tried to distance itself from that bad PR by re-christening their monitor line "Constant Care." The Constant Care 1000 is an entry level model with sound and light display for $25 while the 3000 offers rechargeable batteries, sound and light display, out of range indicator and an intercom feature for $50. New for 2001, Evenflo will debut their first 900 MHz monitor (the 4000, $40) with a compact design. The new models are definitely an improvement over Evenflo's re-hashed Gerry models, but we've noticed they haven't made much of a splash in the marketplace. The monitors are neither innovative nor well-priced, so we'll take a pass on this brand. ***Rating: C-***

First Years *To find a dealer near you, call (800) 225-0382 or (508) 588-1220.* Sometimes, we goof. In our last edition, we recommended First Year's "Crisp & Clear Plus" monitor ($50) as a best bet.

Shopping 'Bots

Okay, you know there are deals on the 'net. But where do you find them, short of searching for hours on baby product web sites. One idea: DealTime (www.dealtime.com). This free service (a shopping robot, or 'bot) has a special baby section. Click on this web site's "Babies & Kids" and do a search for monitors. Whamo! 112 prices for different baby monitors from a slew of different sites (see Figure 1 on the next page). Among the steals: a Fisher Price monitor that retails for $50 for just $27.92 on Overstock.com. DealTime lists sites which have free shipping with corresponding quick links.

And it had some great features: rechargeable batteries, 900 MHz frequency for better reception and a sound/light display. Best of all, the receiver had an all-but-non-existent antenna. The only problem? The unit buzzed, crackled and popped–and those were the unit's *better* days. Our readers carpet-bombed us with emails complaining about this monitor and we listened–First Years is NOT on our monitor recommended list this time out. We don't know if First Years had a bad production batch or what, but the problems seem to center around cellular phone interference. That was strange since our field test of the Crisp & Clear showed it to work fine, without any interference. Go figure. Anyway, First Years will try to redeem itself this year with a new model, the Safe & Sound Monitor with Finder Feature. Yep, this monitor has a pager button so you can find a misplaced parent's unit quickly. The unit also features sound and light display and rechargeable batteries. Not bad for $30, but will it work on the old 49 MHz frequency (an admission that their 900 MHz monitor is a bust? We're not sure). Since the new monitor wasn't out at press time, we can't really comment on the quality but First Year's track record now gives us pause. ***Rating: B-***

Fisher Price *To find a dealer near you, call (800) 828-4000 or (716) 687-3000. Web: www.fisher-price.com* Fisher Price is the market leader for baby monitors and for good reason–these are among the best-made monitors on the market. You want choice? Fisher Price offers an amazing array of SIX models, ranging from $20 to $50 (see a chart on page 250 for comparison of models/features). In 2002, Fisher Price shook up their monitor line with several new models. We were impressed with the new models' innovative features. For example, the Soothing Dreams Monitor ($50), which lets parents activate soothing music with a touch of a button on the

Figure 1: DealtTime.com lets you compare prices for baby products across several sites at once.

parent's unit. The baby's unit then displays a light show on the ceiling above the crib (this turns off after a period of time). Very cool. Also new: The 900 mhz "Vibrating Monitor" ($40) which is the first baby monitor to feature a vibrate feature on the parent's unit when sound in the baby's room reaches a pre-set limit. Finally, we should note FP has introduced the first combination womb sound monitor and baby monitor---the "Womb Listener: Prenatal to Nursery Monitor" ($30). This prenatal monitor comes with a CD with instructions and samples of sounds you might expect to hear. After the baby is born, the unit converts to a full sound and lights monitor. FP will discontinue their Direct Link monitor for 2002. ***Rating: A-***

Graco *To find a dealer near you, call (800) 345-4109, (610) 286-5951. Web: www.rubbermaid.com/graco/* The juvenile products giant best known for strollers and playpens debuted its first baby monitor a few years back and has been slowly expanding its monitor line ever since. The original "UltraClear" monitor ($40 to $50) uses "compander" technology (also used by cordless phones) to reduce interference. The range is about 600 feet and the receiver does have sound and light displays. The Ultraclear comes in two versions: with one or two receivers. New in the past year, Graco

F-P's Monitors

An overview of Fisher Price's monitors

	2 Channels	Sound/Lights	900 MHz	Prenatal listening	Rechargeable batteries	Dual Receiver
Super Sensitive $20	✔					
Sound & Lights $25	✔	✔				
Dual Sound/Lights $35	✔	✔				✔
Prenatal/Nursery $30	✔	✔		✔		
900Mhz Vibrating $40	✔	✔	✔		✔	
Soothing Dreams $50	✔	✔				

Prices quoted are actual street prices seen online or in stores.

also debuted the "Sounds Sleep Monitor" which had two receivers, sound/light display and a hip translucent plastic look (a la the iMac). Graco has been a bit behind in the 900 MHz trend (the original UltraClear monitors were the old 49 MHz band), so they are playing catch up with some new models. This year, expect Graco to roll out two new models: a 900 MHz version of the Ultra Clear ($40) and a Two Way 900 MHz monitor with an intercom feature for $45. There will also be a version of the intercom monitor with two receivers (the Ultra Clear Deluxe, $65). Overall, we found Graco's monitors to be good quality, perhaps just a step or two behind Fisher Price. ***Rating: B+***

Safety 1st *To find a dealer near you, call (800) 962-7233 or (781) 364-3100. Web: www.safety1st.com* Just like Fisher Price, Safety 1st figures more is better with monitors–the company's monitor line has TEN choices, including several innovative combo video/audio monitors. You can find everything from a bare bones model with no sound and light display (Crystal Clear, $20-$25) to elaborate models with rechargeable batteries and 900 MHz technology. So, which is best? We like the Super Clear Rechargeable Nursery Monitor (#49241, $40). Yes, it works on the old 49 MHz frequency, but it does have rechargeable batteries and sound and light display. At $40, it's about $10 less than similar monitors from Fisher Price and First Years. New last year, Safety 1st will debuted the "Sound & Sight TV Monitor," the first combo audio/video monitor we've seen on the market. A wireless camera sends a picture to any television; a regular "audio" monitor can be used separately. Pretty cool for $90, but since it wasn't out at press time, we can't report yet on how well it works.

We should also discuss Safety 1st's other innovative monitor: "Angelcare" is the first sound and breathing monitor for baby—a special device that is slipped under the crib mattress to monitor baby's breathing. If Angelcare (invented by a Canadian company that was acquired by Safety 1st) determines baby has stopped breathing for 20 seconds, the parent's unit sounds an audible alarm. There's also a function that sends an audible tick to the parent's unit with each breath baby takes (this can be turned off). The unit can also be used as a regular baby monitor (sound only) and features a sound/light display. The disadvantages to Angelcare? The unit does not use rechargeable batteries and features a rather skimpy 200 foot range; also some cribs require the placement of a board under the mattress for the AngelCare to work properly. Price: $99. Who would need this? If you have a preemie or a baby with health problems, AngelCare might be a plus. Other than that, it seems like overkill to us.

(We should note that as we went to press in 2002, Safety 1st discontinued the Angelcare . . . but you might still it around on store shelves and online.)

All in all, Safety 1st's wide array of offerings is impressive, but the quality has troubled us. In 1997, the company recalled 25,000 monitors whose rechargeable batteries ruptured in 76 reports to the CPSC. While that might have been an isolated incident, it sums up our feelings about Safety 1st's quality—lots of companies make baby monitors with rechargeable batteries, but only Safety 1st was forced to recall theirs because of this defect. ***Rating: C***

◆ ***Other Brands.*** Like most gadgets that ***Sony*** sells, their "Baby Call" monitor is an attractive unit but grossly overpriced. We liked the rounded antenna (on both the transmitter and receiver), but it's missing a sound-activated light display. And the price ($70+) is too much for what it is. Nonetheless, it has its fans—parents tell us it works well.

What about a baby surveillance camera? Yes, it sounds a bit Orwellian, but you can buy a baby VIDEO monitor. This was a fad that peaked a couple years ago, when there were several models on the market. Yet the trend never caught on, due to the units' high prices (many were $200 to $300). Safety 1st is still trying to crack this market—they debuted the ***Child View Monitor*** last year, the first hand-held color video monitor that can also be used as a television. It's about $200. Also new: last year, Safety 1st introduced a combo audio/video monitor (see their review earlier in this section for details). As for other models, we still occasionally see a Fisher-

Price video monitor (about $150) and Smart Choice's ***BabyCam*** ($280). All of them work the same way: a wireless camera sends a black and white picture (with sound) to a parent's 5" monitor in another room. We tested a Smart Choice Baby Cam and thought it worked OK. A low-light sensor lets you see grainy pictures at night (*Consumer Reports* says that Fisher Price's camera worked somewhat better in low-light situations than the Baby Cam, though). For most parents, however, a video monitor is probably overkill. We found we could tell whether our child really needed us based on his different cries—no picture was necessary. On the other hand, parents who have babies with medical problems that need constant monitoring might find video monitors helpful.

Our Picks: Brand Recommendations

Here are our picks for baby monitors, with one BIG caveat: how well a monitor will work in your house depends on interference sources (like cordless phones), the presence of other monitors in the neighborhood, etc. Since we get so many complaints about this cat-

BABY MONITORS *A quick look at various features and brands*

NAME	MODEL	PRICE
EVENFLO	CONSTANT CARE 1000	$25
	CONSTANT CARE 3000	$50
	CONSTANT CARE 4000	$40
FIRST YEARS	CRISP & CLEAR PLUS	$50
	SAFE & SOUND	$30
GRACO	ULTRACLEAR	$30-$50
	SOUNDS SLEEP	$30
	TWO WAY	$45
SAFETY 1ST	CRYSTAL CLEAR	$20-$25
	SUPER CLEAR	$40
	ANGELCARE	$100

KEY

✔= Yes

SOUND/LIGHT: indicates whether the monitor has a sound and lights display. This additional visual clue helps determine if baby is crying when the receiver is in a noisy environment

egory, it is imperative you buy a monitor from a place with a good return policy. Keep the receipts in case you have to do an exchange.

Good. Fisher Price's "Sound & Lights" is a good deal at $30. Yes, it lacks rechargeable batteries and the design is a little behind the times (it still sports a big antenna). But it has among the best clarity and sensitivity of any monitor on the market. Another good monitor: Graco's Ultraclear for $40 to $50 that sports similar features.

Better. Fisher Price's "900 MHz Vibrating Monitor" adds several nice features for $40, including rechargeable batteries and a vibration feature so you can feel baby crying. (Isn't that special?).

Best. The Fisher Price "Soothing Dreams Monitor" ($50) lets you activate a sound and light show to soothe baby. Very cool. You also get a good sounds and light monitor among other nice features, such as two-way intercom function so you can communicate back and forth from the nursery.

RECHARGEABLE BATTERIES	SOUND/LIGHT	900MHZ	INTERCOM
	✔		
✔	✔		✔
		✔	
✔	✔	✔	
✔	✔		
	✔	✔*	
	✔		
	✔	✔	✔
✔	✔		
	✔		

900MHZ: Most monitors work on the 46-49mhz frequency; some work on the 900mhz frequency, which eliminates interference with cordless phones and extended a monitor's range.

INTERCOM: Does the monitor have a two-way intercom feature?

*One version of the Graco Ultra Clear has 900mhz technology.

Pet meets baby

If you already have a pet and are now expecting a baby, you're probably wondering how your "best friend" is going to react to the new family addition. Doubtless you've heard stories about how a pet became so jealous of its new "sibling" that he had to be given away. How can you avoid this situation? Here are seven tips on smoothing the transition.

For Dogs:

1 **IF THE DOG HASN'T BEEN OBEDIENCE TRAINED, DO IT NOW.** Even if you feel confident that your dog is well trained, a refresher course can't hurt.

2 **DON'T OVERCOMPENSATE.** You may start feeling guilty while you're pregnant because you won't be able to spend as much time with Fido after the baby comes. So what mistake do expectant parents make? They overcompensate and give the dog extra attention before the baby arrives. Do this and then the dog really misses you and resents the new baby. While it might seem counter-intuitive, gradually give your best friend less attention so he or she can adjust before baby comes.

3 **IF YOUR DOG HAS NEVER BEEN AROUND BABIES AND SMALL CHILDREN, now is the time to introduce him**—before your baby is born.

4 **CONSIDER BUYING A BABY DOLL.** Why? If you practice loving and attending to a baby doll for a few weeks prior to your baby's actual arrival, your dog can begin to get used to you paying attention to small bundles wrapped up in blankets. We did this, and our dog ZuZu got over her curiosity about it quickly. By the time the baby arrived, she didn't much care what we were carrying around (as long as it didn't smell like doggie biscuits!).

5 **BEFORE THE BABY COMES HOME FROM THE HOSPITAL,** have a friend or relative bring home a blanket or piece of clothing the new baby has slept on or worn in the hospital. This helps the dog get used to the smell of the new addition before you bring on the actual baby. We put a blanket the baby slept on in our dog's kennel, and we really think it helped smooth the transition. Another idea: one mom told us she had the nursery staff tape the cries of babies in the hospital nursery. She then put the tape inside the crib and let it "cry" for a while. "By the time my son came home, our dogs were so used to hearing a baby's cry, it didn't bother them at all," she said.

6 **STRATEGIES FOR BRINGING BABY HOME.** Make sure your dog is under control (on a leash or under voice command) when you first come home with your new baby. Greet your four-legged friend first, without the baby. This allows your dog to release some of his excitement and jumping (remember he hasn't seen you for a few days), without you

worrying about the dog harming a baby in your arms. Next, Dad should hold the dog by the collar or leash while Mom shows Fido the baby. Give your dog time to sniff a little, but don't let the dog turn the situation into a lick-fest. If everything looks OK, you can release the dog.

7 **NEVER LEAVE THE DOG ALONE WITH THE BABY**—especially if the dog has shown any signs of jealousy toward your child. Don't allow the dog to sleep under the crib (there have been incidents of dogs standing up and pushing the mattress off its supports, causing the mattress to crash to the floor). Always supervise how your baby plays with the dog. For example, when our son was older, he found our Dalmatian very interesting. However, he tended to pull on her ears and tail whenever he got a hold of them. So, we constantly encourage gentle petting.

What about cats?

Cats have recently surpassed dogs in popularity as America's favorite domestic pet. So as not to slight those cat lovers out there, here are three pieces of advice.

1 **BEFORE YOU GET PREGNANT, HAVE YOUR CAT TESTED FOR TOXOPLASMOSIS**, a disease that is caused by a parasitic organism that is transmitted to humans from cat feces. Toxoplasmosis is dangerous and may cause the fetus to become seriously ill or die.

If your cat is infected, have it boarded at a kennel or have someone take care of it for the period of infection (usually about six weeks). It's also best not to get pregnant during this time. You can avoid getting the infection yourself by having someone else clean out your cat's litter box. If you keep your cat indoors and he or she doesn't catch mice or birds outside, chances are the cat won't be infected (outdoor cats are more likely to be exposed to toxoplasmosis). Consult your doctor and your cat's veterinarian if you have any questions about this serious problem.

2 **INTRODUCE YOUR CAT TO THE BABY SLOWLY.** Similar to the way you would introduce a dog to your new baby, keep an eye on your cat's reactions. Don't leave your cat alone with the baby if you suspect any jealousy. Most cats will ignore the new addition with their usual aplomb.

3 **CONSIDER USING A NET OVER YOUR BABY'S CRIB.** Cats love to sleep in warm places and might decide to take up residence with your bundle of joy. The Cozy Crib Tent ($70), manufactured by Tots in Mind (800) 626-0339 web: www.totsinmind.com is a mesh crib topper that attaches to the side railing. It completely encloses the crib, making it impossible for cats to snuggle up to little ones. Another idea: train your cat where not to go by using double sided tape on such items as the crib, changing table, etc. One couple decided to install a screen door on the baby's room. They could see in and hear the baby, but the cat couldn't enter.

Formula

Is there any difference between brands of formula? According to our research, the answer is no. The federal government regulates the ingredients in baby formula. Hence almost all the commercially available baby formula sold in the U.S. and Canada contain the *same* ingredients . . . the only difference is the color of the label on the outside of the can. That's right–the "generic" formula sold at Wal-Mart and Target is no different than pricey Similac.

What about formula brands that claim they are easier to digest? Carnation's "Good Start" says just that, claiming its "Comfort Proteins" are "broken down into smaller pieces to be easy to digest in babies tummies." Sorry, we're not buying it. We think all formula brands are virtually the same, despite the marketing.

What does formula cost these days? First realize that formula comes in three different versions: powder, liquid concentrate and ready to drink. Powder is least expensive, followed by liquid concentrate and then ready to drink. A recent check of grocery stores revealed a 16 ounce of Emfamil with Iron was running about $12. This can makes 118 fluid ounces of formula, so the cost per ounce of formula is 10¢.

Of course, formula makers have tricks to make it difficult to compare prices. Each brand of formula comes in a different size can–Similic powdered formula comes in 14.1 oz cans, so it looks cheaper at $10.69. BUT since this can only makes 105 ounces of formula, the cost per ounce is almost the same as Enfamil (10¢ per ounce of liquid formula.) Adding to the confusion: each brand has a different size scoop, which also frustrates apples to apples comparisons.

Money Saving Tips

1 STAY AWAY FROM PRE-MIXED FORMULA. Liquid concentrate formula and ready-to-drink formula are 50% to 200% more expensivethan powdered formula. Yes, it is more convenient but you pay big time for that. We priced name-brand, ready to drink formula at a whopping 25¢ ounce.

Guess what type formula companies gives out as freebies in doctors' offices and hospitals? Yes, it's often the ready-to-drink liquid formula. These companies know babies get hooked on the particular texture of the expensive stuff, making it hard (if not impossible) to switch to the powdered formula later. Sneaky, eh?

2 CONSIDER GENERIC FORMULA. Most grocery stores and discounters sell "private" label formula at considerable savings, at least 30% to 40%. At one grocery store chain, their generic powdered formula worked out to just 7¢ per fluid ounce of formula, a 30% savings. One great brand of generic formula: BabyMil (800-344-1358; web: www.BabyMil.com), whose formulas are 30% less expensive than national brands. BabyMil sells for $6 to $7 a 16 oz can, versus $10 plus for 16 oz of Enfamil. BabyMil comes both in regular and soy versions (BabySoy); check their web site to find a store near you that sells generic formula.

We should note that some pediatricians are concerned about recommending generic formula—doctors fret that such low-cost formula might discourage breastfeeding. We wonder if it has to more with their lucrative research grants that are handed out by the big name brand formula companies; the more market share generic formula takes from the name brands, the less money for doctors' research projects might be available.

3 BUY IT ONLINE. Yep, you can buy formula online from eBay. You can save big but watch out—some unscrupulous sellers

Formula for disaster: Confusing cans confront soy users

Soy formula now accounts for 15% of the infant formula market. Yet, a case of mistaken identity has led some parents to nearly starve their infants. Apparently, parents mistakenly thought they were feeding their babies soy formula, when in fact they were using soy *milk*. The problem: soy *milk* is missing important nutrients and vitamins found in soy *formula*. As a result, babies fed soy milk were malnourished and some required hospitalization. Adding to the confusion, soy milk is often sold in cans that look very similar to soy formula. The government has asked soy milk makers to put warning labels on their products, but some have still not complied. If you use soy formula, be careful to choose the right can at the grocery store.

Another concern: low-iron formula. A myth among some parents is that the iron in standard formula causes constipation—it does not, says a pediatrician we interviewed. Yes, constipation can be a problem with ALL formulas (although some parents tell us Similac is the least constipating since it was reformulated a couple of years ago). But, babies should NEVER be on low-iron formula unless instructed by a pediatrician.

try to pawn off expired formula on unsuspecting buyers. Be sure to confirm the expiration date before buying formula online. And watch out for shipping charges—formula is heavy and shipping can outweigh any deal, depending on the price you pay. We saw one case of formula go for $53 on eBay. But the $6 shipping charge made the deal less sweet, considering a case would retail for $65!

Baby Formula Manufacturers: Modern Convenience or Sinister Conspiracy?

We got an interesting package in the mail the other day. It was from Enfamil, one of the country's largest formula makers. This wasn't any special treatment because we had authored this book. Nope, it appears to be standard practice. What was inside this special delivery? A case of six cans of formula and, get this, a pamphlet with tips on breastfeeding. We were appalled. It was sort of like Marlboro sending us a booklet on how to quit smoking—along with a case of cigarettes.

We've got nothing against formula, per se. Sure, we're firm believers in breastfeeding, but we realize there are times when formula is the only option for medical reasons. What really bothers us is not formula itself, but the way formula companies market their product. In a word, it's shameful.

The formula company's marketing tactics are very clever. Among the more interesting activities we discovered: formula makers shower hospitals with all kinds of gifts and free samples—all in the hope that the nurses will pass the word to you and other new mothers. One company offers gift incentives to nurses who hand out the most formula packets to new moms. Another firm has even shamelessly produced a video on breastfeeding, with a plug for their formula tactfully inserted at the end. Hospitals get the video free of charge and send one home with each new mom.

You can always spot the new parents when they check out of a maternity ward—they're the ones weighed down with free diaper bags, rattles, and toys, all emblazoned with the fancy logos of the formula makers.

All this makes us think, what kind of message are they trying to send? "Sure, you should breastfeed, but if it seems too challenging, we want to make sure a convenient can of formula is never that far away." One of our favorite examples of this duplicity was a rattle we received as a gift, once again at the hospital. Emblazoned with the name Enfamil, it featured a picture of a rabbit feeding its baby with a bottle! We don't know about you, but we haven't seen any rabbits in the Wild Kingdom who bottle-feed their young.

4 Buy in bulk. We found wholesale clubs had the best prices on name brand formula. For example, Sam's Club (www.samsclub.com) sells a 2.5 pound (40 oz) can of Enfamil for $24. That was 20% less than grocery stores.

5 Ask your pediatrician for free samples. Just make sure you get the powdered formula (not the liquid concentrate or

Consider a recent advertising campaign for Carnation's Good Start formula: a new mom looks into the camera and says something like "Remember, breast milk is best, but Carnation's Good Start is made to be gentle for your baby." Sort of like a beer company saying "Don't drink and drive, BUT if you're going to get sloshed, make it a Spuds Beer."

Frankly, we think the baby formula companies are taking advantage of new mothers, plying us poor souls (who are already short of sleep) with slick pitches for "convenient" solutions to our babies' feeding problems.

Adding insult to injury, several of the formula makers recently pleaded guilty to price-fixing charges. If you've wondered why most formula is marked at about the same price in many stores, it's apparently no accident.

What's our solution to this marketing muddle? Ban direct advertising of formula to consumers. That's what several European countries have done, with no adverse consequences to mothers or babies. A couple of major formula makers (namely, Mead/Johnson and Ross) already restrict their marketing to the medical community, and they don't seem the worse for it. We'd also like to see an end to the promotional freebies that hospitals give out–and strict enforcement of anti-price-fixing laws to keep formula companies from gouging consumers.

Formula companies aren't run by dummies. Ironically, breastfeeding moms are a lucrative profit center for formula makers. When a breastfeeding mother switches to formula within her baby's first year, odds are she will continue formula feeding for the rest of that first year. Contrast that with the fact that moms who never breastfeed often switch to whole cow's milk after just six months (even though that's NOT what's recommended by doctors; cow's milk is only recommended for infants 12 months or older). Hence, it's more lucrative for these companies to target breastfeeding moms, since getting them to switch racks up bigger profits in the long run.

Considering the overwhelming evidence that breastfeeding is infinitely better for babies, it is time this country took a hard look at regulating the out-of-control marketing of baby formula.

ready to pour). One reader in Arizona said she got several free cases from her doctor, who simply requested more freebies from the formula makers.

6 **SHOP AROUND.** Yes, powdered formula at a grocery store can run $10-$12 for a 16 ounce can–but there's no federal law that says you must buy it at full retail. Readers of our first edition noticed that formula prices varied widely, sometimes even at different locations of the same chain. In Chicago, a reader said they found one Toys R Us charged $1.20 less per can for the same Similac with Iron ready-to-feed formula than another Toys R Us across town. "They actually have a price check book at the registers with the codes for each store in the Chicagoland area," the reader said. "At our last visit, we saved $13.20 for two cases (about 30% of the cost), just by mentioning we wanted to pay the lower price."

Another reader noticed a similar price discrepancy at Wal-Mart stores in Florida. When she priced Carnation Good Start powdered formula, she found one Wal-Mart that marked it at $6.61 per can. Another Wal-Mart (about 20 miles from the first location) sells the same can for $3.68! When the reader inquired about the price discrepancy, a customer service clerk admitted that each store independently sets the price for such items, based on nearby competition. That's a good lesson–many chains in more rural or poorer locations (with no nearby competition) often mark prices higher than suburban stores.

Bottles/Nipples

What's the best bottle for baby? Actually, it's not the bottle that's important but the nipple–how the milk is delivered to baby is more important than the container.

When it comes to nipples, there are a myriad of choices. At the low end, Playtex and Gerber are available in just about every grocery store in the U.S. and Canada. Mid-price options like Evenflo and Johnson & Johnson's Healthflow are also widely available, as are the high-end Avent nipples and bottles.

So, which nipple (and bottle) system is best? This is like asking a baseball fan to name their favorite team. For many parents, the bottle/nipple system they start with is the one they stick by. And the low-end options can work just as well as the premium brands.

That isn't to say premium, reusable bottle brands like ***Avent*** don't have their advantages. The company claims its nipples are clinically proven to reduce colic, the endless crying that some infants develop around one month of age. Avent says its nipples are better since their shape mimics the breast–and many readers of this book tell us Avent is superior to the competition. Avent bottles have wide-mouth openings that are easier to fill (for formula) and easier to clean than competing bottles. The thicker plastic Avent uses feels more substantial that that used by other brands; you can definitely re-use these bottles for later children (although the nipples should be replaced after six months of use).

Unfortunately, Avent isn't cheap. Their products can cost twice as much as other less-expensive bottles and nipples. A 9oz Avent bottle with nipple runs $5 at Babies R Us, compared to $4 for a Playtex bottle, $3 for a Johnson and Johnson Health Flow and $2.50 for a an Evenflo bottle (all prices are for a bottle with nipple).

Until a couple of years ago, Avent only made reusable bottles, missing out on the one-third of the market that prefers the convenience of disposable nursers. Well, there's good news to report: Avent's has now also sells a disposable bottle that includes their famous nipple and storage bags that clip on the bottle.

A couple of caveats about Avent: first, you can't use the disposable nipple on the reusable bottle (and vice versa)–you have to buy two separate sets of bottles and nipples. Another bummer: Avent's bottles only come with the newborn nipple, which has a very LOW flow rate. Why the company sells a giant NINE oz. bottle intended for a toddler with a nipple that's for an infant is beyond us–and a rip-off, since then you've got to buy separate nipples.

Remember that many bottles use "proprietary" nipples–hence, an Avent nipple won't work on someone else's bottle. Yes, some manufacturers let you mix and match, but you should check first before assuming compatibility.

One last gripe for Avent: beware of their storage bags for breastmilk. Readers complain that Avent's storage bags leak, frustrating nursing moms who are trying to pump, store and freeze breastmilk for later use. (Gerber's storage bags seem to hold up better and are easier to use, say readers. Also Mother's Milk Mate (800-499-3506; web: www.mothersmilkmate.com) sells a good solution for breast milk storage for under.

Among the more hip products on the bottle front are the "angled nursers." ***Johnson & Johnson's*** Health Flow started the trend, which purportedly keeps baby from gulping too much air and is easier for parents to monitor the amount of liquid baby has consumed. Evenflo has introduced a similar product and several other companies have knocked-off the Health Flow in recent years.

Of course, there are other bottles out there besides the big brands. A reader recommend a new bottle from a company with the scary name of ***BreastBottle*** (www.breastbottle.com). Shaped like, well, a breast, this pricey bottle ($13) is made of soft plastic and is dishwasher safe.

Another neat product: ***The Bottle Burper*** from Tender Moments (800) 699-BURP, which eliminates air from disposable bottles (which can contribute to colic). It's dishwasher safe, fits most disposable bottles and is available in stores like Baby Depot, Toys R Us and more. Cost: $1.50 to $2 each.

Where can you find bottles at a discount? Readers say Avent bottles at Target are $4, about a $1 less than other stores. The web is another source: DrugStore (www.drugstore.com) has great prices on many Avent items. And many of the general baby product sites reviewed in Chapter 11 carry Avent at a discount as well.

Smart Shopper Tip

Smart Shopper Tip #1
Nipple confusion?

"When I check the catalogs and look in baby stores, I see bottles with all different shaped nipples. Which one is best for my baby? How do I avoid nipple confusion?"

Nipple confusion occurs when a baby learns to suck one way at the breast and another way from a bottle. This happens because the "human breast milk delivery system" (i.e., the breast and nipple) forces babies to keep their sucking action forward in their mouth. The result: they have to work harder to get milk from a breast than from a conventional baby bottle.

So if you want to give an occasional bottle, what bottle is least likely to cause nipple confusion? Unfortunately, the answer is not clear–some parents swear that Avent's nipple is best. Others find less expensive options like the Playtex Nurser work fine.

Are there really that many differences between nipples, besides shape? Not really. All major brands are dishwasher-safe, made of the same plastics and have very similar flow rates. The bottom line: you may have to experiment with different nipples/bottles to find one your baby likes.

What about pacifiers? Some experts say early use of pacifiers may interfere with breastfeeding. The best advice: wait until lactation is firmly established before introducing a pacifier. Which type of pacifier is best? There are two types–regular pacifiers have round nipples, while "orthodontic" pacifiers have flat nipples. There's no consensus as to which type is best–consult with your pediatrician for more advice on this topic.

Bottle Warmers & Sterilizers

Like the competition in bottles, ***Avent*** also seems to win the sterilizer war: their "Microwave Steam Sterilizer" ($25-30) holds four bottles of any type and is easy to use—just put in water and nuke for eight minutes. Most parents have been very happy with this product, which is a convenient alternative to boiling bottles. If you don't have a microwave, Avent has an "Electric Steam Sterilizer" for $64 that does much the same thing.

New for 2001, Avent has introduced the "Sterilizer Express," a new model that is even more zippy than their previous sterlizers. The Express comes in both electric ($70) and microwave versions ($27) and can sterilize six bottles in just four to six minutes (the lower figure is for the microwave; the higher one for the electric version).

What about bottle warmers? Avent's old bottle warmer ($40) got mixed reviews from our readers. It only worked with Avent bottles and took about six minutes to warm a bottle—"that's too long when your baby is screaming at the top of his lungs," says one mom. On the upside, it could warm baby food in addition to bottles. To address these complaints, Avent debuted the new "Express Bottle and Baby Food Warmer" ($40) in late 2000—this new model can heat a bottle in four minutes. It also fits baby food and all types of baby bottles (not just Avent).

A better bet for a warmer may be the ***First Years*** "Night & Day Bottle Warmer System" ($30). It steam heats two 8 oz. bottles in under five minutes (one reader said its more like three minutes). For night-time feedings, it can keep two bottles cool for up to eight hours (so there's no need to run to the kitchen). Yes, it fits Avent bottles, both the 4 oz. and 8oz. versions. One bummer: some readers gripe that the warmer sometimes over-warms a bottle (always test the milk/formula on your wrist before giving to a baby, of course). But, overall, folks seem happy with this unit.

Baby Food

At the tender age of four to six months, you and your baby will depart on a magical journey to a new place filled with exciting adventures and never-before-seen wonders. Yes, you've entered the SOLID FOOD ZONE.

Fasten your seat belts and get ready for a fun ride. As your tour guide, we would like to give a few pointers to make your stay a bit more enjoyable. Let's take stock:

Parents in Cyberspace: What's on the Web?

Looking for a schedule of what foods to introduce when? ***Earth's Best's*** web site has a comprehensive chart with suggestions (www.earthsbest.com). ***Gerber's*** slick web site (www.gerber.com) also has baby development info (including when to start different stage foods) and cool "Shockwave" features that let you take a virtual tour of their baby food jars (trust us, it's more interesting than it sounds). We also liked ***Beechnut's*** site (www.beechnut.com), which includes "suggested menus," "feeding FAQ's" and "mealtime pointers." Although it is designed for Canadian parents, ***Heinz*** web site, www.heinzbaby.com contains extensive nutritional advice and other helpful info. Canadians can take advantage of rebate offers and other deals on this site (hopefully, they'll add the rest of North America to the coupon deals soon).

Safe & Sound

1 **FEED FROM A BOWL, NOT FROM THE JAR.** Why? If you feed from a jar, bacterium from the baby's mouth can find their way back to the jar, spoiling the food much more quickly. Also, saliva enzymes begin to break down the food's nutrients. The best strategy: pour the amount of baby food you need into a bowl and feed from there (unless it's the last serving from the jar). And be sure to refrigerate any unused portions.

2 **DON'T STORE FOOD IN PLASTIC BAGS.** If you leave plastic bags on the baby's high chair, they can be a suffocation hazard. A better solution: store left-over food in small, Tupperware-type containers.

3 **DO A TASTE TEST.** Make sure it isn't too hot, too cold, or spoiled. We know you aren't dying to taste the Creamed Ham Surprise from Gerber, but it is a necessary task.

4 **CHECK FOR EXPIRATION DATES.** Gerber's jarred food looks like it would last through the next Ice Age, but check that

expiration date. Most unopened baby food is only good for a year or two. Use opened jars within two to three days.

5 **A FINAL WORD OF ADVICE ON FEEDING BABY:** don't introduce nuts (like peanuts or peanut butter) until your child is at least three years old. This advice comes from a nationally known allergist we interviewed who's a specialist in nut allergies. He points out that nut allergies are potentially fatal and lifelong. So the longer you wait to introduce nuts, the better chance you have of avoiding these deadly allergies.

Smart Shopper Tips

Smart Shopper Tip #1

Tracking Down UFFOs (Unidentifiable Flying Food Objects)

"We fed our baby rice cereal for the first time. It was really cute, except for the part when the baby picked up the bowl and flung it across the kitchen! Should we have bought some special stuff for this occasion?"

Well, unless you want your kitchen to be redecorated in Early Baby Food, we do have a few suggestions. First, a bowl with a bottom that suctions to the table is a great way to avoid flying saucers. Plastic spoons that have a round handle are nice, especially since baby can't stick the spoon handle in her eye (yes, that does happen–babies do try to feed themselves even at a young age). Spoons with rubber coatings are also nice; they don't transfer the heat or cold of the food to the baby's mouth and are easier on the gums. One of our favorite spoons is Munchkin's "Soft Bite Safety Spoon" (call 800-344-2229 or 818-893-5000 to find a dealer near you; web: www.munchkininc.com). This spoon uses new technology to change color when baby's food is too hot (105 degrees or warmer).

Smart Shopper Tip #2

Avoiding Mealtime Baths

"Our baby loves to drink from a cup, except for one small problem. Most of the liquid ends up on her, instead of in her. Any tips?"

Cups with weighted bottoms (about $5) help young infants to get the hang of this drinking thing. A sipping spout provides an interim learning step between bottle and regular cup. When your baby's older, we've found clear plastic cups to be helpful. Why?

Your baby can see out the bottom and not feel like someone has turned out the lights.

No-spill cups are a godsend—Playtex (203) 341-4000 pioneered this category with a cup that doesn't leak when tipped over. Despite the fact that many other companies have jumped into the no-spill cup market in recent years, Playtex's cups are still the gold standard. We also liked the First Years' "Tumble Mates Spill-Proof Cup" (for a dealer near you, call 800-225-0382), which is dishwasher safe and cleans easily.

You don't have to go to a baby store to find these items—we've seen many baby feeding accessories in grocery stores.

Money-Saving Tips

1 **MAKE YOUR OWN.** Let's be honest: baby foods such as mashed bananas are really just . . . mashed bananas. You can easily whip up this stuff with that common kitchen helper, the food processor. Many parents skip baby food altogether and make their own. One tip: make up a big batch at one time and freeze the leftovers in ice cube trays. Check the library for cookbooks that provide tips on making baby food at home. A reader suggestion: the "Super Baby Food" book ($19.95, published by F. J. Roberts Publishing, web: www.superbabyfood.com). This 590-page book is about as comprehensive of a book as you can find on the subject.

2 **BELIEVE IT OR NOT, TOYS R US AND BABIES R US SELL BABY FOOD.** If you think your grocery store is gouging you on the price of baby food, you might want to check out the prices at Toys R Us or their sister store, Babies R Us. We found Gerber 1st Foods in a four-pack of 2.5 ounce jars for $1.13—that works out to about 28¢ per jar or about 5% to 10% less than grocery store prices. Toys R Us also sells four-packs of assorted dinners from Gerber's 2nd and 3rd Food collections.

3 **COUPONS! COUPONS! COUPONS!** Yes, we've seen quite a few cents-off and buy-one-get-one-free coupons on baby food and formula—not just in the Sunday paper but also through the mail. Our advice: don't toss that junk mail until you've made sure you're not trashing valuable baby food coupons. Another coupon trick: look for "bounce-back" coupons. Those are the coupons put in the packages of baby food to encourage you to bounce back to the store and buy more.

4 BUY HEINZ. As noted later in this section, Heinz baby food is often priced 10% to 20% below the competition. The only drawback: it isn't available everywhere. Another problem: Heinz also has more starches and fillers (like sugar) than other brands. Hence, you're saving money, but giving your baby less protein, minerals and vitamins with each spoonful. Look for single food jars without the fillers.

5 SUBSTITUTE COMPARABLE ADULT FOODS. What's the difference between adult applesauce and baby applesauce? Not much, except for the fact that applesauce in a jar with a cute baby on it costs several times more than the adult version. While the adult applesauce isn't fortified with extra vitamins, it probably doesn't matter. Baby will get these nutrients from other foods. Another rip-off: the "next step" foods for older babies. Gerber loves to tout its special toddler meals in its "Graduates" line. What's the point? When baby is ready to eat pasta, just serve him small bites of the adult stuff.

6 GO FOR THE BETTER QUALITY. That's a strange money-saving tip, isn't it? Doesn't better quality baby food cost more? Yes, but look at it this way–the average baby eats 600 jars of baby food until they "graduate" to adult foods. Sounds like a lot of money, eh? Well, that only works out to $300 or so in total expenditures (using an average price of 48¢ to 75¢ per jar). Hence, if you go for the better-quality food and spend, say, 20% more, you're only out another $60. Therefore it might be better to spend the small additional dollars to give baby better-quality food. And feeding baby food that tastes more like the real thing makes transitions to adult foods easier.

E-MAIL FROM THE REAL WORLD

Making your own baby food isn't time consuming

A mom in New Mexico told us she found making her own baby food isn't as difficult as it sounds:

"My husband and I watch what we eat, so we definitely watch what our baby eats. One of the things I do is buy organic carrots, quick boil them, throw them in a blender and then freeze them in an ice cube tray. Once they are frozen, I separate the cubes into freezer baggies (they would get freezer burn if left in the ice tray). When mealtime arrives, I just throw them in the microwave. Organic carrots taste great! This whole process might sound complicated, but it only takes me about 20 minutes to do, and then another five to ten minutes to put the cubes in baggies."

The Name Game: Reviews of Selected Manufacturers

Here's a round-up of some of the best known names in baby food. We should note that while we actually tried out each of the foods on our baby, you may reach different conclusions than we did. Unlike our brand name ratings for clothing or other baby products, food is a much trickier rating proposition. We rated the following brand names based on how healthy they are and how much they approximate real food (aroma, appearance, and, yes, taste). Our subjective opinions reflect our experience–always consult with your pediatrician or family doctor if you have any questions about feeding your baby. (Special thanks to Ben and Jack for their help in researching this topic.)

The Ratings

A EXCELLENT–*our top pick!*
B GOOD– *above average quality, prices, and creativity.*
C FAIR–*could stand some improvement.*
D POOR–*yuck! could stand some major improvement.*

Beech-Nut *(800) BEECHNUT; Web: www.beechnut.com* Beech-Nut was one of the first baby food companies to eliminate fillers (starches, sugar, salt) or artificial colors/flavors in its 120 flavors. While Beech-Nut is not organic, the company claims to have "stringent pesticide standards." Our readers generally give Beech-Nut good marks (some like it better than Gerber). The only bummer: it can be hard to find (not every state has stores that carry it). You can search their web page or call their 800-number to check availability. One bonus: Beech-Nut's web site includes on-line coupons and a rebate offer. (A last bit of good news on Beech-Nut: the company's plan to merge with Heinz was scuttled by anti-trust regulators, which is good news for consumers who want more choice.) ***Rating: B+***

Earth's Best *(800) 442-4221. Web: www.earthsbest.com* Organic food has gone mainstream in the last few years, so there's no surprise you can now buy organic baby food. One of our favorite brands: Earth's Best. Started in Vermont, Earth's Best was sold in 1996 to Heinz, one of the baby food giants. Heinz couldn't figure out what to do with the company and decided to sell it to natural foods conglomerate Hain Celestial (parent of Celestial Tea). Despite all the changes in ownership, Earth's Best still has the largest line of "natural" baby foods on the market—all vegetables and grains are certified to be organically grown (no pesticides are used), and meats are raised without antibiotics or steroids. Another advantage: Earth's Best never adds any salt, sugar or modified starches to its food. And the foods are only made from whole grains, fruits and vegetables (instead of concentrates). Surprisingly, Earth's Best costs about the same as Gerber (around 45¢ to 49¢ for a 2.5 ounce jar). We tried Earth's Best and were generally pleased. Our only complaint: some of the dinners have corn, a highly allergenic food that is not supposed to be introduced until your baby is 12 months old. Another bummer: Earth's Best can be hard to find (it's more likely in health food stores like Whole Foods, but we've seen it in some "regular" grocery stores too). All in all, Earth's Best is a much-needed natural alternative to the standard fare that babies have been fed for far too many years. ***Rating: A***

"Toddler" foods a waste of money

When the number of births plateaued in recent years, the baby food companies began looking around for ways to grow their sales. One idea: make foods for older babies and toddlers who have abandoned the jarred mushy stuff! One company warns parents not to feed "adult" foods to babies too early, saying they won't provide "all the nutrition they need." To boost sales in the $1 billion baby food market, Gerber rolled out "Gerber Graduates" while Heinz debuted "Toddler Cuisine," microwaveable meals for kids as old as 36 months. Heck, even Enfamil rolled out the "EnfaGrow" line of fortified snacks. So, what do nutritionists and doctors think of these foods? Most say they are completely unnecessary. Yes, they are a convenience for parents but, besides that, so-called toddler foods offers no additional nutritional benefit. In their defense, the baby food companies argue that their toddler meals are meant to replace the junk food and unhealthy snacks parents give their babies. We guess we can see that point, but overall we think that toddler foods are a complete waste of money. Once your baby finishes with baby food, they can go straight to "adult food" without any problem—of course, that should be HEALTHY adult food. What's best: a mix of dairy products, fruits, vegetables, meat and eggs. And, no, McDonald's French fries don't count as a vegetable.

Gerber *Web: www.gerber.com* Dominating the baby food business with a whopping 70% market share (that's right, three out of every four baby food jars sold sport that familiar label), Gerber sure has come a long way from its humble beginnings. Back in 1907, Joseph Gerber (whose trade was canning) mashed up peas for his daughter, following the suggestion of a family doctor. We imagine those peas looked quite different from Gerber's peas today. Now, thanks to scientific progress, Gerber's peas are put through such a rigorous canning process that they don't even look like peas . . . instead more like green slime. And it's not just the look, have you actually smelled or tasted any of Gerber's offerings? Yuck. Sure it's cheap (about 49¢ for a 2 1/2 ounce jar of Gerber 1st Foods), but we just can't feed our baby this stuff with a clear conscience. On the upside, Gerber offers parents one key advantage: choice. The line boasts an amazing 200 different flavors. Gerber is sold in just about every grocery store on Earth. And we have to give Gerber credit: a few years ago, the company announced it would respond to parents' concerns and reformulate its baby food to eliminate starches, sugars and other fillers. Gerber also rolled out "Tender Harvest," a line of organic baby food to compete with Earth's Best. The new line is made with "whole grains and certified organic fruits and vegetables" (note that Gerber's regular line still uses fruit and vegetable concentrates). While we like the changes Gerber has made, we still have problems with the brand. First, we think their "Graduates" line of "toddler" foods are a waste of money. And their juice line is overpriced compared to others on the market. ***Rating: C***

Heinz *Web: www.heinzbaby.com* Heinz is probably the best bargain amongst the national baby food brands. A recent price survey revealed Heinz's baby food is typically 10% to 20% cheaper than Gerber. The company has more success selling baby food abroad than here in the U.S.–it's not available in every state. One bummer: while Heinz has removed fillers like sugar or starch from 100 of its foods, there are still another 60 with those extra ingredients. We were also puzzled with Heinz's internet strategy–there isn't a baby food web site for US parents (but we did find one for Canadians). From that Canadian web site, we discovered in 1997 Heinz launched Earth's Best (reviewed earlier) in Canada as well as "Congee," an ethnic line of baby food for Chinese parents that incorporates traditional rice dishes. ***Rating: B+***

◆ ***Another brand.*** Specialty baby food brands seem to come and go, but one company has had some success in this field recently: the ***Well Fed Baby*** (888-935-5333; www.wellfedbaby.com). Started by a self-described "health food fanatic," the Well Fed Baby says it is the first baby food that is frozen, organic, kosher and vegetarian. Well Fed Baby got its start in California health food stores, but has expanded its distribution in recent years. Since their distribution has been rather limited, we haven't heard from any readers who've actually used the product but it does like an interesting alternative. Call them at 888-935-5333 to find a store near you that carries it.

High Chairs

As soon as Junior starts to eat solid food, you'll need this quintessential piece of baby furniture—the high chair. Surprisingly, this seemingly innocuous product generates 6600 injuries each year. So, what are the safest high chairs? And how do you use them properly? We'll share these insights, as well as some money-saving tips and brand reviews in is section.

Safe and Sound

Considering the number of injuries caused by high chairs, it's important to understand how to safely use these products:

1 MOST INJURIES OCCUR WHEN BABIES ARE NOT STRAPPED INTO THEIR CHAIRS. Sadly, four to five deaths occur each year when babies "submarine" under the tray. The safest high chairs now feature a "passive restraint" (a plastic post) under the tray to prevent this. Even if the high chair has a passive restraint, you STILL must strap in baby with the safety harness with EACH use. This prevents them from climbing out or otherwise hurting themselves. Finally, never put the high chair near a wall—babies have been injured in the past when they push off a wall or object, tipping over the chair. This problem is rare with the newest high chairs (as they have wide, stable bases), but you still can tip over older, hand-me-down models.

2 THE SAFETY STANDARDS FOR HIGH CHAIRS ARE VOLUNTARY. In a recent report, *Consumer Reports* claimed that not all high chairs meet these voluntary standards. Perhaps the safest bet: look for JPMA-certified high chairs. The JPMA requires a battery of safety tests, including checks for stability, a locking device to prevent folding, a secure restraining system, no sharp edges, and so on.

3 INSPECT THE SEAT—IS IT WELL UPHOLSTERED? Make sure it won't tear or puncture easily.

4 LOOK FOR STABILITY. It's basic physics: the wider the base, the more stable the chair.

5 CAREFULLY INSPECT THE RESTRAINING SYSTEM. Straps around the hips and between the legs do the trick. The cheapest high chairs have only a single strap around the waist. Expensive models have "safety harnesses" with multiple straps.

6 SOME HIGH CHAIRS OFFER DIFFERENT HEIGHT POSITIONS, INCLUDING A RECLINING POSITION THAT SUPPOSEDLY MAKES IT EASIER TO FEED A YOUNG INFANT. The problem? Feeding a baby solid foods in a reclining position is a choking hazard. If you want to use the reclining feature, it should be exclusively for bottle feeding.

More Money Buys You

Whether you spend $30 or $200, most high chairs do one simple thing—provide you with a place to safely ensconce your baby while he eats. The more money you spend, however, the more comforts there are for both you and baby. As you go up in price, you find chairs with various height positions, reclining seats, larger trays, more padding, casters for mobility and more. From a safety point of view, some of the more expensive high chairs feature five-point restraint harnesses (instead of just a waist belt). Nearly all high chairs feature the under-tray passive restraint mentioned earlier. As for usability, some high chairs are easier to clean than others, but that doesn't necessary correspond to price. Nearly all high chairs sold today are made of plastic and metal, replacing the wooden high chairs that previous generations of babies used.

Smart Shopper Tips for High Chairs

Smart Shopper Tip #1
High Chair Basics 101

"I was looking at those fancy Italian high chairs and trying to figure out why they are so expensive. And does it matter what color you get? I like the white the best."

The high chair market is basically divided into two camps: the domestic-made chairs from companies like Graco and Cosco and the Italian imports from Peg Perego and Chicco. The key differences: styling (the Italian chairs admittedly look better) and quality (the imports are generally better than the domestic brands, but you pay for it).

Peg Perego's Prima Pappa, for example, is a runaway success, thanks to its stylish looks and compact fold for storage. At $160, however, the Pappa is TWICE the price of Graco's top-of-the-line high chair. And, as you'll read later, some readers gripe the Pappa is a nightmare to clean.

Besides the domestic versus import choice, here are some basic features and new trends to keep an eye out for:

◆ ***Tray release.*** Nearly all high chairs now have a "one hand" tray release that enables you to remove easily remove the tray with a quick motion. The problem: not all releases are the same. The more expensive chairs generally have a release that's easier to operate.

◆ ***Snack trays.*** Some new high chairs have two trays–a big one for meals and a smaller one for snacks. Why? We have no idea.

◆ ***Tray wars.*** High chair makers like to battle their competitors by touting the newest gimmick on their trays. Hence, you'll now see trays with cup holders, compartmentalized snack areas and so on. Do you really need a cup holder? Don't worry–your baby will spill their juice, cup holder or not.

◆ ***Less convertibility.*** Here's an ironic twist: while the rest of the baby products market is awash in "convertible" products, high chairs are moving the other way. Gone are the high chairs that converted into a table and chair seat, or some other future use. Parents seem to like high chairs that are, well, high chairs.

◆ ***Washability***. Here's an obvious tip some parents seem to miss: make sure the high chair you buy has a removable washable seat cover OR a seat that easily sponges clean. What color should you get? Answer: anything but white. Sure, that fancy white "leatherette" high chair looks all shiny and new at the baby store, but it will forever be a cleaning nightmare once you start using it. Darker colors and patterns are better. Another tip: avoid high chairs that have lots of cracks and crevices near the tray and seat. (This seems to be the Peg Perego's Prima Pappa's biggest sin).

Smart Shopper Tip #2

Tray Chic and Other Restaurant Tips

"We have a great high chair at home, but we're always appalled at the lack of safe high chairs at restaurants. Our favorite cafe has a high chair that must date back to 1952–no straps, a metal tray with sharp edges, and a hard seat with no cushion. Have restaurateurs lost their minds?

We think so. People who run eating places must search obscure South American countries to find the world's most hazardous high chairs. The biggest problem? No straps, enabling babies to slide out of the chair, submarine-style. The solution? When the baby is young, keep her in her infant car seat; the safe harness keeps baby secure. When your baby is older (and if you eat out a lot), you may want to invest in a portable booster seat like Safety 1st's Fold-Up Booster seat ($20) or the 1st Years Portable 3-in-1 booster seat for $20. You can also use these seats later at home when baby outgrows the high chair, but is too small for a regular chair yet.

The Name Game: Reviews of Selected Manufacturers

Many high-tech high chairs feature height adjustments and extra-large feeding trays. While most are made of plastic and metal, there are still fans out there who like traditional wood chairs. If you want a wood chair, consider offerings from Simmons and Child Craft (yes, they're the same names you saw in Chapter 2 in the crib reviews). Since wood high chairs lack fancy features (you can't adjust the height, they don't fold up, etc.), the majority of high chairs sold in the U.S. and Canada are those reviewed in this section:

The Ratings

- **A EXCELLENT**–*our top pick!*
- **B GOOD**– *above average quality, prices, and creativity.*
- **C FAIR**–*could stand some improvement.*
- **D POOR**–*yuck! could stand some major improvement.*

Carter's. This high chair is made by Kolcraft, see review later.

Chicco *4E Easy Street, Bound Brook, NJ 08805. For a dealer near you, call (877) 4CHICCO or (732) 805-9200.. Web: www.chic-*

cousa.com Considering the phenomenal success of Peg Perego's Prima Pappa high chair (reviewed later in this section), we figured it wouldn't take long for Italy's other major baby product maker (Chicco) to come up with their version. And we weren't wrong. Chicco's version, the "Chicco Mamma" (cute, eh?) is a virtual clone of the Prima Pappa and runs about the same in stores and online ($160 regular retail, lower online). You get a six position height chair with three-position recline and the whole thing folds up for easy storage. But Chicco has gone one step further than Perego by adding some useful features: the chair is 7% wider and 20% taller than the Pappa. The Mamma's pad is easier to remove and clean than the Pappa's; and the tray (which has a cup holder and one-hand release) hooks on the back of the chair for storage. Even better: the Chicco Mamma can fold at any height (the Pappa must be in the top position) and the unit is fully assembled in the box (the Perego requires some assembly). And the Chicco chair avoids the cleaning problems that dog by the Perego model. The only gripe we've heard about Chicco is that some parents find the tray too

Living the High Life

Hook-on chairs and booster seats are close relatives to the familiar high chair. Depending on your needs, each can serve a purpose. Hook-on chairs do exactly what they say–hook onto a table. While some have trays, most do not, and that is probably their biggest disadvantage: baby eats (or spills and throws food) on your table instead of hers. At least they're cheap: about $25 to $40 at most stores. Best use: if your favorite restaurants don't have high chairs (or don't have safe ones) or if you plan to do some road trips with Junior. One caveat: hook-on chairs are only safe when used with tables that have four legs (not pedestals).

Booster seats are more useful. With or without an attached tray, most strap to a chair or can be used on the floor. We use ours at Grandma's house, which spares us the chore of dragging along a high chair or hook-on chair. It's also convenient to do evening feedings in a booster seat in the baby's room, instead of dragging everyone to the kitchen. And you can't beat the price: $18 to $30 at most stores.

Our vote for the coolest booster for toddlers: the BabySmart "Cooshie Booster" ($30 at Babies R Us; www.babysmart.com). This cushy foam booster won't stain or absorb liquid and doesn't slip or slide on a chair. The only thing it is missing is a strap (it's really best for toddlers).

high for smaller infants (you might have to prop them up for the first few weeks). New last year, Chicco added a five-point harness to the Mamma, a fold-away footrest and splash mat (isn't that what pets are for?). So, we'll give the Chicco a big thumbs up. It might have been second to the market, but it out performs the Perego on several counts. ***Rating: A***

Cosco *2525 State St., Columbus, IN 47201. Call (812) 372-0141 for a dealer near you (or 514-323-5701 for a dealer in Canada). Web:* www.coscoinc.com Like most things Cosco makes, their high chairs define the entry-level price point in this market. Simple Cosco high chairs (the Lil' Diner) are bare bones models that sell for $30 to $40 in discount stores like K-Mart. These might make good choices for grandma's house, where occasional use is all that would be required. Cosco's main offering in the full feature high chair category is the Options 5 High Chair ($40 to $50)–a model that has a seven positions recline, four-position tray, removable pad and more. Once again, safety concerns continue to dog Cosco–in late 2000, Cosco recalled one MILLION of the Options 5 High Chairs after they received reports that the seats could separate from the frame and fall to the ground. Cosco and the CPSC received 168 reports of such incidents, including 57 injury reports. We were haunted by the collapse of one Cosco high chair that was captured on home video and played on the local news. As a result, we can't recommend this brand. ***Rating: F***

Evenflo *1801 Commerce Dr., Piqua, OH 45356. For a dealer near you, call (800) 233-5921 or (937) 415-3300. Web: www.evenflo.com* Evenflo has always been an also-ran in the high chair market. Lackluster models are one reason. While we liked the "Phases" or "Steps to Grow" model (it converted from a high chair to a table and chair, $85), no one else seemed to. As a result, Evenflo has gone back to the drawing boards and will debut a new model called the "Easy Comfort" that is, well, just a high chair. Similar to the Graco Neat Seat or Cosco Options 5, the Easy Comfort will feature a four-position recline, permanent snack tray with passive restraint three-point harness, eight height positions and a washable fabric seat. Yet, at $100, it seemed overpriced to us. ***Rating: C***

Fisher-Price *636 Grand Ave., East Aurora, NY 14052. For a dealer near you, call (800) 828-4000 or (716) 687-3000.* Web: www.fisher-price.com. Like Evenflo, Fisher Price isn't a big player in the high chair market–but unlike Evenflo, at least the folks at Fisher Price are trying to do something innovative in the category. Their "Swing 'N'Meals" ($99) is the first product to combine a high chair AND a swing. We

License mania

One thing that always confuses parents is all the licensed baby products out there. For example, Kolcraft licenses the names "Carter's" and "Lennon Baby" to put on their high chairs. Cosco does the same with Eddie Bauer and NASCAR for their car seats and Evenflo with Osh Kosh for strollers and more. Here's a little secret of the baby product biz: licensed products are often IDENTICAL to the same ones made under the manufacturer's own name. At most, there are just different fabric colors or patterns. BUT, you pay for the licensed name—most licensed products are 10% to 30% more expensive them the plain vanilla versions. Whether that premium for a certain color or pattern is worth it is up to you.

were skeptical when we first heard about this product, as most "convertible" products rarely live up to their promises. But, we have to give it to Fisher Price—the thing actually works and works well. The Swing N Meals combines a three-speed swing (with two position recline) and a full-size high chair with three-position tray, footrest, and machine-washable (and reversible) cushion. It also folds for storage. So, what's not to like? Well, readers note the unit has no wheels, which limits its portability. Others complain about the seat's short safety straps and some knock the swing for being somewhat loud (of course, that sound can lull a baby to sleep, so it can be a plus). Finally, other parents tell us there isn't much of a difference between swing speeds and the swing itself tends to eat batteries (rechargeable batteries might be a good investment). Those negatives aside, most parents say they are happy with the Swing N Meals—it will save you about $25 to $50 over buying the products separately. If you get it, make sure you have plenty of room in your kitchen/dining area—the Swing N Meals has a wide base and doesn't fold up very compactly. If you just a good basic high chair, Fisher Price's new " Healthy Care" high chair is well-priced at $70. It features a three-position one-hand seat recline, five point restraint, one-hand tray removal and seven height adjustments. Best of all: the snap-off tray is dish-washer safe. The biggest drawback to this new chair: the fabrics are rather ugly (at least the tan and blue one we saw at a trade show; there is a navy and white version at Babies R Us that should be easier on the eyes). ***Rating: B+***

Graco *Rt. 23, Main St., Elverson, PA 19520. For a dealer near you, call (800) 345-4109, (610) 286-5951. Web: www.gracobaby.com*

Graco is probably the biggest play in the under $100 high chair market. The company offers everything from bare-bones models for $29 to top-of-the-line units with all the bells and whistles for $69. On the low-end, the "Easy Chair" ($30) is a very simple unit–basically a chair and tray. It might make a good back-up chair for grandma's house if you're on a budget. The "Easy Seat" ($30) has a five position height adjustment and larger seat, while the "Neat Seat" comes in several different versions that range from $40 to $70. The top-of-the-line Neat Seat ($70) features a double tray (a large, compartmentalized tray with cup holder and a small snack tray), five point harness, removable, washable pad and footrest. New last year, Graco added a passive under-tray restraint with all their models, as well as one-handed tray releases. Lockable casters also appear on the more expensive models, a feature that was sorely missing on pervious models. So, what about the quality? Graco's high chairs only get average grades from our readers. Many complain that the high chair doesn't feel sturdy compared to the Italian imports and several note the chair recline lever is hard to operate. The one-handed tray release? Readers say it is more like two hands and a lot of effort. We also hear occasional reports about trays breaking on Graco high chairs and others say the seat cover rips way too easily–don't plan on this high chair making it to baby #2. If you get a Graco, plan on having a large kitchen or dining room–the unit doesn't fold up for storage. ***Rating: B-***

Kolcraft 3455 West 31st Pl., Chicago, IL 60623. For a dealer near you, call (773) 247-4494. Web: www.kolcraft.com. Kolcraft's main emphasis in the high chair market is their licensed brands–this company makes both a Carter's high chair and a "collectible" Lennon Baby high chair. Of course, no matter what name is on the chair, it's just a Kolcraft high chair with different fabrics. Prices are $49 for a Kolcraft model, $59 for the Carter's and $69 for the Lennon Baby. Whatever you pay, you basically get the same seat: three-position recline, six-position height adjustment and four-position adjustable tray with one-hand release. While we like the safety T-bar under the tray, we were disappointed in a lack of wheels/casters at this price point. And Kolcraft's high chairs only get average grades when it comes to quality and durability. ***Rating: C+***

Lennon Baby. This high chair is made by Kolcraft, see above.

Martinelli. Peg Perego markets their products in some specialty stores under the name Martinelli. Yet, the Martinelli high chairs are EXACTLY the same as the Perego models, just different colors. See Perego's review below for more details.

Peg Perego *3625 Independence Dr., Ft. Wayne, IN 46808. For a dealer near you, call (219) 482-8191. Web: www.perego.com* Peg Perego has hit a home-run with their "Prima Pappa" high chair. Sure, it does what most high chairs do–it has seven height adjustments, four seat-recline positions, casters for mobility, and a spacious tray with one-handed release. But the Prima Pappa does one trick few other full-feature high chairs do–it folds up! With a couple of quick motions, the chair folds up to a mere 11" in width for storage, a boon for families with small kitchens or eating areas. The downside? It ain't cheap–the Prima Pappa retails for $160, but we've seen it on sale online for as little as $120. In the past year, Perego has added a passive restraint bar under the tray and a five point harness to enhance the chair's safety. New for 2002, Perego will be rolling out a version of the Pappa with two covers–vinyl underneath and fabric on top, so when you move the fabric cover for cleaning, you still have a vinyl seat underneath. (The vinyl seat only version will be $160; the dual fabric version is $180). Also new: a dinner tray that pops off to go into a dishwasher for easier cleaning. In previous editions of this book, we recommended the Pappa as a our top high chair pick. This time out, however, we've knocked Perego down to number two, behind the Chicco Mamma. Why? The list of gripes from our readers is long: many parents complain the Pappa has too many cracks and crevices for food/dirt to hide (and hence, it takes an effort to keep clean). The white leatherette versions have been known to stain, say other readers. Another gripe: the tray on the Pappa sits so high that parents with small babies find it hard to use. And other parents say their babies can kick off the tray with little effort. If you get the Pappa, here's a quick buying tip: Perego also makes a version of the Pappa called the "Roller," which features a bar that helps you roll it about the kitchen and a new storage basket. It's rather striking with a seat covered in black "leatherette" fabric, but beware: "The Roller" does NOT fold up like the Pappa, which is a major negative in our opinion. Our advice: skip the Roller (which costs $30 or more) and get the Pappa. Or better yet, get the Chicco Mamma instead. ***Rating: B***

◆ **Other Brands.** *Playskool* used to be a big player in the high chair market with their affordable 1-2-3 high chair, but the company has withdrawn from the baby products market amid slumping sales. The 1-2-3 was plagued by many recalls, so we'd skip it if you find one second-hand.

Finally, as we went to press, ***Baby Trend*** introduced a fantastic new high chair model that is a knock-off of the Chicco Mamma and Perego Prima Pappa–it basically has all the same features, but only a $90 price tag. This one is definitely worth a look.

Our Picks: Brand Recommendations

Here is our round-up of the best high chair bets.

Good. The Fisher-Price Swing 'N' Meals ($99) is a dark horse in this category, but it really does work both as a swing and high chair. If you were planning to get a swing, this might be a good way to combine the purchases and save money (and space).

Better. Peg Perego's Prima Pappa ($120-$160, depending on where you buy it) was our top pick last time out, but we've bumped it down to number two. The complaints about cleanability and a too-high tray mar what would otherwise be an excellent high chair. Yet, the Pappa is still light years ahead of the low-end Graco models in terms of quality and durability. If you go for the Pappa, do NOT buy the all-white version–it is hardest to keep clean.

Best. Sure the Chicco Mamma ($130 to $160) is a Prima Pappa clone, but it does have some key advantages: the seat is slightly bigger, it can fold up in any position and comes fully assembled. And it is easier to clean.

Special needs. For grandma's house, a simple Graco Easy Chair ($30) should do the trick. For travel, the First Years Portable 3-in-1 Booster folds for travel and is easy to use. What about older babies? For toddlers, we like the Cooshie Booster by BabySmart ($30) as a comfortable place to sit after your baby outgrows the high chair.

Swings

You can't talk to new parents without hearing the heated debate on swings, those battery-operated or wind-up surrogate parents. Some think they're a god-send, soothing a fussy baby when nothing else seems to work. Cynics refer to them as "neglect-o-matics," sinister devices that can become far too addictive for a society that thinks parenting is like microwave dinners–the quicker, the better.

Whatever side you come down on, we do have a few shopping tips. First, ALWAYS try it before you buy. Give it a whirl in the store or borrow one from a friend. Why? Some babies love swings. Others hate 'em. Don't spend $120 on a fancy swing only to discover your little one is a swing hater.

Should you buy a manual (wind-up) or battery operated swing? We've been impressed in the past few years with the improvements in the wind-up swings. These units now work effectively with only

Babee Tenda's "safety" seminar: Anatomy of a Hard Sell

We got an interesting invitation in the mail during our second pregnancy—a company called "Babee Tenda" invited us to a free "safety seminar" at a local hotel. Our curiosity piqued, we joined a couple dozen other expectant parents on a Saturday afternoon to learn their expert safety tips.

What followed was a good lesson for all parents—beware of companies that want to exploit parents' fears of their children being injured in order to sell their expensive safety "solutions." Sure enough, there was safety information dispensed at the seminar. The speaker started his talk with horrific tales of how many children are injured and killed each year. The culprit? Cheap juvenile equipment products like high chairs and cribs, he claimed. It was quite a performance—the speaker entranced the crowd with endless statistics on kids getting hurt and then demonstrated hazards with sample products from major manufacturers.

The seminar then segued into a thinly veiled pitch for their products: the Babee Tenda high chair/feeding table and crib. The speaker (really a salesperson) spent what seemed like an eternity trying to establish the company's credibility, claiming Babee Tenda has been in business for 60 years and only sells its products to hospitals and other institutions. We can see why—these products are far too ugly and expensive to sell in retail stores.

How expensive? The pitchman claimed their crib retailed for $725—but is available for you today at the special price of $489! And what about the high chair/feeding table (which converts into a walker, swing, etc.)? It "regularly" sells for $450, but we'll give you a special deal at $298!

We found Babee Tenda's sales pitch to be disgusting. They used misleading statistics and outright lies to scare parents into thinking they were putting their children in imminent danger if they used store-bought high chairs or cribs. Many of the statistics and "props" used to demonstrate hazards were as much as 20 years old and long since removed from the market. Even more reprehensible were claims that certain popular juvenile products were about to be recalled. Specifically, Babee Tenda claimed the Evenflo Exersaucer was "unsafe and will be off the market in six months," an accusation that clearly wasn't true.

The fact that Babee Tenda had to use such bogus assertions raised our suspicions about whether they were telling the truth about their own products. Sadly, the high pressure sales tactics did win over some parents at the seminar we attended—they forked over nearly $800 for Babee Tenda's items. Since then, we've heard from other parents who've attended Babee Tenda's "safety seminars," purchased the products and then suffered a case of "buyer's remorse." Did they spend too much, they ask?

Yes, in our opinion. While we see nothing wrong per se with Babee Tenda's "feeding table" (besides the fact it's god-awful ugly), you should note it costs nearly twice as much as our top recommended high chair, the very well-made Chicco Mamma. (At some seminars, the price for the feeding table is $400, but you get a free car seat with your purchase. Whoopee). There's nothing wrong with the crib either—and yes, Babee Tenda, throws in a mattress and two sheets. But you can find all this for much less than the $500 or so Babee Tenda asks.

So, we say watch out for Babee Tenda (and other similar companies like Babyhood, who pitches their "Baby Sitter" in hotel safety seminars). We found their "safety seminar" to be bogus, their high pressure sales tactics reprehensible and their products grossly overpriced.

a little effort on part of a parent; so it's a toss-up whether you should get a manual or battery operated swing. You can save $20 with a wind-up instead of a battery-operated model, as well as the additional savings in batteries. Wind-up swings start at $40 and go up to $60; battery operated swings run $60 to $120. Second-hand stores are great places to look for deals on swings; we've seen some in good condition for just $20 (check with for recalls before you buy second hand).

Remember to observe safety warnings about swings, which are close to the top ten most dangerous products as far as injuries go. You must always stay with your baby, use the safety belt, and stop using the swing once your baby reaches the weight limit (about 25 pounds in most cases). Always remember that a swing is not a baby-sitter.

Our picks: Brand recommendations

What's the best brand? We'd give the award to ***Graco***, who's "Open Top" swings (that is, no overhead bar) are best-sellers–they start at $69 and have various do-dads that increase the price (more speeds, more tunes, etc). The top of the line "Gentle Choice" swing ($100 to $120) features six speeds, 15 musical tunes, and (we're not making this up) "cruise control." That last feature adjusts the swing to your baby's weight to ensure consistent speed. There's even an auto shut-off timer. Yes, Graco still sells the old-style swings with overhead bars, but we don't recommend them (you always seem to clunk baby's head on the bar when putting them in the swing).

A good second bet would be the ***"3 in 1 Cradle/Swing" by Fisher Price*** ($80). This unit comes with an infant carrier that can be detached from the swing. The model swings from side to side or front to back and has three speeds. We also like the ***Swing 'N' Meals*** ($99), the combo high chair and swing reviewed in the previous section.

We'd stay away from swings that incorporate a "bassinet" or "cradle" feature–we do not think it's safe to have an infant in a sleeping position in a swing.

Playpens

The portable playpen has been so popular in recent years that many parents consider it a necessity. Compared to the old wooden playpens of years past, today's playpens are made of metal and nylon mesh, fold compactly for portability and offer such handy features as bassinets, canopies, wheels and more. Some shopping tips:

◆ ***Don't buy a second-hand playpen or use a hand-me-down.*** Many playpen models have been the subject of recalls in recent years. Why? Those same features that make them convenient (the collapsibility to make the playpen "portable") worked too well in the past—some playpens collapsed with babies inside. Others had protruding rivets that caught some babies who wore pacifiers on a string (a BIG no-no, but that's another subject). A slew of injuries and deaths has prompted the recall of ten million playpens over the years. Yes, you can search government recall lists (www.cpsc.gov) to see if that hand-me-down is recalled, but we'd skip the hassle and just buy new.

◆ ***Go for the bassinet feature.*** Some playpens feature bassinet inserts which can be used for babies under three months of age (always check the weight guidelines). This is a handy feature that we recommend. Other worthwhile features: wheels for mobility, side-rail storage compartments and a canopy (if you plan to take the playpen outside or to the beach). If you want a playpen with canopy, look for those models that have "aluminized fabric" canopies—they reflect the sun's heat and UV rays to keep baby cooler.

◆ ***Consider alternatives.*** In Chapter 2, we reviewed the "Bedside Co-Sleeper" by Arm's Reach, which is a combo playpen and co-sleeper (sort of a bassinet that attaches to your bed). Want something bigger than the standard playpen? Regalo makes a Safari Square Playard ($130 from BabyCatalog.com) that is 40"x40" wide. Simo (the stroller maker reviewed in Chapter 8) also makes a 40x40 size playpen made from wood (wow, what a concept) for $190.

Our Picks: Brand recommendations

What are the best brands for playpens? Once again, we give it to Graco—their ***Pack 'N Play*** playpens are the best-designed and least-recalled. Last we looked, they had 12 models that ranged from $59 to $139.

For 2001, Graco plans several improvements to the Pack 'N Play line. First, Graco plans to debut a new smaller playard for $39 that will be able to fit through a door. Also new: look for removable "play panels" that hold various activities in their $49-$59 playpens. Graco also plans to roll out a $60 playpen with a changing table attachment that has a new U-shaped design.

If that weren't enough, Graco also plans a new larger (40x40) square playpen for $90 and a "Twins" playpen with two bassinets and extra storage for $150.

So, which model should you get? We like the basic Pak N Play with bassinet attachment for $100. If you plan to use the playpen outdoors, go for one with a canopy that is aluminized to cut down on the heat ($130).

Not to be outdone, Graco's sister company (***Century***) has an entire slate of playpens of their own under the name ***Fold & Go.*** Many of Century's playpens feature a diaper changing station, which is a nice bonus. Century's "Care Center Lite" playpen features a removable bassinet and changing unit but no wheels for $80–not a bad deal. (If you need wheels for portability, Century makes a version of this playpen with casters for $99). The top-of-the-line Century playpens ($120) feature more plush padding, canopies and storage pockets.

What about the other playpen brands? Yes, you can find playpens by Baby Trend, Kolcraft and Fisher Price, but we don't think their quality or features measure up to Graco and Century's offerings.

The Bottom Line: A Wrap-Up of Our Best Buy Picks

In the nursery, we highly recommend the Diaper Genie as the best diaper pail. But we're not too wild about wipe warmers, which have safety concerns.

The best toys for infants include a basic set of stacking cups ($5), an activity center ($15), and a play center ($30). An activity/bouncer seat with a toy bar is a good idea, with prices ranging from $30 to $60–we like the Fisher Price bouncers best. An affordable alternative: adding a $10 toy bar to an infant seat.

Of course, our favorite stuffed animal/rattle is the Flatobearius line–at $10, they make affordable gifts. As for where to shop, the best deals on toys and books are often found at garage sales and second-hand stores.

With baby monitors, look for models with rechargeable batteries, privacy scrambling and compact design (no big antennas) for easier carrying. The best brands are Fisher Price and Graco.

Wal-Mart and Target have great prices on formula. And since all the brands are essentially the same, go for the cheapest price. Another money-saver: generic formula like BabyMil at stores like Wal-Mart.

Our readers say Avent bottles are best–yes, they're pricey, but you can't beat them for quality (both in nipple and bottle design).

What about baby food? If you're on a tight budget and/or have the time, consider making your own. If convenience is more important but you still want that fresh taste, go for Earth's Best. Finally, if you don't care about organic baby food and just want the cheapest stuff, try Heinz.

The best high chair is the Chicco Mama ($130-$160), although the Fisher Price Swing 'N Meals ($99) is a good choice that combines a swing and high chair. Speaking of swings, we like Graco's Open Top swings ($70 to $120) best. And Graco also makes the best playpens (Pack 'N Plays, $59-$139), although the Century line is a good second bet.

CHAPTER 7

Car Seats: Picking the right child safety seat

What's the best car seat for your baby? What is the difference between an infant and a convertible seat? How will the new safety standards affect child safety seats? We'll discuss these issues and more in this chapter. You'll find complete reviews and ratings of the major car seat brands as well as informative charts that compare the best choices.

Here's a sobering figure: last year, motor vehicle crashes killed 1,135 children under age ten and injured another 182,000. While the majority of those injuries and deaths occurred to children who were not in safety seats, the toll from vehicle accidents in this country is still a statistic that can keep you awake all night.

Every state in the U.S. (and every province in Canada) requires infants and children to ride in child safety seats, so this is one of the few products that every parent must buy. In fact you may find yourself buying multiple car seats as your baby grows older–and for secondary cars, grandma's car, a caregiver's vehicle and more.

So, which seat is the safest? Easiest to use? One thing you'll learn in this chapter is that there is not one "safest" or "best" seat. Yes, we will review and rate the various car seat brands and examine their recall/safety history. BUT, remember the best seat for your child is the one that correctly fits your child's weight and size–and can be correctly installed in your vehicle.

And that's the rub: roadside safety checks by police reveal 80% to 90% of child safety seats are NOT installed or used properly. Although the exact figure isn't known, a large number of child fatalities and injuries from crashes are caused by improper use or installation of seats. Realizing that many of today's child safety seats are a failure due to complex installation and other hurdles, the federal government is rolling out a new safety standard for child seats and vowing to fix loopholes in current crash testing. While that might make them easier to use, there will be confusion during the transition from the old type to the new system. We'll try to sort out all the details in this chapter.

Getting Started: When Do You Need This Stuff?

You can't leave the hospital without a car seat. By law, all states require children to be restrained in a child safety seat. You'll want to get this item early (in your sixth to eighth month of pregnancy) so you can practice wedging it into the back seat. Also: some of the best deals on car seats are found online. You'll need to leave a few weeks in shipping time to insure the seat arrives before baby does.

Sources to Find Car Seats

1 **Discounters.** Car seats have become a loss leader for many discount stores. Chains like K-Mart, Target and Wal-Mart sell these items at small mark-ups in hopes you'll spend money elsewhere in the store. The only caveat: most discounters only carry a limited selection of seats, typically of the no-frills brands.

2 **Baby Specialty Stores.** Independent juvenile retailers have all but abandoned car seats to the chains. With the exception of premium brands like Britax, you'll only see a few scattered offerings here.

3 **The Superstores.** Chains like Babies R Us, Toys R Us and Burlington Coat Factory's Baby Depot (reviewed in depth in Chapter 2) tend to carry a wider selection of car seats than discounters. And, sometimes, that includes the better brands. Prices can be a few dollars higher than the chains, but sales often bring better deals.

4 **Mail Order/The Web.** Yes, you can buy a car seat through the mail or online. More on the 'net next. A run-down of other mail order sources appears later in the chapter. Prices are usually discounted, but watch out for shipping–the cost of shipping bulky items like car seats can outweigh the discount in some cases. Use an online coupon (see the previous chapter for coupon sites) to save and look for free shipping specials.

Parents in Cyberspace: What's on the Web?

The web is teeming with both information and bargains on car seats and strollers. Here's the best of what's out there.

◆ ***NHTSA.*** The National Highway Traffic & Safety Administration site (www.nhtsa.dot.gov) is a treasure trove of car seat info—you can read about recalls, the latest news on changing standards and installation tips. The NHTSA's brochure "Buying a Safer Car For Child Passengers" is a must read for any parent. If you don't have web access, you can order it by calling (888) DASH2DOT. You can also contact the government's Auto Safety Hotline at 800-424-9393 to ask car seat related questions.

◆ ***The American Academy of Pediatrics*** (www.aap.org, go to "You and Your Family") is an excellent resource for car seat buying tips.

◆ ***The National Safe Kids Campaign*** (www.safekids.org) has an excellent interactive "car seat locator" that helps you determine which seat is right for the age and weight of the child.

◆ ***Safety Belt Safe USA*** (www.carseat.org) has a good site with tips on picking the best seat for your child, as well as the latest recalls and info on child safety seats.

◆ ***Car Seat Data*** (www.CarSeatData.org) has an "interactive compatibility database" that lets you search for which seats work in which vehicles. Very cool.

◆ ***ParentsPlace*** (www.parentsplace.com) has a car seat FAQ, buying guide and message board dedicated to car seats.

◆ ***Our web site*** has a brochure called "Buying a Better Car Seat Restraint" produced by a Canadian auto insurance institute. This publication (downloadable as a PDF, portable document format) has excellent charts that compare major brands of car seats on ease of installation and other safety factors. Since it was produced in 1999, some of the model info is a bit out of date but it still has valuable info. Go to www.BabyBargainsBook.com and click up the "Updates" section for a link to this car seat guide. See figure 1 on the next page for a screen shot of this brochure.

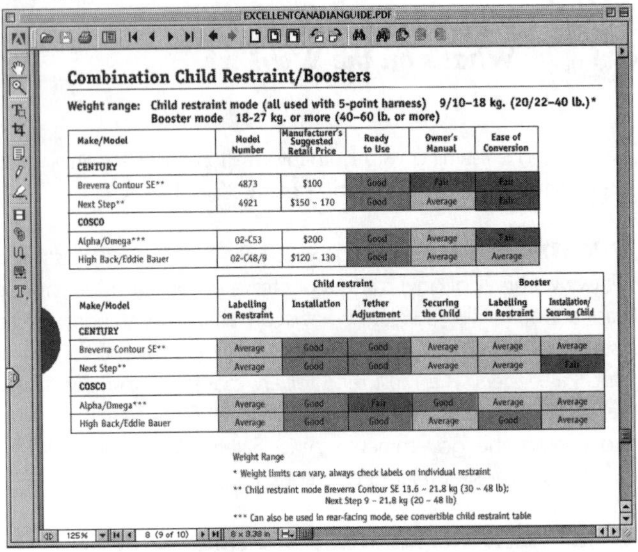
EXCELLENTCANADIANGUIDE.PDF

Combination Child Restraint/Boosters

Weight range: Child restraint mode (all used with 5-point harness) 9/10–18 kg. (20/22–40 lb.)*
Booster mode 18-27 kg. or more (40–60 lb. or more)

Make/Model	Model Number	Manufacturer's Suggested Retail Price	Ready to Use	Owner's Manual	Ease of Conversion
CENTURY					
Breverra Contour SE**	4873	$100	Good	Fair	Fair
Next Step**	4921	$150 ~ 170	Good	Average	Fair
COSCO					
Alpha/Omega***	02-C53	$200	Good	Average	Fair
High Back/Eddie Bauer	02-C48/9	$120 ~ 130	Good	Average	Average

	Child restraint				Booster	
Make/Model	Labelling on Restraint	Installation	Tether Adjustment	Securing the Child	Labelling on Restraint	Installation/ Securing Child
CENTURY						
Breverra Contour SE**	Average	Good	Good	Average	Average	Average
Next Step**	Average	Good	Good	Average	Average	Fair
COSCO						
Alpha/Omega***	Average	Good	Fair	Good	Average	Average
High Back/Eddie Bauer	Average	Good	Good	Average	Good	Average

Weight Range
* Weight limits can vary, always check labels on individual restraint
** Child restraint mode Breverra Contour SE 13.6 ~ 21.8 kg (30 ~ 48 lb);
Next Step 9 ~ 21.8 kg (20 ~ 48 lb)
*** Can also be used in rear-facing mode, see convertible child restraint table

125% 8 (9 of 10) 8 x 8.38 in

Figure 1: Our web site, www.BabyBargainsBook.com has a free brochure that compares many seats.

◆ ***Where to buy online.*** Many of the large baby product web sites (and catalogs) reviewed in Chapter 11 sell car seats at competitive prices. When you find an online coupon for these sites (see Chapter 6 for a list of such sites), the deals can be even better. As for other sites that sell car seats, we found the baby stores on sites like BabyCatalog.com are great for rock-bottom deals on car seats (and often have free shipping specials).

More Money Buys You . . .

As you'll read later in this chapter, all child safety seats are regulated by the federal government to meet minimum safety standards. So whether you buy a $50 seat from K-Mart or a $200 brand from a specialty store, your baby is equally covered. When you pay extra money, however, there are some perks. First, on the safety front, the more expensive seats have built-in locking clips (more on this later) and other design features that give you a rock solid installation in most vehicles. That means the seat doesn't tip, slide or move. The more expensive seats are also more comfortable for the child—they typically feature reclining seats, more padding, pillows and other comforts. For infant seats, when you spend more money, you get an adjustable base (which enables a better fit in vehicles), canopies to block the sun and plush padding.

Smart Shopper Tips

Smart Shopper Tip #1

So many seats, so much confusion

"I'm so confused by all the car seat options out there. For example, are infant car seats a waste of money? Or should I go with a convertible seat? Or one of those models that is good from birth to college?

Children's car seats come in three flavors: "infant," "convertible" and "boosters." Let's break it down:

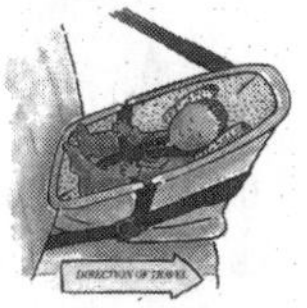

◆ ***Infant*** car seats are just that—these rear-facing seats are designed to be used with infants up to 20 lbs. or so (a new model from Cosco can be used up to 35 lbs. but that is the exception).

◆ ***Convertible*** car seats (see right) can be used for both infants *and* older children (up to 40 lbs.)—infants ride rear facing; older kids ride facing forward.

◆ ***Booster seats*** (not pictured) were once used exclusively to position the auto's safety belt to correctly fit a young child up to 80 pounds (hence, they are called belt-positioning boosters). In recent years, some boosters have added five point harness for use by younger children weighing under 40 pounds (after that time, the five-point harness is removed and the seat is used with the auto's safety belt). These new seats are called "transitional boosters." An example is the Cosco Alpha Omega, which can be used rear-facing from 5 to 30 pounds, then forward-facing to 40 lbs. From 40 lbs. to 80 lbs. the Alpha Omega converts to a booster seat that uses the auto safety belt to restrain an older child.

So does it make more sense to buy one car seat (that is a convertible car seat or transitional booster) and just skip the infant car seat? Nope. Safety experts say it's best for babies under 20 lbs. to be in an *infant* car seat—they're built to better accommodate a smaller body and baby travels in a semi-reclined position, which better supports an infant's head and neck. Yes, some convertible seats recline—but the degree of recline can be affected by the angle of your vehicle's seat back. And certain convertible seats (those with bar shields or t-shields instead of five-point restraints—

more on this later) simply don't work well with infants. Furthermore, most babies don't reach the 20-pound mark until between six and 12 months—and that can be a very long period of time if you don't have an infant car seat.

Why? First, it's helpful to understand that an infant car seat is more than just a car seat—it's also an infant carrier when detached from its base. Big deal, you might say? Well, since infants spend much of their time sleeping (and often fall asleep in the car), this *is* a big deal. By detaching the carrier from the auto base, you don't have to wake the baby when you leave the car. Buy a convertible car seat, and you'll have to unbuckle the baby and move her into another type of carrier (and most likely wake her in the process). Take it from us: let sleeping babies lie and spend the additional $50 to $70 for an infant car seat, even if you use it for just six months.

There is one catch to this. The current thinking among safety advocates is this: babies should be REAR-FACING until they reach one year of age, regardless of weight. And that's the rub: some babies reach the 20 lbs. limit for infant seats long before their first birthday. At that point, you need to switch to a convertible seat that is rear facing. The catch? Some convertible seats are only rear-facing to 20 lbs. Later in this chapter, we'll tell you which seats are rated rear facing to 30 lbs. (which should accommodate even the biggest infant to one year of age).

Smart Shopper Tip #2

New standards, new confusion?

"I hear the federal government is changing car seat standards. Should I wait to purchase my baby's car seat? And what's wrong with the old seats anyway?"

Stop any ten cars on the road with child safety seats and we'll bet eight or nine are not installed or used correctly. That's what road-side checks by local law enforcement in many states have uncovered: a 1998 study by the National Highway Traffic and Safety Administration stopped 4000 drivers in four states and found a whopping 80% made mistakes in installing or securing a child safety seat.

What's causing all the problems?

Our view: current child safety seats have failed parents. Installation of a car seat can be an exercise in frustration—even parents who spend hours with the instructions can still make mistakes. The number one culprit: the auto seat belt—they're great at restraining adults, but not so good at child safety seats. And those seats simply won't work well if they aren't attached to a car correctly . . . that's the crux of the problem. Simply put, thanks to the quirkiness of auto safety belts (different auto makers have different systems), putting a child safety seat in a car is like trying to fit a square peg into a round hole.

The bottom line: some child safety seats simply DON'T FIT in some vehicles. Which cars? Which seats? It's hard to tell. There is one good web site with a car seat compatibility database (www.carseatdata.org), but it doesn't cover every seat and every vehicle. Often, parents find it's trial and error to see what works. Car seat makers are also to blame—many seats aren't designed to work in today's cars with deep bucket seats.

The federal government has pledged to fix this problem—in September 2002. That year, new mandated "uniform" attachments (called LATCH or ISO-FIX) will be required for all vehicles and safety seats. Instead of using the auto's seat belt, car seats will attach to two anchor bars installed in the lower seatback. The result: no more confusing installations, locking clips or other apparatus needed to make sure the seat is correctly attached. (Another part of the new standard: tether straps, which are discussed later in this section).

Some car makers are getting a head start on the new standards, adding the new attachments to their current models. For example, 1999 and 2000 Volkswagen cars, 2000 Ford Windstar minivans and Ford Focus small cars have the new attachments. In spring 2000, some Volvo models and the Chrysler PT Cruiser rolled out the new system. Finally, the General Motors family and Chrysler minivans came on board with LATCH systems with their fall 2000 models. Yet other car makers are still lagging in meeting the new standard.

The car seats are another matter, however. So far, only a handful of LATCH/ISO-FIX seats are on the market, namely models by Fisher Price, Cosco and Evenflo (see reviews later for specifics). Britax announced a LATCH seat for 2000 but ran late and now says their model will be out in 2001. Most frustrating: the biggest car seat makers (Century and Graco) have taken a "wait and see" attitude on new LATCH seats—they probably won't bring such models to market until late 2001 or even 2002.

As you can see, this is all quite confusing. Both car makers and seat manufacturers are phasing in models that meet the requirements. Meanwhile, older seats that use the auto's safety belt will also be on the market. Here is a sum up of frequent questions we get on the new LATCH seats:

◆ ***Are there any LATCH infant seats with stay-in-the-car bases?*** Not as of this writing. All of the LATCH seats available in 2001 are "convertible seats," which can be used rear-facing for infants, of course. There are no infant LATCH seats scheduled to debut in 2001, but there might be some in 2002. Stay tuned.

◆ ***Will I have to junk my old car seat in 2002?*** Of course not.

If you have an older model vehicle and an older (non-LATCH) car seat, that is fine—the law just mandates you use an appropriate safety seat, it doesn't specify a LATCH seat.

◆ ***Will LATCH seats be more expensive then the old ones?*** Yes, car seat makers grumble that the new attachments will force them to raise prices. Yet, they said the same thing about tether straps (see below) and guess what happened? New seats with tether straps were not any more pricey than those without. Why? The market place for car seats is so competitive that no prices increase stuck. We'd guess the same thing will happen with LATCH seats.

◆ ***I just bought a new car that has the new LATCH attachments. Can I use an old seat in the new vehicle?*** Yes . . . but here is our advice: if you have a vehicle that has the new attachments, get a seat that takes advantage of the system. If your new car does NOT have the new attachments, get the best safety seat you can buy (we'll have recommendations later in this chapter) and use it with a tether strap.

◆ ***Will there be retrofit kits so you can use an old car seat with the LATCH system in my new car?*** Good question. One car seat maker (Britax) promised such a kit in 2000, but it never came out. And we're unsure there will be any future retrofit kits (Century did tell us they have plans to offer one for $25 in early 2001 at stores like Wal-Mart and Toys R Us). The better bet: buy a new LATCH seat to use in the new car.

◆ ***I need to move my LATCH seat to a second car that doesn't have the new attachments. Will it work?*** Yes, you should be able to secure a LATCH seat in an older car using the auto's safety belt. But always check the car seat's instructions to make sure this installation is possible.

We'll have continuing coverage of the new LATCH system and seats on our web page at www.BabyBargainsBook.com.

Smart Shopper Tip #3

Strap Me In

"What is a tether strap? Do I want one?"

In 1999, the federal government mandated that all convertible child safety seats be sold with a tether strap—these prevent a car seat from moving forward in the event of a crash. How? One end of the tether strap attaches to top the car seat; the other is hooked to an "anchor bolt" that's permanently installed on the floor (or the back of the back seat) in your car.

And that's the challenge to the whole tether strap thing—getting that anchor bolt installed in your car. Of course, some vehicles are easier than others. Newer vehicles may have pre-drilled anchorage points—just ask your car deal for the "anchor bolt installation kit" (a part number that's listed in your owner's manual in the section on installing child safety seats). You can install the bolt or have the dealer do it.

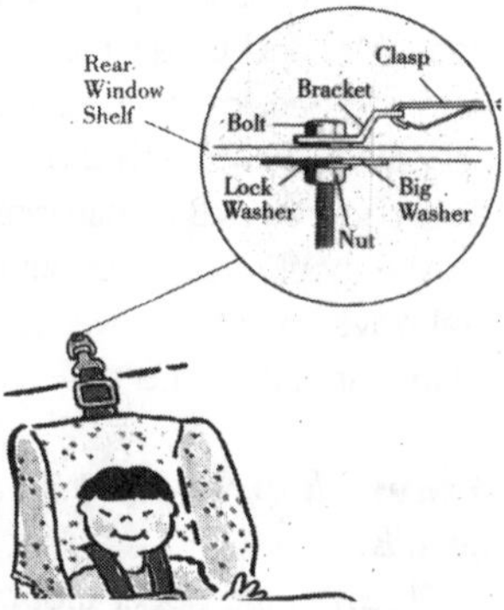

Older cars are trickier—to install the anchor bolt, you may need to drill through your car's sub floor (a job for the car dealer, as you can guess). And just finding out the part number for the anchor bolt can be a challenge; some car dealers are clueless about this issue.

(One tip: call a CANADIAN dealer to find out the part number of the anchor bolt for child safety seats. Why? Tether straps have been required for years in Canada. Hence, car dealers there are more familiar with this request. You can find a Canadian dealer's phone number on most automobile maker's web sites.)

A side note: most car seats can only use tether straps when they are FORWARD-FACING. Only one model (the Britax Roundabout, reviewed later) has a tether which can be used in either the rear or forward-facing position.

So, is the tether strap worth all the hassle? Yes—crash tests show car seats are SAFER when used with a tether strap. The strap keeps the car seat (and hence, your baby's head) from moving forward in a crash, lowering the chance of injury. So are seats used without tethers unsafe? No, the federal government requires seats to be safe even when a tether is not in use. Of course, the tether adds that extra measure of safety and is always preferable to a tether-less installation.

Smart Shopper Tip #4

One Size Does Not Fit All

"My friend has a car seat that just doesn't fit very well into her car. Does anyone put out a rating system that says which seats are most compatible? Safest?"

There is good news on this front. In 2000, Congress passed the Fitzgerald-Shimkus car seat legislation that instructed the Department of Transportation to come up with a rating system for car seats. (What a concept!) After years of complaining from safety advocates, we have to give Congress a hand for passing this legislation (particular thanks to Senator John Fitzgerald R-Ill. and his aide, Evelyn Fortier, for seeing this to fruition).

The new ratings system will provide "practicable, readily understandable, and timely information to consumers for use in making informed decisions in the purchase of child restraints." We hope the new system will be rolled out soon. Again, read the updates on our web page www.BabyBargainsBook.com for the latest details.

We should also point out the new car seat law requires the federal government to develop new crash tests for car seats that simulate rear-impact and side-impact crashes, a long overdue change.

Smart Shopper Tip #5

Recalls

"I saw in the paper that a particular car seat is being recalled. Should I be skeptical of other seats by that manufacturer?"

Here's a sobering fact of car seat shopping: EVERY major brand of car seats has had a recall over the past five years. We've seen recalls on cheap seats sold in K-Mart and $200 car seats sold in specialty stores, so recalls are a fact of life no matter what brand you consider. How can you make a smart decision?

First, realize that some recalls are more serious than others. Some car seats are recalled for minor problems, like incorrect labels. Other companies do voluntary recalls when their own testing reveals a problem. The key issue: look to see if there are any deaths or injuries associated with the defective product. Obviously, car seats that are so defective as to cause injury to babies are much more serious than minor labeling recalls.

Another issue: how does a company handle a recall? Do they fight the government, forcing regulators to order a recall? Or do they voluntarily recall the item and set up an efficient process (toll free phone number) to get replacements or retrofit kits to consumers? As you'll note below, we lowered the rating for one major car seat maker (Evenflo) for the abysmal way they handled a recall for their On My Way infant seat.

When a company announces a recall, the product is typically removed from store shelves (if the recall is for the current production run). If the recall is for a product's previous production run, you may still see it on store shelves (since the defect may have been corrected months before). That's why it is key to see WHEN the recalled product was manufactured. Of course, different car seats in the same manufacturer's line may be totally unaffected by a recall.

Smart Shopper Tip #5

Holding Your Baby Back: Safety Harness Advice

"Which safety harness is best—the 5-point, bar-shield, or T-shield?

Car Seat Lesson 101: Understand the different harness systems available on the market. For INFANT seats, you have two choices: three point or five-point belts. For CONVERTIBLE seats, you have three choices: five-point, bar-shield or t-shield.

Three (or five) point belts refer to number of points in which the belt attaches to the car seat. A t-shield is a plastic shield that buckles in below baby's crotch. A bar shield lowers over the baby's head and snaps into a buckle.

Our recommendation: for INFANT seats, three point systems are fine. Yes, we've noticed many new models that tout the FIVE point systems, but we think it's overkill—crash tests show there's no difference in effectiveness. And it's much easier to buckle a baby into a three-point seat than a five-point one.

For CONVERTIBLE seats, we recommend the five-point version. Why? Safety experts say it's the best choice because you can tighten the belts to securely hold your baby in her seat. T-shields are second in preference (but don't work well for small infants). And bar shields have another problem—some don't adjust well to growing children. Even those expensive models that feature *adjustable* shields only adjust so much—if your child grows quickly, they still might outgrow the car seat. The result? You'll have to move them into a booster seat (making an extra purchase) sooner than you want to.

Another major problem with bar shields: wiggling toddlers can get out of them way too easily. One mom told us she was horrified to look in her rear view mirror one day to find her 18 month old STANDING in his car seat while the vehicle was moving. We think five point harnesses are safer since it is very difficult for baby to wiggle out when the belts are tightened correctly.

Let's be honest, however: the five-point harness is the *least convenient* to use. You have to put each strap around baby's arms, find the lower buckle (which always seems to disappear under their rump) and then snap them in. Bar-shields and t-shields slip over the baby's head in one motion and are easier to buckle.

The fact that the five-point harness is inconvenient is just the way it goes. Simply put, it's the safest choice for your baby. And sometimes as a parent you have to do what's best for your child, even if that makes your life less convenient.

Here are ten more shopping tips for car seats:

◆ ***How easily does it recline?*** Some convertible car seats have a lever in front that makes the seat recline (nice for a sleeping baby). Unfortunately, not all car seats recline equally—some levers are more difficult to work than others. Check it out in the store before you buy.

◆ ***Check the belt adjustments.*** You don't merely adjust the car seat's belts just when your baby gets bigger–if you put Junior in a coat, you'll need to loosen the belts as well. As a result, it's important to check how easily they adjust. Of course, every car seat maker seems to have a different idea on how to do this. The best car seats let you adjust the belts from the *front*. Those models that require you to access the back of the seat to adjust the belts are more hassle.

◆ ***Look at the chest clip.*** The chest clip or harness tie holds the two belts in place. Lower-quality seats have a simple "slide-in" clip–you slip the belt under a tab. That's nice, but some older toddlers can slip out from this type of chest clip. A better bet: a chest clip that SNAPS the two belts together like a seat belt. This is more kid-proof.

◆ ***Are the instructions in Greek?*** Before you buy the car seat, take a minute to look at the set-up and use instructions. Make sure you can make sense of the seat's documentation. Another tip: if possible, ask the store for any installation tips and advice.

◆ ***Is the pad cover machine-washable?*** You'd think this would be a "no brainer," but a surprising number of seats (both convertible and infant) have covers that aren't removable or machine washable. Considering how grimy these covers can get, it's smart to look for this feature.

◆ ***Does the seat need to be installed with each use?*** The best car seats are "permanently" installed in your car. When you put baby in, all you do is buckle them in the seat's harness system. Yet some infant car seats and even a few convertible models need to be installed with each use–that means you have to belt the thing into your car every time you use it. Suffice it to say, that's a major drawback.

◆ ***Watch out for hot buckles.*** Some inexpensive car seats have exposed metal buckles and hardware. In the hot sun, these buckles can get toasty and possibly burn a child.

◆ ***Is it shopping cart compatible?*** Some inexpensive infant car seats do NOT fit into shopping carts. That's a major drawback–check for compatibility before you buy.

◆ ***If the baby comes early,*** many hospitals rent car seats at affordable rates. You can rent one for a few days until you get your own.

◆ ***Buying a new car?*** Consider getting a built-in child safety seat. Yes, you can skip the hassle of buying a separate convertible safety seat if you get a built-in model, which is probably the safest option since they are permanently installed in the car. Not all vehicles offer this option, but it doesn't hurt to ask. The cost varies from car maker to maker, but is about $200 to $400. Remember that the seats can only be used with children one year or older; you'll still need to buy an infant car seat for babies under one year of age.

Smart Shopper Tip #6
Watch the height limit

"My son isn't anywhere near the 20 lb. limit for his infant seat, but he's so tall I think it isn't safe anymore—he has to bend his legs when we put him in!"

Here's a little known limit to most infant seats: in addition to WEIGHT limits, all infant car seats also have HEIGHT limits. And like everything in the car seat world, each seat has different limits (check the sticker on the side of the carrier—by law, the manufacturer must list both height and weight limits). Once your baby exceeds EITHER the height or weight limit, you must move them to a convertible seat.

With the bigger babies everyone seems to be having these days (credit more breastfeeding? Genetically modified foods?), this isn't a moot point. A large infant might exceed the height limit BEFORE he or she passes the weight limit. Here's the scoop: height limits range from 26" for the Graco Snug Ride to 29" for the Fisher Price Stay in View or the Century Smart Fit Plus. Most infant seats have weight limits in the 20lb to 22lb range, although the new Cosco Opus 35 goes up to a whopping 35 lbs. Later in this section, we'll have a chart that lists the height and weight limits of all major infant car seats. See the box on the next page for more on this topic.

Safe & Sound

1 **NEVER BUY A USED CAR SEAT.** If the seat has been in an accident, it may be damaged and no longer safe to use. Bottom line: used seats are a big risk unless you know their history. And the technology of car seats improves every year; a seat that is just five years old may lack important safety features compared to today's models. Another tip: make sure the seat has not been recalled (see phone number and web contact below for the National Highway Traffic Safety Administration). Safety seats made before 1981 may not meet current safety standards (unfortunately, most seats aren't stamped with their year of manufacture, so this may be difficult to determine). The bottom line: risky hand-me-downs aren't worth it. Brand new car seats (which start at $50) aren't that huge of an investment to ensure your child's safety.

How big is normal?

A quick glance at the "average" growth charts for infants makes you realize why kids outgrow their infant seats so quickly. Most infant seats are only rated for babies up to 20 pounds and 26" in height (although a few now go to 22 pounds and 29" height). The average male infant hits 20 pounds at about eight months (at the 50th percentile). But for boys at the top of the growth chart, that could happen at a mere *four months*! Girls are of course a bit behind that curve, hitting 20 pounds on average at ten months of age (at the 50th percentile). Girls at the top of the chart might hit 20 pounds as soon as six months.

When a child outgrows his infant seat, he must go into a convertible seat—and there is the rub. Safety advocates say babies should be rear-facing to one year of age. But some convertible seats (like the Cosco Maxi Cosi) are only rear-facing to 20 pounds . . . odds are the average infant will hit that before one year of age. So, that's why we recommend convertible seats that are rear-facing to at least 30 pounds.

What about height? Boys hit 26" at around 5 months (again the 50th percentile). But some really tall baby boys can hit 26" as soon as *three months*. For girls, the average age when most infants hit 26" is six months, but it can happen as soon as four months. You'll note that on average, babies hit the upper limit for height restrictions for infant seats three or four MONTHS before they outgrow the seat weight-wise. That's why we strongly recommend infant seats with 29" height limits—that milestone typically isn't reached until ten months for boys and 12 months for girls.

Source: National Center for Health Statistics, www.cdc.gov/growthcharts

2 READ THE DIRECTIONS VERY CAREFULLY. Many car accidents end in tragedy because a car seat was installed improperly. If you have any questions about the directions, call the company or return the car seat for a model that is easier to use. Another tip: read your vehicle's owner's manual for any special installation instructions. Consult with your auto dealer if you have any additional questions.

What's the number-one problem with car seat installation? Figuring out what to do with that darn locking clip, perhaps the most misunderstood part of your child's car seat. Vehicles made

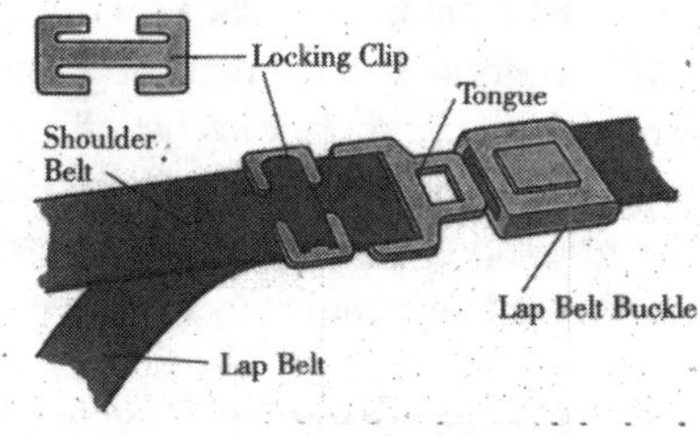

before September 1, 1995 typically require the use of locking clips, a small piece of metal that "locks" the safety belt, attaching right above the buckle. Newer vehicles made after that date may have safety-belt locking features that eliminate the need for locking clips—check your owner's manual for details. Without a locking clip in older cars, the seat could become a projectile, injuring or killing your child. Make sure the safety seat is held firmly against the back of the car seat and doesn't wobble from side to side (or front to back).

Thankfully, some child safety seat makers have woken up to the locking clip problem—two models we'll review later actually have built-in locking clips. Also, the new LATCH or ISO-FIX car seats eliminate the locking clip as well.

Another good idea: the ***Mighty-Tite*** car seat belt tightener, which removes slack and provides for a rock solid seat installation. It's $20 at Babies R Us and other stores, call 888-336-7909 or web: www.mighty-tite.com. We were impressed with this easy-to-use product.

Finally, it's always good to put your knee on the seat and push down with your full weight while you tighten the seat belt. This eliminates belt slack and ensures a snug installation.

3 **USE YOUR CAR SEAT.** Don't make the mistake of being in a hurry and forgetting to (or just not wanting to) attach the restraints. Many parents merely put their child in the seat without hooking up the harness. It is more dangerous to leave your child in a car seat unrestrained by the safety harness than it is to put him or her in a regular seat belt. And always observe weight limits. As we mentioned earlier, children should ride REAR-FACING to one year of age, regardless of weight. Make sure your child's safety seat is able to accommodate her weight in that position.

4 **PUT THE CAR SEAT IN THE BACK SEAT.** Air bags and car seats don't mix—several reports of injuries and deaths have been attributed to passenger side air bags that deployed when a car seat was in the front seat. As a result, the safest place for kids is the back seat. And where is the safest part of the back seat? Safety experts say it's the middle. The only problem with that advice is that some cars have a raised hump in the middle of the back seat that makes it difficult/impossible to safely install a car seat. Another problem: safety seats are best held against the car's back seat by a three-point belt—and most middle seats just have a two-point belt.

5 BUY ANOTHER LOCKING CLIP. If you rent a car, most rental agencies will also rent you a car seat so you don't have to lug your own on the plane. What's the problem? Most forget to give you a locking clip (see earlier for an explanation). As a result, we suggest buying an extra locking clip (available for a few dollars at most stores) and taking it with you whenever you travel.

6 REGISTER YOUR SEAT. Don't forget to send the registration card back to the manufacturer. That's the only way you'll be notified of any recalls or problems that may be discovered in the future.

7 GET YOUR SEAT CHECKED. The National Highway Traffic Safety Administration's web site (www.nhtsa.dot.gov) has a national listing of fitting/inspection stations. Another cool program: Daimler Chrysler has a FREE car seat inspection–just take your car to a Chrysler dealer and they'll check your seat to see if it is safely installed. No, you don't need to have an appointment, nor do you have to own a Chrysler. Call 877-FIT-4-A-KID or web: www.FitForAKid.org to find a local participating Chrysler, Jeep or Dodge near you.

Recalls

The National Highway Traffic Safety Administration (NHTSA) has a toll-free hot line to check for recalls or to report a safety problem. For info, call (800) 424-9393 or (202) 366-0123 (web: www.nhtsa.dot.gov). You can have a list of recalled car seats automatically faxed to you at no charge. Note that this is a different governmental agency than the Consumer Product Safety Commission, which regulates and recalls other juvenile products. (For Canadian recalls and safety seat rules, see the special section at the end of this book for more info).

Money-Saving Secrets

1 IF YOU HAVE TWO CARS, YOU DON'T NEED TO BUY TWO INFANT SEATS. Instead, just buy one seat and then get an extra stay-in-the-car base. While it's not widely known, major infant seat makers like Century and Evenflo sell their auto bases separately for $20 to $30. If you can't find them in stores likes Babies R Us, check out baby web sites that stock them.

2 CHECK WITH YOUR HEALTH INSURANCE CARRIER. Some of these companies offer free car seats (or a car seat at a greatly reduced price) to expectant parents who attend a safety seminar. One parent told us members of the USAA insurance company receive a $25 rebate on the purchase of any new child safety seat.

3 WEB SHOPPING 'BOTS AND COUPONS TO CUT PRICES. Who has the lowest prices on car seats? It depends–stores like Babies R Us and Baby Depot are very competitive on car seat prices. But, the web can have even better deals, especially if you use an online coupon or find a free shipping offer. Again, using a shopping 'bot like DealTime.com (go to the Babies & Kids section) is a good way to compare prices for a model or brand across several sites at once. Look for the free shipping deals for the best bargains, since bulky car seats can be expensive to ship. Before you order, check which sites have coupons (see Chapter 6 for a list of such sites like DotDeals.com and FlamingoWorld.com).

4 EXPENSIVE MODELS AREN'T NECESSARILY BETTER. If you spend $100 on a car seat, are you getting one that's twice as safe as a seat that's $50? Not necessarily. Often, all you get for that additional money is plush padding and extras like pillows. Bottom line: the $50 seat may be just as safe and probably as comfortable for baby.

Outlet

Cosco has an outlet store in Indiana (812-526-0860) at the Prime Outlets at Edinburgh (I-65 at US 31, exit 76B). You can find car seats, play yards and strollers, all at 10% to 60% off retail prices. All the stock is first-quality, including some discontinued colors. You can also find current items. We found the Alpha Omega car seat (current model and fabrics) for just $109 for the five-point version ($119 for either the bar shield version or Eddie Bauer five-point model). That's about $10 to $20 less than we found in other stores. Look for periodic clearance sales for even bigger deals.

The Name Game: Reviews of Selected Manufacturers

Here is our reviews of the major car seat makers sold in the U.S. and Canada. Note: the ratings in this section apply to the ENTIRE line of a company's car seat offerings (both infant and convertible seats). We don't rate each model (although we do comment on individual models within a specific manufacturer's review below). Many of these infant seats are sold as part of stroller/car seat combo products; the strollers are reviewed separately in the next chapter. Of course, you don't have to buy a travel system–nearly all these seats are sold separately.

The Ratings

- **A EXCELLENT**–*our top pick!*
- **B GOOD**– *above average quality, prices, and creativity.*
- **C FAIR**–*could stand some improvement.*
- **D POOR**–*yuck! could stand some major improvement.*

Britax *460 Greenway Industrial Dr., Ft. Mill SC 29715. For a dealer near you, call (888) 4-BRITAX or (803) 802-2022. Web: www.britax.com* European-based Britax came to the U.S. car seat market in 1996 and immediately made a big splash–their convertible seats (particularly the Roundabout) became best sellers thanks to their innovative features. Britax got its start providing child seats for Mercedes and Porsche and translated that Euro safety-know-how into innovative features not seen the in U.S. and Canada. The Roundabout is the only car seat that can use a tether in either the front or rear-facing position (Britax calls this their Versa Tether feature). Britax seats also use a patented "lock-off" clamp that securely attaches the seat to the car's belt. As a result, the seat doesn't require a locking clip, that often misunderstood and poorly installed piece of equipment every other car seat maker requires. Finally, we're impressed that Britax is the only child seat manufacturer with its own state-of-the-art crash test sleds that can certify seats to various government safety requirements.

That said, Britax did hit some speed bumps in 2000. First, the Roundabout was recalled when crash tests showed some seats made in early 1999 failed to meet federal standards (Britax blamed the problem on a supplier that improperly molded the seat's shells). *Consumer Reports* knocked the Roundabout in a review for this reason. Yet, Britax handled the recall professionally, voluntarily recalling the seats and offering a free retrofit kit to affected owners. There were no injuries associated with the problem.

Another Britax fumble: the company failed to come out with a LATCH/ISO-FIX seat in 2000 as promised. In fact, a raft of new products announced for 2000 were delayed, hurting the company's credibility in the marketplace. We were especially upset that Britax took until 2001 to come out with a LATCH seat; as a leader in car seat safety, we expected more from them. (Hence, read the new seat announcements from Britax below with a grain of salt–we're not sure they will come out on schedule). Here is a breakdown of their models.

Convertible seats. Britax promised to redeem themselves with a raft of new products this year. First up is the Expressway ($160, 20-40 pounds forward facing) which debuted in late 2001. This is Britax's forward-only seat and the first one that will work with the

On a Jet Plane

Which car seats can be taken on an airplane? All of the seats reviewed in this section are certified for use in an airplane. But will they fit? That's a tougher question—each airline has different size seats. Hence, large seats like the Century "Smart Move" may not fit (especially if you're required to keep the armrests down for take-off). Check with the airline before you get to the airport if you have questions about car seat compatibility. A better bet: simple seats like the Century Accel or 1000STE (both are narrow and light in weight) usually do the trick. We've used a 1000STE on several airplanes without a problem.

new LATCH attachments.

Also new last year: The King, a unique seat that pops forward so you can more easily thread the auto safety belt. Britax pitches this to parents with compact cars, where seat installation can be difficult. The King is a forward-facing only seat that will eventually replace their existing (and similar) "Freeway" model and sell for about $200.

The best-selling and best-known Britax seat, the Roundabout won't see much in the way of changes. This is by far Britax's best seat—rated rear-facing to 30 pounds, forward facing for 20 to 40 pounds. It has a snap-together chest clip (which some parents complain is too complex), the belt adjustments are very easy and once the seat is properly installed in a car, it is rock solid. No wobbling, no tipping.

The only downside to the Roundabout: it isn't cheap. The basic version (which features a full recline and sculpted base) retails for about $200, making it the priciest car seat on the market. We've seen it on sale for $170 and sometimes web site discounters (see reviews earlier Chapter 11) offer the seat for $200 with free shipping and no sales tax. In the last year, Britax released the Advantage ($240), which is basically a Roundabout with one added feature: an automatic belt height adjustment knob that you can use with baby in the seat (hence, no need to rethread the belts as baby grows). Britax told us a LATCH version of the Roundabout will be out in late 2002.

Adding to Britax's woes in last year was their sorry underestimation of the demand for the Super Elite ($200), a great forward-facing seat that works for children 20 to 80 pounds. What's so cool about the Super Elite? It is the only seat on the market now that lets you use a five-point harness for kids up to 80 pounds. The only problem: Britax made like, oh, seven of these units. And they quickly sold out, as you can guess. The company says a new batch will be ready in summer 2002.

In other news, Britax has also released a special car seat (The Traveller Plus) for special needs children up to 105 pounds. Also new: the company promises to release a travel system for their Handle with Care infant seat. The system will pair the infant seat with a 22 lb. stroller with a large basket, tray and inflated tires (for the back wheels).

Infant seat. Speaking of the infant seat, we should note that while we highly recommend Britax's convertible seats, the Handle With Care infant seat is a loser: it has no snap-in base, which means you must belt in the seat with each use, and it's way overpriced ($150).

Readers who have this seat, however, say its features outweigh any inconvenience. They say you get efficient buckling it with each use after a few tries and the lack of a base means it's easier to move from car to car. The only gripe: the chest clip sometimes slides down during use and the seat is only rated for use up to 20 pounds and 26" in height.

Safety track record: Well, no one's perfect. Besides the Roundabout recall (discussed above), Britax also had a minor recall on the Freeway seat back in 1997. So, is all this talk about Britax's safety just sales hype? No, we still think these are among the best seats on the market. And since these two recalls had no reported injuries associated with them, we'll still give Britax high marks.

Bottom line: It's thumbs down for the infant seat, but a big thumbs up for the convertible seats. ***Rating: A***

Consumer Reports crash tests vs our ratings

Every time *Consumer Reports* comes out with a report on car seats, our phones and email light up—many readers want to know how we sometimes come to different conclusions as to which are the best car seats. It's quite simple: *Consumer Reports* actually crash tests car seats, something we don't have the budget to do here at *Baby Bargains*. When we rate a car seat, we look at the seat's overall features, ease of use and value based on parent feedback and our own hands-on inspections. We also look at the company's recall track record and (if they are available) any *Consumer Report's* crash test reports. Even though we might use different rating methodologies, most of the time we agree with *Consumer Reports*. In the case of a major discrepancy, we'll often comment on this on our web page at www.BabyBargainsBook.com. For more on this topic, see the discussion in Chapter 1.

Century *9600 Valley View Rd., Macedonia, OH 44056. For a dealer near you, call (330) 468-2000. Web: www.centuryproducts.com.* Century was acquired by Rubbermaid (Graco's parent) in 1998 and was merged with Graco. With most mergers, you'd expect one brand to disappear but, oddly enough, Rubbermaid has decided to keep both Century and Graco as separate brands with distinct offerings.

Century is the biggest car seat maker in North America, with a model and style for just about every need. Here is a break-down of their offerings:

Infant car seats. Century's most innovative feature in this category is their "LevelRight" indicator, which helps parents properly position their seat. This has proved so popular that other infant car seat makers have recently copied it.

Century offers FOUR infant seat models. The best one is the Smart Fit Plus ($50-$70), which features an adjustable stay-in-the-car base, cushioned handle and two piece harness tie. Although this model is a few years old, it is very well-designed. The Smart Fit comes in both a three-point and a five-point harness version. As for the other infant car seats, Century has the Assure ($40) which is basically the same as the Smart Fit, except it lacks the car base (hence you have to belt it in with each use). One bummer: readers say the Smart Fit Plus is somewhat hard to find in stores. On the upper end, Century offers the Vante V. Gone are last year's Celestia and Avanta infant seats. (Actually, the Vante V is very similiar to the Celestia). By the time you read this, the Vante V should be on the market for about $80 to $100. One nice feature: the Vante V will be one of the first infant car seats on the market this year with LATCH attachments.

Convertible car seats. Century offers a mind-numbing list of choices in this category. On the low end, the no frills STE car seats are good buys. The 1000 STE Classic ($50) was top-rated in *Consumer Reports* and features five-point harness, two-position recline, level indicator (like the infant seats) and washable/removable seat cover. At $50, it's a very good buy and a great no-frills seat for a second vehicle (or grandma's car). The other STE car seats ($60 to $80) offer more plush fabrics in both T-shield (2000 STE) and bar-shield (3000 STE) versions. The latter features Century's "Room to Grow" feature for the bar shield—four adjustments to accommodate larger children. There will be no changes in the STE line for 2001.

Next up in price are Bravo seats. They feature a snap-together chest clip (that's an upgrade from the STE's) which have the slide-in harness ties). Also, the Bravo seats feature upgraded seat padding, one-hand recline and the "BeltWay" belt routing system, which is basically a trap door that lets you better position the auto safety belt.

You also get more seat padding and extras like removable storage pouches and snap-in adjustable head pillows. The low-end Bravo SE has a pillow for $99, while the LX had more padding and leatherette treatments for $130.

Whew! Are we done yet? Nope, we haven't talked about Century's top-of-the-line seat: the SmartMove. the "first and only rotational convertible car seat." It offers a full recline for infants that "rotates instantly and automatically to an upright protective position in the event of a frontal collision." The super plush car seat is lined with foam for extra comfort. The only bummer to the SmartMove: it's a monster seat that simply doesn't fit into smaller cars or those with limited space in the back seat. At 21 pounds, you won't want to be moving this seat from car to car. One parent told us a car seat technician he consulted called the Smart Move "the bane of his existence" since it is apparently very hard to install tightly in a rear-facing position. When it first came out, the Smart Move was very expensive ($120 to $150), but Century has been lowering the price ever since. As we went to press in 2002, we heard Century was planning to discontinue the Smart Move, although you might see some still on store shelves for $89 to $99.

Finally, we should discuss Century's new class of convertible seats called the "Accel," which debuted in 2000. These new low-price models will eventually replace the STE line. Accel models feature larger seats, higher backs, and two-piece harness ties in both five point ($59-$69) and adjustable bar-shield models ($69-$79). We were very impressed with the Accel; they are Century's best offerings to date in this category.

All of Century's convertible seats are rear-facing to 30 pounds (with the exception of the STE line, which is just 22 pounds) and forward facing to 40 pounds.

While it's not a true convertible seat, the Century "Next Step" does merit a brief mention. It's a combo toddler and booster seat–use it with a five-point harness for children 20 to 40 pounds forward-facing and then as a booster (with the vehicle's safety belt) for 40 to 80 pounds. If your baby has outgrown an infant seat and is at least a year of age, this might be a good choice for $79 to $99. (We will cover Century's other booster seats in a special report available on our web page at www.BabyBargainsBook.com).

Safety track record. Century has had a spotty safety record over the last decade, but it has improved in the last few years. Readers of previous editions of this book may recall our articles on the ill-fated 590 infant seat in the mid 1990's, and Century has continued to have problems with infant seats. That culminated with a recent recall of four million infant seats for defective handles: Century received 2700 reports of handle-related problems, "including handles breaking, cracking or possibly not being locked while the seat is being used as a carrier. In addition to these reports, Century has also received over 200 reports of injuries, including concussions, skull fractures, lacerations, broken bones, bruises and scratches as a result of such handle-related problems." The seats involved in this recall were manufactured *before* 1997; since that time, Century has improved the safety of this line and has had no recalls since (as of this writing).

The bottom line: Despite the bumpy past safety record, Century's current line of infant seats are excellent, with the exception of the too-heavy Celestia/Avanta line. The convertible seats are very good, with the Accel and STE lines as the best bets. Unfortunately, Century has taken a wait and see approach to the new LATCH/ISO-FIX seats; it might be late 2001 or early 2002 before Century rolls out those models. ***Rating: B+***

Cosco *2525 State St., Columbus, IN 47201. Call (812) 372-0141 for a dealer near you (or 514-323-5701 for a dealer in Canada). Web: www.coscoinc.com* Owned by Canadian conglomerate Dorel Industries, Cosco has staged a comeback in the car seat market in recent years. Previously an also-ran in the car seat business, Cosco

Chocolate donuts with sprinkles?

Here's a confusing thing about car seat shopping: most car seat makers offer their models in a plethora of versions. At one point, Century's Smart Fit infant seat had FIVE different versions: the Smart Fit Classic, Plus, Elite, Supreme and the Extra Crispy. Okay, there wasn't an Extra Crispy, but you get the point. The key thing to remember: the Smart Fit was basically the very same seat in each configuration, just with minor cosmetic variations (a extra bit of padding here, a pillow there, etc). Okay, sometimes there are more significant variations like a five-point harness (versus three-point) or an adjustable base. But often there isn't much difference. Think of it this way: car seat makers produce a chocolate donut and top it with different color sprinkles–the rainbow sprinkle version goes to Wal-Mart, the green sprinkle donut goes to K-Mart, etc. That way the companies can offer "exclusives" on certain "models" to their large customers, so they don't have to go head-to-head with other chains on price. Bottom line: don't get caught up in all the version stuff. If the basic seat has the features you want, it doesn't really matter whether you buy the Plus or the Elite. Or the Extra Crispy.

hit a home run with their Alpha Omega seat (described below) and Eddie Bauer-licensed products. Yet, we are still troubled by Cosco's poor safety track record, which we'll discuss at the end of this review.

Before we get to the models, let us point about that Cosco makes three versions of their car seats: one under their own name and versions under the "Eddie Bauer" and "NASCAR" names. Note that in all cases, the seats are just the same, only the colors/fabric patterns have changed. Of course, you will pay extra for the name.

Infant seats. Cosco has three basic models of infant seats: the Arriva and the Designer (which comes in two versions, the 22 and 35).

The entry-level Arriva ($30 to $50; rear-facing to 22 pounds) is sold in versions with and without a stay-in-the-car base. The simplest Arriva has a three-point harness and no base. Next up, is a version that adds a canopy that wraps around the handle. We think this is a rather lousy design, since you then can't carry the carrier under your arm. Cosco also makes an Arriva version with an "adjustable canopy," which is obviously the way to go.

The new Designer 22 ($49 to $79; rear-facing to 22 pounds) features plusher padding, easier to adjust belts and a soft foam carry handle. One version of the Designer 22 has an adjustable base.

The top-of-the-line Designer 35 is the first infant car seat that can be used rear-facing to a whopping 35 pounds. While that sounds good, we seriously wonder how any parent could carry a 35 pound infant in a carrier under their arm—heck even a 22 pounder would stress the average non-steroid using parent. Nonetheless, Cosco pulls out all the stops for this seat—you get plush padding, four position headrest, multi-position canopy and more. The Designer 35 sells for $69 to $79.

Parents of twins or premature babies take note: Cosco is one of very few manufacturers to make a "travel bed." For babies that need to travel lying down, the Cosco "Dream Ride" is about $60.

Convertible seats. Cosco's most successful seat in this category is the Alpha Omega, the first (and so far, only) seat that can be used from 5 pounds up to 80 pounds. First, it is a rear-facing convertible seat for infants up to 35 pounds. Then it is a forward facing seat up to 40 pounds and finally it morphs into a belt-positioning booster for children up to 80 pounds. In order to accommodate growing kids, the harness adjusts with the headrest and there is a one-hand, three position recline feature. The Alpha Omega comes in both five point ($120) and bar shield ($139, adjustable to four positions) and, of course, there is also an Eddie Bauer Alpha Omega for $10 more. We were impressed with the Alpha Omega as were our readers; most complimented the seat for its multiple uses and value. The only criticisms: twisting belts that frustrated some parents and the large

Baby on vacation

Just because you're a parent doesn't mean you'll never take a vacation again. Yet, how do you travel with baby . . . or more importantly, with all baby's stuff? Well, the good news is you don't have to lug all that baby equipment with you on the plane (or in the car). Baby's Away (800) 571-0077 (web: www.BabysAway.com) rents everything you need at many resort and vacation spots in the U.S. and Canada. You can rent name-brand cribs, strollers, high chairs, safety gates, potty seats, toys and more at reasonable rates (either by the day or week).

size of the Alpha Omega means it won't fit in some cars (see the compatibility list on carseatdata.org for specifics). Perhaps the biggest complaint: parents reported that the recline feature was not deep enough for young infants (when the seat is in the rear-facing position). This underscores our earlier point that the best seat for an infants under 20 pounds is an INFANT seat, not a convertible like the Alpha Omega.

Also: *Consumer Reports* criticized the Alpha Omega for the design of its booster seat belt clip and we have to agree–the design can introduce belt slack that could compromise the safety of the seat. As a result, we don't recommend the use of this seat as a booster, which of course is one of its prime selling points.

Of course, the Alpha Omega isn't Cosco's only convertible seat–the company also offers a slew of less pricey seats. The entry-level Touriva ($50 to $75) comes in five-point and bar-shield (which is not adjustable) versions. The next level is the more plush Olympian car seat ($70 to $90), which also comes in five-point and adjustable bar-shield versions. The Regal Ride is basically the same as the Olympian, but adds removable infant insert padding and pillow ($80 to $100).

If you are looking for a LATCH seat, Cosco has one model, the Triad ($80, rear facing to 35 pounds, forward 22 to 40 pounds). This five point seat has a removable infant insert, pillow, two-piece harness tie and mesh storage pockets. It also has color-coded belts to make the LATCH installation easier.

If that weren't enough, Cosco also has a new high-end line of car seats that go under the name "Maxi Cosi." These seats are made in Europe and imported by Cosco. Maxi Cosi Priori seats feature a lock-off clamp that eliminates the need for a locking clip (like the Britax models). We wonder if what some parents like about these seats is the look–Maxi Cosi's fashionable fabrics (the seats are made in Holland) are definitely a cut-above those normally offered by Cosco. There is even a leather version of the Maxi Cosi for a whopping $400. Non-leather Maxi Cosi seats are still $200, which is too expensive since these are forward-only facing seats (20 to 40 pounds). As we went to press in 2002, we heard Cosco was discontinuing the Maxi Cosi line. Too bad–these are good quality seats, even if they are overpriced.

New for 2002 from Cosco: the "Summit" ($90) will be a combo forward-facing seat and booster. It will accommodate children 22-100 lbs.–the first seat to reach that weight limit in US. In other news, Cosco will also market seats under the Safety 1st brand name in 2002. The first Safety 1st car seat will be a high-back booster called the Vantage Point ($80) that will have a five-point harness up to 40 pounds and a belt-positioning booster with an easy-glide open loop belt path. Another note: the "Forerunner" will replace the Triad as a convertible LATCH seat by the time you read this. Basically, it has the same features as the Triad.

Safety track record: We are still quite troubled by Cosco's safety track record, which has been marred by recent recalls–11 at last count since 1990. Among the worst was a 1999 recall involving 670,000 Arriva and Turnabout infant car seats. The seats' handle unexpectedly released in some cases, causing the seat to flip forward and dump out the child. 29 children were injured due to this defect.

Bottom line: Because of Cosco's questionable safety record, we'll pass on recommending Cosco's Alpha Omega, despite its innovative design and features. We'll also take a pass on Cosco's infant seats. ***Rating: C+***

Seat inserts provide head support, warmth

Even though an infant car seat is built to accommodate small babies, newborns may still need some extra support. That's where a seat insert comes in, providing additional head and side support. One of our favorites: Kiddopotamus's "Snuzzler" ($20), an infant insert that has an adjustable/detachable head support, all made of washable fleece. When baby outgrows the infant seat, you can use the insert in a larger car seat or jogging stroller to provide extra support and warmth. The same company also offers several other innovative travel products, including the Sun Shade (a cover-up for infant seats and strollers) and a Fleece Warmer (again for car seats, strollers or carriers). Each is $15 to $30. For more details, call (800) 772-8339 or web: www.kiddopotamus.com.

Eddie Bauer. These seats are made by Cosco; see the previous review for details.

Evenflo *1801 Commerce Dr., Piqua, OH 45356. For a dealer near you, call (800) 233-5921 or (937) 415-3300. In Canada, PO Box 1598, Brantford, Ontario, N3T 5V7. (905) 337-2229. Web: www.evenflo.com* Evenflo is probably the second-largest car seat maker in the U.S. and Canada (after Century). Besides their own name, Evenflo also makes seats under their Osh Kosh license. Like Cosco's Eddie Bauer line, the Osh Kosh seats are exactly the same as Evenflo's models, just with denim fabric.

Infant seats. Evenflo has three infant seat models: First Choice, Discovery and Cozy Carry (which in 2002 replaced the On My Way). The entry-level First Choice ($40) is a very basic seat without a snap-in base (which requires the seat to be belted-in with each use). Step up to the Discovery ($49 to $59) and you get a snap-in base, Z-shaped handle and retractable canopy. Evenflo's top-end infant seat, The Cozy Carry, is available with either three point or five point harness. This infant seat will feature a molded, rubberized handle (Press 'n Go) that is adjustable without having to press any trigger buttons (as was the case on the On My Way). It has three positions: carrying, traveling and feeding. It runs $90 or as part of a travel system for about $145. The Cozy Carry will be LATCH compatible. We've got to hand it to Evenflo: this new infant seat is a vast improvement over past efforts. We liked the extra padding, a low profile base with angle indicator (for correct install) as well as a buckle with an indicator with a visual clue to let parents know it is latched. You also get a retractable canopy and separate head support for infants. BUT, the Cozy Carry does have one big negative: there is NO front adjustment for the harness. And there isn't any extra EPS foam for additional crash protection. Meanwhile, Evenflo's other infant seats (Discovery, etc.) will continue to be sold in 2002 without any changes.

With the new Cozy Carry, Evenflo has improved their infant seat line, but we still note competitors' seats have better features at the same price.

Convertible car seats. Evenflo's convertible seats have been suffering from a lack of innovation–instead of coming out with new seats or features, Evenflo just changes the name of its seats from time to time. This year, the Ultara and Secure Advantage seats have been rechristened "Odyssey." No changes in features, just a name change. What's the point?

Like Century and Cosco, Evenflo sells car seat models in several price ranges. (All of Evenflo's convertible seats are now rear-facing to 30 pounds, forward-facing 20 to 40 pounds). The entry level

Odyssey comes both in five-point and adjustable bar shield versions ($69 to $79). A more plush version of the Odyssey (called Comfort Touch, $89 to $99) has built-in pillows and more padding. All the Odysseys have two-piece chest clips and a three-position one-hand recline feature.

The Conquest is an even more scaled back version of Evenflo's entry level convertible seats, omitting the chest clip and up-front recline handle. The Conquest comes in both five point and adjustable bar shield ($59 to $69).

If you are looking for a LATCH seat, Evenflo offers the Horizon ($69 to $79), a slightly bigger seat than the Odyssey or Conquest with more padding. Once again, Evenflo offers the Horizon in both five point and adjustable bar shield versions. (Be sure to check the box if you want the LATCH version–Evenflo apparently sells the Horizon in both LATCH and non-LATCH versions). And here's a note for Canadian readers: Evenflo's web site warns that even though the Horizon is rated to 30 pounds rear-facing, it can only be used in Canada to 22 pounds rear-facing.

At the very top end, Evenflo sells the ultra-plush "Medallion" series (about $109 to $139), which all feature five-point harnesses. The Medallion V Comfort Touch features built-in pillows and padded harness straps; the Medallion V Fresh Air Gear adds Evenflo's "seat within a seat" for infants.

The Medallion car seat will be sold through the first half of 2002 and then phased out for a new model: the Triumph. Rear-facing 5-30 pounds and forward facing 20-40 pounds, this seat features a harness positioning system that lets you adjust the belt height WITHOUT having to re-thread the belts; five position recline and $130 price tag. The Triumph's biggest problem: the adjustment knob for the harness height is hard to turn when the seat is installed rear-facing (that's because the knob is on the inside, near the child's seat).

Safety track record: In March 1998, Evenflo was forced to recall 800,000 On My Way infant seats after 89 children were injured when the seat's handle failed to lock and the seat tipped forward. What really bothered us was how Evenflo handled this situation–while we realize car seat recalls are an all-too-frequent fact of life, we were miffed that Evenflo first blamed parents for mis-using the product when reports of the problem first surfaced. Only after arm-twisting by the federal government did Evenflo reluctantly recall the seat and admit the production defect. A top safety regulator heavily criticized Evenflo's foot-dragging, calling the company one of "the most difficult to work with" in the industry. That kind of behavior is inexcusable; as a result, we don't recommend any Evenflo car seats.

Bottom line: All in all, we found Evenflo's convertible seats to be disappointing. We see little innovation, just warmed-over models from years past. Evenflo lacks an Alpha Omega-style combo product or the innovative low-end seats like Century's Accel line. And don't look for a seat with built-in locking clips (a la Britax) from these guys. We'll raise their rating slightly for the better push-action handle on the infant seats, but other than that this company is a disappointment. And we still have a sour taste in our mouths from the way Evenflo handled that 1998 infant seat recall. ***Rating: D+***

Fisher-Price Fisher Price withdrew from the car seat market in 2001. That's too bad, because the company had some great models with innovative features. Why did Fisher Price throw in the towel? The company says the car seat line didn't make enough money. If you find a Fisher Price car seat on the clearance rack, snap it up—we hear they are still in some stores. For that reason, here is an overview of what Fisher Price offered:

Infant seat. The Stay in View infant car sat has two innovative features—first it features a "mirrored high-back base" that let you see a rear-facing baby while driving, which is a nice feature. But what we really like about this seat is the handle, or lack thereof. Instead of a bulky handle, the Stay in View had a padded carry strap. This has two advantages: first, it makes seat the lightest infant seat on the market. Second, Fisher Price avoids all the safety problems that have dogged other infant car seat handles in recent years. The Stay in View can be used rear facing to 20 pounds, but up to 29" in height. At $70, the Stay in View isn't cheap but we think it is worth it.

Convertible seats. The Safe Embrace ($109) is Fisher-Price's main entry in this category. We were impressed with the Safe Embrace's innovative features: all-steel frame, five point harness, built-in locking clips (a la Britax), energy-absorbing foam padding and color-coded belt paths for easy installation. The Safe Embrace is rated rear facing to 30 pounds (forward-facing 22 to 40 pounds). Strangely enough, however, the Safe Embrace doesn't recommend use of a chest clip when the seat is in a rear-facing position (which means enterprising infants may wiggle their way out of the seat).

In 2000, Fisher Price rolled out the Safe Embrace II, which is a LATCH seat. At $160, it is a bit pricey compared to other LATCH seats on the market, but still has all the safety features of the original Safe Embrace.

Finally, Fisher-Price offers one product in the transitional booster category, the Futura 20/60 ($89). Similar to the Century Next Step, this model is for forward-facing use for children 20 to 60 pounds. The five-point version of this seat was a great option—you could use the harness for kids up to 60 pounds.

Once again, we should point out that all Fisher Price seats are now all discontinued—but keep an eye out for one in some stores.

Graco *Rt. 23, Main St., Elverson, PA 19520. For a dealer near you, call (800) 345-4109, (610) 286-5951. Web: www.gracobaby.com*

Infant Seat. Graco offers one of the best infant seats on the market: the Snug Ride. We were impressed with the seat's features: it has an adjustable base, level indicator, retractable canopy and a padded, ergonomic carry handle. The seat also weighs less than the Evenflo's On My Way. The basic Snug Ride sells for $59 and the DX5 model adds a five-point harness and front strap-adjuster for $69. You can buy the seat separately or as part of Graco's travel systems. While Graco's seat rated number-one in *Consumer Reports* recent tests, we noted one major complaint from our readers: some parents complained the Snug Ride's straps were too short to accommodate larger infants. Graco fixed that problem in 2001 by including longer straps with the Snug Ride.

In a previous edition of this book, we mentioned the Snug Ride was not shopping cart compatible (hence, it couldn't lock into a shopping cart top basket). As it turns out, that wasn't entirely true. Yes, Graco warns in big bold letters not to use the Snug Ride in a shopping cart basket, but many parents note that it fits just fine. We wonder if Graco's warnings have more to do with fear of lawsuits from cart accidents than whether the seat really works or not in such carts.

One final negative to the Snug Ride: it can only used for infants up to 20 pounds and 26 inches, two pounds and three inches less than the similar Century SmartFit. A word to the wise: if you have a large infant, you might want to skip this seat.

A LATCH compatible Graco Snug Ride infant seat will also be on the market in mid 2002. Meanwhile, Graco has debuted a new base for the Snug Ride that is adjustable AND coutoured for a better fit. This new base appears on the 3pt basic model and the new LX model (with 5 pt). So, now the Graco Snug Ride has THREE bases: the old non-adjustable one, the the old adjustable (but not contoured) one and the new adjustable and contoured one! There will be a quiz on this at the end of this chapter.

Graco doesn't offer any convertible seats, but does have a couple of other niche products. The Cherish Car Bed ($60) is for preemies (up to 9 lbs.) who have to ride in a seat lying down. Besides the Cosco Dream Ride, this is the only other car bed on the market.

Graco also has a transitional booster that is similar to Century's Next Step called the CarGo. This booster has a five-point harness for use from 20 to 40 pounds and then a belt-positioning booster for 40 to 80 pounds. The CarGo comes in three different versions that range from $60 to $80.

Safety track record: As of this writing, Graco has had no recalls on their car seats. While that is good news, remember that Graco

Belt positioners

Here's a common email we get from parents in New York and other urban areas: are there any portable car seats that can be used in taxis? Something that is lightweight, easy to install and collapses to fit inside a small purse when not in use? Well, the answer is no—almost all car seats are designed to be semi-permanently installed in a vehicle. We're not sure the geniuses at the car seat companies have ever considered folks who have to use taxis and public transport. And even the lightest car seat can approach 20 pounds, not something that's easily lugged around in any city.

What about those belt-positioning devices for toddlers? The jury is still out on so-called travel vests (lightweight devices that simply adjust a vehicle's belts to better fit a child). Some safety advocates say they don't provide any protection and the government has no data on them—yet. The National Highway Traffic Safety Administration has pledged to study belt-positioners in 2001, but we're unsure when they'll announce the findings. Stay tuned.

is a newcomer to the car seat market and only sells a limited number of models.

Bottom line. A great infant seat, but not if you have a large baby! ***Rating: A-***

Maxi Cosi. This is an imported line of European seats sold in the U.S. and Canada by Cosco. See Cosco's review earlier in this section for details on these models.

Osh Kosh. These seats are made by Evenflo. See their review earlier for details.

Peg Perego *3625 Independence Dr., Ft. Wayne, IN 46808. For a dealer near you, call (219) 482-8191. Web: www.perego.com* After seeing their stroller sales eaten away by travel systems for years, Peg Perego has finally decided to address this long shortcoming with the debut of an infant seat (and travel system) in 2001.

The Primo Viaggio (also called the Traveller) is a five point car seat that can be detached from its stay-in-the-car base with just one hand. It also has a ratcheting handle, up front belt adjustment, padded straps and head support. And it will have a Perego-like hefty price tag: $100, making it the most expensive infant seat on the market today.

The Perego infant seat is sold separately and as part of travel systems for the Venezia, Milano XL and G-matic strollers.

So, what's the verdict on the Primo Viaggio? Thumbs down, in our opinion. First, we don't like the skimpy 20 pound, 26" limits, which are on the lower end of what's available today. We also noticed the base of the seat is not adjustable or sculpted to fit easier in cars with bucket seats.

Safety track record: Right off the bat in 2001, Perego issued a safety recall for the Primo Viaggio, which underscores our point that this seat isn't ready for prime time.

Bottom line: This product has all the feel of Version 1.0 software–not a bad idea, but lots of rough edges. And way too expensive to recommend, even if it comes in those fancy Italian fashion fabrics. ***Rating: C+***

Safety 1st. These seats are made by Cosco; see the previous review for details.

◆ ***Other brands to consider:*** *Kolcraft* (773) 247-4494 is another player in the car seat market, albeit one who's always far back in the pack when it comes to quality and features. Their "Secura" infant seat is a good example of what's wrong at Kolcraft: this expensive ($75) seat lacks a level indicator, is difficult to remove from its base and has no harness height adjustment. Plus, you can't attach the Secura to a shopping cart and the padding is NOT machine-washable. Verdict: it's a loser.

Kolcraft's convertible seats aren't much better: it's "Auto-Mate" seat won the dubious distinction of being the only car seat to fail *Consumer Reports'* recent crash tests. Kolcraft's other car seats (the bar-shield "Secure Fit" and "Performa" models) are such poor sellers you probably won't see them much in stores. And don't look

Booster seats

As you read this section, you might wonder where are the reviews for booster seats, those seats for older children who've outgrown their convertible seats? Since this book covers products for children age birth to two, we decided to put a special report on this topic for sale on our web page. Go to www.BabyBargainsBook.com for details.

Even though the federal government recommends the use of booster seats to 80 pounds, most states don't require children older than three or four (it varies by state) to be in a child safety seat. The exception is California, which in 2000 passed a new law requiring children to ride in a booster seat until age six or 60 pounds. You can read about each state's laws at SafetyBeltUSA's web site (www.CarSeat.org).

What is the lightest infant car seat carrier?

Here at BABY BARGAINS we have Ivy League-trained scientists who help us determine important stuff like which infant car seat weighs the least (and hence, is easiest to lug around). Oh, we're just kidding. Actually, we the authors just went to our local baby store and stood there in the aisles lifting each infant seat and saying things like "Yep, this one is lighter!" Our official results: the lightest seat is the Fisher Price Stay in View. The next lightest is the Evenflo Discovery followed closely by the Century Smart Fit. The heaviest seats? Graco's Snug Ride and Century's Vante V. Of course, the weight of an infant seat isn't the only factor we used to decide which was best, but it certainly is important.

for Kolcraft online—the company is the only major juvenile products company to lack a web site as of press time.

In contrast to the me-too offerings of Kolcraft, the ***Sit N Stroll*** ($160) from Safeline Corporation (800) 829-1625, (303) 457-4440 (web: www.safelinecorp.com) has won a small but loyal fan base for its innovative car seat/stroller. With one flick of the hand, this convertible car seat morphs into a stroller. Like the Batmobile, a handle pops up from the back and wheels appear from the bottom—presto! You've got a stroller without having to remove baby from the seat.

We've seen a few parents wheel this thing around, and though it looks somewhat strange, they told us they've been happy with its operation. We have some doubts, however. First, unlike the four-in-one car seat/stroller combos reviewed later in this chapter, the Sit N Stroll's use as a stroller is quite limited—it doesn't have a full basket (only a small storage compartment) or a canopy (a "sunshade" is an option). We'd prefer a seat that reclines (it doesn't) and you've got to belt the seat in each time you use it in a car—even if you don't take it along as a stroller. Not only is installation a hassle, but the Sit N Stroll's wide base may also not fit some vehicles with short safety belts or contoured seats. Plus, lifting the 14-pound car seat with a full-size child out of a car to put on the ground is quite a workout. So, we're not sure we can wholeheartedly recommend this seat. On the other hand, we did hear from a flight attendant who loved her Sit N Stroll—it wheels down those narrow plane aisles and is a FAA-certified flight seat. So, it's a mixed bag for the Sit N Stroll. While we salute the maker for their innovation, the product's drawbacks may limit its appeal.

As you can imagine, the child safety seat world changes quickly—check out our web page (www.BabyBargainsBook.com) for the latest updates and changes.

Our Picks: Brand Recommendations

Here are our top picks for infant and convertible seats. Are these seats safer than others? No–all child safety seats sold in the U.S. and Canada must meet minimum safety standards. These seats are our top picks because they combine the best features, usability (including ease of installation) and value. Remember the safest and best seat for your baby is the one that best fits your child and vehicle. Finding the right car seat can be a bit of trial and error; you may find a seat can NOT be installed safely in your vehicle because of the quirks of the seat or your vehicle's safety belt system. Hence it is always wise to buy a seat from a store or web site with a good return policy.

Infant car seats

Good. Let's be honest: if you're on a super-tight budget, consider not buying an infant car seat at all. A good five-point, convertible car seat (see below for recommendations) will work for both

INFANT SEATS

The following is a selection of the better infant car seats and how they compare on features:

MAKER	MODEL	PRICE	WEIGHT/ HEIGHT LIMITS
BRITAX	HANDLE W/CARE	$150	20LBS/26"
CENTURY	SMART FIT PLUS 22	$50-70	22LBS/29"
	VANTE V	$80-100	22LBS/29"
COSCO	ARRIVA	$30-50	22LBS/29"
	DESIGNER 35	$60-80	22LBS/29"
EVENFLO	FIRST CHOICE	$40	20LBS/26"
	DISCOVERY	$50-60	20LBS/26"
	COZY CARRY	$90	20LBS/26"
FISHER-PRICE	STAY IN VIEW***	$70	20LBS/29"
GRACO	SNUG RIDE	$60-90	20LBS/26"
PEG PEREGO	PRIMO VIAGGIO/TRAVELLER	$100	20LBS/26"

KEY

AUTO BASE: Does the seat have a stay-in-the-car auto base?

HARNESS TYPE: Does the seat have a 3 or 5-point harness? "Both" means either type is available, depending on the model.

LEVEL IND.: Does the seat have a level indicator for easier installation?

HARNESS ADJUSTABLE: Is the HEIGHT of the harness straps adjustable?

infants and children. Of course, if you think you can spare $40 to $50, you could get a no-frills infant car seat.

Better. The Century "Smart Fit Plus 22"–it's got all the best features of other seats (level indicator, adjustable base, retractable canopy) and one key advantage: the Smart Fit Plus 22can be used for babies up to 22 pounds and 29" in height, more than most other brands. Price: $50 to $70 and comes in both three point and five point versions. One bummer: this seat can be hard to find in stores.

Best. For $60 to $90, the Graco Snug Ride impressed us with its plush padding, level indicator and padded handle and more. The only downside: the 20 pound weight limit and 26" height limit means big babies might outgrow this seat too soon. If you go for a Snug Ride, get the new base that is adjustable AND coutoured for a better fit. This new base appears on the 3 point basic model and the new LX model (with 5 point harness).

AUTO BASE	LEVEL IND.	HARNESS TYPE	HARNESS ADJUSTABLE	SHOPPING CART COMPATIBLE?
NO	NO	5 POINT	YES	YES
YES	YES	BOTH	YES	YES
YES	YES	BOTH	YES	YES
YES/NO**	NO	BOTH	YES	NO
YES	NO	5-POINT	NO	YES
NO	NO	3 POINT	NO	YES
YES	YES	BOTH	YES	YES
YES	YES	5 POINT	NO	YES
YES	NO	5 POINT	YES	YES
YES	YES	BOTH	YES	YES‡‡
YES	NO	5-POINT	YES	YES

Notes:

*** Cosco's Arriva has models that come with OR without an auto base.*

‡‡ Graco's Snug Ride seat does fit into shopping carts, but unlike its competitors, the seat does NOT lock into place.

****Discontinued but still sold in some stores and online.*

Convertible car seats

Good. For a decent, no-frills car seat, we recommend the Accel DX 5-point, a good seat with level indicator, two-piece harness tie and removable pillow. For $59, it's a good deal. The only bummer: it does not recline, so it would not be appropriate for small infants. But it can be used rear-facing to 30 pounds (then forward-facing to 40 pounds).

Better. There are many seats in the second-tier—with more features than the bare-bones Accel above and not as good as our top pick (the Britax Roundabout). The Cosco Alpha Omega ($100 to $120) has been a big-seller for its versatility, but we don't like the booster seat belt loop design. One dark horse: The Evenflo Triumph. Rear-facing 5-30 pounds and forward facing 20-40 pounds, this seat features a harness positioning system that lets you adjust the belt height *without* having to re-thread the belts. A good bet at $130.

Convertible Seats

The following is a selection of the better convertible car seats and how they compare on features:

			Weight Limits (in pounds)	
Maker	**Model**	**Price**	**Rear**	**Forward**
Britax	Roundabout	$200	30 lbs	40 lbs
Century	1000STE	$50	20	40
	Accel	$60-$80	30	40
	SmartMove SE*	$90-100	30	40
Cosco	Alpha-Omega	$120	35	80
Evenflo	Horizon	$70-80	30	40
	Odyssey	$80-120	30	40
	Medallion V*	$110-140	30	40
Fisher-Price	Safe Embrace*	$110-160	22	40
Safeline	Sit N Stroll	$160	25	40

Key

All of these seats have five-point restraining harnesses.

Model: These are the company's flagship models. For an overview of the company's entire offerings, refer to their review earlier in this chapter.

Recline: Most seats recline, but the reclines are not equal—some

Best. If you can afford it, our top recommendation is Britax's "Roundabout." While it is darn expensive (about $180-$200), it's the only car seat on the market that can use a tether in both forward AND rear-facing positions. We also like the snap-together chest clip, built-in locking clips, the extra foam for crash protection and overall safety design.

LATCH/ISO-FIX seats. Unfortunately, the pickings are slim here–as of press time, the best bet was Britax Expressway, which is NOT a convertible seat (but forward-facing only). We expect more LATCH seats to be on the market later in 2002. The Cosco Triad (now Forerunner) and Evenflo Horizon are two LATCH seats that have performed well. Watch our web page at www.BabyBargainsBook.com for the latest!

Recline	Comment
Yes	Built-in locking clip; Snap-together chest clip
No	Best buy, great for second car, grandma's car
No	Another best buy; 2 piece harness tie, larger back
Full	Rotates to upright position in case of accident
3-pos	Converts to booster seat for toddlers
2-pos	Lowest price latch seat on market
3-pos	Features up-front recline lever
3-pos	The top-of-the-line Evenflo model
No	Built-in locking clips; Latch version is called the "II"
No	Converts to stroller

recline more than others. Generally, the more positions, the more the recline. "3-pos" means a three position recline.

Notes:
** These models have been discontinued but you may still see them on store shelves in 2002.*

CHAPTER 8

Strollers, Diaper Bags, Carriers and other Gear To Go

What are the best strollers? Which brands are the most durable AND affordable? We'll discuss that plus other tips on how to make your baby portable—from front carriers to diaper bags and more. And what do you put in that diaper bag anyway? We've got nine suggestions, plus advice on dining out with baby.

Getting Started: When Do You Need This Stuff?

While you don't need a stroller, diaper bag or carrier immediately after baby is born, most parents purchase them before baby arrives anyway. Another point to remember: some stroller models have to be special-ordered with at least two to four weeks lead time. And some of the best deals for strollers and other to-go gear are found online, which necessitates leaving a week or more lead time for shipping.

Sources to Find Strollers, Carriers

Strollers and carriers are found at similar sources as we mentioned for car seats in the previous chapter. Once again, the discounters like Target and Wal-Mart tend to specialize in just a handful of models from the mass-market companies like Cosco, Kolcraft, Graco and so on. The baby superstores like Babies R Us and Baby Depot have a wider selection and (sometimes) better brands like Peg Perego and Combi. Meanwhile, juvenile specialty stores almost always carry the more exclusive brands like Maclaren, Simo and other euro-manufactured brands.

Yet perhaps the best deals for strollers, carriers and diaper bags are found online—for some reason, this seems to be one area the web covers very well. Perhaps this is because strollers are relatively easy to ship (compared to other more bulky juvenile items). Of course, more competition often means lower prices, so you'll see many deals online. Another plus: the web may be the only way to find certain European-made strollers if you live in certain less-populous parts of the U.S. and Canada (most of their dealers are concentrated on the East and West coasts).

Beware of shipping costs when ordering online or from a catalog—many strollers may run 20 or 30 pounds, which can translated into hefty shipping fees. Use an online coupon (see Chapter 6 for coupon sites) to save and look for free shipping specials.

Parents in Cyberspace: What's on the Web?

Online info on strollers, diaper bags and carriers fall into two categories: manufacturer sites and discounters who sell online. Here's a brief overview:

◆ ***Most manufacturers do not sell online, but you can find a wealth of info on their sites in some cases.*** With stroller makers, you may find fabric swatches and other technical info about different models. This is helpful since most stores don't carry every available fabric, accessory or model. Among the better sites is Combi (www.combi-intl.com), which includes detailed info on their models and even comparison charts so you can compare several models at once. Combi also has an outlet store on their site where they sell discontinued models, overstock and showroom samples—when we last visited, we saw last year's Savvy Z for $155 (it sold in stores for up to $200). Baby Jogger has a similar area (called the Ugly Duckling) on their site for overstocks and customer returns.

◆ ***Discounters.*** Besides previously mentioned web sites like BabyCatalog.com (which has an excellent stroller deals), readers say they've had luck with smaller sites like Lots4Tots (www.lots4tots.com) and JuniorPlace (www.juniorplace. com). Lots4Tots carries top brands like Simo and Peg Perego with discounts on some models up to 20% off retail (look for their specials). JuniorPlace specializes in Emmaljunga and SilverCross carriages—the best deal we saw their was a Emmaljunga model that sells for $300 marked down to just $179.

Of course, any mention of online bargains for strollers wouldn't be complete without mention of eBay (www.eBay.com), the massive bargain bazaar. Go to eBay's baby section and choose both the "general" and "stroller" categories for deals (see Figure 1 on the next page). Sure, there are some dogs here (like Graco or Evenflo models that are virtually worthless for resale), but you'll also find

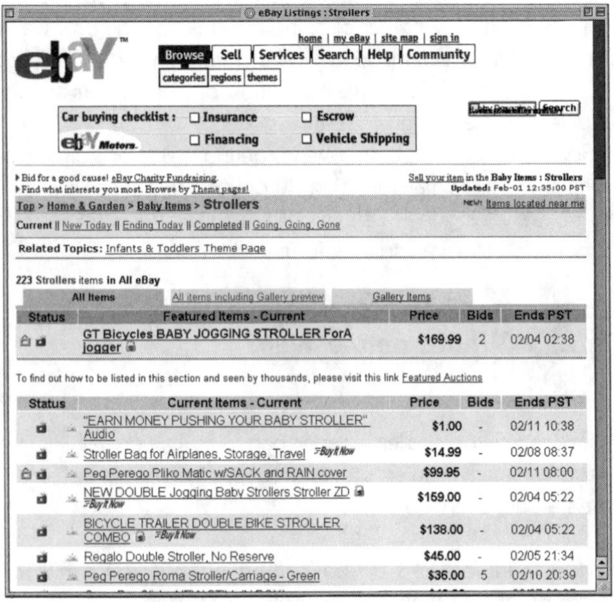

Figure 1: We found 223 strollers for auction on eBay during a recent visit—at prices way below retail.

new-in-the-box Perego models as well as jogging strollers by the score. Do your price research up front (know what things really sell for at retail) and you'll find many 50% off bargains.

Strollers

Baby stores offer a bewildering array of strollers for parents. Do you want the model that converts from a car seat to a stroller? What about a stroller that would work for a quick trip to the mall? Or do you want a stroller for jogging? Hiking trails? The urban jungle of New York City or beaches of LA?

And what about all the different brand names? Will a basic brand found at a discount store work? Or do you need a higher-quality brand from Japan or Europe? What about strollers with anti-lock brakes and air bags? (Just kidding on that last one).

The $180 million dollar stroller industry is not dominated by one or two players, like you might see in car seats or high chairs. Instead, you'll find a couple dozen players offering just about anything on wheels, ranging from $30 for a bare-bones model to $500 for deluxe stroller from Europe. A recent trend: SUV-like strollers from Jeep (made by Kolcraft) and Eddie Bauer (made by Cosco), as well as a boom in joggers.

We hope this section takes some of the mystery out of the stroller buying process. First, we'll look at the six different types of strollers on the market today. Next, we'll zero in on features and help you decided what's important and what's not. Then, it's brand ratings and our picks as the best recommendations for different lifestyles. Finally, we'll go over several safety tips, money saving hints, wastes of money and a couple of mail-order sources that sell strollers.

What Are You Buying?

There are six types of strollers you can buy:

◆ ***Umbrella Strollers.*** The name comes from the appearance of the stroller when it's folded, similar to an umbrella.

WHAT'S COOL: They're lightweight and cheap—that is, low in price (about $25 to $35). We should note that a few European stroller makers (Maclaren and Peg Perego) offer a couple of pricey umbrella strollers that sell for $150 to $200.

WHAT'S NOT: They're cheap—that is, low in quality (well, with the exception of Maclaren and Peg Perego). You typically don't get any fancy features like canopies, storage baskets, reclining seats, and so on. Another problem: most umbrella strollers have hammock-style seats with little head support, so they won't work well for babies under six months of age.

◆ ***Carriage/Strollers.*** A carriage (also called a pram) is like a bed on wheels—most are similar in style to a bassinet. Since this feature is most useful when a baby is young (and less helpful when baby is older), most companies make carriages that convert to strollers.

WHAT'S COOL: If your baby is sleepy, she can lie down. Most combo carriage/strollers have lots of high-end features like reversible handles or seats (so you can push the stroller and see your baby at the same time).

WHAT'S NOT: Hefty weight (not easy to transport or set up) and hefty price tags. Another negative: most Euro-style "prams" have fixed front wheels, which make maneuvering difficult on quick trips. Some carriage/stroller models can top $300 and $400. These strollers once dominated the market but have lost favor as more parents opt for "travel systems" that combine an infant seat and stroller (see below).

◆ ***Lightweight Strollers.*** These strollers are our top recommendation: they're basically souped-up umbrella strollers with many convenience features.

WHAT'S COOL: Most offer easy set-up and fold-down; some even fold up similar to umbrella strollers. Many models have an amazing number of features (canopies, storage baskets, high-quality wheels) at amazingly light weights (as light as seven pounds). Combi's Savvy (see review later) is this category's leader, although many companies (namely Graco) have introduced low-priced, Savvy knock-offs in recent years.

WHAT'S NOT: Can be expensive—most high-quality brands run $200 to $300. Some models are so popular you might have to wait for delivery.

◆ ***Jogging (or Sport) Strollers.*** These strollers feature three big bicycle-tire wheels and lightweight frames—perfect for jogging or walking on rough roads.

WHAT'S COOL: How many other strollers can do 15 mph on a jogging trail? Some have plush features like padded seats and canopies—and the best fold up quickly for easy storage in the trunk. This category has boomed in recent years; now it seems like every stroller maker is rolling out a jogger model.

WHAT'S NOT: They can be darn expensive, topping $200 or even $300. Jogging strollers are a single-purpose item—thanks to their sheer bulk and a lack of steering, you can't use one in a mall or other location. On the plus side, the flood of new models is helping lower prices. New, low-end jogging strollers run $100 to $150. The trade-offs to the new bargain price models: heavier steel frames and a lack of features.

◆ ***All-terrain Strollers.*** The baby equivalent of four-wheel drive sport-utility vehicles, these strollers are pitched to parents who want to go on hikes or other outdoor adventures.

WHAT'S COOL: Big knobby tires and high clearances work better on gravel trails/roads than standard strollers. All-terrain strollers still have convenience features (baskets, canopies, etc.), yet don't cost as much jogging strollers (most are under $100). Besides, they look cool.

WHAT'S NOT: A few models have fixed front wheels, making them a hassle to use—when you want to turn the stroller, you have to lift the entire front half off the ground. Even if the front wheels swivel, the larger wheels make the stroller less maneuverable in tight spaces. All-terrain strollers are wider than other strollers, which could make them troublesome in stores with narrow aisles. Another caveat: new models now boast "pneumatic" (inflated) wheels for a smoother ride. The only bummer—what if you get a flat? While pneumatic-tired strollers seem to be the new hot trend, most folks who really want to go on a hike will opt for a jogging stroller instead of an all-terrain.

◆ ***Travel systems.*** It's the current rage among stroller makers–models that combine infant car seats and strollers (also called "travel systems"). Century kicked off this craze way back in 1994 with its "4-in-1" model that featured four uses (infant carrier, infant car seat, carriage and toddler stroller). Since then, just about every major stroller maker jumped into the travel system market. Travel systems have just about killed sales of carriage strollers; now even carriage stroller king Peg Perego has bowed to the travel system trend. In 2001, Peg Perego is releasing their first travel systems.

WHAT'S COOL: Great convenience–you can take the infant car seat out of the car and then snap it into the stroller frame. Voila! Instant baby carriage, complete with canopy and basket. Later, you can use the stroller as, well, just a stroller.

WHAT'S NOT: The strollers are often junk–especially those by mass market makers Graco, Evenflo and Century. Quality problems plague this category, as does something we call "feature bloat." Popular travel systems from Evenflo and Graco, for example, are so loaded with features that they tip the scales at nearly 30 pounds! The result: many parents abandon their travel system strollers for lighter weight models after baby outgrows their infant seat. And considering these puppies can cost $150 to $250 (some even more), that's a big investment for such short use. On the plus side, quality stroller makers Peg Perego, Maclaren and Combi have jumped into the travel system market, albeit with different solutions (see reviews later in this chapter).

Safe & Sound

Next to walkers, the most dangerous juvenile product on the market today is strollers. That's according to the U.S. Consumer Product Safety Commission, which estimates that over 12,000 injuries a year occur from improper use or defects. The problems? Babies can slide out of the stroller (falling to the ground) and small parts can be a choking hazard. Seat belts have broken in some models, while other babies are injured when a stroller's brakes fail on a slope. Serious mishaps with strollers involved entanglements and entrapments (where an unrestrained baby slides down and gets caught in a leg opening). Here are some safety tips:

1 **NEVER HANG BAGS FROM THE STROLLER HANDLE**–it's a tipping hazard.

2 **DON'T LEAVE YOUR BABY ASLEEP UNATTENDED IN A STROLLER.** Many injuries happen when infants who are lying

down in a stroller roll or creep and then manage to get their head stuck in the stroller's leg openings. Be safe: take a sleeping baby out of a stroller and move them to a crib or bassinet.

3 **THE BRAKES SHOULDN'T BE TRUSTED.** The best stroller models have brakes on two wheels; cheaper ones just have one wheel that brakes. Even with the best brakes, don't leave the stroller unattended on an incline.

4 **FOLLOW THE WEIGHT LIMITS.** Most strollers shouldn't be used for children over 35 pounds.

5 **CHECK FOR THE JPMA CERTIFICATION.** The JPMA (the Juvenile Products Manufacturers Association) has a pretty good safety certification program. They require that strollers must have a locking device to prevent accidental folding and meet other safety standards, such as those for brakes. You can contact the JPMA for a list of certified strollers at (856) 231-8500 or www.jpma.org.

6 **JOGGING STROLLERS ARE BEST FOR BABIES OVER ONE YEAR OF AGE.** Yes, some stroller makers tout their joggers for babies as young as six weeks (or six months) of age. But we think the neck muscles of such small infants can't take the shocks of jogging or walking on rough paths (or going over curbs). Ask your pediatrician if you need more advice on when it is safe to use a jogger.

Recalls: Where to Find Information

The U.S. Consumer Product Safety Commission has a toll-free hotline at (800) 638-2772 (web: www.cpsc.gov) for the latest recall information on strollers and other juvenile products. It's easy to use–the hotline is a series of recorded voice mail messages that you access by following the prompts. The same info is online. You can also report any potential hazard you've discovered or an injury to your child caused by a product. If you prefer, you can write to the US Consumer Products Safety Commission, Washington, D.C. 20207.

Smart Shopper Tips

Smart Shopper Tip #1

Give it a Test Drive

"My friend was thinking of buying a stroller online, sight unseen. Should you really buy a stroller without trying it first?"

Always try before you buy. Most stores have at least one stroller set up as a floor model. Give it a whirl, practice folding it up, and check the steering. Once you've tried it out, shop for price through 'net or mail-order sources. Ask retailers if they will meet or beat prices quoted to you on-line (many quietly do so). What if you live in Kansas and the nearest dealer for a stroller you want is in, say, Texas? Then you may have no choice but to buy sight unseen—but just make sure the web site or catalog has a good return policy.

Smart Shopper Tip #2

What Features are Really Important?

"Let's cut through the clutter here. Do I really need a stroller that has deluxe shock absorbers and four-wheel drive? What features are really important?"

Walk into any baby store and you'll encounter a blizzard of strollers. Do you want a stroller with a reversible handle? Full boot and retractable canopy? What the heck is a boot, anyway? Here's a look at the features in the stroller market today:

Features for baby:

◆ *Reclining seat.* Since babies less than six months of age sleep most of the time and can't hold their heads up, strollers that have reclining seats are a plus. Yet, how much each stroller reclines varies by model. Some have full reclines, a few recline part of the way (120 degrees) and some don't recline at all.

◆ *Front (or napper) bar.* As a safety precaution, many strollers have a front bar (also called a napper bar) that keeps baby secure (though you should always use the stroller's safety harness). Better strollers have a bar that's padded and removable. Why removable? Later, when your baby gets to toddlerhood, you may need to remove the bar to make it easier for the older child to access the stroller.

◆ *Seat padding.* You'll find every possible padding option out there, from bare-bones models with a single piece of fabric to strollers with deluxe-quilted padding made from fine fabrics hand woven by monks in Luxembourg. (Okay, just kidding—the monks actually live in Switzerland). For seating, some strollers have cardboard platforms (these can be uncomfortable for long rides) and other models have fabric that isn't removable or machine washable (see below for more on this).

◆ *Shock absorbers or suspension systems.* Yes, a few strollers do have wheels equipped with shock absorbers for a smoother ride. We're unsure how effective this feature really is—it's not like you could wheel baby over potholes without waking her up. On the other hand, if you live in a neighborhood with uneven or rough sidewalks, they might be worth a look.

◆ ***Wheels.*** In reality, how smooth a stroller rides is more related to the type of wheels. The general rule: the more the better. Strollers with double wheels on each leg ride smoother than single wheels. Most strollers have plastic wheels. In recent years, some stroller makers have rolled out models with "pneumatic" or inflated wheels. These offer a smoother ride.

◆ ***Weather protection.*** Yes you can buy a stroller that's outfitted for battle with a winter in New England, for example. The options include retractable hoods/canopies and "boots" (which protect a child's feet) to block out wind, rain or cold. Fabrics play a role here too—some strollers feature quilted hoods to keep baby warm and others claim they are water repellent. While a boot is an option some may not need, hoods/canopies are rather important, even if just to keep the sun out of baby's eyes. Some strollers just have a canopy (or "sunshade") that partially covers baby, while other models have a full hood that can completely cover the stroller. Look for canopies that have lots of adjustments (to block a setting sun) and have "peak-a-boo" windows that let you see baby even when closed.

Features for parents:

◆ ***Storage baskets.*** Many strollers have deep, under-seat baskets for storage of coats, purses, bags, etc. Yet, the amount of storage can vary sharply from model to model. Inexpensive umbrella strollers may have no basket at all, while other models have tiny baskets. American-made strollers (Graco, etc.) typically have the most storage; other stroller makers have been playing catch-up in the basket game. Japanese-made Combi, for example, has added new models with big storage baskets. One tip: it's not just the size of the storage basket but the access to it that counts. Some strollers have big baskets but are practically inaccessible, tucked under strollers or blocked by a support bar.

◆ ***Removable seat cushion for washing.*** Let's be honest: strollers can get icky real fast. Crushed-in cookies, spilt juice and the usual grime can make a stroller a mobile dirt-fest. Some strollers have removable seat cushions that are machine washable—other models let you remove *all* of the fabric for a washing. Watch out for those models with non-removable fabric/seat cushions—while you can clean these strollers in one of those manual car washes (with a high-pressure nozzle), it's definitely a hassle (especially in the winter).

◆ ***Lockable wheels.*** Some strollers have front wheels that can be locked in a forward position—this enables you to more quickly push the stroller in a straight line.

◆ ***Wheel size.*** You'll see just about every conceivable size wheel out there on strollers today. As you might guess, the smaller wheels are good for maneuverability, but larger wheels handle rough sidewalks (or gravel paths) much better.

◆ ***Handle.*** This is an important area to consider—a few strollers feature a "reversible" handle. Why would you want that? By reversing the handle, you can push the stroller while the baby faces you (better for small infants). Later, you can reverse the handle so an older child can look out while being pushed from behind. Another important factor: consider the handle *height*. Some handles have adjustable heights to better accommodate taller parents (more on this later). A few stroller makers offer "one-touch fold" handles. Hit a button on the stroller and it can be folded up with one motion. Later in this chapter, we'll have a box that lists strollers with height-adjustable handles and one-touch folds.

◆ ***Compact fold.*** Some strollers fold compactly and can fit in a narrow trunk or airline overhead cabin, which is great if you plan to do much traveling. Not only should you consider how compactly a stroller folds, but also how it folds in general. The best strollers fold with just one or two quick motions; others require you to hit 17 levers and latches.

◆ ***Durability.*** Should you go for a lower-price stroller or a fancier European brand? Let's be honest: the lower-priced strollers (say, under $100) have nowhere near the durability of the models that cost $200 to $400. Levers that break, reclining seats which stop reclining and other glitches can make you hate a cheap stroller mighty quick. Yet, some parents don't need a stroller that will make it through the next world war. If all you do is a couple of quick trips to the mall every week or so, then a less expensive stroller will probably be fine. Yet, if you plan to use the stroller for more than one child, live in a tough urban environment with rough sidewalks, or plan extensive outdoor adventures with baby, then invest in a better stroller. Later in this chapter, we'll go over specific models and give you brand recommendations for certain lifestyles.

◆ ***Overall weight.*** Yes, it's a dilemma: the more feature-laden the stroller, the more it weighs. And, the super lightweight strollers are often quite expensive. Yet it doesn't take lugging a 30-pound stroller in and out of a car trunk more than a few times to justify the expense of a lighter-weight design. Carefully consider a stroller's weight before purchase. Some parents end up with two strollers—a lightweight/umbrella-type stroller for quick trips (or air travel) and then a more feature-intensive model for extensive outdoor outings.

One factor to consider with weight: steel vs. aluminum frames. Steel is heavier than aluminum, but some parents prefer steel because it gives the stroller a stiffer feel. Along the same lines, sometimes we get complaints from parents who own aluminum strollers because they feel the stroller is too "wobbly"—while it's lightweight, one of aluminum's disadvantages is its flexibility. One tip for dealing with a wobbly stroller: lock the front wheels so you can push the stroller in a straight line. That helps to smooth the ride.

Smart Shopper Tip #3

The Cadillac El Dorado or Ford Escort Dilemma

"This is nuts! I see cheap umbrella strollers that sell for $30 on one hand and then fancy designer brands for $300 on the other. Do I really need to spend a fortune on a stroller?"

Whether you drive a Cadillac El Dorado or Ford Escort, you'll still get to your destination. And that fact pretty much applies to strollers too—most function well enough to get you and baby from point A to point B.

So, should you buy the cheapest stroller you can find? Well, no. There *is* a significant difference in quality between a cheap $30 umbrella stroller and a name brand that costs $100, $200 or more. Unless you want the endless headaches of a cheap stroller (wheels that break, parts that fall off), it's important to invest in a stroller that will make it through the long haul.

The real question is: do you need a fancy stroller loaded with features or will a simple model do? To answer that, you need to consider *how* you will use the stroller. Do you live in the suburbs and just need the stroller once a week for a quick spin at the mall? Or do you live in an urban environment where a stroller is your primary vehicle, taking all the abuse that a big city can dish out? Climate plays another factor—in the Northeast, strollers have to be winterized to handle the cold and snow. Meanwhile, in Southern California, full canopies are helpful for shading baby's eyes from late afternoon sunshine.

Figuring out how different stroller options fit your lifestyle/climate is the key to stroller happiness. Later in this chapter, we'll recommend several specific strollers for certain lifestyles and climates.

One final note: quality, name-brand strollers actually have resale value. You can sell that $300 stroller on eBay, at a second-hand store, or via the classifieds and recoup some of your investment. The better the brand name (Peg Perego, Combi, Aprica, Maclaren, Emmaljunga), the more the resale value. Unfortunately, the cheap brands like Graco, Century, Evenflo and Kolcraft are worth little or nothing on the second-hand market. Take a quick look at eBay's stroller section to see what we mean.

Smart Shopper Tip #4

Too tall for their own good

"I love our stroller, but my husband hates it. He's six feet tall and

has to stoop over to push it. Even worse, when he walks, he hits the back of the stroller with his feet."

Strollers are made for women of average height. What's that? About 5'6". If you (or your spouse) are taller than that, you'll find certain stroller models will be a pain to use.

This is probably one of the biggest complaints we get from parents about strollers. Unfortunately, just a few stroller models have height-adjustment handles that let a six-foot tall person comfortably push a stroller without stooping over or hitting the back of the stroller with his feet. (See box later in this section for such models). One smart shopping tip: if you have a tall spouse, make sure you take him or her stroller shopping with you. Checking out handle heights in person is the only way to avoid this problem.

Wastes of Money

1 **GIVE THE "BOOT" THE BOOT.** Some expensive strollers offer a "boot" or apron that fits over the baby's feet. This padded cover is supposed to keep the baby's feet dry and warm when it rains or snows. But how many parents walk their baby in the rain or snow anyway? We say save the $20 to $60 extra cost and buy a blanket instead.

2 **SILLY ACCESSORIES.** Entrepreneurs have worked overtime to invent all kinds of silly accessories that you "must have" for your stroller. We've seen stroller "snack trays" ($15) for babies who like to eat on the run. Another company made a clip-on bug repellent which allegedly used sound waves to scare away insects. Yet another money-waster: extra seat cushions or head supports for infants made in your stroller's matching fabric. You can find these same items in solid colors at discount stores for 40% less.

One accessory we do recommend is a toy bar (about $10 to $20), which attaches to the stroller. Why is this a good buy? If toys are not attached, your baby will probably punt them out the stroller. Another affordable idea: Rinky Links ($9, in most chain stores) enable you to snap toys to plastic rings that attach to the stroller. We also like Kelgar's Stroll'r Hold'r cup holder ($7, call 972-250-3838 or web: www.kelgar.com).

What about stroller handle extensions? If you find yourself kicking the back of the stroller as you walk, you might want to invest in one of these $23 devices (sold in catalogs like One Step Ahead 800-274-8440). They add up to 8" in height to your stroller handle.

Money-Saving Tips

1 **CHECK OUT THE DISCOUNTERS.** As we discussed earlier, the web is a great source for stroller bargains. But don't forget stores like Babies R Us and Baby Depot. They sell quality brands (including Peg Perego) and have frequent specials.

2 **WHY NOT A BASIC UMBRELLA STROLLER?** If you only plan to use a stroller on infrequent trips to the mall, then a plain umbrella stroller for $30 to $40 will suffice. One caveat: make sure you get one that is JPMA certified (see above section for details). Some cheap umbrella strollers have been involved in safety recalls.

3 **CONSIDER THE ALTERNATIVES TO BULKY (AND EXPENSIVE) TRAVEL SYSTEMS.** Among the best bets: the Snap N Go (also called Kar Seat Karriage) from Baby Trend (800) 328-7363 or (909) 902-5568 (web: www.babytrend.com). You pop just about any name-brand infant seat carrier into the Snap N Go stroller frame ($20 to $60, depending on which version) and voila! Instant travel system at half the price. Another idea: Combi has the "Perfect Match" feature that lets you attach an infant car seat to their popular line of strollers (see review later in this chapter). Peg Perego is also rolling out an infant seat attachment bar for several of their models. Finally, consider a front carrier or back-pack instead of a bulky stroller. Later in this section, we'll discuss our picks for carriers and back-packs.

4 **CHECK FOR SALES.** We're always amazed by the number of sales on strollers. We've seen frequent sales at the Burlington Coat Factory's Baby Depot, with good mark-downs on Aprica and Peg Perego strollers, to name a few. And just the other week we received a coupon booklet from Toys R Us that featured a $10 off coupon on any Graco stroller over $70. That's nearly a 15% savings. Another reason strollers go on sale: the manufacturers are constantly coming out with new models and have to clear out the old. Which leads us to the next tip.

5 **LOOK FOR LAST YEAR'S MODELS.** Every year, manufacturers roll out new models. In some cases, they add features; other times, they just change the fabric. What do they do with last year's stock? They discontinue it–and then it's sale time. You'll see these models on sale for as much as 50% off in stores and on the web. And it's not like stroller fabric fashion varies much from year to year–is there really much difference between "navy pin dot" and "navy

with a raspberry diamond"? We say go for last year's fabric and save a bundle.

6 **SCOPE OUT FACTORY SECONDS.** Believe it or not, some stroller manufacturers sell "factory seconds" at good discounts–these "cosmetically imperfect" models might have a few blemishes, but are otherwise fine. An example: one reader told us Combi occasionally has "showroom models" that are offered to the public at good discounts on their web site. She found a factory second for just $99–that's much less than the $250 retail price. Call Combi at (800) 992-6624 or (708) 350-0101 for more info (web: www.combi-intl.com). Another reader told us Baby Jogger sells factory seconds at Boolacoc.com. This site sells re-conditioned Baby Joggers used in amusement parks. Sample price: a Baby Jogger Twinkle (12" wheel) for $79.

7 **DON'T FALL VICTIM TO STROLLER OVERKILL.** Seriously evaluate how you'll use the stroller and don't over buy. If a Toyota Camry will do, why buy a Lexus? You don't really need an all-terrain stroller or full-feature pram for mall trips. Flashy strollers can be status symbols for some parents–try to avoid "stroller envy" if at all possible.

8 **SELL YOUR STROLLER TO RECOUP YOUR INVESTMENT.** When you're done with the stroller, consign your stroller in a second-store or sell it in the classifieds. You'd be surprised how much it can fetch. The best brands for resale are, not surprisingly, the better names we recommend in this chapter (Perego, Combi, Aprica, Maclaren).

The Name Game: Reviews of Selected Manufacturers

Here's a wrap-up of many of the stroller brands on the market today. We evaluated strollers based on hands-on inspections, interviews with recent parents, and conversations with juvenile product retailers. For us, the most important attributes for strollers were safety, convenience and durability. Of course, price to value (as reflected in the number of features) was an important factor as well.

Just as we mentioned in the previous chapter, the ratings in this section apply to the ENTIRE line of a company's strollers. No, we don't assign ratings to individual strollers, but we will comment on what we think are a company's best models. Following this section, we will give you several "lifestyle recommendations"–specific models of strollers to fit different parent lifestyles.

The prices quoted here are street prices–that is prices we saw in stores or on the 'net. These are the lowest actual prices we saw quoted on web sites. In some cases, we used manufacturer's estimated retail prices. Yet, prices can fluctuate widely: in areas with heavy competition among stores (like the Northeast or West Coast), prices are lower. In more isolated communities, however, you may find prices in stores to be higher than what's quoted here.

The Ratings

A EXCELLENT–*our top pick!*
B GOOD– *above average quality, prices, and creativity.*
C FAIR–*could stand some improvement.*
D POOR–*yuck! could stand some major improvement.*

Aprica *400 W. Artesia Blvd., Compton, CA 90004. For a dealer near you, call (310) 639-6387 or (201) 883-9800 (web: www.apricausa. com).* Aprica (pronounced Ah-pree-cah) is one of two Japanese-made stroller brands sold in the U.S. (Combi is the other). Readers of the past edition of this book will probably notice our review of Aprica hasn't changed much (if at all) from last year . . . or the year before that–that's because Aprica's strollers haven't changed much either. Why the company seems stuck in neutral is a mystery; Aprica hasn't released new models in two years and fired their North American sales manager in 1998. As we searched for newsworthy items to update this review, all we could find was the addition of a "Five Layered Air Cushion" to Aprica's Prestige line (reviewed below). Aprica claims this new cushion (which debuted in early 1999) absorbs bumps and shocks better than their regular cushion. Besides that (and a few new "Italian-inspired" fabric patterns), there ain't much new here. Yes, Aprica plans to debut one new model in 2001 (the Colo-Pa, reviewed below). And most Aprica strollers still have such neat-o features as height adjustable handles and "one-touch" open/close handles which fold (or unfold) the stroller, but we're disappointed that there's been so little innovation in the last few years.

The models. Aprica divides its line into two categories: Prestige (pricey, lightweight aluminum frame strollers) and Royale (less expensive, heavier steel-frame strollers). In the Prestige line, you can get a G-Impact cushion (that five-layered air cushion mentioned above) as an additional option. The top-of-the line "Windsor Prestige" model (also known as the Intreccio) features the one-touch open/close, plush padding, triple-padded head support, zip-off boot and pop-up head protection. This model (which is based on the old Prima stroller) also has a height adjustable handle and weighs just 13.5 pounds. Price: $370. If you want an even lighter-weight stroller that folds compactly, consider the "Super Zap," which weighs a mere ten lbs. Although it doesn't have as many features as the Windsor Elite, the Super Zap does have a fully reclining seat, one-touch fold, and a height-adjustable handle. A basic Super Zap runs $300, while a Super Zap with a full-length boot is $340. A Super Zap with the G-impact cushion is $365. Two other Prestige models include the Super Mini ($500, which is the same as the Super Zap but includes a reversible handle) and the Flash ($300, a seven-pound stroller with one-touch open/close).

Realizing those prices are hard to swallow, Aprica in 1997 launched a lower-price line (Royale) made with heavier steel frames. Of course, "heavy" is a relative term—many of these strollers are still much lighter than the competition. Basically, the Royale models are based on similar Prestige strollers—the Quantum Royale ($230, 16 lbs.) is similar to the Windsor Elite, the Calais Royale LX ($195 to $225, 14 lbs.) is the same as the Super Zap (but no height-adjustable handle or boot), and the Sprint Royale ($189, 9 lbs.) is similar to the Flash. The entry-level umbrella stroller "Escort" also weighs 9 lbs. but doesn't have a reclining seat or safety bar. It retails for $129. We should also point out that Aprica makes the only tandem stroller (Prestige Embrace) on the market with a reversible handle. It runs about $400.

New in the past year, Aprica released the Colo-Pa, a seven pound stroller with one-handle close, full recline and detachable front bar. It sells for $350.

Our view. Let's be honest: these are feature-packed strollers, but the prices are way too high. The Royale line is a step in the right direction, but Aprica remains a brand that few can afford. As for Aprica's quality and durability, we've received scattered complaints about the brand in recent years—folks complain about the skimpy baskets, shaky suspensions, somewhat complicated folding mechanism (and in one case), a hood that broke off a stroller. At this price level, you'd expect the stroller to be darn near perfect, so Aprica is a disappointment overall. ***Rating: B***

Baby Trend *For a dealer near you, call (800) 328-7363, (909) 902-5568, Web: www.babytrend.com.* Baby Trend's biggest selling stroller isn't really a stroller at all—it's a stroller *frame*. Here's an overview of the line:

The Models. The Snap N Go is such a simple concept it's amazing someone else didn't think of this years ago—basically it's a stroller frame that lets you snap in most major-brand infant car seats. Presto! Instant travel system at a fraction of the price. The original Snap N Go was just a frame and wheels for $30. In the last few years, Baby Trend has improved the line by adding new models: The Snap N Go Lite ($40) sits higher than the original model and the Snap N Go LX ($50 to $60) adds a big basket.

One warning about the Snap N Go: using it may void your infant car seat warranty in case something goes wrong with the seat. Makers of infant seats understandably want you to buy their pricey travel systems, so they aren't wild about folks who use the affordable Snap N Go. One mom found this out when her infant seat broke when removing it from the Snap N Go. The seat's maker disclaimed any warranty. Admittedly, that's a rather rare situation, but we thought you should know.

Also be aware that the Snap N Go doesn't work with ALL infant car seats. Consult Baby Trend's web site for a current list.

Of course, Baby Trend makes more than just the Snap N Go. Their regular stroller line isn't that innovative . . . basically the same features and prices you'd find with other brands like Graco.

Baby Trend's tandem strollers, however, are more interesting—the Sit N Stand LX ($159 to $179) is a concept imported from England. This "pushcart" is a regular stroller (with reclining seat, canopy and basket) that has a place for an older child to stand (or sit in a jump seat) in back. The latest model of this stroller (the LX3, $149 to $179) can also accommodate an infant car seat.

We were also impressed with the functionality of Baby Trend's tandem (front/back) double strollers. The Caravan Lite LX ($199-249) lets you attach one or two infant car seats and gets generally good marks from parents for its features and ease of use.

Baby Trend is a big player in the jogging stroller market (we'll discuss these models later in this chapter in the "Exercise This" section). We should also note that Baby Trend markets their products under the name "Swan" for specialty stores. Basically, these are the same products/models as Baby Trend makes, albeit with a few cosmetic differences (fabric color, etc.).

Our View. We're not sure what to make of Baby Trend—parents seems to love some of their products (particularly the Snap N Go) and loathe others (basically, most of their other strollers). Yes, the jogging strollers get good marks but Baby Trend has been dogged by numerous quality problems when it comes to their tandems and more expensive models. Parents say parts break, wheels fall off and worse—"bad engineering" was how one parent put it when talking about her tandem stroller. So, it's hard to assign a rating. If we were just looking at the Snap N Go or the joggers, we'd give them an A. Yet, the other models would barely earn a C. So, we'll compromise. ***Rating: B-***

Carter's These strollers are made by Kolcraft; see their review at the end of this section in "Other Brands."

Century *9600 Valley View Rd., Macedonia, OH 44056. For a dealer near you, call (216) 468-2000. Web:* www.centuryproducts.com Century shook up the stroller world when they introduced the "4-in-1" system a few years ago. By combining a Century infant car seat

Strollers with height-adustable handles, one-touch folds

Which strollers have height adjustable handles that make life easier for tall folks (basically, anyone over 5'8"?) And which strollers have one-touch folds that make putting the stroller away easier? Here is a list of popular models with such features:

◆ ***Aprica*** models with height adjustable handles: Super Mini Prestige, Super Zap, Flash Prestige, Windsor Prestige, Embrace and Quantum Royale. Aprica models with one touch fold: Super Mini Prestige, Super Zap, Flash Prestige, Windsor Prestige, Sprint Royale, Quantum Royale, Calais Royale.

◆ ***Century's*** Lifestyle strollers feature a one hand fold system.

◆ ***Combi's*** Sprit and Legacy (now discontinued) have height adjustable handles, as does the Convenience stroller line. Savvy Z and Ultra Savvy now have one touch folds.

◆ ***Evenflo.*** All travel systems have one touch fold feature. No height adjustable handles though.

◆ ***Graco***. The CitiSport and MetroLite have one-touch fold. The MetroLite also has a height adjustable handle. Coach rider has one-touch fold, as does the Citi-Sport.

◆ ***Maclaren.*** All models work well for tall parents.

◆ ***Regalo.*** The Evolution has one-touch fold.

◆ ***Simo.*** The Bertini has a height adjustable handle.

◆ ***Perego.*** The Venezia, Milano and Pliko families have height adjustable handles.

Bottom line: while the above models have height adjustable handles, tall parents tell us the best brand is Maclaren.

and a stroller, Century essentially created an affordable carriage system for the masses. Since then, they've refined the concept and introduced several spin-offs, discussed below.

In 1998, Century was bought by Graco's parent, Rubbermaid, which has since merged the two companies. Despite the common ownership, however, the brands are still being marketed separately—hence Century's stroller offerings are different (albeit slightly) from Graco's.

The models. In the past year, Century has redesigned their travel systems and strollers, dubbing the new lines "Travel Solutions" and "Lifestyles." The Travel Solutions travel systems include a basic stroller that enables you to attach a Century infant seat in either a rear or forward facing position. You also get a parent cup holder with storage compartment, extended canopy with peek-a-boo window and three-position reclining seat. As with all Century strollers, you also get an oversized storage basket.

The Travel Solutions travel system line has two models: the Limited and the Take 2. The Travel Solutions Limited ($150) pairs Century's excellent Smart Fit 22 infant car seat with the aforementioned stroller. The Take 2 ($200) is Century's first tandem travel system. It features a stroller with a front attachment for an infant car seat (Century Smart Fit 22), height adjustable handle and toddler jump-seat in back (where a toddler can sit or stand).

The new "Lifestyles" systems feature strollers with several upgrades: five-point harness restraints, "AllWays" handles with one-handed steering and a four position reclined seat (to 150 degrees). The Lifestyles strollers also have a "WonderFold natural fold system" which Century says is easier to use than competitors' strollers.

The Lifestyle travel systems come in four flavors: the "Calypso" ($150) pairs a basic Lifestyle stroller with the Century Celestia infant seat (see the previous chapter for reviews of Century's infant seats). The "Sedona" ($170) features the Celestia seat and an upgraded stroller with bigger wheels. The "Vienna" system ($170) is very similar to the Sedona, except for a few cosmetic differences in the stroller. Finally, the top-of-the-line "Avanta" system includes the Avanta infant seat and "Sedona" stroller for $180.

If you already have a Century infant seat, you can buy just the Calypso or Sedona stroller separately for $90 or $99 respectively.

New for 2002: the Century Solara LX is Century's first stroller that will be able to accept EITHER a Century or Graco car seat. This 23 lbs. steel stroller will feature a full recline and a time/temperature gadget on the handle. Price: $90.

Our view. We've recommended Century's travel systems in previous editions of this book, but this year's line-up is a bit of a disappointment. The best stroller (the Lifestyle) is unfortunately paired with the Celestia or Avanta infant seats, which are way too heavy in our opinion. And the strollers themselves are not light-weight affairs either—most are 21 to 23 pounds *without* an infant seat.

What about quality? While we like Century's Smart Fit Plus 22 infant seat, the travel system strollers are only average in quality. Parents tell us the strollers are too bulky and have other quality problems. While we think the Take 2 tandem is innovative, we find it hard to recommend any other Century travel system this year. ***Rating: B-***

Chicco *4E Easy Street, Bound Brook, NU 08805. For a store near you, call (877) 4-CHICCO or (732) 805-9200. Web: www.chiccousa.com.com* Chicco (pronounced Kee-ko) has a 50-year history as one of Europe's leading juvenile products makers. Along with Peg Perego, Chicco is Europe's biggest producer of strollers and other baby products and toys. In the U.S. and Canada, however, Chicco was always an also-ran while Perego was a top-seller. That changed a couple of years ago when Chicco beefed up their North American efforts. Their first big success was the Chicco Mamma high chair, but the strollers have come quite a ways since we first reviewed them in 1993, Here's an overview:

The models. Chicco offers everything from lightweight umbrella strollers to chrome-frame European-style prams. Like most other strollers makers, however, Chicco has concentrated recently on their lightweight models. A good example: Chicco "Trekking" ($179 to $199), which sort of looks like the Peg Perego "Pliko Matic Sherpa." The Trekking's unique feature: its handles rotates 360 degrees "for (parental) comfort." The all-terrain stroller comes with

Who's who?

A big trend in recent years in strollers are licensed names—stroller makers try to add cache to their strollers by slapping a better-known company's name on it. Here's a run-down of the major licenses and who to look up in this chapter for a review of their parent company:

LICENSE	MADE BY
CARTER'S	KOLCRAFT
EDDIE BAUER	COSCO
JEEP	KOLCRAFT
MARTINELLI	PEG PEREGO
OSHKOSH	EVENFLO
SWAN	BABY TREND

a rainshield that rolls easily into the canopy and features fleece fabric. New for 2001, Chicco will debut the "Fly," a 12 lb. stroller with canopy, five point harness and basket for $99.

Jumping on the jogger craze, Chicco will also sell a Chinese-made jogger called the 3WD Sport for $159. It will feature 16" wheels in back and a 12" wheel up front, aluminum frame, handle brake, and compact fold (the wheels are removable).

In 2002, Chicco will introduce two Chinese-made strollers. The Caddy stroller is a 11 lbs. bare-bones stroller that will sell for $120–it has no basket but does include a rain hood. The Pony is a 15 lb. aluminum stroller with one touch fold, child tray and semi-full recline for $180.

Our view. We knocked Chicco in previous editions of this book for overpriced models that offered few innovative features. Well, the prices are more in line with the market today, even though the line is almost a direct copy of Perego. One major drawback to this line continues to be its limited distribution. Chicco strollers are rarely sold online (despite their own web site's claims to the contrary) and we don't see them much in chain stores like Babies R Us and Baby Depot. As a result, you're likely to only see this line in pricey specialty stores where discounts may be few and far between. As a result, we can't give them a very high rating. ***Rating: C+***

Different versions spark confusion

Here's a common question we get here at the home office: readers go into a chain store like Babies R Us and see a major brand stroller they like. Then, they visit a specialty store and see a *similar* model, but with some cosmetic differences . . . and a higher price tag. What's up with that? Big stroller makers like Graco and Century have to serve two masters–chain stores and specialty retailers. Here's a little trick of the baby biz: stroller makers often take the same basic model of stroller and make various versions for different retailers. Hence, you'll see a Graco stroller with basic fabric in Babies R Us–and then the same model with the name "Graco Baby Classics" and fancier fabric in specialty stores. Peg Perego does the same thing with their Martinelli brand, a specialty store version of their Perego strollers. So is there any real difference besides the fabric color to justify the increase in price? No, not in our research. The strollers are almost exactly the same. Our advice: if you can live with the chain store version look, go for it.

Combi *199 Easy St., Carol Stream, IL 60188. For a dealer near you, call (800) 752-6624, (800) 992-6624, (630) 871-0404; Web: www.combi-intl.com.* Like Aprica, Combi is a Japanese brand that specializes in feature-packed lightweight strollers. And, also like Aprica, Combi divides its line into two parts: expensive aluminum frame models and the more affordable steel frame options. Yet, Combi does have one advantage: its prices are already lower than Aprica and quality is (generally) higher.

The models. Combi's most successful model must be the "Savvy," a terrific 7 lbs. stroller that is among the lightest weight strollers on the market. The compact-folding Savvy comes in three versions: the Travel Savvy ($79, with a steel frame), the Z ($180 to $200, which has removable, washable seat cushions) and the top-of-the-line Ultra Savvy ($269). The Ultra Savvy is the only Savvy with a full-recline seat (hence it can be used with infants). Last year, the Ultra Savvy got a redesigned larger basket, canopy and five-point harness. Parents tell us the Ultra Savvy is a good stroller, although the access to the basket is a bit difficult and the fold is more cumbersome than the Savvy Z.

In the past year, the Savvy Z added an increased handle height, which might help address the common complaint that Combi's are best for short parents. Also new: an entry-level stroller dubbed the "SubV" ($50-$70), a 10 lb. steel stroller with a compact fold, retractable canopy and reclining seat (to 145 degrees). The SubV lacks removable seat cushions and has no napper bar.

So, what's new for Combi in 2002? The company is discontinuing the Savvy Z and replacing it with the Savvy DX ($200). The 12 lb. stroller will have a wider seat base and bigger basket, napper bar (with cup holder) that swings open, a five point harness and extended canopy visor. A stroller storage pack (that fits on the back handle) also comes with the model.

The Ultra Savvy will get a minor make-over for 2002: the stroller will now weigh 13 pounds instead of 10 pounds, thanks to a new extended canopy, snack tray and five-point harness. The price stays the same as last year.

Perhaps the biggest news for Combi last year was their return to the twin stroller market–the new Twin Savvy is a side-by-side model that weighs a mere 15 pounds and sports a removable napper bar, machine washable cushions, a 165-degree reclining seat, a separate canopy and a stroller pack with two insulated bottle holders. At 30" wide, this side by side should fit through most doors. The price is a bit steep, however: about $300 to $320.

As for single strollers, Combi does have a lower-price "Convenience" line of strollers. The 6100 (14 lbs., $79 to $89) is a steel frame model similar to the Travel Savvy, but has a bigger storage basket and larger wheels. The 6510 (15 lbs., $85) is a steel frame stroller with three-position recline, large basket, front snack tray and height adjustable handle. The 6610 (14 lbs., $119) is similar to the 6500, but has an aluminum frame and fabric upgrades.

The most exciting news from Combi last year was the debut of their "Perfect Match Attachment System." Now you can attach an infant car seat (not included) to three of Combi's strollers. The system includes a bar (you swap for the front napper bar) that lets you attach a Century, Graco or Evenflo infant car seat (at press time, it appears Cosco and Kolcraft seats would not be compatible with the system). You'll find the Perfect Match system on the 6500 series, 6600 series and Ultra Savvy models.

In 2002, Combi will debut a new Perfect Match stroller: the 6630. This model will feature a larger "acoustic" canopy, bigger wheels, four wheel suspension and a parent tray, plus five-point harness. Price: $120.

We think the Perfect Match system is an excellent idea–now you can avoid those bulky, poorly-made strollers that come with other company's "travel systems." Just buy the infant seat you want and combine it with a high quality Combi stroller–poof! Instant travel system, at no extra cost compared to other systems. We hope Combi extends this feature to all their stroller models soon.

Finally, we should mention that Combi has decided to discontinue its high-end carriage strollers (the Legacy and Spirit).

Our view. Combi is one of our favorite strollers; the Savvy Z is an all-time bestseller and for good reasons. The light weight is a great plus for a suburban lifestyle (that is, hauling in and out of a trunk). Combi's quality and durability are excellent–even for their lower-price models. Yes, some models have skimpy baskets but overall we think this one of the best stroller brands out there for the dollar. And we have to give Combi kudos for an excellent web site that has detailed info on their models and even an outlet store with bargains on discontinued strollers. ***Rating A***

Cosco *2525 State St., Columbus, IN 47201. Call (812) 372-0141 for a dealer near you (or 514-323-5701 for a dealer in Canada;. Web: www.coscoinc.com* Long an also-ran in the U.S. stroller market, Cosco (owned by Canadian conglomerate Dorel) has recently introduced several new stroller models that are both innovative and affordable. All these models are built in a Chinese factory that is part-owned by Combi, which might explain the cutting-edge design (each model has a contoured arc frame) and up-to-date fashion fabrics (navy blue or hunter green pin dots). Cosco strollers are mostly found at discount stores like Wal-Mart. Here's an overview:

The models. Like most mass-market stroller makers, Cosco's emphasis in recent years has been their travel systems. For 2001, Cosco will debut three new models, from the entry-level Pioneer ($140 to $150) to the more deluxe Toscana ($180), which has inflated wheels. But Cosco's travel systems are hobbled by their infant seats, which didn't impress us when compared with Graco or Century.

As for the strollers themselves, Cosco's flagship model is the "Rock N Roller" stroller which rocks *or* glides to soothe a fussy baby—pretty neat. Cosco makes this stroller in several versions, most of which are $100 to $130.

In the past year, Cosco debuted the "Vanguard," a $100 stroller with a car seat attachment bar (no car seat, though). You get a full reclining seat, parent tray, adjustable handle and one-hand fold. The double basket on this model is also innovative.

Also new: Cosco's first jogging stroller (Two Ways Jogger, $150) features a reversible seat (which is a first in the jogger market). The telescoping handle is quite cool, as is the infant seat attachment system (another first). The steel frame for this model is a bit heavy, but the five-point harness is nice as are the full size (16") rear wheels.

Cosco's double stroller (the Two Ways Tandem, with a front/back seat configuration) has a reversible front seat, so the children can face one another. And the price is hard to beat at $120 to $140, making this one of the lowest price tandem strollers out there.

Of course, this just scratches the surface of Cosco's stroller models. The company makes a dozen different strollers, including the Grand Endeavor ($85) and Phoenix ($90), both of which have a one-hand close. The Phoenix is sort of Cosco's Combi Savvy knock-off, while the Endeavor looks a bit like Graco's LiteRider stroller.

So, what's new here for 2002? Cosco will debut a Safety 1st Travel System with the Designer 22 five-point car seat for $170 this year. The stroller with have a one-touch fold feature, full recline and thermos cooler. Another new stroller for 2002: a Safety 1st jogger for $180 that features a parent tray, two position telescoping handle, odometer and quick release wheels. Among the cooler features of this jogger: baby can ride either forward OR rear facing.

We should note that Cosco makes the Eddie Bauer stroller line as well. Just as we discussed in the previous chapter, the Eddie Bauer strollers and travel systems are identical to Cosco's regular models. The only difference is fabric color and a higher price tag (some 20% to 30% more).

Our view. We have to give it to Cosco—unlike other juvenile product giants who churn out look-alike products year after year, this company is really trying to do something innovative. Their new strollers have piqued our curiosity; but, will they do the same for parents? The early verdict is NO. The limited feedback we received on the Rock N Roller travel system has not been positive–one mom knocked the product for being too heavy and too big when folded. And she was just getting warmed up: we also heard complaints that the model was hard to fold, the canopy falls off and the infant seat doesn't fit into shopping carts. Cosco also suffered a safety recall on the Two Ways Tandem in 1999, when the folding mechanism on the stroller broke during use, causing the strollers to suddenly collapse. Cosco received 250 reports of the strollers collapsing, causing over 200 injuries. So, we just can't give a thumbs-up to this brand. The features are innovative, but the quality is lacking and the safety track record of Cosco is troubling. ***Rating: C-***

Eddie Bauer These strollers and travel systems are made by Cosco. See the above review for more info.

Emmaljunga *Web: www.emmaljunga.com* This Swedish stroller brand withdrew from the U.S. market in 2001; as of this writing, they have no distribution in the U.S. or Canada. You might still see their strollers on eBay and at second-hand stores, but since they are no longer on the market we'll skip them for review in this section.

Evenflo *1801 Commerce Dr., Piqua, OH 45356. For a dealer near you, call (800) 233-5921 or (937) 415-3300. In Canada, PO Box 1598, Brantford, Ontario, N3T 5V7. (519) 756-0210; Web: www.evenflo.com* Evenflo's claim to fame, stroller-wise, is their one-handed steering. All of Evenflo's strollers and travel systems have this feature. Here is a breakdown:

The models. Evenflo offers travel systems for both their entry-level Discovery infant seat or the more deluxe On My Way infant seat. Whatever version you get, the stroller is basically the same–one touch brake, one hand fold, large basket, parent "console" with cup holder and a reclining seat.

The Discovery Travel systems come in two versions: the Discovery Travel System (with three point harnesses in both the infant seat and stroller) and the Discovery Deluxe V Travel System (five-point harnesses in both infant seat and stroller). Both sell for about $160.

The Easy Comfort travel systems include the On My Way car seat and come in four versions: The basic Easy Comfort Deluxe includes the On My Way seat and the same stroller as found in the Discovery travel systems ($160). The Easy Comfort Advantage V ($179) includes the On My Way Position Right V infant seat and a stroller with a few upgrades like a two-piece chest clip. The Ultra V ($189) is basically the same thing with more padding. The top of the line Comfort Dimensions Travel System ($229) includes even more padding ("Comfort Touch" pads for the infant seat and stroller that provide head support) and storage basket that slides out for easier access.

You can buy the Easy Comfort Plus Stroller separately for $120 or so. There is also a version of the Easy Comfort (called the Prodigy) with bigger wheels and a beefed up suspension.

Breaking from their line of feature-laden carriage strollers, Evenflo introduced the Light & Easy stroller last year, which is Evenflo's knock-off of Combi's Savvy. The Light & Easy is an aluminum frame stroller (9.5 lbs.) with one-hand, compact fold for $90.

As with infant seats, Evenflo also makes Osh Kosh versions of their strollers and travel systems—these have the exact same features, just denim fabric and a different name. And the price is about $20 higher.

So, what's on tap for Evenflo in 2002? Evenflo is replacing their travel systems with the new Comfort Dimensions this year. This system pairs the Cozy Carry infant seat (described in the car seat section) with a 22 lb. stroller that includes a giant slide-out basket with pockets inside and a parent console with privacy lid. The stroller also has a Comfort Glide wheel system with suspension for a smoother ride. The travel system comes in three versions: the Plus (basic model) for $159, the Premier (added storage pockets in the basket) for $179 or the Ultra (more plush padding) for $199. The stroller is sold separately for $79.

Evenflo will also debut another travel system in 2002: the Featherlight. This system will pair the Cozy Carry with a lightweight stroller (13 pounds) that will feature one-hand folding, a large storage basket, parent console with cup holders and front wheel suspension. The Featherlight comes in two versions: the Plus $149 and the Premier (which adds full suspension and a removable head support). The stroller is sold separately for $79 (Plus) or $99 (Premier).

The final stroller in Evenflo's 2002 line-up is the InSight, a 20lb. stroller designed to fit infants through toddlers (something unique in the market). The higher seat will enable older children to use the stroller longer; the stroller also has a parent console with cup holders, one-hand fold feature, height adjustable handle and larger wheels. The Insight holds all Evenflo infant seats, as well as those by Graco, Cosco and Century. The InSight will come three versions: basic Plus $59, a Premier model (adding pockets on the sides and rear of the basket) for $69 and Ultra. The Ultra will have a aluminum frame (which subtracts 2-3 pounds off the Plus or Premier versions) and includes a zippered cargo bag on the side of the basket as long as removable diaper pouch on the seat back. The InSight Ultra will sell for $89.

Our View. Can you say "feature bloat"? Evenflo is perhaps the worst offender when it comes to the weight game—these strollers often weigh in 24 pounds empty! Add an infant seat and you've got 40 to 45 pounds even before you've added a baby.

Evenflo's previous travel systems were hampered by quality problems according to complaints from our readers. We received numerous gripes about the wheels on Evenflo strollers, which seemed to get stuck when the stroller was loaded with a baby over 20 pounds. And we still have a lingering bad taste in our mouths for the way Evenflo handled the recall of 800,000 infant car seats in 1998 (see the previous chapter for details).

While the quality of Evenflo's models have improved a bit over the past few years (and as a result we've raised their rating slightly to reflect this), we still think these strollers are too heavy and poorly made. ***Rating: C-***

Graco *Rt. 23, Main St., Elverson, PA 19520. For a dealer near you, call (800) 345-4109, (610) 286-5951; Web: www.gracobaby.com* Graco is a great example of what's right (and wrong) with American-made strollers today. The company (a division of Rubbermaid) is probably the market-leader in strollers, with affordable models that are packed with features like oversized baskets. You'll find Graco everywhere: discount stores, baby superstores, specialty shops and more. But, as we'll discuss later in this review, those low prices often mean low quality. Graco's line is huge, so let's get to the highlights:

The models. Graco divides their stroller line into four areas: CoachRiders, Compact Strollers, LightRiders and Tandems.

The CoachRider is sort of Graco's pram, with a reversible seat, one hand fold and a reclining seat to 180 degrees. This top of the line stroller features lots of padding and other goodies like a removable canopy. The stroller is $150 and available as a travel system with the Snug Ride infant (called the Chauffeur) for $229.

The compact stroller category includes Graco's knock-off's of Combi's Savvy Z (does it seem like all the mass market stroller makers decided to do this in the last year?). The CitiLite ($89) is a 10.8 pound stroller with one-hand fold and removable, washable seat pads. New for 2001, Graco will release a new compact stroller (the MetroLite) which is an upgraded version of the CitiLite. The MetroLite will feature a larger basket, kid snack tray, adjustable handle and more. The MetroLite will come in both three-point ($99) and five-point versions ($129), the latter of which has larger wheels and a head support cushion. There will also be travel system versions of the MetroLite, again both in three-point ($189) and five-point ($219) models.

The best-selling stroller in Graco's line has to be the LiteRider. It is relatively lightweight (19lbs.), has a reclining seat, an easy fold and a huge storage basket. As you'd expect, Graco makes the LiterRider in a zillion versions, from $39 to $99. We've heard very good feedback on this stroller from parents, who like its convenience and low price.

Graco offers several travel system versions that pair the LiteRider with the Snug Ride infant seat–the Breeze ($120), Cirrus ($149), Glider ($169-$179) and Sterling ($199). As you might expect, the difference in price depends on the plushness of the car seat/stroller. The top-of-the line Chauffeur system features a reversible seat ($230).

Finally, double strollers are Graco's other major forte–the DuoRider ($130) is Graco's side-by-side model, while the DuoGlider ($150) is a front/back tandem. Graco's claim to fame in the tandem market is their "stadium seating," where the rear seat is elevated. Of course, you get all the standard features: huge storage baskets, removable canopies, etc. Graco also offers the DuoGlider in a travel system that will now accept two infant car seats (note to parents of twins) for $229 (but that price just includes one infant seat).

New for 2002, Graco will debut an UltraLite Duo side by side stroller at 17 lbs for $159. Also new: Graco's first jogging stroller (Leisure Sport Travel System) which will have 12" tires, parent tray, storage basket and one-hand fold. You'll be able to buy this jogger as a travel system for $200 to $230. The stroller features parent's tray, child's tray, five point harness, quick release wheels, easy fold, hand brake and large basket. The stroller will be sold with either a five point or three point Graco Snug Ride car seat. And, finally, Graco will jump on the inflated tire trend with the Air Six ($230), a LiteRider stroller with pneumatic tires, boot and rain guard.

Our view. The adage "you get what you pay for" unfortunately applies to Graco. Sure, they're affordable and packed with goodies. That's the good news. The bad news: Graco strollers suffer from far too many quality problems. Yes, they are $100 or $200 less than similar European or Japanese brands, but these strollers just aren't as durable–levers break, reclining seats stop reclining, retractable canopies stop retracting, etc. That's probably why we see many parents who used a Graco for their first child buy a better brand for child #2. Another bummer: these strollers are far too heavy. Many full-feature Graco models tip the scales at over 30 lbs., which may have you cursing the thing in a parking lot. Yet, if all you need is a very light-duty stroller that doesn't have to survive more than one child, a Graco is not a bad choice. The LiteRider would make a good budget stroller for quick trips to the mall. As one parent pointed out, even if the thing breaks, you can go through three LiteRiders before you approach the cost of a Combi Savvy Z.

We also have to compliment Graco for their new models–the MetroLite travel system in particular is a winner. We were also impressed with the CitiLite stroller as a credible Savvy Z knock-off. Whether the new models will fare better than other Graco strollers quality-wise remains to be seen, however. ***Rating: C***

Kolcraft *3455 West 31st Pl., Chicago, IL 60623. For a dealer near you, call (773) 247-4494; Web: www.kolcraft.com.*

The models. Kolcraft has always been an also-ran in the stroller business, thanks to their lackluster travel systems. The Secura travel system ($130) uses the inferior Secura infant car seat in a lousy stroller–this is one to avoid. Almost all of Kolcraft strollers get poor reviews from parents we interviewed, who knock their low quality. Yes, they are cheap but, in this case, you get what you pay for. The exception to the rule: the Kolcraft Grand Sport ($50), a Graco LiteRider knock-off–quality-wise, this stroller is the only Kolcraft model that rises above mediocrity.

Realizing their own questionable standing in the marketplace, Kolcraft has licensed different brand names to hawk their products: Carter's and Jeep. The Carter's strollers (and other products) are exactly the same as Kolcraft's models, albeit with nicer looking fabric. A more interesting license is Jeep–Kolcraft has an entire line of Jeep strollers, complete with SUV-like knobby wheels, beefed up suspension, and sporty fabrics at affordable prices ($49 to $109). The Jeep Wrangler stroller is $49 and is basically a souped-up umbrella stroller. The more deluxe Cherokee and Grand Cherokee ($89 to $109) have toy steering wheels, bigger seats and four wheel independent suspension. These strollers looked rather amazing (our favorite detail: simulated lug nuts on the wheels), but we're still leery about recommending the Jeep strollers given Kolcraft's quality track record. A better bet: Kolcraft has a knock-off of Baby Trend's Snap & Go called the Universal Car Seat System for $40. This stroller frame will accommodate most car seats and have a large basket and one-hand fold.

Kolcraft will continue to expand their Jeep line of strollers in 2002. New models include a tandem that will fit any infant car seat brand for $170. The Rubicon stroller will feature pneumatic wheels, one hand steering and fold, parent's tray and toy bar with sounds. Price: $150, which includes a cooler bag. Also new: the Liberty stroller, a three wheel stroller with steer-able front wheel for $120.

Our view. Okay, the Jeep strollers do look cool but watch out–Kolcraft's previous quality track record is nothing to brag about. ***Rating: C-***

Jeep These strollers are made by Kolcraft. See the previous review for details.

Maclaren *4 Testa Place, S. Norwalk, CT 06854. For a dealer near you, call (877) 504-8809 or (203) 354-4400; Web:www.maclaren-baby.com* Maclaren is a British-made brand that sells 500,000 strollers each year in 30 countries worldwide. Their specialty? High-quality umbrella strollers made from lightweight aluminum. Maclaren's distribution is limited to the East Coast and the brand has many fans in New York City and Boston. You might wonder whether these parents (who fork over $200 to $300 for a Maclaren) have lost their minds—can't they just go down to a discount store and buy an umbrella stroller for $30? Well, unlike the cheap-o umbrella strollers you find at Toys R Us, Maclaren strollers are packed with good features, are ultra light weight and are built to last, withstanding all the abuse an urban jungle can dish out.

The models. Maclaren's entry-level model, the "Day Tripper," (formerly called the Sprinter, $169 to $189) weighs ten pounds and features a fully enclosed protective hood. If you want a model with a reclining seat, check out the "Mistral" (formerly called the Concorde, $199 to $229, 12 lbs.). It has a three-position, partially reclining seat, full hood and extendible leg rest. An upgraded version of the Mistral is called the Vogue 2001 ($250). In the past year, Maclaren debuted the top-of-the-line "Opus VI" ($300, 17 lbs.), which replaces the old Cruiser. The Opus features a new, thickly padded seat that's fully reclining (the fabric is removable for machine washing), a bigger canopy, boot and six-inch wheels.

To catch the all-terrain stroller craze, Maclaren recently debuted the "Techno" ($12 lbs, $299) with larger wheels, fully reclining seat, reflective ergonomic handles and extra padding. (Memo to Bill Gates: Maclaren also makes a version of the Techno with leather seats and a titanium frame for a mere $1500 to $2000).

If you need a side-by-side double stroller (preferred by parents of twins), Maclaren offers the Day Tripper, Vogue 2000 and Opus models in "duo" versions ($300 to $450).

In the past year, Maclaren debuted a new lightweight (6 lb.) stroller, Volo. This stripped down model (no basket or hood) features a five-point harness and aluminum frame for $100 to $125.

Finally, the biggest news at Maclaren will be their first model that can be used with an infant seat. The "Global" ($300, 16.7 lbs.) is basically a Techno stroller with an infant seat attachment bar that will fit Century, Evenflo or Graco infant seats. After your baby outgrows the infant seat, the attachment bar is replaced with a removable napper bar.

Also new for 2002: the Volo, a bare-bones mesh seat stroller that weighs 8.2lbs and has a five-point harness and basket. The Volo will sell for $100; an optional canopy, rain cover and seat liner will run $50 extra. A revamped Techno stroller will also be out in 2002 (just minor changes there). As a side note, all Maclaren strollers are now made in China (they used to made in the UK). Also: Maclaren will debut a namesake baby carrier (made for them by Theodore Bean) for $70 in late 2001. There are no major other changes for this line in 2002.

Our view. While those prices are a bit high compared to Combi, Maclaren does get excellent marks from parents we've interviewed. We can understand why parents on Manhattan's Upper West Side think they're well worth the money—few strollers can maneuver around Zabar's and outlast those giant potholes on Broadway. We do have one criticism, though: what happened to the napper bar? Almost all strollers come with this important safety feature to keep baby safe inside a stroller? With the exception of the Global stroller, none of the Maclaren models include this important safety feature. Another bummer: Maclaren's customer service could stand improvement. We occasionally hear from parents who've found Maclaren's customer service department to be lacking in the "service" quotient. Getting replacement parts seems to be especially troublesome. Maclaren has shifted its customer service among three different companies in the last three years and we're sure that has contributed to the chaos. But we expect more from a company that sells $300 strollers. ***Rating: B+***

Martinelli These strollers are made Peg Perego. See their review later in this section.

Osh Kosh These strollers are made by Evenflo. See their review earlier in this chapter for more details.

Peg Perego *3625 Independence Dr., Ft. Wayne, IN 46808. For a dealer, call (219) 482-819;. Web: www.perego.com* Perhaps the biggest frustration with buying a Peg Perego stroller is simply deciding what model to purchase—this hot-selling Italian brand offers a bewildering list of two dozen different models, from simple compact-folding strollers to prams to strollers for twins or triplets. Adding to the confusion: the company rapidly discontinues models, coming out with slightly different versions only months later. Perego goes through more models than Italy goes through governments.

Yet, why is Peg Perego so popular? In a word: quality. These are possibly the best-made strollers on the planet, loaded with features to please both parent and baby. And, unlike other European brands, Perego doesn't overprice their strollers (prices start at about $200). Peg Perego's durability has made it a favorite in New York City, where strollers are your primary vehicle and take quite a beating. In fact, we recently walked into a Barnes & Noble there and noticed the cafe looked like a Peg Perego showroom—quite a testimonial. Since we don't have the space to review every Perego model here, we'll hit the highlights of the line.

The models. The biggest news at Perego is their new travel systems. In the "better late than never" category, Perego has finally woken up and realized that parents love the convenience of systems that combine an infant seat and stroller.

Interestingly, Perego has decided to take a hybrid approach to the travel system–first, they debuted their own infant seat (reviewed in the last chapter). This seat is paired with strollers in three versions: the Giro, the Primo Viaggio and Pliko travel systems.

Unfortunately, the prices are very high–the Giro weighs in at $400, while the Primo Viaggio and Pliko systems aren't far behind. On the plus side, at least Perego is trying to do something innovative: the Giro includes the car seat (with stay-in-the-car base), a 13 lb. aluminum stroller frame with storage basket AND a separate G-matic stroller seat (8.5 lbs.) which has an adjustable hood, boot, washable upholstery. The only glaring omission: a canopy on the stroller frame itself.

The Primo Viaggio travel system ($350) debuts an entire new stroller with large basket, washable cushions, full reclining seat, plush boot, aluminum chassis, all-terrain wheels and the aforementioned infant car seat. Want a lightweight travel system? Try the Pliko travel system ($325), which will pair a Pliko stroller (see review below) and Perego's infant car seat.

In 2002, Perego is planning to replace the Primo Viaggio system with the Atlantico. It features a new parent's tray, larger basket and boot. For the first time, Perego will actually offer a parent tray/cup holder with their Atlantico model. A "Trek" version of the Atlantico will come with a child's tray and rain canopy for about the same price.

Not impressed with Perego's infant seat? (We sure weren't.) Well, Perego seems to be hedging their bets with the travel systems by offering a new accessory–attachment bars that work with other name-brand infant seats. These bars ($20) will work on the Milano, Venezia and Pliko strollers. Let's discuss these models next.

The "Venezia" (21 lbs., $289-319) is Perego's entry-level carriage stroller. This stroller/carriage features fully reclining seat, reversible handle, and removable boot that snaps and folds back plus a height adjustable handle. Like all Perego's, the Venezia has a decent size storage basket and stylish fabrics. If that doesn't excite you, Perego offers a more plush carriage stroller called the Milano XL ($349, 20 lbs.), which is larger and adds a boot that has a zip-out top portion. (Memo to Perego: for $300, how come you can't add a cup holder to these strollers?)

Looking for a European-style pram? Perego has several offerings that combine a bassinet and stroller–the Arianna, Sabrina, Coupee G Matic and Culla ($300 to $450). The Coupee G Matic ($330) was introduced last year and features removable bassinet and bigger, all-terrain wheels.

In recent years, Perego has greatly expanded their lightweight, umbrella strollers (the Pliko family). The Pliko stroller line (16 lbs) features a five-point safety harness, storage basket, full reclining seat, adjustable leg rest, adjustable height handle, removable/washable seat cushions. Perego makes the Pliko in several versions: the basic Plikomatic ($200) has smooth wheels, while the Pliko Sherpa ($229) and Trek ($249) feature knobby wheels (for rougher sidewalks). The Trek adds a raincover that rolls into the canopy, while the Pliko Sherpa Bubble ($249) has a detachable rain cover.

For parents looking for double strollers, Perego offers the Tender Twin tandem ($329-$399). The Micro Twin side-by-side stroller ($300), was discontinued last year. On the plus side, Perego will debut the new Duette double (tandem) stroller ($450) this year that will allow parents of twins to attach TWO infant car seats to the G-matic frame. Basically, this is a double version of the Primo Viaggio travel system described above. (And there is also a new "Triplette" version of this stroller that will debut in 2001 as well).

Last year, Perego debuted a new lightweight (9.9 lb.) stroller that is their Combi Savvy Z knock-off—the "Aria" ($179) will feature a seat that reclines to 150 degrees, decent size storage basket, canopy and a five-point restraint. What's missing? The Aria will not have a car seat attachment bar (like all other Perego models). Another bummer: unlike the Savvy Z and other umbrella strollers, the Aria does NOT fold compactly (it folds over on itself).

New for 2002, the lightweight Aria stroller will accept a infant seat. Also new in the Aria line: a twin (side-by-side) version of the Aria that is 32" wide and will sell for $290.

Whew! Is that it? Nope, Perego also markets an entire line of strollers called "Martinelli." These models will have limited distribution (just fancy specialty stores) and feature upgraded fabrics and leather trim. We previewed this line at a recent trade show and weren't impressed—Martinelli strollers are EXACTLY the same as Perego models, just different names. What's the point? We assume this line is only meant to give specialty stores a different brand name that would be hard to comparison shop.

Our view. Perego strollers are the best you can buy, quality-wise. We are consistently impressed with how durable and functional these models are. Yet, Peg Perego's popularity has been a double edged sword—there are often shortages of popular Perego models. The company also seems perpetually behind in production and slow shipping from Italy doesn't help either. Each year, Perego promises juvenile retailers it's going to step up production and fix the shortage problem . . . and each year, nothing happens. We wonder if they don't intentionally short-ship the U.S., artificially creating shortages to give this brand cache. And speaking of bogus cache, the Martinelli line looks like an excuse for retailers to sell Perego strollers at steeper mark-ups.

On the upside, we are amazed at all of Perego's new products for this year—the travel systems are amazing, albeit at too high a price. We'd skip Perego's loser of an infant seat and just get a model that has the car seat attachment bar (basically, any model but the Aria). And speaking of the Aria, nice first try but we'd like to see Version 2.0.

Bottom line: we still think Peg Perego's strollers are tops. We give them our top recommendation. ***Rating: A***

Regalo *5740 Wayzata Blvd., Minneapolis, MN 55416. For a dealer near you, call (800-521-2234; Web: www.regalo-baby.com* This relative newcomer to the stroller market first distributed Chicco strollers before launching their own line. We weren't impressed with their first offerings when they debuted in 1996 but they've steadily improved.

The models. Regalo prices its strollers between Graco and the expensive brands (like Peg Perego)—most are between $100 and $200 and feature all aluminum frames. The "Evolution" stroller ($129), for example, weighs 13.5 lbs. and features an easy one-step fold, storage basket and aluminum frame. (Basically, it is similar to Graco's LiteRider). We liked Regalo's new jogging strollers, which ranged from $189 to $239 and their new tandem line (the "Discovery," $129 to $199), which features all-terrain wheels and full canopies.

Our view. Regalo is a rather obscure brand, hard to find in most baby stores or on the 'net. The few parent comments we hear about their strollers could be charitably described as mixed: those who like Regalo think the strollers are feature-packed for the price. Yet others knock Regalo for quality problems and other woes. One parent complained about a Discovery tandem that broke after six months of use (a wheel fell off) and had little legroom for the rear-seated child. Others complain about skimpy storage baskets and other quality problems. So, it is a mixed review for Regalo—these strollers are a bit better than Graco's offerings, but that isn't saying much. As a result of parent feedback, we've lowered Regalo's rating this time out. ***Rating: C+***

Safety 1st These strollers and travel systems are made by Cosco. See the above review for more info.

Simo *142 Hamilton Ave., Stamford, CT 06902. For a dealer near you, call (800) SIMO4ME or (203) 348-SIMO; Web: www.simostrollers.com* Simo may be new to the U.S., but the brand has been a best-seller in Norway for years. As with other European brands imported to the U.S., Simo's emphasis is on high-quality prams. We reviewed the line recently and were impressed: all strollers come with a two-year warranty and feature steel frames, water proof fabrics and a bassinet that fits inside the stroller seat.

The Models. The "Nordic Cruiser" ($370) is Simo's flagship stroller–this 35 lb. steel frame model converts from a pram to a stroller and features a fully reclining seat and full boot (an optional bassinet is $150 more). Last year, Simo rolled out the innovative "Bertini" model ($400). This Euro style carriage had four *turnable* wheels (the Nordic Cruiser, like most prams, has fixed wheels).

New this year, Simo is introducing the "Shuttle" ($299, 22 lbs.), another steerable pram with a two-position reclining seat, rain cover, inflated wheels, adjustable handle, larger basket and compact fold. Also new: Simo is rolling out a second child's seat ($55) that can be attached to the front of the Bertini so it can accommodate two children. Also new: the "Super Cruiser," a close cousin to the Nordic Cruiser that features larger wheels and an easier to operate foot brake.

Our view. If you're interested in a Euro-style pram/carriage, this is a great brand to consider. Yes, the offerings are similar to Emmaljunga, but we thought the fabrics and features were better. Since Simo is new to the U.S., we have limited feedback from parents on this brand; but the little we've heard has been very positive. ***Rating: B+***

Swan. This brand is made by Baby Trend. See their review earlier in this section.

◆ ***Other brands to consider.*** Parents of multiples should check out ***Inglesina*** *(877-486-5112 or 973-746-5112; web: www.inglesina.com)*, an Italian-made brand of strollers with options for twins, triplets and even quadruplets (and you thought you had challenges with just one). Like other European brands, Inglesina offers traditional European-style prams, combo strollers/carriages, and the aforementioned strollers for multiples (overall, prices range from $300 to $550). Inglesina's side-by-side duo (Twin Jet $419) is a compact-folding model with four-position reclining seats and full boot. In the last year, Inglesina rolled out a new umbrella-type stroller (the Ace, $150, 10 lbs.) and a carriage model (the Max Evo, $229, 14 lbs.). For 2001, Inglesina is rolling out knock-offs of Perego's Sherpa strollers–the "Planet" ($299, 16 lbs.) is a brightly colored umbrella stroller with removable cushions, canopy, rain shield and a big storage basket. The new "Easy" ($199-$229, 16 lbs.) is a jazzed up version of the Ace with new handles and a five-point harness. These are great strollers, but the prices are too high.

KidCo (800-553-5529, 847-970-9100, www.kidcoinc.com) got its start distributing Maclaren strollers but now has their own line that goes under the name BebeCar. Basically, these strollers are knock-offs of Maclaren and Perego. We were impressed with their offerings, but these strollers have so little distribution, we don't have much feedback from parents on their quality or durability. New for 2001, KidCo will roll out the "Raider A/T Plus" ($399, 19 lbs.). This hybrid pram/carriage has 12" removable, inflated wheels that steer. A Pliko-like stroller (the Spice) is $269, but most of KidCo's carriage models are $300 to $400. New this year, KidCo will roll out several Maclaren-like umbrella strollers that run $129 to $399; double (side by side) versions of these models will run $249-$389.

You can lump strollers by ***Spectrum, J. Mason*** (818-993-6800; web: www.jmason.com) and ***Safety 1st*** (made by Delta, 718-385-1000) into the same category as Kolcraft and Cosco—cheap strollers made for discount stores. We found the quality and durability of these Asian-made strollers to be below average.

Our Picks: Brand Recommendations

Unlike other chapters, we've broken up our stroller recommendations into several "lifestyle" categories. Since many parents end up with two strollers (one that's full-featured and another that's lighter for quick trips), we'll recommend a primary stroller and a secondary option. For more specifics on the models mentioned below, read each manufacturer's review earlier in this chapter. Let's break it down:

Mall Crawler

You live in the suburbs and drive just about everywhere you go. A stroller needs to be packed with features, yet convenient enough to haul in and out of a trunk. Mostly the stroller is used for the mall or for quick trips around the block for fresh air.

In the past, we recommended buying a travel system that combined an infant seat and stroller. This time we have one word of advice when it comes to travel systems: DON'T. Don't waste your money on those huge, bulky systems from mass market brands like Graco, Century, or Evenflo. Why? Parents repeatedly tell us the stroller parts of these travel systems are aggravating to use, thanks to low quality and hefty weight. Many readers tell us they usually chuck the stroller when their baby outgrows the infant seat.

Instead, consider one of the great new alternatives to the massive travel system—first, look at stroller frames like ***Baby Trend's Snap & Go LX*** for $50. Snap in any major brand car seat and you've got a travel system without the expense. Of course, if you go this route, you'll have to buy a second stroller after baby outgrows the infant seat (we'll have some thoughts on this in just a second).

Another idea: go for a stroller that has a car seat attachment bar. Now, the better brands of strollers (namely, Combi, Perego and Maclaren) finally have models that have infant car seat attachment bars! This is a great improvement over previous years. ***Combi's "Perfect Match"*** system is available on strollers that start at $85. (for example, the ***Combi 6510,*** a 14 lb. stroller for $85). Want something a bit more plush? Go for a ***Peg Perego Pliko***, which starts at about $200 and include an infant seat attachment bar.

Second stroller. If you buy a Combi or Perego with a car seat attachment bar, you won't need a second stroller. But if you decide to add a second stroller to your collection, go for something that is ultra lightweight and folds compactly. At the budget end, the ***Graco LiteRider*** ($39-$99) boasts a large number of features at an affordable price.

If you plan to do air travel with baby or just desire something better, consider investing in the 800 lb. gorilla of the lightweight stroller category–the ***Combi Savvy Z***. Yes, every other stroller maker tries to knock off this one, but the Savvy Z is still tops. The Combi Savvy Z ($180 to $200) is a 7.7 lbs. stroller that's a clear win-

STROLLER ROUND-UP

Here's our round-up of some of the best stroller models by the following manufacturers.

MAKER	MODEL	WEIGHT	PRICE	RECLINE
APRICA	SUPER ZAP	10 LBS	$300	FULL
CHICCO	TREKKING	18.5	$200	FULL
COMBI	CONVENIENCE 6510	15.0	$85	FULL
	SAVVY Z	7.0	$180-200	PARTIAL
EMMALJUNGA	EC SPORT	21.0	$360-400	FULL
EVENFLO	LIGHT & EASY	9.5	$90	PARTIAL
GRACO	CITILITE	15.0	$90	PARTIAL
JEEP/KOLCRAFT	CHEROKEE	21.0	$90	FULL
MACLAREN	DAY TRIPPER	10.0	$170-190	NONE
PEG PEREGO	VENEZIA	20.6	$290-320	FULL
	PLIKO MATIC	16.0	$200	FULL
REGALO	EVOLUTION	13.5	$130	PARTIAL
SIMO	NORDIC CRUISER	35.0	$370	FULL

***BEST FOR:** See our lifestyle categories for more info on these classifications

ner. Too much money? Combi makes a scaled-down ***Travel Savvy*** for $79 or try the new SubV (10 lbs.) for $50 to $70.

Urban Jungle

When you live in a city like New York City, Boston or Washington D.C., your stroller is more than just baby transportation—it's your primary vehicle. You stroll to the market, on outings to a park or longer trips on weekend getaways. Since you're not lugging this thing in and out of a trunk as much as suburbanites, weight is not as much of a factor. (On the other hand, strollers can't weigh TOO much—lugging a 30-pound stroller up a flight of subway stairs ain't fun). This stroller better take all the abuse a big city can dish out—giant potholes, uneven sidewalks . . . you name it.

We have two words for you: Peg Perego. A full-featured model like Perego's ***Venezia*** (21 lbs., $289-$319) is plush, yet weatherized to fight the elements. Shock absorbers make for a smooth ride. The only problem—it's too wide to fit down the check-out aisles at some of those grocery stores in New York City (sorry, you can't have everything). Of course, Perego makes a wide range of models in several price levels—the ***Milano XL*** is a larger version of the Venezia with a more deluxe boot for $349.

FRAME	BEST FOR*	COMMENTS
ALUMINUM	MALL CRAWL	ONE-TOUCH FOLD
STEEL	GREEN ACRES	HANDLES ROTATE 360°
STEEL	MALL CRAWL	CAN SNAP IN INFANT SEAT
ALUMINUM	MALL CRAWL	NEW: INCREASED HANDLE HEIGHT
ALUMINUM	URBAN JUNGLE	FIXED FRONT WHEELS
ALUMINUM	MALL CRAWL	ONE-HAND FOLD
ALUMINUM	MALL CRAWL	ONE-HAND FOLD
STEEL	MALL CRAWL	SUV STYLING, SUSPENSION
ALUMINUM	URBAN JUNGLE	FULLY ENCLOSED HOOD
STEEL	URBAN JUNGLE	HEIGHT-ADJUSTABLE HANDLE
STEEL	URBAN JUNGLE	5 PT HARNESS; ADJUSTABLE HANDLE
ALUMINUM	MALL CRAWL	ONE-STEP FOLD
STEEL	URBAN JUNGLE	PRAM/CARRIAGE

How about a pram? These full-featured and weatherized strollers are made for the urban jungle, especially for lengthy walks. The best brands are Simo and Emmaljunga. Specifically, we like the ***Simo Bertini*** ($400), the first pram with steerable wheels.

Second stroller. While Peg Peregos and prams are all nice, they do have one disadvantage. They're heavy (many are 20 to 40 pounds) and most don't fold compactly. Sometimes, all you need is a lightweight stroller that can withstand big-city abuse YET quickly folds like an umbrella so you can quickly get in a taxi or down a set of subway stairs. (Just try lugging a Perego up the stairs at a T stop in Boston). The solution: Maclaren–their strollers weigh just ten to 14 pounds and fold compactly, yet offer top-quality construction and durability. The ***Maclaren "Mistral"*** ($199 to $229) has all the features you'd need (including a partially reclining seat) yet weighs a mere 12 lbs. Of course, the ***Combi Savvy Z*** (see mention in the previous section) is a contender for this category as well.

While it's easy to spend less money than a Maclaren or Peg Perego, don't be penny-wise and pound foolish. Less-expensive strollers lack the durability and weather-proofing that living in an East Coast city requires. And since baby spends more time in the stroller than tots in the suburbs, weatherized fabrics and padding are more of a necessity than a luxury.

Travel Systems

Round up of popular travel systems, which combine a infant car seat and stroller.

Maker	Rating	Model	Price	Infant Seat
Century	B-	Limited	$150	Smart Fit 22
		Calypso	$150	Celestia
		Sedona	$170	Celestia
		Vienna	$170	Celestia
		Avanta	$180	Avanta
Evenflo	C-	Discovery	$160	Discovery
		Deluxe	$160	On My Way
		Advantage V	$180	On My Way V
		Comfort	$230	On My Way V
Graco	C	Sterling	$200	Snug Ride DX5
		Chauffeur	$230	Snug Ride DX5
Perego	A	Pliko	$325	Primo Viaggio
		Viaggio	$350	Primo Viaggio
		Giro	$400	Primo Viaggio

Green Acres

If you live on a dirt or gravel road or a neighborhood with no sidewalks, you need a stroller to do double duty. First, it must handle rough surfaces without bouncing baby all over the place. Second, it must be able to "go to town," folding easily to fit into a trunk for a trip to a mall or other store.

This is a tough category to recommend a stroller for—there are many so-called "all-terrain" strollers on the market. Yet, we found those made by the big guys (Century, Graco, Jeep) were just pretenders. Yeah, the box says "all-terrain" and they have larger wheels and shock absorbing suspension, but we just don't think most of them could really cut it in the real world. Like faux-SUV's that couldn't handle two inches of snow, these strollers are long on promise and short on delivery.

So, that leaves us with two other possibilities: jogging (or sport) strollers and pram/carriages. Both have MUCH larger wheels than the so-called all-terrain models. Jogging strollers have the same tires as bicycles; prams have large "balloon" style wheels that are fixed (better to go over objects).

We'll review jogging strollers in depth in the next section. Both our top brand picks (Baby Jogger and Kool Stop on the top end, Baby Trend and InStep on the lower end) have "mini-version" models with 12" wheels—these would make great strollers for gravel roads.

COMMENTS
EXTENDED CANOPY, 3 POS. RECLINE SEAT, PARENT TRAY WITH CUPHOLDER
ADDS: 5 PT HARNESS, 4 POSITION RECLINE SEAT, ONE-HAND STEERING
ADDS: UPGRADED STROLLER WITH BIGGER WHEELS, SUSPENSION
ADDS: A FEW COSMETIC UPGRADES, BUT VERY SIMILAR TO THE SEDONA
COMES WITH SAME STROLLER AS SEDONA
ONE-HAND FOLD/STEERING, LARGE BASKET, PARENT CONSOLE, RECLINING SEAT
SAME STROLLER AS ON DISCOVERY TRAVEL SYSTEMS
ADDS: 2-PC CHEST CLIP AND A FEW OTHER UPGRADES
ADDS: MORE PADDING, SLIDE-OUT STORAGE BASKET
STROLLER WITH 5-POINT HARNESS, EXTRA STORAGE, ONE HAND FOLD
TOP-OF-THE-LINE: REVERSIBLE SEAT, FULL RECLINE, DELUXE PADDING
5 PT HARNESS, FULLY RECLINING SEAT, ADJUSTABLE HEIGHT HANDLE
ALL-TERRAIN WHEELS, FULLY RECLINING SEAT, ALUMINUM CHASSIS
13LB ALUMINUM STROLLER WITH SEPARATE SEAT; ADJUSTABLE HOOD

As for more specific models, ***Baby Jogger's*** (call 509-457-0925 for a store near you; web: www.babyjogger.com) ***"Twinkle"*** ($169) model has 12" wheels, retractable canopy, and one-motion folding with no pins. Kool Stop (800-586-3332, 714-738-4973; web: www.koolstop.com) has the ***"Kool-Stride Junior"*** ($270) with a 12" front wheel and 16" rear wheels. It features a height-adjustable handle, reclining seat, mesh storage pocket and retractable canopy.

If that's too much, you can try out the ***Baby Trend Expedition*** for $109, which features five-point harness, canopy and two-position seat recline.

Oddly enough, European-style prams also do well in a Green Acres-type of environment. Their brawny steel frames and fixed wheels with serious suspension have that "go anywhere" attitude. The downside is cost: the ***Emmaljunga EC Sport***, for example, is $359 to $399. A better bet may the ***Zooper*** strollers, reviewed in the next section.

Exercise This: Jogging and Sport Strollers

This year must be the year of the jogging stroller—just about every major stroller maker is rolling out so-called "sport" or jogging models. Even Graco and Cosco are jumping on the jogging bandwagon.

So, what's all the fuss about? Most jogging or sport strollers have three wheels and are built like bicycles—they boast large rubber wheels with rugged tread that can handle any terrain, yet move smoothly along at a fast clip. Folks who like to jog or even walk for fitness favor joggers over regular strollers for that reason.

How young can you put a baby in a jogger? First, determine whether the seat reclines (not all models do). If it doesn't, wait until baby is at least six months old and can hold his or her head up. If you want to jog or run with the stroller, it might be best to wait until baby is at least a year old since all the jostling can be uncomfortable for a younger infant.

Before heading out to buy a jogging stroller, consider how you'll use it. Despite their name, few parents actually use a jogging stroller for jogging. If you just plan to use the stroller for walks in the neighborhood, a lower price model (we'll have specific recommendations below) with 12" wheels will do fine. If you really plan to run with a sport stroller, go for 20" wheels for a smoother glide and a higher-quality brand name for durability.

Another decision area: frame material. The cheapest strollers (under $120) have plastic frames. Steel frames are seen on mid-price models (under $200)—they're strong but also heavy (and that could be a drawback). The most expensive models ($200 to $350) have aluminum frames, which are the lightest in weight. Once again, if you plan casual walks, a plastic or steel frame is fine. Runners should go for aluminum.

Check the seat fabric carefully. The best strollers use Dupont Cordura, which is also used in backpacks for its durability and strength. As for other features, go for a model that has a hand brake on the handle (the cheapest models omit this). The brake is used to slow the stroller when you are going down a steep incline. And always check the folding feature: some are easier than others. Quick release wheels are also a must if you have a small trunk.

Until a few years ago, there were just a couple of brands of sport strollers out there–and the price was so high ($200 and up), only serious enthusiasts bought joggers.

That's all changed with the flood of new entrants to the market. Here's an overview of the new players (in alphabetical order):

Dreamer Design (formally Fitness First, 509-574-8085; web: www.dreamerdesign.net) has joggers designed for young infants that are sold under the name ***Boogie Deluxe***. Their Deluxe 16" wheel stroller ($280) has an insert ($36) for small children as young as six weeks of age. The Deluxe comes with a canopy, rear foot brake and pin-free fold. Dreamer also makes an attachment kit that lets you snap an infant seat into the stroller frame for $80. Dreamer also makes strollers with 12" wheels.

Gozo (415-388-1814; web: www.getgozo.com) offers the only tandem jogging stroller on the market–their stroller frame can be configured to carry one or two seats. The strollers (21 lbs. with one seat, 26 pounds for two) feature quick-release 16" wheels, three-position reclining seats, sun canopies, five-point harness, removable/washable seat covers, a storage basket and aluminum chassis. The stroller itself is $335 to $350, while the second seat is $135. We were very impressed with these innovative strollers.

Kelty (303-530-7670, web: www.kelty.com) is best known for their backpacks, but they are jumping in the jogger market for 2001. Kelty will have a single jogger (the Joy Rider, $300) that will be available with either 12", 16" or 20" wheels and a double jogger (Deuce Coupe, $400) with 16" or 20" wheels. The Kelty strollers will have five-point harnesses, a unique umbrella-style fold, quick release wheels, storage basket but no reclining seats.

Zooper (503-248-9469; web: www.zooperstrollers.com) makes an excellent stroller that is a hybrid between a traditional carriage and a jogger. The "Walk Air" ($250) features inflated wheels and has a carriage stroller seat with five-point harness, full recline and height adjustable handle. We also loved Zooper's traditional jogger (the Buddy, $250) which as extra padding, rain cover, nice suspension and a height adjustable handle. The top of the line Zooper Air ($350) comes with a carry cot and reversible seat. These are amazing strollers.

Whew! And those were just the new guys. So, which jogging stroller do we recommend? Let's break that down into two categories: low-end and high-end.

At the affordable end, there are really just two choices. ***InStep*** and ***Baby Trend***. InStep (800-242-6110; web: www.instep.net) offers models in just about every price range, from a $90 steel frame stroller (the 5K) to a $200 aluminum model (the Elite). Baby Trend's affordable joggers are sold in Babies R Us and other chain stores. The entry-level Expedition ($109) has five-point harnesses, canopy and two-position seat recline. These steel frame strollers will do fine for occasional walks and other light-duty use.

What if you really want to jog or run with a sport stroller? Or you plan to use it intensively for exercise (say more than two times a week)? Or go for hikes? Then go for the gold standard of baby joggers: Baby Jogger.

Baby Jogger (509-457-0925; web: www.babyjogger.com) is the company that pioneered this category back in the early 1980's. Their flagship "Baby Jogger II" ($250 to $300) comes with 12", 16" or 20" wheels, five-point harness, aluminum frame, hand brake, and thorn resistant tubes. The only bummer: the fold isn't pin-free, making it a bit cumbersome. Other small complaints: the seat doesn't recline and is a bit snug for older kids. On the plus side, Baby Jogger makes extra tall strollers for "vertically blessed" parents over 6'3."

Of course, Baby Jogger has a plethora of different models besides the II. The new Joggeroo ($379) has 16" wheels, five-point harness and one-hand fold that is pin free. Also new: the Citi Jogger with swivel front wheels for $279. As for the other models, the Zipper and Twinkle have smaller 12" wheels. And Baby Jogger makes double and triple versions of their strollers. If Baby Jogger's prices sound

SPORT STROLLERS

How top sport/jogging strollers compare:

MODEL	CAPACITY	PRICE	HARNESS
BABY JOGGER II 16" ALLOY	75 LBS.	$270	5-POINT
BABY TREND EXPEDITION	50 LBS.	$110	5-POINT
BOB SPORT UTILITY	70 LBS.	$360	5-POINT
GOZO 1X2	55 LBS.	$335	5-POINT
INSTEP 5K 16"	50 LBS.	$90	5-POINT
KELTY JOYRIDER 16"	75 LBS.	$300	5-POINT
KOOL STRIDE JR 16"	75 LBS.	$270	5-POINT
ZOOPER BUDDY 12"	44 LBS.	$250	5-POINT

too high, remember Baby Jogger is often discounted online.

Besides Baby Jogger, there are two other excellent brands of high-end joggers: Kool Stop and BOB.

We were impressed by ***Kool Stop*** (800-586-3332, 714-738-4973; www.koolstop.com). Each Kool Stride has a five-point safety harness, reclining seat, and retractable hood. Another plus: Kool Stop's rear wheels are angled by five degrees for improved tracking. Quick release wheels and simple fold up make the stroller easy to transport. Like Baby Jogger, Kool Stop makes both single and double models. Their flagship mode is the "Senior" ($320) with an all-steel frame, reclining seat and quick release wheels. Yes, Kool Stop may be a bit harder to find, but we think it's worth the effort. New for 2001, Kool Stride will debut a "Baby Strider" ($250) with a lockable front wheel that swivels. Kool Stride will also debut a wire frame accessory ($60) that will let you attach an infant seat to their strollers.

If you want to go whole hog, check out the ***BOB*** "Sport Utility Stroller" (805-541-2554; web: www.bobtrailers.com) It's got a fully padded reclining seat, pin-free folding mechanism and "multi-position coil spring shock absorbers." Yea, it's $359 but it's the Mercedes of jogging strollers. New for 2001, Bob will roll out a double stroller for $399.

So, what's best–Baby Jogger, Kool Stop or BOB? That's a toss-up based on our research, but some parents prefer the Baby Jogger's easy fold, quick release wheels and standard alloy wheels. From a safety standpoint, both the BOB, InStep and Baby Trend joggers were involved in recalls in 2000, although these were minor and involved a small number of strollers.

The same advice for brands applies to double joggers–the better brands for single joggers are the same as the ones for doubles.

Most of the above models can be found in both bike stores and

SUSPENSION	SEAT RECLINE	SUN SHADE	PIN-FREE FOLDING
		✔	
	✔	✔	
✔	✔	✔	✔
	✔	✔	✔
	✔	✔	
		✔	✔
	✔	✔	
✔	✔	✔	✔

baby shops. A great discount source is ***Agee's Bikes*** (804) 672-8614 (web: www.ageebike.com). This Richmond, Virginia based retailer offers great discounts on jogging strollers, available via mail order from their web site. (In fact, the prices quoted in this section are from Agee's site, which were the lowest we could find).

Plan to take your jogger out in the cold weather? Instead of bundling up baby, consider a stroller blanket. The ***Cozy Rosie*** by Sew Beautiful ($50-$55, 877-744-6367 or 914-244-6367; web: www.cozyrosie.com) fits over the stroller and is made of washable polar fleece with Velcro fasteners.

Double The Fun: Strollers for two

There are two types of strollers that can transport two tikes: tandem models and side-by-side styles. For the uninitiated, a tandem stroller has a "front-back" configuration, where the younger child rides in back while the older child gets the view. These strollers are best for parents with a toddler/older child and a new baby.

Side-by-side strollers, on the other hand, are best for parents of twins. In this case, there's never any competition for the view seat. The only downside: many of these strollers are so wide, they can't fit through narrow doorways or store aisles. Another bummer: few have napper bars or fully reclining seats, making them impractical for infants.

Double strollers can be frustrating—your basic choices are low-price (and low-quality) duos from Graco, Cosco or Baby Trend or high-price doubles like those from Perego, Maclaren or Combi. There doesn't seem to be much in between the low-price ones (at $150) and the high-end ($300 and up).

After seeing the $300+ price tags of high-end double strollers, many parents are tempted to go with a Graco or Cosco duo and who can blame 'em? But, remember a double stroller takes twice the weight (and abuse) compared to a single stroller. Given the poor track record of the low-end brands, we're very hesitant in recommending anything that's $150 or less for fear it will break in under six months. So, here's a round-up of the best choices:

As for tandem strollers, the best choice is ***Peg Perego's Tender Twin*** ($329-$399, 27 lbs.). For the money, it's a top-quality stroller with plush fabric and a compact fold. Another good model: ***Aprica's "Embrace"*** ($350, 26 lbs.) which has a reversible handle. If you can't spend over $150, the ***Graco DuoGlider*** is probably the best low-end option, but with the caveat that you might have to buy more than one when the first one breaks.

What about side by side strollers? For parents of twins, we'd recommend the new ***Combi Twin Savvy***. This 15-pound stroller is pricey ($300-$320) but feature-packed, including removable napper bars, reclining seats and more. The Maclaren side-by-side strollers are also excellent: the ***Opus Duo*** might break the bank at $440, but you are getting a stroller that will last for years, not months.

Do It By Mail

THE BABY CATALOG OF AMERICA.

To Order Call: (800) PLAYPEN or (203) 931-7760; Fax (203) 933-1147
Web: www.babycatalog.com
Or write to: 738 Washington Ave., West Haven, CT 06516.
Credit Cards Accepted: MC, VISA, AMEX, Discover.

This web site won't win any design awards (the main stroller section is just a list of models with no thumbnails), but what they lack in graphics is made up for in selection. Baby Catalog has it all—three dozen models from such brand names as Peg Perego, Combi, Baby Jogger and more. Prices are rock-bottom, about 20% to 30%

E-MAIL FROM THE REAL WORLD
Biting the bullet on a pricey twin stroller

Cheapo twin strollers sounds like a good deal for parents of twins, but listen to this mother of multiples:

"Twins tend to ride in their strollers more often and longer, and having an unreliable, bulky or inconvenient stroller is a big mistake. As you suggest, it's a false economy to buy an inexpensive Graco or other model, as these most likely will break down before you're done with the stroller. My husband and I couldn't believe that we'd have to spend $400 on a stroller, but after talking to parents of multiples we understand why it's best to just bite the bullet on this one. We've heard universally positive feedback about the Maclaren side-by-side for its maneuverability, durability and practicality. It fits through most doorways and the higher end model (Opus Duo) also has seats that fully recline for infants. We've heard much less positive things about front-back tandems for twins. These often are less versatile, as only one seat reclines, so you can't use them when both babies are small (or tired). And when the babies get bigger, they're more likely to get into mischief by pulling each others' hair and stuff."

below retail. Once you click to each stroller's page, you'll find detailed pictures and fabric swatches that make shopping easy.

Baby Catalog has been in business since 1992, first as a printed catalog and now primarily a web site (don't waste your time with the printed catalog as it is only produced sporadically and the web site has more up to date stuff). The company has a good (but not spotless) record when it comes to customer service—most folks are happy with their orders. The complaints we get focus on backordered items (one customer was charged for an item that was back-ordered for over a month) and mis-described items on the site (where an item ships in a different color/pattern than what's displayed online). And the baby gift registry also has a few kinks left to be ironed out (readers complain about mistakes with orders, etc.).

Fortunately, these complaints are few and far between—most of the time, Baby Catalog does a good job.

Of course, this site sells much more than strollers—they also discount Avent bottles, Dutailier gliders, designer bedding and more.

One tip: you can save an additional 10% off the site's prices by purchasing a membership, $25 for a year (or $49.95 for three years). With each membership, you also get three "associate" memberships for friends/relatives to purchase items for you at the same discount. Interestingly, this is a clever way to get a premium brand that is rarely discounted online—for some reason, manufacturers who don't allow sites to discount their products don't seem to mind when Baby Catalog offers their members that 10% discount.

Bike Trailers & Seats

Bike Trailers. Yes, lots of companies make bike trailers, but the gold standard is ***Burley*** (800-311-5294; web: www.burley.com). Their trailers (sold in bicycle stores) are considered the best in the industry. A good example is the ***Burley "d'Lite."*** It features a multi-point safety harness, built-in rear storage, 100 lb. carrying capacity and compact fold (to store in a trunk). Okay, it's expensive at $350 but check around for second-hand bargains. All Burley trailers have a conversion kit that enables you to turn a trailer into a jogging stroller (although we hear mixed reviews on the Burley as a jogging stroller for its wobbly steering).

If that's too much, check out the ***Schwinn "JoyRider"*** ($300; call 1-800-SCHWINN ; web: www.schwinn.com). This model features quick release alloy wheels, five-point restraints, extra storage and a carrying capacity of 125 lbs. A less-expensive version of the JoyRider called the "JoyMag" features molded plastic wheels (instead of metal) for $269.99. Agee Bike's site (www.ageebike.com) sells this model online if you can't find a local dealer.

There will be several new bike trailers on the market in 2001, including several from Kool Stop (the jogger company reviewed earlier in this chapter).

What about the "discount" bike trailers you see for $150 to $200? ***InStep*** makes several of these models (Duo Cruiser, Duo Sport). What do you give up for the price? First, the wheels aren't bicycle tires with metal spokes, but molded plastic with rubber inserts. The InStep Duo Cruiser and Duo Sport are made of steel frames and hence are heavier then the Burleys or Schwinns (which are made of aluminum). And the cheaper bike trailers don't fold as easily or compactly as the Burleys, nor do they attach as easily to a bike.

To be fair, we should note InStep makes two aluminum frame bike trailers, the Ride N Stride and the Turbo Elite for $250 to $325.

The key feature to look for with any bike trailer is the ease (or lack thereof) of attaching the stroller to a bike. Quick, compact fold is important as well. Look for the total carrying capacity and the quality of the nylon fabric.

So, should you spring for an expensive bike trailer or one of the $150 ones? Like jogging strollers, consider how much you'll use it. For an occasional (once a week?) bike trip, we'd recommend the cheaper models. Plan to do more serious cycling, say two or three times a week? Then go for a Burley, Schwinn or Kool Stop. Yes, they are expensive but worth it if you really plan to use the trailer extensively.

Hint: this might a great item to buy second-hand on eBay. We saw several used Burley trailers for sale on eBay (www.eBay.com) for $50 to $200, or 30% to 60% off retail.

Bike seats. When shopping for a bike seat, consider how well padded the seat is and what type of safety harness the unit has (the best are five-points are bar shields; less expensive seats just have three-point harnesses). The more expensive models have seats that recline and adjust to make a child more comfortable.

One good model is the ***Rhode Limo Child Seat*** ($130) by Rhode Gear (www.rhodegear.com), which has a safety bar and a reclining seat that adjusts to various positions. A simpler version of this seat is called the ***Rhode Taxi*** for $95 which lacks the reclining seat. REI (www.rei.com) sells this seat. We've not seen any safety problems with the cheaper bike seats sold in discount stores; they just tend to lack some of the fancier features (padding, reclining seats) that make riding more comfortable for a child.

LL Bean (www.llbean.com) is a good source for outdoor items—their web site stocks bicycle carriers, a bike seat, the Baby Jogger strollers and Kelty carriers.

The Well-Stocked Diaper Bag

We consider ourselves experts at diaper bags—we got *five* of them as gifts. While you don't need five, this important piece of luggage may feel like an extra appendage after your baby's first year. And diaper bags are for more than just holding diapers—many include compartments for baby bottles, clothes, and changing pads. With that in mind, let's take a look at what separates great diaper bags from the rest of the pack. In addition, we'll give you our list of nine items for a well-stocked diaper bag.

Smart Shopper Tips

Smart Shopper Tip #1
Diaper Bag Science
"I was in a store the other day, and they had about one zillion different diaper bags. Some had cute prints and others were more plain. Should I buy the cheapest one or invest a little more money?"

The best diaper bags are made of tear-resistant fabric and have all sorts of useful pockets, features and gizmos. Contrast that with low-quality brands that lack many pockets and are made of cheap, thin vinyl—after a couple of uses, they start to split and crack. Yes, high-quality diaper bags will cost more ($30 to $40 versus $15 to $20), but you'll be much happier in the long run.

Here's our best piece of advice: buy a diaper bag that doesn't *look* like a diaper bag. Sure those bags with dinosaurs and pastel animal prints look cute now, but what are you going to do with it when your baby gets older? A well-made diaper bag that doesn't look like a diaper bag will make a great piece of carry-on luggage later in life. The best bets: Lands' End's or Eddie Bauer's high-quality diaper bags (see reviews later).

What's the hip new fabric for diaper bags this year? Two words: micro fiber. You'll see more of this super-soft fabric appearing as diaper bags in the months to come.

Smart Shopper Tip #2
Make your own
"Who needs a fancy diaper bag? I just put all the necessary changing items into my favorite backpack."

That's a good point. Most folks have a favorite bag or backpack that can double as a diaper bag. Besides the obvious (wipes and diapers), put in a large zip-lock bag as a holder for dirty/wet items. Add a couple of receiving blankets (as changing pads) plus the key items listed below, and you have a complete diaper bag.

Another idea: check out the ***"Diaper Bag Essentials" from Mommy's Helper*** (call 800-371-3509 or 316-684-2229 for a dealer near you; web: www.mommyshelperinc.com). This $30 kit is basically everything for a diaper bag but the bag—you get an insulated bottle holder, changing pad, dirty duds bag, toiletry kit, etc. That way you can transform your favorite bag or backpack into a diaper bag.

Top Nine Items for a Well-Stocked Diaper Bag

After much scientific experimentation, we believe we have perfected the exact mix of ingredients for the best-equipped diaper bag. Here's our recipe:

1 **TWO DIAPER BAGS**—one that is a full-size, all-option big hummer for longer trips (or overnight stays) and the other that is a mini-bag for a short hop to dinner or the shopping mall. Here's what each should have:

The full-size bag: This needs a waterproof changing pad that folds up, waterproof pouch or pocket for wet clothes, a couple compartments for diapers, blankets/clothes, etc. Super-deluxe brands have bottle compartments with Thinsulate (a type of insulation) to keep bottles warm or cold. Another plus: outside pockets for books and small toys. A zippered outside pocket is good for change or your wallet.

The small bag: This has enough room for a couple diapers, travel wipe package, keys, wallet and/or checkbook. Some models have a bottle pocket and room for one change of clothes. If money is tight, just go for the small bag. To be honest, the full-size bag is often just a security blanket for first-time parents—they think they need to lug around every possible item in case of a diaper catastrophe. But, in the real world, you'll quickly discover schlepping that big full-size bag everywhere isn't practical. While a big bag is nice for overnight or long trips, we'll bet you will be using the small bag much more often.

2 **EXTRA DIAPERS.** Put a dozen in the big bag, two or three in the small one. Why so many? Babies can go through quite a few in a very short time. Of course, when baby gets older (say over a year), you can cut back on the number of diapers you need for a trip. Another wise tip: put whole packages of diapers and wipes in your car(s). We did this after we forgot our diaper bag one too many times and needed an emergency diaper. (The only bummer:

here in Colorado, the wipes we keep in the car sometimes freeze in the winter!)

3 **A TRAVEL-SIZE WIPE PACKAGE.** A good idea: a plastic Tupperware container that hold a small stack of wipes. You can also use a Ziplock bag to hold wipes. Some wipe makers sell travel packs that are allegedly "re-sealable"; we found that they aren't.

4 **BLANKET AND CHANGE OF CLOTHES.** Despite the reams of scientists who work on diapers, they still aren't leak-proof—plan for it. A change of clothes is most useful for babies under six months of age, when leaks are more common. After that point, this becomes less necessary.

5 **A HAT OR CAP.** We like the safari-type hats that have flaps to cover your baby's ears (about $10 to $20). Warmer caps are helpful to chase away a chill, since the head is where most babies lose the most heat.

6 **BABY TOILETRIES.** Babies can't take much direct exposure to sunlight—sunscreen is a good bet for babies over six months of age (doctors advise against it for younger infants). Besides sunscreen, other optional accessories include bottles of lotion and diaper rash creme. The best bet: buy these in small travel or trial sizes.

7 **DON'T FORGET THE TOYS.** We like compact rattles, board books, teethers, etc.

8 **SNACKS.** When your baby starts to eat solid foods, having a few snacks in the diaper bag (a bottle of water or milk, crackers, a small box of Cheerios®) is a smart move.

9 **YOUR OWN PERSONAL STUFF.** Be careful of putting your wallet or checkbook into the diaper bag—we advise against it. We've left ours behind one too many times before we learned this lesson. Put your name and phone number in the bag in case it gets lost.

Our Picks: Brand Recommendations

We've looked the world over and have come up with two top choices for diaper bags: Land's End and Eddie Bauer (plus a couple of other smaller brands worthy of consideration). They both meet our criteria for a great diaper bag—each offers both full-size and smaller bags, they don't look like diaper bags, each uses high-quality materials and, best of all, they are affordably priced. Let's take a look at each:

Land's End (800) 356-4444 (web: www.landsend.com) sells not one but three diaper bags: The Do-It-All Diaper bag ($34.50), the Deluxe ($49.50), and the Little Tripper ($24.50). Lands' End also has two diaper backpacks (Backpack Diaper Bag, $39.50 and the Little Tripper Backpack Diaper Bag, $29.50).

The Do-It-All features a large main compartment for diapers and wipes, a clip for your keys, and a detachable waterproof pouch for wet clothes. Then there's another zippered compartment for a blanket or change of clothes, a waterproof changing pad and an expandable outside pocket for books and small toys. Outside, you'll find a zippered pocket on the other side and a small pouch with a Velcro closure. And, if that weren't enough, the bag also has two large pockets for bottles on each end of the bag.

For 2001, Lands End has added several improvements to the Do-It-All, including a new parent pocket to stow a wallet and cell phone and a bigger water-resistant pouch for "when disaster strikes."

Whew! That's a lot of stuff. But how does it work in the real world? Wonderful, as a matter of fact. We've spoken to parents who've hauled this thing on cross-country airline trips, on major treks to the mountains, and more. At $34.50, it isn't cheap, but considering the extra features and durability, we think it's worth the money. (Don't forget to check Lands End's outlet stores for diaper bag bargains).

How about those quick trips to the store? We bought the Little Tripper for this purpose and have been quite happy. It has a changing pad, waterproof pouch and bottle pocket. With just enough room for a few diapers, wipes and other personal items, it's perfect for short outings. New this year, Lands End has also added a parent's pocket to the Little Tripper. And, at $24.50, it's a good value.

In case you need more room, the Deluxe is a bigger version of the Do-It-All (about 30% larger). It has a bigger changing pad, two zippered pouches for wet clothes and other items, a zippered compartment on the outside, built-in toiletry kit and larger bottle pockets lined with Thinsulate to keep food cool or warm.

This might be a good place to plug the "Overstocks" page on Lands End's web site (www.landsend.com). This regularly updated section has some fantastic bargains (up to 50% off) on all sorts of Lands End items, including their kids clothing, bedding, diaper bags and more. You can also sign up for their newsletter which updates you on the site.

Not to be outdone, ***Eddie Bauer*** (800) 426-8020 (web: www.eddiebauer.com) offers three diaper bags–the Diaper Tote ($40), Diaper Daypack (backpack, $48) and Diaper Shoulder Bag ($48).

Each is made of high-quality nylon that's easy to clean and contains a removable changing pad, two exterior bottle pockets, and a detachable pocket for damp items. The *Wall Street Journal* called Bauer's offering "the most manly diaper bag available" and we have to agree—the look does not scream baby.

Besides Lands End and Eddie Bauer, readers say they've had success with Baby Bjorn's Diaper Backpack ($56), but it looked a bit bulky and cumbersome to us.

A dark horse contender in the diaper bag wars is ***Combi***, the stroller maker mentioned earlier in this chapter. Their four offerings have been surprising hits—the Deluxe Backpack ($40), Traditional ($38-$44), Fashion Bag ($34) and Deluxe Tote Bag ($30). New for 2001, Combi will debut the "Urban Sling Messenger" diaper bag for $48. We like the backpack model best—it features all the doodads you'd expect from a diaper bag, including two insulated bottle pockets, zipper side pocket for parents, diaper changing bad and more. Plus it looks just as fashionable as the Kenneth Cole diaper bag at half the price.

Speaking of which, those oh-so-hip ***Kenneth Cole*** bags are our least favorite in this category. Running as much as $90 for vinyl or $200 for leather, these bags feature fancy styling but lack some of the functional accessories and storage space you see in Lands End and Eddie Bauer. Hence, it's more style than substance. And did we mention it is twice the price of Land's End's bags?

What about all those other diaper bag brands out there? Yes, you'll see a myriad of cheaper bags out there from brands as diverse as Gerber to Nicole Miller. Bottom line: stick with Lands End, Eddie Bauer or Combi for the best combo of price and features.

Carriers

Strollers are nice, but you'll soon discover that your baby doesn't want to sit in one for a long time. No, they really want to be with you. So, how do you cart around a baby for long distances without throwing out your back?

Several companies have come to the rescue with dozens of different carriers, all designed to make your little one more portable. Carriers come in two flavors: soft carriers (for everyday use) and backpack carriers (for outdoor adventures, especially for older children).

As for the soft carriers, one of the more famous is Nojo's ***Baby Sling*** (about $40; call 714-858-9496 for a dealer near you; web: www.nojo.com). The Sling enables you to hold your baby horizontally or upright. Babies seem to either love or hate the Baby Sling—we used one and found that our baby would go to sleep in it if he was really tired. However, he was less thrilled about the Sling when he was awake. And that experience pretty much paralleled the experiences of the parents we interviewed–some had babies who loved the Sling and others panned it.

Another sling that parents praise is the ***Maya Wrap Sling*** ($35; www.mayawarp.com), which can be used in various positions on the front, back, hip, nursing and more.

So, what's the best soft carrier on the market? We have two words for you: ***Baby Bjorn***. Quite simply, we love this thing! In a Bjorn, baby can face forward or backward and is positioned for easy carrying. Adjusting the straps is also easy, since everything is up front. And best of all, you can snap off the front of the Bjorn to put a sleeping baby down. Imported from Europe by Regal Lager (for a store near you, call 800-593-5522; web: www.babybjorn.com), the Baby Bjorn isn't cheap (about $75 to $80 retail) but it's vastly superior to other carriers on the market. There is also a "tall" version of the Bjorn for vertically-blessed parents.

New this year, Bjorn has added a "washable leather" carrier for $180. Obviously, we don't recommend THAT version–besides being so expensive, we can't imagine how hot a leather carrier would be to use. Yea, Bjorn has added ventilation holes into the carrier but we can see a bunch of sweating moms in Beverly Hills trying to use this thing in summer . . . and that isn't pretty.

One note of caution on the Bjorn: a recall in 1999 fixed a design problem with the Bjorn's leg openings. Bjorns made between 1991 and October 1998 had leg openings that were too large; as a result, a small infant (under two months) could slip out of the carrier. The company fixed the problem with a redesign and offered a retrofit kit for parents with the older model. If you get a hand-me-down Bjorn, make sure you have this kit (call toll-free 877-242-5676 to get one).

What about the other brands? We've heard mixed reviews about carriers by ***Kapoochi*** and ***Snugli***. The only carrier parents unanimously can agree on is the Bjorn. Parents do praise the ***Over the Shoulder Baby Holder*** ($30 to $40), a sling that has a myriad of adjustments. Another great carrier: ***Theodore Bean*** (877-68TBEAN; web: www.theodorebean.com). Their basic Sport Carrier is $55 (we saw it online at www.travelingtykes.com) and has a myriad of adjustments and comfort features. Theodore Bean also makes leather and micro fiber versions of their carriers.

Canadian parents write to us with kudos for the ***Baby Trekker*** (800-665-3957; web: www.babytrekker.com). This 100% washable cotton carrier has straps that around the waist for support. Canucks like the fact a baby can be dressed in a snowsuit and still fit in the Baby Trekker. The carrier ($80 US, $102 Canada) is available in baby stores in Canada or via the company's web site for folks in the U.S.

Going hiking? Just because you have a baby doesn't mean you can never go hiking again. Outdoor companies like ***Kelty*** (800-423-2320, web: www.kelty.com) and ***Madden*** (303-442-5828, web: www.maddenusa.com) have come to the rescue of parents with full lines of high-quality back and front pack carriers. Kelty's soft front carrier the Kangeroo ($75) is sort of like the outdoor version of the Bjorn—high quality and well-designed. If you want a frame carrier, Kelty offers five models, including the new Expedition ($275) that has all the bells and whistles. New for 2001, Kelty will debut a new combo backpack stroller (basically a Town pack with wheels) for $150 that weighs just 8.5 lbs.

Madden offers only frame carriers such as the Caravan. This carrier ($250) has aluminum frames and suspension systems to take the strain off your back. What most impressed us with Kelty and Madden is their quality—these are real backpack makers who don't skimp on details. Backpack carriers made by juvenile product companies are wimpy by comparison.

If those prices are a bit hard to swallow, check out the ***Tough Traveler Kid Carrier*** ($157, call 800-GO-TOUGH, web: www.toughtraveler.com). Adjustable for just the right fit, the Tough Traveler features cushioned pads, tough nylon cloth, and two-shoulder harnesses for baby. A comfortable seat provides head and neck protection for smaller children—you even get a zippered pouch for storage. Tough Traveler has several other models that combine great quality and decent pricing.

So, what's the best back-pack among Kelty, Madden or Tough Traveler? That's a tough one—each has great features. Readers give the slight edge to the Tough Traveler for its quick and easy adjustments, light weight (less bulk) and great storage. Madden makes a great carrier, but it doesn't fit smaller moms as well.

A good source for outdoor baby gear is the ***Campmor*** catalog (800) 226-7667. You can also find this gear at outdoor retailers like REI.

So, how do you decide which carrier is best for you and your baby? The best advice is to borrow different models from your friends and give them a test drive.

The Bottom Line: A Wrap-Up of Our Best Buy Picks

Strollers are a world unto themselves, with prices ranging from $30 for a cheap umbrella style to $500 or more for a deluxe foreign model with all the bells and whistles. The key message here is to buy the right stroller for your lifestyle (see specific recommendations earlier in this chapter). No one model works best for all situations.

In general, the best stroller brands are Peg Perego, Combi and Maclaren. For jogging strollers, the Baby Jogger is our top pick while we liked Burley bike trailers best in that category.

Who's got the best deals on car seats and strollers? We use web sites and online coupons for the best pricing. But we have to give it to stores like Babies R Us and Baby Depot—their prices are competitive and the sales can't be beat.

For diaper bags, we love Lands End and Eddie Bauer best, although Combi offers a decent alternative.

Baby Bjorn runs away with the crown for best carrier; for outdoor enthusiasts, check out the offerings from Kelty and Madden.

CHAPTER 9

Affordable Baby Proofing

Inside this chapter, you'll discover how to baby proof your home on a shoe-string budget. We've got room-by-room advice and several money-saving tips that might surprise you. Which devices work best? We'll give you the answers and share four mail-order catalogs that will save you time and money. Finally, learn what items should be in your baby's first aid kit.

Getting Started: When Do You Need This Stuff?

Whatever you do, start early. It's never too soon to think about baby proofing your house. Everyone we talked to admitted they waited until their baby "almost did something" (like playing with extension cords or dipping into the dog's dish) before they panicked and began childproofing.

Remember Murphy's Law of Baby Proofing: your baby will be instantly attracted to any object that can cause permanent harm. The more harm it will cause, the more attractive it will be to him or her. A word to the wise: start baby proofing as soon as your child begins to roll over.

Safe &Sound: Smart Baby Proofing Tips

The statistics are alarming—each year, 100 children die and millions more are injured in avoidable household accidents. Obviously, no parent wants their child to be injured by a preventable accident, yet many folks are not aware of common dangers. Others think if they load up their house with safety gadgets, their baby will be safe. Yet, there is one basic truth about child safety: safety devices are no substitute for adult supervision. While this chapter is packed with all kinds of gizmos and gadgets to keep baby out of harm's way, you still have to watch your baby at all times.

Where do you start? Get down on your hands and knees and look at the house from your baby's point of view. Be sure to go room by room throughout the entire house. As you take your tour, here are some points to keep in mind.

General Tips

◆ *Throw away plastic bags and wrappings*—these are a suffocation hazard. And there are more plastic bags and packing in your

What are the most dangerous baby products?

The Consumer Product Safety Commission releases yearly figures for injuries and deaths for children under five years old related to juvenile products. The latest figures from the CPSC are for 2000 and show a decrease overall in the number of injuries. The following chart details the statistics:

PRODUCT CATEGORY	INJURIES	DEATHS
WALKERS/JUMPERS	9,340	8
STROLLERS/CARRIAGES	12,600	12
INFANT CARRIES/CAR SEATS*	12,820	18
CRIBS, BASSINETS, CRADLES**	10,240	106
HIGH CHAIRS	6,660	5
BABY GATES/BARRIERS	1,470	0
PLAYPENS	1,470	42
CHANGING TABLES	2,120	1
OTHER	8,680	69
TOTAL	**65,400**	**261**

Key:
Deaths: Total deaths from 1995 to 1997.
*excludes motor vehicle incidents
** including crib mattresses and pads

Our Comments: The large number of deaths associated with cribs almost exclusively occurs in cribs that are so old they don't meet current safety standards. We encourage parents to avoid hand-me-down, antique and second hand cribs.

As for walkers, we continue to request that the CPSC ban walkers. As you can see by the statistics, they cause the most injuries of any juvenile product. Keep in mind that these are statistics of injuries that require a *hospital visit,* not just minor bruises.

house than you might realize–dry cleaning bags, grocery bags and bubble pack are all prime suspects.

◆ ***Check out the 'Net for sites like SafetyAlerts.com (www.safetyalerts.com).*** Although this isn't the easiest site to navigate, they offer some wonderful information on safety, recalls and more. You'll find categories like allergies, child car seats, clothing, drugs and medicine, infant and child and more. In the section on infant and child we found articles on baby food, cribs, bedding, even pacifiers. For example, they listed a recall of First Alert plastic safety gates which can break into small pieces. You can sign up for email alerts in specific categories so you don't have to check back with the site frequently. SafetyAlerts is dilligent about sending out recall notices as fast as the government issues them.

◆ ***Put window guards on any windows you plan to open.*** In June of 2000, the Consumer Product Safety Commission issued new standards for window guards. Each year about 12 children die in falls from windows while another 4,000 require hospital visits. You have two options with windows. You can place a stopper on the window frame so the window can only be raised up to four inches or you can install a guard. Window guards screw into the window frame and have bars no more than four inches apart. The guards come in two flavors: stationary or removable. If your windows are in a standard two story house (up to the sixth floor of an apartment building), you'll need a barrier that can be opened by an adult or older child in case of a fire. If you live in an apartment above the sixth floor, you'll need a permanently mounted option. Most window guards sell for $10 to $30 although some catalogs sells them for an outrageous $55 to $70.

◆ ***Mini-blind cords can be a strangulation hazard.*** Put them high off the floor or buy cord shorteners (available from many of the catalogs and web sites we review later in this chapter). Another money-saver: inexpensive "cleats" from hardware stores let you wrap up the cords, keeping them far from baby's reach.

◆ ***Always use gates at the TOP and BOTTOM of stairs.*** Placing a gate two or three steps up from the bottom allows your child to practice climbing without the danger. Gates at the top of the stairs should be permanently mounted (instead of pressure gates). If you have wrought iron railings or other challenging railings, consider gates from ***KidCo*** (800-553-5529 for a dealer near you, www.kidcoinc.com). KidCo makes adapter kits to make any gate compatible with wood banisters, hollow walls and wrought iron railing.

Our Picks for Best Gates

When you look at the options available in baby gates, you can get easily overwhelmed. KidCo, Safety 1st, Evenflo, SuperGate and First Years are just a few of the brands available. And you'll see metal, plastic, fabric padded, tall, short, wide, permanent mount, pressure mount and more. So, what to get? The temptation of many parents (including us) is to buy what's cheapest. But after buying and using at least six gates, here are our picks and tips:

Your best option from the start is to stick with the metal or wooden gates. Plastic never seems to hold up that well and looks dirty in short order from all those sticky finger prints. Our favorite brand is ***KidCo***. They make the Gateway, Safeway and Elongate models plus a variety of extensions and mounting kits. We used the permanent mount gate (the Safeway $55) which expands from 24 inches to 43 inches. We thought it was fairly easy to install and simple to use. The Gateway ($60) is the pressure mounted version. The Elongate ($80) fits spaces from 45 inches to 60 inches wide. All three gates can be expanded further with inexpensive extensions.

Another interesting option for a pressure gate is the ***First Years' Hands Free Gate*** ($50). This metal gate has a foot pedal that adults can step on to open. If you have your hands full, this is a great way to get in and out. Soft gates have recently entered the market including the ***Soft n' Wide from Evenflo*** ($35). It is a stationary gate (does not swing open) with nylon covered padding at the top and bottom to protect baby from the metal frame. This is useful if you don't want to move the gate often and don't need to open the gate for access. Otherwise swinging gates are a better bet.

Finally, check out the plastic ***Supergate*** from North State Industries ($37), a gate our readers have recommended. This gate expands up to 60 inches and slides together and swings out of the way so you can easily clear a path. It is a hard mounted gate so it can be used at the top of stairs. You may also notice a new gate, the ***Kiddy Guard***, that opens and retracts like a window blind. At $110, however, it's a bit on the expensive side.

◆ ***Eliminate pool hazards.*** Pools are among the most dangerous outdoor hazards for a toddler; about 350 children under five drown each year according to the Consumer Product Safety Commission (CPSC). The CPSC actually studied the effectiveness of pool alarms in a report released in 2000. They looked at three types of alarms: floating alarms that detect waves on the surface, underwater products that detect waves under the surface and a wristband alarm worn by children that activates when wet.

The CPSC found that, in general, underwater alarms performed most consistently with less likelihood of false alarms (one surface alarm also performed well). The CPSC points out that underwater alarms can also be used in conjunction with a pool cover–surface alarms cannot. The wristband alarm was most impractical of all the devices since it requires a care giver to remember to put it on a child. Here are the alarms they recommended–for underwater alarms, ***Poolguard*** (PBM Laboratories, www.poolguard.com) and ***Sentinel LINK*** (Lambo Products; we found it on www.babyproofingplus.com). A good surface alarm: ***PoolSOS*** by Allweather (www.allweather.ca) Here are additional tips from the CPSC for safety around your pool:

1. ***Fences and walls should be at least four feet high and installed completely around the pool.*** Fence gates should be self-closing and self-latching. The latch should be out of a small child's reach.

2. ***If your house forms one side of the barrier to the pool,*** then doors leading from the house to the pool should be protected with alarms that produce a sound when a door is unexpectedly opened.

3. ***A power safety cover*** (a motor-powered barrier that can be placed over the water area) can be used when the pool is not in use.

4. ***For above-ground pools, steps/ladders to the pool should be secured and locked,*** or removed when the pool is not in use.

5. ***If a child is missing, always look in the pool first. Seconds count in preventing death or disability.*** Keep rescue equipment by the pool, and be sure a phone is poolside with emergency numbers posted. You or someone in your household should know CPR.

◆ ***Keep your child out of garages and basements.*** There are too many items stored in these areas that can be dangerous (like pesticides and gardening equipment). If you don't want to install a keyed lock to basement stairs, consider a hook and eye closure at the top of the door. This allows adults to open the door easily.

◆ ***Put the cat's litter box up off the floor.*** Even better: install a cat-sized pet door in the laundry room, put the litter box in there, and keep the door closed.

◆ ***Keep pet food dishes and water dishes out of baby's reach.*** Besides eating dog or cat food (and maybe choking on it), some pets jealously guard their food and might snap at an eager toddler. Water dishes are a drowning hazard.

◆ ***Fireplaces can be a major problem.*** Never leave your child unattended around a fire. Even if there is no fire in the fireplace, the soot left behind is a toxic snack. Fireplace tools aren't good play toys either; put them away in a locked cabinet. Consider buying a bumper pad to go around the hearth to prevent injuries.

◆ ***Cover outlets.*** You have two choices: outlet PLUGS that stick directly into receptacles and outlet COVERS, which are an entire face plate that is mounted over each pair of outlets. You can buy outlet covers from hardware stores or safety catalogs. Safety experts caution that those cheap outlet plugs are a potential choking hazard. Consider moving heavy furniture in front of some of your outlets as well. If you have a computer and other peripherals, consider a kid-proof outlet strip. We've seen such strips with covers that slide over unused outlets, and other models that keep baby from unplugging any cords (see the safety catalogs later in this chapter for more info).

◆ ***Fire escape ladder.*** If you live in a two-story home, purchase a portable fire escape ladder. These ladders fold up compactly for under-bed or closet storage. They cost about $100 depending on the length. We actually saw the Kidde fire escape ladder in Costo warehouse stores for a mere $28. Just shows you you can find the weirdest stuff in the most surprising places if you keep your eyes open.

◆ ***Keep top-loading freezers locked.*** An enterprising toddler can get a chair and climb inside if it's not locked.

◆ ***Going to the grocery?*** Consider this: according to the Consumer Product Safety Commission 16,000 children under age five were injured in falls from shopping carts in 1996 (latest years' data). Sixty-six percent of those injuries were head trauma. And don't think all those injuries were from the seat. In fact, 49% fell out of the basket. Makes you think twice before putting your baby in a cart. If you're concerned about your toddler's safety consider buying a special shopping cart strap. The Baby Comfy Strap (made by Dex and available in Babies R Us) is an affordable option for under $10 which features a washable pad with strap. You'll see other shopping cart inserts in stores and catalogs. At the very least, use the straps in the cart and DON'T leave your child unattended.

Bathrooms

◆ ***Toilets make a convenient stepping stool and can be used to reach the bathroom countertop.*** Take hair dryers and curling irons off the counter and put them in a locked cabinet.

◆ ***Secure tub spouts or nozzles with protective covers.***

◆ ***Set your hot water heater to a lower setting.*** The best temperature for baby-friendly bathrooms is 120 degrees or less. As an alternative, you can purchase an anti-scalding device that attaches to showers or sink faucets. The ScaldSafe line of faucet anti-scald devices is an excellent safeguard. The shower version sells for $22 and the sink model for $9.50. It shuts the water off immediately when it reaches 114 degrees. We found them on Efficient Home's web site (www.efficienthome.com)

◆ ***Hide medication (including vitamins), mouthwash, perfume, and anything else containing alcohol in a cabinet with a latch.*** Don't think that a childproof cap is really childproof. Junior is much smarter than those rocket scientists at the drug companies think he is. Keeping all items that pose a hazard out of reach is your best defense. Each year, one million children accidentally ingest medicines or chemicals. Sadly, 50 of those cases are fatal.

◆ ***Get a toilet lock for all the toilets*** (about $10 from hardware stores and safety catalogs). Toddlers are fascinated with the water in the bowl. If they fall in head first, they won't be able to get themselves out. Also, don't use those colored deodorant products in the toilet. Not only are they toxic and therefore inherently dangerous, but they also make the toilet water a more enticing blue color.

◆ ***Check bath rugs and mats.*** Get non-skid versions or buy rubber backing to keep baby from slipping when she starts walking.

◆ ***Never leave buckets of water around,*** in the bathroom or anywhere in the home. If your baby should fall in head first, the weight of his head makes it impossible for him to leverage himself out. The result could be a tragic drowning, even in an inch or two of water.

◆ ***Separate your medicine and vitamins from the baby's.*** You don't want to make any mistakes in the middle of the night, when you're sleepy and trying to get your baby's medication.

◆ ***Don't store non-medicines in the medicine cabinet.*** You might grab a bottle of rubbing alcohol instead of cough syrup by accident.

◆ ***Bath rings and seats can be dangerous.*** Yes, these items (which are attached to a bath with suction cups) are pitched to parents as a safe way to bathe baby. But, they are not foolproof. *Never* leave any child under five years old alone in the bathtub or with an older sibling. Remember that a young infant can drown in less than an inch of water.

Kitchen

◆ ***Remember the dishwasher is a fun toyland, filled with all kinds of interesting objects.*** The best advice: keep it locked at all times. Another tip: never put dishwasher detergent in the dishwasher until you're ready to use it (and clean up any left over blobs after it's done). Dishwasher detergents are highly toxic.

Lock the oven door as well. However, as one reader wrote us, you can get "burned" following this tip: "My husband fixes appliances and received a frantic call on Thanksgiving Day. A mother had her turkey in the oven and had locked it to ensure that her enterprising toddler didn't open the door. Unfortunately, when you lock an oven door during use it will not unlock until the oven temp drops below a certain degree. It thinks you're trying to do a high temp clean. The frantic mother had a house full of people and turkey burning in the oven." Sounds like something we'd do!

◆ ***Put all cleaning supplies and poisons into an upper, locked cabinet.***

◆ ***Use safety latches on drawers with sharp cutlery and utensils.***

◆ ***Latch any cabinets containing glassware.***

◆ ***Lock up garbage in a place that's out of sight.***

◆ ***Unplug those small appliances–you*** don't want Junior playing with the Cuisinart.

◆ ***Protect your child from the stove.*** The best bargain tip here is to simply remove the knobs and keep them in a drawer until you are ready to use the stove. Another alternative is to use knob covers, sold in most chain stores.

◆ ***Keep stools/chairs away from countertops, stoves, and sinks.***

◆ ***Tablecloths can be yanked off your table by an overzealous toddler***, bringing dishes crashing down on her head. Use placemats instead when you're eating at the table; otherwise, the table should be cleared.

◆ ***Get a fire extinguisher rated ABC*** (which can handle any type of fire). If you have a two-story house, a second fire extinguisher upstairs would be a good idea as well.

Living Rooms

◆ ***Forget using that coffee table for just about anything–remove any small objects and potential missiles.*** If it's breakable, it should go up on a high shelf or in a locked cabinet. Pad that coffee table with bumpers–especially if it's made of glass.

◆ ***Anchor bookcases to the wall with nails or brackets.*** Shelves present a temptation to budding rock climbers who might pull them over on themselves.

◆ ***Inspect your house plants and get rid of poisonous ones.*** Consult your local nursery or agricultural extension office for a list of poisonous plants. Of course, even a "safe" plant should be placed out of reach. And don't forget to check silk plants and trees to make sure leaves cannot be detached and swallowed.

◆ ***Extension cords are a notorious hazard.*** Use as few cords as possible and hide them behind (or under) furniture.

◆ ***Make sure any TV or stereo cart can't be pulled over.*** Babies also love to play disc jockey, so your stereo equipment should be moved far out of reach.

◆ ***Consider buying a VCR lock*** to keep your little one from feeding the tape player her Cheerios.

Bedrooms

◆ ***Don't leave small objects like coins, jewelry, cosmetics, or medications on dressers or bureaus.***

◆ ***Storing items under the bed is a no-no.*** These are easy pickings for a baby.

◆ ***Check how easily drawers in dressers can be pulled out.*** Once babies can open the drawers, they may try using them as stepladders.

◆ ***If you're concerned about your cat climbing into baby's crib, consider a crib tent***. The Cozy Crib Tent ($90), manufactured by Tots in Mind (call 800-626-0339 for a dealer near you), is a mesh crib topper that attaches to the side railing. It completely encloses the crib, making it impossible for cats to snuggle up to little ones.

Money-Saving Secrets

1 **OUTLET COVERS ARE EXPENSIVE.** Only use them where you will be plugging in items. For unused outlets, buy cheap plate covers (these blank plates have no holes and are screwed into the wall over the plugs). Another option: put heavy furniture in front of unused outlets. What type of outlet cover should you buy? We like the Safe-Plate ($5 from the Right Start catalog; web: www.rightstart.com), which requires you to slide a small plate over to access the receptacle. In contrast, those that require you to rotate a dial to access the outlet are more difficult to use.

2 **MANY DISCOUNTERS LIKE TARGET, K-MART, AND WAL-MART SELL A LIMITED SELECTION OF BABY SAFETY ITEMS.** We found products like gates, outlet plugs, and more at prices about 5% to 20% less than full-priced hardware stores.

3 **SOME OF THE MOST EFFECTIVE BABY PROOFING IS FREE.** For example, moving items to top shelves, putting dangerous chemicals away, and other common sense ideas don't cost any money and are just as effective as high-tech gadgets.

Do It By Mail

ONE STEP AHEAD.

To Order Call: (800) 274-8440; Fax (847) 615-7236.
Web: www.onestepahead.com
Shopping Hours: 24 hours a day, seven days a week.
Or write to: One Step Ahead, PO Box 517., Lake Bluff, IL 60044.
Credit Cards Accepted: MC, VISA, AMEX, Discover, Optima.

One Step Ahead has a convenient index that lets you zero-in on any product. The catalog's five pages of babyproofing products include such items as gates, "Tot Lok" cabinet latches ($12.95 for two locks a key), and Toddler Shield coffee table bumpers. They even offer TV/VCR guards, power strip covers and appliance safety latches. We especially like their child-safe medicine cabinet. Prices are basically retail, but they've beefed up the selection.

CHILD SAFETY SOTRE

To Order Call: (800) 282-3836
Web: www.childsafetystore.com
Or write to: 1085 SW 15 AVE. E-3, Delray Beach, FL 33444
Credit Cards Accepted: MC, VISA, AMEX, Discover.

This geat web site is organized by room, product or brand. For example, you can search for just kitchen safety items or zero on Kidco's Gateway gates. We liked the section on pool alarms, as well as cabinet locks. Sample price: $10 for the Tubbly Bubbly spout cover by Kel-Gar. Their email newsletter includes promotions and coupons, as well as other helpful tips. Our only complaint: the site is slow to load and contains annoying banner ads.

RIGHT START CATALOG.

To Order Call: (800) 548-8531); Fax (800) 762-5501.
Web: www.rightstart.com
Shopping Hours: 24 hours a day, seven days a week.
Or write to: 5388 Sterling Center Dr., Unit C, Westlake Village, CA 91361.
Credit Cards Accepted: MC, VISA, AMEX, Discover.

The Right Start Catalog seems to have added substantially to their safety items in the past years. Beyond the usual (Tot-Loks cabinet locks, stove guards and fireplace bumpers) they sell the Mighty Tight seat belt tightener ($20), heat sensitive bath tub mats ($5.50) and driveway warning signs (Kids at Play, $11). Prices are regular retail but be sure to check their web site for special deals. They also have quite a few stores (usually in major malls across the country). Sales seem more frequent although the stores usually have a more limited selection than the catalog.

Wastes of Money

Waste of Money #1

Outlet plugs

"My friend thought she'd save a bundle by just using outlet plugs instead of fancy plate covers. Unfortunately, her toddler figured out how to remove the plugs and she had to buy the plates anyway."

It doesn't take an astrophysicist to figure out how to remove those cheap plastic outlet plugs. While the sliding outlet covers are pricier, they may be well worth the investment. Another problem: outlet plugs can be a choking hazard. If baby removes one (or an adult removes one and forgets to put it back), it can end up in the mouth.

Waste of Money #2

Plastic corner guards

"The other day I was looking through a safety catalog and saw some corner guards. It occurred to me that they don't look a whole lot softer than the actual corner they cover. Are they worth buying?"

You've hit (so to speak) on a problem we've noticed as well. Our advice: the plastic corner guards are a waste of money. They aren't very soft—and they don't have air bags that pop out when you hit them either. So what's the solution? If you're worried about Junior hitting the corner of your coffee table, you can either store it for a while or look into getting a soft bumper pad ($30 to $65 in catalogs). Similar bumpers are available for your fireplace as well. On the other hand, you may decide that blocking off certain rooms is a more affordable option.

Waste of Money #3

Appliance safety latches

"I can't imagine that my daughter is going to be able to open

the refrigerator any time soon. So why do they sell those appliance latches in safety catalogs, anyway?"

There must be some super-strong kids out there who have enough torque to open a full-sized refrigerator. At this point, ours isn't one of them so a $6 refrigerator latch isn't on our shopping list. One point to remember: many appliances like stoves and dishwashers have locking mechanisms built in. And, keep all chairs and stools away from the laundry room to prevent your baby from opening the washing machine and dryer.

How safe is Safety 1st?

If you ran a company named "Safety 1st," you'd think it would turn out products that were, well, safe. Yet we were troubled to notice Safety 1st (which controls a whopping 70% of the baby proofing market) fared poorly in a test by *Consumer Reports*. In its January 1997 issue, the magazine evaluated 24 Safety 1st products, from cabinet locks to stove guards. While six products were rated good, very good or excellent, the majority (ten products) were rated only "fair." We were surprised that one product rated poor and three more "not acceptable."

How could these safety products be so unsafe? Unfortunately, no government agency tests safety products to make sure they actually work. Only after a product causes an accident or injury will the government consider an investigation.

To be fair, these problems aren't unique to Safety 1st—many companies that make "low-cost" (read: cheap) safety products suffered poor ratings from *Consumer Reports*. Many of these items are made of flimsy plastic or other materials that simply don't work in the real world.

We should note that Safety 1st has new owners—they were acquired by Dorel (Cosco's parent) in 2000. While we hope that the new ownership might fix some of Safety 1st's problems, unfortunately Dorel/Cosco doesn't have a stellar safety record themselves after suffering several major recalls in the past couple years.

So, what's a parent to do? Use high-quality safety products like the ones featured in the mail-order catalogs listed in this chapter. Another idea: consider calling a professional baby-proofer who is a member of the International Association for Child Safety (to find a member near you, call 888-677-IACS; web: www.iafcs.com). These folks sell high-quality baby proofing items and offer installation, or you can do-it-yourself.

A Baby First Aid Kit

Wonder what should be in your baby first aid kit? Honestly, as a childless couple, we were probably lucky to find a couple of plastic bandages and an ancient bottle of Bactine in our medicine cabinet. Now that you're Dr. Mom (or Nurse Dad) it's time to take a crash course on baby medicine etiquette. Here's a run-down of essentials.

◆ ***Acetaminophen*** (one brand name of this drug is Tylenol). If you suspect your child may have an allergy to flavorings, you can buy a version without all the additives. You may also want to keep acetaminophen infant suppositories in your medicine cabinet in case your infant persists in vomiting up his drops. Or refuses to take them at all. Do NOT keep baby aspirin in your house. Aspirin has been linked to Reyes Syndrome in children and is no longer recommended by the medical community.

◆ ***Children's Benadryl.*** To relieve minor allergic reactions.

◆ ***Antibiotic ointment*** to help avoid bacterial infection from cuts.

◆ ***Baking soda*** is great for rashes.

◆ ***A bulb syringe*** to remove mucus from an infant's nose when she's all stuffed up. One of the top 15 fun parenting activities that no one tells you about.

◆ ***Calamine lotion*** to relieve itching.

◆ ***A cough and cold remedy*** recommended by your pediatrician.

◆ ***A good lotion.*** Unscented and unmedicated brands are best.

◆ ***Measuring spoon*** or cup for liquid medicine. For small infants, you may want a medicine dropper or syringe.

◆ ***Petroleum jelly***, which is used to lubricate rectal thermometers.

◆ ***Plastic bandages*** like Band-Aids.

◆ ***Saline nose drops*** for stuffy noses.

◆ ***Tweezers.*** For all kinds of fun uses.

◆ ***A card with the number for poison control.*** You may want to call your local poison control center and ask them what poison remedies they recommend having on hand. It use to be that everyone recommended Syrup of Ipecac to induce vomiting. However, many poison experts and doctors think this may do more harm than good. Find out what your local center thinks of this issue (they may recommend activated charcoal instead) and always call the center if your child ingests a dangerous substance. DON'T try to remedy the situation by yourself.

◆ ***Thermometer.*** There are four types of thermometers you can use to take baby's temperature. A rectal thermometer, the old stand-by, is probably the most accurate. On the other hand, an ear thermometer is certainly the most convenient yet can give inaccurate readings if not used properly. The third possibility, especially for infants, is an underarm thermometer—again easy to use, but not as accurate as rectal ones. Some thermometers can be used either rectally or underarm. Finally, we've seen a new entrant to the thermometer category: forehead thermometers. These take a temperature from applying the sensor to your baby's forehead.

When it comes to ear thermometers, certainly the most famous brand is ***Braun's Thermoscan*** ($40 to $60 in stores like Target). They've really improved the accuracy in recent years and added new features including memory storage, beeping when it's done and more.

First Years has a new high speed digital thermometer ($10) that gives a rectal temp in 20 seconds and an underarm in 30 seconds. It comes in a unique oval shape for easy of use.

Safety 1st has added a new forehead thermometer this year, the ***Hospital's Choice*** for $50. They claim it takes accurate temperature readings in only three seconds, and has a memory button to recall eight previous temps, automatic shut off, five year battery, and more. While it sounds amazing, it was not available at press time and we don't have any feedback on how well it works.

Top Ten Safety Must Haves

To sum up, here's our list of top safety items to have for your home (in no particular order).

◆ ***Fire extinguishers,*** rated "ABC," which means they are appropriate for any type of fire.

◆ ***Outlet covers.***

◆ ***Baby monitor***—unless your house or apartment is very small, and you don't think it will be useful.

◆ ***Smoke alarms.*** The best smoke alarms have two systems for detecting fires—a photoelectric sensor for early detection of smoldering fires and a dual chamber ionization sensor for early detection of flaming fires. An example of this is the ***First Alert "Double System"*** ($25 to $35). We'd recommend one smoke alarm for every bedroom, plus main hallways, basement and living rooms. And don't forget to replace the batteries twice a year. Both smoke alarms and carbon monoxide detectors can be found in warehouse clubs like Sam's and Costco.

◆ ***Carbon monoxide detectors.*** These special detectors sniff out dangerous carbon monoxide (CO) gas, which can result from a malfunctioning furnace. Put one CO detector in your baby's room and another in the main hallway of your home.

◆ ***Cabinet and drawer locks.*** For cabinets and drawers containing harmful cleaning supplies or utensils like knives, these are an essential investment. For fun, designate at least one unsecured cabinet or drawer as "safe" and stock it with pots and pans for baby.

◆ ***Spout cover for tub.***

◆ ***Bath thermometer or anti-scald device.***

◆ ***Toilet locks***—so your baby doesn't visit the Tidy Bowl Man. One of the best we've seen in years is KidCo's toilet lock ($15). They won an award from the Juvenile Products Manufacturers Association product competition. Check their web site at www.kidcoinc.com for a store that carries it.

◆ ***Baby gates.*** See the box earlier for recommendations.

The Bottom Line: A Wrap-Up of Our Best Buy Picks

Some of the most affordable baby-proofing tips are free—lowering the setting on your water heater to 120 degrees or less, moving heavy furniture in front of outlets, not leaving plastic bags lying around, etc. Instead of buying expensive outlet covers for EVERY outlet in your home, just buy blank plates (less than $1) for unused outlets.

Most of the brands of baby-proofing products were pretty similar. Safety 1st is probably the best known, although we have mixed feelings about their products. Mail-order catalogs and web sites are good places to shop, with ChildSafetyStore.com as one of the most comprehensive.

CHAPTER 10
Best Gifts for Baby

What was the best baby gift you received? That was the question we posed to new parents across the U.S. In this chapter, we'll report on the results, some of which might surprise you. In addition to top gifts, we'll fill you in on "gift don'ts," advice on how to avoid wasting money. Finally, learn how to save money on baby announcements and discover a company that custom-designs announcements.

Top 10 Best Baby Gifts

What are the best gifts for baby? Here are our thoughts on what most new moms and dads would really use.

We should note that these are the "best gifts," not necessary the best gift *bargains*. You'll note some of our picks here are under $50; yet we will also recommend a few more extravagant purchases (a $200 stroller or $250 backpack). We assume that some of your gift-givers (or grandparents reading this book) might want to splurge on the baby, so here are some options. Of course, you can use the baby product web sites listed in the next chapter to order most of these items at a discount.

One of the best tips we can give the gift-giver is save the receipts. In fact, many retail stores offer "gift receipts" which make it easy for your friend to return something. The price isn't printed on a gift receipt, so unless they return your gift, they won't know how much you spent. Also keep return info for mail order and web purchases.

◆ ***Quilt.*** Here's a gift that offers both warmth and beauty. Quilts can be used as wonderful wall décor, a throw over a rocker, a play mat or a snuggle up blankie. And you'll find some of the best in the Garnet Hill catalog (800-622-6216; www.garnethill.com). How about goofy animals, dinosaurs, whimsical villages and more? The quilts are well made, machine washable (line dry, however) and thin enough to be used safely to sleep under (when your baby is older). Prices vary depending on design; the dinosaur quilt was $98 for a crib size.

◆ ***Tiny Love's "Symphony in Motion" mobile*** for $45 is our pick as best mobile. It plays three classical tunes and has a unique rotating bar that sends toys/characters along a funky path to keep baby entertained.

◆ ***Innovative Décor.*** Forget buying one of those pink piggy banks or a designer airplane lamp for your friend's baby, instead give them room décor in a box. "Transfer-mations" by Camp Kazoo has to be one of the best new products we've discovered (call 303-526-2626 for a store near you; web: www.boppy.com). Using innovative iron-on transfers, this product lets parents create paint-by-number masterpieces in their baby's room. Paint an eight-by-ten foot mural or just add some decorative borders. Cost: $30 (plus the cost of paints). And if you're giving it as a gift, you can offer to lend a hand decorating the nursery!

◆ ***The 7 lb. Stroller.*** Yes, lots of companies make cheap umbrella strollers. The trick is making one that's both low in weight AND high in quality. The answer: Combi's "Savvy Z," is a terrific 7 pounder with removable, washable seat cushions, a basket, larger canopy and partial recline. For $180 to $200, this stroller makes an excellent gift for the suburban baby on the go. (If you want to go whole hog, the Combi "Ultra Savvy" features a full reclining seat for $279) For a dealer near you, call (800) 752-6624, (800) 992-6624, (630) 871-0404. web: www.combi-intl.com.

◆ ***Baby Mozart.*** For all those grandparents convinced their grandchild is the next Beethoven, check out Neurosmith's Music Blocks toy (call 562-434-9856 for a dealer near you; web: www. neurosmith.com). This cool $70 "smart toy" lets babies create complex musical compositions by simply mixing and matching colored blocks.

◆ ***Chicco Mama High Chair.*** Here's something new parents won't be buying right away but will love as a gift. It's wider, taller and easier to clean than it's closest competitor, comes completely assembled and folds up in any position. The ultimate feeding chair at $160. For a dealer near you, call (877) 4CHICCO or (732) 805-9200; web: www.chiccousa.com.

◆ ***Baby Bjorn.*** Quite simply, it's the best baby carrier on the market. For $77, you get a carrier that lets baby ride facing forward or backward, is well-designed and easy to use. The Baby Bjorn has wide shoulder straps to distribute the weight comfortably and evenly, a head support for newborns—heck, even the front snaps off so you can put a sleeping baby down without waking it. They also offer a version in extra large ($80) for tall parents. And just to mirror the extravagance of the millennium, they've added a leather version for a whopping $180. Yes, it's washable and perforated for better air flow but . . . Don't call us if you buy the leather version and it's hot and sweaty. The Baby Bjorn is 100% cotton and machine washable. To find a store near you, call Regal+Lager at (800) 593-5522 or (770) 955-5060.

◆ ***Fire Escape Ladder.*** It weighs only nine pounds, but this portable fire escape ladder can save the lives of you and your children. When unfurled and hung on a window sill, the ladder instantly positions itself on your home's outside wall. The Perfectly Safe Catalog (800) 837-KIDS sells both a two-story ($80) and three-story ($120) versions. Both fold up compactly for storage.

◆ ***Something for Mom.*** How about a coupon for a night off? What about a visit to a day spa? Even a casserole dinner would be welcome in those first months. And if you visit and offer to "help" with anything, be prepared to do it. We've heard of friends giving a housecleaner for a day, a book of babysitting coupons, restaurant gift certificates and more. And remember, the first time mom will love it, but the second and third time mom will probably put you in her will for such thoughtfulness!

◆ ***The Ultimate Baby Back Pack.*** Just because you're a parent doesn't mean you can't go for a nature hike with your baby. The "Caravan" backpack from hip outdoor equipment maker Madden is the ultimate in baby backpacks–aircraft-quality aluminum frame, sophisticated suspension system to carry 65 pounds of child and other stuff, high-tech waterproof fabrics and more. Price: $250. For a dealer near you, call (303) 442-5828, web: www.maddenusa.com.

Gift Don'ts:

Unless specifically requested, these items are gift don'ts:

1 **Diaper bags.** As far as gifts go, this one has "been there, done that." People have different ideas about what's useful, so ask before you buy. Better yet, buy something else and leave the choice up to the parents. We've also seen those cheapie diaper bags that are stuffed with baby bottles and other miscellaneous items. They almost never put high quality products in these "gift bags" so try to resist them.

2 **Bottle Feeding System.** This may be offensive to a breast feeding mom who might feel that her choice to nurse is being undermined (remember, new moms have very sensitive feelings!).

3 **Gender Specific Clothes For Girls.** Just because your friend is having a girl, don't rush out and buy lacy, frilly dress-

es in cotton-candy pink. Some moms prefer more toned down or less gender-cliché gifts.

4 **BABY FLATWARE.** A friend of ours received an Oneida Love Lasts baby flatware set that includes utensils for first-time eaters up to toddlers. This gift is useless until a baby is 4 to 6 months old, and even then we wonder about the practicality of baby flatware. Plastic spoons and forks are much more useful because they are gentler on the gums and will get tossed on the floor.

5 **WALKERS**. This product is an absolute no-no. There are too many injuries every year (over 9300) involving walkers. And walker alternatives aren't much better. Studies have show that walkers and walker alternatives can contribute to developmental delays in babies who use them (see Chapter 6 for more details).

6 **THE RIGHT GIFT FOR THE WRONG SEASON.** Your friend gives birth to a bouncing baby boy in August. Wouldn't a cute shorts and shirt outfit be a perfect gift? The answer is no, if you bought a six-month size. When the baby is the right size to fit into this outfit, it will be the dead of winter. Instead, buy the baby a summer outfit for next summer (in a 12 to 18 month size range).

What if you receive one of the "gift don'ts" for your baby? Don't despair. Consign it at a local thrift shop and buy something you really need. Make sure to keep all the packaging, instructions, tags, etc.—it helps the consignment shop sell the item that much quicker.

Do it By Mail

Here's a selection of catalogs that offer gifts for baby:

CHINABERRY

To Order Call: (800) 776-2242; Fax (619) 670-5203
Web: www.chinaberry.com
Shopping Hours: 24 hours a day, seven days a week.
Or write to: 2780 Via Orange Way, Suite B, Spring Valley, CA 91978
Credit Cards Accepted: MC, VISA, AMEX, Discover.

"A cozy place for buying books" is Chinaberry's mission and it delivers—this simple black and white catalog is well-organized and very detailed. Each book gets lavish treatment, including comments from parents. If you're not familiar with children's books, this is a great resource. The catalog features board books for babies, books on tapes, parenting tomes and more. Check out the full color web site. Well organized along the same lines as the catalog, it's a great place to shop.

EXPOSURES

To Order Call: (800) 222-4947; Fax (920) 231-6942.
Web: www.exposuresonline.com
Shopping Hours: 8 am-Midnight, seven days a week.
Or write to: Exposures, 1 Memory Ln., P.O. Box 3615, Oshkosh, WI 54903.
Credit Cards Accepted: MC, VISA, AMEX, Discover.

If you're like us, you'll probably snap 10,000 pictures of your baby before she turns one. When our baby was born, the stock price of Kodak must have tripled overnight. But where to put all these wonderful snapshots? Call Exposures, a fantastic catalog that sells an amazing variety of picture frames and photo albums. You'll also find photo-related gifts, curio cabinets, and photograph storage systems.

We love Exposure's photo albums, from the basic leather styles to funky leather and wood combinations. Scrapbooks are also scattered throughout, including oversized options capable of storing 11" x 14" photos. On their web site you can click on the kids' section and find funky frames, coat hooks, shelves and keepsake boxes.

Our only complaint: the service from Exposures can be inconsistent. The company had so many problems shipping orders one Christmas that they told us in early December that orders wouldn't arrive until January. Phone operators also tend to be a little gruff. Because the catalog's offerings are so unique, we hope they can iron out these wrinkles.

LILLY'S KIDS (LILLIAN VERNON)

To Order Call: (800) 285-5555; Fax (804) 430-1010
Shopping Hours: 24 hours a day, seven days a week.
Or write to: Lillian Vernon, Virginia Beach, VA 23479.
Credit Cards Accepted: MC, VISA, AMEX, Discover, Diner's.

An offshoot of the popular Lillian Vernon catalog, Lilly's Kids is a collection of gifts and toys just for kids. At 80 pages, Lilly's Kids is chock full of interesting items.

MUSIC FOR LITTLE PEOPLE

To Order Call: (800) 346-4445.
Web: www.musicforlittlepeople.com
Shopping Hours: Monday through Friday, 8:30am to 6:30pm Eastern.

Or write to: P.O. Box 1460, Redway, CA 95560-1460.
Credit Cards Accepted: MC, VISA.

You'll find compact discs, videos and musical instruments (guitars, recorders, etc.). There's a nice selection of classical music, as well as options from Raffi and Tony Bennett. Compilations from a vast array of artists from Los Lobos to Dan Fogelberg make for an eclectic selection.

The Seven Most Ridiculous Baby Products

In our official capacity as your ambassadors to the world of baby stuff, we attend juvenile product trade shows where manufacturers ply us with large amounts of liquor and expensive trinkets.

Just kidding! Actually, we usually collect less-glamorous things like press kits and catalogs. And it's in those kits and catalogs that we discover some of the darnedest things—products that make you wonder aloud "What were these guys thinking?!!"

As a public service, we have compiled a list of the items that are truly hilarious. Fortunately, this year there's been a bumper crop of crazy baby stuff. For your entertainment and amusement, won't you join us as we proudly present the ***Official Fields List of The Seven Most Ridiculous Baby Products:***

1 **GUCCI'S WHITE MINK COAT FOR BABY**. Chase away baby's chill for just $4250! Too much? How about a $1500 baby leather jacket or $90 baby booties, all with that Gucci logo! Don't forget to get that $800 Gucci diaper bag or baby carrier.

2 **CASABLANCA PLUME WROUGHT IRON CRIB.** Why buy a normal crib when you can have one topped with ostrich feathers? By Bratt Décor; price: $1050.

3 **AROMATHERAPY FOR TOTS.** "Fussytime Calming Baby Bath Aromatherapy" by Baby Spa, $8.30 for two ounces. Got a cranky baby? Use the "pure essential oils of Roman chamomile and lavender to help calm overtired or colicky babies."

4 **CASHMERE BABY BLANKET.** Just $390 from Vermont luxury linen maker Anichini.

5 **ESTEE LAUDER'S ORIGINS NATURAL RESOURCES DIAPER "BALM."** Let Estee Lauder chase away those diaper rash blues for just $10 for a 3.50 oz tube!

6 **TITANIUM STROLLER.** Steel strollers are so yesterday. Why not go titanium? Maclaren's "TI Techno" boasts a titanium frame and a leather seat for $1500 to $2000.

7 **BABY PERFUME.** Is your infant a bit stinky after that diaper change? Spritz them with Musti, a $27 bottle of French cologne for babies.

If you've run across a truly ridiculous baby product, feel free to share it with us and our readers. Call us at (303) 442-8792 or e-mail your suggestion to authors@BabyBargainsBook.com. We won't stop until we've uncovered every last silly baby product available on Planet Earth.

Announcements

Getting Started: When Do You Need This Stuff?

Most printers take between five days and two weeks for delivery of standard baby announcements. (A good tip: most printers can provide the envelopes early so you can get a head start on the addressing). You'll want to begin shopping for your design in advance, preferably when you're six or seven months pregnant. If you know the sex of your baby ahead of time, you can pick just one design. If it's going to be a surprise, however, you may want to either select two designs or one that is suitable for both sexes. When the baby is born, you phone in the vital statistics (length, weight, date, and time), and it's off to the printing presses.

Parents in Cyberspace: What's on the Web?

Stationers abound on the web, but we've discovered a couple that specialize in birth announcements.

Babies N Bells

Web site: www.babiesnbells.com
What it is: Low cost stationery site.
What's cool: Here's a site that offers online samples of all their birth announcements. You can search their designs by themes (Noah's Ark, Sports) or by sex (Baby Boy, Baby Girl). Online ordering is available, the company will send free samples and they offer free proofs of your

order. A reader raved about their "wonderful customer service." ***Needs work:*** Unfortunately, there is no listing of actual manufacturers' names. The designs are all coded–what's the secret? We also found the navigation somewhat cumbersome. The samples are sometimes fuzzy as well.

Celebrate Invitations

Web site: www.celebrateinvitations.com
What it is: A discount birth announcement source.
What's Cool: One of the few sites that specializes in discounting high quality printers like Encore, William Arthur, Checkerboard and many more. They offer a free price quote on brands and have added retail prices to their price sheets. Be sure to note that Celebrate offers a 10% discount on the prices you see if you order on the web or by fax. A search option is also available.
Needs work: Since our last edition they've added samples (thumbnails and expanded views) to their site making it easier to get an idea of what you want. They've also posted prices on line–a huge improvement in our opinion. The tough part is finding the one you want. We recommend shopping around before you use this site so you know which brands and styles you want. The quality of the on line samples is not as good as what you see in a store.

Stork Avenue

Web site: www.storkavenue.com, see Figure 1 on the next page.
What it is: Affordable designer quality announcements resource.
What's Cool: Cute and affordable announcement cards for a mere $1.10 to $1.20 each. For only 15¢ more per card they'll add return addresses to the envelopes. They also offer free priority mail on all on line orders and 24 to 48 hour turnaround. We saw 27 different options for announcements from bears with balloons to antique toys to a big yellow crescent moon.
Needs work: It's a bit confusing to use the graphics on the home page. The roll overs aren't as clear as we'd like (you don't even know that's what you're doing at first), but once you get into the site, it works well with clear and simple graphics.

◆ ***Other sites to consider: Announcements by Jeannette*** is online at www.announcingit.com and offers six collections of announcement stock. The categories range from "elegant" to "doo-dads." What makes this site cool is you can order the cards printed or blank.

Card Creations (www.cardcreations.com) offers some unique options for photo announcements. Prices are pretty reasonable: $75 for 50 cards incorporating one photo and including any touch ups you might need.

Figure 1: Stork Avenue offers quantity discounts for their announcements–email the site for details.

The ***Fairy Godmother*** (www.thefairygodmother.com) carries some impressive designs from such manufacturers as Blue Mug. Prices are a bit higher than other sites at about $2.50 each.

AlphaBit Soup (www.alphabitsoup.com) is another site with beautiful options, both photo and regular announcements. Look for pretty bows and even vintage backgrounds on these affordable (about $50 for 50) announcements.

Afrocentric announcements can be found on ***Celebrating Children's*** web site (www.CelebratingChildren.com). Both custom designs and fill-in-the-blank options are available as well as terrific articles on different holidays and special occasions like Kwanzaa, Christmas, baby showers and even Grandparent's Day.

Money Saving Secrets

1 **ORDER 10% TO 20% MORE THAN YOU NEED.** Odds are you will forget that long lost friend or relative. Going back for additional announcements will be very expensive–most companies have minimums of at least 25 pieces. Ordering 75 announcements at the outset will be about 50% cheaper than ordering 50, forgetting some relatives, and then going back for another 25.

2 **CHECK YOUR LOCAL NEWSPAPER FOR SALES.** Many stationers have periodic sales with 10% to 20% discounts.

3 LOOK FOR DISCOUNT STATIONERS IN YOUR AREA. Discount Bridal Service, a company we review in our wedding books, has 500 reps across the country. While their main business is selling bridal apparel, DBS reps often have a discount invitations and baby announcements business too. You can find discounts of 20% to 40% off name brand manufacturers like Elite, Encore, William Arthur, Chase and many others. Call (800) 874-8794 for a dealer near you.

4 COMPARE MAIL-ORDER PRICES. At the end of this section, we list a couple of catalogs that offer affordable options for baby announcements.

5 LASER IT YOURSELF. Consider ordering a box of 100 sheets of specialty laser paper, designing the announcement on a computer, and then printing it out on a desktop printer. Paper Direct catalog (800-272-7377; www.paperdirect.com) has a wonderful selection of appropriate stationery. We like the "Sweet Dreams" (order #DT3041) design, with its adorable bear and toy border. Price: $22 for a box of 100. Coordinating envelopes are $17 for 25. All in all, there are a half dozen designs that would be appropriate. This requires a little more effort than the standard baby announcement but might be a fun project if you're so inclined. Another source: Kinko's copy shops sells laser compatible papers you could use for birth announcements. The cost is 19¢ per sheet and each sheet has two or four post-card size announcements. Matching envelopes are 10¢ each. With a little effort, you could do all of your baby announcements for under $10.

6 GET CREATIVE. Check out that do-it-yourself maven, Martha Stewart for ideas. On a recent visit to her web site, www.marthastewart.com, we saw several cute birth announcement samples. For example, we thought the diaper pocket idea was great. Using a template (downloaded from the site), you take left-over wallpaper from baby's room (or wrapping paper) and create a diaper shaped pocket. Then you slip a card with the vital info into the diaper pocket.

Other ideas can be found on craft sites like Michaels (www.michaels.com) and Hobby Lobby (www.hobbylobby.com). Check the articles archives on baby sites like Parent Soup (www.parentsoup.com).

7 TRY SOMETHING SWEET YET SIMPLE. How about sending your friends and relatives a chocolate bar announcement? You can order wrappers to fit a regular Hershey's candy bar that say "Here She Is" or "Here He Is." Hershey's offers 36 wrappers and candy bars in a keepsake box for $19.95 (plus shipping). Call (800) 544-1347 or check their web site at www.hersheys.com. Another company, Carson Enterprises (800-995-2288; web: www.carsonenterprises.com), sell the whole candy bar and wrapper for $1 per full size bar with a minimum of 24 bars per order. Miniature bars are 45¢ each (minimum 70). You can also buy the wrappers only. Homestead can print the vital statistics on the back of the wrapper with cute tags like "Baked: November 14, 1999, Serving Size: 20 inches, Delivery of Goods: 9:28 am." A wide variety of wrapper designs are available. Finally, Angel Bars (www.angelbars.com) sells wrappers as well.

The Name Game: Reviews of Selected Printers

While dozens of companies print baby announcements, we think the six companies reviewed in this section are the best of the best. We should note that these printers do not sell directly to the public–you must place your order through one of their dealers (usually a retail stationary store). Call the phone numbers below to find the name of a dealer near you.

Carlson Craft *For a dealer near you, call (800) 328-1782 (web: www.carlsoncraft.com).* Carlson Craft can deliver your baby announcements in as little as seven days (although expect a 10-day wait for most orders). They cost on average $49 to $89 for 50 announcements. Carlson Craft has wonderful designs; we saw die-cut bunnies and border designs with cartoon baby clothes scattered about. ***Rating: B+***

Chase *For a dealer near you, call (508) 478-9220.* Chase's baby announcements include cute cartoons, twin announcements, and more–at very reasonable prices. Prices range from $42 to $92 for 50 announcements. The only negative: Chase takes a whopping three weeks for delivery. ***Rating: B***

NRN Designs *For a dealer near you, call (714) 898-6363.* California-based NRN Designs offers a unique option for baby announcements. While the printer doesn't have fancy die-cut designs, embossing or ribbons and bows, they do offer wonderful graphic designs. We were especially impressed with their Noah's Ark announcement–a hard-to-find design. Some of the envelopes even have coordinating graphics, creating a complete look from start to finish. NRN's prices aren't cheap, but you can buy them in any increment so you don't have to waste money buying more than you need. You can purchase as few as 25 announcements with coordinating envelopes for $3 each. ***Rating: A-***

William Arthur *For a dealer near you, call (800) 985-6581, (207) 985-6581 (web: www.williamarthur.com).* No discussion of birth announcements would be complete without the classic look of William Arthur. These higher quality card stocks feature sophisticated type styles, linings, ink colors and bows. One particular standout: a Beatrix Potter design in the palest of colors, suitable for boy or girl. Although 50 of these were $98, prices start at $75. One note of caution: if you choose the pink parfait ink, select a heavier type style. This ink is a bit too pale for delicate type styles. ***Rating: A***

If I had a million dollars . . .

Looking for a unique announcement? Is money no object? Consider checking out ***Elite*** (800) 354-8321) and ***Encore*** (800) 526-0497 (web: www.encorestudios.com). These printers have fabulous designs with real ribbons and beautiful embossing–we even spotted a die-cut baby shoe with real laces.

Encore's prices start at $73 and range up to $435 for 50 announcements. They require a minimum 50-piece purchase. Elite's designs are priced from $74 to $389 for 50, with a minimum order of 25.

If you don't have a million dollars but want announcements that make you look like you do, consider a stationery discounter. Our recommendation: Marcy Slachman of ***Invitation Hotline*** (800-800-4355; web: www.invitationhotline.com). With discounts up to 25% on brand names like William Arthur, Encore, Elite and more, this is one cool place to shop.

Do it By Mail

HEART THOUGHTS

To Order Call: (800) 524-2229; Fax (800) 526-2846.
Web: www.heart-thoughts.com
Shopping Hours: 8am to 5pm Monday through Friday, Central .
Or write to: Heart Thoughts, 6200 E. Central #100, Wichita, KS 67208.
Credit Cards Accepted: MC, VISA, Discover, AMEX.

Heart Thoughts offers affordable baby announcements in over

100 different styles. Their recent catalog included "classic" birth announcements with black and white line drawings, formal cards with ribbon details, and the usual cutesy, cartooned designs. All are available with quick shipment—just two business days, depending on the design (add an extra day if you want ribbons tied onto the cards).

Heart Thoughts' announcements are very affordable. At the bottom of the price range are the "classic" designs ($35 for 50 announcements); at the top are the "Ribbons & Lace" cards ($90 per 50). Included in the price are colored inks and ribbons, as well as a choice of eight typefaces. Heart Thoughts will even address them for you, plus print your return address on the back flap for an additional cost. Ribbon tying is also available for as little as $9 for 50. Shipping prices are reasonable: for example, it costs just $10 for next day air delivery.

In addition to announcements, Heart Thoughts also carries parenting books, pregnancy exercise videos, and other gift items. Although they do have a web site, at the time of this writing they did not have their catalog on line.

Adoption Announcements

Sure, standard baby announcements are cute, but what if you adopt? Many sites and manufacturers we review above offer announcements appropriate for adoptions. Here's a recommended web site specifically for adoption announcements:

◆ ***Artitudes***, PO Box 12408 Cincinnati, OH 45212. (800) 741-0711 or (513) 351-5412 (web: www.miracleofadoption.com). We saw a few samples of these invitations and were pleased. The sentiments are sweet and the graphics attractive. Pricewise, they are an affordable $1.10 each. Look for other adoption related items like t-shirts and prints.

◆ Another site to check out is ***Adoption World Specialties*** at www.adoptionstuff.com. They have several fill-in-the-blank cards for $7.50 per eight invites.

CHAPTER 11

Etcetera: Catalogs, The 'Net, Child Care & More

How can you be a savvy mail order shopper? What about cyberspace—how can you use the Internet to get expert parenting advice, browse discount catalogs or simply chat with other parents? We'll look at all this, plus discuss day care hints, tips and advice.

Online and Mail Order Shopping

Tired of the mall? Think those sky-high prices at specialty stores are highway robbery? Sit back in your favorite chair and do all your shopping for your baby by phone or computer. With over 8000 mail-order catalogs (and more web sites) out there, you can buy everything from bedding to furniture, clothes to safety items.

Yet before you pick up the phone (or fire up the web browser), a word on being a smart catalog shopper. Ordering from a mail-order company or web site that's miles away from you can be a nerve-racking experience–we've all heard the stories of scamsters who bilk money from unsuspecting consumers. As a result, there are a few precautions any smart shopper should take:

1 **ALWAYS USE YOUR CREDIT CARD.** Federal consumer protection laws cover credit card purchases. Basically, the law says if you don't get what you were promised, you must get a refund. Technically known as Federal Regulation C, the rule says you have 60 days to dispute the charge with the company that issued your credit card–but first you must try to work out the problem with the merchant directly. Call your credit card company to determine the exact procedures for disputing a charge.

What if you pay with cash or a check? If the company goes out of business, you're out of luck. We've interviewed some consumers who feel squeamish about giving out their credit card number over the phone or online. While you always have to be careful, ordering from a reputable mail-order or web company (like the ones reviewed throughout the book) with a credit card is very safe, in our opinion. And the consumer protection benefits of using a credit card far outweigh any risks.

2 If you're buying a high dollar item (anything over $200), it pays to buy from a well-known vendor. If you aren't familiar with a vendor, check with the Better Business Bureau or state attorney general's office in the state where they do business. Don't buy from a business located overseas unless you're very confident in their reputation.

One caveat: watch out for sales tax. Some catalogs and e-tailers will require you to pay sales tax if they have a bricks and mortar store in your state. An example: the Right Start. With their wide network of stores, you may find yourself paying tax plus shipping.

3 Read a web site's privacy policy. Check on whether a catalog sells it's mailing list. If you don't want to find yourself on other emailing lists or catalog mailing lists, be sure to check the company's policy and inform the company you don't want your info sold to others.

4 Watch out for sites that ask for more info than you're comfortable giving. In most cases, your password, credit card number and shipping information are the only information a company should require to take your order.

5 If an Internet company requires a password to buy an item, don't use the same password as you use to log on your computer. In fact, you should change passwords every time you register with a new site. Keep a list of passwords and corresponding sites handy so you don't have to re-register.

6 Order Only on a Secure Server. Buy only from web vendors that protect your financial information when you order online. To confirm that you're on a secure server, look for an unbroken key or padlock at the bottom of the browser window. These symbols mean that the information you are sending is encrypted–turned into a secret code–or online transmission.

7 Most companies have return policies that enable you to get a refund or credit within a specified period of time. Make sure to confirm this before you order. Also ask who pays for the shipping on a returned item–some companies pay, while others don't. One tip: NEVER refuse an item that you've ordered but decided you don't need or want. This always delays your refund. Accept the package and contact the company about return procedures.

When you place an order, the customer service rep or web site usually tells you when to expect delivery. Sellers are required by the Federal Trade Commission to ship items as promised, and no more than 30 days after the order date. If an item is back ordered and can't be shipped within either the stated deadline or the 30-day deadline, the company must notify you, give you a chance to cancel your order and send a full refund if you've chosen to cancel. The site can cancel your order unilaterally at that time and refund your money as well.

8 **ALWAYS KEEP ALL INVOICES, RECEIPTS, AND ORDER CONFIRMATIONS.** Inspect all packages thoroughly upon arrival and keep the original packing, just in case you decide to return the item. For equipment, keep all boxes, documentation and instructions for at least 30 days. When purchasing clothing, wash the items immediately following the care label instructions. That way you can confirm the item does not shrink, etc.

9 **KEEP A LOG OF WHOM YOU SPOKE TO AT THE COMPANY.** Get any names and order confirmation numbers and keep them in a safe place. If you order online, print out any order confirmations or email receipts. The key issue: record the DATE when you ordered the item and estimated shipping times. That way you can track down overdue items that might have been backordered.

10 **CONFIRM DELIVERY METHODS.** Some companies use United Parcel Service to deliver merchandise. The problem? UPS can't deliver to post office boxes and often requires you to be present when the package is delivered. If you're not at home, they leave a call slip, and you've got to go to the nearest UPS office (which could be a long drive) to pick up the item. A possible solution: give your work address and specify any floor, suite number, or building location for the delivery. Or you could request delivery by the U.S. Postal Service (USPS). The downside to the USPS: most packages that go via parcel post or first class mail do NOT have tracking numbers. If it's an expensive purchase (say, over $50), request shipping via a method that can be tracked. Remember, most catalogs and many web sites ship only to the U.S. and sometimes Canada. Folks outside North America may be out of luck.

11 **THE TIME REQUIRED FOR SHIPPING WILL VARY WIDELY.** Some companies offer two to three-day delivery, while others may take weeks. Customized items (like monogrammed bedding) take the longest. As for the cost, mail-order catalogs use a variety of methods to determine shipping charges. Some charge a flat fee, while others use a sliding scale based on the dollar amount of the order or the weight of the package. Please note that mail order prices we quote in this book do not include shipping.

12 Use that 24-hour fax number. Not all catalogs have operators standing by around the clock. However, many have fax numbers that you can use to place an order at any time. When you fax, request the company call you back to confirm they received the order.

13 Nearly all mail-order catalogs are free for the asking. Even though some have a price printed on the cover, we've never had to pay for one. (The only exception in this book is the Chock clothing catalog mentioned in Chapter 4, which does require a small fee).

14 Be prepared to wait. Some catalogs take weeks to arrive, so plan ahead. Don't wait until baby arrives to request catalogs that look interesting. While you're waiting, you can always check out the catalog's web site. Not all have online shopping, but you can usually browse through some items, learn about specials, etc.

15 Get a copy of Wholesale by Mail. If you're serious about mail order shopping, you need Wholesale By Mail (by the Gail Bradney, $20, HarperPerrenial). This thick book (available in bookstores nationwide) gives mail-order sources for just about anything you need to buy.

General Baby Product Catalogs

Kids Club

To Order Call: (800) 363-0500; Fax (330) 492-8290. Web: www.kidsstuff.com
Shopping Hours: 24 hours a day, seven days a week.
Or write to: 7835 Freedom Avenue, N.W., North Canton, Ohio 44720.
Credit Cards Accepted: MC, VISA, Discover, AMEX.

Kids Club (owned by the same parent company as Perfectly Safe and Natural Baby) offers two prices: "catalog price" and "club price," which is about 10% to 30% less. To get the club price, you buy an $18 yearly membership, which also includes a free monthly newsletter. When we visited their web site they were offering a free 90 day trial membership. We found the prices in Kids Club to be excellent, comparable to or lower than prices in other discount stores or catalogs. Kids Club carries bath items, toys and safety items not to mention car seats, high chairs, nursery decor and more. Overall, this is a wonderful catalog–the full-color photos let you see most products clearly and the prices can't be beat.

ONE STEP AHEAD

To Order Call: (800) 274-8440. Web: www.onestepahead.com
Shopping Hours: 24 hours a day, seven days a week.
Or write to: P.O. Box 517, Lake Bluff, IL 60044
Credit Cards Accepted: MC, VISA, AMEX, Optima.
Outlet store: Deerfield, IL (847) 714-1940

Illinois-based One Step Ahead is a jack-of-all-trades catalog that covers everything from clothes to toys, car seats to organizational items. Similar to the Right Start catalog, One Step Ahead has a slightly heavier emphasis on around-the-house items, as well as clothing, shoes, and linens. We also saw baby monitors, nursery decor, carriers, and thermometers, including many of the brand names we review in this book. The catalog is easy to use and features large pictures and helpful graphics. The customer service and delivery from this catalog is above average.

RIGHT START CATALOG

To Order Call: (800) LITTLE-1 (800-548-8531); Web: www.rightstart.com
Shopping Hours: 24 hours a day, seven days a week.
Or write to: PO Box 1259, Camp Hill, PA, 17011.
Credit Cards Accepted: MC, VISA, AMEX, Discover.
Retail stores: The Right Start has 60+ retail stores in major malls; call the above number for a location near you.

Is it a store? A catalog? A website? Actually, all of the above–the Right Start has built an empire by selling high-quality baby products like Perego high chairs, Britax car seats and more. The only bummer: prices are typically full retail, although sometimes the stores do have sales. New this year, we see an increased emphasis on educational toys and car seats. What we like best about the Right Start is their emphasis on cutting-edge products–if it's hip and new, you'll probably see it in their stores or catalog first. Even if you don't buy anything at the stores, it's nice to see, touch and try-out products in person.

Top 5 Things You Didn't Know You Could Do with the Web as a Parent-To-Be

1 **GET YOUR FREE BABY NAMES HERE.** Used to be, in the old days, expectant parents had to go to the library or a book store and pick up a baby name book. If you were looking for something unusual, you probably had to make it up yourself because you

didn't have access to a wide variety of names beyond the usual Michael and Jennifer. But today, forget those giant tomes. You can check out a myriad of free web sites with baby name suggestions.

One of the top sites to visit is ***Babynames.com*** (www.babynames.com). Here you can search alphabetically or by meaning, vote your opinion of different names and even make "name art" (whatever that means). The site is free, but for $19 the site will even pick names for you! That's right, you tell them what kinds of names you like and they'll develop a list of six for you. We're sure you can handle this on your own. Don't forget to check out their message boards, especially ones like "unusual names."

Sites like ***Parent Soup*** (www.parentsoup.com), ***Parenthood Web*** (www.parenthoodweb.com), ***Baby Center*** (www.babycenter.com), and ***Baby Zone*** (www.babyzone.com) have baby name sections as well. For unique names we found a site called ***Alphabette Zoope*** (www.zoope.com). And the Social Security Administration has several reports on most popular names from the 20th Century. To find these reports, go to the ***Social Security Administration's*** web site at www.ssa.gov. Once there, enter a search for Note 139 (the name of the reports). You'll get a list of 15 reports organized by date. No surprise, but when we looked up most popular names for 1900 to 1910 topping the list was John and Mary. But names like Mildred, Bessie, Viola were interesting to see as well. Try finding a Mildred at a daycare center these days.

2 RECALLS AS THEY HAPPEN. Tired of hearing only a couple words on the nightly news about a serious recall of car seats, playpens or toys? Want the details and fast? Consider a couple options. The ***Consumer Product Safety Commission*** (cpsc.gov) has a great web site you can use to look up past recalls. But even better, you can sign up to have recall info immediately emailed to you as it is released to the public. Plus you get more details on the recall (was it life threatening, was anyone injured or killed as a result, was it voluntary or did the company have to be forced to recall the item, how many items were sold, what kinds of remedies are available like retrofit kits, how to contact the manufacturer and more).

A similar service is offered by ***Safety Alerts*** (www.safetyalerts.com). They add in other topics like food allergy recalls, drug and medicine recalls and more. Both web sites allow you to report a problem with a baby product as well. We highly recommend that if you have discovered a problem with a baby product you report it to the CPSC as soon as possible.

3 MAKE NEW (PREGNANT) FRIENDS. If you're looking for other parents in the same situation as you, then the Internet has the answer. Back in the early days of the Internet, you signed up to be on a mailing list with a group of other parents whose babies were due in the same month. The only disadvantage to the mailing lists: every single email anyone in the group sent came to your address. This means you could get quite a bit of email. Today, you can also join "expecting clubs" or visit message board. All these options are organized by due date and the plus is you can get involved when you want to without getting oodles of email. ***Parents Place*** (www.parentsplace.com), ***Parent Soup*** (www.parentsoup.com), ***ePregnancy*** (www.epregnancy.com) and many of the large baby sites we review later in this chapter have message boards as well. Although they aren't organized by due date, we have our own message boards at www.babybargainsbook.com. You can post questions or comments on a variety of topics.

4 **COUPONS FOR SPECIAL DEALS.** The Internet has quite an array of sites whose sole goal in life is to find coupons and special deals. ***Amazing Bargains*** (www.amazingbargains.com), ***Bizrate*** (www.bizrate.com), ***Save a Bundle*** (www.save-a-bundle.com) and ***Total Deals*** (www.totaldeals.com) are just a few of the options out there. Check Chapter 6 for details.

5 **COMPARE PRICES AT THE CLICK OF YOUR MOUSE.** Consider using shopping bots to help you find great deals. Shopping bots are merely search engines that compare prices on the same product from different sites. Plug in a stroller brand and model, for example, and the bot will find every appearance of that item on the web and the cost. You then click on the site with the best price to buy or research further. Some of the most common shopping bots include: ***My Simon*** (www.mysimon.com), ***Shop Best*** (www.shopbest.com), ***Smart Bots*** (www.smartbots.com), ***Price Scan*** (www.pricescan.com), and ***Deal Time*** (www.dealtime.com).

Parents in Cyberspace

Baby Center

Web site: www.babycenter.com
What it is: Baby information and shopping site.
What's cool: Right off the bat when you pull up Babycenter.com, you'll be able to check on your baby's development (before or after birth). It's a neat idea to pull you into the site which emphasizes its articles and tips with general topic areas like "prepregnancy," "toddler" and more. The "Shop at our store" area leads you off to an

easy-to-navigate page with every product area imaginable. They also list weekly specials, clearances and membership info. We like the clear shipping button ($5 on most orders), the links to the gift registry and new items and the variety of the most popular products.
Needs work: No matter how hard we looked, we couldn't find much to complaint about on Baby Center's web site. They have a well organized, easy-to-use site with a wide selection of items. ***A major caveat to BabyCenter:*** as we were going to press, it was unclear as to whether BabyCenter's parent eToys.com, was going to survive. See our web site for updates on this.

Baby Style

Web site: www.babystyle.com
What it is: Estyle.com's baby oriented off shoot.
What's cool: Estyle has always tried to position themselves as a hip, upper end site catering to style conscious folks. And that carries through to their attractive baby products web site. You'll see high dollar designers and manufacturers like Wendy Belissimo (bedding), DKNY baby (clothing), and Emmaljunga (strollers) to name a few. Navigation on the site is simple and clear.
Needs work: In many categories, this web site has only a few items available. The ads from manufacturers can be a bit irritating although they've tried to make them discreet. Prices are regular retail meaning that some items are quite expensive but they have an extensive sales page for each category.

◆ ***Other sites:*** There are a myriad of web sites targeting new and expecting parents. One of the more promising entries into the market is ***Baby Ant*** (www.babyant.com), a whimsical site with items ranging from safety gates to humidifiers to clothing.

Baby Super Center (www.babysupercenter.com) offers more than 17,000 baby products. Their site has a newsletter, assembly tips and news articles on pregnancy, childbirth and children. Another option, ***the Baby Warehouse*** (www.thebabywarehouse.com) offers great deals brand names like Cottontale, Britax and Peg Perego.

A less sophisticated site, ***Baby Products Online*** (www.babyproductsonline.com) offers extensive line listings of products by brand, age, price and category. They even sell all terrain vehicles (a mere $1789). They offer free shipping within the U.S. ***Baby Bundle*** (www.babybundle.com) on the other hand, has a more limited selection and a more upscale price range. We saw a bassinet set, for example, for almost $500!

Specializing in the more popular mass market brands like Graco strollers and Cosco car seats, ***Baby Super Mall*** (www.babysupermall.com) offers closeouts mixed in with regular priced mer-

National Parenting Center

Looking for more consumer information on the latest baby products? The National Parenting Center is a California-based group that produces a "Seal of Approval" product report three times a year (spring, fall and holiday times). The 30-page book reviews the latest infant products like furniture, toys, music, computer software and educational items. A one-year membership for $19.95 ($17.95 for online users) gets you this report, a monthly subscription to the "Parent Talk" newsletter, and various discounts on child-rearing products. For more information, call (800) 753-6667 or (818) 225-8990 or write to The National Parenting Center, 22801 Ventura Blvd., Suite 110, Woodland Hills, CA 91367 (web: www.tnpc.com).

chandise. They also carry bedding, clothing and toys. ***Just Babies*** (www.justbabies.com) is another general site carrying everything from maternity clothes to breast pumps to crib bedding and more.

Baby Universe (www.babyuniverse.com) is a pleasing site with products for health, safety, diapering, feeding and much more. In fact, they cover over 15 different topics. Likewise, ***Baby Age*** (www.babyage.com) stocks an amazing assortment of products. Users can peruse baby bathtubs, playpens, even kid size rockers and potty seats. Check their specials for deals. We saw an On My Way Position Right infant seat on sale for $55 (regularly $70 to $80).

BabyPressConference.com broadcasts live, streaming Web video of your newborn right from the hospital. The webcast is free; BabyPressConference.com makes its money by selling copies of the webcast to family members or a digital picture of the newborn. The site also owns UrbanBaby (www.urbanbaby.com) which has resource guides and an online store.

◆ ***All purpose sites with good baby sections:*** Many web sites offer a few items to parents shopping for baby products, but one of the best is ***Overstock.com*** (www.overstock.com). They sell exactly what it sounds like: overstocks and clearance items. We saw accessories, clothing, and bedding from makers like NoJo. An Amy Coe duvet set was a mere $166. How do they get such deals? You've probably heard about the flameouts of so many baby e-tailers in recent months. These guys failed at trying to sell juvenile products at low prices. While that's bad news for consumers who enjoyed the low prices, in the short term, you can often find deals on liquidator's sites like Overstock and another site to watch, ***Smart Bargains*** (www.smartbargains.com).

◆ ***Bricks and Clicks.*** These are web sites that have both real stores and great cyber sites. Examples include Baby Depot, Babies R Us, Walmart, Kmart, and Target. Many of these sites are reviewed in detail in Chapter 2. Each of the major discounters include a baby section on their general site. These sections are small and include mainly mass market brands. The best bets: ***Baby Depot*** (www.babydepot.com) and ***Babies R Us*** (www.babiesrus.com).

◆ ***Feedback sites.*** With the myriad of baby product web sites out there, how do you really know who's reputable? Which sites have high satisfaction ratings from consumers? Feedback sites are a great way to take a quick pulse on which e-tailers to

DOT-COM GOOD VS. EVIL

What makes a great baby products web site? Here's our list of what's good and what's bad.

GOOD DOT-COM

SHIPPING COSTS	UP FRONT DISCLOSURE—EASY TO USE CHART OR CHARGE IS IMMEDIATELY ADDED TO ORDER.
STOCK STATUS	IMMEDIATE INFO ON THE SITE OF WHAT'S IN STOCK AND WHAT'S BACKORDERED. REMOVE OUT OF STOCK OR DISCONTINUED ITEMS PROMPTLY FROM THE WEB SITE.
PAYMENT	WAIT TO CHARGE YOUR CARD UNTIL THE ITEM(S) SHIPS. ONLY CHARGE FOR ITEMS SENT ON PARTIAL ORDERS.*
CONTACT INFORMATION	EASY TO FIND BUTTON LEADS YOU TO PHONE NUMBERS, EMAIL AND PHYSICAL ADDRESS.
REFUNDS	IMMEDIATE CREDITS WHEN ITEMS ARE RETURNED OR ORDERS ARE CANCELLED.
TRACKING	EASY TRACKING VIA WEB SITE USING A TRACKING NUMBER OR CODE. TRACKING IS ALWAYS AVAILABLE.
EXCUSES	NONE. WHEN THEY SCREW UP THEY ADMIT IT, APOLOGIZE AND CORRECT THE PROBLEM.
CUSTOMER SERVICE	QUICK REPLIES TO EMAIL QUERIES, LIVE CHAT, AND LIVE HUMANS ANSWERING PHONES PROMPTLY.

** Federal law does NOT prohibit mail order companies from charging a card*

trust. One example is ***Planet Feedback*** (www. planetfeedback.com) where you can look up company report cards for various sites in their "news and ratings" section. You can also read "shared letters" from consumers that either complain about or praise companies. To test the site, we looked up the ratings on the notorious e-tailer BabyGear.com, a bankrupt baby products supplier. They earned a dismal D+ on the site. By contrast BabyStyle.com earned an A.

Another site, ***UGetHeard*** (www.ugetheard.com), rates both manufacturers and e-tailers. You can also file complaints and read consumer stories. Our only caveat to these sites: sometimes with the small number of comments on these companies, it's hard to place any real confidence in the ratings' significance. You also have to take some of the complaints with a grain of salt. Read with skepticism and verify with other sites, friends, etc.

Or one you want to take a rocket launcher to?

Bad Dot-Com
No mention of cost until you step all the way through or go through several step registration process.
No information. They let you place the order even if they are out of stock then take days/weeks/never to tell you the item is back ordered. Never seem to remove out of stock or discontinued items from the site.
Charge your card immediately whether the item ships or not. Worse case scenario: The item you want is never shipped, forcing you to argue with the site over a refund.
Where is it? Can't find any button for customer service that gives phone numbers or addresses. Sometimes the only way to contact anyone is to send an email to an unknown human.
All you get is foot dragging and excuses, then weeks or months go by. Customer is forced to dispute charge with credit card company.
No tracking number or the number never works. Tracking function is always down.
Anything you can think of: it's the supplier's fault, the warehouse is having problems, their dog ate your order, etc.
What service? Emails go unanswered, phone calls to customer service require one hour waits on hold.

before shipping goods. The best dot-coms only charge when they ship.

Childcare

"It's expensive, hard to find and your need for it is constantly changing. Welcome to the world of child care," said a recent *Wall Street Journal* article–and we agree. There's nothing more difficult than trying to find the best child care for your baby.

With 59% of moms with children under age one back in the workforce today, wrestling with the choices, costs and availability of childcare is a stark reality. Here's a brief overview of the different types of childcare available, questions to ask when hiring a provider and money-saving tips.

What are you buying?

On average, parents pay 7.5% of their pre-tax income for childcare. And if you live in a high-cost city, expect to shell out even more. As you'll read below, some parents spend $20,000 or more per year. Whatever your budget, there are three basic types of child care:

◆ ***Family Daycare.*** In this setting, one adult takes care of a small number of children in her home. Sometimes the children are of mixed ages. Parents who like this option prefer the lower ratio of children to providers and the consistent caregiver. Of course, you'll want to make sure the facility is licensed and ask all the questions we outline later. One drawback to family daycare: if there is only one caregiver, you might have to scramble if that person becomes ill. How much does it cost? Family daycare typically runs $3000 to $10,000 per year–with bigger cities running closer to the top figure. For example, in New York City or San Francisco, family daycare can run $200 to $250 per week (that's $10,000 to $13,000 a year).

◆ ***Center Care.*** Most folks are familiar with this daycare option–commercial facilities that offer a wide variety of childcare options. Convenience is one major factor for center care; you can often find a center that is near your (or your spouse's) place of work. Other parents like the fact that their children are grouped with and exposed to more kids their own age. Centers usually give you a written report each day which details your baby's day (naps, diaper changes, mood). On the downside, turnover can be a problem–some centers lose 40% or more of their employees each year. A lack of consistency can upset your child. Yet center care offers parents the most flexibility: unlike nannies or family care, the day care center doesn't take sick or vacation days. Many centers offer drop-off care, in case you need help in a pinch. The cost: $3000 to $13,000 per year, yet some pricey centers can cost over $20,000 in the biggest cities. As with family daycare, the cost varies depending on how many days a week your baby needs care. We pay about $4000 per year for 20 hours of daycare per week for one child in Boulder, CO.

◆ ***Nanny Care.*** No, you don't have to be super-rich to afford a nanny. Many "nanny-referral" services have popped up in most major cities, offering to refer you to a pre-screened nanny for $100 to $200 or so. Parents who prefer nannies like the one-to-one attention, plus baby is taken care of in your own home. The cost varies depending on whether you provide the nanny with room and board. Generally, most nannies who don't live in run $8 to $15 per hour. Hence, the yearly cost would be $10,000 to $20,000. And the nanny's salary is just the beginning—you also must pay social security and Medicare taxes, federal unemployment insurance, plus any state-mandated taxes like disability insurance or employment-training taxes. All this may increase the cost of your $20,000 nanny by another $3500 or more per year. And the paperwork hassle for all the tax reporting can be onerous. The other downside to nannies? You're dependent on one person for childcare. If she gets sick, needs time off or quits, you're on your own.

Money Saving Tips

1 ASK YOUR EMPLOYER ABOUT DEPENDENT CARE ACCOUNTS. Many corporations offer this great benefit to employees. Basically, you can set aside pretax dollars to pay for child-care. The maximum set aside per child is $5000 and both parents can contribute to that amount. If you're in the 31% tax bracket, that means you'll save $1550 in taxes by paying for childcare with a dependent care account. Consult with your employer for the latest rules and limits to this option.

2 SHARE A NANNY. As we noted in the above example, a nanny can be expensive. But many parents find they can halve that cost by sharing a nanny with another family. While this might require some juggling of schedules to make everyone happy, it can work out beautifully.

3 GO FOR A CULTURAL EXCHANGE. The U.S. government authorizes a foreign nanny exchange program. "Parents can hire a young European to provide as much as 45 hours of child care a week as part of a yearlong cultural exchange," said a recent *Wall Street Journal* article. The wages are fixed at $138 per week for a nanny arriving after 1996, although that amount may adjust with any change in the federal minimum wage. You also agree to pay for the nanny's room and board, but the fixed fee is good for any number of children. Eight "au pair" agencies are authorized by the federal government to place foreign nannies in homes (call Au Pair in America 800-727-2437 x6188 for more details). These agencies charge placement fees of $3700 to $4200 which cover health insurance, training and other support services. When you factor this and other fees, an au pair runs about $200 a week (plus room/board) or $11,000 a year.

4 **TAKE A TAX CREDIT.** The current tax code gives parents a tax credit for childcare expenses. The amount, which varies based on your income, equals about 20% to 30% of childcare costs up to a certain limit. The credit equals about $500 to $1500, depending on your income. Another tax break: some states also give credits or deductions for child care expenses. Consult your tax preparer to make sure you're taking the maximum allowable credit/deduction.

Questions to Ask

1 **WHAT ARE THE CREDENTIALS OF THE PROVIDER(S)?** Obviously, a college degree in education and/or child development is preferred. Additional post-college training is also a plus.

2 **WHAT IS THE TURNOVER?** High turnover is a concern since consistency of care is one of the keys to successful childcare. Any turnover approaching 40% is cause for concern.

3 **WHAT IS THE RATIO OF CHILDREN TO CARE PROVIDERS?** The recommended national standard is one adult to three babies (age birth to 12 months). After that, the ratios vary depending on a child's age and state regulations. With some day care centers, there is one primary teacher and a couple of assistants (depending on the age of the children and size of class). Compare the ratio to that of other centers to gain an understanding of what's high and low.

4 **DO YOU HAVE A LICENSE?** All states (and many municipalities) require childcare providers to be licensed. Yet, that's no guarantee of quality—the standards vary so much from locale to locale that a license may be meaningless. Another point to remember: the standards for family daycare may be lower than those for center daycare. Educate yourself on the various rules and regulations by spending a few minutes on the phone with your state's child care regulatory body. Check on the center's file with the state to make

sure there are no complaints or violations on record. Some states are putting this info on the web.

5 May I visit you during business hours? The only way you can truly evaluate a childcare provider is an on-site visit. Try to time your visit during the late morning, typically the time when the most children are being cared for. Trust your instincts—if the facility seems chaotic, disorganized or poorly run, take the hint.

6 Discuss your care philosophy. Sit down for a half-hour interview with the care provider and make sure they clearly define their attitudes on breast feeding, diapers, naps, feeding schedules, discipline and any other issues of importance to you. The center should have established, written procedures to deal with children who have certain allergies or other medical conditions. Let's be honest: child-rearing philosophies will vary from culture to culture. Make sure you see eye to eye on key issues.

7 Do you have liability insurance? Don't just take their word on it—have them provide written documentation or the phone number of an insurance provider for you to call to confirm coverage.

8 Does the center conduct police background checks on employees? It's naive to assume that just because employees have good references, they've never been in trouble with the law.

9 Is the center clean, home-like and cheerful? While it's impossible to expect a child care facility to be spotless, it is important to check for basic cleanliness. Diaper changing stations shouldn't be overflowing with dirty diapers, play areas shouldn't be strewn with a zillion toys, etc. Another tip: check their diaper changing procedures. The best centers should use rubber gloves when changing diapers and wipe down the diapering area with a disinfectant after each change. Finally, ask how often toys are cleaned. Is there a regular schedule for washing children's hands?

10 What type of adjustment period does the center offer? Phasing in daycare isn't easy—your child may have to have time to adjust to the new situation. Experienced providers should have plans to ease the transition.

Sources For The Best Child Care Facilities. Which childcare centers have the highest standards? The National Association of Family ChildCare (800) 359-3817 (web: www.nafcc.org) and the National Association for the Education of Young Children (800) 424-2460 (www.naeyc.org) offers lists of such facilities to parents in every state.

CONCLUSION

Chapter 12

What Does it All Mean?

How much money can you save if you follow all the tips and suggestions in this book? Let's take a look at the average cost of having a baby from the introduction and compare it with our Baby Bargains budget.

Your Baby's First Year

Item	Average	Baby Bargains Budget
Crib, mattress, dresser, rocker	$1500	$1280
Bedding / Decor	$300	$200
Baby Clothes	$500	$340
Disposable Diapers	$600	$300
Maternity/Nursing Clothes	$1200	$540
Nursery items, high chair, toys	$400	$225
Baby Food/Formula	$900	$350
Stroller, Car Seat, Carrier	$300	$200
Miscellaneous	$500	$500
TOTAL	$6200	$3935
TOTAL SAVINGS:		***$2265***

WOW! YOU CAN SAVE OVER $2000! We hope the savings makes it worth the price of this book. We'd love to hear from you on how much you saved with our book–feel free to email, write or call us. See the "How to Reach Us" page at the back of this book.

What does it all mean?

At this point, we usually have something pithy to say as we end the book. But, as parents of two boys, we're just too tired. We're going to bed, so feel free to make up your own ending.

And thanks for reading *Baby Bargains*.

Appendix A
Canada

If you walk into a baby store in Canada, you'll see many of the same baby products that are for sale in the U.S. One reason for the overlap: Canada sees about 380,000 births a year, which is less than 10% the U.S. rate. As a result, Canada only has 15 baby product manufacturers (compared to hundreds in the U.S.). To fill the gap, many U.S. companies export their goods to Canada.

While many products are the same, there is one exception: car seats. Canada requires child safety seats to meet slightly different safety standards than the U.S. Perhaps the biggest difference is the tether strap, which is used to keep the car seat from flying forward in the event of a head-on crash. One end of the tether strap attaches to the car seat while the other end is bolted to the back seat of the car.

Any child safety seat made after 1987 is required to have tether strap hardware. Furthermore, any *car* made after 1989 that's sold in Canada must have tether anchorage points provided. For older cars, check your owner's manual or car dealership for more info.

Using the tether strap is not an option in Canada; all provinces have laws that not only require a child to be in an approved safety seat but also that the seat be anchored with the tether strap. Although the US has caught up to Canada requiring all car seats be sold with tether straps, there is no mandate requiring parents to use it.

What if you have two cars but only one child safety seat? You can purchase an additional anchor bolt at most baby stores and juvenile retailers in Canada.

As a result of these special rules, not all car seats sold in the U.S. will be available in Canada. For more information on this and other issues regarding child safety seats, contact Transport Canada's Road Safety Office at (613) 990-2309 or on the internet at *www.tc.gc.ca/*.

The Canadian Automobile Association (CAA) also works closely with Transport Canada to provide child safety seat info. Contact their headquarters at www.caa.ca for more details or check your phone book for the number of a local CAA office. We noticed the British Columbia Automobile Association (604-268-5000) operates a web site (www.bcaa.bc.ca) that provides basic safety tips plus recall notices.

General Safety Info

If you have a question about a juvenile product or a safety concern, contact any of these regional branches of the Canada Consumer and Corporate Affairs Product Safety Office:

LOCATION	PHONE
Ottawa/Hull (headquarters)	(819) 953-8082
Halifax	(902) 426-6328
St. John's	(709) 772-4050
Moncton	(506) 851-6638
Montreal	(514) 283-2825
Quebec	(418) 648-4327
Toronto	(416) 973-4705
Hamilton	(416) 572-2845
Winnipeg	(204) 983-3293
Saskatoon	(306) 975-4028
Edmonton	(403) 495-7198
Calgary	(403) 292-5613
Vancouver	(604) 666-5006

Recap of Canadian Sources

Many of the sources mentioned earlier in this book sell or ship to Canada. Here's a recap of specific Canadian juvenile product manufacturers (all prices are in U.S. dollars):

CANADA COSTS

What does it cost to raise a child in Canada? These figures are from Manitoba, but are a good general guide for most Canadian parents. Costs of raising a child to age two (total cost for two years):

FOOD	$2049
CLOTHING	2118
HEATH CARE	290
PERSONAL CARE	101
RECREATION	438
CHILD CARE	10,600
SHELTER	3971
TOTAL	**$19,567**

Figures are for 2000 in Canadian dollars. Source: Manitoba government web page (http://www.gov.mb.ca/agriculture/homeec/).

Cribs

A.P. Industries. *346 St. Joseph Blvd., Laurier Station, Quebec, Canada, Call (800) 463-0145 or (416) 728-2145.* A.P. Industries' (also known as Generations) stylish cribs and case pieces are available in five styles in nine different collections. Al the items are made in Quebec of solid birch (although one collection is made of beech). Sample price: $500 to $600 for a crib with hidden hardware and a knee-push rail release. We thought A.P had the best look of all the Canadian cribs we reviewed, although the rail release does make a rather loud "click" when it is locked into position (at least on one model we tested). Another plus: A.P. makes some very affordable dressers; a reader spied an A.P. hi-low dresser for just $309 at Baby Depot. If you plan to splurge on a crib, this is a good choice. ***Rating: A-***

Morigeau/Lepine *3025 Washington Rd., McMurray, PA 15317. Call (800) 326-2121 or (724) 941-7475 or (970) 845-7795 for a dealer near you. Web: www.morigeau.com* Based in Quebec, Canada, this family-run juvenile furniture company has been in business for over 50 years. Like other Canadian manufacturers, Morigeau/Lepine's specialty is stylish cribs and dressers that look like adult furniture. The quality is impeccable, but you're going to pay for it–cribs run $500 to $700 and a simple dresser can run $600. What do you get for those bucks? Solid wood construction (Morigeau even runs its own sawmill to process the maple and beech it uses in the furniture), drawers with dove-tailed joints and cribs with completely hidden hardware with self-lubricating nylon tracks, which makes Morigeau cribs some of the quietest on the market. Safety-wise, Morigeau's dressers have side-mounted glides with safety stops. We also liked the fact that most of Morigeau's dressers are oversized with 21" deep drawers to give you extra storage. The styling of the line is quite sophisticated–in fact, this is probably the most "adult" looking baby furniture on the market today. We weren't wild about some of the new, darker finishes Morigeau has introduced in the past year, but we think some of the new, oversize pieces (like a large armoire for $2000) were rather amazing in their design. We should note that Morigeau's sister line is "Lepine," a smaller collection of cribs at slightly lower prices (cribs are $450 to $660). All in all, we liked Morigeau–the prices are high, but so is the quality. Perhaps the biggest beef we've heard about Morigeau is their slow delivery; some retailers complain it can take forever to get in special order items. ***Rating: A-***

Ragazzi *8965 Pascal Gagnon, St. Leonard, Quebec H1P 1Z4. Call (514) 324-7886 for a dealer near you. Web: www.ragazzi.com* Readers of past editions of this book may remember that Ragazzi wasn't our favorite crib brand (to put it charitably). Our biggest beef with Ragazzi was their high prices–many of their cribs sell for $500, $600 or more (although some of our sharp-eyed readers have seen them on sale for $400 or so). You spend that much money and get exposed hardware on the crib rails? Yea, it is a very quiet release but if you paying this much money, you'd least expect the Canucks to figure out how to match the Italians for their hidden hardware and styling. (Ragazzi will finally correct this long-standing deficit in 2001 with a new, completely hidden hardware system on their new models). All that said, our position on Ragazzi has softened in recent years. Parents who've bought Ragazzi acknowledge the high prices, but say the quality is worth it–they like high-quality construction and hip styling. Like Morigeau and other Canadian-based crib makers, Ragazzi's styling emphasis is on fancy adult-like looks. Founded by the son of an Italian carpenter, Ragazzi started out in 1972 making TV consoles (of all things), then segued into cribs and juvenile furniture in 1991. The company's "3 child or 15-year warranty" is unique in the industry and we have to admit their web site is very cool. Yet, we still can't get past the snob quotient with this line–we still think the prices are too high. You can buy the same quality crib from Babi Italia, MIBB or Sorelle for at least $100 or $200 less. And those cribs would have completely hidden hardware. ***Rating: B***

Status *571 Lepine Ave., Dorval, Quebec, Canada, H9P 2R2 . For a dealer near you, call (514) 631-0788. Web: www.statusfurniture.com* Yet another Canadian juvenile furniture maker that's recently come to the U.S., Status offers several coordinating sets of cribs and dressers. We liked the neo-shaker looks, as well as the French Country motifs. New this year are several sleigh style cribs (six in all). The oversized dressers with bun feet echo similar looks in the adult furniture market. The quality of Status is very good–the cribs use a knee-push rail release and are made from hardwoods like maple and birch. Prices for a crib are $400 to $700. The only disappointment: the rail hardware isn't completely hidden (a plastic track is visible when the rail is in the lower position). Yes, it is similar to Ragazzi's rail release but we weren't impressed by that either. And watch for some of Status' case pieces. One dresser we noticed was painted MDF (medium density fiberboard) instead of wood. While we liked the styling of this group, we'd rather get solid maple or birch wood instead of MDF at these prices. ***Rating: B+***

Stork Craft *11511 No. 5 Road, Richmond, British Columbia, Canada, V7A4E8. For a dealer near you, call (604) 274-5121. Web: www.storkcraft.com* Unlike other Canadian crib makers that concentrate on the upper-end markets, Stork Craft's cribs are priced for the rest of us. Most are in the $150 to $250 range (although a few reach $400) and are sold in such places as Babies R Us and other chain stores. Manufactured in Mississauga, Ontario (just outside Toronto), Stork Craft has three collection. The entry-level "Fisher Price" brand cribs sell for $129 to $299 and feature very simple styling, painted MDF construction (not solid wood) and wood mattress platforms (no springs). The middle-level cribs (Signature) feature mixed species of wood and a bit more fancy styling (as well as spring mattress platforms). The top-end "Diamond" cribs are solid maple. All Storkcraft cribs now feature knee-push rail release (gone are the foot-bar rail releases wit exposed hardware). The hardware on Storkcraft is similar to Ragazzi and Status—the rail release glides up and down on a plastic track. As a result of the new hardware, we've decided to up Stork Craft's rating this year. ***Rating: B***

◆ ***Other Canadian manufacturers include: Meubles*** (418-428-3746) is a Quebec-based crib maker with three styles of cribs (made of solid birch) that sell for $450 to $500. The hardware of these cribs is similar to Ragazzi. The same can be said for ***E.G. Furniture*** (418-325-2050; web: www.egfurniture.com), another Quebec-based crib manufacturer. Finally, ***Forever Mine*** (800-356-2742 or 819-297-2000; web: www.forevermine.com) recently debuted their convertible cribs on the market for about $400. We weren't impressed with hinged drop-gate drop side on some of their models, but they are solid maple and made in Quebec. One unique aspect to Forever Mine: they sell direct from their web site. A reader who ordered a convertible crib, three drawer dresser with changing table and a four drawer dresser from Forever Mine was very impressed with the quality and easy of assembly. The best part: the total price was just $845 for all three pieces including shipping. A reader in Toronto emailed us with a rave for ***Mother Hubbard's Canada***, a Toronto based children's furniture manufacturer (416) 661-8201. "I saw a four-drawer dresser for $377 and an armoire for $466; the pieces seemed to be well made."

Rocker-Gliders

We're not talking about the rocking chair you've seen at grandma's house. No, we're referring to the high-tech modern-day rockers that are so fancy they aren't mere rockers—they're "glider-rockers."

Thanks to a fancy ball-bearing system, these rockers "glide" with little or no effort.

Quebec-based ***Dutailier*** (call 800-363-9817 or 450-772-2403; web: www.dutailier.com), is to glider-rockers what Microsoft is to software–basically, they own the market. Thanks to superior quality and quick delivery, Dutailier probably sells one out of every two glider rockers sold in the U.S. and Canada each year.

Dutailier has an incredible selection of 45 models, seven finishes, and 80 different fabrics. The result: over 37,000 possible combinations. All wood is solid maple or oak and features non-toxic finishes. You have to try real hard to avoid seeing Dutailier–the company has 3500 retail dealers, from small specialty stores to major retail chains.

Prices for Dutailier start at about $200 for a basic model. Of course, the price can soar quickly from there–add a swivel base, plush cushions or leather fabric and you can spend $500. Or $1000. (The fancier Dutailier's are in the "AvantGlide" line).

If we had to criticize Dutailier on something, it would have to be their cushions. Most are not machine washable (the covers can't be zipped off and put into the washing machine). As a result, you'll have to take them to a dry cleaner and pay big bucks to get them looking like new. A few of our readers have solved this problem by sewing slip covers for their glider-rockers (most fabric stores carry pattern books for such items). Of course, if the cushions are shot, you can always order different ones when you move the glider-rocker into a family room.

It can take 10-12 weeks to order a custom Dutailier rocker, but the company does offer a "Quick Ship" program–a selection of 17 chair styles in two or three different fabric choices that are in stock for shipment in two weeks.

Unfortunately, Dutailier's web site lacks a product catalog. But there is good news: Dutailier is one of those products that is easy to research (and buy) online. Several sites carry the brand at a discount, including ***BabyCatalog.com***. Two sites that have a great selection of Dutailier are ***CribNCarriage*** (www.cribncarriage.com) and ***Rocking Chairs*** 100% (www.rocking-chairs.com; 800-4-ROCKER), a web site offshoot of the Corte Madera, CA store of the same name. The latter site is easy to navigate, with thumbnails of different models and little color chips for available colors.

An optional accessory for glider rockers is the ottoman that glides too. These start at $99 without a cushion, but most cost $125 to $150 with cushion. We suggest forgetting the ottoman and ordering an inexpensive "nursing" footstool (about $30 to $40 in catalogs like ***Motherwear*** 800-950-2500. Why? Some moms claim the ottoman's height puts additional strain on their backs while breastfeeding. While the nursing footstool doesn't rock, it's lower height puts less strain on your back.

Is a glider-rocker a waste of money? Some parents have written to us with that question, assuming you'd just use the item for the baby's first couple of years. Actually, a glider-rocker can have a much longer life. You can swap the cushions after a couple of years (most makers let you order these items separately) and move the glider-rocker to a family room.

Outlet Stores

A great source for outlet info is Outlet Bound magazine, which is published by Outlet Marketing Group ($9.95 plus $3.50 shipping, 800-336-8853). The magazine contains detailed maps noting outlet centers for all areas of the U.S. and Canada, as well as store listings for each outlet center. We liked the index that lists all the manufacturers, and they even have a few coupons in the back. Outlet Bound also has an excellent web site (www.outletbound.com) with the most up-to-date info on outlets in Canada.

A reader called in this outlet find: the ***Snugabye*** outlet in Toronto (188 Bentworth Ave., 416-783-0300), which sells infant clothing at prices way below those in department stores.

Layette Items and Diapers

If you're looking for great shoes for your little one, reader Teri Dunsworth recommends Canadian-made ***Robeez*** (800) 929-2623 or (604) 929-6818; web: www.robeez.com. "They are the most AWESOME shoes—I highly recommend them," she said in an email. Robeez are made of leather, have soft skid-resistant soles and are machine washable. They start at $22 for a basic pair. "My baby wears nothing else! They have infant and toddler sizes and oh-so-cute patterns." Another reader recommended New Zealand made ***Bobux*** shoes (www.bobuxusa.com). These cute leather soft soles "do the trick" by staying on extremely well according to our reader.

A Canadian clothing manufacturer to look for in stores near you is ***Baby's Own*** by St. Lawrence Textiles (613) 632-8565.

The Mercedes of the cloth diaper category is Canada-made ***Mother-Ease*** (www.mother-ease.com), a brand that has a fanatical following among cloth diaper devotees. Suffice it to say, they ain't cheap but the quality is excellent. Mother-Ease sells both fitted diapers and covers; the diapers run $9 to $10 a pop, while the covers are about $9.75. Before you invest $73 to $375 in one of Mother-Ease's special package deals, consider trying their "introductory offer" (see details below in our money-saving tips section).

Other parents like ***Kushies*** (800) 841-5330 (web: www. kushies.com), another Canadian product. This brand offers several models.

One note: both Kushies and Mother-Ease are sold via mail-order only. Yes, you can sometimes find these diapers at second-hand or thrift stores, but most parents buy them via a catalog or on the 'net. Kushies are trying to branch out into retail stores–check your local baby specialty shop.

One great catalog and web site for cloth diaper and breast-feeding products and information is ***Born to Love*** (416-499-8309; web: www. borntolove.com). They have won numerous fans for their low prices. You'll see page after page of cloth diaper systems (including such name brands as Mother-Ease and Nikki's). Heck, there are even NINE pages of accessories, plus selections of nursing bras, breast pumps, toys, safety products and more. Yes, the web site is a jumbled mess, but there's lots of useful info, articles and links when you sift through it all.

TC KidCo (888) 825-4326 is another Canadian catalog that sells "Indisposables" all-in-one cloth diapers and diaper covers. You can buy from the catalog or from their direct representative. The catalog also has nursing bras, blankets, bibs and more.

Feel guilty about using disposables? The ***Diaper Club*** offers to recycle disposable diapers for a small fee for parents in the Toronto area. Call 800-566-9278 for details and info.

Maternity

Canuks looking for the world's best maternity bras need to look no further than their own backyard. Toronto-based ***Bravado Designs*** (for a brochure, call 800-590-7802 or 416-466-8652; web: www.bravadodesigns.com) makes a maternity/nursing bra of the same name that's just incredible. "A godsend!" raved one reader. "It's built like a sports bra with no underwire and supports better than any other bra I've tried . . . and this is my third pregnancy!" raved another. The Bravado bra comes in three support levels, sizes up to 42-46 with an F-G cup and a couple of wonderful colors/patterns (you can also call them for custom sizing information). Another. Available via mail order, the bra costs $32 U.S. (or $33.50 Canadian). Another plus: the Bravado salespeople are knowledgeable and quite helpful with sizing questions. Some of our readers have criticized the Bravado for not providing enough support, especially in the largest sizes. If you have doubts, just try one at first and see if it works for you before investing in several.

A reader recommend Montreal-based ***Thyme Maternity*** (514-729-3333, web: www.maternity.ca) which offers "decent maternity clothes at very reasonable prices." Another reader chimed in with her kudos, saying their "Bootleg Ottoman Pants" with adjustable waistband were excellent. Thyme has stores throughout Canada and a web site with online ordering.

What about nursing fashions in Canada? The Toronto-based ***Breast is Best*** catalog sells a wide variety of nursing tops, blouses and dresses as well as maternity wear. For a free catalog and fabric swatches, call (877) 837-5439 toll free or check out their web site at www.breastisbest.com.

Looking for plus-size maternity or petites? Canadian maternity maker ***Maternal Instinct*** has a catalog and web site (www.maternal-instinct.com; 877-MATERNAL). The line is also sold in a dozen stores in Canada (and another dozen or so in the U.S.). "They don't have a huge catalog inventory," writes one Vancouver mom, "but it's a nice, simple selection of plus-size and petite work and casual maternity clothes with a few pieces of formalwear thrown in."

Baby Food Web Site

Heinz has a Canadian-based web site (www.heinzbaby.com) which contains extensive nutritional advice and other helpful info. What makes this site great for Canadians are the coupons and rebate offers.

Car Seats

On a recent trip to Toronto, we noticed many of the same car seat brands that are sold in the U.S. are offered in Canada as well. Hence, it will be helpful to review Chapter 7 to get a complete picture of the car seat market. The following review of Cosco (which is owned by Canada conglomerate Dorel), a common brand of car seats sold in Canada.

Cosco *2525 State St., Columbus, IN 47201. Call (812) 372-0141 for a dealer near you (or 514-323-5701 for a dealer in Canada). Internet: www.coscoinc.com* Owned by Canadian conglomerate Dorel Industries, Cosco has staged a comeback in the car seat market in recent years. Previously also-ran in the car seat business, Cosco hit a home-run with their Alpha Omega seat (described below) and Eddie Bauer-licensed products. Yet, we are still troubled by Cosco's poor safety track record, which we'll discuss at the end of this review. Before we get to the models, let us point about that Cosco makes three versions of their car seats: one under their own name and versions under the "Eddie Bauer" and "NASCAR" names. Note that in all cases, the seats are just the same, only the colors/fabric patterns have changed. Those Eddie Bauer seats are the same as Cosco's models, just with taupe and blue fabric. Of course, you're going to pay extra for the name.

Infant seats. Cosco has three basic models of infant seats: the Arriva, the Designer 22 and the Opus 35, which of course is named after the penguin in the Bloom County cartoon series. (Just kidding).

The entry-level Arriva ($30 to $50; rear-facing to 22 pounds) is sold in versions with and without a stay-in-the-car base. The simplest Arriva has a three-point harness and no base. Next up, is a version that adds a canopy that wraps around the handle. We think this is a rather lousy design, since you then can't carry the carrier under your arm. Cosco also makes an Arriva version with an "adjustable canopy," which is obviously the way to go.

The new Designer 22 ($49 to $79; rear-facing to 22 pounds) features plusher padding, easier to adjust belts and a soft foam carry handle. One version of the Designer 22 has an adjustable base.

The top-of-the-line Opus 35 is the first infant car seat that can be used rear-facing to a whopping 35 pounds. While that sounds good, we seriously wonder how any parent could carry a 35 pound infant in a carrier under their arm–heck even a 22 pounder would stress the average non-steroid using parent. Nonetheless, Cosco pulls out all the stops for the Opus 35–you get plush padding, four position headrest, TWO bases, a "Turnabout" handle with soft grip, multi-position canopy and a full-wrap around cover and removable boot. It's almost as if the marketing guys at Cosco thought if they through EVERYTHING at parents, they'd have to break down and buy the seat. We do have to admit the two bases (in one version, they are adjustable) and the no-thread belt path for easy installation are cool features, but we seriously doubt the 35 pound thing.

The Opus 35 comes in both three point and five point versions and will sell for $79 to $99. And just to confuse you, Cosco will also market a 35 pound rated version of their Designer seat (the Designer 35), which will be a scaled down version of the Opus–no fancy handle and no second base ($69-$79).

Parents of twins or premature babies take note: Cosco is one of very few manufacturers to make a "travel bed." For babies that need to travel laying down, the Cosco Dream Ride is about $60.

Convertible seats. Cosco's most successful seat in this category is the Alpha Omega, the first (and so far, only) seat that can be used from 5 pounds up to 80 pounds. First, it is a rear-facing convertible seat for infants up to 35 pounds. Then it it's a forward facing seat up to 40 pounds and finally it morphs into a belt-positioning booster for children up to 80 pounds. In order to accommodate growing kids, the harness adjusts with the headrest and there is a one-hand, three position recline feature. The Alpha Omega comes in both five point ($120) and bar shield ($139, adjustable to four positions) and, of course, there is also a Eddie Bauer Alpha Omega for $10 more. We were most impressed with the Alpha Omega as were our readers; most complimented the seat for its multiple uses and value. The only criticisms: twisting belts that frustrated some parents and the large size of Alpha Omega means it won't fit in some cars (see the compatibility list on carseatdata.org for specifics). Perhaps the biggest complaint: the recline feature was not deep enough for young infants (when the seat is in the rear-facing position). This underscores our earlier point that the best seat for an infants under 20 pounds is an INFANT seat, not a convertible like the Alpha Omega.

Of course, the Alpha Omega isn't Cosco's only convertible seat—the company also offers a slew of less pricey seats. The entry-level Touriva ($50 to $75) come in five-point and bar-shield (which is not adjustable) versions. The next level is the more plush Olympian car seat ($70 to $90), which also comes in five-point and an adjustable bar-shield version. The Regal Ride is basically the same as the Olympian, but adds a removable infant insert padding and pillow ($80 to $100).

If you are looking for a LATCH seat, Cosco has one model, the Triad ($80, rear facing to 35 pounds, forward 22 to 40 pounds). This five point seat has a removable infant insert, pillow, two-piece harness tie and mesh storage pockets. It also has color-coded belts to make the LATCH installation easier.

If that weren't enough, Cosco also has a new high-end line of car seats that go under the name "Maxi Cosi." We guess this is Cosco's answer to Britax's euro-designed seats—Maxi Cosi Priori seats feature a lock-off clamp that eliminates the need for a locking clip (like the Britax models). We wonder if what some parents like about these seats is the look—Maxi Cosi's fashionable fabrics (the seats are made in Holland) are definitely a cut-above those normally offered by Cosco. There is even a leather version of the Maxi Cosi for a whopping $400. Non-leather Maxi Cosi seats are still $200, which is too expensive since these are forward-only facing seats (20 to 40 pounds; you can't use them rear-facing for younger infants under one year of age).

Safety track record: We are still quite troubled by Cosco's safety track record, which has been marred by recent recalls—11 at last count since 1990. Among the worst was a 1999 recall involving 670,000 Arriva and Turnabout infant car seats. The seats' handle unexpectedly released in some cases, causing the seat to flip forward and dump out the child. 29 children were injured due to this defect.

Bottom line: Despite Cosco's questionable safety record, we'll still recommend Cosco's Alpha Omega seat for its innovative design and features. Although this seat doesn't recline far enough for infants, we still like it as a combo convertible and booster seat. We'll take a pass on Cosco's infant seats, however. Rating: C+

◆ ***Car seat safety info.*** Our web site has a brochure called "Buying a Better Car Seat Restraint" produced by a Canadian auto insurance institute. This publication (downloadable as a PDF, portable document format) has excellent charts that compare major brands of car seats on ease of installation and other safety factors. Since it was produced in 1999, some of the model info is a bit out of date but it still has valuable info. Go to www.BabyBargainsBook.com and click up the "Updates" section for a link to this car seat guide.

Carriers

Mountain Equipment Co-operative (MEC; web: www.mac.ca) is a unique, not-for-profit member owned co-op that sells baby carriers (among other outdoor products). A reader in Ottawa emailed us a rave for their "excellent" backpack carriers that are "renown for their excellent quality." At C$159, the MEC backpack carrier "clearly beats Kelty Kids and other U.S.-made carriers" at a much lower price. MEC has stores in major cities in Canada; call 800-747-7704 for details.

Canadian parents also write to us with kudos for the ***Baby Trekker*** (800) 665-3957; web: www.babytrekker.com. This 100% washable cotton carrier has straps that around the waist for support. Canucks like the fact a baby can be dressed in a snowsuit and still fit in the Baby Trekker. The carrier ($80 US, $102 Canada) is available in baby stores in Canada.

Baby Proofers

Looking for help baby proofing your house? Consider calling a professional baby-proofer who is a member of the ***International Association for Child Safety*** (to find a member near you, 888-677-IACS). These folks sell high-quality baby proofing items and offer installation, or you can do-it-yourself. There are about 50 members of the association in both the U.S. and Canada.

Web Resources

Yes, we have a large list of web sites that sell baby products in Chapter 11 (Do it My Mail and Online). One caveat for Canucks, however: not all sites ship to Canada. And that info is usually buried somewhere on their site that requires some digging. And remember prices are almost always in the U.S. dollar, not Canadian dollars. Given recent exchange rates and shipping costs, cross-border shopping is a bit painful as you can understand.

Canadian Parents Online (www.canadianparents.com) is a great resource, with advice columns, chat/discussion areas and recall info for Canadian parents. We liked their "Ask an Expert" areas, which included advice on childbirth, lactation and even fitness.

The ***Childcare Resources and Research Unit*** (www.childcare-canada.org) has great info and statistics on childcare costs in Canada.

Sears may not have a catalog any more in the U.S., but the Canadian version of ***Sears*** (www.sears.ca) has both a web site and printed catalog with baby products and clothes. A reader said the catalog has a nice selection of products and is a great resource for Canadian parents who might live outside the major metro areas.

Figure 1: CanadianParents.com is a giant portal to a myriad of sites for Canuck parents.

Appendix B

Sample registry

Here's the coolest thing about registering for baby products at Babies R Us—that neato bar code scanner gun. You're supposed to walk (waddle?) around the store and zap the bar codes of products you want to add to the registry. This is cool for about 15 seconds, until you realize you have to make DECISIONS about WHAT to zap.

What to do? Yes, you could page through this book as you do the registry, but that's a bit of a pain, no? To help speed the process, here's a list of what stuff you need and what to avoid. Consider it *Baby Bargains* in a nutshell:

The order of these recommendations follows the Babies R Us Registry form:

Car Seats/Strollers/Carriers/Accessories

◆ ***Full Size Convertible Car Seat.*** Basically, we urge waiting on this one—most babies don't need to go into a full-size convertible seat until they outgrow an infant seat (that could be four to six months or as much as a year). In the meantime, new models are always coming out with better safety features. Hence, don't register for this and wait to buy it later.

If want to ignore this advice, go for the ***Britax Roundabout*** ($180-$200) or ***Evenflo Triumph*** $130. If you have a LATCH-ready car (see Chapter 7 for details), go for the ***Britax Expressway*** ($160).

◆ ***Infant car seat.*** Best bets: the ***Century "Smart Fit Plus"*** ($50 to $70) and the ***Graco "Snug Ride"*** ($60 to $90; the LX is a good option).

◆ ***Strollers.*** There is no "one size fits all" recommendation in this section. Read the lifestyle recommendations in Chapter 8 to find a stroller that best fits your needs. In general, stay away from the pre-packaged "travel systems"—remember that many of the better stroller brands now can be used with infant seats.

◆ ***Baby Carriers.*** *Baby Bjorn* ($75 to $80). You really don't need another carrier (like a backpack) unless you plan to do serious outdoor hikes. If that is the case, check Chapter 8 for suggestions.

◆ ***Misc.*** Yes, you should buy an infant head support pad for your infant seat or stroller, but there really isn't a specific brand preference in this category (all basically do the same thing). As for stroller and car seat accessories, that's purely optional.

Travel Yards/High Chairs/Exercisers/Accessories

◆ **Gates.** The best brand is ***KidCo*** (which makes the Gateway, Safeway and Elongate). But this is something you can do later–most babies aren't mobile until at least six months of age.

◆ ***Travel Yard/Playard.*** Graco's ***Pack 'N Play*** and Century's ***Fold & Go*** playpens are best bets. Go for one with a bassinet feature.

◆ ***High Chair.*** The best high chair is the Chicco Mamma ($130-$160), although the Fisher Price Swing 'N Meals ($99) is a good choice that combines a swing and high chair.

◆ ***Walker/Exerciser.*** Skip this. See Chapter 6 for details.

◆ ***Swing.*** We like Graco's ***Open Top*** swings ($70 to $120) best.

◆ ***Hook on high chair.*** Not really necessary; if you want one, get it later.

◆ ***Infant jumper.*** Too many injuries with this product category; pass on it.

◆ ***Bed rail.*** Don't need this either.

◆ ***Bouncer.*** Fisher Price (www.fisher-price.com) makes the most popular one on the category–their ***"Soothing Bouncer Seat"*** is about $30 to $35 (it comes in a couple different versions).

Cribs/Furniture

◆ ***Crib.*** For cribs, you've got two basic choices: a simple model that is, well, just a crib or a "convertible" model that eventually morphs into a twin or full size bed. In the simple category for best buys, ***Child Craft's 10171*** is a basic maple crib with single-drop side for just $200 to $250. In a similar vein, a basic ***Simmons*** model at Baby Depot ran $240. Other features that are nice (but not necessary) for cribs include a double drop side, a quiet rail release and hidden hardware. If you fancy an imported crib, there are few bargains but we found that ***Sorelle/C&T*** and ***Babi Italia*** have reasonable prices ($250 to start) for above average quality.

◆ ***Bassinet.*** Skip it. See Chapter 2 for details. If you buy a playpen with bassinet feature, you don't need a separate bassinet.

◆ ***Dressing/changing table.*** Skip it. Just use the top of your dresser as a changing area. (See dresser recommendation below.)

◆ ***Glider/rocker and ottoman.*** In a word: ***Dutailier***. Whatever style/fabric you chose, you can't go wrong with that brand. Hint: this is a great product to buy online at a discount, so you might want to skip registering for one.

◆ ***Dresser.*** Dressers and other case pieces by ***Rumble Tuff*** were great deals–they exactly match the finishes of Child Craft and Simmons, but at prices 10% to 25% less than the competition. We liked their three-drawer combo unit that combines a changing table and a dresser for $500 to $600. Unfortunately, Rumble Tuff isn't sold in chain stores like Babies R Us (see chapter 2 for details).

◆ ***Misc.*** Babies R Us recommends registering for all sorts of miscellaneous items like cradles, toy boxes and the like. Obviously, these are clearly optional.

Bedding/Room Décor/Crib Accessories

◆ ***Crib set.*** Don't–don't register for this waste of money. Instead, just get two or three good crib sheets and a nice cotton blanket. See Chapter 3 for brands.

◆ ***Bumper pads, dust ruffle, diaper stacker.*** Ditto–a waste.

◆ ***Lamp, mobile.*** These are optional, of course. We don't have any specific brand preferences.

◆ ***Mattress.*** We like the foam mattresses from Colgate ($90 for the Classica I). Or, for coil, go for a Sealy (Kolcraft) 150 coil mattress for $60 at Babies R Us. Unfortunately, Babies R Us and other chains don't sell foam mattresses but you can find them online.

◆ ***Misc.*** Babies R Us has lots of miscellaneous items in this area like rugs, wallpaper border, bassinet skirts and so on. We have ideas for décor on the cheap in Chapter 3.

Infant Toys, Care & Feeding

◆ Toys: All of this (***crib toys, bath toys, blocks***) is truly optional. We have ideas for this in Chapter 6.

◆ ***Nursery monitor.*** In general, the ***Fisher Price*** line is best but keep the receipt–many baby monitors don't work well because of electronic interference in the home.

◆ ***Humidifier.*** The ***Holmes/Duracraft*** line sold in Target is best. Avoid the "baby" humidifiers sold in baby stores, as they are overpriced.

◆ ***Diaper pail.*** Two words: *Diaper Genie*.

◆ ***Bathtub.*** While not a necessity, a baby bath tub is a nice convenience (especially if you are bathing baby solo). As a best bet, we suggest the ***First Years' "Bath Tub/Bath Seat Combo"*** (800) 225-0382 or (508) 588-1220–it's a $20 bath tub that later converts to a bath seat. For $20, it's a good deal.

◆ ***Bottles.*** *Avent* is the best bet, according to our readers.

◆ ***Bottle Warmer.*** Avent's new ***Express Bottle and Baby Food Warmer*** ($40) can heat a bottle in four minutes. ***The First Years "Night & Day Bottle Warmer System"*** ($30) is an alternative. It steam heats two 8 oz. bottles in under five minutes (one reader said its more like three minutes). For night-time feedings, it can keep two bottles cool for up to eight hours (so there's no need to run to the kitchen). Yes, it fits Avent bottles, but one reader said just the small 4 oz ones, not the 8 oz variety.

◆ ***Sterilizer.*** Although it's an optional device, ***Avent's "Microwave Steam Sterilizer"*** ($25-30) is a good choice. It holds four bottles of any type and is easy to use–just put in water and nuke for eight minutes.

◆ ***Thermometer.*** *First Years* has a new high speed digital thermometer ($10) that gives a rectal temp in 20 seconds and an underarm in 30 seconds. That's the best budget choice; ***Braun's "Thermoscan"*** and ***Safety's 1st's "Hospital's Choice"*** are not bad if you want to go whole hog with an ear or forehead model.

◆ ***Breast pump.*** There isn't a "one size fits all" recommendation here. Read Chapter 5 Maternity/Nursing for details.

◆ ***Misc.*** In this category, Babies R Us throws in items like bibs, hooded towels, washcloths, pacifiers and so on. See Chapter 4 "Reality Layette" for ideas in this category.

Diapers/Wipes

◆ ***Diapers.*** For disposables, the best deals are in warehouse clubs like ***Sam's*** and ***Costco***. Generic diapers at ***Wal-Mart*** and ***Target*** are also good deals. We have a slew of deals on cloth diapers in Chapter 4.

◆ ***Wipes.*** Don't go generic here. Brands like ***Pampers Baby Fresh*** and ***Huggies*** are the better bets.

Clothing/Layette

◆ See the "Reality Layette" list (Ch. 4) for suggestions on quantities/brands.

APPENDIX C
Multiples advice

Yes, you are the parent-to-be of twins and that can mean double trouble when it comes to buying for baby. Here's our round-up of what products are best for parents of multiples:

Cribs

Since twins tend to be smaller than most infants, parents of multiples can use a bassinet or cradle for an extended period of time. We discuss this category in depth in Chapter 2, but generally recommend looking at a portable playpen (Graco Pak N Play is one popular choice) with a bassinet feature as an alternative. A nice splurge if your budget allows it: the ***Arm's Reach Co-Sleeper***.

Bedding

Take our advice here and save by just getting high quality sheets and a good cotton blanket. Skip those fancy bedding sets–the last thing you need is to waste money on quilts, diaper stackers and other frills in a $300 bedding set.

Nursing help

Check out ***EZ-2-NURSE's pillow*** (800-584-TWIN; we saw it on www.everythingmom.com). A mom told us this was the "absolute best" for her twins, adding "I could not successfully nurse my girls together without this pillow. It was wonderful." Cost: $56.

New at Wal-Mart is a breastfeeding collection with ***Lansinoh*** products (including their amazing nipple cream). Check the special displays in the store or on their web site at www.walmart.com.

Yes, nursing one baby can be a challenge, but two? You might need some help. To the rescue comes ***Mothering Multiples: Breastfeeding & Caring for Twins and More*** by Karen Kerkoff Gromada ($14.95; available on the La Leche League web site, www.lalecheleague.com). This book was recommend to us by more than one mother of twins for its clear and concise advice.

Car seats

Most multiples are born before their due date. The smallest infants may have to ride in special "car beds" that enable them to lie flat (instead of car seats that require an infant to be at least five or six pounds and ride in a sitting position). The car beds then rotate to become regular infant car seats so older infants can ride in a sitting position.

For years, the only choice in this category was ***Cosco's Ultra Dream Ride*** ($50-$55, www.coscoinc.com). Now, Graco has introduced the ***Cherish Car Bed***, which can be used up to nine pounds (up to 20 inches). Unlike Cosco Ultra Dream Ride ($40), the Cherish Car Bed has a "fabric hook and loop harness for a soft, snug fit."

Bottom line: while the Cosco is $10 to $15 more expensive than the Graco unit, it is the better bet. The Graco bed does NOT convert into a regular infant seat, so you'll be out another $50 or more when your baby surpasses nine pounds. The Cosco bed can be used up to 20 pounds and 26 inches. The only criticism we heard of the Cosco bed: sometimes it is a bit difficult to put in a smaller car when in the car bed position.

Strollers

Our complete wrap-up of recommendations for double strollers is in Chapter 8 (see Double the Fun in the lifestyle recommendations). In brief, we should mention that the new ***Graco DuoGlider*** accepts two infant seats ($229 for a travel system that includes one infant seat). We should also note Baby Trend's tandem (front/back) double strollers. The ***Caravan Lite LX*** ($199-249) lets you attach one or two infant car seats and gets generally good marks from parents for its features and ease of use.

New for 2001: Perego will debut the new ***Duette*** double stroller ($450) that will allow parents of twins to attach TWO infant car seats (included) to the G-matic frame. Basically, this is a double version of the ***Primo Viaggio travel system*** described in Chapter 8. (And there is also a new ***"Triplette"*** version of this stroller that will debut in 2001 as well).

Those strollers are great since they can handle two infant car seats, but most parents of twins find that side-by-side strollers do better for them than tandem (front/back) models. Why? Tandem strollers typically only have one seat that fully reclines (when parents of twins find they need two reclining seats). And the front/back configuration seems to invite more trouble when the twins get older—the back passenger pulling the front passenger's hair, etc.

Unfortunately, the brand choices here are rather limited. The best choices (Maclaren or Combi) in the side-by-side category are rather pricey. Graco and Cosco offer side-by-side models in the under $200 price range, but they are much less reliable.

In the dark horse category, consider the ***Double Decker***

Stroller (941-543-1582; www.doubledeckerstroller.com), a jogging stroller than can accommodate two infant car seats. It runs $235.

As for other jogging strollers, the side-by-side versions of ***Baby Jogger*** and ***Kool Stop*** are probably best if you really plan to exercise with a sport stroller. The new tandem jogger by ***Gozo*** (again, see Chapter 8) is an interesting alternative as well.

Carrier

A mom of twins emailed us to rave about the ***MaxiMom*** carrier. She found it easier to use and adjust. The best feature: you adjust it to be a sling and nurse a baby in it. We saw this carrier on TwinStuff (www.twinstuff.com) for $75 to $80; a triplet version is $109.

Freebies

◆ Get a ***FREE Diaper Genie from Playtex*** when you send proof of multiple births to Playtex (800) 222-0453; www.playtex.com.

◆ ***Kimberly Clark Twins Program:*** Get a gift of "high-value coupons" for Huggies diapers by submitting birth certificates or published birth announcements. (800) 544-1847).

◆ ***The First Years*** offers free bibs and rattles for parents of multiples when you send in copies of birth certificates. Web: www.thefirstyears.com.

◆ ***Heinz/Beechnut***: Get coupons for baby food by calling 800-872-2229 in the US or 800-565-2100 in Canada. Web: www.heinz.com.

Source: Twins Magazine is a bi-monthly, full-color magazine published by The Business Word (800) 328-3211 or (303) 290-8500 (www.twinsmagazine.com). Remember that offers can change at any time. Check with the companies first before sending any info.

Miscellaneous

BabyBeat is a fetal monitoring device that lets you listen to your babies' heartbeats as early as 10-12 weeks. Best of all, BabyBeat lets you rent the device instead of buying–$30 to $50 per month depending on the model. You can also buy the unit at $445 to $549. For details, call 888-758-8822 or www.babybeat.com. Unlike cheaper ultrasound monitors that are low-quality, BabyBeat is similar to the Doppler instruments found in doctor's offices.

Appendix D

Phone/Web Site Directory

Wonder where these contact names appear in the book? Check the index for a page number. Remember that many of these contacts do not sell to the public directly; the phone numbers are so you can find a dealer/store near you. Refer to the chapter in which they are mentioned to see which companies offer a consumer catalog, sell to the public, etc.

We've divided this section into two parts: general baby product makers and a chapter-by-chapter listing of companies. The general listing is for companies that appear in multiple places in the book (see the index for specific page numbers). Note: we've omitted the "www." prefix before the web address for space reasons.

Contact Name	Toll-Free	Phone	Web Site
General Baby Product Manufacturers			
Baby Trend	(800) 328-7363	(909) 773-0018	babytrend.com
Century		(330) 468-2000	centuryproducts.com
Chicco	(877) 4-CHICCO		chiccousa.com
Cosco	(800) 457-5276	(812) 372-0141	coscoinc.com
Evenflo	(800) 233-5921	(937) 415-3229	evenflo.com
First Years	(800) 225-0382	(508) 588-1220	thefirstyears.com
Fisher Price	(800) 828-4000	(716) 687-3000	fisher-price.com
Graco	(800) 345-4109	(610) 286-5951	gracobaby.com
Peg Perego		(219) 482-8191	perego.com
Safety 1st	(800) 962-7233	(781) 364-3100	safety1st.com
Introduction			
Alan & Denise Fields (authors)		(303) 442-8792	babybargainsbook.com
Chapter 2: Nursery Necessities			
JCPenney	(800) 222-6161		jcpenney.com
CPSC	(800) 638-2772		cpsc.gov
Bus Van (2 locations)		(415) 981-1405 , (415) 752-5353	
Baby Furniture Outlet	(800) 613-9280	(519) 649-2590	
Buy Buy Baby			buybuybaby.com
Scarsdale, NY		(914) 725-9220	
Rockville, MD		(301) 984-1122	
Paramus, NJ		(201) 599-1900	
Huntington Station, NY		(631) 425-0404	
Babies R Us	(888) BABYRUS		babiesrus.com
Baby Depot	(800) 444-COAT		coat.com
Cosco (outlet)		(812) 526-0860	
Child Craft (outlet)		(812) 524-1999	
Kiddie Kastle (outlet)		(502) 499-9667	
Baby Boudoir (outlet)	(800) 272-2293	(508) 998-2166	
Pottery Barn (outlet)		(901) 763-1500	
Baby Catalog America		(800) PLAY-PEN	babycatalog.com
Baby Style			babystyle.com

Pottery Barn Kids			PotteryBarnKids.com
Danny Foundation			dannyfoundation.org
Great Beginnings	(800) 886-9077	(301) 417-9702	childrensfurniture.com
Baby Furniture Outlet	(800) 613-9280	(519) 649-2590	babyfurnitureoutlet.com
Good Night Ben			goodnightben.com

Crib manufacturers

Angel Line	(800) 889-8158	(856) 863-8009	angelline.com
AP Industries	(800) 463-0145	(418) 728-2145	apindustries.com
Baby's Dream	(800) TEL-CRIB	(912) 649-4404	babysdream.com
Bassett		(540) 629-6000	bassettfurniture.com
Bellini	(800) 332-BABY	(516) 234-7716	bellini.com
Berg		(908) 354-5252	bergfurniture.com
Bonavita	(888) 266-2848	(732) 346-5150	bonavita-cribs.com
Child Craft		(812) 883-3111	childcraftind.com
Generation 2	(800) 736-1140	(334) 792-1144	childdesigns.com
Delta		(718) 385-1000	deltaenterprise.com
Legacy (see Child Craft)			
Little Miss Liberty	(800) RND-CRIB	(310) 281-5400	crib.com
MIBB		(212) 279-9222	
Million Dollar Baby	(877) 600-6688	(323) 728-9988	milliondollarbaby.com
Morigeau/Lepine	(800) 326-2121	(724) 941-7475	morigeau.com
Pali	(877) 725-4772		paliItaly.com
Pottery Barn	(800) 430-7373		potterybarnkids.com
Ragazzi		(514) 324-7886	ragazzi.com
Simmons		(920) 982-2140	simmonsjp.com.
Sorelle	(888) 470-1260	(201) 461-9444	sorellefurniture.com
Status		(514) 631-0788	statusfurniture.com
Stork Craft		(604) 274-5121	storkcraft.com
Tracers		(914) 686-5725	
Vermont Precision		(802) 888-7974	vtprecision.com
Corsican Kids	(800) 421-6247	(323) 587-3101	corsican.com
Lexington	(800) 539-4636	(336) 249-5300	lexington.com
Mondi		(630) 953-9519	mondibaby.com
Muebles		(418) 428-3746	
E.G. Furniture		(418) 325-2050	egfurniture.com
Forever Mine	(800) 356-2742	(819) 297-2000	forvermine.com
Moosehead		(207) 997-3621	kynd.com/~moosehed
Todd Parr Furniture		(416) 924-0766	funtimedesigns.com
Stephanie Anne	(888) 885-6700		stephanieanne.com

IKEA		(610) 834-0180	ikea.com
JPMA		(856) 439-0500	jpma.org
Arm's Reach	(800) 954-9353		armsreach.com
Ethan Allen	(888) EAHELP-1		ethanallen.com
Mother Hubbard's Cupboard		(416) 661-8201	
Colgate		(404) 681-2121	colgatekids.com
Babies Boutique			babiesboutique.com
Halo Crib Mattress		(218) 525-5158	halosleep.com
SIDS Alliance			SidsAlliance.org
maker Jupiter Industries			bopeepnurseryproducts.com

Sleep Tight Soother	(800) NO-COLIC		colic.com
Burlington Basket Co.	(800) 553-2300	(319) 754-6508	
Container Store	(800) 733-3532		
Rumble Tuff	(800) 524-9607	(801) 226-2648	rumbletuff.com
Camelot Furniture		(714) 283-4194	
Dutailier	(800) 363-9817	(450) 772-2403	dutailier.com
CribNCarriage			cribncarriage.com
Rocking Chairs 100%	(800) 4-ROCKER		rocking-chairs.com

Brooks	(800) 427-6657	(423) 626-1111	
Conant Ball	(800) 363-2635	(819) 566-1515	
Relax-R	(800) 850-2909		
Towne Square	(800) 356-1663		gliderrocker.com
Home Base		(949) 442-5000	homebase.com
American Health	(800) 327-4382		foryourbaby.com
Closet Maid	(800) 874-0008		closetmaid.com
Storage Pride	(800) 441-0337		
Lee Rowan	(800) 325-6150		leerowan.com
Hold Everything	(800) 421-2264		holdeverything.com
Closet Factory	(800) 692-5673		closetfactory.com
California Closets	(800) 274-6754		californiaclosets.com
Sassy		(616) 243-0767	sassybaby.com
Shades of Light	(800) 262-6612		shades-of-light.com

Chapter 3: Bedding & Décor

Baby Bedding Online			babybeddingonline.com
Best For Babies			bestforbabies.com
Kid's Etc		(949) 495-5828	kids-etc.com
Country Lane			countrylane.com
Basic Comfort	(800) 456-8687		basiccomfort.com
Kiddopotamus	(800) 772-8339		kiddopotamus.com
Michaels Arts & Crafts	(800) MICHAELS		michaels.com
Transfer-Mations		(303) 526-2626	boppy.com
Bumpa Bed	(800) 241-1848	(509) 457-0925	babyjogger.com
Stay Put safety sheet			babysheets.com

Outlets

Garnet Hill		(802) 362-6198	
House of Hatten		(512) 392-8161	
The Interior Alternative		(413) 743-1986	
Laura Ashely		(703) 494-3124	
Nojo		(949) 858-9496	
Quiltex		(718) 788-3158	

Bedding Manufacturers

Amy Coe		(203) 221-3050	amycoe.com
Baby Guess		(714) 895-2250	crowncraftsinfantproducts.com
Bananafish	(800) 899-8689	(818) 727-1645	
Beautiful Baby		(903) 295-2229	bbaby.com
Brandee Danielle	(800) 720-5656	(714) 957-1240	brandeedanielle.com
California Kids	(800) 548-5214	(650) 637-9054	
Carters	(800) 845-3251	(803) 275-2541	caters.com
Celebrations		(310) 532-2499	baby-celebrations.com
Cotton Tale	(800) 628-2621	(714) 435-9558	
CoCaLo		(714) 434-7200	cocalo.com
Crown Crafts		(714) 895-9200	crowncraftsinfantproducts.com
Gerber	(800) 4-GERBER		gerber.com
Glenna Jean	(800) 446-6018	(804) 561-0687	
Hoohobbers		(773) 890-1466	hoohobbers.com
House of Hatten	(800) 542-8836	(512) 819-9600	
Infantino	(800) 365-8182	(858) 689-1221	
Judi's	(800) 421-9433		judis.com
KidsLine		(310) 660-0110	kidslineinc.com
Lambs & Ivy	(800) 345-2627	(310) 839-5155	lambsivy.com
Luv Stuff	(800) 825-BABY	(972) 278-BABY	
Martha Stewart			kmart.com
My Dog Spot		(858) 259-7200	mydogspot4kids.com

Nava's Design		(818) 988-9050	navasdesigns.com
Nojo	(800) 854-8760	(310) 763-8100	nojo.com
Patchkraft	(800) 866-2229	(973) 340-3300	patchkraft.com
Pine Creek		(503) 266-6275	pinecreekbedding.com
Quiltex	(800) 237-3636	(212) 594-2205	
Red Calliope	(800) 421-0526	(310) 763-8100	redcalliope.com
Sumersault	(800) 232-3006	(201) 768-7890	sumersault.com
Sweet Pea		(626) 578-0866	
Wendy Bellissimo		(818) 348-3682	wendybellissimo.com
Riegal	(800) 845-3251	(803) 275-2541	parentinformation.com
Springs		(212) 556-6300	springs.com
Vicarage	(888) VICARAGE		
Ruby & Coco	(800) 316-2772	(610) 869-4830	rubycoco.com
Bebe Chic		(201) 941-5414	bebechic.com
Kimberly Grant		(714) 546-4411	kimberlygrant.com
Groovy Baby		(973) 748-0606	groovybaby.com
Creative Images	(800) 784-5415	(904) 825-6700	crimages.com
Eddie Bauer	(800) 426-8020		eddiebauer.com
Michel & Co/Charpent		(310) 390-7655	
Beacon		(828) 686-3861	
Couristan	(800) 223-6186		
Sunworthy Wallcover	(800) 535-7811		
Gund	(800) 448-4863	(732) 248-1500	gund.com
Biobottoms	(800) 766-1254		biobottoms.com
The Company Store	(800) 323-8000		companykids.com
Garnet Hill	(800) 622-6216		garnethill.com
Graham Kracker	(800) 489-2820		grahamkracker.com
The Land of Nod	(800) 933-9904		landofnod.com
Lands' End	(800) 345-3696		landsend.com
Pottery Barn Kids	(800) 430-7373		potterybarnkids.com
Kids Club	(800) 363-0500		
Seventh Generation	(800) 456-1177		

Chapter 4: Reality Layette

Little Princess			royalbaby.com
One of a Kind Kids			oneofakindkids.com
Preemie.com			preemie.com
SuddenlyMommies			suddenlymommies.com
Poling Polars			polingpolars.com
Internet Resale Directory			secondhand.com
Nat'l Assoc. Resale & Thrift			narts.org
Ebay			ebay.com
Minnetonka Moccasins		(718) 365-7033	minnetonka-by-mail.com
Robeez shoes	(800) 929-2623	(604) 435-9074	robeez.com
Bobux shoes			bobuxusa.com)
Once Upon a Child		(614) 791-0000	onceuponachild.com
Outlets			
Carter's	(888) 782-9548	(770) 961-8722	
Esprit		(415) 648-6900	
Flapdoodles		(970) 262-9351	
Florence Eiseman		(414) 272-3222	FlorenceEiseman.com
Hanna Andersson		(503) 697-1953	
Hartstrings		(610) 687-6900	
Health-Tex	(800) 772-8336	(914) 428-7551	vfc.com
JcPenney outlet	(800) 222-6161		jcpenney.com
Osh Kosh		(920) 231-8800	oshkoshbgosh.com
Talbot's Kids	(800) 543-7123	(781) 740-8888	talbots.com
Outlet Bound mag	(800) 336-8853		outletbound.com

Clothing Manufacturers

Alexis	(800) 253-9476		alexisusa.com
Baby Gap	(800) GAPSTYLE		
babygap.com			
Cotton Tale Originals	(800) 628-2621		
Earthlings	(888) GOBABYO		earthlings.net
Flap Happy	(800) 234-3527		
Flapdoodles		(302) 731-9793	
Florence Eisman		(414) 272-3222	florenceeiseman.com
Good Lad of Philadelphia		(215) 739-0200	goodlad.com
Gymboree	(800) 990-5060		gymboree.com
Hartstrings		(610) 687-6900	hartstrings.com
Jake and Me		(970) 352-8802	jakeandme.com
Little Me			littleme.com
Mini Classics		(201) 569-7357	
Mother-Maid		(770) 479-7558	
Mulberri Bush (Tumbleweed too)			mulberribush.com
OshKosh B'Gosh			oshkoshbgosh.com
Patsy Aiken		(919) 872-8789	patsyaiken.com
Pingarama			pingarama.com
Sarah's Prints	(888) 4-PRINTS		sarasprints.com
Skivvydoodles		(212) 967-2918	skivvydoodles.com
Sweet Potatoes and Spudz		(510) 527-7633	sweetpotatoesinc.com
Wes & Willy			wesandwilly.com
Carter's		(770) 961-8722	carters.com
Fisher Price	(800) 747-8697		fisher-price.com
Good Lad of Philadelphia		(215) 739-0200	goodlad.com
Le Top	(800) 333-2257		

Catalogs

Biobottoms	(800) 766-1254		biobottoms.com
Childrens Wear	(800) 242-5437		cwkids.com
Chock	(800) 222-0020	(212) 473-1929	chockcatalog.com
Fisher Price	(800) 747-8697		fisher-price.com
Hanna Andersson	(800) 222-0544		hannaandersson.com
Lands End	(800) 963-4816		landsend.com
LL Kids	(800) 552-5437		llbean.com
Oilily	(800) 977-7736		
Olsen's Mill Direct	(800) 537-4979		olsensmilldirect.com
Patagonia Kids	(800) 638-6464		patagonia.com
Talbot's Kids	(800) 543-7123		talbots.com
Wooden Soldier	(800) 375-6002	(603) 356-7041	
Warner Bros. Catalog	(800) 223-6524		
Disney Catalog	(800) 237-5751		disneystore.com
Fitigues	(800) 235-9005		
Campmor	(800) 226-7667		campmor.com
Sierra Trading Post	(800) 713-4534		sierratradingpost.com

Diapers

All Together Diaper Company			clothdiaper.com
Baby Lane			thebabylane.com
Diapers 4 Less			diapers4less.com
Drug Emporium			.drugemporium.com
CVS Pharmacy			cvspharmacy.com
Baby's Heaven			babysheaven.com
Diaper Site			diapersite.com
Costco			costco.com
A Bottom Line			abottomline.com
Baby J			babyj.com
Huggies			huggies.com
Luvs			luvs.com

Cloth Diaper Resources

Diaper Changes book	(800) 572-1826		homekeepers.com
Mother-Ease			motherease.com
Kushies	(800) 841-5330		kushies.com
DiaperDance			diaperdance.com
All Together		(801) 566-7579	clothdiaper.com
Bumkins	(800) 338-7581		bumkins.com
Indisposables	(800) 663-1730		
Baby Town			eskimo.com/~babytown
Baby Bunz	(800) 676-4559		
Sams Club			samsclub.com
BJ's			bjswholesale.com
Baby Works	(800) 422-2910		babyworks.com
Born to Love		(905) 725-2559	borntolove.com
Natural Baby	(800) 388-2229		kidsstuff.com
Nurtured Baby	(888) 564-BABY		nurturedbaby.com
TC Kidco	(888) 825-4326		
Weebees			weebees.com

Chapter 5: Maternity/Nursing

Playtex	(800) 537-9955		playtex.com
Motherwear	(800) 950-2500		motherwear.com
Anna Cris Maternity			annacris.com
Little Koala			littlekoala.com
Maternity 4 Less			maternity4less.com
Mom Shop			momshop.com
One Hot Mama			onehotmama.com
Fit Maternity			fitmaternity.com
From Here to Eternity			fromheretomaternity.com
Just Babies			justbabies.com
Lattesa			Lattesa.com
Liz Lange Maternity			lizlange.com
Mothers In Motion			mothers-in-motion.com
Naissance Maternity			naissancematernity.com
On'na Maternity			onnamaternity.com
Pumpkin Maternity			pumpkinmaternity.com
Style Maternity			stylematernity.com
That Glow			ThatGlow.com
Thyme Maternity			maternity.ca
Twinkle Little Star			twinklelittlestar.com
Plus maternity sources			
Baby Becoming			babybecoming.com
Baby Becoming			babybecoming.com
Expecting Style			expectingstyle.com
Imaternity			imaternity.com
JCPenney			jcpenney.com
Maternal Instinct			maternal-instinct.com
MomShop			momshop.com
Motherhood			maternitymall.com
One Hot Mama			onehotmama.com
Plus Maternity			plusmaternity.com
Plus Size Mommies			plussizemommies.com
Majamas			majamas
Bravado Designs	(800) 590-7802	(416) 466-8652	bravadodesigns.com
One Hanes Place	(800) 300-2600		onehanesplace.com
Decent Exposures	(800) 524-4949		decentexposures.com
Fit Maternity		(530) 938-4530	fitmaternity.com
Title 9 Sports		(510) 655-5999	titleninesports.com
Hue		(212) 947-3666	

Motherwear	(800) 950-2500		motherwear.com
Elizabeth Lee Designs		(435) 454-3350	elizabethlee.com

Outlets

Motherhood outlets	(800) 466-6223		
Mothertime Outlets		(773) 481-3180	mothertime.com
Motherwear outlet		(413) 586-2175	

Maternity Chains

Dan Howard	(800) 966-6847	(312) 263-6700	dan-howard.com
Japanese Weekend	(800) 808-0555	(415) 621-0555	japaneseweekend.com
Mothercare		(312) 263-6700	imaternity.com
Motherhood	(800) 4MOM2BE		maternitymall.com

Catalogs

Garnet Hill	(800) 622-6216	(603) 823-5545	garnethill.com
Breast Is Best	(877) 837-5439		

Breastfeeding

La Leche League	(800) LALECHE		lalecheleague.org
Nursing Mothers' Council		(408) 272-1448	nursingmothers.org
Int'l Lactation Consultants Assoc		(703) 560-7330	iblce.org
Bosom Buddies	(888) 860-0041	(720) 482-0109	bosombuddies.com
Avent	(800) 542-8368		aventamerica.com
Medela	(800) 435-8316		medela.com
Bosom Buddies			bosombuddies.com
White River Concepts	(800) 824-6351		
Ameda Egnell	(800) 323-4060		hollister.com
My Brest Friend	(800) 555-5522		zenoffproducts.com
EZ-2-Nurse	(800) 584-TWIN		everythingmom.com
MedRino			breastpumps-breastfeeding.com
Nursing Mothers Supplies			nursingmotherssupplies.com
Baily Medical			bailymed.com

Chapter 6: Around the House

Kel-Gar		(972) 250-3838	kelgar.com
Comfy Kids	(888) 529-4934		comfykids.com
BabySmart	(800) 756-5590	(908) 766-4900	baby-smart.com
Nature Company			naturecompany.com
Container Store	(800) 733-3532		containerstore.com
Diaper Genie	(800) 843-6430		playtexbaby.com
Duracraft humidifiers	(800) 5-HOLMES		holmesproducts.com
Learning Curve	(800) 704-8697		learningtoys.com
Dolly mobiles	(800) 758-7520		dolly.com
Infantino	(800) 365-8182		infantino.com
Gymfinity		(972) 404-9335	todayskids.com
Gymini	(800) 843-6292		tinylove.com
Children on the Go	(800) 345-4109		gracobaby.com
Neurosmith		(562) 296-1100	neurosmith.com
North American Bear	(800) 682-3427	(312) 329-0020	nabear.com
EZ Bather Deluxe	(800) 546-1996		dexproducts.com
Discovery Toys	(800) 426-4777		discoverytoysinc.com
Green Peace			greenpeace.org
Wal-Mart			wal-mart.com

Coupon sites

BabyDollar			babydollar.com
Deal of the Day			dealoftheday.com
EDealFinder			eDealFinder.com
ImegaDeals			imegadeals.com
Big Big Savings			bigbigsavings.com
Fat Wallet			fatwallet.com
Clever Moms			clevermoms.com
Image Deals			imagedeals.com
DotDeals			dotdeals.com

Catalogs

Back to Basics Toys	(800) 356-5360		backtobasicstoys.com
Constructive Play.	(800) 832-0572	(816) 761-5900	constplay.com
Edutainment	(800) 338-3844		mattelinteractive.com
Kaplan Co	(800) 533-2166		kaplanco.com
Playfair Toys	(800) 824-7255		playfairtoys.com
Sensational Begin.	(800) 444-2147		sensationalkids.com
Toys to Grow On	(800) 542-8338		toystogrowon.com
Totally Thomas' Toy	(800) 30-THOMAS		totallythomas.com
Thomas The Tank Engine			thomasthetankengine.com
FAO Schwarz	(800) 426-8697		faoschwarz.com
Hearthsong	(800) 325-2502		heathsong.com
Imagine/Challenge	(888) 777-1493		imaginetoys.com
Leaps & Bounds	(800) 477-2189		leapsandboundscatalog.com
Smarter Kids			smarterkids.com
Earthwise Toys			naturaltoys.com
Cozy Crib Tent	(800) 626-0339		totsinmind.com
DealTime			dealtime.com
Overstock			overstock.com

Baby Formula

BabyMil	(800) 344-1358		babymil.com
Mothers Milk Mate	(800) 499-3506		mothersmilkmate.com
Bottle Burper	(800) 699-BURP		

Bottles

Munchkin	(800) 344-2229	(818) 893-5000	munchkininc.com
Playtex		(203) 341-4000	
BreastBottle			breastbottle.com
DrugStore.com			drugstore.com

Baby Food

Beech-Nut	(800) BEECHNUT		beechnut.com
Earth's Best	(800) 442-4221		earthsbest.com
Gerber			gerber.com
Heinz			heinzbaby.com
Well Fed Baby	(888) 935-5333		wellfedbaby.com
Super Baby Food book			superbabyfood.com

Chapter 7: Car Seats

NHTSA	(888) DASH2DOT	(202) 366-0123	nhtsa.dot.gov
American Academy of Pediatrics			aap.org
National Safe Kids Campaign			safekids.org
Safety Belt Safe USA			carseat.org
Car Seat Data			carseatdata.com
ParentsPlace			parentsplace.com
Auto Safety Hotline	(800) 424-9393		
Might Tite	(888) 336-7909		might-tite.com
Fit for a Kid	(877) FIT4AKID		fit4akid.org
Britax	(888) 4-BRITAX	(803) 802-2022	childseat.com
Kolcraft		(773) 247-4494	kolcraft.com
Safeline SitNStroll	(800) 829-1625	(303) 457-4440	safelinecorp.com
Baby's Away	(800) 571-0077		babysaway.com
Kiddopotamus	(800) 772-8339		kiddopotamus.com

Chapter 8: Strollers & To-Go Gear

Lots4Tos			lots4tots.com
Aprica		(310) 639-6387	apricausa.com
Baby Trend	(800) 328-7363		babytrend.com
Combi	(800) 752-6624	(630) 871-0404	combi-intl.com
Emmaljunga		(760) 597-1565	emmaljunga.com
Maclaren	(877) 504-8809	(203) 354-4400	maclarenbaby.com
Regalo	(800) 521-2234		regalo-baby.com
Simo	(800) SIMO4ME	(203) 348-SIMO	simostrollers.com

Ingelsina	(877) 486-5112	(973) 746-5112	ingelsina.com
Kidco	(800) 553-5529	(847) 970-9100	kidcoinc.com
J Mason		(818) 993-6800	jmason.com
Safety 1st		(718) 385-1000	
Baby Jogger		(509) 457-0925	babyjogger.com
Kool Stop	(800) 586-3332	(714) 738-4973	koolstop.com
Dreamer Design		(509) 574-8085	dreamerdesign.net
Gozo		(415) 388-1814	getgozo.com
Zooper		(503) 248-9469	zooperstrollers.com
InStep	(800) 242-6110		instep.net
BOB		(805) 541-2554	bobtrailers.com
Agee's Bikes		(804) 672-8614	ageebike.com
Cozy Rosie	(877) 744-6367	(914) 244-6367	CozyRosie.com
Burley	(800) 311-5294		burley.com
Schwinn	(800) SCHWINN		schwinn.com
Rhode Gear			rhodegear.com
REI			rei.com

Diaper Bags

Mommy's Helper	(800) 371-3509	(316) 684-2229	mommyshelperinc.com

Carriers

Maya Wrap			mayawrap.com
Baby Bjorn	(800) 593-5522		babybjorn.com
Theodore Bean	(877) 68-TBEAN		theodorebean.com
Baby Trekker	(800) 665-3957		babytrekker.com
Kelty		(303) 530-7670	kelty.com
Madden		(303) 442-5828	maddenusa.com
Tough Traveler	(800) GO-TOUGH	(518) 377-8526	toughtraveller.com

Chapter 9: Safety

SafetyAlerts			safetyalerts.com
Child Recalls			childrecalls.com
PoolGuard			poolgaurd.com
PoolSOS			allweather.ca
Efficient Home			effcienthome.com
Perfectly Safe		(800) 837-5437	perfectlysafe.com
Intl Assoc Child Safety	(888) 677-IACS		iafcs.com

Chapter 10: Best Gifts

Gift Catalogs

Chinaberry	(800) 776-2242		chinaberry.com
Exposures	(800) 222-4947		exposures.com
Lilly's Kids	(800) 285-5555		lillianvernon.com
Music Little People	(800) 346-4445		musicforlittlepeople.com

Announcement Sources

Babies N Bells			babiesnbells.com
Celebrate Invitations			celebrateinvitations.com
Stork Avenue			storkavenue.com
Announcements by Jeannette			announcingit.com
Card Creations			cardcreations.com
Fairy Godmother			thefairygodmother.com
AlphaBit Soup			alphabitsoup.com
Celebrating Children			celebratingchildren.com
Paper Direct	(800) 272-7377		paperdirect.com
Hershey's wrappers	(800) 544-1347		hersheys.com
Homestead wrappers	(800) 995-2288		carsonenterprises.com
Angel Bars			angelbars.com

Announcement Printers

Carlson Craft	(800) 328-1782		carlsoncraft.com
Chase		(508) 478-9220	

NRN Designs		(714) 898-6363	
William Arthur	(800) 985-6581	(207) 985-6581	williamarthur.com
Elite	(800) 354-8321		
Encore	(800) 526-0497		encorestudios.com
Invitations Hotline	(800) 800-4355		invitationhotline.com
Heart Thoughts	(800) 524-2229		miracleofadoption.com
Artitudes	(800) 741-0711		miracleofadoption.com
Adoption World			adoptionstuff.com

Chapter 11: Etc.

Catalogs

Kid's Club	(800) 363-0500		kidsstuff.com
One Step Ahead	(800) 274-8440		onestepahead.com
Right Start Catalog	(800) LITTLE-1		rightstart.com

BabyNames

Babynames			babynames.com
Parentsoup			parentsoup.com
Alphabette Zoope			zoope.com

Shopping Bots

My Simon			mysimon.com
Shop Best			shopbest.com
PriceScan			pricescan.com

Baby Products Web Sites

Babycenter			babycenter.com
BabyStyle			babystyle.com
Baby Ant			babyant.com
Baby Super Center			babysupercenter.com
Baby Warehouse			thebabywarehouse.com
Baby Bundle			babybundle
Baby Super Mall			babysupermall
Just Babies			justbabies.com
Baby Universe			babyuniverse.com
Baby Age			babyage.com
BabyPressConference			babypressconference.com
Comfort Living			comfortliving.com
Overstock			overstock.com
Smart Bargains			smartbargains.com
Planet Feedback			planetfeedback.com

Nat'l Parenting Ctr	(800) 753-6667	(818) 225-8990	tnpc.com
Catalogs			catalogsite.com
Au Pair in America	(800) 727-2437 x6188		
Nat'l Assoc Family Child Care	(800) 359-3817		nafcc.org
Nat'l Assoc Educ Young Child.	(800) 424-2460		naeyc.org

Appendix A: Canada

Transport Canada		(613) 990-2309	tc.gc.ca
Canadian Auto. Assoc			caa.ca
British Columbia AAA		(604) 268-5000	bcaa.bc.ca
Canadian Parents Online	(877) 325-8888		canadianparents.com
Maternal Instinct	(877) MATERNAL		maternal-instinct.com
Mountain Equip Coop			mac.ca
Child Resources			childcarecanada.org

Appendix C: Twins

Twins Magazine	(800) 328-3211	(303) 290-8500	twinsmagazine.com
Baby Beat	(888) 758-8822		babybeat.com
Kimberly Clark Twins	(800) 544-1847		
Double Decker Stroller		(941) 543-1582	doubledecker.com
Maxi Mom Carrier			twinsstuff.com

INDEX

How to Reach the Authors

Have a question about

Baby Bargains?

Want to make a suggestion?

Discovered a great bargain you'd like to share?

Contact the Authors, Denise & Alan Fields in one of five flavorful ways:

1. By phone:
(303) 442-8792

2. By mail:
436 Pine Street, Suite 600,
Boulder, CO 80302

3. By fax:
(303) 442-3744

4. By email:
authors@BabyBargainsBook.com

5. On our web page:
www.BabyBargainsBook.com

If this address isn't active, try one of our other URL's: www.DeniseAndAlan.com or www.WindsorPeak.com. Or call our office at 1-800-888-0385 if you're having problems accessing the page.

What's on our web page?

- *FREE updates on this book.*
- *NEW BARGAINS suggested by our readers.*
- *CHECK out our reader "Mail Bag" for great ideas!*
- *CORRECTIONS and clarifications.*
- *Sign up for a FREE E-NEWSLETTER!*

Our Other Books

By Denise & Alan Fields

Your New House

The alert consumer's guide to buying and building a quality home.
$15.95 (4th Edition)

As seen on ABC's 20/20
"This is, by far, the best book available on how to buy and build a new home!"
—Robert Bruss
Chicago Tribune

Bridal Bargains

Secrets to throwing a fantastic wedding on a realistic budget
$14.95 (5th Edition)

As seen on DATELINE NBC
Oprah and People Magazine

Call toll-free to order!
1-800-888-0385

*Additional information on all our books is available on our home page **www.windsorpeak.com***
Mastercard, VISA, American Express and Discover Accepted!
Shipping to any U.S. address is $3 ($4 for Canada)

MONEY BACK GUARANTEE

If this book doesn't save you at least

$250

off your baby expenses, we'll give you a complete refund on the cost of this book!

NO QUESTIONS ASKED!

Just send the book and your mailing address to

Windsor Peak Press • 436 Pine Street, Suite T Boulder, CO, 80302.

If you have any questions, please call (303) 442-8792.

Look at all those other baby books in the bookstore—no other author or publisher is willing to put their money where their mouth is! We are so confident that *Baby Bargains* will save you money that we guarantee it in writing!

SMART SHOPPER TIPS

Reprinted from
The *Baby Bargains* book • Fields

CRIBS

- ❑ Evaluate the mattress support: springs? straps? bars? cardboard?
- ❑ How easy does the side rail release?
- ❑ Evaluate the mattress height adjustment: screws or hooked bracket?
- ❑ How stable is the crib?
- ❑ Is the crib JPMA safety-certified?
- ❑ How easy is the crib to assemble?
- ❑ Does the store offer delivery and set-up?
- ❑ Are there any danger signs: sharp edges? Fold-down railings? Attached dressers?

BEDDING

- ❑ What is the thread count of the sheets?
- ❑ Is the appliqué stiching tight, smooth?
- ❑ Is there a tag with maker contact info?
- ❑ Is the bedding sewn with cotton/poly thread (versus nylon)?
- ❑ Are there ties on the top and bottom of the bumper pads?
- ❑ Is the design printed on the fabric? Or merely stamped?
- ❑ Are the ruffles folded over for double thickness?

LAYETTE (CLOTHING)

- ❑ Choose sizes based on your child's weight and length (not age).
- ❑ Evaluate the fiber content (all cotton versus blends).
- ❑ Is the item pre-shrunk?
- ❑ Are snaps on a reinforced band?
- ❑ Check for easy diaper access.
- ❑ Avoid outfits with detachable decoration.
- ❑ Remove any drawstrings.
- ❑ Recommended layette:

Quantity	Item
❑ 6	T-shirts/onesies (over the head)
❑ 6	T-shirts (side snap or side tie)
❑ 4-6	Sleepers
❑ 1	Blanket Sleeper
❑ 2-4	Coveralls
❑ 3-4	Booties/socks
❑ 1	Sweater
❑ 2	Hats (safari and caps)
❑ 1	Snowsuit/bunting
❑ 4	Large bibs (for feeding)
❑ 3 sets	Wash cloths and towels
❑ 7-8	Receiving blankets

High chairs

- ❑ Does the chair have a stable, wide base?
- ❑ How easily does the tray release?
- ❑ Is the chair height adjustable?
- ❑ How easy it is to clean?
- ❑ Is there any protection to keep the baby from sliding under the tray?

Car Seats

- ❑ Check your vehicle's owner manual to see if you need additional hardware.
- ❑ How easily do the belts adjust?
- ❑ Are the installation instructions clear?
- ❑ Is the pad cover machine washable?
- ❑ Does it require installation with each use?
- ❑ New rules to take effect soon! Check our web page at *www.babybargainsbook.com* for the latest on changing safety standards.

Strollers: key features to look for

For Baby: ❑ Reclining seat. ❑ Front Bar. ❑ Seat Padding. ❑ Weather protection.

For Parents: ❑ Roomy storage basket. ❑ Compact fold. ❑ Removable cushion. ❑ Lockable wheels. ❑ Handle height. ❑ Reversible handle. ❑ Overall weight.

Top Ten Safety must haves

- ❑ Outlet covers.
- ❑ Baby monitor.
- ❑ Smoke alarms.
- ❑ Toilet locks.
- ❑ Cabinet/drawer locks
- ❑ Tub Spout cover.
- ❑ Bath thermometer or anti-scald device.
- ❑ Carbon monoxide detectors.
- ❑ Fire extinguishers, rated "ABC."
- ❑ Baby gates.

Question to ask a child care provider

- ❑ What are the credentials/education of the provider(s)?
- ❑ What is the turnover?
- ❑ What is the ratio of children to care providers?
- ❑ Do you have a license? Verify.
- ❑ May I visit you during business hours?
- ❑ Discuss your care philosophy.
- ❑ Do you have liability insurance? Ask for written verification.
- ❑ Does the center conduct police background checks on employees?
- ❑ Is the center clean, home-like, cheerful?
- ❑ What type of adjustment period does the center offer?